Health, Safety, and Nutrition for the Young Child

Health, Safety, and Nutrition for the Young Child

Eighth Edition

Lynn R. Marotz, RN, Ph.D.
University of Kansas

WADSWORTH
CENGAGE Learning™

Australia • Brazil • Japan • Korea • Mexico • Singapore • Spain • United Kingdom • United States

WADSWORTH
CENGAGE Learning

Health, Safety, and Nutrition for the Young Child, Eighth Edition
Lynn R. Marotz

Executive Publisher: Linda Schreiber-Ganster

Executive Editor: Mark D. Kerr

Senior Developmental Editor: Lisa Mafrici

Assistant Editor: Beckie Dashiell

Media Editor: Media Editor: Elizabeth Momb

Editorial Assistant: Genevieve Allen

Marketing Manager: Kara Kindstrom

Marketing Assistant: Dimitri Hagnéré

Marketing Communications Manager: Tami Strang

Content Project Manager: Samen Iqbal

Art Director: Maria Epes

Print Buyer: Mary Beth Hennebury

Rights Acquisitions Specialist: Don Schlotman

Production Service: Lindsay Schmonsees, MPS Limited, a Macmillan Company

Text and Cover Designer: tani hasegawa

Photo Researcher: Scott Rosen, Bill Smith Group

Text Researcher: Sarah D'Stair

Copy Editor: Cathy Albano

Cover Image: Diana Ong/SuperStock/Getty Images

"Girl biting an orange" image: Meg Takamura/IZA Stock/Getty Images

Compositor: MPS Limited, a Macmillan Company

Library of Congress Control Number: 2010925892

Student Edition
ISBN-13: 978-1-111-29837-1
ISBN-10: 1-111-29837-8

Loose-leaf Edition:
ISBN-13: 978-1-111-35580-7
ISBN-10: 1-111-35580-0

Wadsworth
20 Davis Drive
Belmont, CA 94002-3098
USA

Cengage Learning is a leading provider of customized learning solutions with office locations around the globe, including Singapore, the United Kingdom, Australia, Mexico, Brazil, and Japan. Locate your local office at **www.cengage.com/global.**

Cengage Learning products are represented in Canada by Nelson Education, Ltd.

To learn more about Wadsworth, visit **www.cengage.com/wadsworth**

Purchase any of our products at your local college store or at our preferred online store **www.cengagebrain.com**.

Printed in Canada
1 2 3 4 5 6 7 14 13 12 11 10

Brief Contents

Preface xi

UNIT 1 Promoting Children's Health: Healthy Lifestyles and Health Concerns 1

Chapter 1 Children's Well-Being: What It Is and How to Achieve It / 2
Chapter 2 Daily Health Observations / 39
Chapter 3 Assessing Children's Health / 54
Chapter 4 Common Chronic Medical Conditions Affecting Children's Health / 84
Chapter 5 The Infectious Process and Environmental Control / 114
Chapter 6 Communicable and Acute Illness: Identification and Management / 136

UNIT 2 Keeping Children Safe 171

Chapter 7 Creating High-Quality Environments / 172
Chapter 8 Safety Management / 207
Chapter 9 Management of Injuries and Acute Illness / 237
Chapter 10 Maltreatment of Children: Abuse and Neglect / 267
Chapter 11 Planning for Children's Health and Safety Education / 290

UNIT 3 Foods and Nutrients: Basic Concepts 317

Chapter 12 Nutritional Guidelines / 318
Chapter 13 Nutrients That Provide Energy (Carbohydrates, Fats, and Proteins) / 337
Chapter 14 Nutrients That Promote Growth of Body Tissues (Proteins, Minerals, and Water) / 353
Chapter 15 Nutrients That Regulate Body Functions (Vitamins, Minerals, Protein, and Water) / 368

UNIT 4 Nutrition and the Young Child 387

Chapter 16 Feeding Infants / 388
Chapter 17 Feeding Toddlers and Young Children / 409

Chapter 18 Planning and Serving Nutritious and Economical Meals / 430
Chapter 19 Food Safety / 457
Chapter 20 Nutrition Education Concepts and Activities / 484

Epilogue 507

Looking Ahead...Making a Difference / 507

Appendices 509

A National Health Education Standards / 510
B Monthly Calendar: Health, Safety, and Nutrition Observances / 514
C Federal Food Programs / 518
D Children's Book List / 520
E Nutrient Information: Fast-Food Vendor Websites / 525

Glossary 527

Index 535

Contents

Preface xi

UNIT 1 Promoting Children's Health: Healthy Lifestyles and Health Concerns 1

Chapter 1 **Children's Well-Being: What It Is and How to Achieve It / 2**

Learning Objectives / 2 The Preventive Health Concept / 3 Health, Safety, and Nutrition: An Interdependent Relationship / 7 Children's Growth and Development / 12 Promoting a Healthy Lifestyle / 15 Summary / 32 Terms to Know / 32 Chapter Review / 33 Case Study / 33 Application Activities / 34 Helpful Web Resources / 34 References / 35

Chapter 2 **Daily Health Observations / 39**

Learning Objectives / 39 Promoting Children's Health / 40 Observation as a Screening Tool / 41 Daily Health Checks / 42 Family Involvement / 47 Health Education / 48 Summary / 51 Terms to Know / 51 Chapter Review / 51 Case Study / 52 Application Activities / 52 Helpful Web Resources / 53 References / 53

Chapter 3 **Assessing Children's Health / 54**

Learning Objectives / 54 Health Records / 55 Screening Procedures / 58 Sensory Development / 59 Vision Screening / 59 Hearing Screening / 65 Speech and Language Evaluation / 69 Nutritional Assessment / 71 Referrals / 75 Summary / 78 Terms to Know / 78 Chapter Review / 78 Case Study / 80 Application Activities / 80 Helpful Web Resources / 81 References / 81

Chapter 4 **Common Chronic Medical Conditions Affecting Children's Health / 84**

Learning Objectives / 84 Common Chronic Diseases and Medical Conditions / 85 Allergic Diseases / 85 Asthma / 90 Anemia / 92 Childhood Cancers / 94 Diabetes / 96 Eczema / 98 Excessive Fatigue / 99 Lead Poisoning / 100 Seizure Disorders / 102 Sickle Cell Disease / 104 Summary / 107 Terms to Know / 108 Chapter Review / 108 Case Study / 109 Application Activities / 109 Helpful Web Resources / 110 References / 110

Chapter 5 The Infectious Process and Environmental Control / 114

Learning Objectives / 114 Communicable Illness / 115 Stages Of Illness / 117 Control Measures / 118 Summary / 131 Terms to Know / 132 Chapter Review / 132 Case Study / 133 Application Activities / 133 Helpful Web Resources / 134 References / 134

Chapter 6 Communicable and Acute Illness: Identification and Management / 136

Learning Objectives / 136 Communicable Childhood Illnesses / 137 Common Acute Childhood Illnesses / 148 Summary / 166 Terms to Know / 166 Chapter Review / 166 Case Study / 167 Application Activities / 167 Helpful Web Resources / 168 References / 168

UNIT 2 Keeping Children Safe 171

Chapter 7 Creating High-Quality Environments / 172

Learning Objectives / 172 Locating High-Quality Programs / 173 Licensing / 175 Features of High-Quality Programs / 176 Guidelines for Safe Environments / 182 Summary / 202 Terms to Know / 202 Chapter Review / 202 Case Study / 203 Application Activities / 203 Helpful Web Resources / 204 References / 205

Chapter 8 Safety Management / 207

Learning Objectives / 207 What Is Unintentional Injury? / 208 Risk Management: Principles and Preventive Measures / 212 Implementing Safety Practices / 217 Legal Implications / 227 Summary / 231 Terms to Know / 231 Chapter Review / 232 Case Study / 233 Application Activities / 233 Helpful Web Resources / 233 Videos / 234 References / 234

Chapter 9 Management of Injuries and Acute Illness / 237

Learning Objectives / 237 Emergency Care vs. First Aid / 240 Life-Threatening Conditions / 240 Non-Life-Threatening Conditions / 254 Summary / 263 Terms to Know / 263 Chapter Review / 264 Case Study / 265 Application Activities / 265 Helpful Web Resources / 265 References / 266

Chapter 10 Maltreatment of Children: Abuse and Neglect / 267

Learning Objectives / 267 Historical Developments / 268 Discipline vs. Punishment / 268 Abuse and Neglect / 269 Understanding the Dynamics of Abuse and Neglect / 274 Protective Measures for Programs and Teachers / 276 Reporting Laws / 277 The Role of the Teacher / 279 Summary / 285 Terms to Know / 285 Chapter Review / 285 Case Study / 286 Application Activities / 287 Helpful Web Resources / 287 References / 287

Chapter 11 Planning for Children's Health and Safety Education / 290

Learning Objectives / 290 Family Involvement in Health and Safety Education / 291 The Role of Teacher Inservice In Health and Safety Education / 292 Effective Instructional Design / 292 Activity Plans / 298 Summary / 312 Terms to Know / 313 Chapter Review / 313 Case Study / 314 Application Activities / 314 Helpful Web Resources / 314 References / 315

UNIT 3 Foods and Nutrients: Basic Concepts 317

Chapter 12 Nutritional Guidelines / 318

Learning Objectives / 318 Dietary Reference Intakes (DRIs) / 319 Dietary Guidelines for Americans / 320 The Food Guide Pyramid / 324 Food Labels / 329 Summary / 333 Terms to Know / 333 Chapter Review / 333 Case Study / 334 Application Activities / 334 Helpful Web Resources / 335 References / 335

Chapter 13 Nutrients That Provide Energy (Carbohydrates, Fats, and Proteins) / 337

Learning Objectives / 337 Food as an Energy Source / 338 Carbohydrates as Energy Sources / 340 Fats as Energy Sources / 344 Proteins as Energy Sources / 347 Summary / 348 Terms to Know / 349 Chapter Review / 349 Case Study / 350 Application Activities / 350 Helpful Web Resources / 351 References / 351

Chapter 14 Nutrients That Promote Growth of Body Tissues (Proteins, Minerals, and Water) / 353

Learning Objectives / 353 Children's Growth / 354 Proteins for Growth / 354 Minerals For Growth / 357 The Role of Water / 360 The Supporting Role of Vitamins / 361 Summary / 363 Terms to Know / 364 Chapter Review / 364 Case Study / 365 Application Activities / 365 Helpful Web Resources / 366 References / 366

Chapter 15 Nutrients That Regulate Body Functions (Vitamins, Minerals, Protein, and Water) / 368

Learning Objectives / 368 Vitamins as Regulators / 369 Minerals as Regulators / 375 Proteins as Regulators / 379 Water as a Regulator / 380 Nutrient Functions: A Recap / 381 Summary / 383 Terms to Know / 384 Chapter Review / 384 Case Study / 384 Application Activities / 385 Helpful Web Resources / 385 References / 385

UNIT 4 Nutrition and the Young Child 387

Chapter 16 Feeding Infants / 388

Learning Objectives / 388 Profile of an Infant / 388 Meeting the Infant's Nutritional Needs / 389 Feeding Time for the Infant / 394 Introducing Semi-Solid (Pureed) Foods / 397 Some Common Feeding Concerns / 401 Summary / 405 Terms to Know / 405 Chapter Review / 406 Case Study / 406 Application Activities / 406 Helpful Web Resources / 407 References / 407

Chapter 17 Feeding Toddlers and Young Children / 409

Learning Objectives / 409 Developmental Profile of Toddlers, Preschoolers, and School-Aged Children / 409 The Challenge of Feeding Toddlers / 411 As the Toddler Becomes a Preschooler / 415 Healthy Eating Habits / 418 Health Problems Relating to Eating

Habits / 419 Summary / 426 Terms to Know / 426 Chapter Review / 427 Case Study / 427 Application Activities / 428 Helpful Web Resources / 428 References / 428

Chapter 18 Planning and Serving Nutritious and Economical Meals / 430

Learning Objectives / 430 Meal Planning / 430 Writing Menus / 445 Nutritious Snacks / 445 Serving Meals / 446 The Menu Must Stay Within the Budget / 448 Summary / 452 Terms to Know / 453 Chapter Review / 453 Case Study / 454 Application Activities / 454 Helpful Web Resources / 455 References / 455

Chapter 19 Food Safety / 457

Learning Objectives / 457 Food Safety Depends on Sanitation / 457 Food-Borne Illnesses / 472 Conditions for Bacterial Growth / 477 Summary / 480 Terms to Know / 481 Chapter Review / 481 Case Study / 481 Application Activities / 482 Helpful Web Resources / 482 References / 482

Chapter 20 Nutrition Education Concepts and Activities / 484

Learning Objectives / 484 Basic Concepts of Nutrition Education / 485 Responsibility for Nutrition Education / 486 Rationale for Nutrition Education in the Early Years / 488 Planning a Nutrition Education Program / 488 Guidelines and Safety Considerations for Nutrition Education Activities / 490 Developing Lesson Plans for Nutrition Activities / 494 Additional Food Information Sources / 501 Summary / 504 Terms to Know / 504 Chapter Review / 504 Case Study / 505 Application Activities / 505 Helpful Web Resources / 505 References / 506

Epilogue 507

Looking Ahead...Making a Difference / 507

Appendices 509

A National Health Education Standards / 510

B Monthly Calendar: Health, Safety, and Nutrition Observances / 514

C Federal Food Programs / 518

D Children's Book List / 520

E Nutrient Information: Fast-Food Vendor Websites / 525

Glossary 527

Index 535

Preface

Children's state of wellness has an unquestionable effect on their development and ability to learn. Our understanding of factors that shape and influence well-being, such as diet, environmental safety, and mental health, is continually improving as a result of new research findings. This information has led to noteworthy changes in our views about health, approaches to health care, and the critical importance of addressing health education. It has also contributed to the development of functional resources that currently guide personal and classroom practices with respect to children's health, safety, and nutrition. The National Health Education Standards, National Association for the Education of Young Children's (NAEYC) Standards for Early Childhood Professional Preparation, the Food Guide Pyramid, and the new Dietary Guidelines for Americans are several examples. In addition, our knowledge of wellness and its promotion draws increasing attention to the pivotal role teachers play in identifying children's health needs, creating high-quality environments that are safe and support learning, and providing comprehensive health education in schools.

Health, Safety, and Nutrition for the Young Child, now in its eighth edition, has become the standard text in the early childhood field based on its well-documented student/teacher-oriented focus. This best-selling, full-color text provides students and teachers with a fundamental understanding of children's health, safety, and nutrition needs and guides them in implementing effective classroom practices. It emphasizes the importance of respecting and partnering with families to help children establish healthy lifestyles and achieve their learning potential. It accomplishes this by addressing all three essential components of children's wellness in one book:

- promoting children's ***health*** through awareness, effective practices, and sound health education
- creating and maintaining ***safe learning environments***
- meeting children's essential ***nutritional needs*** through thoughtful meal planning, food safety, and nutrition education

Extensive resources, lesson plans, checklists, references, and links to additional sources are provided throughout the book to aid busy students and practicing teachers in making a difference in children's lives.

The Intended Audience

First and foremost, *Health, Safety, and Nutrition for the Young Child* is written on behalf of young children everywhere. Ultimately, it is the children who benefit from having families and teachers who understand and know how to protect and promote their safety and well-being. The term *families* is used throughout the text in reference to the diverse caring environments in which children are currently being raised and that may or may not include their biological parents. The term *teachers* is used inclusively to describe all adults who care for and work with young children—including educators, therapists, coaches, camp leaders, administrators, health care providers, legislators, and concerned citizens, whether they work in early education centers, home-based programs, recreation activities, public schools, community agencies, or after-school programs. The term *teacher* also acknowledges the important educational role that families play in their children's daily lives. Its use also acknowledges the educators who dedicate their lives to children's learning.

Health, Safety, and Nutrition for the Young Child is intended for students, new and experienced teachers, families, and colleagues who work in any role that touches children's lives. The material is based on current research in health, safety, and nutrition and its application in varied settings. After reading and studying the material addressed in this book, I hope you will understand, value, and accept the important responsibilities and roles you play in helping young children achieve their goals and learning potential.

Organization and Key Content

Three major topical areas are addressed in this new edition: promoting children's health (Unit 1); creating high-quality, safe environments (Unit 2); and, children's nutrition (basic and applied) and healthy eating behaviors (Units 3 and 4). This arrangement maximizes student learning and offers instructors flexibility in designing their courses. However, the interrelatedness of these three subject areas must not be overlooked despite their artificial separation.

The eighth edition of *Health, Safety, and Nutrition for the Young Child* is written in a clear, concise, and thought-provoking manner. It reflects the latest developments and research regarding children and wellness and continues to reinforce the importance of diversity and partnering with families to promote children's well-being. Important information on key topics, such as the National Health Education Standards, children's mental health, bullying, fostering resilience and social-emotional competence, chronic and acute health conditions, SIDS, childhood obesity, food safety, and menu planning has been expanded and updated. Additional information about children with special challenges and school-aged children can be found throughout the book. This comprehensive book is a resource that no teacher (new or experienced) should be without!

Several changes and additions have been incorporated into this edition in response to emerging trends, improved knowledge of how young children learn and grow, and efforts to prepare successful and effective teachers:

- **Lesson Plans Aligned with the National Health Education Standards for Students (Grades PreK–2 and 3–5)**—The concept of health promotion is built on a foundation of ongoing, developmentally appropriate, evidence-based learning experiences for children. The National Health Education Standards for Students provide a unified framework that can be used to guide educational opportunities in the areas of health, safety, and nutrition. Relevant standards are noted in each *Classroom Corner* lesson plan to help teachers achieve meaningful learning outcomes. A complete list of the standards and behavioral indicators is located in Appendix A and on the inside of the back cover.
- **National Association for the Education of Young Children Professional Preparation Standards Linked to Chapter Content**—NAEYC standards are identified at the onset of each chapter to help students understand how chapter content is linked to the association's professional education framework. These standards serve as a reference for ensuring that future and current teachers are prepared to work with diverse families, facilitate children's learning, and share values consistent with their professional role. A complete list of the standards and their key elements is located on the inside front cover of this book.
- **New Chapters**—Several chapters have undergone significant restructuring in response to changes in the field and reviewer suggestions. Chapters 1 and 2 have been combined into a new Chapter 1, *"Children's Well-Being: What It Is and How to Achieve It"* to strengthen the message and implementation of health promotion. Chapter 4, *"Common Chronic Medical Conditions Affecting Children's Health"* has also been reorganized to focus more specifically on the chronic medical conditions teachers are most likely to encounter in their classrooms.

- **New, Expanded and Updated Content**— The material in each chapter has been updated to reflect the most current knowledge, research findings, and references available at the time of this revision. Many key topics, such as *childhood obesity, children's mental health, bullying, resilience, chronic and acute health conditions, environmental quality, cultural competence, children with special medical needs* and *healthy eating* have been expanded. Additional resources and web links have also been incorporated throughout the book to assist teachers in accessing a wealth of useful tools and information.
- **Reorganization and Strengthening of Chapter Pedagogy**—The pedagogy in each chapter has been reorganized to improve learning outcomes. Learning objectives and point-by-point summaries reflect the major concept presented in each chapter. NAEYC standards are identified at the beginning of each chapter to show students how the content is aligned. The terms to know, chapter reviews, case studies, and application activities are designed to foster active, student-centered learning.

Special Features

The eighth edition continues to include features, tables, and checklists designed to reinforce learning and expand the reader's ability to apply fundamental concepts in contemporary educational settings:

- **Focus on Families**—provides busy teachers with information about lifestyle topics that can be shared with families in newsletters, program handbooks, website postings, on bulletin boards or during conferences and parent meetings. Teachers are encouraged to identify additional topics that may be of unique interest to the children, families, and communities they serve.

> **Focus On Families** Poison Prevention in the Home
>
> Children under the age of 6 are the most frequent victims of unintentional poisonings. Their curiosity and limited understanding often lead them unknowingly into risky situations. In many households, items such as cleaning products, garden chemicals, automobile waxes, charcoal lighter, lamp oil, and medications are commonly left in places accessible to young children. Often, simple precautions can be taken to make children's environments safe.
>
> - Always place potentially dangerous substances in a locked cabinet. Don't rely on your child's ability to "know better."
> - Supervise children closely whenever using harmful products. Take them with you if the doorbell rings or if you must leave the room.
> - Teach children not to put anything into their mouths unless it is given to them by an adult.

- **Teacher Checklists**—are included in every chapter to provide teachers with quick, efficient access to critical information about key issues and best practices. Beginning practitioners will find these concise reference lists especially helpful in learning new material. Experienced teachers and administrators will find them useful for personal reference and staff training purposes.

Table 9–4 Teacher Checklist: Foods Commonly Linked to Childhood Choking

raw carrots	seeds (sunflower), peanuts, and other nuts
hot dogs	chewy cookies
pieces of raw apple	cough drops
grapes (whole)	raisins
fruit seeds and pits	pretzels
gummy or hard candies	popcorn
peanut butter sandwich	chewing gum

- **Classroom Corner…Teacher Checklists**—showcases lesson plans alignedwith the National Health Education Standards. Learning and evaluation objectives, materials lists, and step-by-step procedures help teachers translate chapter content into meaningful learning and applying activities for children and reinforce the importance of ongoing, integrated learning experiences that promote healthy lifestyle behaviors.

> **Classroom Corner** Teacher Activities
>
> **Preventing Burns** (PreK–2; National Health Education Standards 5.2.1 and 5.2.2)
>
> **Concept:** There are things that are safe to touch and play with and other things that can hurt you.
>
> **Learning Objectives**
>
> - Children will be able to identify items that are safe to touch and other items that are not safe.
> - Children will explain what to do if they aren't sure that an item is safe to touch.
>
> **Supplies**
>
> - pictures of a stove, lighter, matches, campfire, candle, barbeque grill, ball, car, apple, crayons, a stuffed toy, and a block

- **Reflective Thoughts**—offer thought-provoking questions for individual learning and/or class discussion. Students and teachers are encouraged to examine personal beliefs and professional practices through self-reflection.

> ***Reflective Thoughts***
>
> When you place an emergency telephone call, it is important to remain calm and stay on What information should you be prepared to give the dispatcher? Why shouldn't you han making a report? What emergency telephone numbers should be posted in schools and c facilities? Where should they be posted? What emergency numbers should children lear

- **Issues to Consider**—encourage readers to relate basic theory and principles of health, safety, and nutrition to everyday situations and settings. Thought-provoking questions are included for individual consideration and/or group discussion.

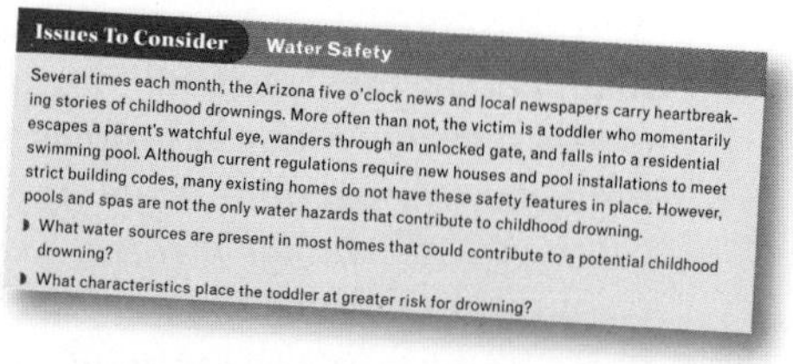
Issues To Consider Water Safety

Several times each month, the Arizona five o'clock news and local newspapers carry heartbreaking stories of childhood drownings. More often than not, the victim is a toddler who momentarily escapes a parent's watchful eye, wanders through an unlocked gate, and falls into a residential swimming pool. Although current regulations require new houses and pool installations to meet strict building codes, many existing homes do not have these safety features in place. However, pools and spas are not the only water hazards that contribute to childhood drowning.
- What water sources are present in most homes that could contribute to a potential childhood drowning?
- What characteristics place the toddler at greater risk for drowning?

- **Monthly Calendar of National Health, Safety, and Nutrition Observances**—provides a month-by-month listing of national observances and website resources to aid teachers in planning meaningful learning experiences for children. This information is located in Appendix B.

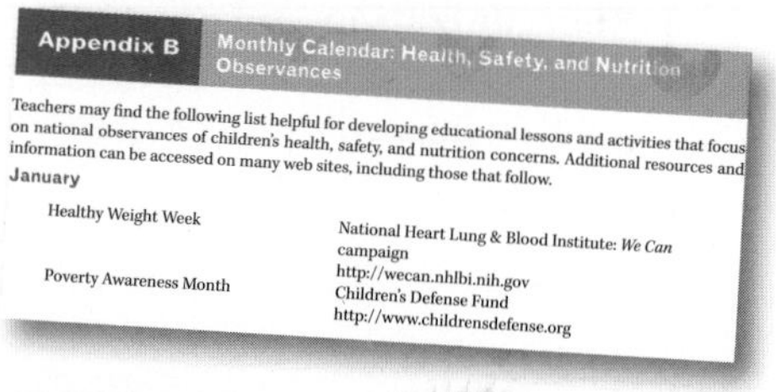
Appendix B Monthly Calendar: Health, Safety, and Nutrition Observances

Teachers may find the following list helpful for developing educational lessons and activities that focus on national observances of children's health, safety, and nutrition concerns. Additional resources and information can be accessed on many web sites, including those that follow.

January

Healthy Weight Week	National Heart Lung & Blood Institute: *We Can* campaign http://wecan.nhlbi.nih.gov
Poverty Awareness Month	Children's Defense Fund http://www.childrensdefense.org

- **Children's Book List**—is an extensive, updated collection of children's books that can be used for teaching about health, safety, and nutrition while also encouraging literacy skills. This resource is located in Appendix D and includes titles that address topics such as dental health, mental health, self-care, safety, nutrition, special needs, and physical activity.

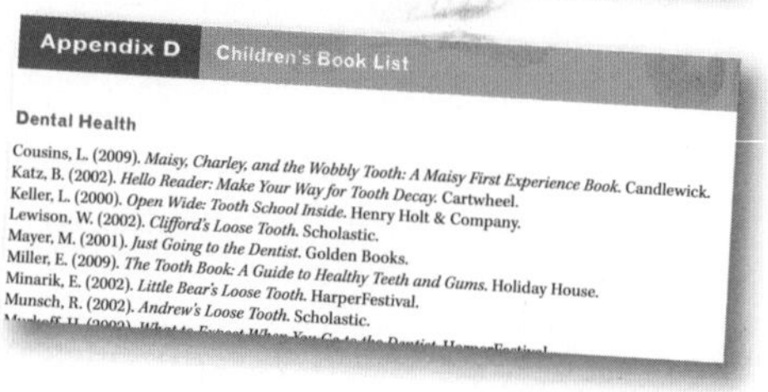
Appendix D Children's Book List

Dental Health

Cousins, L. (2009). *Maisy, Charley, and the Wobbly Tooth: A Maisy First Experience Book.* Candlewick.
Katz, B. (2002). *Hello Reader: Make Your Way for Tooth Decay.* Cartwheel.
Keller, L. (2000). *Open Wide: Tooth School Inside.* Henry Holt & Company.
Lewison, W. (2002). *Clifford's Loose Tooth.* Scholastic.
Mayer, M. (2001). *Just Going to the Dentist.* Golden Books.
Miller, E. (2009). *The Tooth Book: A Guide to Healthy Teeth and Gums.* Holiday House.
Minarik, E. (2002). *Little Bear's Loose Tooth.* HarperFestival.
Munsch, R. (2002). *Andrew's Loose Tooth.* Scholastic.

Pedagogy and Learning aids

Each chapter includes pedagogical features based on sound educational principles that encourage active student-centered learning, mastery, and application. The features also reflect student differences in learning needs, abilities, and styles:

- ***New* NAEYC Standards Chapter Links** are identified at the beginning of each chapter to help students understand how the content relates to national quality standards and prepares them for a professional role.

- **Learning Objectives** appear at the beginning of each chapter to draw students' attention to key points and concepts.

- **Bulleted lists** are used throughout the book to present important information in a concise, easy-to-access format.

- **Multicultural color photographs** taken on location at centers and schools show children as they work and play in developmentally appropriate settings.

- **Full-color illustrations** and tables reinforce and expand on important chapter content.

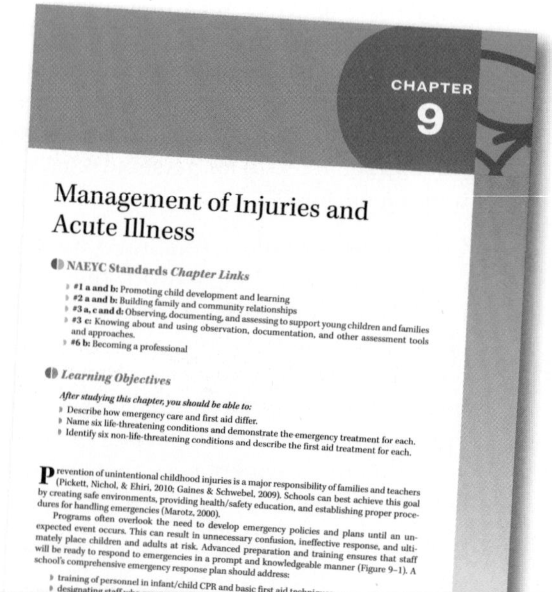
CHAPTER 9

Management of Injuries and Acute Illness

NAEYC Standards *Chapter Links*
- **#1 a and b:** Promoting child development and learning
- **#2 a and b:** Building family and community relationships
- **#3 a, c and d:** Observing, documenting, and assessing to support young children and families
- **#3 c:** Knowing about and using observation, documentation, and other assessment tools and approaches.
- **#6 b:** Becoming a professional

Learning Objectives

After studying this chapter, you should be able to:
- Describe how emergency care and first aid differ.
- Name six life-threatening conditions and demonstrate the emergency treatment for each.
- Identify six non-life-threatening conditions and describe the first aid treatment for each.

Prevention of unintentional childhood injuries is a major responsibility of families and teachers (Pickett, Nichol, & Ehiri, 2010; Gaines & Schwebel, 2009). Schools can best achieve this goal by creating safe environments, providing health/safety education, and establishing proper procedures for handling emergencies (Marotz, 2000).

Programs often overlook the need to develop emergency policies and plans until an unexpected event occurs. This can result in unnecessary confusion, ineffective response, and ultimately place children and adults at risk. Advanced preparation and training ensures that staff will be ready to respond to emergencies in a prompt and knowledgeable manner (Figure 9–1). A school's comprehensive emergency response plan should address:
- training of personnel in infant/child CPR and basic first aid techniques
- designating staff who are responsible for administering emergency care
- obtaining contact information and notarized permission that authorizes emergency medical treatment from each child's parent/guardian. (Note: Most medical facilities will not treat minor children without the notarized consent of their legal parent or guardian.)
- having an accessible telephone

- A bulleted **Summary** concludes each chapter and recaps the main points of discussion.
- **Terms to Know** are highlighted in color throughout the chapters. Each term is defined on the page where it initially appears and also in a comprehensive glossary located at the end of the book.
- **Chapter Review**—offers thought-provoking questions to reinforce learning and comprehension. Questions can also be used for group discussion.
- **Case Studies**—current, real-life situations challenge students to analyze and apply basic theory to solving everyday problems.
- **Application Activities**—provide additional opportunities for students to practice and reinforce what they have learned.
- **Helpful Web Resources**—take advantage of technology to extend student learning beyond the pages of this book and to access valuable resource materials.

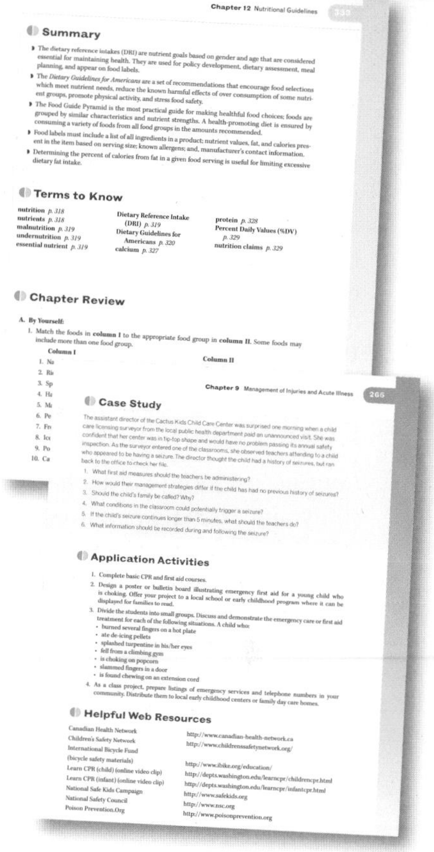

Ancillaries

Instructor's Manual

The Instructor's Manual that accompanies the eighth edition includes answers to chapter review questions and case studies. Additional questions are provided to guide class discussions or to be used for testing purposes. A new feature integrates TeachSource Video Cases with questions for classroom discussion. A list of multimedia resources is also included.

Test Bank

The Test Bank contains multiple choice, true/false, short answer, completion, and essay questions for each chapter.

PowerLecture w/ExamView CD

This one-stop digital library and presentation tool includes preassembled Microsoft® PowerPoint® lecture slides that can be used with this book. In addition to a full Instructor's Manual and Test Bank, PowerLecture also includes ExamView® testing software with all the test items from the Test Bank in electronic format, enabling you to create customized tests in print or online, and media resources in one place including an image library with graphics from the book itself and TeachSource Video Cases.

Web Tutor

The Web Tutor to accompany the eighth edition of *Health, Safety, and Nutrition for the Young Child* allows you to take learning beyond the classroom. This online courseware is designed to complement the text and allows students to better manage their time, prepare for exams, organize their notes, communicate, and much more. Special features include Chapter Learning Objectives,

Online Course Preparation, Study Sheets, Glossary, Discussion Topics, Frequently Asked-Questions, Online Class Notes, Online Chapter Quizzes, and Web Links related to chapter content. Printing features allow students to print their own customized study guides.

A benefit for instructors as well as students, the Web Tutor allows for online discussion with the instructor and other class members, real-time chat to enable virtual office hours and encourage collaborative learning environments, a calendar of syllabus information for easy reference, e-mail connections to facilitate communication among classmates and between students and instructors, and customization tools that help educators tailor their course to fit their needs by adding or changing content.

WebTutor allows you to extend your reach beyond the classroom and is available on either the WebCT or Blackboard platform.

Education CourseMate

Cengage Learning's Education CourseMate brings course concepts to life with interactive learning, study, and exam preparation tools that support the printed textbook. Access an integrated eBook, learning tools including flashcards and practice quizzes, printable forms and charts displayed in the book, web activities and exercises, web links, videos including the TeachSource Video Cases, and more in your Education CourseMate, accessed through www.CengageBrain.com. The accompanying instructor website offers access to password-protected resources such as an electronic version of the instructor's manual and PowerPoint® slides. Instructors can access this site by visiting www.CengageBrain.com.

About the Author

Lynn R. Marotz received a Ph.D. from the University of Kansas, an M.Ed. from the University of Illinois, and a B.S. in nursing from the University of Wisconsin. She has served as the health and safety coordinator and associate director of the Edna A. Hill Child Development Center (University of Kansas) for 30 years. In addition, she teaches undergraduate and graduate courses in the Department of Applied Behavioral Science that include issues in parenting, health/safety/nutrition for the young child, administration, and foundations of early childhood education. She also provides frequent inservice training in first aid, safety, child abuse, and identification of children's health problems for early childhood students and community educators.

Lynn has authored invited chapters in early childhood, international food industry, and law books. In addition, she is the co-author of *Developmental Profiles—Pre-Birth to 12 Years, Motivational Leadership*, and *By the Ages*. She has been interviewed for a number of articles about children's nutrition and well-being that have appeared in national trade magazines, and has served as a consultant for children's museums and training film productions. Her research activities focus on childhood obesity and children's health, safety, and nutrition. She has delivered numerous presentations at international, national, and state conferences and held appointments on national, state, and local committees and initiatives that advocate on children's and families' behalf. However, it is her daily interactions with children and their families, students, colleagues, and her beloved family that bring true insight, meaning, and balance to the material in this book.

Acknowledgments

A special thank you is extended to the instructors, students, and colleagues who use *Health, Safety, and Nutrition for the Young Child* in their classes and professional endeavors. Their suggestions continue to influence and improve each new edition. I would also like to recognize the contributions of dedicated teachers and families everywhere who strive to better children's lives.

I am grateful to have had the opportunity to work with Lisa Mafrici, who served as my faithful guide, visionary, and developmental editor. Her professional expertise and encouragement not only helped to keep me on track, but also to produce an attractive and improved edition. I would also like to thank the production staff at Wadsworth Cengage Learning who exercised their "Cinderella effect" by turning pages and pages of manuscript into a thing of worth and beauty! Thank you, too, to the many other individuals who contribute so much to getting the word out!

I want to thank my husband and family for their patience and understanding during times when writing took precedence over times spent together.

I also offer my sincere appreciation to the following reviewers for sharing so many constructive suggestions:

Amber Aguillard
Louisiana State University, Baton Rouge

Lisa Alastuey
Texas A and M University, Commerce

Vanese Delahoussaye
Houston Community College

Dawn McCrumb
Barton College

Melanie Rothchild
Tri County Community College

Adele Ruszak
Millersville University

Kyle Taft
East Central Technical College

Cynthia Waters
Upper Iowa University

UNIT 1

Promoting Children's Health: Healthy Lifestyles and Health Concerns

CHAPTER 1

Children's Well-Being: What It Is and How to Achieve It

NAEYC Standards *Chapter Links*

- **#1 a and b:** Promoting child development and learning
- **#2 a, b, and c:** Building family and community relationships
- **#4 a, b, c, and d:** Using developmentally effective approaches to connect with children and families
- **#5 a, b, and c:** Using content knowledge to build a meaningful curriculum
- **#6 b, c, d, and e:** Becoming a professional

Learning Objectives

After studying this chapter, you should be able to:

- Explain how the preventive health concept differs from traditional ideas about health care.
- Identify and describe several national programs that address children's health needs.
- Discuss how health, safety, and nutrition are interrelated.
- Describe typical growth and developmental characteristics of infants, toddlers, preschool-age, and school-age children.
- Discuss ways that teachers can be proactive in promoting children's wellness in the areas of injury prevention, dental health, physical activity, and mental health.

Our ideas about health, disease, and the health care system have undergone significant change in recent years. Public attention is gradually shifting from a mode of dependency on the medical profession for treating diseases and chronic illnesses to a realization that individuals must assume some personal responsibility for their own well-being. In part, this change is being fueled by escalating medical costs, lack of health insurance, and disabling conditions for which there are no present cures. In addition, and perhaps even more significant, are the research findings that demonstrate positive health outcomes when people adapt healthy lifestyle behaviors (Butterfoss & Cohen, 2009; DeVault et al., 2009; Mirvism & Clay, 2008).

The Preventive Health Concept

The concept of **preventive health** recognizes that individuals are able to reduce many factors that threaten personal wellness (Figure 1–1). It implies that children and adults are able to make choices and engage in behaviors that improve the quality of life and lessen the risk of disease (Guyer et al., 2009). This includes practices such as establishing healthful dietary habits (eating more fruits, vegetables, whole grains), practicing safety behaviors (wearing seat belts, limiting sun exposure), engaging in daily physical activity, and seeking early treatment for occasional illness and injury.

The early years are an ideal time for children to begin establishing preventive behaviors that will foster a healthy, productive lifetime. Young children are often more receptive to new ideas and have fewer unhealthy habits to overcome. Teachers and families can also capitalize on children's endless curiosity and take advantage of learning opportunities throughout the day—planned as well as spontaneous—to teach positive health, safety, and nutrition practices.

Although the preventive approach emphasizes an individual role in health promotion, it also implies a shared responsibility for addressing social and environmental issues that affect the quality of everyone's well-being, including:

- poverty and homelessness
- **food insecurity**
- inequitable access to medical and dental care
- adverse effects of media advertising
- substance abuse (e.g., alcohol, tobacco, drugs)
- food safety
- air and water pollution
- discrimination based on diversity
- unsafe neighborhoods

Figure 1–1 **Examples of preventive health practices.**

A preventive health approach involves a combination of personal practices and national initiatives.

On a personal scale:

- eating a diet low in animal fats
- consuming a wide variety of fruits, vegetables, and grains
- engaging in aerobic and muscle-strengthening activities regularly
- practicing good oral hygiene
- using proper hand washing techniques
- avoiding substance abuse (e.g., alcohol, tobacco, drugs)
- keeping immunizations up-to-date

On a national scale:

- regulating vehicle emissions
- preventing chemical dumping
- inspecting food supplies
- measuring air pollution
- providing immunization programs
- fluoridating drinking water
- monitoring disease outbreaks

---

preventive health – *engaging in behaviors that help to maintain and enhance one's health status; includes concern for certain social issues affecting the populations' health and environment.*

food insecurity – *uncertain or limited access to a reliable source of food.*

Children can begin to develop preventive health behaviors.

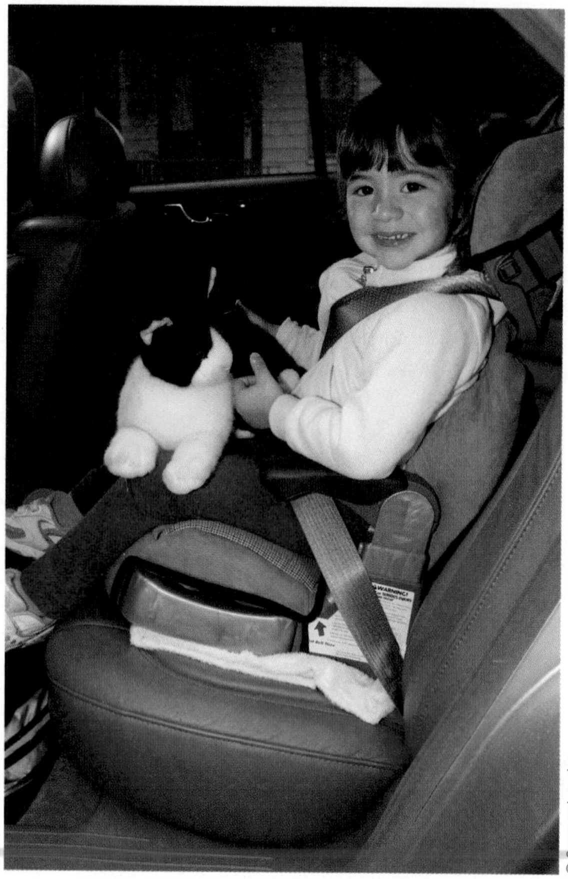

In addition to helping children learn about these complex issues, adults must also demonstrate their commitment by supporting social actions, policies, and programs that contribute to healthier environments and lifestyles for society as a whole.

National Health Initiatives

The positive health outcomes that are achievable through preventive practices continue to gain increased public interest, especially with respect to young children. Poor standards of health, safety, and nutrition have long been acknowledged as significant barriers to children's ability to learn and to ultimately become healthy, productive adults. As a result, a number of large-scale programs have been established in recent years to improve children's access to preventive services. Descriptions of several initiatives follow; information about federal food programs for children is located in Appendix C.

Healthy People 2020 In 1990, the U.S. Department of Health and Human Services issued an agenda entitled *Healthy People 2000: National Health Promotion and Disease Prevention Objectives*, which outlined twenty-two national health priorities, many of which addressed the needs of children (Office of Disease Prevention & Health Promotion, 2000). The purpose of the original document was aimed at improving the nation's standard of health through increased public awareness, dissemination of health information, interagency collaboration, and community participation. It placed significant emphasis on the need for individuals of all ages and backgrounds to assume active responsibility for their personal well-being.

The latest revision, *Healthy People 2020*, continues to uphold and strengthen the philosophy of health promotion and disease prevention. Health priorities identified in the revised initiative focus on newly emerging public health risks as well as a continuation of existing concerns, such as heart disease, obesity, and diabetes. Emphasis is placed on the importance of assuming personal responsibility for well-being and the need for improved access to preventive health services through agency collaboration and coordination (Table 1–1). The *Healthy People 2020* goals and objectives continue to have direct application for schools and early childhood programs and can easily be incorporated into existing efforts to promote children's health and development. For example, teaching children positive ways to manage anger, incorporating more physical activity into daily classroom schedules, and creating safe learning environments reflect teachers' commitment to the ideals highlighted in the *Healthy People 2020* initiative.

National Children's Agenda A similar Canadian proposal aimed at health promotion for children is outlined in a report entitled, *A National Children's Agenda: Developing a Shared Vision.* This document presents a comprehensive agenda of goals and objectives for addressing children's critical health care and safety needs. It also embraces the importance of the early years and supports the vision of creating a unified approach to helping children achieve their full potential.

Table 1–1 Healthy People 2020 Objectives

Areas targeted for improving children's health include the following:	
• physical activity and fitness	• immunizations and infectious diseases
• nutrition—overweight and obesity	• oral health
• substance abuse	• maternal and infant health
• mental health	• access to health services
• sleep	• health education
• elimination of lead poisoning	• vision, hearing, and communication disorders
• injury and violence prevention	

Children's Health Insurance Program (CHIP) The Children's Health Insurance Program (previously known as the State Children's Health Insurance Program or SCHIP) was recently reauthorized and expanded to serve an additional four million uninsured income-eligible children and pregnant women (U.S. DHHS, 2009a). Revised eligibility guidelines also increased the number of families that qualify for assistance. This program is administered in each state through annual appropriations from the federal government and requires the states to submit a Child Health Plan describing how the program will be implemented, how eligibility will be determined, and how eligible children will be located.

Approximately 7.4 million children and 335,000 adults were enrolled in CHIP-sponsored plans during 2008 (U.S. DHHS, 2009a). Services covered by this plan include free or low-cost medical and dental care, immunizations, prescriptions, mental health treatment, and hospitalization. Improving children's access to preventive health care contributes to a better quality of life and ability to learn. It also results in significant cost-saving benefits that can be attributed to early identification and treatment of children's medical and developmental problems (Simpson & Fairbrother, 2009).

Healthy Child Care America The primary objective of the Healthy Child Care America (HCCA) Initiative is quality improvement in early childhood programs. HCCA, supported by the U.S. Department of Health and Human Services, the Child Care Bureau, and the Maternal and Child Health Bureau, was established in 1995 to coordinate the mutual interests of health professions, early education professionals, and families in addressing children's health and safety needs in out-of-home programs. The program is administered by the American Academy of Pediatrics (AAP) and has been instrumental in launching several large-scale educational campaigns, including Moving Kids Safely in Child Care, Tummy Time, Back to Sleep (for parents), and Back to Sleep in Child Care Settings. Grant-supported offices, located in every state, have been established to evaluate and strengthen existing community infrastructure and to assist with new initiatives for improving children's health and safety in early childhood programs and access to preventive health care. Extensive resource information is provided on their website (http://www.healthychildcare.org).

National Health and Safety Performance Standards for Child Care National concern for children's welfare led to a collaborative project between the American Academy of Pediatrics (AAP), the American Public Health Association (APHA), and the National Resource Center for Health and Safety in Child Care and Early Education (NRC) to develop health, safety, and nutrition guidelines for out-of-home child care programs. The resulting document, *Caring for Our Children: National Health and Safety Performance Standards: Guidelines for Out-of-Home Child Care* (2002), provides detailed quality standards and procedures for ensuring children's health and safety while they attend organized care (Table 1–2) (APHA & AAP, 2002). The current system of child care regulation allows individual states to establish their own licensing standards, which has resulted in significant differences in quality. This project was an attempt to address regulatory inconsistencies

Table 1–2 National Health and Safety Performance Standards

Comprehensive guidelines address the following areas of child care:

- staffing – child staff ratios, credentials, and training
- activities for healthy development – supervision, transportation, behavior management, partnerships with families, health education
- health promotion and protection – sanitation, special medical conditions, illness management
- nutrition and food services – nutritional requirements, food safety, nutrition education
- facilities, supplies, equipment, and transportation – space and equipment requirements, indoor/outdoor play, maintenance, transportation
- infectious diseases – respiratory, bloodborne, skin
- children with special needs – inclusion, eligibility for special services, facility modifications, assessment
- administration – health/safety policies, personnel policies, documentation, contracts
- recommendations for licensing and community action – regulatory agencies, policy

by proposing a set of uniform standards based on what research has identified as best practices. The National Association for the Education of Young Children (NAEYC) adopted similar guidelines for their quality accreditation program in 2006 (NAEYC, 2006).

No Child Left Behind (NCLB) The importance of children's health and learning during their earliest years received one of its strongest endorsements with the passage of the No Child Left Behind Act of 2001. This bill authorized significant reforms of the K–12 educational system and strengthened partnerships with Head Start, Even Start, and early education programs in center- and home-based settings. It acknowledges families as children's first and most important teachers, the educational contributions of early childhood programs, and the importance of fostering early literacy skills (understanding and using language) to ensure children's readiness for, and success in, schools. The bill also authorized additional funding to cover child care costs for low-income families, health care coverage for eligible children, and prenatal services for pregnant women. Subsidies for parent education programs and for research focused on quality improvement in early education were also addressed in this legislation. The No Child Left Behind bill is currently undergoing review and calls for reform in preparation for the next reauthorization.

Coordinated School Health Program (CSHP) In 1988, the Centers for Disease Control and Prevention (CDC) proposed a new school health services model called the Coordinated School Health Program. At the time, teachers were being pressured to ensure children's success in school while studies demonstrated a strong association between children's health and academic outcomes. It became clear that traditional delivery methods were failing to address children's complex health needs and that a different approach was needed.

The Coordinated School Health program assumes a preventive health approach and emphasizes the collaborative involvement of teachers, administrators, staff, students, families, media, and community partners to improve the health of children and schools. The model identifies eight interactive components and outlines the expectations for each (Figure 1–2). Additional information regarding this program can be accessed from the website listed at the end of this chapter.

The National Children's Study One of the most comprehensive studies of children's health ever undertaken in the United States is currently in progress (National Children's Study, 2009). The National Institutes of Child Health and Human Development (NICHD) is coordinating this longitudinal study, which will follow over 100,000 children from birth to age 21 to examine the interaction of environmental effects on children's health and how they might contribute to

Figure 1–2 Coordinated school health program components.

© Dmitriy Shironosov/Shutterstock.com

disease. The study will eventually yield one of the most expansive information databases ever compiled about children's growth and development, differences in access to health care, and the incidence of disease. Data from the study will be used for future policy formulation, funding, and service interventions.

Numerous states and professional organizations, such as Head Start, Parents as Teachers, and Zero to Three have developed similar initiatives that focus on young children's health and nutritional needs. Schools, school districts, and private and public agencies are also creating programs that target children's wellness in response to increasing concerns about childhood health problems and obesity.

Many schools have developed programs to improve children's eating and physical activity.

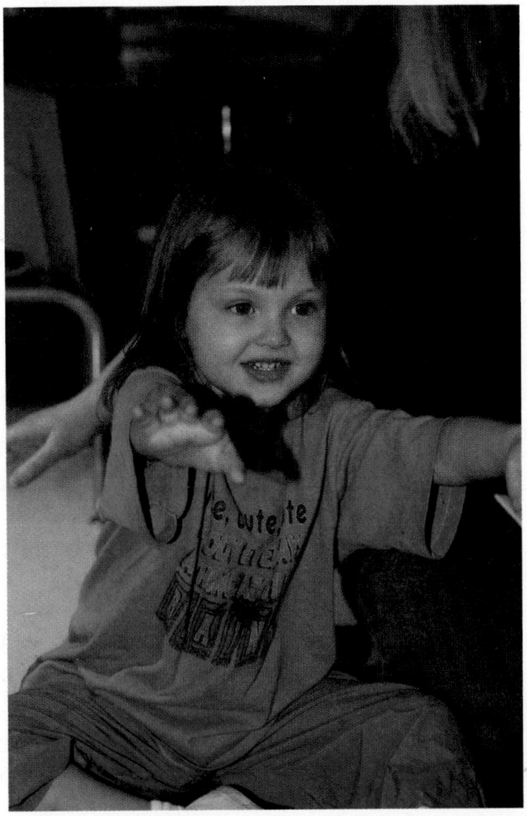

© Cengage Learning

Health, Safety, and Nutrition: An Interdependent Relationship

Health, safety, and nutrition are closely intertwined and dependent on one another. The status of each has a direct effect on the quality of the others. For example, children who receive all essential nutrients from a healthful diet are more likely to reach their growth potential, benefit from early learning opportunities,

Reflective Thoughts

The word *diversity* appears frequently in the media and conversation. What does the term *diversity* mean to you? What biases do you have that would influence your attitudes toward people of diverse backgrounds? Why do you think you have developed these feelings? Consider how you might go about changing any personal biases. What steps can you take to help children develop positive attitudes toward all people?

experience fewer illnesses, and have ample energy for play. In contrast, a child whose diet lacks critical nutrients such as iron may develop anemia, which can lead to fatigue, diminished alertness, growth failure, and loss of appetite. Disinterest in eating is likely to further compromise the child's iron intake. In other words, nutritional status has a direct effect on children's health and safety, which, in turn, influences the dietary requirements needed to restore and maintain well-being.

A nutritious diet also plays an important role in injury prevention. The child or adult who arrives at school having eaten little or no breakfast may experience low blood sugar, which can result in fatigue, decreased alertness, and slowed reaction times and, thus, increase an individual's risk of accidental injury. Similarly, overweight children and adults are more likely to sustain injuries because excess weight may restrict physical activity, slow reaction times, and increase fatigue with exertion.

What Is Health?

Definitions of **health** are as numerous as the factors that affect it. In the past, the term referred strictly to an individual's physical well-being and the absence of illness.

Contemporary definitions of health view it from a broader perspective and recognize it as a state of physical, emotional, social, economic, cultural, and spiritual well-being. Each interactive component is assumed to make an equally important contribution to health and to have an effect on the others. For example, a stressful home environment may be contributing to a child's frequent illnesses, stomachaches, or headaches; in turn, a child's repeated illnesses or chronic disability can have a profound effect on the family's emotional, financial, social, and physical stability and well-being.

The current definition of health also recognizes that children and adults are active participants in multiple groups, including family, peer, neighborhood, ethnic, cultural, recreational, religious, community, and so on. Consider, for example, recent outbreaks of H1N1 flu or E. coli and how quickly these communicable illnesses spread as a result of personal contact in multiple group settings. In each case, the environment served as an influential factor in both the spread and control of the disease.

What Factors Influence Children's Health?

Health is a complex state determined by ongoing interactions between an individual's genetic makeup and everyday environmental factors (Figure 1–3). For example, a baby's immediate and long-term health is affected by the mother's personal health and daily practices during pregnancy: her diet; use or avoidance of alcohol, tobacco, and certain medications; routine prenatal care; and exposure to communicable illnesses. Mothers who ignore healthy practices during pregnancy are more likely to give birth to infants who are born prematurely, have low birth weight, or experience a range of special needs (Polakowski, Akinbami, & Mendola, 2009). These children also face a significantly higher risk of lifelong health problems and possibly early death. In contrast, a child who is

---

health – *a state of wellness. Complete physical, mental, social, and emotional well-being; the quality of one element affects the state of the others.*

born healthy, grows up in a nurturing family, consumes a nutritious diet, lives in a safe environment, and has numerous opportunities for learning and recreation is more likely to enjoy a healthy life.

Heredity Characteristics transmitted from biological parents to their children at the time of conception determine all of the genetic traits of a new, unique individual. **Heredity** sets the limits for growth, development, and health potential. It explains, in part, why children in one family are short while those from another family are tall or why some individuals have allergies or require glasses while others do not.

Understanding how heredity influences health can also be useful for predicting an inherited tendency, or **predisposition**, to certain health problems, such as heart disease, deafness, cancer, diabetes, allergies, or mental health disorders. However, it should be noted that a family history of heart disease or diabetes, for example, does not necessarily predict the development of these conditions. Many lifestyle factors, including physical activity, diet, sleep, and stress levels, interact with genetic material (genes) to determine whether a child will ultimately develop heart disease or any number of other chronic health conditions.

Environment Although heredity provides the basic building materials that predetermine the limits of one's health, environment plays an equally important role. Environment encompasses a combination of physical, psychological, social, economic, and cultural factors that collectively influence the way individuals perceive and respond to their surroundings. In turn, these responses shape a person's behaviors and potential outcomes. For example, two cyclists set off on a ride: One wears a helmet, the other does not. The choices each has made could potentially have quite different outcomes if they were to be involved in a collision. In turn, if the cyclist who decided not to wear a helmet sustained injuries, he or she is likely to experience significant health, economic, social, and psychological consequences.

Examples of environmental factors that promote healthy outcomes include:

- following a nutritious diet
- participating in daily physical and recreational activities
- getting adequate rest
- having access to medical and dental care
- reducing stress

Figure 1–3 Health is an interactive and continuously changing state.

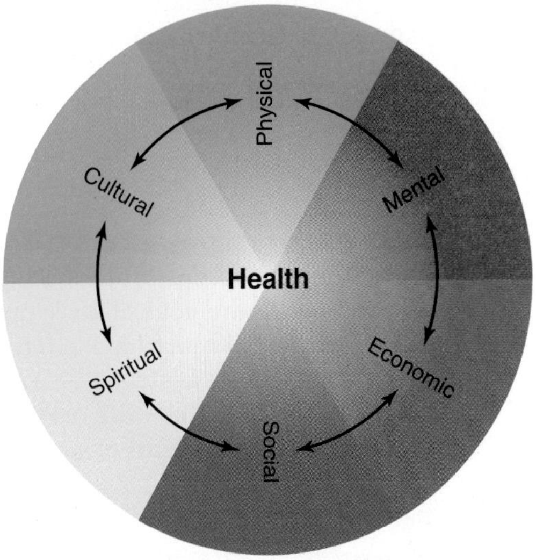

Heredity sets the limits for growth, development, and health potentials.

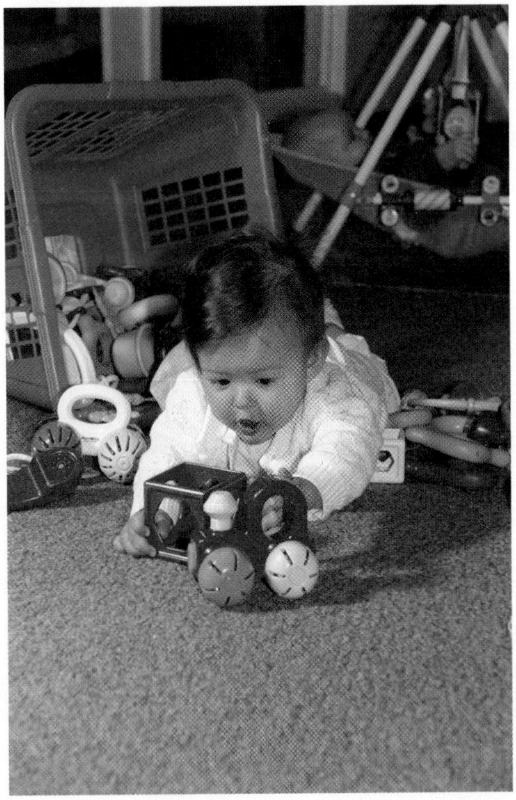

heredity – *the transmission of certain genetic material and characteristics from biological parents to child at the time of conception.*
predisposition – *having an increased chance or susceptibility.*

- residing in homes, child care facilities, schools, and workplaces that are clean and safe
- having opportunities to form stable and respectful relationships

There are also many environmental factors that have a negative effect on health. For example, exposure to chemicals and pollution, abuse, illness, obesity, prenatal alcohol, **sedentary** lifestyles, poverty, stress, food insecurity, violence, or unhealthy dietary choices can interfere with children's optimal growth and development.

Safety

Safety refers to the behaviors and practices that protect children and adults from unnecessary harm. Young children are at especially high risk for sustaining serious injuries because their developmental skills are not well developed. As a result, unintentional injuries are the leading cause of death among children from birth to 14 years in the United States and Canada and, sadly, many of these instances are avoidable (Forum on Child & Family Statistics, 2009; Safe Kids Canada, 2009). Every adult who works with, or cares for, young children, has a significant responsibility to maintain the highest standards of supervision and environmental safety (Mytton et al., 2009).

Factors Affecting Children's Safety Protecting children's safety requires a keen awareness of their skills and abilities at each developmental stage (Allen & Marotz, 2010). For example, knowing that an infant enjoys hand-to-mouth activities should alert teachers to continuously monitor the environment for small objects or poisonous substances that could be ingested. Understanding that toddlers are spontaneous and exceedingly curious should cause adults to take extra precautions to prevent children from wandering away or straying into unsupervised sources of water. Children who have developmental disabilities or sensory disorders are also at increased risk of sustaining unintentional injury and must be monitored continuously (Lee et al., 2008). An in-depth discussion of environmental safety and safety management will be covered in Chapters 7 and 8.

Nutrition

The term *nutrition* refers to the science of food, its chemical components (**nutrients**), and their relationship to health and disease. It includes all of the processes, from the ingestion and digestion of food to the absorption, transportation, and utilization of nutrients, and finally the excretion of unused end products. Nutrients are essential for life and have a direct effect on a child's nutritional status, behavior, health, and development.

They play critical roles in a variety of vital body functions, including:

- supplying energy
- promoting growth and development
- improving resistance to illness and infection
- building and repair of body tissue

Meeting the body's need for essential nutrients depends on consuming a wide variety of foods in recommended amounts. However, environmental and family factors such as financial resources, transportation, geographical location, cultural preferences, convenience, and nutrition knowledge can also influence a child's dietary quality. Most children in the United States live in a time and place where food is reasonably abundant. Yet, there is increasing concern about the number of children who may not be getting enough to eat or whose diets do not include the right types of foods (Metallinos-Katsaras, Sherry & Kallio, 2009; Tarasuk & Vogt, 2009). Also, because many young

sedentary – *unusually slow or sluggish; a lifestyle that implies inactivity.*
nutrients – *the chemical substances in food.*

children spend the majority of their waking hours in out-of-home child care programs or school classrooms, care must be taken to ensure that their nutrient needs are being met in these settings.

Children's Nutrition and Its Effect on Behavior, Learning, and Illness Children's nutritional status has a significant effect on behavior and cognitive development. Well-nourished children are typically more alert, attentive, physically active and better able to benefit from learning experiences (Rose-Jacobs et al., 2008). Poorly nourished children may be quiet and withdrawn, or hyperactive and disruptive during class activities (Benton, 2009; Melchior et al., 2009). They are also more prone to accidental injury because their levels of alertness and reaction times may be considerably slower. Children who are overweight also face a range of social, emotional, and physical challenges, including difficulty participating in physical activities, ridicule, emotional stress, and peer exclusion (Wang et al., 2009). Additional information about children's specific nutrient needs and the challenges associated with over- and under-consumption of foods will be addressed in-depth in Chapters 12 through 20.

Children's **resistance** to infection and illness is also directly influenced by their nutritional status (Katona & Katona-Apte, 2008). Well-nourished children are generally more resistant to illness and able to recover quickly when they are sick. Children who consume an unhealthy diet are more susceptible to infections and illness and often take longer to recuperate. Frequent illness can interfere with children's appetites which, in turn, may limit their intake of nutrients important for the recovery process. Thus, poor nutrition can create a cycle of increased susceptibility to illness and infection, nutritional deficiency, and prolonged recovery.

Nutritional status also affects children's behavior.

resistance – *the ability to avoid infection or illness.*

Teachers have an exceptional opportunity to protect and promote children's well-being. Their knowledge of children's development and health, safety, and nutritional needs can be applied when planning learning activities, classroom environments, meals and snacks, and supervision. In addition, teachers can implement sanitation and early identification practices to reduce children's unnecessary exposure to illness and infection. Furthermore, they can support the concept of preventive health by serving as positive role models and providing children with learning experiences that encourage a healthy lifestyle.

Children's Growth and Development

When teachers understand typical growth and developmental patterns, they are better able to identify and address children's diverse needs and to help children master critical skills (Charlesworth, 2011). They can create learning experiences and set goals for children that are developmentally appropriate and foster positive self-esteem. They are able to design high-quality environments that are safe and encourage children's mastery of new skills. In addition, they are able to use this knowledge to promote children's well-being by identifying health problems and abnormal behaviors and teaching healthy practices.

Discussions of growth and development often make reference to the "average" or "normal" child; however, such a child probably does not exist. Every child is a unique individual—a product of diverse experiences, environments, interactions, and heredity. Collectively, these factors can lead to significant differences in the rate at which children grow and acquire various skills and behaviors (Allen & Marotz, 2010).

Norms for children's growth and development have been established to serve as useful frames of reference. They represent the average or approximate age when the majority of children demonstrate a given skill or behavior. Thus, the term **normal** implies that while many children are able to perform a given skill by a specific age, some will be more advanced and others may take somewhat longer, yet they are still considered to be within the normal range.

Growth

The term **growth** refers to the many physical changes that occur as a child matures. Although the growth process takes place without much conscious control, there are many factors that affect both the quality and rate of growth:

- genetic potential
- level of emotional stimulation and bonding
- cultural influences
- socioeconomic factors
- adequate nutrition
- parent responsiveness
- health status (i.e., illness)

Infants (0–12 months) The average newborn weighs approximately 7 to 8 pounds (3.2–3.6 kg) at birth and is approximately 20 inches (50 cm) in length. Growth is rapid during the first year; an infant's birth weight nearly doubles by the fifth month and triples by the end of the first year. For example, an infant who weighs 8 pounds (3.6 kg) at birth will weigh approximately 16 pounds (7.3 kg) at 5 months and 24 pounds (10.9 kg) at 12 months.

norms – *an expression (e.g., weeks, months, years) of when a child is likely to demonstrate certain developmental skills.*
normal – *average; a characteristic or quality that is common to most individuals in a defined group.*
growth – *increase in size of any body part or of the entire body.*

An infant's length increases by approximately 50 percent during the first year. Thus, an infant measuring 21 inches (52.5 cm) at birth should reach an approximate length of 31.5 inches (78.7 cm) by 12 months of age. A majority of this gain occurs during the first 6 months when an infant may grow as much as 1 inch (2.5 cm) per month.

Other physical changes that occur during the first year include the growth of hair and eruption of teeth (four upper and four lower). The infant's eyes begin to focus and move together as a unit by the third month, and vision becomes more acute. Special health concerns for infants include the following:

- nutritional requirements
- adequate provisions for sleep
- **attachment**
- early brain development
- safety and injury prevention
- identification of birth defects and health impairments

Maternal practices during pregnancy (such as diet, smoking, ingestion of alcohol or drugs, and infections) have a significant effect on the genetic makeup of an infant's brain (Shenassa et al., 2009; Kaiser & Allen, 2008). During the weeks and months following birth, the infant's brain undergoes rapid growth and development in response to early learning experiences. New and repetitive experiences create complex electrical connections that transform the infant's brain from an otherwise disorganized system to one capable of profound thought, emotions, and learning (Zhu et al., 2009). The majority of this transformation occurs during the first 5 years, when the brain appears to be more receptive to shaping and change. Researchers have also discovered what they believe to be certain "critical periods," or windows of opportunity, when some forms of learning and sensory development are more likely to take place (Spolidoro et al., 2009). Families and teachers can use this knowledge to provide infants and young children with environments and varied experiences that are enriching and will foster healthy brain development. For example, hanging pictures and mobiles where infants can see and reading to them often promotes early visual and cognitive development.

An infant's head appears large in proportion to the rest of the body due to rapid brain growth. **Head circumference** is measured at regular intervals to monitor brain development and to ensure that it is proceeding at a rate that is neither too fast nor too slow. Measurements should reflect a gradual increase in size; head and chest circumferences will be almost equal by age 1.

Toddlers (12–30 months) The toddler continues to make steady gains in height and weight, but at a much slower rate than during infancy. A weight increase of 6 to 7 pounds (2.7–3.2 kg) per year is considered normal and reflects a total gain of nearly four times the child's birth weight by the age of 2. The toddler grows approximately 3 to 5 inches (7.5–12.5 cm) in height per year. Body proportions change and result in a more erect and adult-like appearance.

Eruption of "baby teeth," or **deciduous teeth**, is complete by the end of the toddler period. (Deciduous teeth consist of a set of twenty temporary teeth.) Toddlers can begin learning how to brush their new teeth as an important aspect of preventive health care, although considerable adult supervision is still needed. Special attention should also be paid to providing foods that promote dental health; are colorful, appealing, and easily chewed; and include all of the essential nutrients. Foods from all food groups—fruits, vegetables, dairy, protein, whole-grains—should be part of the toddler's daily meal pattern.

---

attachment – *an emotional connection established between infants and their parents and/or primary caregivers.*

head circumference – *the distance around the head obtained by measuring over the forehead and bony protuberance on the back of the head; it is an indication of normal or abnormal growth and development of the brain and central nervous system.*

deciduous teeth – *a child's initial set of teeth; this set is temporary and gradually begins to fall out at about 5 years of age.*

Toddlers need plenty of sleep to meet their high energy demands.

High activity levels make it essential for toddlers to get at least 10 to 12 hours of uninterrupted nighttime sleep. In addition, most toddlers continue to nap 1 to 2 hours each day. Safety awareness and injury prevention continue to be major concerns that demand close adult supervision.

Preschoolers/Early School-Age (2 1/2–8 years) During the preschool and early school-age years, a child's appearance becomes more streamlined and adult-like in form. Head size remains relatively constant, while the child's trunk (body) and extremities (arms and legs) continue to grow. Gradually, the head appears to separate from the trunk as the neck lengthens. Legs grow longer and at a faster rate than the arms, adding extra inches to the child's height. The toddler's characteristic chubby body shape becomes more streamlined as muscle tone and strength increase and results in straighter posture and a flatter abdomen.

Gains in weight and height are relatively slow but steady throughout this period. By 3 years of age, children weigh approximately five times their weight at birth. An ideal weight gain for a preschool child is approximately 4 to 5 pounds (1.8–2.3 kg) per year. However, children grow more in height than in weight during this period, gaining an average of 2 to 2.5 inches (5.0–6.3 cm) per year. By the time children reach 6 years of age, they have nearly doubled their original birth length (from approximately 20 inches to 40 inches [50–100 cm]). By age 7, girls are approximately 42–46 inches (105–115 cm) tall and weigh 38–47 pounds (19.1–22.3 kg); boys are 44–47 inches (110–117.5 cm) tall and weigh 42–49 pounds (17.3–21.4 kg). This combination of growth and muscle development causes children to appear longer, thinner, and more adult-like.

Adequate nutrition continues to be a prime consideration (Insel, Turner, & Ross, 2009). High activity levels replace the rapid growth of earlier years as the primary demand for calories. A general rule for estimating a child's daily caloric needs is to begin with a base of 1,000 calories and add an additional 100 calories per birthday. (For example, a 7-year-old would need approximately 1,700 calories). However, because the preschool years are often marked by decreased appetite and inconsistent eating habits, families and teachers must continue to monitor children's food intake and encourage healthy eating habits.

Adequate sleep is also required for children's optimal growth and development. When days are long and tiring or unusually stressful, children's need for sleep may be even greater. Most preschool and school-aged children require 8 to 12 hours of uninterrupted nighttime sleep in addition to daytime rest periods, although bedtime and afternoon naps often become a source of adult-child conflict. Preschool children have a tendency to become so involved in play activities that they are reluctant to stop for sleep. Nevertheless, young children benefit from brief rest breaks during their normal daytime routine. Planned quiet times, with books, puzzles, quiet music, or a small toy, may be an adequate substitute for older children.

By the time children reach school-age, they begin to enjoy one of the healthiest periods of their lives. They generally experience fewer colds and upper respiratory infections due to improved resistance and physical maturation. Visual acuity continues to improve, gains in linear growth (height) are fairly rapid, and muscle mass increases to give children a more adult-like appearance.

Development

In the span of 1 year, remarkable changes take place in the infant's **development.** The child progresses from a stage of complete dependency on adults to one marked by the acquisition of language and the formation of rather complex thought patterns. Infants also become more social and outgoing near the end of the first year, and seemingly enjoy and imitate the adults around them (Allen & Marotz, 2010).

The toddler and preschool periods reflect a continued refinement of language, perceptual, motor, cognitive, and social achievements. Improved motor and verbal skills enable the toddler to explore, test, and interact with the environment for the purpose of determining personal identity, or autonomy.

Developmental gains enable the preschool-aged child to perform self-care and fine motor tasks with improved strength, speed, accuracy, control, and ease. The beginning of a conscience slowly emerges and is an important step in the socialization process because it allows children to exercise some control over their emotions. Friendships with peers become increasingly important as preschool children begin to expand their sphere of acquaintances beyond the scope of family members.

Preschoolers can manage most of their own self-care.

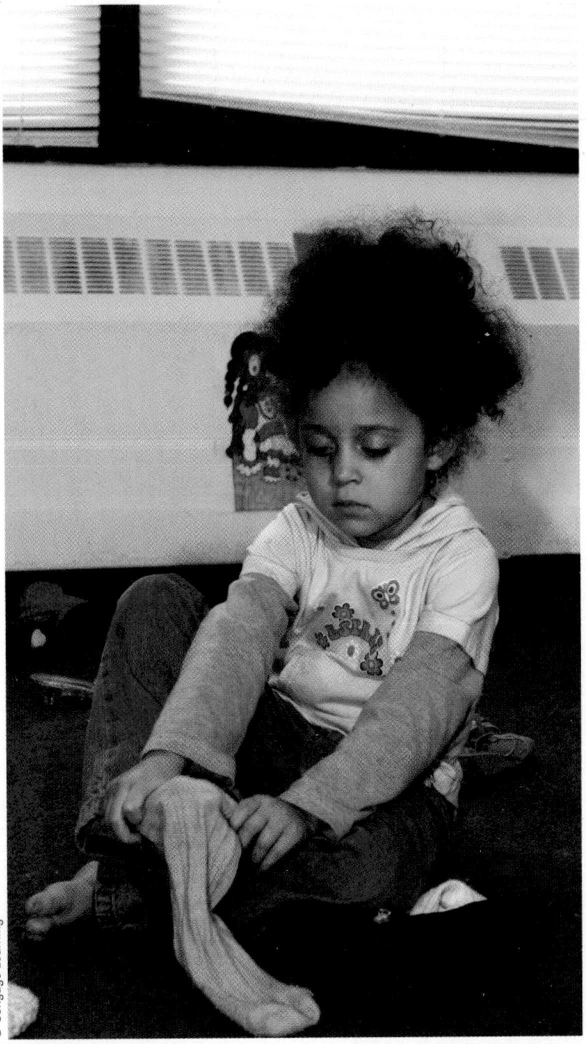

© Cengage Learning

A strong desire to achieve motivates 6-, 7-, and 8-year-olds. Participation in sports and other vigorous activities provides opportunities for children to practice and improve motor skills. Adult approval and rewards continue to serve an important role in helping children build self-confidence and self-esteem. During this stage, children also begin to establish gender identity through meaningful social interactions.

A summary of major developmental achievements is presented in Table 1–3. It should be remembered that such a list represents accomplishments that a majority of children can perform at a given age. It should also be noted that not every child achieves all of these tasks. Many factors, including nutritional adequacy, opportunities for learning, access to appropriate medical and dental care, a nurturing environment, cultural expectations and family support, exert a strong influence on children's skill acquisition.

Promoting a Healthy Lifestyle

Today, concern for children's health and welfare is a shared vision. Changes in current lifestyles, family structures, cultural diversity, trends, and expectations have shifted some responsibilities for children's health to the collaborative efforts of families, teachers, and service providers. Communities are also valued members of this partnership and must assume a proactive role in creating environments that are safe, enriching, and healthy places for children to live.

---

development – *commonly refers to the process of intellectual growth and change.*

Table 1–3 Major Developmental Achievements

Age	Achievements
2 months	• lifts head up when placed on stomach • follows moving person or object with eyes • imitates or responds to smiling person with occasional smiles • turns toward source of sound • begins to make simple sounds and noises • grasps objects with entire hand; not strong enough to hold on • enjoys being held and cuddled
4 months	• has good control of head • reaches for and grasps objects with both hands • laughs out loud; vocalizes with coos and giggles • waves arms about • holds head erect when supported in a sitting position • rolls over from side to back to stomach • recognizes familiar objects (e.g., bottle, toy)
6 months	• grasps objects with entire hand; transfers objects from one hand to the other and from hand to mouth • sits alone with minimal support • deliberately reaches for, grasps, and holds objects (e.g., rattles, bottle) • plays games and imitates (e.g., peek-a-boo) • shows signs of teeth beginning to erupt • prefers primary caregiver to strangers • babbles using different sounds • raises up and supports weight of upper body on arms
9 months	• sits alone; able to maintain balance while changing positions; picks up objects (e.g., bits of cracker, peas) with pincer grasp (first finger and thumb) • begins to crawl • attempts to say words such as "mama" and "dada" • is hesitant toward strangers • explores new objects by chewing or placing them in mouth
12 months	• pulls up to a standing position • may "walk" by holding on to objects • stacks several objects one on top of the other • responds to simple commands and own name • babbles using jargon in sentence-like form • uses hands, eyes, and mouth to investigate new objects • can hold own eating utensils (e.g., cup, spoon)
18 months	• crawls up and down stairs one at a time • walks unassisted; has difficulty avoiding obstacles in pathway • is less fearful of strangers • enjoys being read to; likes toys for pushing and pulling • has a vocabulary consisting of approximately 5–50 words, can name familiar objects • helps feed self; manages spoon and cup
2 years	• runs, walks with ease; can kick and throw a ball; jumps in place • speaks in two- to three-word sentences (e.g., "Dada", "bye-bye"); asks simple questions; knows about 200 words • displays parallel play • achieves daytime toilet training • voices displeasure

Table 1–3 Major Developmental Achievements *(continued)*

Age	Achievements
3 years	• climbs stairs using alternating feet • hops and balances on one foot • feeds self • helps dress and undress self; washes own hands and brushes teeth with help • is usually toilet trained • is curious; asks and answers questions • enjoys drawing, cutting with scissors, painting, clay, and make-believe • can throw and bounce a ball • states name; recognizes self in pictures
4 years	• dresses and undresses self; helps with bathing; manages own tooth brushing • enjoys creative activities: paints, draws with detail, models with clay, builds imaginative structures with blocks • rides a bike with confidence, turns corners, maintains balance • climbs, runs, and hops with skill and vigor • enjoys friendships and playing with small groups of children • enjoys and seeks adult approval • understands simple concepts (e.g., shortest, longest, same)
5 years	• expresses ideas and questions clearly and with fluency • has vocabulary consisting of approximately 2,500–3,000 words • substitutes verbal for physical expressions of displeasure • dresses without supervision • seeks reassurance and recognition for achievements • engages in active and energetic play, especially outdoors • throws and catches a ball with relative accuracy • cuts with scissors along a straight line; draws in detail
6 years	• plays with enthusiasm and vigor • develops increasing interest in books and reading • displays greater independence from adults; makes fewer requests for help • forms close friendships with several peers • exhibits improved motor skills; can jump rope, hop and skip, ride a bicycle • enjoys conversation • sorts objects by color and shape
7 and 8 years	• enjoys friends; seeks their approval • shows increased curiosity and interest in exploration • develops greater clarity of gender identity • is motivated by a sense of achievement • begins to reveal a moral consciousness
9–12 years	• uses logic to reason and problem-solve • energetic; enjoys team activities, as well as individual projects • likes school and academic challenge, especially math • learning social customs and moral values • is able to think in abstract terms • enjoys eating any time of the day

Adapted from Allen, K. E., & Marotz, L. R. (2010). *Developmental Profiles* (6th ed.). Belmont, CA: Wadsworth Cengage Learning.

How can families and teachers determine whether or not children are healthy? What qualities or indicators are commonly associated with being a healthy or a **well child**? Growth and developmental norms always serve as a starting point. Again, it must be remembered that norms simply represent an average, not exact, age when most children are likely to achieve a given skill. Healthy children are more likely to exhibit characteristic behaviors and developmental skills appropriate for their age. They tend to be well-nourished, have energy to play, experience continued growth, and have fewer illnesses. Developmental norms are also useful for anticipating and addressing children's special health needs, including injury prevention, posture and physical activity, oral health, and mental health.

Injury Prevention

Unintentional injuries, especially those involving motor vehicles, pose the greatest threat to the lives of young children (Borse et al., 2009; Rowe & Maughan, 2009). They are responsible for more than one-half of all deaths among children under 14 years of age in the United States. Each year an additional one million children sustain injuries that require medical attention, and many are left with permanent disabilities (Berry & Schwebel, 2009).

Close supervision of children's activities is important for their safety.

© Cengage Learning

An understanding of normal growth and development is also useful when planning for children's safety. Many characteristics that make children delightful to work with are the same qualities that make them prone to injury. Children's skills are seldom as well developed as their determination, and in their zealous approach to life, they often fail to recognize inherent dangers. Their inability to judge time, distance, and speed accurately contributes to many injuries, especially those resulting from falls, as a pedestrian, or while riding on a bike (Hotz et al., 2009). Limited problem-solving abilities make it difficult for children to anticipate the consequences of their actions. This becomes an even greater challenge when infants or children with developmental disabilities are present. Adults have an obligation to provide continuous supervision and to maintain safe environments for all children at all times. Safety considerations and protective measures will be discussed in greater detail in Chapter 7.

Posture and Physical Activity

Correct posture, balance, and proper body alignment are necessary for many physical activities that children engage in, such as walking, jumping, running, skipping, standing, and sitting. Teaching and modeling appropriate body mechanics can help children avoid problems related to poor posture that may develop later in life. Early recognition and treatment of ear infections is also important to consider because they can affect children's balance and coordination.

well child – *a child who enjoys a positive state of physical, mental, social, and emotional health.*

Orthopedic problems (those relating to skeletal and muscular systems) are not common among young children. However, there are several conditions that warrant early diagnosis and treatment:

- birth injuries, such as hip dislocation, fractured collarbone
- abnormal or unusual walking patterns, such as limping or walking pigeon-toed
- bowed legs
- knock-knees
- flat feet
- unusual curvature of the spine
- unequal length of extremities (arms and legs)

Some irregularities of posture disappear spontaneously as young children mature. For example, it is not uncommon for infants and toddlers to have bowed legs or to walk slightly pigeon-toed. By age 3 or 4, these problems should correct themselves. However, if they persist beyond the age of 4, children should be evaluated by a health professional to prevent permanent deformities.

Children's posture is an excellent topic for classroom discussions, demonstrations, rhythm and movement activities, games, and art projects (Obeng, 2010). Information about appropriate body mechanics and movement can also be shared with families in newsletters or posted on bulletin boards or a website so that correct practices can be reinforced at home. Children can begin to learn basic body mechanics, including:

- Sitting squarely in a chair, resting the back firmly against the chair back and with both feet flat on the floor.
- Sitting on the floor with legs crossed (in front) or with both legs extended straight ahead. Children should be discouraged from kneeling or sitting in a "W" position because this can place additional stress on developing hip joints and interfere with proper development overtime. Have children sit in a chair with feet planted firmly on the ground or provide them with a small stool that can be straddled (one leg on each side); this eliminates adult nagging and forces children to sit in a correct position. Alternative seating supports may be required for children who have muscular or neurological disabilities.
- Standing with the shoulders square, the chin up, and the chest out. Distribute body weight evenly over both feet to avoid placing added stress on one or the other hip joints.
- Lifting and carrying heavy objects using the stronger muscles of the arms and legs rather than weaker back muscles. Standing close to an object that is to be lifted with feet spread slightly apart to provide a wider support base. Stooping down to lift (with your legs); bending over at the waist when lifting places strain on back muscles and increases the risk of injury.

Children should be discouraged from sitting in the "W" position.

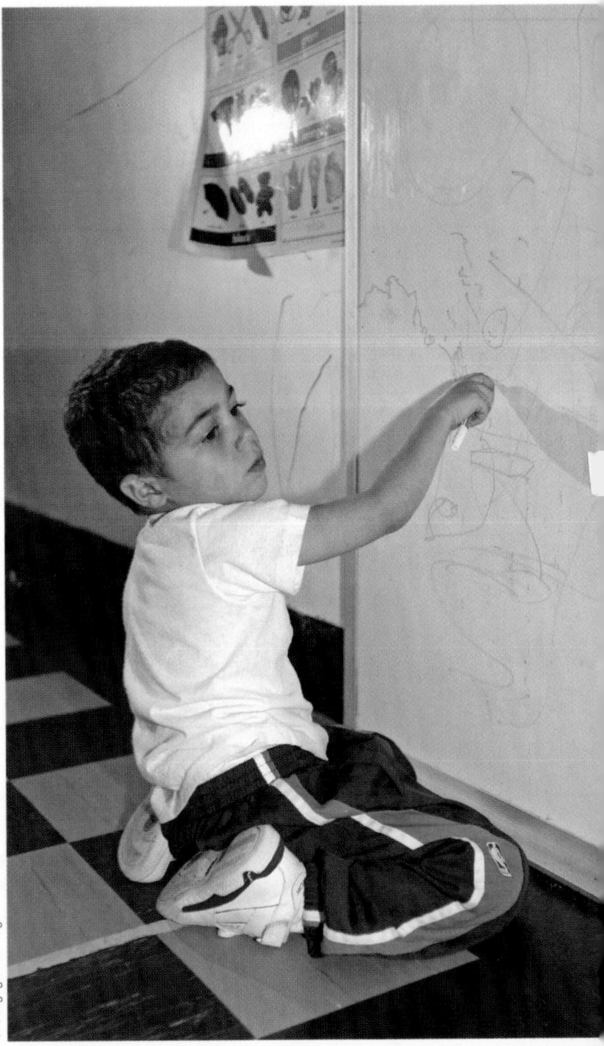

Correct posture and body mechanics are also important skills for parents and teachers to practice (Table 1–4). Because they perform many bending and lifting activities throughout the day, using proper technique can reduce

Table 1–4 Proper Body Mechanics for Adults

- Use correct technique when lifting children; flex the knees and lift using leg muscles; avoid lifting with back muscles, which are weaker.
- Adjust the height of children's cribs and changing tables to avoid bending over.
- Provide children with step stools so they can reach water fountains and faucets without having to be lifted.
- Bend down by flexing the knees rather than bending over at the waist; this reduces strain on weaker back muscles and decreases the risk of possible injury.
- Sit in adult-sized furniture with feet resting comfortably on the floor to lessen strain on the back and knees.
- Transport children in strollers or wagons rather than carrying them.
- Exercise regularly to improve muscle strength, especially back muscles, and to relieve mental stress.
- Lift objects by keeping arms close to the body versus extended; this also reduces potential for back strain.

chronic fatigue and work-related injury. Exercising regularly also improves muscle strength and makes demanding physical tasks easier to complete.

Vigorous physical activity should be an essential part of every child's day. It has a positive effect on children's growth, mental health, weight management, and behavior problems by relieving excess energy, stress, and boredom (Vadiveloo, Zhu, & Quatromoni, 2009). Introducing young children to a variety of sports, games, and other forms of physical activity also provides them with early opportunities to discover those they enjoy and are likely to continue. Teachers should review classroom schedules and look for ways to incorporate more physical activity into daily routines. Current guidelines recommend that children get a minimum of 60 minutes of moderate aerobic activity each day (CDC, 2008). Families and teachers must serve as positive role models for children by also engaging in regular physical activity (Pica, 2009).

Oral Health

Children's oral health continues to be a major goal in the Healthy People 2020 objectives. Dental problems can affect children's general health, development, appearance, and self-esteem in addition to causing considerable pain and expense. Yet, there are many children who seldom visit a dentist because their families cannot afford dental insurance or costly preventive care. Children from low-income and minority groups are twice as likely to experience tooth decay and a lack of dental treatment (Casamassimo et al., 2009). Neglected dental care can result in painful cavities and infected teeth, affect children's behavior, and interfere with concentration and academic performance. There are many adults who erroneously believe that "baby teeth," or deciduous teeth, do not require treatment because they will eventually fall out (Levine, 2008). This belief is unfortunate because temporary teeth are necessary for:

- chewing
- the spacing of permanent teeth
- influencing the shape of the jaw bone
- the development of speech

Advancements in pediatric dentistry and educational efforts have resulted in significant improvements in children's dental care. The importance of consuming a nutritious diet during pregnancy, scheduling regular dental visits, the use of sealants, and the addition of fluoride to water supplies, toothpastes, and direct applications have collectively reduced the incidence of children's dental caries and gum disease (Kagihara, Niederhauser, & Stark, 2009). Proper dental care should be practiced from birth, with special attention given to:

- diet
- hygienic practices—e.g., tooth brushing, flossing

- dental examinations scheduled at recommended intervals
- prompt treatment of dental problems

Diet has an unquestionable effect on children's dental health (Nunn et al., 2009). Proper tooth formation depends on an adequate intake of protein and minerals, particularly calcium and fluoride. One of the most devastating influences on diet, however, is the excessive consumption of highly refined and sticky carbohydrates (Sheller et al., 2009). These are commonly found in cakes, cookies, candies, gum, soft drinks, sweetened cereals, and dried fruits (for example, raisins, dates, and prunes). Families and teachers can encourage children to adopt healthy dietary habits by limiting the frequency and amounts of sweets they are served and by substituting nutritious foods. Because many children's medications and chewable vitamins are sweetened with sugars, tooth brushing should always be encouraged following their ingestion.

Oral hygiene practices implemented early in children's lives promote healthy tooth development. Food particles can be removed from an infant's gums and teeth by wiping them with a small, wet washcloth. A small, soft brush and water can be used for cleaning an older infant's teeth.

Most toddlers can begin to brush their own teeth at around 15 months of age. Tooth brushing can be accomplished by using a soft brush and water to clean the teeth. However, the use of toothpaste is not recommended before age 2; most toddlers do not like its taste and are unable to spit it out after brushing. When a child is first learning tooth brushing skills, an adult should brush over the teeth after at least one of the brushings each day to be sure all areas are clean. Teeth can also be kept clean between brushings by rinsing with water after meals and eating raw foods such as apples, pears, and celery, which

Children's oral health is a major goal of Healthy People 2020.

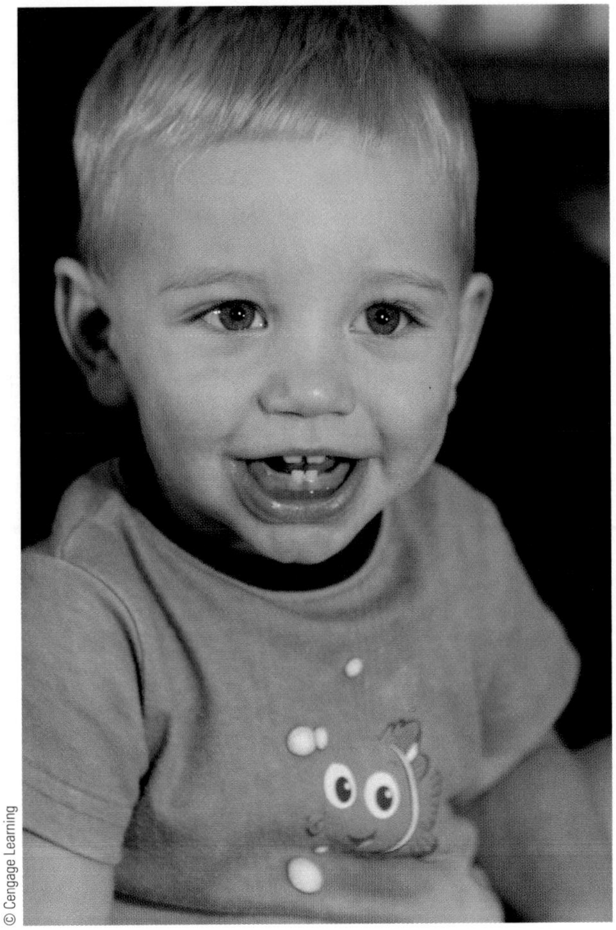

Reflective Thoughts

Baby bottle tooth decay (BBTD) is a preventable condition that occurs when a baby's teeth are exposed to sugary substances, including juices, formula, and breast milk, for prolonged periods. Practices such as putting an infant to bed with a bottle or allowing them to nurse for extended periods at night, and giving a toddler a bottle or sippy cup with fruit juice to carry around can prove harmful to children's teeth (Freeman & Stevens, 2008). Because saliva flow is decreased during sleep, it is less effective in keeping teeth clean.

- What cautions would you offer to new parents who want to prevent their infants from developing BBTD?
- What practices can a mother who wants to feed her infant on demand use to avoid BBTD?
- What practices can parents use to promote older children's oral health?

provide a natural cleansing action. Several additional steps teachers and families can take to increase children's interest in brushing their teeth include:

- purchasing a small, soft toothbrush in the child's favorite color
- storing the toothbrush where the child can reach it
- providing a footstool or chair so the child can reach the sink

⚠ **Caution: Supervise the child closely to prevent slipping or falling.**

- demonstrating the tooth brushing procedure so the child knows what to expect
- helping the child to brush at least twice daily—once in the morning and again before going to bed
- constructing a simple chart where children can place a check each time they brush their teeth; reinforcing children's efforts encourages sound tooth brushing habits

Preschool children are generally able to brush their teeth with minimal supervision, but it may still be advisable for an adult to provide a quick follow up brushing. Although children's technique may not always be perfect, they are beginning to establish a lifelong tooth brushing habit. Proper brushing technique and fluoride-based toothpastes (pea-size application) have proven to be effective in reducing dental cavities. However, children must be supervised closely so they do not swallow the toothpaste. Too much fluoride can result in dental **fluorosis**, which may cause white or brown spots to form on developing teeth (Iida & Kumar, 2009).

The question of whether young children should learn to floss their teeth is best answered by the child's dentist. Although the practice is regarded as beneficial, much depends on the child's maturity and fine motor skills. Flossing is usually recommended once the permanent teeth begin to erupt and spaces between teeth disappear. Parents should assist children who are too young to manage this procedure by themselves. Routine dental checkups are an important component of preventive health care, but they are not a substitute for daily oral hygiene practices and a healthful diet. Children's first visit to the dentist should be scheduled at around 12 to 15 months of age. Initial visits should be pleasant experiences that acquaint children with the dentist, routine examinations, and cleanings without having to undergo painful dental work. Children are more likely to maintain a healthy attitude toward dental care and to approach visits with less fear and anxiety when early experiences are positive.

During routine examinations, dentists look for signs of dental problems and also review the child's tooth brushing technique, diet, and personal habits, such as thumb sucking or grinding that may affect the teeth. Cleaning and a fluoride varnish application are generally included in children's preventive examinations, which are recommended every 6 to 12 months. The addition of fluoride to municipal water supplies has also contributed to a significant decrease in children's tooth decay (Yeung, 2008). Sealants (a plastic-like material applied over the grooves in permanent molars) are also used to prevent future decay.

Reflective Thoughts

Making friends is an important part of growing up. Gaining acceptance and respect from peers helps shape one's sense of self-esteem. However, friendships are not always easy for children to establish. What social skills are required for making friends? What behaviors are likely to alienate friends? Should families get involved in their children's friendships? As a parent, what would you do if your child became friends with someone you didn't care for?

---

fluorosis – *white or brown spots that form on children's teeth due to excessive fluoride intake.*

Self-Esteem and Social-Emotional Competence

The wellness model recognizes a close relationship between children's emotional and physical well-being (Pachter & Coll, 2009; Rasmussen, Scheier, & Greenhouse, 2009). This association is receiving increased attention as the incidence of behavior problems, school dropout rates, substance abuse, violence, gang membership, depression, and child suicide continues to escalate. At present, approximately one in five children in the United States experience mental health problems, and one in ten have disorders that seriously interfere with learning (U.S. DHHS, 2009b). Children who live in dysfunctional or economically challenged families or who have disabilities are at highest risk for developing mental health problems (Copeland et al., 2009).

How children view themselves and the ways in which they believe others perceive them form the basis of **self-concept.** Young children typically define themselves strictly in terms of physical qualities, such as having brown hair, blue eyes, or being able to run fast. However, children's concept of who they are and how they fit in gradually broadens with experience. By 5 or 6 years of age, children's self-characterization is no longer limited to physical features but begins to include comparisons with peers—being able to run faster than Tyshan, build higher towers than Mei, or draw flowers better than Abetzi. Nine- and 10-year-olds are becoming more analytical and reflect a higher order of self-evaluation: "I like to play baseball, but can't field or hit the ball as well as Tori so they probably won't want me on their team." Children's self-image is formed and continuously redefined by the ways in which they are talked to and treated. In turn, these collective experiences influence children's sense of worth or **self-esteem** and form the basis of self-concept.

Teachers have many opportunities to promote children's mental health by teaching them important social skills.

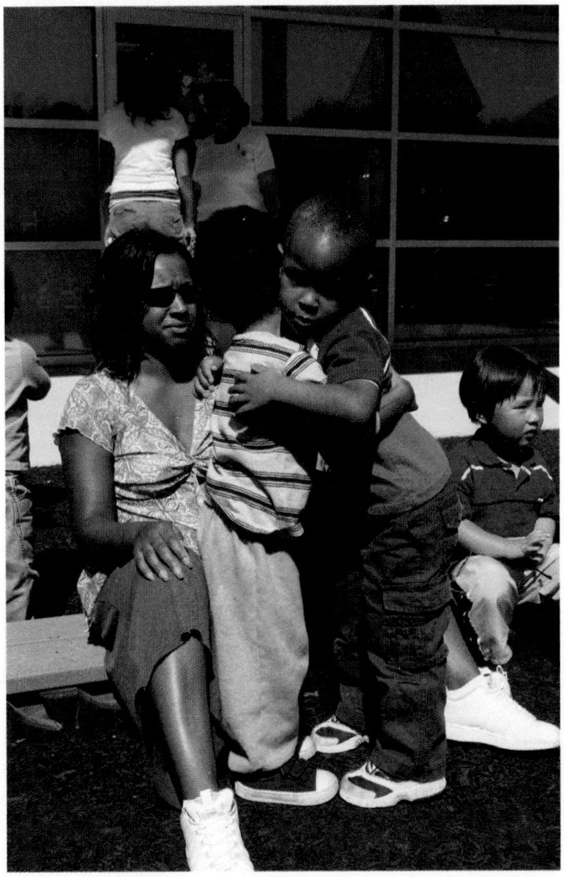

Promoting Children's Self-Esteem Families and teachers play a major role in shaping children's self-esteem (Erwin et al., 2009; Ferkany, 2008; Szente, 2007). They improve children's chances for achieving success by acknowledging and building on their developmental strengths. When adults set realistic goals and expectations for children, they are more likely to experience success and take pride in their accomplishments. Even when children are unsuccessful, their efforts should be acknowledged. Failures and mistakes must be accepted as part of the learning process and should be viewed as occasions for offering guidance and positive support. In doing so, children begin to learn important lifelong lessons about initiative, risk-taking, problem-solving, and handling adversity. However, caution must be exercised never to judge children solely on their accomplishments (or failures) or to make comparisons with other children, but to recognize each child as a unique and valued individual.

---

self-concept – *a person's concept of who they are and how they fit in.*
self-esteem – *an individual's sense of value or confidence in himself or herself.*

Teachers also occupy a strategic position for reinforcing children's development of social-emotional competence. They are able to create opportunities for children to acquire and practice effective communication, behavior management, and decision-making skills in a supportive environment (Caldarella et al., 2009; Petty, 2009). Teachers also foster children's social-emotional competence by creating respectful classrooms that convey positive attitudes, address children's individual needs, provide constructive feedback, and are conducive to learning. In addition, they play an integral role in:

- practicing sound mental health principles — by being responsive and supportive.
- preventing emotional problems — teaching children effective social, communication, anger management, and problem-solving skills.
- identifying and referring children who may exhibit signs of emotional problems, such as excessive or uncontrollable frustration, aggressive behavior, or difficulty making and keeping friends.
- working collaboratively with families to find appropriate community resources (Upshur, Wenz-Gross, & Reed, 2009).

When children develop positive self-esteem and have confidence in their own abilities, they are more likely to experience a trajectory of personal and academic success.

Adults as Role Models Adults must never overlook their importance as role models for young children. Their personal behaviors and response styles exert a powerful and direct influence on children's social-emotional development.

Teachers must carefully examine their own emotional state if they are to be successful in helping children achieve positive self-esteem. They, too, must have a strong sense of self-worth and confidence in what they are doing. They should be aware of personal biases and prejudices, be able to accept constructive criticism, and recognize their strengths and limitations. They must have effective communication skills and be able to work collaboratively with families of diverse backgrounds, community service providers, health care professionals, and other members of the child's educational team.

If teachers are to serve as positive role models, they must be able to exercise the same control over their emotions that they expect of children. Personal problems and stressors must remain at home so that full attention can be focused on the children. Teachers must respect children as individuals—who they are, and not what they are able or not able to do—because every child has qualities that are endearing and worthy of recognition. Teachers must also be impartial in their treatment of children; favoritism cannot be tolerated.

Working with young children can be rewarding, but it can also be stressful and demanding in terms of the patience, energy, and stamina required. Noise, children's continuous requests, long hours, staff shortages, mediocre wages, and occasional conflicts with families or co-workers are everyday challenges. Physical demands and unresolved stress can gradually take their toll on teachers' health, commitment, and daily performance. Eventually, this can lead to job burnout and negative interactions with colleagues and children (Huang & Waxman, 2009). For these reasons, teachers should make an effort to identify sources of stress in their jobs and take steps to address, reduce, or eliminate them to the extent possible (Marotz & Lawson, 2007). (See Table 1–5.)

Emotional Climate The emotional climate of a classroom—the positive or negative feelings one senses—has a significant impact on children's social-emotional development (Maxwell & Chmielewski, 2008; Haas-Foletta & Ottolini-Geno, 2006). Consider the following situations and decide which classroom you would find most inviting:

> Kate enters the classroom excited and eager to tell her teacher about the tooth she lost last night and the quarter she found under her pillow from the "tooth fairy." Without any greeting, the teacher hurries to check Kate in and informs her that she is too busy to talk right now, "but maybe later." When they are finished, the teacher instructs Kate to find something to do without getting into trouble. Kate quietly walks away to her cubbie.

Table 1–5 Strategies for Managing Teacher Stress

- Seek out training opportunities where you can learn new skills and improve your work effectiveness.
- Learn and practice time management techniques.
- Develop program policies and procedures that improve efficiency and reduce sources of tension and conflict.
- Join professional organizations; expand your contacts with other child care professionals, acquire new ideas, advocate for young children.
- Take care of your personal health—get plenty of sleep, eat a nutritious diet, and participate in some form of physical exercise several times each week.
- Develop new interests, hobbies, and other outlets for releasing tension.
- Practice progressive relaxation techniques. Periodically, concentrate on making yourself relax.
- Plan time for yourself each day—read a good book, watch a movie or favorite TV program, go for a long walk, paint, go shopping, play golf, or participate in some activity that you enjoy.

> Ted arrives and seems reluctant to leave his mother for some reason this morning. The home provider immediately senses his distress and walks over to greet Ted and his mother. "Ted, I am so glad that you came today. We're going to learn about farm animals and build a farm with the wooden blocks. I know that blocks are one of your favorite activities. Perhaps you'd like to build something small for your mother before it's time for her to go home." Ted eagerly builds a barn with several "animals" in the yard around it and proudly looks to his mother for approval. When Ted's mother is ready to leave, he waves good-bye.

Clearly, the teacher's actions in each example created a classroom atmosphere that had a different effect on each child's behavior. Children are generally more receptive and responsive to teachers who are warm, nurturing, and sensitive to their needs. Exposure to negative adult responses, such as ridicule, sarcasm, or threats is harmful to children's emotional development and simply teaches inappropriate behaviors. However, an emotional climate that encourages and supports mutual cooperation, respect, trust, acceptance, and independence will encourage children to gain positive social-emotional competence.

A teacher's communication style and understanding of cultural differences also affects the emotional climate of a classroom. Treating all children as if they were the same is insensitive and can encourage failure, especially if a teacher's expectations are inconsistent or incompatible with the child's cultural background. For example, knowing that children in some Hispanic cultures are taught primarily through non-verbal instruction (modeling) may explain why a child who is only given verbal directives may not respond to this approach (Hardin et al., 2009). Some children are reluctant to participate in group activities or to answer a teacher's question because this is counter to the way they have been raised. Unless the teacher understands these cultural differences, such behaviors could easily be misinterpreted as defiance or inattention. When teachers make an effort to learn about individual children and their families they are able to create a climate that supports learning and healthy social-emotional development.

The way in which the curriculum is planned and implemented also contributes to the emotional climate. Children's chances for achieving success are improved when learning activities are developmentally appropriate and matched to children's individual needs and interests (Hoogeveen, van Hell, & Verhoeven, 2009).

Stress Prolonged or intense stress in children's lives will sooner or later affect their emotional and physical well-being. Stressful situations, such as abusive treatment, poverty, unrealistic adult demands, chronic illness, unsafe neighborhoods, being left alone for long periods, or natural disasters (floods, fires, earthquakes, tornadoes), can have a serious impact on children's emotional state (Fairbank & Fairbank, 2009). Poverty, food insecurity, maternal depression, and parental substance abuse are also correlated with an increase in children's mental health

The classroom atmosphere has a direct effect on children's behavior and development.

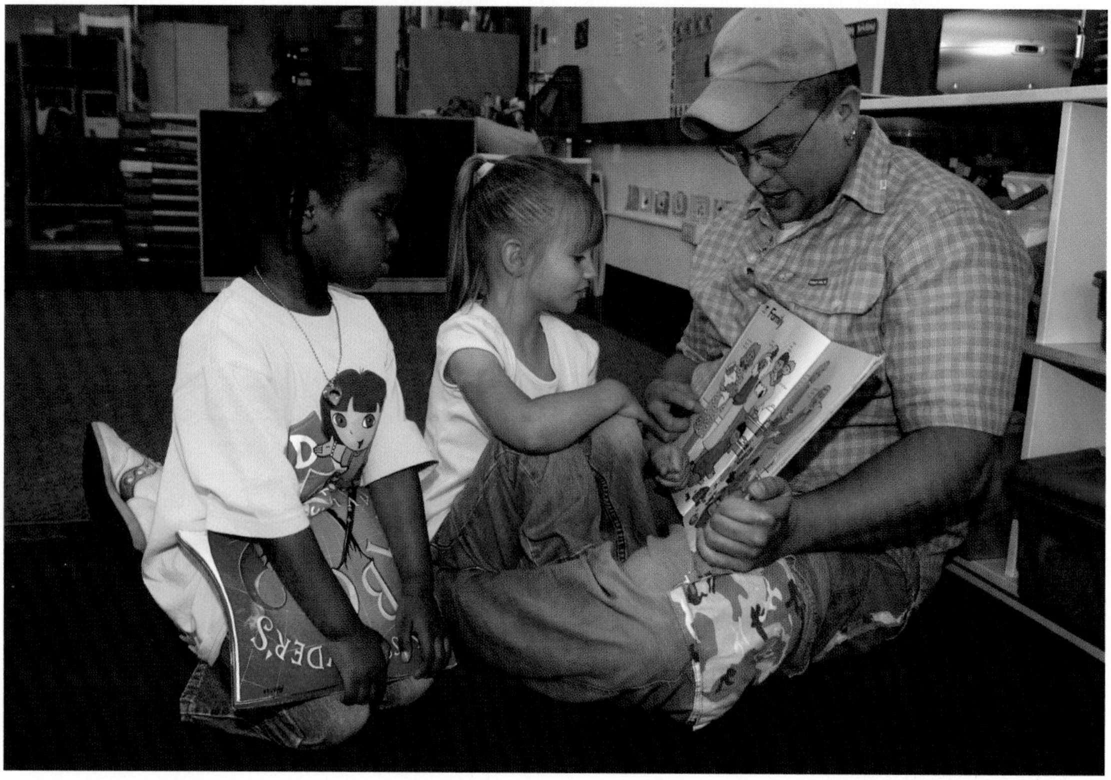

problems (Evans & Schamburg, 2009). Some children experience undue stress and anxiety in response to everyday events such as:

- separation from families
- new experiences—for example, moving, enrollment in a new early childhood program, mother going to work, birth of a sibling, having a new teacher, being left with a sitter
- chronic illness and hospitalization
- divorce of parents
- death of a pet, family member, or close friend
- conflict of ideas; confrontations with family, friends, or teachers
- overstimulation due to hectic schedules, participation in numerous extracurricular activities
- learning problems

Immature coping mechanisms, personal experiences, and temperament influence a child's response to stress and their ability to manage it in a healthy manner (Berk, 2009). Sudden behavior changes are often an early indication that a child is experiencing significant tension or inner turmoil. Signs may range from less serious behaviors—nail biting, hair twisting, excessive fear, prolonged sadness, anxiety—to those that are of significant concern—repeated aggressiveness, destructiveness, withdrawal, depression, nightmares, psychosomatic illnesses, or poor performance in school.

Teachers can help children who are experiencing acute or chronic stress by showing additional patience, understanding, and support. Children also find comfort in knowing they are safe and secure and that they can count on teachers and parents to be accepting even at times when their emotional control may fail. Additional suggestions for helping children to cope are outlined in Table 1–6.

Table 1–6 Stress Management for Children

1. Encourage children to talk about what is causing them to feel tense or upset.
2. Empower children by helping them to identify and express feelings appropriately.
3. Nurture positive thinking and an "I know I can do this" attitude.
4. Prepare children for stressful events (e.g., doctor's visit, moving, flying for the first time, attending a new school) by role-playing or rehearsing what to expect. Practice "what if's": "What should you do if you get lost?", "What can you do if you're afraid?"
5. Maintain predictable schedules, including mealtimes and bedtimes as much as possible.
6. Make sure children are getting a nutritious diet and brief periods of vigorous physical activity (an effective stress reliever).
7. Schedule unstructured play time when children are free to do what they want.

Childhood Depression Some children are unsuccessful or unable to cope with chronic stress and may develop a sense of extreme and persistent sadness and hopelessness that begins to affect the way they think, feel, and act. These may be early signs of childhood depression and can include:

- apathy or disinterest in activities or friends
- loss of appetite
- difficulty sleeping
- complaints of physical discomforts, such as headaches, stomachaches, vomiting, diarrhea, ulcers, repetitive tics (twitches), or difficulty breathing (Dufton, Dunn, & Compas, 2009).
- lack of energy or enthusiasm
- indecision
- poor self-esteem
- uncontrollable anger

Children who have learning and behavior disorders or a family history of mental health conditions are at an increased risk for depression (Boulet, Boyle, & Schieve, 2009). Even children as young as 3 may begin showing early signs of depression particularly when their mothers are also suffering from this condition (Leckman-Westin, Cohen, & Stueve, 2009; Luby et al., 2009).

The onset of childhood depression may occur abruptly following a traumatic event, such as parental divorce, death of a close family member or friend, abusive treatment, or chronic illness. However, it can also develop slowly over time, making the early signs more difficult to notice. In either case, teachers must be knowledgeable about the behaviors commonly associated with childhood depression so children can be referred for professional care. Depression requires early identification and treatment to avoid serious and debilitating effects on children's social, emotional, and cognitive development and to prevent long-term mental health disorders (Lack & Green, 2009; Luby, 2009).

Childhood Fears Most childhood fears and nightmares are a normal part of the developmental process and are eventually outgrown as children mature. Basic fears are relatively consistent across generations, although they vary somewhat from one developmental stage to the next (Burnham, 2009). For example, a 3-month-old infant is seldom fearful of anything, whereas a 3-year-old may awake during the night because of "monsters under the bed." Fears that reflect real-life events, such as fire, kidnapping, thunderstorms, or homelessness, tend to be experienced by 5- and 6-year-olds, whereas 10- and 11-year-olds are more likely to express fears related to appearance and social rejection (Allen & Marotz, 2010). Some fears are unique to an individual child and stem from personal experiences, such as witnessing a shooting, car accident, abusive discipline, or being frightened by a vicious dog.

Fears and nightmares are often accentuated during the preschool years, a time when children have a heightened imagination and are attempting to make sense of their world. Children's literal interpretation of the things they see and hear can easily lead to misunderstanding and fear. For example, children often believe that an adult who says, "I'm going to give you away if you misbehave one more time" will actually do so.

It is important for adults to acknowledge children's fears and understand they are real to the child. Children need consistent adult reassurance and trust to overcome their fears, even though it may be difficult to remain patient and supportive when a child repeatedly awakens at 2 AM every morning. Children may also find comfort in talking about the things that frighten them or rehearsing what they might do, for example, if they were to become lost at the supermarket or if it began to thunder.

Poverty and Homelessness Nearly 41 percent of U.S. children younger than age 6 currently live in families that fall below the national poverty level (National Center for Children in Poverty, 2009). The adults in many of these families are either unemployed or working in low-wage jobs, recent immigrants, classified as minorities (especially Hispanic, Native American, and African American), or are a single parent — usually a mother. Living in a single- versus a two-parent family places children at the highest economic risk for poverty. Children residing in rural areas also experience significant poverty, but they comprise a group that is often overlooked. Economic problems and high unemployment have recently forced many rural families into bankruptcy (Huddleston-Casas, Charnigo, & Simmons, 2009). Collectively, these developments have caused families with young children to become the new majority of today's homeless population.

Poverty places additional burdens on the already challenging demands of parenting. Struggles to provide children with basic food, clothing, shelter, health care, and attention are often compromised by increased stress, fear, and conflict. Ultimately, these pressures can contribute to parental tension, domestic violence, abusive treatment of children, and an inability to provide the nurturing and support that children require.

The impact of poverty on children's growth and development has both immediate and long-term consequences. Children born into poverty experience a higher rate of birth defects, early death, and chronic illnesses, such as anemia, asthma, and lead poisoning (Allen & Marotz, 2010). In addition, their dietary quality, access to health and dental care, and mental health status is often compromised (Melchior et al., 2009). Children living in poverty are also more likely to experience abuse, learning and behavior problems, teen pregnancy, substance abuse, higher dropout rates, and reduced earning potential as adults. Ultimately, the cumulative effects of poverty can threaten children's chances of growing up to become healthy, educated, and productive adults (Mello, 2009).

Violence Children today live in a world where daily exposure to violence is not uncommon. The incidence of crime, substance abuse, gang activity, and access to guns is often greater in neighborhoods where poverty exists and can result in unhealthy urban environments where children's personal safety is at risk. Children living in these settings are also more likely to become victims of child abuse or to witness domestic violence. Their families exhibit a higher rate of dysfunctional parenting skills, are often less responsive and nurturing, and use discipline that is either lacking, inconsistent, or punitive and harsh (Owen et al., 2009). Parents are also less likely to be supportive of children's education or to assume an active role in school activities. As a result, many children who grow up in poverty are at greater risk of experiencing learning problems, becoming violent adults, and/or developing serious mental health disorders (Whiting et al., 2009). Teachers who understand this potential can be instrumental in helping children overcome adversity by reaching out and strengthening their resiliency skills as well as assisting families in locating supportive community resources. (See Table 1–7.)

Children growing up in violent and disadvantaged environments not only face challenges at home, but also at school. Younger children are more likely to attend child care programs that are of

Issues To Consider Children and Bullying

Most school-age children report that they have been subjected to occasional verbal or physical bullying from their peers (Bowes et al., 2009). Bullying differs from children's occasional name-calling and social rejection in that it is usually intentional, repetitive, and ongoing. Girls tend to rely on verbal taunting directed toward another girl whereas boys are more likely to engage in physical intimidation of other males. Contrary to what has long been assumed about children who bully others, researchers have identified two types of bullies: those who are self-assured, impulsive, lacking empathy, angry, and controlling; and those who are passive and willing to join in once another child initiates the bullying (Larsson, Viding, & Plomin, 2008). Children who bully often come from homes where poverty, domestic violence, inconsistent supervision, and lack of social support or parental concern are common. As a result, children may have poor interpersonal skills, impulse control, and problem-solving abilities.

Victims of bullying behavior are sometimes singled out because they are perceived to be socially withdrawn or loners, passive and lacking in self-confidence, having a disability or special needs, not likely to stand up for themselves, and easily hurt (emotionally). In addition, they are more often from economically disadvantaged families, smaller in physical size than their peers, and seen as having fewer friends (Bowes et al., 2009). It is becoming increasingly apparent that bullying behaviors have immediate and long-term negative consequences on children's personal, emotional, and academic development. Early signs that a child is being subjected to bullying may include frequent complaints of health problems, reluctance to attend school, and declining academic performance.

Prevention programs have been implemented in many schools to reduce bullying behavior and to create environments where children feel safe. Educational efforts address both the victims and perpetrators and are designed to teach mutual respect, reinforce effective social and communication skills, reduce harassment, and improve children's self-esteem. Children who are being bullied learn how to respond in these situations by avoiding bullies, walking away, practicing conflict resolution, and always informing an adult.

- What can families do to decrease the likelihood that their child will engage in bullying behavior?
- What factors might contribute to children's inability to control their anger and/or impulsive behaviors?
- How can families help children who are being bullied?
- Should children who harass other children be expelled from school?
- What is cyber bullying and are the consequences for victims any different than in face-to-face encounters?

poorer quality than their counterparts in higher income areas (Burchinal et al., 2009). In addition, children of all ages may have fewer opportunities to engage in learning and enrichment experiences at home. Researchers have observed that children from disadvantaged households typically have delayed language development and literacy skills due to less parent-child interaction and a lack of available reading materials (Pungello et al., 2009). This combination sets many children up for early school failure.

Children are also exposed to additional sources of extreme violence and death in movies, video games, cartoons, on television, and the Internet. Researchers have noted an increase in children's aggressive behaviors as the result of witnessing media violence, but no direct link has been established with involvement in adult criminal activity (Barlett & Rodeheffer, 2009; Strassburger, 2009).

Table 1–7 Strategies for Increasing Children's Resilient Behaviors

- Be a positive role model for children; demonstrate how you expect them to behave.
- Accept children unconditionally; avoid being judgmental.
- Help children develop and use effective communication skills.
- Listen carefully to children to show that you value their thoughts and ideas.
- Use discipline that is developmentally appropriate and based on natural or logical consequences.
- Use and enforce discipline consistently.
- Help children understand and express their feelings; encourage them to have empathy for others.
- Avoid harsh physical punishment and angry outbursts.
- Help children establish realistic goals, set high expectations for themselves, and have a positive outlook.
- Promote problem-solving skills; help children make informed decisions.
- Reinforce children's efforts with praise and encouragement.
- Give children responsibility; assign household tasks and classroom duties.
- Involve children in activities outside of their home.
- Encourage children to believe in themselves, to feel confident rather than seeing themselves as failures or victims.

However, repeated exposure to media violence and death has been shown to desensitize children to their dysfunctional significance (Fanti et al., 2009; Huesmann, 2007). Families are encouraged to limit children's media viewing, closely monitor what they are watching, and help children to understand that media is a form of creative entertainment and not reality.

Resilient Children

Children face many challenges while growing up in this complex world. Stress, violence, uncertainty, and negative encounters are everywhere. What makes some children more vulnerable to the negative effects of stress and aversive treatment or more likely to develop inappropriate behaviors? Many factors, including genetic predisposition, malnutrition, prenatal exposure to drugs or alcohol, poor attachment to primary caregivers, physical and/or learning disabilities, and/or an irritable personality have been suggested as possible explanations. Researchers have also looked at home environments and parenting styles that may make it difficult for some children to achieve normal developmental tasks and positive self-esteem (Guajardo, Snyder, & Petersen, 2009).

Why are other children better able to overcome the negative effects of an impoverished, traumatic, violent, or stressful childhood? This question continues to be a focus of study as researchers attempt to learn what conditions or qualities enable some children to be more **resilient** in the face of adversity. Although much remains to be understood, several important protective factors have been identified. These include having certain personal characteristics (such as above-average intelligence, positive self-esteem, and effective social and problem-solving skills), having a strong and dependable relationship with a parent or parent substitute, and having a social support network outside of one's immediate family (such as a church group, local recreation center, organized sports, Boys and Girls clubs, or youth groups).

Competent parenting is, beyond a doubt, one of the most important factors necessary for helping children manage adversity and avoid its potentially damaging consequences. Children who grow up in an environment where families are caring and emotionally responsive, provide meaningful supervision and discipline that is consistent and developmentally appropriate, offer encouragement and praise, and help their children learn to solve problems in a peaceful way are more

---

resilient – *the ability to withstand or resist difficulty.*

likely to demonstrate resilient behavior (Campbell-Sills, Forde & Stein, 2009; Ungar, 2007). Teachers, likewise, can promote resiliency by establishing classrooms where children feel accepted, respected, and supported in their efforts.

Management Strategies Understandably, all children undergo occasional periods of emotional instability or undesirable behavior. Short-term or one-time occurrences are usually not cause for concern. However, when a child consistently demonstrates abnormal or antisocial behaviors, an intervention program or counseling therapy may be necessary.

Classroom Corner — Teacher Activities

The Importance of Friendship (PreK-2, National Health Education Standard 4.2.1)

Concept: It is fun to do things with friends.

Learning Objectives

- Children will learn that there are many activities to do with friends.
- Children will learn that friendship requires sharing and turn taking.
- Children will learn that working together can be a lot of fun.

Supplies

- a variety of colors of construction paper cut into large hearts (each heart should then be cut in half in a variety of ways so that the two heart pieces can be put back together to form a large heart); glue sticks; various art supplies (glitter, feathers, puff balls, foam shapes, etc.); adhesive tape; large piece of bulletin board paper (large enough to display all of the hearts)

Learning Activities

- Read and discuss one of the following books:
  - *What Is a Friend?* by Josie Firmin
  - *Winnie the Pooh Friendship Day* by Nancy Parent
  - *I Can Share* by David Parker
  - *Pooh Just be Nice to Your Little Friends!* by Caroline Kenneth
- Explain to the children that they are going to make a friendship quilt.
  - Have the children come up and pick a heart half. After they have all selected half of a heart, pair the two children together whose heart halves fit together. Provide art supplies and one glue stick per pair of children to encourage sharing and cooperation. When each pair of children has finished decorating their heart half, tape the two halves together. Label each heart set with the names of both children. Arrange the completed hearts on a large sheet of bulletin board paper to create a friendship quilt that can be hung up in your classroom.
- Talk about the experience, including what it means to work with a partner and to make a friendship quilt.

Evaluation

- Children will work together and take turns.
- Children will name activities they like to do with their friends.

Additional lesson plans for grades 3–5 are available on this text's website.

At times, it may be difficult for families to recognize or acknowledge abnormal behaviors in their own children. Some emotional problems develop slowly over time and therefore may be difficult to distinguish from normal behaviors. Some families may find it difficult to talk about or admit that their child has an emotional disturbance. Others, unknowingly, may be contributing to their children's problems because of dysfunctional (e.g., abusive, unrealistic, inconsistent, or absent) parenting styles.

For whatever reasons, it may be teachers who first identify children's abnormal social and emotional behaviors based on their understanding of typical development, careful observations, and documentation of inappropriate conduct. They also play an instrumental role in promoting children's emotional health by providing stable and supportive environments that foster children's self-esteem and self-confidence and teach socially appropriate behaviors (Bodrova & Leong, 2008). Children who develop conflict resolution, problem-solving, and effective communication skills have powerful resources to help them cope effectively with daily problems. In addition, teachers can use their expertise to help families acknowledge children's problems, counsel them in appropriate behavior management techniques, strengthen parent-child relationships, and assist them in making arrangements for professional counseling or other needed services. Although most families welcome an opportunity to improve their parenting skills, the benefit to high-risk or dysfunctional families may be even greater.

Summary

- The concept of preventive health care:
  - recognizes that health attitudes and practices are learned behaviors.
  - encourages individuals to assume an active role in developing and maintaining practices that promote health.
  - suggests that childhood is an important time when positive health behaviors and habits are being established
- A child's health is determined by the interplay of genetic makeup and environment.
  - Health is a dynamic state of physical, mental, and social well-being that is continuously changing as a result of lifestyle decisions.
  - Children's growth and development potentials are influenced by the interactions of health, safety, and nutrition.
  - Health promotion begins with a sound understanding of children's growth and development.
  - Aspects of children's health that require special adult attention include safety and injury prevention, posture and physical activity, dental health, and mental health including fostering self-esteem, social-emotional competence, and resilience.

Terms to Know

preventive health *p. 3*
food insecurity *p. 3*
health *p. 8*
heredity *p. 9*
predisposition *p. 9*
sedentary *p. 10*
nutrients *p. 10*
resistance *p. 11*
norms *p. 12*
normal *p. 12*
growth *p. 12*
attachment *p. 13*
head circumference *p. 13*
deciduous teeth *p. 13*
development *p. 15*
well child *p. 18*
fluorosis *p. 22*
self-concept *p. 23*
self-esteem *p. 23*
resilient *p. 30*

Chapter Review

A. By Yourself:

1. Define each of the *Terms to Know* listed at the end of this chapter.
2. Explain how genetics and environment influence the quality of a child's well-being.
3. Why are young children at high risk for unintentional injury?
4. What preventive practices are beneficial in promoting children's oral health?
5. Discuss why children living in poverty may experience lower self-esteem?
6. What things can families do to help children build resilient skills?

B. As a Group:

1. Discuss how an individual's lifestyle decisions can have either a positive or negative effect on health.
2. Describe how teachers can use their knowledge of children's development for health promotion.
3. Explain why an abundant food supply does not always ensure a healthy diet.
4. Discuss why it is important to involve and include families in children's health education activities. What steps can a teacher take to be sure that children's cultural beliefs are respected?
5. Explain how incorporating more physical activity into daily classroom schedules benefits children and teachers. Describe several ways that teachers can modify routine activities to make them more aerobic.
6. Define the term self-concept. Provide specific examples of things teachers might do that could have a positive or negative effect on children's self-esteem.
7. Discuss what effects a teacher's mental health state could potentially have on children.

Case Study

Jose, 7 years old, and his mother live alone in a one-bedroom apartment close to his school. Most afternoons Jose walks home alone, lets himself into their apartment, and watches television until his mother comes home from work. His favorite after-school snack consists of potato chips and a soda or fruit drink. For dinner, Jose's mother usually brings something home from a local fast food restaurant because she is "too tired to cook." She knows this isn't good for either one of them. Jose's mother is currently being treated for high blood pressure, and the pediatrician has expressed concern about Jose's continued weight gain. However, Jose's mother doesn't see how she can change anything given her work schedule and limited income.

1. How would you describe Jose's short- and long-term health potential?
2. What concerns would you have about Jose's safety?
3. What potential health problems is Jose likely to develop if he does not change his current behavior?
4. What environmental risk factors may be contributing to the family's health problems?
5. If you were working with this family, what suggestions would you have for improving their health?

Application Activities

1. Observe at least four children while they are eating lunch or dinner. What foods does each child eat? What foods are refused? Based on your observations, do you think the children are developing healthy eating habits? If adults are present, observe their eating behaviors. Do you think the adults are modeling healthy eating habits? Do the adults' food preferences seem to have any influence on what children are willing to eat? Explain.
2. Observe a small group of preschool-aged children during free-play or outdoor times for two 15-minute intervals. For each observation, select a different child and record the number of times that child engages in cooperative play. Repeat this observation procedure with a group of toddler or school-age children. Describe the differences.
3. Contact local law enforcement, fire, public school authorities, and community service organizations to learn more about the educational safety programs they offer for children. Volunteer your time and assist with one or more of these events. Discuss how appropriate and effective you thought the programs were based on your knowledge of child and curriculum development.
4. Contact your local public health department. Arrange to observe a routine well-child visit. What preventive health information was given to families? Was it presented in a way that families could understand and use?
5. Select and read ten children's books from the Mental Health section in Appendix D. Prepare a brief annotation for each book, including the topic, theme, and recommendations. Describe how you would use each book to develop a learning activity that promotes children's social-emotional competence.
6. Research and read more about the national health initiatives described in this chapter. Find out if they are available in your area and what services are provided. Are the programs/services meeting the needs of children in your community? If not, what recommendations would you offer for improvement?
7. Develop a month-long series of classroom learning activities focused on children's oral health. Conduct several of your lessons with children and evaluate their effectiveness in terms of learning outcomes. What changes or improvements would you make the next time?
8. Modify the "Classroom Corner" activity on friendship to meet the National Health Education Standard 4.5.3. (Demonstrate non-violent strategies to manage or resolve conflict.) Design and describe at least three classroom activities that would teach and reinforce positive resolution techniques.

Helpful Web Resources

American Academy of Pediatric Dentistry	http://www.aapd.org
American Institute of Stress	http://www.stress.org
Children's Television Workshop Online	http://www.ctw.org
Coordinated School Health Program	http://www.cdc.gov/HealthyYouth/CSHP/
Council for Exceptional Children	http://www.cec.sped.org
Healthy Schools, Healthy Youth	http://www.cdc.gov/HealthyYouth/
Indian Health Service	http://www.ihs.gov
National Academy for Child Development	http://www.nacd.org
National Center for Children in Poverty	http://asp.cumc.columbia.edu
National Mental Health Association	http://www.nmha.org
National SAFE KIDS Campaign	http://www.safekids.org

You are just a click away from additional health, safety, and nutrition resources! Go to www.CengageBrain.com to access this text's Education CourseMate website, where you'll find:

- characteristics of healthy preschool children
- glossary flashcards, activities, tutorial quizzes, videos, web links, and more

References

Allen, K., & Marotz, L. (2010). *Developmental profiles: Pre-birth through twelve* (6th ed.). Belmont, CA: Wadsworth Cengage Learning.

American Public Health Association (APHA) & American Academy of Pediatrics (AAP). (2002). *Caring for our children. National health and safety performance standards: Guidelines for out-of-home care.* Washington, DC.

Barlett, C., & Rodeheffer, C. (2009). Effects of realism on extended violent and nonviolent video game play on aggressive thoughts, feelings, and physiological arousal, *Aggressive Behavior*, 35(3), 213–224.

Benton, D. (2009). The influence of children's diet on their cognition and behavior, *European Journal of Nutrition*, 47(3), 25–37.

Berk, L. (2009). *Child development* (8th ed.). Boston: Allyn & Bacon.

Berry, J., & Schwebel, D. (2009). Configural approaches to temperamental assessment: Implications for predicting risk of unintentional injury in children, *Journal of Personality*, 77(5), 1381–1410.

Bodrova, E., & Leong, D. (2008). Developing self-regulation in kindergarten, *Young Children*, 63(2), 56–58.

Borse, N., Gilchrist, J., Dellinger, A., Rudd, R., Ballesteros, M., & Sleet, D. (2009). Unintentional childhood injuries in the United States: Key findings from the CDC childhood injury report, *Journal of Safety Research*, 40(1), 71–74.

Boulet, S., Boyle, C., & Schieve, L. (2009). Health care use and health and functional impact of developmental disabilities among US children, 1997–2005, *Archives of Pediatric & Adolescent Medicine*, 163(1), 19–26.

Bowes L., Arseneault, L., Maughan, B., Taylor, A., Caspi, A., & Moffitt, T. (2009). School, neighborhood, and family factors are associated with children's bullying involvement: A nationally representative longitudinal study, *Journal of the American Academy of Child & Adolescent Psychiatry*, 48(5), 545–553.

Burchinal, M., Nelson, L., Carlson, M., & Brooks-Gunn, J. (2009). Neighborhood characteristics and child care type and quality, *Early Education & Development*, 19(5), 702–725.

Burnham, J. (2009). Contemporary fears of children and adolescents: Coping and resiliency in the 21st century, *Journal of Counseling & Development*, 87(1), 28–35.

Butterfoss, F., & Cohen, L. (2009). Prevention works, *Health Promotion Practice*, 10(2 Suppl.), 81S–85S.

Caldarella, P., Christensen, L., Kramer, T., & Kronmiller, K. (2009). Promoting social and emotional learning in second grade students: A study of the Strong Start curriculum, *Early Childhood Education Journal*, 37(1), 51–56.

Campbell-Sills, L., Forde, D., & Stein, M. (2009). Demographic and childhood environmental predictors of resilience in a community sample, *Journal of Psychiatric Research*, 439(12), 1007–1012.

Casamassimo, P., Thikkurissy, S., Edelstein, B., & Maiorini, E. (2009). Beyond the dmft: The human and economic cost of early childhood caries, *Journal of the American Dental Association*, 140(6), 650–657.

Centers for Disease Control & Prevention (CDC). (2008). How much physical activity do children need? Accessed on October 18, 2009, from http://www.cdc.gov/physicalactivity/everyone/guidelines/children.html.

Charlesworth, R. (2011). *Understanding child development* (8th ed.). Belmont, CA: Delmar Cengage Learning.

Copeland, W., Shanahan, L., Costello, E., & Angold, A. (2009). Configurations of common childhood psychosocial risk factors, *Journal of Child Psychology & Psychiatry*, 50(40), 451–459.

DeVault, N., Kennedy, T., Hermann, J., Mwavita, M., Rask, P., & Jaworsky, A. (2009). It's all about kids: Preventing overweight in elementary school children in Tulsa, OK, *Journal of the American Dietetics Association*, 109(4), 680–687.

Dufton, L., Dunn, M., & Compas, B. (2009). Anxiety and somatic complaints in children with recurrent abdominal pain and anxiety disorders, *Journal of Pediatric Psychology*, 34(2), 176–186.

Erwin, E., Brotherson, M., Palmer, S., Cook, S., Weigel, C., & Summers, J. (2009). How to promote self-determination for young children with disabilities, *Young Exceptional Children*, 12(2), 27–37.

Evans, G., & Schamberg, M. (2009). Childhood poverty, chronic stress, and adult working memory, *Proceedings of the National Academy of Sciences* of *the United States of America*, 106(16), 6545–6549.

Fairbank, J., & Fairbank, D. (2009). Epidemiology of child traumatic stress, *Current Psychiatry Reports*, 11(4), 289–295.

Fanti, K., Vanman, E., Henrich, C., & Avraamides, M. (2009). Desensitization to media violence over a short period of time, *Aggressive Behavior*, 35(2), 179–187.

Ferkany, M. (2008). The educational importance of self-esteem, *Journal of Philosophy of Education*, 42(1), 119–132.

Forum on Child and Family Statistics. (2009). *Child Injury and Mortality.* America's Children: Key National Indicators of Well-Being, 2009. *Accessed on September 29, 2009, from* http://www.childstats.gov/AMERICASCHILDREN/phenviro6.asp.

Freeman, R., & Stevens, A. (2008). Nursing caries and buying time: An emerging theory of prolonged bottle feeding. *Community Dentistry & Oral Epidemiology*, 36(5), 425–33.

Guajardo, N., Snyder, G., & Petersen, R. (2009). Relationships among parenting practices, parental stress, child behaviour, and children's social-cognitive development, *Infant and Child Development*, 18(1), 37–60.

Guyer, B., Ma, S., Grason, H., Frick, K., Perry, D., Sharkey, A., & McIntosh, J. (2009). Early childhood health promotion and its life course health consequences, *Academic Pediatrics*, 9(3), 142–149.

Hardin, B., Mereoiu, M., Hung, H., Roach-Scott, M. (2009). Investigating parent and professional perspectives concerning special education services for preschool Latino children, *Early Childhood Education Journal*, 37(2), 93–102.

Hass-Foletta, K., & Ottolini-Geno, L. (2006, March/April). Setting the stage for children's success: The physical and emotional environment in school-age programs, *Exchange*, 168, 40–43.

Hoogeveen, L., van Hell, J., & Verhoeven, L. (2009). Self-concept and social status of accelerated and nonaccelerated students in the first 2 years of secondary school in the Netherlands, *Gifted Child Quarterly*, 53(1), 50–67.

Hotz, G., Kennedy, A., Lutfi, K., & Cohn, S. (2009). Preventing pediatric pedestrian injuries, *The Journal of Trauma: Injury, Infection, and Critical Care*, 66(5), 1492–1499.

Huddleston-Casas, C., Charnigo, R., & Simmons, L. (2009). Food insecurity and maternal depression in rural, low-income families: A longitudinal investigation, *Public Health Nursing*, 12(8), 1133–1140.

Huesmann, L. (2007). The impact of electronic media violence: Scientific theory and research, *Journal of Adolescent Health*, 41(6), S6–13.

Iida, H., & Kumar, J. (2009). The association between enamel fluorosis and dental caries in U.S. schoolchildren, *Journal of the American Dental Association*,140(7), 855–62.

Insel, P., Turner, R., & Ross, D. (2009). *Discovering nutrition* (3rd ed.). Sudbury, MA: Jones & Bartlett.

Kagihara, L., Niederhauser, V., & Stark, M. (2009). Assessment, management, and prevention of early childhood caries, *Journal of the American Academy of Nurse Practitioners*, 21(1), 1–10.

Kaiser, L., & Allen, L. (2008). Position of the American Dietetic Association: Nutrition and lifestyle for a healthy pregnancy outcome, *Journal of the American Dietetics Association*, 108(3), 553–561.

Katona, P., & Katona-Apte, J. (2008). The interaction between nutrition and infection, *Clinical Infectious Diseases*, 46(10), 1582–1588.

Lack, C., & Green, A. (2009). Mood disorders in children and adolescents, *Journal of Pediatric Nursing*, 24(1), 13–25.

Larsson, H., Viding, E., & Plomin, R. (2008). Callous-unemotional traits and antisocial behavior: Genetic, environmental and early parenting characteristics, *Criminal Justice & Behavior*, 35(2), 197–211.

Leckman-Westin, E., Cohen, P., & Stueve, A. (2009). Maternal depression and mother child interaction patterns: Association with toddler problems and continuity of effects to late childhood, *Journal of Child Psychology & Psychiatry*, 50(9), 1176–1184.

Lee, L., Harrington, R., Chang, J., & Connors, S. (2008). Increased risk of injury in children with developmental disabilities, *Research in Developmental Disabilities*, 29(3), 247–255.

Levine, R. (2008). How should we manage caries in deciduous teeth?, *Dental Update*, 35(6), 406–408.

Luby, J. (2009). Early childhood depression, *American Journal of Psychiatry*,166(9), 974–979.

Luby, J., Belden, A., Sullivan, J., Hayen, R., McCadney, A., & Spitznagel, E. (2009). Shame and guilt in preschool depression: Evidence for elevations in self- conscious emotions in depression as early as age 3, *Journal of Child Psychology & Psychiatry*, 50(9), 1156–1166.

Marotz, L., & Lawson, A. (2007). *Motivational Leadership.* Clifton Park, NY: Thomson Delmar Learning.

Maxwell, L., & Chmielewski, E. (2008). Environmental personalization and elementary school children's self-esteem, *Journal of Environmental Psychology*, 28(2), 143–153.

Melchior, M., Caspi, A., Howard, L., Ambler, A., Bolton, H., Mountain, N., & Moffitt, T. (2009). Mental health context of food insecurity: A representative cohort of families with young children, *Pediatrics,* 124(4), e564–572.

Mello, Z. (2009). Racial/ethnic group and socioeconomic status variation in educational and occupational expectations from adolescence to adulthood, *Journal of Applied Developmental Psychology*, 30(4), 494–504.

Metallinos-Katsaras, E., Sherry, B., & Kallio, J. (2009). Food insecurity is associated with overweight in children younger than 5 years of age, *Journal of the American Dietetics Association,* 109(10), 1790–1794.

Mirvism, D., & Clay, J. (2008). Health and economic development: Reframing the pathway, *Journal of Health & Human Services Administration,* 31(1), 134–155.

Mytton, J., Towner, E., Brussoni, M., & Gray, S. (2009). Unintentional injuries in school- aged children and adolescents: Lessons from a systematic review of cohort studies, *Injury Prevention,* 15(2), 111–124.

National Association for the Education of Young Children. (2006). NAEYC accreditation criteria. Accessed on October 26. 2009, from http://www.naeyc.org/accreditation.

National Center for Children in Poverty. (2009). Child poverty. Accessed on October 21, 2009, from http://www.nccp.org/topics/childpoverty.html.

National Children's Study. (2009). Accessed on October 26, 2009, from http://www.nationalchildrensstudy.gov/Pages/default.aspx.

Nunn, M., Braunstein, N., Krall, K., Dietrich, T., Garcia, R., & Henshaw, M. (2009). Healthy eating index is a predictor of early childhood caries, *Journal of Dental Research* 88(4), 361–366.

Obeng, C. (2010). Physical activity lessons in preschool, *Journal of Research in Childhood Education,* 24(1), 50–59.

Office of Disease Prevention & Health Promotion. (2000). *Healthy People.* Accessed on December 18, 2009, from http://www.healthypeople.gov/.

Owen, A., Thompson, M., Shaffer, A., Jackson, E., & Kaslow, N. (2009). Family variables that mediate the relation between intimate partner violence (IPV) and child adjustment, *Journal of Family Violence,* 24(7), 433–445.

Pachter, L., & Coll, C. (2009). Racism and child health: A review of the literature and future directions, *Journal of Developmental & Behavioral Pediatrics,* 30(3), 255–263.

Petty, K. (2009). Using guided participation to support young children's social development, *Young Children,* 64(4), 80–85.

Pica, R. (2009). *Experiences in music and movement: Birth to age 8* (4th ed.). Clifton Park, NY: Delmar Cengage Learning.

Polakowski, L., Akinbami, L., & Mendola, P. (2009). Prenatal smoking cessation and the risk of delivering preterm and small-for-gestational-age newborns, *Obstetrics & Gynecology,* 114(2), 318–325.

Pungello, E., Iruka, I., Dotterer, A., Mills-Koonce, R., & Reznick, S. (2009). The effects of socioeconomic status, race, and parenting on language development in early childhood, *Developmental Psychology,* 45(2), 544–557.

Rasmussen, H., Scheier, M., & Greenhouse, J. (2009). Optimism and physical health: A meta-analytic review, *Annals of Behavioral Medicine,* 37(3), 239–256.

Rose-Jacobs, R., Black, M., Casey, P., Cook, J., Cutts, D., Chilton, M., Heeren, T., Levenson, S., Meyers, A., & Frank, D. (2008). Household food insecurity: Associations with at-risk infant and toddler development, *Pediatrics,* 121(1), 65–72.

Rowe, R., & Maughan, B. (2009). The role of risk-taking and errors in children's liability to unintentional injury, *Accident Analysis & Prevention,* 41(4), 670–675.

Safe Kids Canada. (2009). Accessed on September 28, 2009, from http://www.safekidscanada.ca/safekidsCanada.

Sheller, B., Churchill, S., Williams, B., & Davidson, B. (2009). Body mass index of children with severe early childhood caries, *Pediatric Dentistry,* 31(3), 216–221.

Shenassa, E., Buka, S., Niaura, R., Rosenblith, J., & Lipsitt, L. (2009). Maternal smoking during pregnancy and neonatal behavior: A large-scale community study, *Pediatrics,* 123(5), e842–848.

Simpson, L., & Fairbrother, G. (2009). How health policy influences quality of care in pediatrics, *Pediatric Clinics of North America,* 56(4), 1009–1021.

Spolidoro, M., Alessandro, S., Berardi, N., & Maffel, L. (2009). Plasticity in the adult brain: Lessons from the visual system, *Experimental Brain Research,* 192(3), 335–341.

Strassburger, V. (2009). Children, adolescents and the media: What we know, what we don't know and what we need to find out (quickly)!, *Archives of Disease in Childhood,* 94(9), 655–657.

Szente, J. (2007). Empowering young children for success in school and in life, *Early Childhood Education Journal,* 34(6), 449–453.

Tarasuk, V., & Vogt, J. (2009). Household food insecurity in Ontario, *Canadian Journal of Public Health,* 100(3), 184–188.

Ungar, M. (2007). The beginnings of resilience: A view across cultures, *Education Canada,* 47(3), 28–32.

Upshur, C., Wenz-Gross, M., & Reed, G. (2009). A pilot study of early childhood mental health consultation for children with behavioral problems in preschool, *Early Childhood Research Quarterly,* 24(1), 29–45.

U.S. Department of Health & Human Services (DHHS), Medicare & Medicaid Services. (2009a). The children's health insurance program (CHIP). Accessed on October 15, 2009, from http://www.cms.hhs.gov/lowcost healthinsfamchild.

U.S. DHHS, Mental Health Information Center. (2009b). Child and adolescent mental health. Accessed on Oct. 13, 2009, from http://mentalhealth.samhsa.gov/publications/allpubs/CA-0004/default.asp.

Vadiveloo, M., Zhu, L., & Quatromoni, P. (2009). Diet and physical activity patterns of school-aged children, *Journal of the American Dietetic Association*, 109(1), 145–151.

Wang, F., Wild, T., Kipp, W, Kuhle, S., & Veugelers, P. (2009). The influence of childhood obesity on the development of self-esteem, *Health Reports*, 20(2), 21–27.

Whiting, J., Simmons, L., Havens, J., Smith, D., & Oka, M. (2009). Intergenerational transmission of violence: The influence of self-appraisals, mental disorders, and substance abuse, *Journal of Family Violence*, 24(8), 639–648.

Yeung, C. (2008). A systematic review of the efficacy and safety of fluoridation, *Evidence-Based Dentistry*, 9(2), 39–43.

Zhu, B., Yadav, N., Rey, G., & Godavarty, A. (2009). Diffuse optical imaging of brain activation to joint attention experience, *Behavioural Brain Research*, 202(1), 32–39.

CHAPTER 2

Daily Health Observations

NAEYC Standards *Chapter Links*

- **#1 a and b:** Promoting child development and learning
- **#2 a, b, and c:** Building family and community relationships
- **#3 a, b, c, and d:** Observing, documenting, and assessing to support young children and families
- **#6 b:** Becoming a professional

Learning Objectives

After studying this chapter, you should be able to:

- Discuss ways in which programs can promote children's health.
- Explain why it is important for teachers to conduct daily health observations.
- Perform a daily health check.
- Discuss how teachers can involve children's families in the health appraisal process.
- Explain how daily health checks can be used to teach children about their health.

The *Healthy People 2020* national initiative reinforces the important relationship that exists between children's health and their ability to learn (U.S. Department of Health & Human Services, 2010). It also recognizes that not all children have equal access to medical and dental care or to environments that promote a healthy lifestyle. It underscores the collaborative effort necessary for ensuring children's health and educational success, and challenges communities to address these problems. Teachers and health professionals play a critical role in this process through their early identification of children's health problems, assistance in helping families obtain necessary medical treatment, and collaboration with families to promote children's growth and development.

When children are healthy and well-nourished, they are able to benefit from participation in learning experiences. However, an acute or chronic illness, undetected health **impairment**, inadequate diet, or emotional problem can interfere with a child's level of interest, involvement, and performance in school. For example, a mild hearing loss may distort a child's perception of letter sounds, pronunciations, and responsiveness. If left undetected, it can have a profound and long-term effect on a child's language development and ability to learn. However, health problems do

---

impairment – *a condition or malfunction of a body part that interferes with optimal functioning.*

not have to be obvious or complex to have a negative effect. Even a simple cold, toothache, allergic reaction, or chronic tonsillitis will disrupt a child's energy level, cooperation, attention span, interest, and enjoyment of learning. Thus, it is imperative that teachers be continuously aware of children's health status. Recognizing the early signs of health conditions and arranging for early intervention can limit the negative impact these problems would otherwise have on children's development and learning.

Issues To Consider **The Impact of Health on Learning**

High drop-out rates among school-age children continue to attract national attention. According to several recent studies, many of these children have undiagnosed health problems, such as vision and hearing impairments, allergies, asthma, and anemia, which interfere with their ability to learn and perform adequately in school. After years of struggle and failure, some children simply choose to abandon the source of their frustration.

The visionary founders of Head Start clearly understood the importance of early identification of children's health problems to ensure that they were ready and able to learn upon entering school. This fundamental principle is again acknowledged in the updated *Healthy People 2020* goals and continues to reinforce the essential role teachers play in assessing and promoting children's well-being.

- Should inservice and teacher education programs include more training about children's health needs? Explain.
- Do state child-care licensing regulations support this important role?
- What right does a teacher have to insist that children receive treatment for their health problems? Explain.
- What health care options exist for children whose families cannot afford needed treatments?

Promoting Children's Health

Early childhood programs make a significant contribution to children's well-being by providing on-site health care, educational programs, safe learning environments, and nutritious meals. Quality programs employ a variety of techniques, including teacher observations and daily health checks, to continually monitor children's health status and identify potential health needs. It is important that this process be ongoing because children's health status changes continuously, as illustrated in the following example:

> Joshua bounded into the classroom and greeted his classmates with the usual "Hi guys." However, by 10:00 AM his teacher noticed that Joshua had retrieved his blanket and was lying quietly in the book area. Despite several minutes of coaxing, Joshua vehemently refused to budge. His teacher continued to observe Joshua for the next few minutes and noted that he was holding his hand over his left ear and whimpering. When the teacher took Joshua's temperature, it was 103°F and he complained of an earache.

Teachers must always be alert to changes in children's appearance and behavior throughout the day. These early signs may be the first indication of an impending acute illness or **chronic** health problem and should prompt the teacher to take action.

---

chronic – *frequent or repeated incidences of illness; can also be a lengthy or permanent status, as in chronic disease or dysfunction.*

Gathering Information

Information about children's health can be obtained from a variety of sources, including:

- dietary assessment
- health histories
- results of medical examinations
- teacher observations and daily health checks
- dental examinations
- family interviews
- vision and hearing screenings
- speech evaluations
- psychological testing
- developmental evaluations

Several of these assessment tools can be administered by teachers or volunteers, while others require the skills of specially trained health professionals. Often, the process of identifying a specific health impairment requires the cooperative efforts of specialists from several different fields:

- pediatric medicine
- nursing
- speech
- dietetics
- dentistry
- psychology
- education
- ophthalmology
- social work
- audiology

Changes in children's appearance and behavior may be early signs of an illness.

Health information should always be collected from a variety of sources before any final conclusions about the child's condition are reached. Relying on the results of a single **health assessment** may present a biased and unrealistic picture of the child's problem (Allen & Cowdery, 2009). Children sometimes behave or respond in ways that are **atypical** when confronted with new surroundings or an unfamiliar adult examiner, thereby making it difficult to determine if the results are reliable. When information is gathered from multiple sources, an accurate assessment of the illness or impairment and its effect on the child is more likely to be achieved. For example, combining teacher and family observations with the results of a child's hearing evaluation may confirm the need for referral to a specialist.

Observation as a Screening Tool

Teachers are valuable members of a child's comprehensive health team. Their knowledge of children's developmental patterns and involvement with children in a classroom setting places them in an excellent position for observing potential health problems. Information obtained from

---

health assessment – *the process of gathering and evaluating information about an individual's state of health.*
atypical – *unusual; different from what might commonly be expected.*

Teachers can observe and note children's health problems while they are engaged in daily classroom activities.

daily **observations** provides a useful baseline for determining what is typical behavior and appearance for each child. When combined with an understanding of normal growth and development, this information allows teachers to quickly note any changes or deviations (Bentzen, 2009).

Health observations are a simple and effective screening tool readily available to teachers. Many of the skills necessary for making objective health observations are already at their disposal. Sight, for example, is one of the most important senses; much can be learned about children's health by merely watching them in action. A simple touch can detect a fever or enlarged lymph glands. Odors may indicate lack of cleanliness or an infection. Careful listening may reveal breathing difficulties or changes in voice quality. Problems with peer relationships, eating habits, self-esteem, or abuse in the child's home may be detected during a conversation. Utilizing one's senses to the fullest—seeing children as they really are, hearing what they really have to say, and responding to their true needs—is a skill that requires time, patience, and practice to perfect.

As with any form of evaluation, conclusions drawn from teacher observations should be made with caution. It must always be remembered that a wide range of normal behavior and skill attainment exists at each developmental stage. Norms merely represent the average age at which most children are able to perform a given skill. For example, many 3-year-olds can reproduce the shape of a circle, name and match primary colors, and walk across a balance beam. However, there will also be some 3-year-olds who will not be able to perform these tasks. This does not imply that they are not "normal." Some children simply take longer than others to master certain skills. Developmental norms are useful for identifying children who may be experiencing health problems, as well as those who may simply require additional time and support in acquiring these skills. However, an abrupt change or prolonged delay in a child's developmental progress should be noted and prompt further evaluation.

Daily Health Checks

Assessing children's health status on a daily basis provides valuable information about their well-being and readiness to learn. Health checks require only a minute or two to complete. They enable teachers to detect early signs and symptoms of many common illnesses and health impairments and should, therefore, be conducted as part of ongoing observations. Daily health checks also

observations – *to inspect and take note of the appearance and behavior of other individuals.*

help teachers become familiar with each child's typical appearance and behavior so that changes are easily recognized. This is especially important for teachers who have children with chronic health conditions or other special needs in their classrooms (Hewitt-Taylor, 2009; Raymond, 2009). Because these children are often more susceptible to infections and communicable illnesses, daily health checks can be beneficial for the early identification and removal of sick children.

Parents should be encouraged to remain with their child until the health check has been completed. Children may find comfort in having a family member nearby. Families are also able to provide information about conditions or behaviors the teacher has observed. In addition, parents may feel less apprehensive if they have an opportunity to witness health checks firsthand and to ask their own questions. However, if a parent is unavailable, it may be advisable to have a second teacher witness the procedure so as to avoid any potential allegations of misconduct.

Method

A quiet area set aside in the classroom is ideal for performing health checks. A teacher may choose simply to sit on the floor with the children or provide a more structured setting with a table and chairs. Conducting health checks in the same designated area each day also helps children become familiar with the routine.

Performing health checks in a systematic manner will improve the teacher's efficiency and ensure that the process is consistent and thorough each time. Table 2–1 illustrates a simple observation checklist that can be used for this purpose. It is organized so that observations are conducted from head to foot, first looking at the child's front- and then backside. However, this procedure can easily be modified to meet a program's unique needs in terms of setting and children being served. For example, teachers who work with school-age children might use the checklist to develop a similar tool for observing signs and symptoms rather than for performing a hands-on health check.

Table 2–1 Health Observation Checklist

1. *General appearance*—note changes in weight (gain or loss), signs of fatigue or unusual excitability, skin tone (pallor or flushed), and size for age group.
2. *Scalp*—observe for signs of itching, head lice, sores, hair loss, and cleanliness.
3. *Face*—notice general expression (e.g., fear, anger, happiness, anxiety), skin tone, and any scratches, bruises, or rashes.
4. *Eyes*—look for redness, tearing, puffiness, sensitivity to light, frequent rubbing, styes, sores, drainage, or uncoordinated eye movements.
5. *Ears*—check for drainage, redness, and appropriate responses to sounds or verbal requests.
6. *Nose*—note any deformity, frequent rubbing, congestion, sneezing, or drainage.
7. *Mouth*—look inside and at the teeth; note cavities (brown or black spots), sores, red or swollen gums, mouth-breathing, or unusual breath odor.
8. *Throat*—observe for enlarged or red tonsils, red throat, white patches on throat or tonsils, or drainage.
9. *Neck*—feel for enlarged glands.
10. *Chest*—watch the child's breathing and note any wheezing, rattles, shortness of breath, or coughing (with or without other symptoms).
11. *Skin*—observe the chest and back areas for color (pallor or redness), rashes, scratches, bumps, bruises, scars, unusual warmth, and perspiration.
12. *Speech*—listen for clarity, stuttering, nasality, mispronunciations, monotone voice, and appropriateness for age.
13. *Extremities*—observe posture, coordination; note conditions such as bowed legs, toeing-in, arms and legs of unequal length, or unusual gait.
14. *Behavior and temperament*—note any changes in activity level, alertness, cooperation, appetite, sleep patterns, toileting habits, irritability, or uncharacteristic restlessness.

A teacher should begin daily health checks by observing children as they first enter the classroom. Clues about a child's well-being, such as personal cleanliness, weight change, signs of illness, facial expressions, posture, skin color, balance, and coordination can be noted quickly. The nature of parent–child interactions and their relationship with one another can also be observed and may help to explain why some children exhibit certain behaviors. For example, does the parent have a tendency to do everything for the child—take off boots, hang up clothing, pick up items the child has dropped—or is the child encouraged to be independent? Is the child allowed to answer questions or does the parent always respond?

Following these initial observations, a flashlight should be used to inspect the inside of the mouth and throat. A quick look inside alerts the teacher to a child with an unusually red throat, swollen or infected tonsils, dental cavities, sores, or unusual breath odors. Observations of the hair and face, including the eyes, ears, and nose, can provide additional clues about the child's general hygiene as well as any communicable illness.

Reflective Thoughts

Daily health checks serve many important functions. Teachers can use them to closely monitor children's health, and also for teaching children about important personal health topics. How can teachers get children interested and involved in this process? What can children be expected to learn from this experience? What health and safety topics might be appropriate for teachers to discuss with children during daily health checks? What strategies can a teacher use to improve a child's cooperation? How might families be involved? What cautions would you offer to new parents who want to prevent their infants from developing baby bottle tooth decay?

Next, the child's clothing can be lifted and any rashes, unusual scratches, bumps or bruises, and skin color on the chest, abdomen, and arms noted. Because many rashes associated with communicable disease begin on the warmer areas of the body, such as the chest, back, neck, and forearms, these parts should be inspected carefully. Patches of blue discoloration, called Mongolian spots, are sometimes visible on the lower back of children with darker skin pigment, particularly children of Asian, Native American, and Middle Eastern origin. These spots appear similar to bruises, but do not undergo the color changes typical of an injury. Mongolian patches tend to disappear gradually as children approach 8 or 9 years of age. Finally, the teacher can turn the child around and complete similar observations of the head, hair, and back.

Teachers should continue their observations after the health check has been completed. For example, balance, coordination, and posture can easily be noted as an infant crawls away or an older child walks over to join his or her friends. Information gathered from daily health checks and teacher observations contributes to a well-rounded picture of a child's health status—physical, mental, emotional, and social well-being (Table 2–2).

With time and practice, teachers become skilled in conducting daily health checks and making valuable observations. They are able to recognize the early signs and **symptoms** of illnesses and health conditions and know when to refer a child for further evaluation.

Recording Health Observations

Teachers are indispensable as observers and recorders of information concerning children's health. Through their skilled questioning, careful listening, keen observation, understanding of children's

---

symptoms – *changes in the body or its functions that are experienced by the affected individual.*

development, and precise recording skills, they are able to gather information that may also be useful to health care professionals. Teachers should record their observations immediately following the health check. Checklists are ideal for this purpose and ensure that daily health checks are conducted and recorded in a systematic manner. Attendance records or a form developed specifically for this purpose can also be used to record **anecdotal** information (see this textbook's website for a downloadable example). These records should be placed in each child's permanent health file (electronic or hard copy) or a designated notebook. Any additional changes in a child's condition, such as a seizure, uncontrollable coughing, or diarrhea, that are noted throughout the day should also be documented on this form and reported to the family.

Teachers' observations can provide valuable clues about children's health.

© Cengage Learning

Observations must be recorded in a clear, accurate, and precise manner to be meaningful to others. To say that a child "looks sick" is vague and open to individual interpretation. However,

Table 2–2 Teacher Checklist: Potential Warning Signs of Mental Health Problems

Occasional responses to stress and change are to be expected. However, children who experience excessive or frequent episodes of the following behaviors may need to be referred for professional evaluation and treatment:

- *tearfulness or sadness*
- *preference for being alone*—is withdrawn; reluctant to play with others
- *hostility or excessive anger*—overreacts to situations; has frequent tantrums
- *difficulty concentrating*—has trouble staying focused, remembering, or making decisions
- *aggressiveness*—initiates fights, hurts animals or others, destroys property
- *irritability*—seems anxious, restless, or overly worried; continuous fidgeting
- *unexplained change in eating and/or sleeping habits*—refusal to eat; compulsive eating; persistent nightmares; difficulty sleeping
- *excessive fear*—exhibits fear that is excessive or unwarranted
- *feelings of worthlessness*—self-critical; undue fear of failure; unwilling to try new things
- *refusal to go to school*—fails repeatedly to complete work; performs poorly in school
- *complains of physical ailments*—experiences frequent stomachaches, headaches, joint aches, or fatigue without any reasonable cause
- *engages in substance abuse (for older children)*—uses drugs and/or drinks
- *talks about suicide*—is overly curious about suicide

anecdotal – *brief notes describing a person's observations.*

Information in children's health records is confidential and should be shared with certain school personnel only.

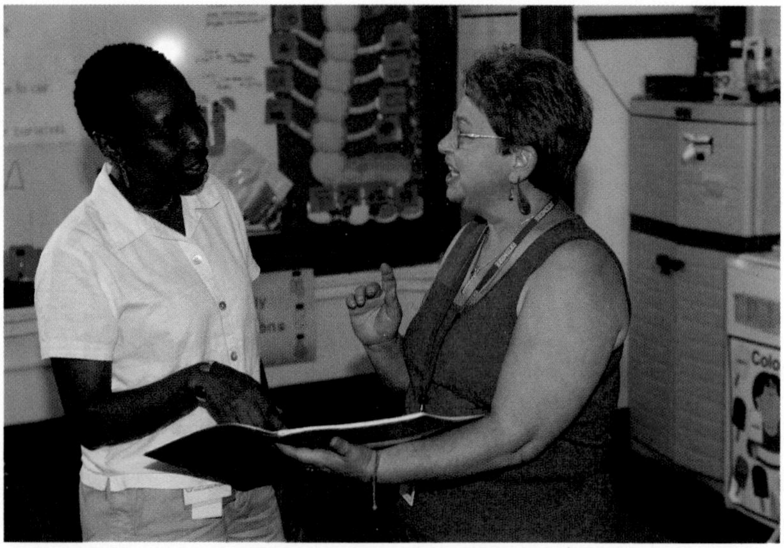

© Cengage Learning

stating that a child is flushed, has a fever of 101°F (38.3°C), and is covered with a fine red rash on his torso is definitive and a meaningful description that families can convey to the child's physician (Dotger, 2009; Seitsinger et al., 2008).

Confidentiality of Health Information

Information obtained from daily health checks and teacher observations should be treated with utmost confidentiality and not remain out where it may be visible to other families or staff members. Anecdotal records and health checklists should be kept in a notebook or folder to protect children's identity until the information can be transferred to their personal files. Additionally, this information must never be released to another individual or organization without first obtaining written parental permission (Rosenbaum, Abramson, & MacTaggart, 2009). However, federal law guarantees families the right to access information in their child's health file at any time and to request the correction of any perceived errors (U.S. Department of Education, 2009).

Benefits of Health Observations

Monitoring children's health status on a regular basis offers several distinct advantages. First, teachers are obligated, professionally and morally, to protect the health of all children in a group setting (Aronson, 2002). Observations and daily health checks provide an effective way to achieve this goal. For example, a teacher may note changes in a child's appearance or behavior that signal the onset of a communicable illness. This information can be used to determine if a child is too ill to remain in the classroom based on the program's exclusion policies. Sending a sick child home reduces the risk of exposing other children to an illness and often allows the child to recuperate more quickly.

The descriptive information teachers compile during their daily observations can also be useful to health care professionals when they are evaluating a child's condition. A teacher's perspective adds a unique dimension in terms of understanding how a health problem, such as a hearing loss or allergies, may be affecting a child. Early identification of any health condition can reduce its negative effect on a child's development and improve the success rate of treatment and intervention strategies.

⚠ **Caution: Responsibility for interpreting signs and symptoms of an illness or health condition and establishing a final diagnosis always belongs to trained health care professionals.**

---

diagnosis – *the process of identifying a disease, illness or injury from its symptoms.*

Additional benefits derived from daily health checks include the individualized attention given to children's well-being and opportunities for providing informal health education. The goal is to help children begin to develop an interest in their own personal well-being and also to become less apprehensive during visits with their health care provider.

Patterns of illness or significant behavioral changes may also be detected from an examining daily health records. For example, knowing that children have been exposed to chicken pox or that an outbreak of head lice has occurred in the school should alert teachers to be even more vigilant in the coming weeks.

Reflective Thoughts

Family involvement in children's education has been shown to have a positive effect on their development. Finding ways to increase family participation is, therefore, important.

How do children benefit from family involvement? What are some ways that families can become more involved in children's programs? What strategies can teachers use to successfully increase family participation? How can teachers help families who are uncomfortable in a school setting to feel more valued and welcomed?

Family Involvement

Daily health checks also provide an excellent opportunity for involving families in children's preventive health care. Frequent contact with families can help build a stronger relationship of understanding and trust with staff (Dotger, 2009). Some families may be hesitant, at first, to initiate contacts with the teacher regarding their child's health needs. However, through repeated encouragement, interest, and assistance, effective lines of communication can gradually be established (Grant & Ray, 2009).

During the health check procedure, parents should be encouraged to ask questions and voice concerns about their child's behavior, physical condition, habits, or adjustment to care. At the same time, teachers can advise families about any communicable illness outbreaks, signs and symptoms to watch for, and preventive measures that can be taken. Parents may also be able to provide simple explanations for problems the teacher observes. For example, a child's fatigue or aggressiveness may be the result of a new puppy, a grandmother's visit, a new baby in the home, or a seizure the night before. Allergies or a red vitamin taken at breakfast may explain a questionable red throat. Without this direct sharing of information, such symptoms might otherwise be cause for concern.

Family-school collaboration is essential for addressing children's health care needs.

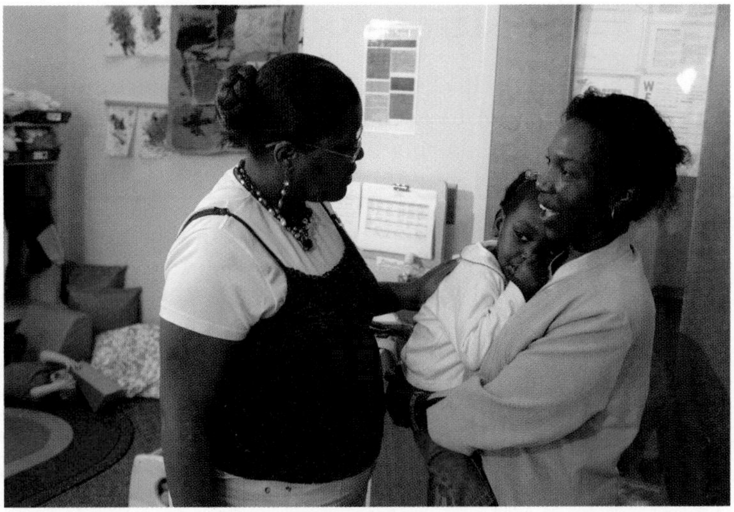

The Family's Responsibility

Primary responsibility for a child's health care *always* belongs to the family. They are ultimately responsible for maintaining their child's well-being, following through with recommendations, and obtaining any necessary evaluations and medical treatments.

Often families are the first to sense that something is wrong with their child (Allen & Marotz, 2010). However, they may delay seeking professional advice, either denying that a problem exists or hoping the child will eventually outgrow it. Some parents may not understand that health problems can have serious consequences on children's development and learning potential. Others may not be able to determine the exact nature of a child's problem or know where to obtain appropriate diagnosis and treatment.

Occasionally, families fail to take the initiative to provide for any type of routine health care. Some have difficulty understanding the need for medical care when a child does not appear to be sick, while others simply cannot afford preventive health care. With today's rising medical care costs, it is easy to understand why this might occur. Cost, however, must not discourage families from obtaining necessary medical attention. Health insurance is now available for income-eligible children through the national Children's Health Insurance Program (CHIP) to improve their access to health care. In addition, most communities offer a variety of free or low-cost health services for young children, including:

- Head Start
- Child Find screening programs
- Medicaid assistance
- Well-child clinics
- University-affiliated training centers and clinics
- Public health immunization centers
- Community centers
- Interagency Coordinating Councils

These agencies and services can generally be located in the telephone directory, on the Internet, or by contacting the local public health department.

Teachers can be supportive and instrumental in helping families understand the importance of scheduling routine health care for children. They should also become familiar with community resources and assist families in securing appropriate health care services (Allen & Cowdery, 2009).

Health Education

Daily health checks also provide many opportunities for teaching children about health. Teachers can begin to encourage children's awareness of practices that promote healthy lifestyle behaviors by sharing information about a range of topics such as dental hygiene, nutrition, physical activity, and sleep. For example:

- "Sandy, did you brush your teeth this morning? Brushing helps to keep teeth healthy and chases away the mean germs that cause cavities."
- "Mario, have you had a drink of water yet today? Our bodies need water to grow and to stay healthy just like the plants in the classroom."

School-age children can be engaged in discussions that are more advanced. For example:

- "Yolanda, how many different fruits and vegetables have you eaten today? What vitamins and minerals does our body get from fruits and vegetables?"

- "Raja, did you put on sunscreen before playing outdoors? Why is this important? What else can we do to protect ourselves from the sun's harmful rays?"

When health education is linked to everyday situations, children are better able to comprehend its importance and application to their personal lives. They are also more likely to follow through and implement what they have learned.

Family Education

Daily health checks also provide an effective opportunity for sharing information with families. Many topics relevant to children's health care and education lend themselves to informal discussions with families during the daily health check assessment, such as:

- new safety alerts and equipment recalls
- the importance of eating breakfast
- nutritious snack ideas

Focus On Families — Children's Oral Health

Oral health and a bright smile are important components of children's well-being. Teeth are essential for chewing, speech, maintaining proper space for permanent teeth, and appearance. Decay and infection can cause discomfort and make it difficult for children to focus on school. Unfortunately, tooth decay continues to affect many young children today despite increased public education and improved dental treatments. However, families can implement many practices at home to promote children's oral health.

- Keep baby's gums clean by wiping them with a damp washcloth after each feeding.
- Dampen a soft toothbrush and use twice daily to clean baby's first teeth.
- Don't put babies to bed with a bottle containing juice, formula, or breast milk. These solutions can pool around gums and teeth and lead to early decay. Offer water if your baby takes a bottle to bed. Also, stop breastfeeding once baby falls asleep.
- Apply a pea-sized dab of toothpaste to a soft brush and encourage toddlers to begin brushing their own teeth. Follow up their efforts by "going once around the block."
- Purchase fluoride toothpaste to help reduce dental decay. Fluoride is also added to the water supply in many cities. Your doctor or dentist may prescribe fluoride drops or tablets if your local water supply does not contain adequate fluoride.
- Continue to supervise preschool children's twice-daily tooth brushing. Discourage children from swallowing fluoride toothpaste, which can cause white or brown spots to form on permanent teeth.
- Schedule your child's first routine dental check between 1 and 2 years of age. If you can't afford dental care, contact local public health personnel for information about free or low-cost options in your community. Reduced-cost dental insurance is also available to eligible families in some states.
- Serve nutritious meals and snacks. Include fresh fruits and vegetables, dairy products, whole-grain breads, crackers and cereals, and limit sugary foods and drinks.
- Offer children water when they are thirsty. Limit their consumption of carbonated beverages, fruit drinks, and sport drinks, which tend to be high in sugars.

- ideas for increasing children's involvement in physical activity
- hand washing
- sun protection
- dental hygiene
- new vaccines

Families are able to support and reinforce a program's health education goals for children when efforts are made to reach out and to include them. This step also improves the consistency of information and practices between school and the child's home.

Classroom Corner Teacher Activities

Hear With My Ears... (PreK–2; National Health Education Standard 1.2.1)

Concept: You use your ears to hear sounds.

Learning Objectives

- Children will learn that ears are used for hearing sounds.
- Children will learn that there are many sounds all around.

Supplies

- Various musical instruments (need two of each); a divider or a barrier

Learning Activities

- Read and discuss one of the following books:
    - *You Hear with Your Ears* by Melvin and Gilda Berger
    - *The Ear Book* by Al Perkins
    - *Hearing (The Five Senses)* by Maria Ruis, J. M. Parramon, & J. Pig
- Explain to the children that their ears are for hearing sounds. Ask them some of the sounds that they hear each day.
- Place the musical instruments where the children can see them and play each one so they can become familiar with the sound each instrument makes.
- Next, place one of each instrument in front of the barrier/divider and one of each behind the barrier/divider.
- Call up one child to go behind the divider and pick an instrument to play. While he/she is playing the instrument, call on another child to come up and pick the instrument that makes the matching sound to the instrument the child is playing behind the barrier.
- Continue until each child has had a turn, and then have the children play all the instruments at once.
- Talk about why it is important to take good care of our ears so we can hear.

Evaluation

- Children can name which body part is used for hearing.
- Children will name some different sounds in their environment.
- Children can match sounds.

Additional lesson plans for grades 3–5 are available on the textbook's website.

Summary

- Good health is essential for effective learning.
  - Health problems can interfere with children's growth, development, and ability to learn.
- Teachers play a valuable role in promoting children's health.
  - Their observations provide information about children's physical, mental, social, and emotional well-being.
  - Their daily health checks yield additional information that is useful for identifying changes in children's health status, including communicable illness.
  - They must never attempt to diagnose children's health problems; this is the health professional's responsibility.
  - They can help families understand the need for professional health care, and assist them in locating appropriate and affordable community services.
- Information gathered from daily health checks and teacher observations can be useful to health professionals for diagnosing and/or ruling out children's health problems.
- Families must always be involved in children's health care and health education.

Terms to Know

impairment *p. 39*
chronic *p. 40*
health assessment *p. 41*
atypical *p. 41*
observations *p. 42*
symptoms *p. 44*
anecdotal *p. 45*
diagnosis *p. 46*

Chapter Review

A. By Yourself:

1. Define each of the *Terms to Know* listed at the end of this chapter.
2. Explain how a child's health and ability to learn influence each other.
3. List the reasons why teachers should conduct daily health checks.
4. Describe how an elementary teacher might modify the health check procedure to use with school-age children.
5. Examine your feelings about conducting daily health checks. Describe your thoughts in a reflective journal entry. Do you think all beginning teachers have similar feelings? Outline several steps you might take to improve your skills and boost your self-confidence in recognizing children's health problems.

B. As a Group:

1. Describe the sources available to teachers for gathering information about a child's health.
2. Describe the health check routine. What are some of the common health problems/conditions that teachers should be looking for?
3. Discuss how you might respond to a parent who objects to the daily health checks conducted by her child's teacher.
4. What benefits do daily health checks have for the child?
5. What suggestions would you have for a preschool teacher who says he is too busy to conduct daily health checks?
6. What are some things teachers can do to get families more involved in their child's preventive health care?

Case Study

Chris, the head teacher in the Sunflower classroom, has recently had some concerns about Lynette's vision. He has noticed that during group story time, Lynette quickly loses interest, often leaves her place in the circle, and crawls closer to him in an apparent effort to see the pictures in books he is holding up. Chris has also observed that when Lynette is working on puzzles, manipulatives, or an art project, she typically lowers her head close to the objects. Lynette's parents have also expressed concern about her clumsiness at home.

The results of two vision screening tests, administered by the school nurse on different days, suggest that Lynette's vision is not within normal limits. The nurse shared these findings during a conference with Lynette's parents, and encouraged them to arrange for a follow-up evaluation with an eye specialist. However, because Lynette's father was recently laid off from his job, they no longer have health insurance and cannot afford a doctor's visit at this time. The nurse continued to work closely with the family and helped them locate two reduced-fee health clinics in their community that provided the type of services Lynette required.

1. What behaviors did Lynette exhibit that made her teacher suspect some type of vision disorder?
2. Identify the sources from which information concerning Lynette's vision problem was obtained before she was referred to an eye specialist.
3. If the teacher suspected a vision problem, why didn't he just go ahead and recommend that Lynette get glasses?
4. What responsibilities do teachers have when they believe a child has a health impairment?
5. If you were the nurse advising Lynette's parents, what free or low cost health service options could you recommend in your community?

Application Activities

1. Develop a health observation checklist. With another student, role-play the daily health check procedure. Use the checklist to record your findings, and discuss your reactions to the experience. What suggestions would you have for the "teacher" who conducted the observation?
2. Invite a public health nurse from a well-child clinic or a local pediatrician to speak to the class about preventive health care for children birth to 12 years.
3. Visit several early childhood programs in your community. Note whether health checks are conducted as children arrive. Describe the method you observed at each center. Also, briefly discuss how this information was recorded.
4. Develop a list of available resources in your state and local community for children who have vision and/or hearing impairments, speech problems, cerebral palsy, autism, and learning disabilities. Be creative in your search; consider child care options, schools, special equipment needs, availability of special therapists, transportation needs, family financial assistance, and so on.
5. Modify the Classroom Corner feature activity so that a child who is severely hearing impaired could participate.

Helpful Web Resources

Canadian Pediatric Society	http://www.caringforkids.cps.ca
Child Development Institute	http://www.cdipage.com
Early Head Start National Resource Center	http://www.ehsnrc.org
U.S. Department of Health & Human Services	http://www.acf.hhs.gov
Tufts University	http://www.cfw.tufts.edu
Zero to Three: National Center for Infants, Toddlers, and Families	http://www.zerotothree.org

You are just a click away from additional health, safety, and nutrition resources! Go to www.CengageBrain.com to access this text's Education CourseMate website, where you'll find:

- a health observation recording form
- a health observation checklist
- glossary flashcards, activities, tutorial quizzes, videos, web links, and more

References

Allen, K. E., & Cowdery, G. (2009). *The exceptional child: Inclusion in early childhood education.* (6th ed.). Clifton Park, NY: Delmar Cengage Learning.

Allen, K. E., & Marotz, L. R. (2010). *Developmental profiles: Pre-birth through twelve.* (6th ed.). Clifton Park, NY: Delmar Cengage Learning.

Aronson, S. (2002). *Healthy young children: A manual for programs.* (4th ed.). Washington, DC: NAEYC.

Bentzen, W. R. (2009). *Seeing young children: A guide to observing and recording behavior.* (6th ed.). Clifton Park, NY: Delmar Cengage Learning.

Dotger, B. (2009). From a medicinal to educational context: Implementing a signature pedagogy for enhanced parent-teacher communication, *Journal of Education for Teaching: International Research and Pedagogy*, 35(1), 93–94.

Grant, K., & Ray, J. (2009). *Home, school, and community collaboration: Culturally responsive family involvement.* Thousand Oaks, CA: Sage Publications.

Hewitt-Taylor, J. (2009). Children who have complex health needs: Parents' experiences of their child's education, *Child: Care, Health and Development*, 35(4), 521–526.

Raymond, J. (2009). The integration of children dependent on medical technology into public schools, *The Journal of School Nursing*, 25(3), 186–194.

Rosenbaum, S., Abramson, S., & MacTaggart, P. (2009). Health information law in the context of minors, *Pediatrics*, 123 (Suppl.), S116–S121.

Seitsinger, A., Felner, R., Brand, S., & Burns, A. (2008). A large-scale examination of the nature and efficacy of teachers' practices to engage parents: Assessment, parental contact, and student-level impact, *Journal of School Psychology*, 46(4), 477–505.

U.S. Department of Education. (2009). Family educational rights and privacy act (FERPA). (2009). Accessed on September 10, 2009 from http://www.ed.gov/policy/gen/guid/fpco/ferpa/index.html.

U.S. Department of Health & Human Services (HHS). (2010). *Healthy people 2020.* Office of Disease Prevention and Health Promotion. Accessed April 21, 2010 from http://www.healthypeople.gov.

CHAPTER

3

Assessing Children's Health

NAEYC Standards *Chapter Links*

- **#1 a and b:** Promoting child development and learning
- **#2 a, b, and c:** Building family and community relationships
- **#3 a, b, c, and d:** Observing, documenting, and assessing to support young children and families
- **#4 a, b, and c:** Using developmentally effective approaches to connect with children and families
- **#5 b:** Using content knowledge to build meaningful curriculum
- **#6 b:** Becoming a professional

Learning Objectives

After studying this chapter, you should be able to:

- Describe how teachers can use information in children's health records to improve learning.
- Identify and describe five screening procedures that can be used to assess children's health.
- Name and discuss three vision impairments.
- Explain why early detection of hearing disorders is important in terms of children's development.
- Discuss why speech assessments should always include a hearing screening.
- Describe two methods used to evaluate children's dietary status.

Teachers understand that health problems can interfere with a child's ability to learn and that early detection improves the success of many interventions. Several screening procedures are available for identifying children who may require additional evaluation. Information collected in an objective manner and from a combination of screening procedures yields: (1) reliable data for health promotion, (2) clues that can aid in the early detection of conditions that affect children's growth and development, and (3) an opportunity to modify programs and environments to meet a child's unique needs.

Health Records

Careful recordkeeping is not always a priority in many early childhood programs. However, when information in children's files is current and sufficiently detailed, it can be used to promote their well-being (Table 3–1). The types of records schools are required to maintain are usually mandated by state departments of education. Child care licensing divisions in each state issue similar regulations for licensed centers and home-based programs. However, because these regulations typically reflect only minimal standards, programs may want to consider keeping additional forms of documentation. Unlicensed programs are not obligated to maintain any records.

Forms and records should be designed to gather information that is consistent with a program's goals and philosophy and that protects the legal rights of the children and staff. This information serves many purposes, including:

- determining children's health status
- identifying patterns and potential problem areas
- developing **intervention** programs
- evaluating the outcome of special services, e.g., speech therapy, occupational therapy
- coordinating services
- making **referrals**
- following a child's progress
- research

Health records often include private information about children and their families. Thus, only information that is needed to work effectively with a child should be shared with teachers and staff. Personal details about a child or family should remain confidential and must never serve as topics of conversation outside of the classroom. No portion of a child's health record should ever be released to another agency, school, health professional, or clinician until written permission has been obtained from the child's parent or legal guardian. A special release form, such as the one shown in Figure 3–1, can be used for this purpose. The form should clearly indicate the nature of information to be released and the agency or person to whom it is to be sent. It must also be dated and signed by the parent or legal guardian, and a copy retained in the child's folder.

Recordkeeping is most efficient when one person is responsible for maintaining all health-related records. However, input from all members of the teaching team is important for determining

Table 3–1 Children's Health Records

Children's permanent health records should include:

- child/family health history
- copy of a recent medical assessment (physical examination)
- immunization records
- emergency contact information
- record of dental examinations
- attendance data
- school-related injuries
- documentation of family conferences concerning the child's health
- screening results, e.g., vision, hearing, speech, developmental
- medications administered while the child is at school

intervention – *practices or procedures implemented to modify or change a specific behavior or condition.*
referrals – *directing an individual to other sources, usually for additional evaluation or treatment.*

Figure 3–1 Sample information release form.

INFORMATION RELEASE FORM

I understand the confidentiality of any personally identifiable information concerning my child shall be maintained in accordance with the Family Education Rights and Privacy Act (P.L.93-380), federal and state regulations, and used only for the educational benefit of my child. Personally identifiable information about my child will be released only with my written consent. With this information, I hereby grant the

____
(Name of program, agency, or person)

permission to release the following types of information:

Medical information ________________
Assessment reports ________________
Child histories ________________
Progress reports ________________
Clinical reports ________________
(Other) ________________

to:____
(Name of agency or person to whom information is to be sent)

regarding ____________________ __________ _____
Child's Name Birthdate Gender

____
Signature of Parent or Guardian

____
Relationship of Representative

____
Date

how health problems may be affecting a child and for monitoring children's progress. Because health records are legal documents, schools and early childhood programs should retain them for at least 5 years.

Child Health Histories

Health histories include information about children's backgrounds, past medical conditions, as well as current developmental status and health problems. Questions about family history are generally included to provide a better understanding of the child's strengths and special needs. Families should complete the health history form at the time of enrollment and update it annually to reflect any changes.

The nature of information requested on health history forms varies from program to program. Unless a standardized form is required by a licensing agency or school district, programs may wish to develop their own format. Sample forms can often be obtained from other programs or state agencies and modified to meet a program's specific needs. Health history questionnaires should be designed to gather basic information about:

- circumstances related to the child's birth
- family structure, such as siblings and their ages, family members, predominant language spoken, and legal custody issues
- major developmental milestones
- previous injuries, illnesses, surgeries, or hospitalizations
- daily habits, such as toileting, eating habits, and napping
- family concerns about the child, such as behavior problems, social development, and speech delays
- any special health conditions, such as allergies, asthma, seizures, diabetes, vision disorders, hearing loss, and medications

Information included in a health history questionnaire contributes to a better understanding of each child's uniqueness, including past health events and potential health risks. It can also be helpful for assessing a child's current state of health and aid teachers in establishing appropriate goals and expectations. Teachers can also use this information for modifying children's environments and activities to accommodate any special needs, such as dietary restrictions or the use of a wheelchair. However, caution must be exercised not to set expectation levels unnecessarily low for children based on this information alone. A child's potential for learning must never be discounted unless an impairment has been confirmed and is known to restrict performance. Lowering goals and expectations may otherwise limit what a child is willing to attempt, for often children will achieve only what is expected and may lack the incentive to progress or work to their full potential.

Child health histories also provide teachers with insight into the type of medical supervision a child receives. This information may reflect the value a family places on preventive health care and can be useful when making future referrals.

Medical and Dental Examinations

Most states require children to have a complete health assessment and current immunizations before they can attend school or an early childhood program. Some states require an annual examination, while others request it only at the time of admission. Health care providers recommend that infants continue to have well-child checkups every 2 to 3 months. Families are encouraged to have their 2- and 3-year-olds examined by a physician every 6 months; children 4 and older should be examined annually. More frequent medical supervision may be necessary if children have existing health problems or new conditions develop.

Current information is obtained from the family and child during the course of the health examination. Families may also be asked to complete a brief developmental questionnaire to better help medical personnel assess all aspects of the child's health. The child's immunization record is reviewed and additional doses are administered as indicated. Body parts and systems, such as the heart, lungs, eyes, ears, **skeletal** and **neurological** development, and gastrointestinal function (stomach and intestines) are carefully examined. Head circumference is routinely measured on all infants and children until 3 years of age to be certain that head size continues to increase at an acceptable rate. Height, weight, and blood pressure readings (after age 3) are also recorded and compared to prior measurements to determine if a child's growth is progressing satisfactorily. Growth failure, especially in height, may be an indication of other health problems that need to be investigated. Specialized tests, such as blood tests for anemia, sickle cell disease, or lead poisoning, may be ordered to identify or rule out any of these conditions. Urinalysis, tuberculin testing, vision

---

skeletal – *pertaining to the bony framework that supports the body.*
neurological – *pertaining to the nervous system, which consists of the nerves, brain, and spinal column.*

Height and weight measurements yield important information about children's health.

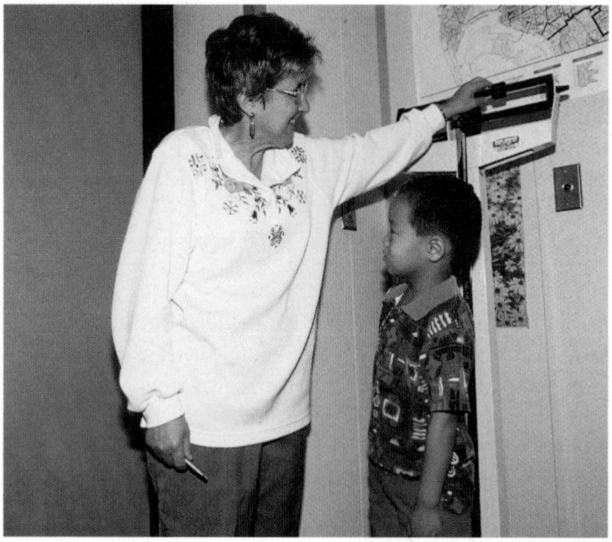

© Cengage Learning

screening, and hearing evaluation may also be completed.

Although dental examinations are seldom required for enrollment in early childhood programs, their benefits are unquestionable. Families are encouraged to arrange routine dental checks and preventive care for children, including visual inspection of the teeth, cleaning, and fluoride applications every 6 to 12 months.

Screening Procedures

Screening tests are also an essential component of the comprehensive health assessment process. They support the preventive care philosophy through the early detection of health problems and impairments that could otherwise interfere with a child's ability to learn.

Most screening procedures are relatively quick, inexpensive, and efficient to administer to groups of young children. Some tests can be conducted by teachers, while others require the services of professional clinicians. Screening tests are designed only to identify children who may have a condition that requires professional evaluation, *never* to diagnose or confirm a specific impairment. Test results simply provide additional information about a child that can be used in combination with family and teacher observations, assessments of growth and development, and the results of daily health checks.

Measurements of Height and Weight

The first 5 years of life are an important period of rapid growth. Increases in height and weight are most dramatic during infancy, and continue at a slower, but steady, rate throughout the preschool and school-age years (Allen & Marotz, 2010). Height measurements are a reliable indicator of a child's general health and nutritional status. Weight often fluctuates in response to recent illness, infection, emotional stress, or overeating and, thus, is not considered a dependable reflection of long-term health.

Teachers and families must understand that a child's growth potential is ultimately governed by genetics. This is especially important to remember when working with children from different cultures and ethnic backgrounds. The Centers for Disease Control & Prevention (CDC) have updated their standard growth charts to more accurately represent the diverse child population in the United States, although they still may not be appropriate for all ethnicities. The World Health Organization (WHO) also released international Child Growth Standards for children birth to 19 years (WHO, 2006) (www.who.int/childgrowth/en). Their charts include developmental milestones (Windows of Achievement) based on an extensive study of children, birth to age 5, from around the world and may more accurately reflect the growth and developmental patterns typical of today's children.

Ideally, children's height and weight should be measured at 4- to 6-month intervals and recorded in their permanent health file. A single measurement is unlikely to identify the child who is experiencing a growth disturbance related to physical illness, stress, or an eating disorder. Rather, what is most important is the pattern of changes that occur over a period of time. Measurements recorded on standardized growth charts allow comparisons to be made with previous data and can be useful

Reflective Thoughts

Children enjoy being weighed and measured. Monitoring their growth is important for ensuring good health. Teachers can use this activity for periodic assessment of children's well-being and to reinforce their learning of sound health practices. However, ethnic differences must be taken into consideration when using standardized tables (available on the premium website for this text) to evaluate children's height and weight measurements. Data in these tables are based on middle-class, Caucasian children and do not always account for ethnic variations in body structure. How would you determine if an Asian or Hispanic child's growth was appropriate for his or her age? What effects does a child's nutritional status have on growth? What classroom activities (science, art, language, motor) might you plan to reinforce children's understanding of a healthy lifestyle? In what ways can teachers include children's families in health education activities? What Internet sites provide reliable health and nutrition information for young children?

for determining if a child's growth is progressing satisfactorily. Growth charts are available from the Centers for Disease Control & Prevention (CDC) (http://www.cdc.gov/growthcharts) or they can be downloaded from the premium website for this book.

The Body Mass Index (BMI) is a relatively new screening tool that provides a height-for-weight ratio. It is appropriate to use with children 2 years and older to determine their risk of being **underweight**, healthy weight, **overweight**, or **obese**. Gender-specific charts for plotting children's BMI-for-age can be accessed at www.cdc.gov/parents/children or downloaded from the premium website for this book.

Sensory Development

The sensory system affects all parameters of a child's growth and development. Five special senses comprise the sensory system: vision, hearing, smell, touch, and taste. Children depend on these senses to receive, interpret, process, and respond to information in their environment. Optimal functioning of the sensory system is, therefore, of critical importance, especially during the early stages of growth and development. Of the five senses, vision and hearing are most critical for young children, since much of their early learning depends on what they are able to see and hear (Pittman, Vincent, & Carter, 2009).

Vision Screening

It is often falsely assumed that young children naturally have perfect vision. However, approximately one in twenty preschoolers and one in four school-age children has a vision impairment that interferes with learning (Prevent Blindness America, 2006). Some conditions, such as cataracts or blindness, may be present at birth. Others can develop as the result of an injury or infectious illness, such as meningitis. Vision problems are also more common in children who have other disabilities, such as cerebral palsy, Down syndrome, or fetal alcohol syndrome (FAS) (Bruce et al., 2009). For

---

underweight – *a BMI of less than 18.5.*
overweight – *a BMI greater than 25.*
obese – *a BMI over 30.*

Often it is the teacher who first notices signs of a child's vision problem.

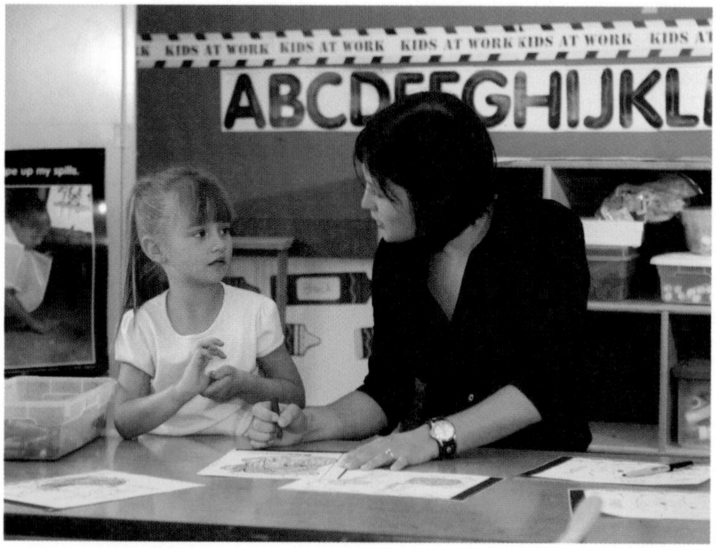

© Cengage Learning

this reason, an infant's eyes should be examined for abnormalities and muscle imbalance during routine well-child checkups to reduce permanent vision loss. It is also recommended that all children have a professional eye evaluation performed by an **ophthalmologist** or **optometrist** before starting kindergarten. Early detection of vision impairments improves the success of medical treatments and a child's readiness for school (Ethan & Basch, 2008).

Often, it is the teacher who first notices clues in a child's behavior that suggest a vision disorder. Young children are seldom aware that they are not seeing well, especially if their vision has not been normal in the past. However, vision problems may become more apparent during the school years when children are required to complete academic work with greater accuracy and detail. A combination of teacher observations and screening test results may reveal a vision problem and the need to refer a child for professional evaluation.

Special attention should be paid to children who have other known physical disabilities or who are repeatedly unsuccessful in achieving tasks that depend on visual cues (Allen & Cowdery, 2009). Delays in identifying vision problems can seriously affect the learning process and reduce the chance for successful treatment. Undiagnosed vision problems can also lead to children being inappropriately labeled as learning disabled or mentally retarded when, in fact, they simply cannot see well enough to learn (Allen & Marotz, 2010). The following case study illustrates the point:

> In many ways, Tina is a typical 4-year-old, although the teachers have been puzzled by some of her recent behaviors. Tina seems easily frustrated and unable to complete many of the pre-academic tasks that her peers enjoy, such as puzzles, tracing, threading beads, and simple object labeling. She trips over toys, runs into children, and is often reluctant to join her classmates in outdoor games. Tina's teachers are concerned that she may have a learning disability and have begun developmental testing. They also arranged with the school health consultant to have Tina's vision checked and were surprised to learn that it was only 20/100. Tina's mother was encouraged to make an appointment with an eye specialist and, after further testing, it was determined that Tina needed corrective glasses. The teachers have been amazed by the changes Tina's improved ability to see has made in her behavior, social interaction, and academic progress.

Methods of Assessment

Early detection of visual impairments requires observing children carefully for specific behavioral indicators (Tables 3–2 and 3–3). Any noted concerns should be discussed with a child's family and may confirm a teacher's suspicions. Some vision problems are more difficult to detect because there are no visible signs or symptoms. Also, vision problems are not outgrown, nor do they usually improve without treatment. For these reasons, children's vision should be closely monitored to ensure proper development.

ophthalmologist – *a physician who specializes in diseases and abnormalities of the eye.*
optometrist – *a specialist (nonphysician) trained to examine eyes and prescribe glasses and eye exercises.*

An infant's vision can be tested informally by holding an object, such as a rattle, 10 to 12 inches away and observing the infant's ability to focus on (fixation) and track (follow) the object as it is moved in a 180-degree arc around the child's head. The infant's eyes should also be observed for any uncoordinated movements as the object is brought closer (convergence) and farther away from the face. In addition, the blink reflex (sweep hand quickly in front of the eyes; observe for blinking), and pupil response (shine a penlight, held 4 to 6 inches away, into the eye; pupil should become smaller) should also be checked. A child showing abnormal responses should be referred for professional evaluation.

Teachers and volunteers can be trained by health professionals to administer many of the standardized visual acuity tests (Table 3–4) (Proctor, 2009). Printable versions of the Eye Tests for Children (HOTV charts for near and distance vision) are also available on the Prevent Blindness America website (www.preventblindness.org) or by contacting the organization's headquarters (211 West Wacker Drive, Chicago, IL, 60606). Children's eyes should also be checked for:

- convergence
- depth perception (Titmus Fly test)
- binocular fusion (Worth 4-Dot test; Random Dot E)
- deviations in pupil position (Test by holding a penlight 12 inches from the child's face, direct light at the bridge of the nose; the light reflection should appear in the same position on both pupils; any discrepancy requires professional evaluation.)

Early detection and treatment of vision problems improves children's learning success.

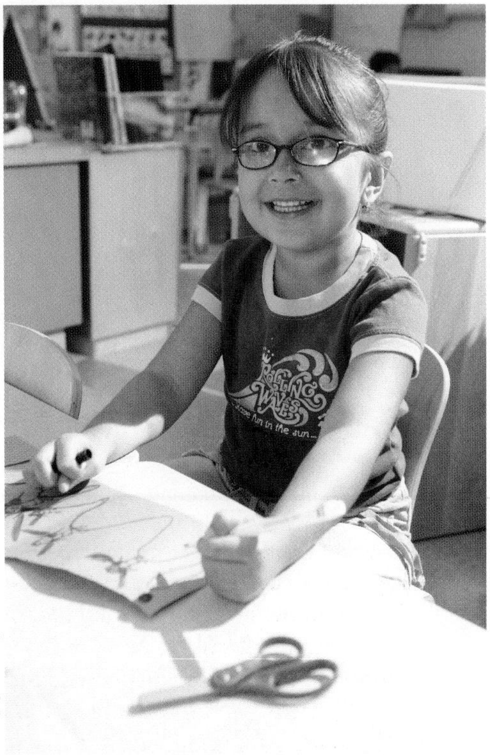

Photoscreening is a relatively new screening tool that is increasingly being used with young children, especially those who are preverbal, nonverbal, or have developmental delays or disabilities that would make it difficult for them to complete conventional screening procedures (Kirk et al., 2008). A special camera records a small beam of light as it is reflected on the eyeball, and is especially useful for the early detection of amblyopia and strabismus. Although it is an efficient and effective screening technology, the equipment is relatively expensive and the test requires special training to administer.

Table 3–2 Early Signs of Visual Abnormalities in Infants and Toddlers

Observe the infant closely for:

- roving eye movements that are suggestive of blindness
- jerky or fluttering eye movements
- eyes that wander in opposite directions or are crossed (after 3 months)
- inability to focus or follow a moving object (after 3 months)
- pupil of one eye larger than the other
- absence of a blink reflex
- drooping of one or both lids
- cloudiness on the eyeball
- chronic tearing

Table 3–3 Signs of Visual Acuity Problems in Older Children

- rubs eyes frequently
- attempts to brush away blurs
- is irritable with close work
- is inattentive to distant tasks, e.g., watching a movie, catching a ball
- strains to see distant objects, squints, or screws up face
- blinks often when reading, holds books too close or far away
- is inattentive with close work, quits after a short time
- closes or covers one eye to see better
- tilts head to one side
- appears cross-eyed at times
- reverses letters, words
- stumbles over objects, runs into things
- complains of repeated headaches or double vision
- exhibits poor eye-hand coordination
- experiences repeated styes, redness, or watery eyes

Table 3–4 Examples of Acuity Tests for Preschool Children

- Denver Eye Screening Test (DEST)
- HOTV Symbols Visual Acuity Test
- Screening Test for Young Children and Retardates (STYCAR) (This test can be used with children who have developmental delays.)
- Snellen "Tumbling" E chart
- Allen Card Test
- Teller Acuity Cards
- Cover-Uncover Test
- Lea Symbols Visual Acuity Test
- Random Dot E Stereoacuity Test

It is important that children understand the instructions and expected method of response before any screening test is administered or the results may be invalid. Children who fail an initial screening should be retested within 2 weeks. If a second screening is failed, testing results should be shared with the child's family and a referral made to a professional eye specialist for a comprehensive assessment.

Early detection and successful treatment of vision impairments in children has been targeted as a major goal in the *Healthy People 2020* initiative. Efforts to increase public awareness and to reach children in medically underserved areas are aimed at combating unnecessary and irreversible vision loss. Information concerning symptoms of visual impairments, testing procedures, and treatments is available on many professional organization websites, including Prevent Blindness America (http://www.preventblindness.org), American Academy of Ophthalmology (http://www.aao.org), American Academy of Pediatrics (http://www.aap.org), and the American Association of Pediatric Ophthalmology and Strabismus (http://www.aapos.org).

Common Disorders

Vision screening programs are designed to detect three common disorders in young children, including:

- amblyopia
- strabismus
- myopia

Amblyopia, or "lazy eye," affects approximately 2 percent of all children younger than 10 years. Children born to mothers who smoke seem to be at higher risk for developing this and other vision disorders (Ip et al., 2008). Amblyopia is caused by a muscle imbalance or childhood cataracts that result in blurred or double vision. The child's brain is confused by this distortion and begins to recognize only images received from the stronger eye while ignoring (suppressing) those from the weaker or "lazy" eye. Sight is gradually lost in the weaker eye as a result of disuse. This also causes a loss of depth perception, which requires comparable sight in both eyes.

Early identification and treatment of amblyopia is critical for preventing a permanent loss of vision. Because the child's eyes appear to be normal, amblyopia is often overlooked and treatment delayed. Seldom are children aware that anything is wrong with their vision so they are unlikely to tell an adult. For these reasons, it is important that young children have periodic routine screenings and comprehensive eye examinations. If amblyopia is diagnosed before the age of 6 or 7, a significant portion of the child's eyesight can often be restored. Even greater improvements may be achieved when this condition is diagnosed and treated before the age of 2 years (National Eye Institute, 2009). However, new research suggests that children as old as 12 may still be able to regain some lost sight (O'Connor, 2009).

Several methods are used to treat amblyopia. One of the more common treatments involves patching the child's stronger (unaffected) eye for several hours each day until muscles in the weaker (affected eye) gradually become stronger. Other treatment methods include corrective glasses, eye drops, special eye exercises, and surgery. Teachers may be asked to administer treatments while children are in school. They must understand the importance of maintaining a child's treatment schedule and be supportive when children resist or are embarrassed by having to wear special glasses or a patch. Added safety precautions, such as clearing obstacles from pathways and guiding children through unfamiliar spaces, may need to be taken to avoid injury during treatments. Teachers can also use these opportunities to help children become more respectful and accepting of individuals with special needs.

Strabismus interferes with children's ability to see properly.

Strabismus, commonly referred to as crossed eyes, is another vision impairment that affects approximately 3 to 5 percent of young children (Optometrists Network, 2009). Strabismus causes an observable misalignment of the child's eyes (for example, both eyes may turn inward or, one eye may turn inward or outward) that occurs intermittently or consistently. Because children's eyes are not able to work together as a unit, they may experience symptoms similar to those of amblyopia, including double or blurred vision, images from the weaker eye being ignored by the brain, and gradual loss of vision.

---

amblyopia – *a condition of the eye commonly referred to as "lazy eye"; vision gradually becomes blurred or distorted due to unequal balance of the eye muscles. There are no observable abnormalities of the eyes when a child has amblyopia.*

strabismus – *a condition of the eyes in which one or both eyes appear to be turned inward (crossed) or outward (walleye).*

Early recognition and treatment of strabismus is essential for restoring normal vision. Today, even infants are being treated aggressively for this condition. Although uncoordinated eye movements are common in very young infants, their eyes should begin to move together as a unit by 4 months of age. Methods used to treat strabismus include surgical correction, patching of the unaffected eye, and eye exercises.

Myopia, or nearsightedness, can affect young children, but is more common in school-aged children. A child who is nearsighted sees near objects clearly, but has poor distant vision. This condition is especially problematic for young children because they tend to move about quickly and engage in play that involves running, jumping, and climbing. As a result, children who have myopia may appear clumsy, and repeatedly stumble or run into objects. Squinting is also common as children attempt to bring distant objects into focus. Teachers can be instrumental in noting these behaviors and referring children for comprehensive screening.

Farsightedness, or **hyperopia**, is thought to be a normal occurrence in children under the age of 5, and is caused by a shortness of the eyeball (Lempert, 2008). This condition often corrects itself as children mature and the eyeball enlarges and changes shape. Children who are farsighted see distant objects clearly but have difficulty focusing on near objects. Older children may struggle academically, be poor readers, have a short attention span, and complain of headaches, tired eyes, or blurred vision following periods of close work. Because hyperopia can be difficult to detect with most routinely administered screening procedures, teacher and parent observations may provide the best initial clues to this disorder. A child who exhibits signs of hyperopia should be referred to a professional eye specialist for evaluation.

Color blindness affects a small percentage of children and is generally limited to males. Females are carriers of this hereditary defect but are rarely affected. The most common form of color blindness involves the inability to discriminate between red and green. Testing young children for color blindness is difficult and often omitted because learning is not seriously affected and there is no corrective treatment.

Management

When a child is suspected of having vision problems, families should be counseled and encouraged to arrange for professional screening (Ethan & Basch, 2008). Teachers can assist families in locating services and reinforce the importance of following through with any recommendations. Arrangements for vision testing can often be made through pediatricians' offices, "well-child" clinics, public

Reflective Thoughts

Children who experience vision problems may require extra care and direction in the classroom (Shaw & Trief, 2009; Li, 2004). They may not be able to complete tasks as quickly or precisely as other children. Some children have difficulty tolerating treatments, such as patching or wearing modified glasses for amblyopia, because their visual field is temporarily distorted. Daily application and removal of adhesive patches can cause skin irritation and may attract peer attention and curiosity. How can teachers turn this opportunity into a positive learning experience for young children? What strategies can teachers use in the classroom to help a child with vision problems? How might vision problems affect children' play in outdoor settings? What observable behaviors would suggest that a child may be experiencing a vision disorder?

---

myopia – *nearsightedness; an individual has good near vision but poor distant vision.*

hyperopia – *farsightedness; a condition of the eyes in which an individual can see objects clearly in the distance but has poor close vision.*

health departments, professional eye doctors, and public schools. Local service organizations, such as the Lions Clubs, may assist qualified families with the costs of professional eye examinations and glasses.

Children who do not pass an initial vision screening should be retested. Failure to pass a second screening necessitates referral to a professional eye specialist for comprehensive evaluation and diagnosis. However, results obtained from routine vision screening tests should be viewed with caution because they do not guarantee that a problem does or does not exist. Also, most routine screening procedures are not designed to test for all types of vision impairments. Consequently, there will always be some over-referral of children who do not have a vision disorder, while other children may be missed. It is for this reason that the observations of teachers and families are extremely important. Visual acuity also changes over time, so it is important that adults be continuously vigilant of children's visual performance.

Hearing Screening

Each year approximately 12,000 babies are born in the United States with a hearing loss (CDC, 2009b). Because **language** development, speech patterns, and most other facets of learning depend on the ability to hear, undetected hearing losses can have a profound effect on children's social interactions, emotional development, and school performance (Pittman, Vincent, & Carter, 2009). When children do not hear properly, they may respond and behave in seemingly unacceptable ways and end up being labeled as slow learners, cognitively challenged or as having behavior problems. Early diagnosis of a chronic hearing impairment or severe loss is, therefore, extremely critical.

Methods of Assessment

Inappropriate responses and behaviors may be the first indication that a child is not hearing properly (Easterbrooks, Lederberg, & Miller, 2008). Additional signs of hearing loss range from very obvious problems to those that are subtle and difficult to identify (Table 3–5).

Hospitals in most states now comply with Universal Infant Hearing Screening recommendations (see Reflective Thoughts) (Sininger et al., 2009). Trained hospital personnel test infants' hearing shortly after birth to detect deafness so that early intervention services can be initiated. An interactive map listing state-by-state testing sites and services is available at http://www.infanthearing.org/states/index.html.

An infant's hearing development should continue to be monitored by checking behavioral responses such as eye blinking or attempts to locate sounds (e.g., stop crying, turn head, interrupt sucking) (Table 3–6). Older infants and toddlers can be tested by observing as they search for sounds (often emitted through speakers in formal testing procedures), as well as by the appropriateness of their responses and language development. Although these procedures can be useful for identifying some children with hearing disorders, they are not effective for detecting all forms of hearing loss.

Children's hearing should be evaluated by a trained specialist, such as a nurse or **audiologist**, at least once during the preschool and school-age years and more often if a hearing problem is suspected. Hearing tests evaluate a child's ability to hear the normal range of tones used in everyday conversation.

Most children are able to complete routine hearing screening with little trouble. However, an unfamiliar situation involving new people, instruments and equipment, a novel task, a lack of

---

language – *form of communication that allows individuals to share feelings, ideas, and experiences with one another.*
audiologist – *a specially prepared clinician who uses nonmedical techniques to diagnose hearing impairments.*

Table 3–5 Behavioral Indicators of Potential Hearing Loss

Families and teachers may observe behaviors that suggest a possible hearing loss, such as:

- frequent mouth breathing
- failure to turn toward the direction of a sound
- delays in acquiring language; development of poor speech patterns
- difficulty understanding and following directions
- asking to have statements repeated
- rubbing or pulling at ears
- mumbling, shouting, or talking loudly
- reluctance to interact with others; quiet or withdrawn
- using gestures rather than words
- excelling in activities that do not depend on hearing
- imitating others at play
- responding to questions inappropriately
- mispronouncing many word sounds
- having an unusual voice quality—one that is extremely high, low, hoarse, or monotone
- failing to respond to normal sounds and voices

Table 3–6 Early Signs of Hearing Abnormalities in the Infant and Toddler

Observe the infant closely for:

- absence of a startle response to a loud noise
- failure to stop crying briefly when adult speaks to baby (3 months)
- failure to turn head in the direction of sound, such as a doorbell or a dog barking (4 months)
- absence of babbling or interest in imitating simple speech sounds (6–8 months)
- no response to adult commands, such as "no" or "come"

Hearing screenings are conducted by an audiologist or specially trained personnel.

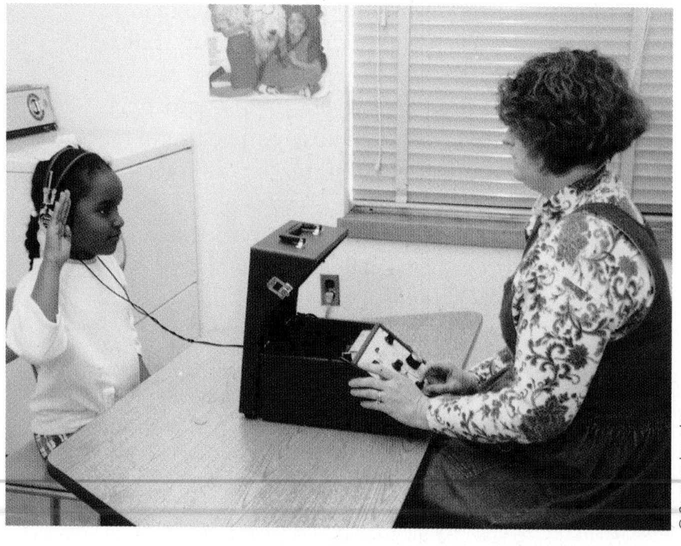

understanding, or failure to cooperate may occasionally interfere with a child's performance and yield unreliable test results. These factors must be taken into consideration if an initial screening is failed, and arrangements made to have the child retested in order to confirm or disprove the initial findings. Children who pass a hearing test yet continue to exhibit behaviors suggestive of a hearing loss should continue to be monitored.

Teachers and families can prepare and train young children in advance for hearing screenings. Play activities that require children to listen carefully or involve the use of headphones—telephone operators, airplane pilots, radio announcers, or musicians—will help them become more comfortable with screening procedures.

Reflective Thoughts

Universal Newborn Hearing Screening and Intervention programs are currently available in every state (ASHA, 2009). Many countries around the world are also making efforts to adapt and implement similar screening initiatives. These programs are designed to evaluate newborn infants for significant hearing loss before they are discharged from the hospital nursery or maternity center so that arrangements for additional testing and medical intervention can be made if indicated. At present, more than 90 percent of all infants in the United States are tested following birth (MCHB, 2009).

Trained staff administer the hearing test in a matter of minutes by placing small electrodes on the scalp and measuring the baby's response (brain waves) to soft sounds emitted through a tiny earpiece. Babies experience no discomfort during this test, and parents can learn the results within minutes. The average cost for this testing is approximately $30 to $40 and is often covered by insurance plans. Numerous studies have demonstrated the unquestionable advantage of identifying infants with hearing loss and initiating appropriate intervention before 6 months of age (McCann et al., 2009). Yet not every hospital offers this screening; some reserve it only for infants considered at high risk for having a hearing impairment (such as low birth weight, prematurity, family history, maternal infection during pregnancy, presence of other disabilities). Why is the early identification of hearing loss so important to young children's development? Why are hearing impairments often not diagnosed before the age of 2 to 3 years? What areas of development are most likely to be affected by hearing loss? What community resources are typically available to families who may have concerns about their child's hearing? Should all insurance companies be required to pay for newborn hearing screening? Explain.

Teachers should also make an effort to determine what response method (such as raising one hand, pressing a button, pointing to pictures, or dropping a wooden block into an empty can) children will be expected to use during the screening and practice this activity in advance. If a special room is to be used for testing purposes, children should be given an opportunity to visit the facilities and equipment beforehand. This will help to reduce their anxiety and increase the reliability of test results.

Common Disorders

Children who are born with any physical disability have an increased risk of also experiencing hearing problems (Allen & Marotz, 2010). Temporary and permanent hearing losses can involve one or both ears and are commonly associated with:

- a family history of hearing problems
- prenatal exposure to maternal infections, such as herpes, German measles, or cytomegalovirus
- prematurity, low birthweight
- bacterial meningitis, measles, mumps
- allergies
- frequent colds and ear infections (otitis media)
- birth defects, such as Down syndrome, Fetal Alcohol syndrome (FAS), cleft lip/cleft palate, cerebral palsy
- head injuries
- exposure to excessive or prolonged noise

Any parent who expresses concern about his or her child's hearing should always be listened to carefully and encouraged to seek professional advice. The most common forms of childhood hearing loss are:

- **Conductive loss** affects the volume of word tones. For example, this child will be able to hear loud, but not soft sounds. Conductive hearing loss occurs when sound waves are not being transmitted properly from the external ear to structures in the middle ear (Figure 3–2). Foreign objects, excess wax, and fluid accumulation in the child's middle ear following an infection are common causes of conductive hearing loss.
- **Sensorineural loss** results when the structures of the inner ear (cochlea) or the auditory nerve (which connects to the brain) have been damaged or do not function properly. This type of hearing loss is permanent and affects a child's ability to understand speech and to hear sounds. Children who have a sensorineural loss are considered to have a learning disability that requires special educational management.
- **Mixed hearing loss** refers to a disorder that involves a combination of conductive and sensorineural hearing losses. Structures in both the outer or middle ear and the inner ear or auditory nerve have either been damaged or are not functional.

Management

Some hearing impairments can be successfully treated if they are identified in the early stages. Treatment approaches depend on the underlying cause, and can range from prescription ear drops and antibiotic therapy to surgery (Grijalva, Nuorti, & Griffin, 2009; O'Brien et al., 2009). Some children who experience permanent hearing loss benefit from hearing aids, while others may receive cochlear implants or eventually learn sign language.

Figure 3–2 Diagram of the ear.

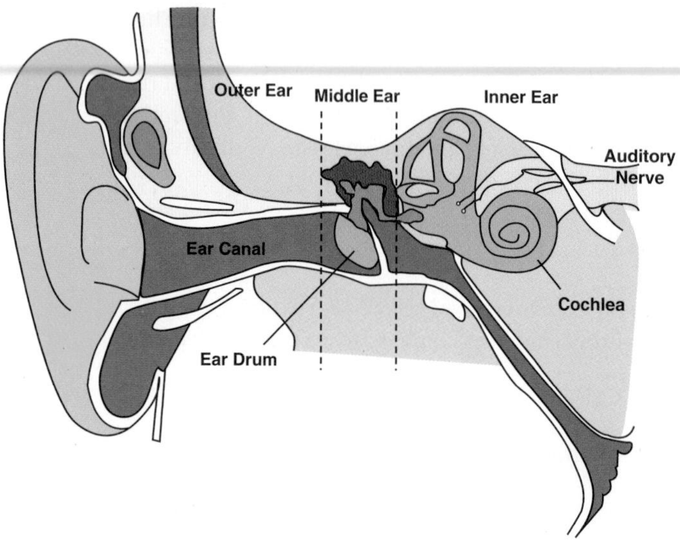

A child who experiences a sudden or gradual hearing loss should be referred to a family physician for medical diagnosis or to an audiologist for a comprehensive hearing evaluation. Families can arrange for this testing through the child's doctor, a speech and hearing clinic, public health department, public schools, or an audiologist.

Teachers who understand how various impairments affect children's ability to hear can take appropriate steps to improve communication and modify learning environments (Table 3–7). Additional information about hearing impairments, testing procedures, and resources for families can be obtained from:

American Association of Speech-Language-Hearing
2200 Research Boulevard
Rockville, MD 20850-3289
www.asha.org

---

conductive loss – *affects the volume of word tones heard, so that loud sounds are more likely to be heard than soft sounds.*
sensorineural loss – *a type of loss that occurs when sound impulses cannot reach the brain due to damage of the auditory nerve, or cannot be interpreted because of prior brain damage.*
mixed hearing loss – *a disorder that involves a combination of conductive and sensorineural hearing losses.*

Table 3–7 Teacher Checklist: Strategies for Improved Communication with Hearing-Impaired Children

- Reduce background noises, such as musical tapes, radio, motors, or fans that can interfere with a child's limited ability to hear.
- Provide individualized versus group instructions.
- Face and stand near the child when speaking.
- Bend down to the child's level; this makes it easier for the child to hear and understand what is being said.
- Speak slowly and clearly.
- Use gestures or pictures to illustrate what is being said; for example, point to the door when it is time to go outside.
- Demonstrate what the child is expected to do; for example, pick up a bead and thread it on a shoestring.

Speech and Language Evaluation

Throughout the early years, children make impressive gains in the number of words they understand (receptive vocabulary) and use to express themselves (expressive vocabulary) (Table 3-8). Children's receptive vocabulary develops earlier and is usually more extensive than their expressive vocabulary. For example, most toddlers can understand and follow simple directions long before they use words to verbalize their wants or needs. Children's language becomes increasingly fluent and complex with time and considerable practice.

Although many factors influence children's **speech** and language development, the ability to hear is especially important during the early years when children are learning to imitate sounds, words, and word patterns. Hearing disorders can jeopardize the normal acquisition of speech and language development and lead to long-term speech impairments. Whenever there is concern about the progress of a child's language development, a comprehensive hearing evaluation is always recommended.

It is also important to consider a child's home environment when evaluating language development. Families who engage children in conversation, read stories to their children, and reinforce children's efforts to express themselves are encouraging early literacy and language development. Homes where these opportunities are lacking may limit children's ability to experience and practice communication skills.

Young children also acquire early speech and language skills by imitating speech that is heard in their homes (Dale, Roche & Duran, 2008; Swanwick & Watson, 2005). For example, children who have a parent with an unusual voice inflection or speech impairment are likely to exhibit similar qualities. Children who live in bilingual homes may also take longer to acquire language skills because they must learn to think and speak in multiple languages. Cultural values and variations also exert a strong influence on children's language usage, style, and speech patterns (Trawick-Smith, 2010).

Methods of Assessment

Families are often aware of their child's speech problems but may not know what to do about them. Many adults also believe erroneously that children will eventually outgrow these impairments, so they take no action. Indeed, some children have developmentally appropriate **misarticulations** that will improve. For example, many 3-year-olds mispronounce "r" as "w" as in "wabbit" (rabbit) or "s" as "th" as in "thong" (song); by age 4 or 5 they are able to correctly pronounce these letter sounds. Nevertheless, children who demonstrate speech or speech patterns that are not developmentally appropriate

---

speech – *the process of using words to express one's thoughts and ideas.*
misarticulations – *improper pronunciations of words and word sounds.*

Table 3–8 Speech and Language Developmental Milestones

Infants	
birth–4 months	• turns to locate the source of sound • begins to coo and make babbling sounds: *baa, aah, ooh* • imitates own voice and sounds
4–8 months	• repeats syllables in a series: *ba, ba, ba* • "talks" to self • responds to simple commands: *no, come*
8–12 months	• recognizes labels for common objects: shoe, blanket, cup • "talks" in one word sentences to convey ideas or requests: *cookie* (meaning, "I want a cookie")
Toddlers	
12–24 months	• follows simple directions • knows and uses 10–30 words • points to pictures and body parts on request and asks frequently, "What's that?" "Why?" • enjoys being read to • understands 200–300 words • speaks in two–three word sentences • 65–70% of speech is intelligible
24–36 months	• refers to self as "me": "Me do it myself." • uses language to get desired attention or object • understands simple concepts when asked: "Find the small ball." • follows simple directions: "It's time to get dressed." • understands and uses 50–300 new words • 70–80% of speech is intelligible
Preschoolers	
3–6 years	• answers simple questions appropriately • describes objects, events, and experiences in fairly detailed terms • sings simple songs and recites nursery rhymes • carries on detailed telephone conversations • enjoys making up and telling stories; acquires a vocabulary of approximately 10,000–14,000 words by age 6 • uses verb tenses and word order correctly
School-age	
6–8 years	• enjoys talking and conversing with adults • uses language, in place of physical aggression, to express feelings • loves to tell jokes and riddles • understands complex statements and performs multistep requests • finds pleasure in writing stories, letters, and e-mail messages • expresses self fluently and in elaborate detail
9–12 years	• talks nonstop • understands grammatical sequences and uses them appropriately • speaks in longer, complex sentences • uses and understands irony and sarcasm • achieves mastery of language development • becomes a thoughtful listener

Adapted from: *Developmental profiles: Pre-birth through twelve (6th Ed.)*, by K. Eileen Allen & L. Marotz, 2010, Belmont, CA: Wadsworth Cengage Learning.

should be referred to a speech therapist for evaluation (Justice et al., 2009). A hearing test should be included in this evaluation to rule out the possibility of a hearing loss that could be affecting the child's speech. Speech and hearing clinics are often affiliated with colleges and universities, medical centers, child development centers, public health departments, public schools, and Head Start programs. Certified speech and hearing specialists can be located in telephone directories or Internet listings or by contacting local school districts or the American Speech, Language, and Hearing Association.

Common Disorders

The term *speech impairment* has many different meanings to persons working with children. For some, the term refers only to more obvious problems, such as stuttering, lisping, or unintelligent speech patterns. For others, a wide range of conditions are cause for concern, such as a monotone voice, nasality, improper pitch of the voice, a voice tone that is too high or too low, omissions of certain letter sounds, or misarticulations of word sounds.

Delayed language development or abnormal speech patterns that persist for more than a few months should be evaluated, and include:

- no speech by 2 years of age
- stuttering
- substitution of word sounds
- rate of speech that is too fast or unusually slow
- monotone voice
- no improvement in speech development
- speech by age 3 that is difficult to understand
- inattentive behavior or ignoring others

Management

Families and teachers serve as important role models and promote children's acquisition of speech and language skills through frequent communication opportunities and experiences. In addition, teachers can be instrumental in identifying and referring children with speech and language patterns that may not be developmentally appropriate or that interfere with effective communication. Children are often able to achieve significant improvements when speech and language disorders are recognized and treated in their earliest stages.

Nutritional Assessment

The quality of children's diets has an unquestionable effect on behavior and health. Rising costs and economic struggles have forced many families to sacrifice the quantity and nutritional value of foods they purchase and, in turn, is raising concerns about children's over- and underconsumption of essential nutrients (Monsivais & Drewnowski, 2009). Television advertising, fast food consumption, and the availability of prepackaged and convenience foods are contributing to a further decline in the quality of children's diets at a time when obesity rates are increasing (McCool, 2009).

Valuable clues about a child's nutritional status can be obtained during daily health observations. Signs, such as facial **pallor**, dry skin, bleeding gums, or **lethargy** may reflect poor eating habits. In contrast, a healthy, well-nourished child has:

- height appropriate for height
- weight appropriate for height

---

pallor – *paleness.*
lethargy – *a state of inaction or indifference.*

- bright, clear eyes—no puffiness, crusting, or paleness of inner lids
- clear skin—good color; no pallor or scaliness
- teeth—appropriate number for age; no caries or **mottling**
- gums—pink and firm; not puffy, dark red, or bleeding
- lips—soft, moist; no cracking at corner of mouth
- tongue—pink; no cracks, white patches or bright red color

Assessment Methods

Selecting an appropriate method for assessing children's nutritional status depends upon the child's age, reason for evaluation, type of information desired, and available resources. Common methods include:

- dietary assessment—is used to determine the nutrient adequacy and areas of nutrient deficiencies in the child's eating patterns. Food intake is recorded for a specified time period (24 hours, 3 days, 1 week) (Figure 3–3). The data is then analyzed using one of several methods, such as the Food Guide Pyramid, nutrient analysis software, or Reference Daily Intakes (RDIs). (See Chapter 12.)
- anthropometric assessment—is based on simple measurements of height, weight, and head circumference and comparisons made with standardized norms. **Skinfold** thickness and mid-arm circumference measurements may also be taken to estimate body fat percentage.
- clinical assessment—involves observing a child for signs of nutritional deficiency (Table 3–9). This is not considered a reliable method because of its subjective nature and the fact that physical symptoms typically do not appear until a deficiency is severe.
- biochemical assessment—involves laboratory testing of various body tissues and fluids, such as urinalysis or hemoglobin (testing for iron level) to validate concerns related to over- or underconsumption of nutrients. These tests are usually ordered by a health care provider and performed by trained laboratory technicians.

Common Disorders – Malnutrition and Obesity

Teachers and families should be alert to several nutritional problems that have a direct effect on children's health and development. Malnutrition, for example, occurs when children's diets lack essential nutrients, especially protein, vitamins A and C, iron, and calcium for prolonged periods. Inadequate nutrition knowledge, unhealthy food choices, poverty, and food insufficiencies may leave children malnourished simply because they do not get enough to eat or are consuming unhealthy foods (Dave et al., 2009). Long-term use of certain medications, such as steroids, aspirin, antibiotics, and laxatives or lack of sunshine can interfere with nutrient absorption and leave children depleted. Children who are malnourished often fail to reach typical growth standards and are at greater risk for communicable illness and infection, chronic irritability, anemia, fatigue, and learning problems. However, not all malnourished children are thin and emaciated. Some overweight children are also malnourished because their diets lack proteins, vitamins, and minerals essential for healthy growth and development.

Obesity presents another serious nutritional challenge to children's health. Approximately 20 to 25 percent of all children in the United States are considered overweight for their age (CDC, 2009a). Inactivity and unhealthy eating habits have been identified as primary causes of the childhood obesity epidemic (Vadiveloo, Zhu, & Quatromoni, 2009). Children who are overweight or obese are likely to remain so as adults and, thus, are at greater risk for developing life-threatening health problems including heart disease, stroke, sleep apnea, asthma, and diabetes.

---

mottling – *marked with spots of dense white or brown coloring.*
skinfold – *a measurement of the amount of fat under the skin; also referred to as fat-fold measurements.*

Figure 3–3 Sample questionnaire for obtaining information about a child's eating habits.

NUTRITIONAL ASSESSMENT

Dear Parent:

Nutrition is a very important part of our program. In order for us to plan appropriate nutrition-education activities and menus to meet your child's needs, we need to know your child's eating patterns. This information will also help us obtain an overview of the eating habits of young children as a group. Please take the time to fill out the questionnaire carefully.

NAME ______________________ AGE ________ DATE __________

1. How many days a week does your child eat the following meals or snacks?
   - a morning meal ________
   - a lunch or midday meal ________
   - an evening meal ________
   - a midmorning snack ________
   - a midafternoon snack ________
   - an evening snack ________
   - snack during the night ________
2. When is your child most hungry?
   - morning ________
   - noon ________
   - evening ________
3. What are some of your child's favorite foods? ______________________
4. What foods does your child dislike?
   ____
5. Is your child on a special diet? Yes ________ No ________
   If yes, why? ______________________
   Describe diet ______________________
   Diet prescribed by whom? ______________________
6. Does your child eat things not usually considered food e.g., paste, dirt, paper? ________
   If yes, how often? ______________________
   What is eaten? ______________________
7. Is your child taking a vitamin or mineral supplement?
   Yes ________ No ________ If yes, what kind? ________
8. Does your child have any dental problems that might create a problem when eating certain foods? ________
9. Has your child ever been treated by a dentist? ________
10. Does your child have any diet-related health problems?
    Diabetes ________ Allergies ________ Other ________
11. Is your child taking any medication for a diet-related health problem?
    ____
12. How much water does your child normally drink throughout the day?
    ____
13. Please list as accurately as possible what your child eats and drinks on a typical day. If yesterday was a typical day, you may use those foods and drinks.

TIME	PLACE	FOOD	AMOUNT

Table 3–9 Physical Signs of Malnutrition

Tissue	Sign	Cause
Face	Pallor	Niacin, iron deficiency
	Scaling of skin around nostrils	Riboflavin, B6 deficiency
Eyes	Hardening of cornea and lining: pale lining	Iron deficiency
	Foamy spots in cornea	Vitamin A deficiency
Lips	Redness; swelling of mouth and lips; cracking at corners of mouth	Riboflavin deficiency
Teeth	Decayed or missing	Excess sugar (or poor dental hygiene)
	Mottled enamel	Excess fluoride
Tongue	Red, raw, cracked, swollen	Niacin deficiency
	Magenta color	Riboflavin deficiency
	Pale	Iron deficiency
Gums	Spongy, red, bleeding	Vitamin C deficiency
Skin	Dry, flaking	Vitamin A deficiency
	Small underskin hemorrhages	Vitamin C deficiency
Nails	Brittle, ridged	Iron deficiency

Increasing children's physical activity is an effective weight management strategy.

Management

Obesity in young children cannot be ignored. Although prevention is always ideal, steps can be taken to help children of any age implement healthy eating and activity behaviors (Kalich, Bauer, & McPartlin, 2009; Gartrell & Sonsteng, 2008). For maximum success, weight management approaches must include the collaborative efforts of the child, family, teachers, and health care personnel, and target:

- meal planning and nutritious eating habits.
- strategies for increasing children's daily activity level. (For example, children can be asked to run errands, walk a pet, help with daily household chores, or ride their bike to school.)
- acquainting children with new outside interests, hobbies, or activities, such as hiking, swimming, dancing, playing neighborhood baseball, or learning to ride a bike. (Involvement in fun activities can divert children's attention away from food.)
- finding ways to help children experience success and develop a positive self-image. (For example, acknowledging children's efforts can boost self-esteem. For many children, positive adult attention replaces food as an important source of personal satisfaction.)

Childhood obesity will be discussed throughout the book because of its current significance, complexity, and serious health consequences.

Issues To Consider **Children's Health**

The U.S. Census Bureau has redefined the term poverty so that it more accurately reflects today's economic standards (U.S. Census Bureau, 2009). However, current guidelines exclude many families whose income is often not adequate to meet even minimal requirements for food, clothing, shelter, and health care. Data show that the adults in a majority of these families are employed, but often in minimum wage jobs. Health care and insurance are luxuries that many cannot afford. Changes in eligibility guidelines for various government assistance programs (food, cash, medical care, and housing) have further reduced some families' access to resources that affect children's health. Increasing poverty has also contributed to more homelessness, especially among families with children—currently the fastest growing segment of the homeless population (U.S. Conference of Mayors, 2008).

- Why is it important for teachers to be aware of changes in national fiscal policy and federal programs?
- How does increasing poverty and homelessness affect a teacher's role in monitoring children's health and making referrals?
- In what ways can teachers become stronger advocates for children's preventive health care?
- How do partnerships with families contribute to the improvement of children's health?

Long-term weight management is achieved by attending to all aspects of a child's well-being—physical, emotional, spiritual, and social (Kalich, Bauer, & McPartlin, 2009; Wang et al., 2009). Placing children on weight reduction plans is not advisable unless they are under a doctor's or nutritionist's supervision. Careful attention must be given to planning weight reduction programs that meet children's critical nutrient needs for sustained growth and development. Adults who model healthy eating and activity lifestyles are also in a position to have a positive influence on children's preferences and weight management behaviors. Additional ideas for healthy eating and physical activities will be addressed throughout the book and are also available on numerous websites, including the American Council for Fitness (www.acfn.org), My Pyramid for Kids (www.mypyramid.gov), and the Division of Adolescent and School Health (www.cdc.gov/nccdphp/dash).

Referrals

The initial step in making successful referrals involves gaining the family's trust and cooperation. Referrals are of little use unless families are willing and able to follow through with recommendations. Knowing something about their beliefs, customs, values, and community resources improves a teacher's ability to make effective referrals. For example, mistrust of the medical profession, poverty, job conflicts, religious beliefs, a lack of transportation, or limited education will undoubtedly affect a family's capacity and willingness to follow through with recommendations.

Meeting with the child's family, or calling them on the telephone, is often the most effective method for making referrals:

> ***Teacher:*** "I am concerned about Ryan's vision. On several occasions, I have noticed that his right eye turns inward more than the left eye and that he holds his head close to materials when he is working. Have you observed any of these behaviors at home?"
>
> ***Parent:*** "Yes, but we didn't think it was anything to worry about. We thought he was just tired or trying to be funny."
>
> ***Teacher:*** "I can't be sure that anything is wrong with Ryan's eyesight, but the behaviors I have observed can sometimes be an indication of vision problems and they need to be evaluated by an

eye specialist. If I can be of assistance in locating a doctor or making an appointment, please let me know. I will also give you a written copy of my observations to take along. Please let me know the date of Ryan's appointment when you have scheduled it."

Although a face-to-face meeting with the child's family is always preferable, a well-written letter may be the only way to reach some families. Copies of all screening test results should be given to families so they can be shared with the child's doctor. Having access to this information improves the referral process and helps medical personnel understand how the child's behavior is being affected. Teachers can also alleviate some of the family's frustration by offering information about local resources, such as hospitals, clinics, health departments, medical specialists, public and private agencies, volunteer organizations, and funding sources where services can be obtained.

Follow-up contact should be made after several days to determine if families have been successful in arranging for professional evaluation or to learn the outcome of diagnostic testing. Teachers can use these findings to make adjustments in the child's instructional program and learning environment. Follow-up contacts are also beneficial for reinforcing a family's efforts to obtain necessary services and to convey the teacher's genuine interest in the child's well-being.

Focus On Families — Children's Eye Safety

Each year, thousands of children sustain eye injuries as the result of hazardous conditions at home or school. The majority of these eye injuries are preventable through proper supervision, careful selection of toys and equipment, and the use of appropriate eye protection. Families play a major role in identifying potentially dangerous situations and taking measures to eliminate children's exposure to unnecessary risk. Adults should also take similar precautions to protect their own eye safety and serve as positive role models for children.

- Never shake a baby! Vigorous shaking can cause serious eye damage and blindness.
- Insist that children wear sunglasses whenever they play outdoors to limit exposure to ultraviolet (UV) light. Over time, UV exposure increases the risk of developing a number of serious eye conditions, including macular degeneration and cataracts. Purchase sunglasses that fit closely, wrap around the entire eye area, and provide UV-A and UV-B protection.
- Keep children indoors whenever mowing or edging the lawn. Stones, sticks, and small debris can become dangerous projectiles.
- Select toys and play equipment based on your child's age and abilities. Avoid toys with projectile parts, such as darts, slingshots, pellet guns, and missile-launching devices.
- Stones, rubber bands, balls, wire coat hangers, and fish hooks also pose a serious eye danger.
- Supervise children closely whenever they are using a sharp item, such as a fork, pencil, toothpicks, wire, paperclips, scissors, or small wooden dowels.
- Keep children away from fireworks. Do not allow them to light fireworks or to be around anyone who is doing so.
- Lock up household cleaners, sprays, paints, paint thinners, and chemicals such as garden fertilizers and pesticides that could injure children's eyes.
- Make sure children wear appropriate protective eyewear, such as goggles or a helmet with a face guard, when participating in sports.
- Don't allow children to shine a laser pointer or aim a squirt gun or spray nozzle toward someone's eyes.
- Remind children to avoid touching their eyes with unwashed hands.

Classroom Corner Teacher Activities

My Five Senses... (PreK–2, National Health Education Standard 1.2.2)

Concept: Seeing, hearing, tasting, touching, and smelling are your five senses.

Learning Objectives

- Children will learn to name all five senses.
- Children will learn which body parts go with which senses: see with eyes, hear with ears, taste with tongue, touch with fingers and skin, and smell with nose.

Supplies

- Small blanket; various objects (items that children can label—plastic foods, animals, people, and so on); small paper cups; tin foil; various scents or foods (vanilla, orange peel, ketchup, peppermint, chocolate, ranch dressing, green pepper, etc.); tape recording of children's and teachers' voices; feely box; various items with shapes that children can recognize (ball, pine cone, banana, block, plate, cup, and so on); salty (crackers), sweet (mandarin orange), sour (lemon), and bitter (unsweetened chocolate) items; hand wipes; plates; forks

Learning Activities

- Read and discuss the following books:
  - *Your Five Senses* by Bobbi Katz
  - *My Five Senses* by Aliki
- Each day discuss one of the senses and have the children participate in an activity.
- Seeing—Tell the children that you are going to play a game called "What's Missing?" This is a game that uses their sense of seeing. Place four to five objects out on the floor in front of the children. Name each item, and then line the items up in a way so that all the children can see them. Place the towel over the items. Remove one of the items and wrap it in the towel. Ask children to guess which item is missing. Call on children one at a time; if they name the missing item, they can come up and hide the next item. Continue until all children have had a turn. Vary the toys to keep children interested.
- Smelling—Tell the children that you are going to do an activity to learn about their sense of smell. Make "smelling cups": for liquid scents, put a few drops on a cotton ball and place it in the cup. Cover the cup with foil in which holes have been poked. Pass the cups around. Have children smell each cup and try to guess what the smell is. After each child has had a chance to smell each cup, remove the foil so they can see if they were correct.
- Hearing—Make a recording of the teachers and children while they are playing. On another day, tell the children that they will use their sense of hearing for this activity. Play the tape and see if the children can guess whose voices they are hearing on the tape.
- Feeling—Tell the children that this activity will involve using their sense of touch. Place various items in a feely box. Have each child reach in and use their sense of touch to determine what the object is.
- Tasting—Tell the children you are going to have them taste some different items to see if they are sweet, sour, salty, or bitter. Tell them that their tongue has little things called taste buds on it that help them know what a food tastes like. Next, have all the children wash their hands

(*continued*)

Classroom Corner **Teacher Activities** *(continued)*

with a wipe. Place a cracker, a mandarin orange, a small piece of lemon, and bit of unsweetened chocolate on each plate, and set a plate in front of each child. Have the children taste one item at a time and talk about the different tastes.

Evaluation

- Children will name each of the five senses.
- Children will name which body parts are associated with each sense.

Additional lesson plans for grades 3–5 are available on the textbook's website.

Summary

- Teachers play an important role in the health assessment of young children.
  - Information obtained from various screening procedures, including observations, health records, screening procedures, daily health checks, and interactions with families, can be used for monitoring children's health.
  - Assessment information is also useful for identifying children who require professional evaluation and for modifying learning experiences to address their special needs.
- Results of screening procedures are not always accurate and can be affected by children's comfort level and ability to respond.
- Teachers can initiate the referral process after gathering and evaluating data from multiple sources.
- Referrals should be followed up to learn about assessment outcomes, treatment interventions, and any classroom modifications that may be needed.

Terms to Know

intervention *p. 55*
referrals *p. 55*
skeletal *p. 57*
neurological *p. 57*
underweight *p. 59*
overweight *p. 59*
obese *p. 59*
ophthalmologist *p. 60*
optometrist *p. 60*
amblyopia *p. 63*
strabismus *p. 63*
myopia *p. 64*
hyperopia *p. 64*
language *p. 65*
audiologist *p. 65*
conductive loss *p. 68*
sensorineural loss *p. 68*
mixed hearing loss *p. 68*
speech *p. 69*
misarticulations *p. 69*
pallor *p. 71*
lethargy *p. 71*
mottling *p. 72*
skinfold *p. 72*

Chapter Review

A. By Yourself:

1. Define each of the *Terms to Know* listed at the end of this chapter.
2. Select the screening test that is recommended for children with the following behaviors, signs, or symptoms. Place the appropriate code letter in each space for questions 1–15.

H	Hearing screening
V	Vision screening
D	Developmental screening
HW	Height and weight
Dt	Dental screening
S	Speech evaluation
N	Nutrition evaluation

______ 1. frequent blinking; often closes one eye to see

______ 2. stutters whenever tense and in a hurry to speak

______ 3. usually listless; appears very small for chronological age

______ 4. stumbles over objects in the classroom; frequently walks into play equipment in the play yard

______ 5. very crooked teeth that make his speech difficult to understand

______ 6. seems to ignore the teacher's requests; shouts at the other children to get their attention

______ 7. awkward; has great difficulty running and climbing; tires easily because of obesity

______ 8. a 5-year-old who has trouble catching a ball, pedaling a bicycle, and cutting with scissors

______ 9. appears to focus on objects with one eye while the other eye looks off in another direction

______10. multiple cavities; in recent weeks has not been able to concentrate on any task

______11. is extremely shy and withdrawn; spends the majority of her time playing alone, imitating the actions of other children

______12. seems extremely hungry at snack time; always asks for extra servings and takes food left on other children's plates when the teacher isn't looking

______13. becomes hoarse after shouting and yelling during outdoor time

______14. arrives at school each morning with potato chips, candy, or a cupcake

______15. a 4½-year-old who whines and has tantrums to get his own way

B. As a Group:

1. Identify and describe the vision disorders that are most common among young children. What behavioral indicators might a teacher observe? How is each typically treated?
2. Discuss how teachers might use information in health records to improve learning experiences for children with special sensory needs?
3. Discuss how the learning activities outlined in the Classroom Corner feature could be modified for a child who is blind or has low vision. How might they be modified for a child with significant hearing loss?
4. Brainstorm ways that teachers could incorporate more physical activity into classroom routines to help children achieve the recommended 60 minutes of vigorous activity each day.
5. Debate whether or not teachers should calculate children's BMI and inform families if a child is overweight. Role-play how a teacher might share this information with an unreceptive parent and offer suggestions for improving the child's nutrition and physical activity. Critique each other's responses.
6. If a family asks you where they can get their 2-year-old's hearing tested, what resources in your community would you recommend?

Case Study

A friend encouraged Mrs. Howard to take her son to the developmental screening clinic being held this week at the community recreation center. Parker is nearly 2 years old and speaks only a few words that are understandable. He has few opportunities to play with other children his age because he spends most days with his grandmother while his mother works at a nearby hospital. On the day of the developmental screening, team members checked Parker's height, weight, vision, hearing, speech, cognitive abilities, and motor skills. The team leader also read through the child history form that Mrs. Howard had completed and noted that Parker had several food allergies, as well as frequent upper respiratory and ear infections. All of Parker's screening results proved to be within normal limits, with the exception of his hearing tests, which revealed a significant loss in one ear and a moderate loss in the other.

1. Is Parker's speech development appropriate for his age? Explain.
2. What significance do Parker's ear infections have to his hearing loss? How might his food allergies be contributing to his hearing loss?
3. Should the screening team's recommendation for Parker include a referral to his physician? Why?
4. What behavioral signs of hearing loss might you expect Parker to exhibit?
5. What strategies might the developmental team suggest to Parker's mother and grandmother for improving his speech development and communication skills?

Application Activities

1. Locate and read instructions for administering the Snellen Tumbling E and one additional acuity screening test. Pair up with another student and practice testing each other. What advantages does each test offer? Disadvantages? Did you encounter any problems administering the test? How would you modify your instructions to a child based on this experience?
2. Devise a monitoring system for recording the daily food intakes of individual children in a group setting. Be sure to address the following questions:
   a. What nutritional information do you want to collect? In what form?
   b. Who will be responsible for collecting this data?
   c. How can this information be obtained efficiently?
   d. How can teachers and families use this data to improve children's eating habits?
   e. What other ways might teachers use this information to promote children's health?
3. Collect samples of child history forms from several schools and/or early childhood programs in your area. Review the type of information that is requested most often. Design your own form and distribute it to several families for their comments and suggestions.
4. Attend a signing class. Learn to say "hello" and "good-bye" and ten additional words in sign language.
5. Make arrangements with a local school or early childhood program to conduct a comparison study of children's growth. Measure and record the heights and weights of fifteen children, ages 3 to 6 years, on the standard Growth Charts (download from the text's premium website). Then, determine each child's BMI and plot this information on the BMI-for-age charts. Which method provides the most accurate information about children's growth? What did you learn about the

children's potential risk for becoming overweight? Learn more about the BMI measure and initiatives for preventing childhood obesity at the CDC website (http://www.cdc.gov).

6. Obtain an audiometer. Have a nurse or audiologist demonstrate the technique for testing a person's hearing. Practice administering the test with a partner. In what ways did this experience change your ideas about how to prepare children for testing?
7. Research the Internet or contact the American Heart Association for educational programs designed to improve children's cardiovascular health. Are the materials/programs developmentally appropriate? How is improvement determined?

Helpful Web Resources

American Speech, Language, and Hearing Association (ASHA)	http://www.asha.org
Children with Special Needs	http://www.napcse.org
KidSource (Parent's guide to middle ear fluid in children)	http://www.kidsource.com
National Eye Institute	http://www.nei.nih.gov
National Institutes of Health	http://www.health.nih.gov
Prevent Blindness America	http://www.preventblindness.org
Action for Healthy Children	http://www.actionforhealthykids.org/

You are just a click away from additional health, safety, and nutrition resources! Go to www.CengageBrain.com to access this text's Education CourseMate website, where you'll find:

- an information release form
- a nutritional assessment form
- growth and BMI charts
- glossary flashcards, activities, tutorial quizzes, videos, web links, and more

References

Allen, K. E., & Cowdery, G. (2009). *The exceptional child: Inclusion in early childhood education.* (6th ed.). Belmont, CA: Wadsworth Cengage Learning.

Allen, K. E., & Marotz, L. R. (2010). *Developmental profiles: Pre-birth through twelve.* (6th ed.). Belmont, CA: Wadsworth Cengage Learning.

American Speech, Language, & Hearing Association (ASHA). (2009). Status of State universal newborn and infant hearing screening legislation and laws. Accessed September 20, 2009, from http://www.asha.org/advocacy/state/issues.

Bruce, B., Biousse, V., Dean, A., & Newman, N. (2009). Neurologic and ophthalmic manifestations of fetal alcohol syndrome, *Reviews of Neurological Diseases*, 6(1)13–20.

CDC. (2009a). *Child overweight.* National Center for Chronic Disease Prevention and Health Promotion. Accessed September 20, 2009, from http://www.cdc.gov/HealthyYouth/obesity/index.htm.

CDC. (2009b). Early hearing detection and intervention (EHDI) program. Accessed on September 20, 2009, from http://www.cdc.gov/ncbddd/ehdi.

Dale, R., Roche, J., & Duran, N. (2008). Language is complex, *International Journal of Psychology & Psychological Therapy*, 8(3), 351–362.

Dave, J., Evans, A., Saunders, R., Watkins, K., & Pfeiffer, K. (2009). Associations among food insecurity, acculturation, demographic factors, and fruit and vegetable intake at home in Hispanic children, *Journal of the American Dietetic Association*, 109(4), 697–701.

Easterbrooks, S., Lederberg, A., & Miller, E. (2008). Emergent literacy skills during early childhood in children with hearing loss: Strengths and weaknesses, *Volta Review*, 108(2), 91–114.

Ethan, D., & Basch, C. (2008). Promoting healthy vision in students: Progress and challenges in policy, programs, and research, *Journal of School Health*, 78(8), 411–416.

Gartrell, D., & Sonsteng, K. (2008). Guidance matters: Promote physical activity — It's proactive guidance, *Young Children*, 63(2), 51–53.

Grijalva, C., Nuorti, J., & Griffin, M. (2009). Antibiotic prescription rates for acute respiratory tract infections in US ambulatory settings, *JAMA*, 302(7), 758–766.

Holstrum, W., Biernath, K., McKay, S., & Ross, D. (2009). Mild and unilateral hearing loss: Implications for early intervention, *Infants & Young Children*, 22(3), 177–187.

Ip, J., Robaei, D., Kifley, A., Wang, J., Rose, K., & Mitchell, P. (2008). Prevalence of hyperopia and associations with eye findings in 6- and 12-year-olds, *Ophthalmology*, 115(4), 678–685.

Justice, L., Bowles, R., Turnbull, P., Khara, L., & Skibbe, L. (2009). School readiness among children with varying histories of language difficulties, *Developmental Psychology*, 45(2), 460–476.

Kalich, K., Bauer, D., & McPartlin, D. (2009). "Early Sprouts": Establishing healthy food choices for young children, *Young Children*, 64(4), 49–55.

Kirk, V., Clausen, M., Armitage, M., & Arnold, R. (2008). Preverbal photoscreening for amblyogenic factors and outcomes in amblyopia treatment: Early objective screening and visual acuities, *Archives of Ophthalmology*, 126(4), 489–492.

Lempert, P. (2008). Retinal area and optic disc rim area in amblyopic, fellow, and normal hyperopic eyes; A hypothesis for decreased acuity in amblyopia, *Ophthalmology*, 115(12), 2259–2261.

Li, A. (2004). Classroom strategies for improving and enhancing visual skills in students with disabilities. *Teaching Exceptional Children*, 36(6), 38–46.

Maternal and Child Health Bureau (MCHB). (2009). Universal newborn hearing screening. Accessed on September 23, 2009, from http://mchb.hrsa.gov/programs/specialneeds/unhs.htm.

McCann, D., Worsfold, S., Law, C., Mullee, M., Petrou, S., Stevenson, J., Yuen, H., & Kennedy, C. (2009). Reading and communication skills after universal newborn screening for permanent childhood hearing impairment, *Archives of Disease in Children*, 94(4), 293–297.

McCool, J. (2009). The role of the media in influencing children's nutritional perceptions, *Qualitative Health Research*, 19(5), 645–654.

Monsivais, P., & Drewnowski, A. (2009). Lower-energy-density diets are associated with higher monetary costs per kilocalorie and are consumed by women of higher socioeconomic status, *Journal of the American Dietetic Association*, 109(5), 814–822.

National Eye Institute. (2009). Amblyopia. Accessed on September 20, 2009, from http://www.nei.nih.gov/health/amblyopia/index.asp.

O'Brien, M., Prosser, L., Paradise, J., Ray, G., Kulldorff, M., Kurs-Lasky, M., Hinrichsen, V., Mehta, J., Colborn, D., & Lieu, T. (2009). New vaccines against otitis media: Projected benefits and cost-effectiveness, *Pediatrics*, 123(6), 1452–1463.

O'Connor, M. (2009). Patching vs. atropine to treat amblyopia in children aged 7 to 12 years, *Evidence-Based Ophthalmology*, 10(2), 82–83.

Optometrists Network. (2009). Strabismus. Accessed on September 24, 2009, from http://www.strabismus.org/.

Pittman, A., Vincent K., & Carter L. (2009). Immediate and long-term effects of hearing loss on the speech perception of children, *Journal of the Acoustical Society of America*, 126(3), 1477–1485.

Prevent Blindness America. (2006). Common eye problems in children. Accessed September 20, 2009 from http://www.preventblindness.org/children/index.html.

Proctor, S. (2009). Vision screening: New and time-honored techniques for school nurses, *NASN School Nurse*, 24(2), 62–68.

Shaw, R., & Trief, E. (2009). *Everyday activities to promote visual efficiency: A handbook for working with young children with visual impairments.* New York: AFB Press.

Sininger, Y., Martinez, A., Eisenberg, L., Christensen, E., Grimes, A., & Hu, J. (2009). Newborn hearing screening speeds diagnosis and access to intervention, *Journal of the American Academy of Audiology*, 20(1), 49–57.

Swanwick, R., & Watson, L. (2005). Literacy in the homes of young deaf children: Common and distinct features of spoken language and sign bilingual environments. *Journal of Early Childhood Literacy*, 5(1), 53–78.

Trawick-Smith, J. (2010). *Early childhood development: A multicultural perspective.* (5th Ed.). Upper Saddle River, NJ: Pearson.

U.S. Census Bureau. (2009). *How the Census Bureau measures poverty.* Housing and Household Economic Statistics Division. Accessed September 21, 2009, from http://www.census.gov/hhes/www/poverty/povdef.html.

U.S. Conference of Mayors. (2008). *A status report on hunger and homelessness in America's cities.* Accessed on September 21, 2009, from http://usmayors.org/pressreleases/documents/hungerhomelessnessreport_121208.pdf.

Vadiveloo, M., Zhu, L., & Quatromoni, P. (2009). Diet and physical activity patterns of school-aged children, *Journal of the American Dietetic Association,* 109(1), 145–151.

Wang, F., Wild, T., Kipp, W., Kuhle, S., & Veugelers, P. (2009). The influence of childhood obesity on the development of self-esteem, *Health Reports,* 20(2), 21–27.

World Health Organization (WHO). (2006). The WHO child growth standards. Accessed on September 18, 2009, at http://www.who.int/childgrowth/en/.

CHAPTER 4

Common Chronic Medical Conditions Affecting Children's Health

NAEYC Standards *Chapter Links*

- **#1 a, b, and c:** Promoting child development and learning
- **#2 a, b, and c:** Building family and community relationships
- **#3 a, b, c, and d:** Observing, documenting, and assessing to support young children and families
- **#4 a, b, and c:** Using developmentally effective approaches to connect with children and families
- **#5 c:** Using content knowledge to build meaningful curriculum
- **#6 b:** Becoming a professional

Learning Objectives

After studying this chapter, you should be able to:

- Explain why it is important for teachers to have an understanding of common chronic diseases and medical conditions that affect children's health.
- Discuss why some chronic conditions are difficult to identify in children.
- Name and describe the symptoms and management strategies for common medical conditions that children may experience.

Children who have disabilities, medical conditions, and chronic diseases are often present in early childhood and school-age classrooms. This means that teachers must be able to respond to children's educational, health, and medical needs. Teachers also play an instrumental role in identifying children who may have undiagnosed conditions that require medical evaluation and treatment. Early identification, referral to appropriate professionals, and intervention strategies have proven to be successful in minimizing the negative effects of undiagnosed health conditions on children's developmental progress (Guralnick, 2004; Nelson, 2000; Ramey & Ramey, 1998) and their ability to learn (Allen & Cowdery, 2009). The purpose of this chapter is to provide brief descriptions of several chronic health conditions and their management strategies, which can help to prepare teachers for these important roles.

Common Chronic Diseases and Medical Conditions

Some chronic conditions and diseases such as sickle cell anemia and diabetes may be difficult to recognize because children may have had them since birth. Other conditions, such as allergies, asthma, and lead poisoning, may present few early symptoms and develop slowly over time so that even the child may not be aware that anything is wrong. This means that from time to time teachers are likely to encounter children who have chronic medical disorders that have not yet been diagnosed (Lieberman et al., 2009; Nelson et al., 2009).

An ideal starting point for teachers to consider is children's environmental circumstances. These factors may contribute to a child's health condition and/or serve as barriers to treatment and can include:

- location—living in an urban neighborhood, rural area, or being homeless
- family's financial situation, which, in turn, may affect dietary quality, living arrangement, and access to medical care
- exposure to environmental pollutants in air or water, such as noise or chemicals
- presence of stress, trauma, or domestic violence
- disruption of the traditional family unit

Teachers can also learn more about children's chronic diseases and/or medical conditions by accessing information on the Internet or through local libraries. Community health professionals are often willing to answer questions and provide expert guidance. Health consultants may be available to train and work directly with classroom teachers in some early childhood programs. School nurses in public and some private schools provide similar assistance, and are often responsible for administering medications and medical procedures. Additional resources and support may also be available to teachers serving children who have an individualized education plan (IEP).

The remainder of this chapter is devoted to an overview of several common chronic diseases and medical conditions that teachers may encounter in their classrooms. Note that developmental and genetic disabilities have not been included here because they are topics addressed extensively in special education courses and specialized textbooks.

Allergic Diseases

Allergies are the leading cause of chronic disease among young children in the United States and may affect as many as one in every five children (AAFA, 2009a). There is significant concern about the increasing incidence of allergic disease and the number of substances to which children are reacting. Although many allergic disorders can be successfully treated and controlled, it is estimated that more than 50 percent of children with symptoms remain undiagnosed (Nelson et al., 2009). Allergic reactions range in severity from mildly annoying symptoms to those that may severely restrict a child's activity or even result in unexpected death.

Many children have allergies that can cause a range of physical and behavioral symptoms.

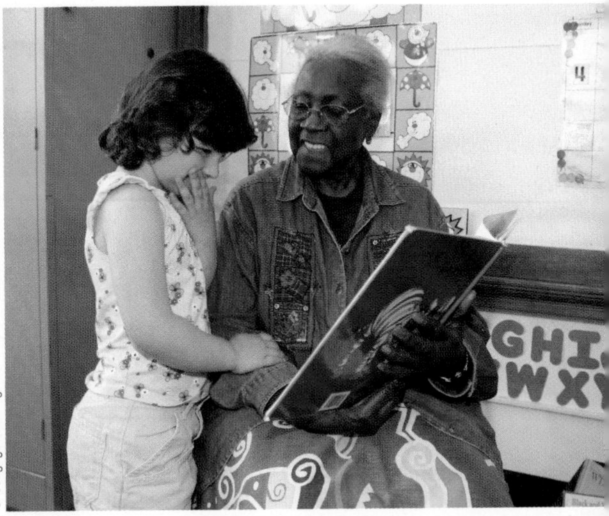

Signs and Symptoms

A substance capable of triggering an allergic reaction is called an *allergen*. An inherited error in the body's immune system causes it to overreact to otherwise harmless environmental substances, such as dust, pollen, foods, chemicals, or medicines (Krauss-Etschmann et al., 2009; Nordling et al., 2008).

Allergic reactions are generally classified according to the body site where contact with the allergen occurs and where symptoms most commonly develop:

- ingestants—cause digestive upsets and respiratory problems. Common examples include foods such as milk, citrus fruits, eggs, wheat, chocolate, tree nuts, peanuts, and oral medications.
- inhalants—affect the respiratory system causing a runny nose, cough, wheezing, and itchy, watery eyes. Examples include pollens, molds, dust, particulate matter, animal dander, and chemicals, such as perfumes and cleaning products.
- contactants—cause skin irritations, rashes, hives, and eczema. Common contactants include soaps, cosmetics, dyes, fibers, latex, medications placed directly on the skin, and some plants, such as poison ivy, poison oak, and grass.
- injectables—trigger respiratory, digestive, and/or skin disturbances. Examples of injectables include medications that are injected directly into the body and insect bites, especially those of bees, wasps, hornets, spiders.

Children who have chronic allergies often experience irritability and malaise in addition to the discomfort that accompanies an acute reaction. To understand how allergies affect children on a day-to-day basis, a simple comparison can be made to the generalized fatigue and uneasiness that one feels during the onset of a cold. Certainly, children cannot benefit fully from learning when they are not feeling well. For these reasons, allergic disorders may contribute to children's behavior and learning problems, including disruptive behaviors, hyperactivity, fatigue, general disinterest, irritability, and difficulty concentrating, and should be investigated.

Teachers can be instrumental in recognizing the early signs of children's allergic conditions. Daily observations and anecdotal records may reveal patterns of repetitious symptoms that may otherwise be overlooked (Table 4–1). Common signs and symptoms of allergic disorders include:

- frequent colds and ear infections
- chronic congestion, such as runny nose, cough, or throat clearing; mouth-breathing
- headaches
- frequent nosebleeds
- unexplained stomachaches
- hives, eczema, or other skin rashes
- wheezing or shortness of breath
- intermittent or permanent hearing losses
- reactions to foods or medications

Table 4–1 Cold or Allergy: How to Tell?

	Cold	Allergy
Time of year	More likely in fall and winter	Depends on what child is allergic to—may be year round or seasonal (fall, spring)
Nasal drainage	Begins clear; may turn color after 2–3 days	Remains clear
Fever	Common with infection	No fever
Cough	May become loose and productive	Usually not productive; nasal drainage irritates throat causing frequent throat clearing and shallow cough
Itchy eyes	No	Typical
Muscle aches	May be present during first 1–2 days	None
Length of illness	7–10 days	May last an entire season or year round

Reflective Thoughts

Examine your feelings regarding children with chronic health disorders. Are you more apprehensive about working with these children? Do you consider them to be different in some way from children who don't have long-term health problems? Do you respond to them differently in the classroom? Do you expect less of these children or are you more likely to be protective? What do you see as your role in helping children adjust to chronic health problems? Why is communication with their families even more important in these situations?

- dark circles beneath the eyes
- mottled tongue
- frequent rubbing, twitching, or picking of the nose
- chronic redness of the throat
- red, itchy eyes; swollen eyelids
- irritability, restlessness, lack of energy or interest

Food Allergies Fewer than 2 percent of all children have an inherited immune disorder resulting in a true food allergy that is not outgrown (AAFA, 2009b). However, many children experience unpleasant reactions to certain foods that parents commonly refer to as food allergies. This type of response is called a **food intolerance** or insensitivity and affects an estimated 8 percent of infants and children younger than 4 years of age. Unlike a food allergy, the symptoms of food intolerances are not likely to be life-threatening and may eventually be outgrown (Gupta et al., 2009). Common symptoms of food allergies include:

- hives, skin rashes
- flushed or pale face
- cramps, vomiting, and/or diarrhea
- runny nose, watery eyes, congestion, and/or wheezing
- itching or swelling around the lips, tongue, or mouth
- anxiousness, restlessness
- shock
- difficulty breathing

Symptoms of an allergic reaction can develop within a few minutes or several hours following the ingestion of an offending food. Foods that most commonly trigger allergic reactions are listed in Table 4–2. The Food Allergen Labeling & Consumer Protection Act (2004) requires food

Table 4–2 Common Food Allergens

Foods that are most likely to trigger an allergic reaction include:
• eggs • milk and milk products such as cheese and ice cream • fish and shellfish • peanuts • tree nuts, such as almonds, cashews, and pecans • wheat and wheat products • soybeans

food intolerance – *unpleasant reactions to particular foods that do not involve an immune response and are usually outgrown.*

Figure 4–1 Precautions must be taken to protect children from known food allergies.

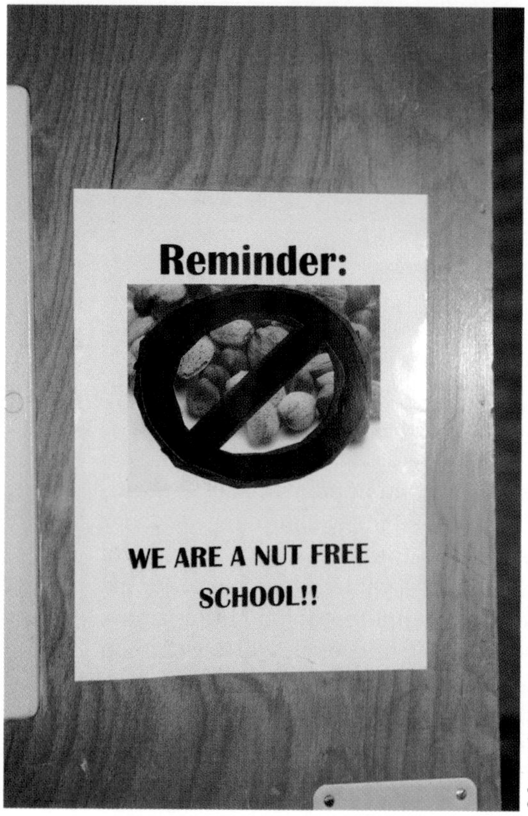

© Cengage Learning

manufacturers to clearly indicate on the label if any of these substances are present in a product or if the product has been exposed to any of these ingredients during its preparation.

Because some food allergies can be severe and potentially life-threatening, school administrators and teachers must take steps to safeguard the child's well-being (Figure 4–1) (Muñoz-Furlong & Weiss, 2009; Young, Muñoz-Furlong, & Sicherer, 2009). They must work closely with the child's family to develop a plan of action in the event of an allergic reaction. A downloadable food allergy action plan is available in multiple languages from the Food Allergy & Anaphylaxis Network website (www.foodallergy.org) in addition to extensive information about children's food allergies. A program's plan should include emergency telephone numbers and directives for actions to be taken in an emergency. All staff members should be familiar with the child's plan and review it often; this step is especially important for new or substitute teachers. If injectable medications, such as an EpiPen, have been ordered by the child's physician, teachers should be trained to administer them properly.

Teachers must consider children's food allergies whenever planning lessons, celebrating holidays or special occasions, or taking field trips. It is also imperative that the cook read food labels carefully and avoid cross-contamination (with other children's food) when preparing the child's meals. Any special food items should be labeled with the child's name and stored away from other foods. A list of children and the foods to which they are allergic should be posted inside the classroom. One teacher should be responsible for monitoring, checking, and serving all foods to children who have known allergies to prevent mistakes from occurring. Everyone should wash their hands carefully following a meal or snack to avoid spreading potential food allergens. Teachers should also spend time educating the other children so they understand why these precautions are necessary and why food items must not be exchanged.

Management

At present, there are no known cures for allergic conditions, only **symptomatic control**. In some cases, the substances to which a child is allergic may change over time. Although this gives the impression that an allergy has disappeared, it may redevelop at a later time or the child may become allergic to different substances

Symptoms and complications of allergies are generally less severe and easier to control if they are identified early. Treatment is aimed at limiting a child's exposure to annoying allergens that, in some cases, involves completely removing the substance(s) from the child's environment. For example, if a child is allergic to milk, all dairy products should be eliminated from the child's diet. If the pet dog is the source of a child's allergies, the dog should be kept outside or at least out of the child's bedroom and frequent hand washing practiced. In other cases, such as dust or pollen allergies, it may only be feasible to control the amount of exposure. Smoking must always

symptomatic control – *treatment that controls symptoms but does not cure the condition.*

be avoided around children with respiratory allergies because it is known to aggravate and intensify their breathing problems (Baena-Cagnani et al., 2009). Left untreated, allergies can lead to more serious health problems, including chronic bronchitis, permanent hearing loss, sinusitis, asthma, and emphysema (Smith et al., 2009).

Antihistamines, decongestants, bronchodilators, and anti-inflammatory nasal sprays are commonly used to treat the symptoms of respiratory allergies. Many children also receive medication through aerosol breathing treatments (Schueepp et al., 2009). Although these medications provide effective control of symptoms, the relief is only temporary. Children taking antihistamines and decongestants often experience drowsiness, difficulty concentrating, and excessive thirst and should, therefore, be supervised closely, especially during outdoor times or when activities involve risk. Some children also experience restlessness or agitation from their medications. These side effects make it particularly difficult for children to pay attention and learn, especially if the medications are prescribed for an extended time. Teachers must observe these children carefully and discuss any concerns about the medication's effectiveness or side effects with the child's family. Sometimes a different medication with fewer side effects can be prescribed.

⚠ **Caution: Teachers should always obtain approval from the child's physician and receive proper training before administering aerosol breathing treatments or any other form of medication therapy.**

In some cases, allergy shots (desensitization therapy) are given when other treatments have been unsuccessful in controlling the child's symptoms. Many children experience some improvement, but the full effect may take 12 to 18 months to achieve.

Most allergic conditions are not considered to be life threatening. However, bee stings, medications, and certain foods can lead to a condition known as **anaphylaxis** in children who have a severe allergic reaction to these substances (Table 4–3) (Muñoz-Furlong & Weiss, 2009). This life-threatening response requires urgent medical attention because it causes the body to go into shock and the air passages to swell closed.

⚠ **Caution: An ambulance should be called at once if anaphylaxis occurs.**

Children who have a history of severe allergic reactions may keep an EpiPen at school. EpiPens are an auto-injecting device that administers a single dose of epinephrine when quickly pressed against the skin (usually the upper thigh) (Figure 4–2) (Stecher et al., 2009). However, this medication provides only temporary relief, so it is essential that emergency medical assistance also be summoned.

The emotional effect that allergies can have on the quality of children's and families' lives cannot be overlooked (Meltzer et al., 2009). Families may overprotect children or subject them to frequent

Table 4–3 Symptoms of Anaphylaxis

Life-threatening symptoms can develop suddenly and include:
• wheezing or difficulty breathing • swelling of the lips, tongue, throat, and/or eyelids • itching and hives • nausea, vomiting, and/or diarrhea • anxiety and restlessness • blue discoloration around the mouth and nail beds

anaphylaxis – *a severe allergic reaction that may cause difficulty breathing, itching, unconsciousness, and possible death.*

Figure 4–2 **An EpiPen auto-injector.**

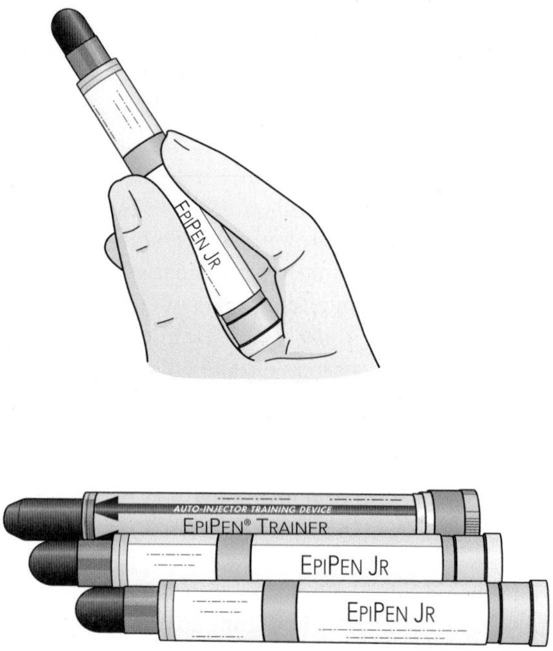

reminders to avoid offending allergens. Some children may also be sensitive about their appearance—frequent sneezing, runny nose, rashes, red and swollen eyes—along with feeling moody, irritable, or even depressed. In other cases, severe allergies may limit a child's participation in physical activity. Collectively, these feelings can lead to fear, withdrawn behaviors, poor self-esteem, and other maladjustment problems if children's allergies are not addressed in a positive manner.

It is also important that children not be allowed to use their allergies as a means for gaining attention or special privileges. Instead, adults can help children become more independent and self-confident in coping with their problems. Teachers can often help children make simple adjustments in their daily lifestyles so they can lead normal, healthy lives. Also, parenting classes, individual counseling, and information posted on professional websites can help family members learn how to foster children's self-esteem and independence. Community clinics and hospitals may also offer special classes to help families and children cope with allergic disease.

Asthma

Asthma is a chronic disease that affects over six million children and is a primary cause of school absenteeism (CDC, 2009a; Lim, Wood & Cheah, 2009). For many young children, asthma is both a chronic and acute respiratory disorder affecting boys twice as often as girls (Lux, Awa, & Walter, 2009). It is a form of allergic response that is most often seen in children who also have other allergic conditions. Like allergies, asthma tends to be an inherited tendency that can become progressively worse without treatment. Children who are overweight or obese are also at increased risk for developing asthma, which can further compromise their health (Ahmad et al., 2009; Tai, Volkmer, & Burton, 2009).

Numerous theories are being investigated to determine why the incidence of asthma is increasing at such an alarming rate. Researchers are looking at multiple factors, including the quality of indoor environments, early infant feeding practices, sanitation standards, and increased air pollution (Liu et al., 2009). Mothers are being encouraged to breastfeed and to withhold solid foods until infants reach 6 months of age to decrease the potential risk of childhood allergies (Meyer, 2009). Women are also being urged to not smoke during pregnancy or to expose infants to second-hand smoke after they are born; infants born to mothers who smoke are more likely to develop asthma later in life (Keil et al., 2009). Recent studies have also found the rate of asthma to be significantly higher among children of minority backgrounds and those living in poverty (Bryant-Stephens, 2009). Acute asthma attacks are thought to be triggered by a number of factors, including:

- airborne allergens, such as pollen, animal dander, dust, molds, perfumes, cleaning chemicals, paint, ozone, cockroaches (Phipatanakul & Gaffin, 2009)
- foods, such as nuts, wheat, milk, eggs
- second-hand cigarette smoke
- respiratory infections, such as colds and bronchitis
- stress (especially anger) and fatigue
- changes in temperature or weather, such as cold, rain, or wind
- vigorous exercise (Lee et al., 2009).

Signs and Symptoms

Acute asthma attacks are characterized by episodes of wheezing, coughing, and difficulty breathing (especially exhalation) that are caused by spasms and swelling in the respiratory tract (bronchial tubes) (Figure 4–3). As mucus collects in the airways, breathing becomes labored, it becomes more difficult to expel air, and the child begins to breathe faster. Many children outgrow acute asthma attacks as the size of their air passageways increases with age.

Figure 4–3 Swelling and excess mucus in the airways make breathing difficult during an asthma attack.

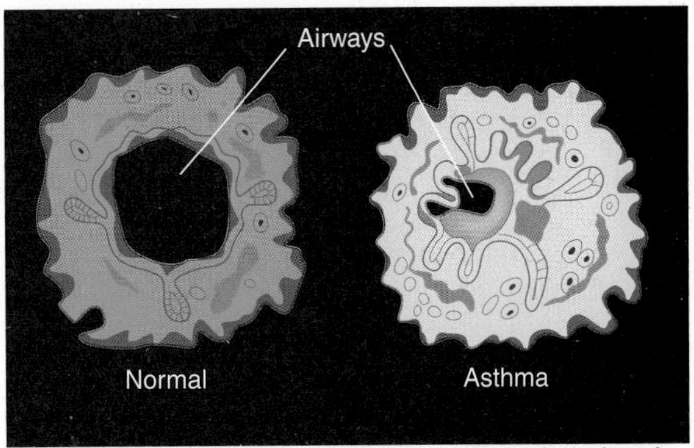

An artist's representation of bronchial tubes, or airways in the lung, in cross section. The normal airway, left, is open. The airway affected by asthma, right, is almost completely closed off. The allergic reaction characteristic of asthma causes swelling, excess mucus production, and muscle constriction in the airways, leading to coughing, wheezing, and difficult breathing.

From: http://www.niaid.nih.gov

Management Asthma treatment is aimed at identifying and removing any substance(s) from the child's environment that may trigger an attack. In cases where complete removal is not feasible, as with dust or pollen, steps can be taken to limit the child's exposure. For example, it may be necessary to dust and vacuum a child's environment daily to address an airborne allergy. Furnace filters should be replaced on a regular basis or an electrostatic air purifier installed to help remove offending particles from the air. Adults should avoid smoking around children and limit the use of chemicals such as cleaning supplies, paints, and fragrances. Some families choose to enroll children who have asthma in smaller-sized early childhood programs because the environment can be monitored more closely and there is less exposure to respiratory infections. Medications, such as anti-inflammatory drugs and bronchodilators, may be administered in the form of an inhaler or aerosol breathing treatment to decrease swelling and open air passages (Stingone & Claudio, 2009).

A meeting should always be arranged with the family when a child with asthma is first enrolled (McWhirter, McCann, & Coleman, 2008). This enables the teacher to better understand the child's condition—what symptoms the child shows, what substances are likely to trigger an attack, what, when, and how medications are to be administered, and what emergency plan of action is needed (Tables 4–4 and 4–5). This information should be written down, posted where teachers can access it quickly, and reviewed frequently with the child's family to note any changes.

Table 4–4 Strategies for Managing Children's Asthma Attacks

- If you know that certain substances trigger a child's attack, remove the child from the environment (cold air, fumes).
- Encourage the child to remain quiet. Do not leave the child alone.
- Allow the child to assume a position that makes breathing easier; sitting upright is usually preferred.
- Administer any medications prescribed for the child.
- Offer small sips of room-temperature liquids (not cold).
- Contact the child's family if there is no relief from medications or if the family requests to be notified in the event of an attack.
- Do not delay calling for emergency medical assistance if the child shows any signs of struggling to breathe, fatigue, anxiety, restlessness, blue discoloration of the nail beds or lips, or loss of consciousness.
- Record your observations—child's condition prior to, during, and following an attack, factors that appeared to trigger the attack, medications that were administered, that parents were contacted.
- Stay calm; this helps to put the child at ease and makes breathing easier.

Table 4–5 Teacher's Checklist: Children with Allergies and Asthma

- Be familiar with the symptoms of a child's allergic reaction.
- Keep children's emergency information located where it is readily accessible; make sure that others know where to find it.
- Post emergency telephone numbers next to the telephone.
- Know where emergency medications are stored and learn how to administer them.
- Review your program's emergency policies and procedures.
- Monitor all food or other sources of allergens (such as animals, plants, lotions, or cleaning supplies) that are brought into the classroom.
- Have the family review and update information about the child's condition periodically.

Reflective Thoughts

Some medications used to treat the symptoms of allergies and asthma can cause undesirable side effects, including restlessness, nervousness, trembling, thirst, difficulty sleeping, drowsiness, nausea, headache, dilated pupils, difficult urination, and decreased appetite. What should you do if you observe any of these effects? What actions would you take if a child began developing difficulty breathing? How might these medications affect children's classroom behaviors and social interactions? What can teachers do to help children adjust to chronic health problems, such as asthma and allergies?

Many children develop anemia because of food insufficiency or unhealthy eating habits.

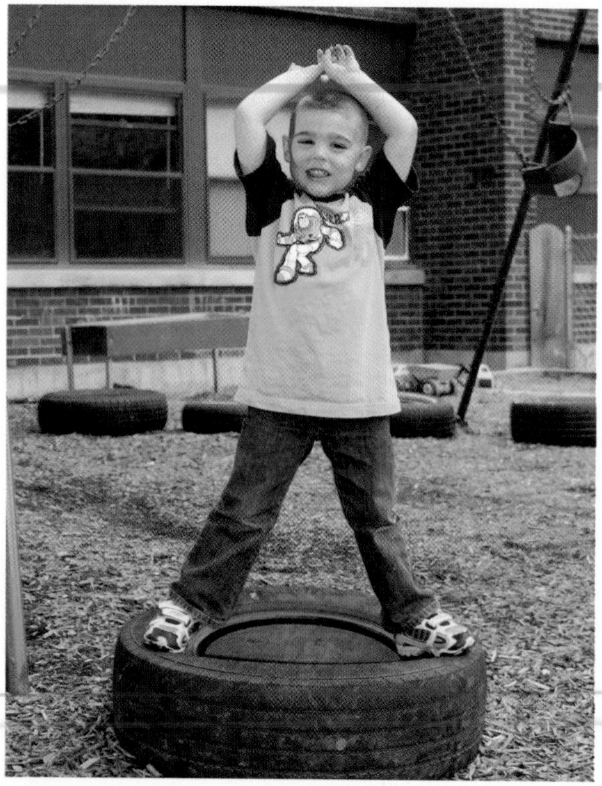

If weather triggers an attack, children may need to remain indoors on days when there are abrupt temperature changes. However, children should be encouraged to participate in regular activities as much as their condition permits. If asthma attacks are caused by strenuous play, teachers should monitor children's activity level and encourage them to rest or to play quietly until the symptoms subside. In any event, teachers should always be prepared to respond quickly in the event that a child develops any difficulty breathing. (See Chapter 9.)

Anemia

Anemia is a common blood disorder that develops when too few red blood cells are available to deliver oxygen to the body's cells. This can be caused by a significant blood loss, decreased production of red blood cells, or their abnormal destruction. Approximately 11 percent of all children under age 5 years experience anemia; however, this rate is greater than 22 percent among black children (CDC, 2008). Many young children are affected by this disorder because of

Issues To Consider **Childhood Asthma**

It is 10 A.M. and six children are lined up on small plastic chairs in the director's office at the Wee Care 4 Kids Child Care Center. Steam hisses from clear plastic masks being held by older children over their noses and mouths while a teacher assists those who are still too young to manage the procedure alone. All of these children have one thing in common—asthma. Twice each day, teachers must administer breathing treatments to increasing numbers of young children who suffer from frequent bouts of wheezing. Unfortunately, this scene is not uncommon in many schools today as the reported incidence of childhood asthma continues to soar.

- What is asthma?
- Why are more children than ever experiencing this chronic condition?
- Why does the incidence of asthma appear to be higher among minorities and children living in poverty?
- Should teachers be responsible for administering medical procedures?
- What steps should you take to prevent administering the procedure incorrectly, and thus protect yourself from liability?

insufficient food or unhealthy dietary patterns (Chilton & Rose, 2009; Cogswell et al., 2009). Additional causes include:

- deficient nutrient intake (iron, folic acid, B-12)
- hereditary disorders, such as sickle cell disease
- chronic infections, such as hepatitis and HIV
- some forms of cancer, such as leukemia
- radiation, chemotherapy, and some medications
- chemical exposure, such as lead poisoning

It is important to understand that anemia is not itself a disease but a symptom of some other condition that requires medical attention. In the majority of cases, anemia is a temporary condition caused by nutrient deficiencies in the child's diet, especially iron intake, and is relatively easy to treat (Eicher-Miller et al., 2009).

Signs and Symptoms

Excessive fatigue is a classic symptom of anemia and is caused by the lack of oxygen cells are receiving. However, the body is often able to compensate for low oxygen levels in the early stages so that the child may not realize that anything is amiss until the condition progresses. As a result, anemia can sometimes be difficult to identify in young children. Common signs of anemia include:

- excessive, prolonged fatigue or lack of energy
- pale skin color; blue discoloration of nail beds
- irritability
- complaints of feeling cold
- rapid heart beat
- dizziness or headache
- feeling short of breath
- decline in school performance
- difficulty concentrating

- loss of appetite
- swollen or sore tongue
- failure to grow

Not every child will experience all of these signs and may present others depending on the underlying cause. Diagnosis requires a complete medical examination and blood tests to determine red blood cell count. For this reason, any concern about a child's health and vitality should be evaluated by a health care professional.

Management

Treatment for anemia is determined by the cause. If the child's diet is deficient, vitamin supplementation may be prescribed along with modifications in nutrient intake (Black, 2009). If the anemia is due to chronic infection, antibiotics may be prescribed. In extreme cases, blood transfusion, surgery, or bone marrow transplant may be necessary.

It is important that families keep teachers informed about their child's condition and treatments so that similar adjustments can be made at school. Any dietary requirements should be addressed during meal planning. Children may need to be given additional opportunities to rest during the day or to participate in less physically demanding activities. Because anemia reduces children's ability to resist infection, frequent hand washing and cleaning practices are important to implement. Teachers should also monitor children's play more closely, as fatigue, low energy, and lack of concentration may increase their vulnerability to unintentional injury.

Childhood Cancers

Childhood cancers are the leading cause of death from disease among children 1 to 14 years of age with over 100,000 new cases diagnosed each year (U.S. Cancer Statistics Working Group, 2009). Young children (1 to 4 years) have the highest incidence of newly reported cases. Adolescents (15 to 19 years) experience the highest death rate due to leukemia while children (5 to 9 years) have the highest death rate from brain tumors.

The term childhood cancer is used inclusively in reference to a broad range of cancer types. Most often, cancers target areas of children's bodies that are undergoing rapid growth, such as the circulatory (blood) system, brain, bones, and kidneys. Leukemia (a cancer of the blood and bone marrow that is more common in boys) accounts for more than 30 percent of all childhood cancers, followed by brain and central nervous system tumors (Jemal et al., 2009). Numerous causes, including environmental chemicals, radioactivity, and prenatal conditions, continue to be under investigation but have yielded only limited conclusive evidence to date. Some children appear to be at higher risk for developing cancer, including those who have HIV infections, certain genetic disorders such as Down syndrome, or those who have parents who smoke (Chang, 2009; Linabery et al., 2008).

Signs and Symptoms

Although childhood cancers are relatively rare, families should never hesitate to seek medical consultation if they have concerns. Many symptoms are unique to a specific form of cancer, while others are more general and easily mistaken for common infectious illnesses, such as the flu. Early warning signs can include:

- loss of appetite, unexplained weight loss
- excessive fatigue that doesn't improve with rest
- painful joints
- unusual bruising, bleeding gums, or small broken blood vessels under the skin
- night sweats or fever
- enlarged glands (in neck, armpits, or groin)

- frequent infections
- persistent headaches
- unexplained cough or difficult breathing
- lumps or masses
- unusual colored urine
- seizures

In most cases, children who present these symptoms will not have cancer. However, if symptoms appear suddenly or if they persist or cause the child unusual discomfort, medical evaluation should be sought. Early diagnosis significantly improves recovery and survival.

Children's return to school following treatment is an important step in their recovery process.

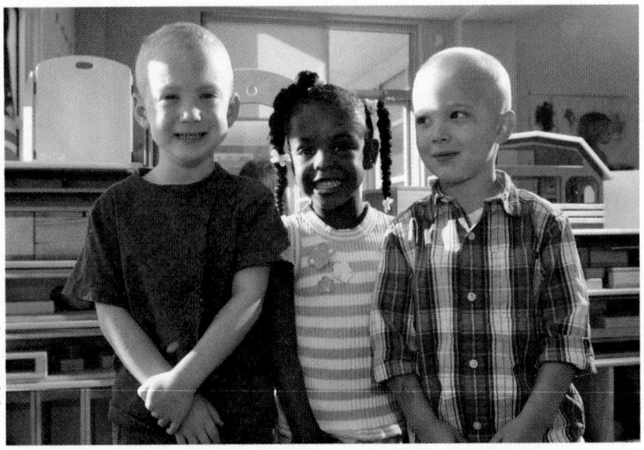

Management

Advances in diagnosis and treatment have resulted in dramatic improvements in children's survival rates. Many children are able to return to school after they have completed and recovered from their treatments. However, this transition requires careful planning and coordination between the child's family, doctors, and school personnel (Harris, 2009; Moore et al., 2009). Children may be sensitive about changes in their appearance, such as surgical scars or hair loss resulting from chemotherapy and/or radiation treatments. Weight loss or gain, fatigue, pain, and generalized weakness may make it difficult for children to participate fully in class activities. Extra precautions must be taken to protect children from communicable illnesses and other infectious conditions because their immune systems are often compromised by chemotherapy and radiation therapies. Children's hearing may also be affected by radiation treatments to the head or high doses of antibiotics that have been administered to fight infection.

Children's return to school is an important step in helping them to resume a near normal lifestyle. Peer interactions can also be beneficial for boosting children's morale and self-esteem. However, teachers must work closely with families to better understand the child's limitations and what adjustments may be needed (Gorin & McAuliffe, 2009). If there are medications to be administered, proper forms and signatures must be obtained. In some cases, children may have an Individualized Education Plan (IEP) to assist with additional services and resources.

It is highly likely that teachers will encounter children who have or are recovering from cancer as treatment success rates continue to improve. Teachers can use these opportunities to better understand childhood cancers and, in turn, to help all children learn about these conditions, accept children with differences, and discover ways they can support their peers (Table 4–6). Initially, children may be apprehensive about a classmate whose appearance and/or ability to play may have changed. Preparing children in advance and encouraging them to talk about their concerns

Table 4–6 Teacher's Checklist: Children with Cancer

- Maintain close communication with the child's family. Find out how much they want other children to know about their child's condition.
- Keep children's emergency contact information located where it is readily accessible; make sure that others know where to find it.
- Determine what, if any, accommodations are needed when the child returns to school, such as dietary modifications, a place to rest, or a change in seating arrangement.
- Review and implement sanitation and hand washing practices.
- Adjust activities and expectations to acknowledge children's limitations, e.g., short attention span, memory problems, learning difficulties, low energy.
- Secure additional resources and services to help children be successful.

can reduce or even eliminate some of these feelings. The American Cancer Society (www.cancer.org) has created a family-friendly website (*Children diagnosed with cancer: Returning to school*), designed to inform and assist families in their efforts to cope with this disease. Although the site is geared toward families, teachers will also find much of the information useful.

Diabetes

Approximately 25 percent of people diagnosed with diabetes, particularly type 2, are children and data suggest this disease is reaching epidemic proportions, especially as obesity rates continue to climb. At present, roughly 10 percent of children 2 to 5 years of age and 30 percent of children ages 6 through 17 are considered to be overweight (CDC, 2009c). Obesity is considered a major factor that places children at greater risk for developing type 2 diabetes. Additional risk factors include having a family history of the disease, **gestational diabetes**, and ethnicity (Kaufman, Gallivan, & Warren-Boulton, 2009). Minority groups, particularly Native Americans, Hispanic/Latinos, and African Americans experience diabetes at a rate that is more than twice that of Caucasian populations (CDC, 2009c).

It is important for teachers to be familiar with the signs, symptoms, and treatment of diabetes, as many of these children will be enrolled in their classrooms. Successful management of childhood diabetes requires careful regulation, which is often challenged by children's frequent exposure to respiratory infections and unpredictable growth changes, activity levels, and eating habits (Hockenberry, 2008).

Signs and Symptoms

Type 1 diabetes is a chronic, incurable, and often hereditary condition that occurs when the pancreas fails to produce an adequate amount of the insulin **hormone**. Type 2 diabetes, often referred to as adult-onset or insulin-resistant diabetes, occurs when the pancreas produces an insufficient amount of insulin or when cells in the body are unable to use the insulin properly. Insulin is necessary for the metabolism of carbohydrates (sugars and starches) and the storage and release of glucose (blood sugar/energy). If insulin is absent or the amount is insufficient, glucose continues to circulate freely in the bloodstream instead of being stored as glycogen in the liver. This condition is known as **hyperglycemia**, which can lead to serious complications, including coma and death, if it is not treated. The onset of type 1diabetes in children usually occurs abruptly, and includes early symptoms such as:

- rapid weight loss
- fatigue and/or weakness
- nausea or vomiting
- frequent urination
- **dehydration**
- excessive thirst and/or hunger
- dry, itchy skin

Symptoms associated with type 2 diabetes are similar, but they tend to develop more slowly and over a longer period of time.

---

gestational diabetes – *a form of diabetes that occurs only during pregnancy; affects the way the mother's body utilizes sugars in foods and increases health risks for the baby.*
hormone – *special chemical substance produced by endocrine glands that influences and regulates certain body functions.*
hyperglycemia – *a condition characterized by an abnormally high level of sugar in the blood.*
dehydration – *a state in which there is an excessive loss of body fluids or extremely limited fluid intake. Symptoms may include loss of skin tone, sunken eyes, and mental confusion.*

Management

Teachers must be aware of each child's individualized situation and treatment regimen—whether the child has type 1 or type 2 diabetes, what dietary restrictions the child requires, and what medical treatments (urine testing, insulin injections, medications) must be administered. Children who have type 1 diabetes must be given insulin injections several times each day, have their glucose levels checked, and closely regulate their diet and activity. Although insulin pumps are being used successfully in adults, their use in young children is still relatively limited (Churchill, Ruppe, & Smaldone, 2009). Some children with type 2 diabetes may also require insulin injections, although many are able to regulate their condition through careful dietary management and/or medications to help their bodies utilize glucose. Increasing children's activity level has also proven effective in reducing the risk of type 2 diabetes and in its management (Bobo et al., 2009; McCall & Raj, 2009). In addition to learning about children's treatment regimens, teachers must also become familiar with the signs of complications associated with diabetes. For example, a child who receives an insulin dose that is too large or too small will exhibit different symptoms and require quite different emergency care. (See Chapter 9: insulin shock, diabetic coma.)

Children with diabetes type 1 must follow special dietary restrictions.

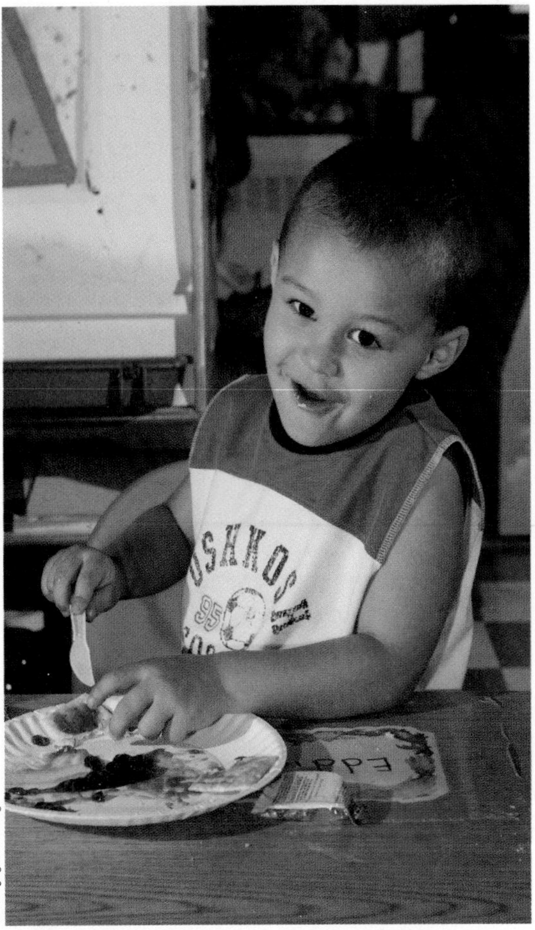

Arrangements should be made to meet with the families of children who are diabetic before they begin to attend school or an out-of-home program. Families can provide teachers with valuable information about their child's condition and how to identify changes in behavior and appearance that may signal an impending complication (Tolbert, 2009). Teachers should also be made aware of dietary restrictions and medical procedures so they can be followed carefully while the child is in school. Plans for handling medical emergencies must also be worked out with families ahead of time and reviewed often.

When teachers are familiar with children's condition and management plans, they are better prepared to respond efficiently and effective to diabetic emergencies (Table 4–7). This can be reassuring

Table 4–7 Teacher's Checklist: Children with Diabetes

- Meet with the family regularly to review the child's progress and treatment procedures.
- Be familiar with the symptoms of hypoglycemia (low blood sugar) and hyperglycemia (high blood sugar) and know how to respond.
- Keep children's emergency information where it is readily accessible; make sure others also know where to find this information.
- Post emergency numbers near the telephone.
- Know where emergency medications are stored and learn how to administer them. Also learn how to check children's blood sugar and train additional staff members to perform these tests.
- Be mindful of any changes in meal schedules, length of outdoor play, or impromptu field trips that might affect the child's insulin needs.
- Review your program's emergency policies and procedures.

Table 4–8 Coping Strategies for Children Who Have Diabetes

Teachers can be instrumental in helping children:
• Learn about their diabetes in simple terms (and not to be ashamed, afraid, or embarrassed). • Understand the importance of maintaining healthy eating habits. • Recognize the relationship between healthy eating habits and feeling well. • Learn to enjoy physical activity. • Assist with their own medical management, e.g., practice good hand washing before glucose tests (finger sticks), cleansing the injection site. • Participate in opportunities that help build positive self-esteem.

for families who may be reluctant to leave children in the care of others. Teachers are also in a unique position to help diabetic children accept and manage their condition and to help their peers learn more about diabetes (Grey et al., 2009) (Table 4–8).

Eczema

Eczema is a chronic inflammatory skin condition. Early symptoms usually appear in infants and children younger than 5, and affect 10 to12 percent of all children (Hockenberry, 2008). Eczema often disappears or significantly improves between the ages of 5 and 15 years in approximately 50 percent of affected children.

Signs and Symptoms

Eczema is caused by an abnormal immune system response and is commonly associated with allergies, especially to certain foods (e.g., eggs, wheat, and milk) and substances that come in contact with the skin (e.g., wool, soaps, perfumes, disinfectants, and animal dander) (Ker & Hartert, 2009). Often there is strong family history of allergy and similar skin problems.

Reddened patches of irritated skin may initially appear on an infant's or toddler's cheeks, forehead, scalp, or neck. Older children may develop dry, itchy, scaly areas on the knees, elbows, wrists, and/or back of hands. Repeated scratching of these areas can lead to open, weeping skin that can become infected. Weather changes can trigger an eczema flare-up or cause it to worsen, especially during summer heat or in winter cold when full-length clothing is likely to be worn. Older children may be reluctant to wear short-sleeved shirts and shorts when warmer weather arrives because they are self-conscious about their appearance.

Management

Eczema is not curable, but it can be controlled through a number of preventive measures. Eliminating environmental allergens is always the preferred and first line of defense. However, in some cases these substances may not yet be known or are difficult to eliminate, such as dust or pollen, but steps can be taken to reduce the child's exposure. Reminding children not to scratch irritated skin and keeping their skin moisturized, especially after bathing or washing, is also helpful.

Avoiding extreme temperature changes can also be effective for controlling symptoms. Keeping children cool in warm weather prevents sweating, which can increase skin irritation. Reducing room temperatures, dressing infants and children in light clothing, and wiping warm areas of their body (creases in neck, elbow, knees, and face) with cool water can improve the child's comfort. Teachers may also be asked to administer antihistamines or topical cortisone ointments that the child's doctor has prescribed. Reducing children's exposure to stress and helping them to develop a healthy self-image are also important strategies for reducing flare-ups.

Signs and Symptoms

Seizures are generally classified according to the pattern of symptoms a child presents, with the most common types being:

- febrile
- absence (previously known as petit mal)
- partial seizures (previously called focal)
- generalized or tonic-clonic (formerly called grand mal)

Approximately 3 to 5 percent of infants and children between the ages of 6 months and 5 years experience *febrile seizures,* with the majority of incidences occurring between 6 to 12 months of age (National Institute of Neurological Disorders & Stroke, 2009). Febrile seizures are thought to be triggered by a high fever, and may cause a child to lose consciousness and experience involuntary jerking movements involving the entire body (Gordon et al., 2009). The child's seizures typically end once the fever subsides and, thus, are not thought to be serious or to result in any permanent damage.

Teachers may be the first to notice the subtle, abnormal behaviors exhibited by children with *absence seizures* (Hughes, 2009). This type of seizure is characterized by momentary lapses of attention that may be observed as:

- repeated incidences of daydreaming
- staring off into space
- a blank appearance
- brief fluttering of the eyes
- temporary interruption of speech or activity
- twitching or dropping of objects

Absence seizures occur most commonly in children 4 to 10 years of age and cause a brief loss of consciousness that lasts between 10 to 20 seconds (Sadleir et al., 2008). Children may abruptly stop an activity and resume it almost as quickly once the seizure subsides. They also are unlikely to recall what has occurred. Teachers should report their observations to the family so they can consult with the child's physician unless the condition has already been diagnosed.

Partial seizures, the most common form of seizure disorder, are characterized by involuntary movements that range from momentary muscle weakness to unusual behaviors such as lip smacking, arm waving, or hysterical laughter, to convulsive tremors affecting the entire body. The child may or may not lose consciousness during the seizure and may have no recall of the event when it is over.

Rhythmic, jerky movements involving the entire body are characteristic of *generalized* or *tonic-clonic seizures.* Some children experience an aura or warning immediately before a seizure begins. This warning may be in the form of a specific sound, smell, taste, sensation, or visual cue. Sudden rigidity or stiffness (tonic phase) is followed by a loss of consciousness and uncontrollable muscular contractions or tremors (clonic phase). When the seizure ends, children may awaken briefly, appear confused, and complain of a headache or dizziness before falling asleep from exhaustion, but they will not remember the event.

Management

Most seizures can be controlled with medication. It is vital that children take their medications every day, even after seizures are under control. Children may initially experience undesirable side effects to these drugs, such as drowsiness, nausea, and dizziness, but the problems tend to disappear with time. Children should be monitored closely by their physician to ensure that prescribed

Table 4–12 Information to Include in a Child's Seizure Report

- child's name
- date and time the seizure occurred
- events preceding the seizure
- how long the seizure lasted
- nature and location of convulsive movements (What parts of the body were involved?)
- child's condition during the seizure, e.g., difficulty breathing, loss of bladder or bowel control, change in skin color (pallor, blue discoloration)
- child's condition following the seizure, e.g., any injuries, complaints of headache, difficulty with speech or memory, desire to sleep
- name of person who observed and who prepared the report

medications and dosages continue to be effective in controlling seizure activity and do not interfere with learning.

Whenever a child experiences a seizure, families should be notified. If the nature of the seizures changes, or if they begin to recur after having been under control, families should be encouraged to consult the child's physician. Teachers should also complete a brief, written report documenting their observations during the seizure and place it into the child's permanent health file (Table 4–12). This information may also be useful to the child's physician for diagnosing a seizure disorder and evaluating current medical treatments.

Teachers play an important role in facilitating the inclusion of children with seizure disorders in classrooms (Frueh, 2008). By arranging safe environments and mastering emergency response techniques (see Chapter 9), teachers can support children's full involvement in all activities. Teachers can build children's confidence and self-esteem by helping them to accept and to cope with their seizure disorder. They can also use the opportunity to teach all children about seizures and to encourage healthy attitudes toward people who may experience them. A teacher's own reactions and displays of genuine acceptance go a long way in teaching children understanding and respect for anyone with special health conditions.

Sickle Cell Disease

Sickle cell disease is an inherited disorder that interferes with the red blood cells' ability to carry oxygen (Hockenberry, 2008). Approximately 1 in every 600 African-American infants and 1 in every 1,200 Hispanic-American infants will be born with this genetic disorder (American Heart Association, 2008). Individuals of Mediterranean, Middle Eastern, and Latin American descent also have the sickle cell gene. Approximately 10 percent of African Americans have the trait for sickle cell disease but do not necessarily develop the disorder; these people are called carriers. When both parents have the sickle cell trait, some of their children may be born with the actual disease, while others may be carriers.

Signs and Symptoms

The abnormal formation of red blood cells in sickle cell anemia causes chronic health problems for the child (American Heart Association, 2008). Red blood cells develop in the shape of a comma or sickle rather than their characteristic round shape (Figure 4–3). As a result, blood flow slows throughout the body and occasionally becomes obstructed. Symptoms of the disease do not usually appear until sometime after the child's first birthday.

Clumping of deformed blood cells results in periods of acute illness called *crisis.* A crisis can be triggered by infection, injury, strenuous exercise, dehydration, exposure to temperature extremes (hot or cold) or, in some cases, for no known reason. Symptoms of a sickle cell crisis include fever, swelling of the hands or feet, severe abdominal and leg pain, vomiting, and ulcers (sores) on the arms and legs. Children are usually hospitalized during a crisis, but they may be free of acute symptoms between flare-ups. Children who have sickle cell disease are also at high risk for having a stroke, which is characterized by muscle weakness, difficulty speaking, and/or seizures (Roberts et al., 2009). In addition, chronic infection and anemia may cause children to be small for their age, irritable, fatigued, and at risk for cognitive delays (Mitchell et al., 2009). They are also more susceptible to infections, a fact that families should consider when placing young children in group care.

Figure 4–4 **Normal and abnormal blood cells in sickle cell disease.**

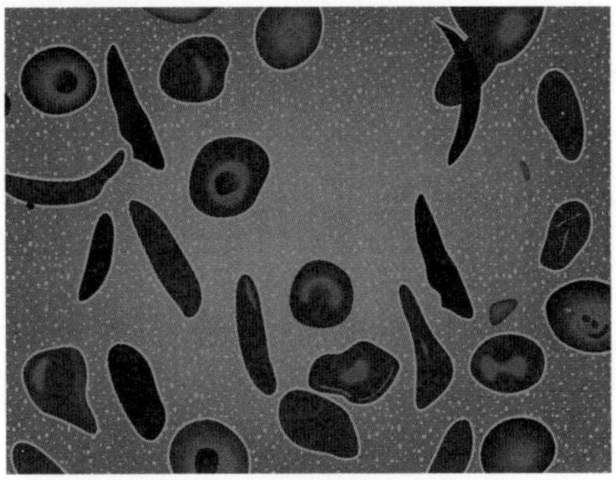

Management

At present there is no known cure for sickle cell disease. Genetic counseling can assist prospective parents who are carriers in determining their probability of having a child with this condition. Hospitals in many states are beginning to screen newborns for the disease before they are sent home. Early diagnosis and medical intervention can help to lessen the frequency and severity of crises and also reduce mortality. Several new drugs are being tested for use with children but final approval has not yet been granted. Children may be given daily antibiotics to reduce the risk of infections, which are a common cause of death. Studies have also shown that frequent blood transfusions may be helpful in preventing acute crises (Wahl & Quirolo, 2009).

Children who have sickle cell disease are living longer today as the result of improved diagnosis and treatments. Although children may appear to be perfectly normal between acute episodes, they often experience a high rate of absenteeism due to flare-ups, infections, and respiratory illnesses, which can interfere with their developmental and academic progress (Schwartz, Radcliffe, & Barakat, 2009). Illness and pain may also disrupt children's intake of essential dietary nutrients. When teachers understand this disease and its effects on children's health, they can work collaboratively with families to help children cope with the condition and continue to progress in school (Table 4–13).

Table 4–13 **Teacher's Checklist: Children with Sickle Cell Disease**

- Meet with the family regularly to review the child's progress and treatment procedures.
- Be familiar with the symptoms of acute complications, such as fever, pain, difficulty breathing, or signs of a stroke (muscle weakness, difficulty speaking, and/or seizures).
- Keep children's emergency information in a place where it is readily accessible; make sure that others know where to find this information.
- Post emergency telephone numbers near the telephone.
- Collaborate with the child's family and provide learning materials that can be used at home.
- Maintain strict sanitation procedures (e.g., hand washing, sanitizing of surfaces and materials) in the classroom to protect children from unnecessary infections.
- Monitor the child's physical activity and provide frequent rest periods to avoid fatigue.
- Protect the child from temperature extremes (heat or cold); arrange for the child to stay indoors when conditions are not favorable.
- Encourage children to eat a healthful diet and drink adequate fluids. (Allow them to use the restroom whenever necessary.)
- Review your program's emergency policies and procedures.

Focus On Families — Protecting Children from West Nile Virus

The West Nile virus is transmitted to humans through the bite of an infected mosquito. Although the number of identified cases remains relatively low, the infection continues to spread. Few people who are bitten will actually develop symptoms of the disease, which include fever, headache, body aches, skin rash, and swollen lymph glands. Some victims experience chronic health problems that persist beyond the acute infection. For these reasons, preventive steps should be taken to protect children against this infectious disease.

- Eliminate sources of standing water in bird baths, plants, fountains, tire swings, buckets, and wading pools.
- Keep children indoors during early-morning hours, or at dusk when mosquitoes are more active.
- Dress children in light-colored, protective clothing, such as a long-sleeved shirt, long pants, and hat.
- Apply insect repellant containing no more than 10 percent DEET sparingly to exposed skin or clothing. Do not apply around the eyes, nose, or mouth, and wash hands carefully when you are finished. Be sure to wash the repellant off when children come indoors. Do not use DEET repellants on children younger than 2 years or if you are pregnant.
- Install or repair screens on doors and windows.
- Keep grass cut short and eliminate areas of overgrown vegetation.
- Contact a physician if your child develops any early signs of the West Nile virus.

Classroom Corner — Teacher Activities

Everyone Is Special

(PreK-2, National Health Education Standard 1.2.2)

Concept: People may be different, but everyone is special.

Learning Objectives

- Children will learn that people are more alike than different.
- Children will learn why it is important to show others respect.

Supplies: unbreakable mirror; sheets of white paper; crayons or markers; shoebox and magazine pictures of children (different ethnicities and abilities); ball of string or yarn

Learning Activities

- Read and discuss any of the following books about children who have special qualities:
  - *That's What Friends Do* by K. Cave (general)
  - *Someone Special, Just Like You* by Tricia Brown (general disabilities)
  - *Be Quiet, Marina!* by Kristen De Bear (cerebral palsy, Down syndrome)
  - *Listen for the Bus: David's Story* by P. McMahon (vision and hearing impaired)
  - *It's Okay to Be Different* by T. Parr (general)
  - *Russ and the Firehouse* by J. E. Rikert (Down syndrome)
  - *A Book of Friends* by D. Ross (diversity)
  - *Andy and His Yellow Frisbee* by M. Thompson (autism)
  - *Susan Laughs* by Jeanne Willis (wheelchair)

(*continued*)

Classroom Corner **Teacher Activities** *(continued)*

- Ask the children to help you describe the word *respect.* Have them suggest other words that mean the same thing (e.g., being kind, treating a person kindly, doing things together, not making fun of a person).
- Have children sit in a circle. Give the first child a ball of string or yarn; ask him/her to name something special about the person sitting next to him/her. The first child should hold onto the end of the yarn and pass the ball to the person they have just described. Continue around the circle with each child describing something about the person sitting next to them and holding onto the string/yarn as it is passed to the next child. When everyone has had a turn, explain how the yarn/string illustrates that we are all connected by many of the same qualities and the things we need or like to do. (We are more alike than different and that makes everyone special.)
- As a group, make a list of things that everybody likes and needs (e.g., food, sleeping, playing, having friends).
- One at a time, have children look in a mirror and describe one quality that makes them special.
- Place the pictures of children in a shoebox. One at a time, have children pull a picture out of the box and describe why they think this person would be special.

Evaluation

- Children will name several different ways that people are the same and different.
- Children will explain why it is important to treat all people with respect and kindness.

Additional lesson plans for grades 3–5 are available on the textbook's website.

Summary

- Many children in group care settings and schools experience a range of chronic diseases and medical conditions.
  - Teachers play an important role in early detection, referral, and management of children's health needs in the classroom.
- Chronic diseases and medical conditions discussed in this chapter include:
  - Allergies: are caused by an abnormal response to substances called allergens. Symptoms can include nasal congestion, headaches, eczema, rashes, asthma, and behavioral changes. Treatment is aimed at identifying offending substances and controlling symptoms.
  - Asthma: involves an allergic response and is becoming increasingly more common for unknown reasons. Management is based on avoiding triggers (such as smoke, chemicals, infection) and administering medications during acute episodes.
  - Anemia: occurs when there are too few red blood cells or they are unable to carry adequate oxygen to body cells. Treatment involves identifying and treating the underlying cause; infection, unhealthy diet, disease.
  - Childhood cancers: are relatively uncommon. Symptoms and treatment vary according to the type of cancer involved; leukemia is the most common form experienced by children.

- Diabetes: is caused by an inadequate amount or lack of the hormone insulin. Early symptoms include weight loss, frequent urination, fatigue, and excessive thirst. Treatment includes daily insulin injections and careful regulation of diet and activity.
- Eczema: is an inflammatory skin condition commonly seen in children who have allergies; it is sometimes outgrown. Treatment is aimed at limiting exposure to offending substances and reducing skin irritation.
- Excessive fatigue: is not common among children, but can be caused by chronic infection, unhealthy diet, anemia, lead poisoning, and other serious conditions. Treatment is directed at eliminating the cause.
- Lead poisoning: continues to be a public health issue. Caused by ingestion of lead from contaminated items. (See Table 4–10.) Elevated blood lead levels can result in impaired cognitive abilities, headaches, loss of appetite, fatigue, and behavior problems. Treatment is aimed at eliminating the source, correcting dietary deficiencies, and administering medication if needed.
- Seizure disorders: caused by abnormal electrical activity in the brain. Symptoms depend on the type of seizure and range from brief inattention to convulsive movements involving the entire body. Medication is usually prescribed to control seizure activity.
- Sickle cell disease: a genetic disease that affects certain ethnic groups; abnormally shaped red blood cells are unable to carry adequate oxygen to cells. Treatment involves avoiding infection and stress; blood transfusions may also be needed.

Terms to Know

food intolerance *p. 87*
symptomatic control *p. 88*
anaphylaxis *p. 89*
gestational diabetes *p. 96*
hormone *p. 96*
hyperglycemia *p. 96*
dehydration *p. 96*
sleep apnea *p. 99*
endocrine *p. 99*
seizures *p. 102*

Chapter Review

A. By Yourself:

1. Define the following terms:
   a. chronic
   b. anaphylaxis
   c. allergen
   d. insulin
   e. hyperglycemia
   f. sleep apnea
2. Explain why some chronic health conditions may be difficult to recognize.
3. Describe the ways in which febrile, absence, partial, and tonic-clonic seizures differ.
4. What are the early warning signs of diabetes? What resources are available in your community to help teachers improve their understanding of this condition and also learn how to administer injections?
5. Explain how you can determine if a child's symptoms are due to a cold or an allergy.

B. As a Group:

1. Divide into small groups. Each group should develop a case study to illustrate one of the chronic health conditions described in this chapter. The case study should include a description of the condition—its

cause, symptoms, effects on the child and family, and classroom strategies for ensuring the child's successful inclusion. Have groups take turns reading and discussing each other's case studies.

2. Develop an emergency response plan for a child who has a seizure disorder and discuss how it would be implemented in the classroom.
3. Discuss why the incidence of childhood allergies and asthma appears to be increasing.
4. Explain how a child's environment may contribute to the development and progression of chronic health conditions.
5. Discuss what teachers can do to support a child who has recently undergone cancer treatment and is ready to return to school.

Case Study

Read the case study and answer the questions that follow.

Mr. Lui arranged to take his first grade class on a field trip to a nearby nature park after they had spent several weeks learning about small mammals living in the wild. The day was warm and sunny, and the children were bubbling with excitement as they completed a short hike around the beaver ponds. As they headed back to the picnic shelter for lunch, one of the children who had run ahead let out a sudden shriek and fell to the ground. The teacher quickly ran to the child and observed that she was unconscious and her arms and legs were jerking violently. Mr. Lui sent one of the other children to get the park ranger, calmed the rest of the children down, and then used his cell phone to call 911 for emergency medical assistance. Within minutes, the seizure ended and the child regained consciousness. When the paramedics arrived, they checked the child over carefully and were satisfied that she required no additional treatment at the time. Mr. Lui contacted the child's family and learned that her doctor had recently prescribed a new seizure medication.

1. What type of seizure was this child probably experiencing?
2. What indication did the child give of a preceding aura?
3. What signs, in addition to the jerky movements, might you expect to observe during and immediately following this type of seizure?
4. Should Mr. Lui have called for emergency assistance? Would you expect his response to be different if he had known that the child was being treated for a seizure disorder?
5. What steps should Mr. Lui take when the child's seizure ends?
6. How can Mr. Lui turn this event into a learning experience for the other children?

Application Activities

1. Locate and read at least eight children's books written about several of the chronic diseases and medical conditions discussed in this chapter.
2. Interview teachers in three different educational settings. Inquire about the types of allergies they encounter most often and how they manage children's health needs in the classroom. Develop a simple, five-day snack menu for a toddler who is allergic to milk and milk products, chocolate, and eggs.
3. Design a poster for classroom teachers that illustrates, step-by-step, how to administer an EpiPen.

4. Conduct an online search and compile a list of sources that could potentially expose children to lead poisoning.
5. Go to the website *Bubbliboo* (http://www.bubbliboo.com) and click through each of the sections on childhood asthma. If you were a child, would you find the site attractive? Based on what you have learned in this chapter, is the information accurate and presented in a way that children would understand?

Helpful Web Resources

Asthma and Allergy Foundation of America	http://www.aafa.org
American Cancer Society	http://www.cancer.org
American Diabetes Association	http://www.diabetes.org
American Lung Association	http://www.lungusa.org
Canadian Pediatric Society	http://www.cps.ca
Centers for Disease Control and Prevention	http://www.cdc.gov
Center for Health and Health Care in Schools	http://www.healthinschools.org
Indian Health Service	http://www.ihs.gov
KidsHealth–Nemours Center for Children's Health Media	http://www.kidshealth.org
National Childhood Cancer Foundation	http://www.curesearch.org
National Diabetes Education Program	http://www.ndep.nih.gov

You are just a click away from additional health, safety, and nutrition resources! Go to www.CengageBrain.com to access this text's Education CourseMate website, where you'll find:

- glossary flashcards, activities, tutorial quizzes, videos, web links, and more

References

Ahmad, N., Biswas, S., Bae, S., Meador, K., Huang, R., & Singh, K. (2009). Association between obesity and asthma in US children and adolescents, *Journal of Asthma*, 46(7), 642–646.

Allen, K. E., & Cowdery, G. (2009). *The exceptional child: Inclusion in early child hood education.* (6th ed.). Belmont, CA: Wadsworth Cengage Learning.

American Heart Association. (2008). Sickle cell disease. Accessed on November 6, 2009, from http://www.strokeassociation.org/presenter.jhtml?identifier=3034962.

Asthma & Allergy Foundation of America (AAFA). (2009a). Allergy facts and figures. Accessed on October 30, 2009, from http://www.aafa.org/display.cfm?id=9&sub=20&cont=286.

AAFA. (2009b). Food allergies. Accessed on November 7, 2009, from http://www.aafa.org/display.cfm?id=9&sub=30.

Baena-Cagnani, C., Gómez, R.; Baena-Cagnani, R., & Canonica, G. (2009). Impact of environmental tobacco smoke and active tobacco smoking on the development and outcomes of asthma and rhinitis, *Current Opinion in Allergy & Clinical Immunology*, 9(2), 136–140.

Black, M. (2009). Micromineral deficiencies and child development, *Nutrition Today*, 44(2), 71–74.

Bobo, N., Shantz, S., Kaufman, F., & Kollipara, S. (2009). Lowering risk for type 2 diabetes in high-risk youth, *American Journal of Health Education*, 40(5), 282–285.

Bryant-Stephens, T. (2009). Asthma disparities in urban environments, *Journal of Allergy & Clinical Immunology*, 123(6), 1199–1206.

Centers for Disease Control & Prevention (CDC). (2009a). Asthma. Accessed on October 30, 2009 from http://www.cdc.gov/HealthyYouth/Asthma.

CDC. (2009b). Lead and candy. Accessed on October 30, 2009 from http://www.cdc.gov/nceh/lead/tips/candy.htm.

CDC (2009c). Office of Minority Health & Health Disparities (OMHD), Eliminate disparities in diabetes. Accessed on October 30, 2009 from http://www.cdc.gov/omhd/AMH/factsheets/diabetes.htm.

CDC. (2008). 2008 Pediatric nutrition surveillance. Accessed on December 11, 2009 from http://www.cdc.gov/pednss/pednss_tables/pdf/national_table18.pdf.

Chang, J. (2009). Parental smoking and childhood leukemia, *Methods in Molecular Biology*, 472, 103–137.

Chilton, M., & Rose, D. (2009). A rights-based approach to food insecurity in the United States, *American Journal of Public Health,* 99(7), 1203–1211.

Churchill, J., Ruppe, R., & Smaldone, A. (2009). Use of continuous insulin infusion pumps in young children with type 1 diabetes: A systematic review, *Journal of Pediatric Health Care*, 23(3), 173–179.

Cogswell, M., Looker, A., Pfeiffer, S., Cook, J., Lacher, D., Beard, J., Lynch, S., & Grummer-Strawn, L. (2009). Assessment of iron deficiency in US preschool children and nonpregnant females of childbearing age: National health and examination survey, 2003-2006, *American Journal of Clinical Nutrition*, 89(5), 1334–1342.

Eicher-Miller, H., Mason, A., Weaver, C., McCabe, G., & Boushey, C. (2009). Food insecurity is associated with iron deficiency anemia in US adolescents, *American Journal of Clinical Nutrition*, 90(5), 1358–1371.

Epilepsy Foundation. (2009). Epilepsy and seizure statistics. Accessed on November 6, 2009 from http://www.epilepsyfoundation.org/about/statistics.cfm.

Frueh, E. (2008). Seizure management for school-age children, *Education Digest*, 73(6), 38–40.

Gordon, K., Dooley, J., Wood, E., & Bethune, P. (2009). Is temperature regulation different in children susceptible to febrile seizures?, *Canadian Journal of Neurological Sciences*, 36(2), 192–195.

Gorin, S., & McAuliffe, P. (2009). Implications of childhood cancer survivors in the classroom and the school, *Health Education*, 109(1), 25–48.

Gozal, D., & Kheirandish-Gozal, L. (2009). Obesity and excessive daytime sleepiness in prepubertal children with obstructive sleep apnea, *Pediatrics*, 123(1), 13–18.

Gracia, R., & Snodgrass, W. (2007). Lead toxicity and chelation therapy, *American Journal of Health-System Pharmacology*, 64(1), 45–53.

Grey, M., Whittemore, R., Jaser, S., Ambrosino, J., Lindemann, E., Liberti, L., Northrup, V., & Dziura, J. (2009). Effects of coping skills training on school-age children with type 1 diabetes, *Research in Nursing & Health*, 32(4), 405–418.

Gupta, R., Kim, J., Springston, E., Smith, B., Pongraciec, J., Wang, X., & Holl, J. (2009). Food allergy knowledge, attitudes, and beliefs in the United States, *Annals of Allergy, Asthma & Immunology*, 103(1), 43–50.

Guralnick, M. (2004). The effectiveness of early intervention for vulnerable children: A developmental perspective. In M. Feldman (Ed.), *Early intervention: The essential readings*, Hoboken, NJ: Wiley-Blackwell.

Harris, M. (2009). School reintegration for children and adolescents with cancer: The role of school psychologists, *Psychology in the Schools*, 46(7), 579–592.

Hockenberry, M. (2008). *Wong's essentials of pediatric nursing.* (8th ed.). St Louis: Mosby.

Hornung, R., Lanphear, B., & Dietrich, K. (2009). Age of greatest susceptibility to childhood lead exposure: A new statistical approach, *Environmental Health Perspectives*, 117(8), 1309–1312.

Hudson, J., Gradisar, M., Gamble, A., Schniering, C., & Rebelo, I. (2009). The sleep patterns and problems of clinically anxious children, *Behaviour Research & Therapy,* 47(4), 339–344.

Hughes, J. (2009). Absence seizures: A review of recent reports with new concepts, *Epilepsy & Behavior*, 15(4), 404–412.

Jemal, A., Siegel, R., Ward, E., Hao, Y., Xu, J., & Thun, M. (2009). Cancer statistics 2009, *CA: A Cancer Journal for Clinicians*, 59(4), 225–249.

Kaufman, J., Gallivan, M., & Warren-Boulton, E. (2009). Overview of diabetes in children and teens, *American Journal of Health Education* 40(5), 259–264.

Keil, T., Lau, S., Roll, S., Grüber, C., Nickel, R., Niggemann, B., Wahn, U., Willich, S., & Kulig, M. (2009). Maternal smoking increases risk of allergic sensitization and wheezing only in children with allergic predisposition: Longitudinal analysis from birth to 10 years, *Allergy*, 64(3), 445–451.

Ker, J., & Hartert, T. (2009). The atopic march: What's the evidence?, *Annals of Allergy, Asthma & Immunology*, 103(4), 282–289.

Krauss-Etschmann, S. Niedermaier, S., Beyer, J., Campoy, C., Escolano, V., Decsi, T., Jakobik, V., Schendel, D., Demmelmair, H., & Heinrich, J. (2009). Current use of room disinfectants and allergic symptoms at the age of 4 years, *Journal of Allergy & Clinical Immunology*, 123(5), 1176–1178.

Lee, S., Kim, H., Yu, J., & Hong, S. (2009). Exercise-induced asthma in children, *Expert Review of Clinical Immunology*, 5(2), 193–207.

Lieberman, L., Kirby, M., Ozolins, L., & Mosko, J. (2009). Initial presentation of unscreened children with sickle cell disease: The Toronto experience, *Pediatric Blood & Cancer*, 53(3), 397–400.

Lim, J., Wood, B., & Cheah, P. (2009). Understanding children with asthma: Trouble and triggers, *Childhood Education*, 85(5), 307–313.

Linabery, A., Blair, C., Gamis, A., Olshan, A., Heerema, N., & Ross, J. (2008). Congenital abnormalities and acute leukemia among children with Down syndrome: A Children's Oncology Group study, *Cancer Epidemiology, Biomarkers, & Prevention*, 17(10), 2572–2577.

Liu, L., Poon, R., Chen, L., Frescura, A., Montuschi, P., Ciabattoni, G., Wheeler, A., & Dales, R. (2009). Acute effects of air pollution on pulmonary function, airway inflammation and oxidative stress in asthmatic children, *Environmental Health Perspectives*, 117(4), 668–675.

Lux, R., Awa, W., & Walter, U. (2009). An interdisciplinary analysis of sex and gender in relation to the pathogenesis of bronchial asthma, *Respiratory Medicine*, 103(5), 637–649.

McCall, A., & Raj, R. (2009). Exercise for prevention of obesity and diabetes in children and adolescents, *Clinical Sports Medicine*, 28(3), 393–421.

McWhirter, J., McCann, D., & Coleman, H. (2008). Can schools promote the health of children with asthma?, *Education Research*, 23(6), 917–930.

Meltzer, E., Blaiss, M., Derebery, M., Mahr, T., Gordon, B., Sheth, K., Simmons, A., Wingertzahn, M., & Boyle, J. (2009). Burden of allergic rhinitis: Results from the Pediatric Allergies in America survey, *Journal of Allergy and Clinical Immunology*, 124(3), S43–S70.

Meyer, R. (2009). Infant feeding in the first year, *Journal of Family Health Care*, 19(2), 47–50.

Mitchell, M., Carpenter, G., Crosby, L., Bishop, C., Hines, J., & Noll, J. (2009). Growth status in children and adolescents with sickle cell disease, *Pediatric Hematology & Oncology*, 26(4), 202–215.

Moore, J., Kaffenberger, C., Goldberg, P., Oh, K., & Hudspeth, R. (2009). School reentry for children with cancer: Perceptions of nurses, school personnel and parents, *Journal of Pediatric Oncology Nursing*, 26(2), 86–99.

Muñoz-Furlong, A., & Weiss, C. (2009). Characteristics of food-allergic patients placing them at risk for a fatal anaphylactic episode, *Current Allergy & Asthma Reports*, 9(1), 57–63.

National Institute of Neurological Disorders & Stroke. Febrile seizure fact sheet. Accessed on November 1, 2009 from http://www.ninds.nih.gov/disorders/febrile_seizures/detail_febrile_seizures.htm#1 20733111.

Nelson, B., Awad, D., Alexander, J., & Clark, N. (2009). The continuing problem of asthma in very young children: A community-based participatory research project, *Journal of School Health*, 79(5), 209–215.

Nelson C. (2000). The neurobiological bases of early intervention. In: *Handbook of of Early Childhood Intervention* (2nd ed.) (eds. J.P. Shonkoff & S.J. Meisels), pp. 204–277. Cambridge: Cambridge University Press.

Nordling, E., Berglind, N., Melén, E., Emenius, G., Hallberg, J., Nyberg, F., Pershagen, G., Svartengren, M., Wickman, M., & Bellander, T. (2008). Traffic-related air pollution and childhood respiratory symptoms, function and allergies, *Epidemiology*, 19(3), 401–408.

Phipatanakul, W., & Gaffin, J. (2009). The role of indoor allergens in the development of asthma, *Current Opinion in Allergy & Clinical Immunology*, 9(2),128–135.

Ramey, C., & Ramey, S. (1998). Early intervention and early experience, *American Psychologist*, 53(2), 109–120.

Raymond, J., Anderson, R., Feingold, M., Homa, D., & Brown, M. (2009). Risk for elevated blood lead levels in 3- and 4-year-old children, *Maternal & Child Health Journal*, 13(1), 40–47.

Roberts, L., O'Driscoll, S., Dick, M., Height, S., Deane, C., Goss, D., Pohl, K., & Rees, D. (2009). Stroke prevention in the young child with sickle cell anaemia, *Annals of Hematology*, 88(10), 943–946.

Sadleir, L., Scheffer, I., Smith, S., Carstensen, B., Carlin, J., Connolly, M., & Farrell, K. (2008). Factors influencing clinical features of absence seizures, *Epilepsia*, 49(12), 2100–2107.

Schueepp, K., Devadason, S., Roller, C., Minocchieri, S., Moeller, A., Hamacher, J., & Wildhaber, J. (2009). Aerosol delivery of nebulised budesonide in young children with asthma, *Respiratory Medicine*, 103(11), 1738–1745.

Schwartz, L., Radcliffe, J., & Barakat, L. (2009). Associates of school absenteeism in adolescents with sickle cell disease, *Pediatric Blood & Cancer*, 52(1), 92–96.

Smith, K., Warholak, T., Armstrong, E., Leib, M., Rehfeld, R., & Malone, D. (2009). Evaluation of risk factors and health outcomes among persons with asthma, *Journal of Asthma*, 46(3), 234–237.

Stecher, D., Bulloch, B., Sales, J., Schaefer, C., & Keahey, L. (2009). Epinephrine auto-injectors: Is needle length adequate for delivery of epinephrine intramuscularly?, *Pediatrics*, 124(1), 65–70.

Stingone, J., & Claudio, L. (2009). Components of recommended asthma care and the use of long-term control medication among urban children with asthma, *Medical Care*, 47(9), 940–947.

Tai, A., Volkmer, R., & Burton, A. (2009). Association between asthma symptoms and obesity in preschool (4–5 year old) children, *Journal of Asthma*, 46(4), 363–365.

Tolbert, R. (2009). Managing type 1 diabetes at school: An integrative review, *Journal of School Nursing*, 25(1), 55–61.

U.S. Cancer Statistics Working Group. (2009). Childhood cancers. *United States Cancer Statistics: 1999–2005 Incidence and Mortality Web-based Report.* Atlanta: U.S. Department of Health and Human Services, Centers for Disease Control and Prevention and National Cancer Institute. Accessed on February 5, 2010 from http://apps.nccd.cdc.gov/uscs/Table.aspx?Group=TableChild&Year=2005&Displa y=n.

Wahl, S., & Quirolo, K. (2009). Current issues in blood transfusion for sickle cell disease, *Current Opinion in Pediatrics*, 21(1), 15–21.

Wengrovitz, A., & Brown, M. (2009). Recommendations for blood lead screening of Medicaid-eligible children aged 1–5 years: An updated approach to targeting a group at high risk, *Morbidity & Mortality Weekly Report*, 58(RR09), 1–11.

Young, M., Muñoz-Furlong, A., & Sicherer, S. (2009). Management of food allergies in schools: A perspective for allergists, *Journal of Allergy & Clinical Immunology*, 124(2), 175–182.

CHAPTER

5

The Infectious Process and Environmental Control

NAEYC Standards *Chapter Links*

- **#1 a, b, and c:** Promoting child development and learning
- **#3 a, c, and d:** Observing, documenting, and assessing to support young children and families.

Learning Objectives

After studying this chapter, you should be able to:

- Discuss why young children experience frequent communicable illness.
- Explain what factors are required for an illness to be communicable.
- Identify the stages of a communicable illness.
- Name and describe four control measures that teachers can use to reduce communicable illnesses in the classroom.

Young children, especially those under 3 years of age, are highly susceptible to communicable illness (Mink & Yeh, 2009). Frequent upper respiratory infections are common, especially during a child's first experiences in group settings. Several factors contribute to this increased risk. First, young children are more vulnerable to infections because they have had limited exposure to communicable illnesses and, thus, fewer opportunities to develop protective **antibodies**. Physical disabilities and chronic conditions, such as diabetes, sickle cell anemia, and asthma further reduce children's resistance and may put them at even greater risk.

Second, immature development of children's body structures also contributes to a higher rate of illness. For example, shorter distances between an infant's or toddler's ears, nose, and throat encourage frequent respiratory infections.

Third, group settings, such as home- and center-based early childhood programs and elementary school classrooms, are ideal environments for the rapid spread of illness (Bright, Boone & Gerba, 2010; Sandora, Shih, & Goldman, 2008). Children are also exposed to communicable illnesses in numerous other places, including grocery stores, shopping centers, churches, libraries, and restaurants where groups of people are present. Many of children's habits, such as sucking on fingers, mouthing toys, carelessness with bodily secretions (runny noses, drool, urine, stool), and an

---

antibodies – *special substances produced by the body that help protect against disease.*

abundance of physical contact also encourage the rapid spread of communicable illness. For these reasons, every attempt must be made to establish and implement policies, practices, and learning experiences that will help to protect young children from unnecessary exposure.

Communicable illnesses can be spread when children mouth toys and other objects.

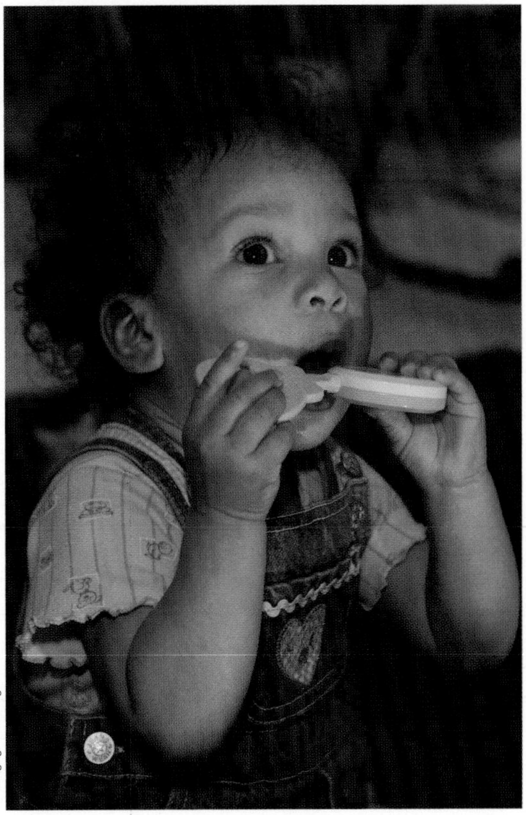

© Cengage Learning

Communicable Illness

A **communicable** illness is an infection that can be transmitted or spread from one person or animal to another. Three factors, all of which must be present at approximately the same time, are required for this process to occur (Figure 5–1).

- a pathogen
- a susceptible host
- a method of transmission

First, a **pathogen** or disease-causing agent, such as a bacteria, virus, or parasite, must be present and available for transmission. These invisible germs are specific for each illness and are most commonly located in discharges from the respiratory (nose, throat, lungs) and intestinal tract of infected persons. They can also be found in the blood, urine, and discharges from the eyes and skin. Most pathogens require a living host for their survival, with the exception of the organism that causes tetanus; it is able to survive in soil and dust for several years.

Second, there must be a **susceptible host** or person who can become infected with the pathogen. The communicable illnesses that children most commonly experience usually enter their new host through either a break in the skin, the **respiratory tract**, or digestive tract. The route of entry depends on the specific illness or disease involved.

Not every child who is exposed to a particular virus or bacteria will become infected. Conditions must be favorable to allow an infectious organism to successfully avoid the body's defense systems, multiply, and establish itself. Children who are well rested, adequately nourished, **immunized**, and healthy are generally less susceptible to infectious organisms. Some children will have immunity as a result of having experienced a prior case of the same illness. However, the length of this protection varies with the illness and can range from several days to a lifetime. For example, a child who has had chickenpox will have permanent immunity to the

Figure 5–1 **Communicable illness model.**

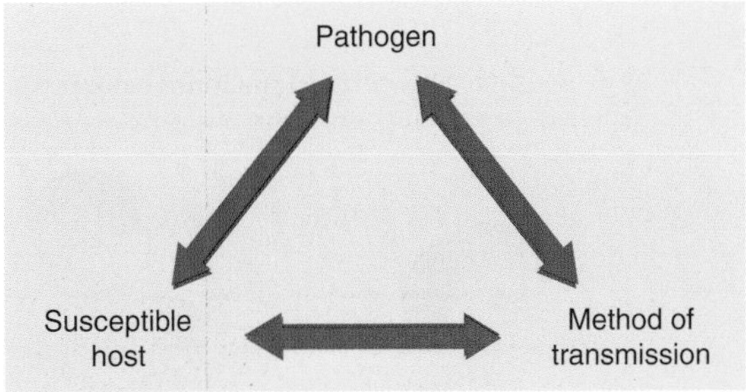

communicable – *a condition that can be spread or transmitted from one individual to another.*
pathogen – *a microorganism capable of producing illness or infection.*
susceptible host – *an individual who is capable of being infected by a pathogen.*
respiratory tract – *pertains to, and includes, the nose, throat, trachea, and lungs.*
immunized – *a state of becoming resistant to a specific disease through the introduction of living or dead microorganisms into the body, which then stimulates the production of antibodies.*

disease. Children who are carriers or who experience a very mild case of some communicable diseases may also develop immunity without knowing that they have been infected.

Third, a method for transmitting the infectious agent from the original source to a new host is necessary to complete the communicable process. Infectious agents are most commonly spread via **airborne transmission in school settings.** Disease-causing pathogens are carried on tiny droplets of moisture which are expelled during coughs, sneezes, or while talking (Figure 5–2). Influenza, colds, meningitis, tuberculosis, and chickenpox are examples of infectious illnesses spread in this manner.

Fecal-oral transmission is the second-most common route by which infectious illnesses are spread in group settings, particularly when there are infants and toddlers in diapers. Teachers who fail to wash their hands properly after changing diapers or assisting children with toileting needs are often responsible for spreading disease-causing germs, especially if they also handle food. For this reason, it is advisable to assign diaper changing and food preparation responsibilities to different teachers. Children's hands should always be washed after diaper changes or after using the bathroom because their hands often end up in their mouths. Appropriate hand-washing procedures should be taught and monitored closely to be sure children are washing correctly. Pinworms, hepatitis A, salmonella, and giardiasis are examples of illnesses transmitted by fecal-oral contamination.

A third common method of transmission involves direct contact with body fluids, such as blood or mucus, or an infected area on another person's body. The infectious organisms are transferred directly from the original source of infection to a new host. Ringworm, athlete's foot, impetigo, Hepatitis B, and conjunctivitis (pinkeye) are a few of the conditions spread in this manner.

Communicable illnesses can also be transmitted through indirect contact. This method involves the transfer of infectious organisms from an infected individual to an intermediate object, such as water, milk, dust, food, toys, towels, eating utensils, animals, or insects, and finally to the new susceptible host. It is also possible to infect oneself with certain bacteria and viruses, such as those causing colds and influenza, by touching the moist linings of the eyes, nose and/or mouth with contaminated hands.

Eliminating any one of these factors (pathogen, host, or method of transmission) will interrupt the spread of a communicable illness. This is an important concept for families and teachers to understand when trying to control outbreaks of communicable illness, especially in group settings. It can also be beneficial for reducing the number of illnesses that teachers may experience or carry home to their families.

Figure 5–2 How infectious illnesses are spread.

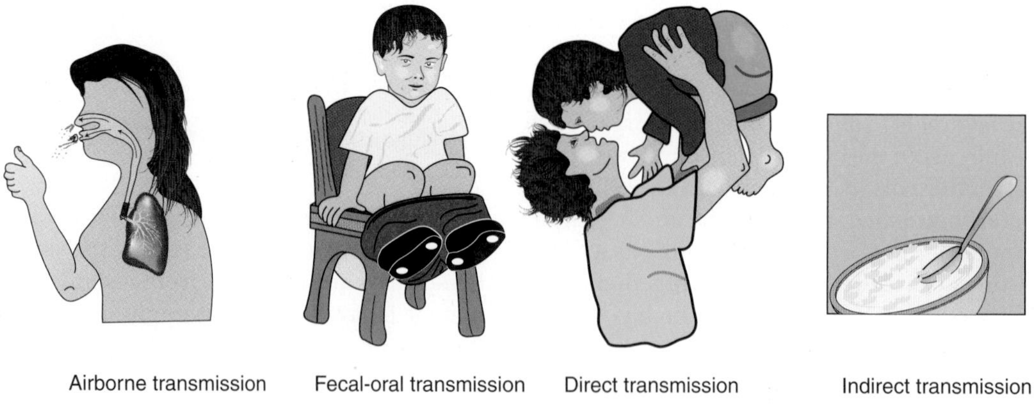

airborne transmission – *when germs are expelled into the air through coughs/sneezes, and transmitted to another individual via tiny moisture drops.*

fecal-oral transmission – *when germs are transferred to the mouth via hands contaminated with fecal material.*

Stages Of Illness

Communicable illnesses generally develop in predictable stages:

- incubation
- prodromal
- acute
- convalescence

Because these stages sometimes overlap, it may be difficult to identify when each begins and ends. The length of each stage also varies for different illnesses.

The **incubation** stage includes the time between exposure to a pathogen and the appearance of the first signs or symptoms of illness. During this period, the infectious organisms enter the body and multiply rapidly in an attempt to establish themselves and overpower the body's defense systems. The length of the incubation stage is described in terms of hours or days and varies for each communicable disease. For example, the incubation period for chickenpox ranges from 2 to 3 weeks following exposure, while for the common cold it is thought to be only 12 to 72 hours. Many infectious illnesses are already communicable near the end of this stage. The fact that children are often **contagious** before any symptoms are apparent makes the control of infectious illness in the classroom challenging, despite teachers' careful observations.

The **prodromal** stage begins when an infant or young child experiences the first nonspecific signs of infection and ends with the appearance of symptoms characteristic of a particular communicable illness. This stage may last from several hours to several days. However, not all communicable diseases have a prodromal stage. Early symptoms commonly associated with the prodromal stage may include headache, unexplained fatigue, low-grade fever, a slight sore throat, and a general feeling of restlessness or irritability. Many of these complaints are so vague that they can easily go unnoticed. However, because children are highly contagious during this stage, teachers and parents must understand that these subtle changes could signal an impending illness.

Fatigue and irritability may be the first indications of a communicable illness.

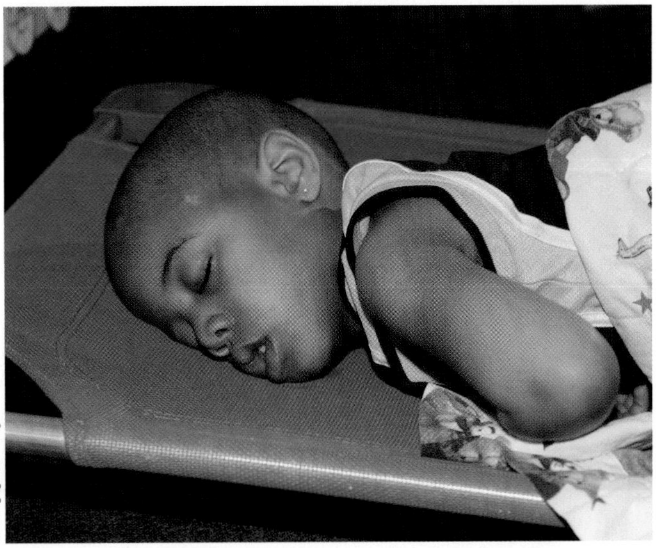

During the **acute** stage an infant or child is definitely sick and highly contagious. The onset of this stage is marked by the appearance of symptoms characteristic of the illness and it ends as the person begins to slowly recover. Some of the early symptoms such as fever, sore throat, cough, runny nose, rash, or enlarged lymph glands are common to many infectious diseases.

---

incubation – *the interval of time between exposure to infection and the appearance of the first signs or symptoms of illness.*
contagious – *capable of being transmitted or passed from one person to another.*
prodromal – *the appearance of the first nonspecific signs of infection; this stage ends when the symptoms characteristic of a particular communicable illness begin to appear.*
acute – *the stage of an illness or disease during which an individual is definitely sick and exhibits symptoms characteristic of the particular illness or disease involved.*

However, there are also characteristic patterns and variations of these symptoms that can be useful for identifying a specific communicable illness.

The **convalescent** or recovery stage generally follows automatically unless complications develop. During this stage, symptoms gradually disappear, children begin to feel better, and they are no longer considered to be contagious.

Control Measures

Teachers have an obligation and responsibility to help protect young children from communicable illnesses. Although many illnesses are simply an inconvenience, others can cause serious complications. Because classrooms are ideal settings for the rapid spread of many infectious conditions, control measures must be practiced diligently to limit their spread.

Observations

Teachers' daily health observations are effective for identifying children in the early stages of a communicable illness. By removing sick children from group settings, a direct source of infection can be eliminated. However, it is important to remember that many illnesses are communicable before the characteristic symptoms appear, so not all spread can be avoided. Early recognition of sick children requires that adults develop a sensitivity to changes in children's normal appearance and behavior patterns (Aronson, 2002). This process is facilitated by the fact that young children generally look and behave differently when they are not feeling well. Their actions, facial expressions, skin color, sleep habits, appetite, and comments provide valuable warnings of impending illness. Other signs may include:

- unusually pale or flushed skin
- red or sore throat
- enlarged **lymph glands**
- nausea, vomiting, or diarrhea
- rash, spots, or open lesions
- watery or red eyes
- headache or dizziness
- chills, fever, or achiness
- fatigue or loss of appetite

However, these same signs and symptoms may not always warrant concern in all children. For example, a teacher who knows that Tony's allergies often cause a red throat and cough in the fall, or that Shadra's recent irritability is probably related to her mother's hospitalization, would not be alarmed by these observations. Teachers must be able to distinguish between children with potentially infectious illnesses and those with health problems that are explainable and not necessarily contagious. Knowing that some illnesses are more prevalent during certain times of the year or that a current outbreak exists in the community can also be useful for identifying children who may be infectious.

Policies

Written policies offer another important method for controlling infectious illnesses (Mink & Yeh, 2009; Copeland & Shope, 2005). Policies should be consistent with state regulations, and in place before a program begins to enroll children. Frequent review of policies with staff members ensures their familiarity with the information, and that enforcement will be more consistent.

---

convalescent – *the stage of recovery from an illness or disease.*
lymph glands – *specialized groupings of tissue that produce and store white blood cells for protection against infection and illness.*

General health and exclusion policies should also be described in handbooks that are given to families. Collaborative partnerships are strengthened when families know in advance what to expect if their child does become ill. Exclusion and inclusion policies should establish clear guidelines for when sick children should be kept home, when they will be sent home due to illness, and when they are considered well enough to return (Figure 5–3).

Opinions differ on how restrictive exclusion policies should be (Alkon et al., 2008). Some experts believe that children with mild illnesses can remain in group care, while others feel that children who exhibit symptoms should be sent home. Because many early signs of communicable illnesses are nonspecific, teachers and families may have difficulty distinguishing between conditions that warrant exclusion and medical attention and those that do not. Consequently, programs may decide to set exclusion policies that are fairly restrictive unless they are prepared to care for sick children.

It is also important for programs to adopt policies about notifying families when children are exposed to communicable illnesses. This measure enables parents to watch for early symptoms and to keep sick children home (Figure 5–4). Immunization requirements should also be addressed in program policies, as well as actions the program will take if children are not in compliance. Local public health authorities can provide useful information and guidance to programs when they are formulating new policies or are confronted with a communicable health problem about which they are unsure.

Guidelines for Teacher Illness Teachers are exposed to many infectious illnesses through their daily contact with young children. They often experience an increased frequency of illness—especially during the initial months of employment—that is similar to what young children do when they enroll in a new program or school. However, over time, teachers gradually build up their resistance to many of these illnesses. They can also take steps to minimize their risk by obtaining a pre-employment health assessment, having a tuberculin test, updating immunizations, following a healthy lifestyle, and practicing frequent hand washing. Teachers who are pregnant may want to temporarily reconsider working around young children because some communicable illnesses, such as cytomegalovirus (CMV) and German measles can affect the fetus, especially during the early months.

When teachers are ill and trying to decide whether or not they should go to work, they must follow the same exclusion guidelines that apply to sick children. Adults who do not feel well will not be able to meet the rigorous demands necessary for working with young children and also face an

Figure 5–3 Sample exclusion policy.

EXCLUSION POLICY

Control of communicable illness among the children is a prime concern. Policies and guidelines related to outbreaks of communicable illness in this center have been developed with the help of the health department and local pediatricians. In order to protect the entire group of children, as well as your own child, we ask that families assist us by keeping sick children at home if they have experienced any of the following symptoms *within the past 24 hours:*

- a fever over 100°F (37.8°C) orally or 99°F (37.2°C) axillary (under the arm)
- signs of a newly developing cold or uncontrollable coughing
- diarrhea, vomiting, or an upset stomach
- unusual or unexplained loss of appetite, fatigue, irritability, or headache
- any discharge or drainage from eyes, nose, ears, or open sores

Children who become ill with any of these symptoms will be returned home. We appreciate your cooperation with this policy. If you have any questions about whether or not your child is well enough to attend school or group care that day, please call the center *before* bringing your child.

Figure 5–4 Sample letter notifying families of their child's exposure.

Date________________________

Dear Parent:

There is a possibility that your child has been exposed to chickenpox. If your child has not had chickenpox, observe carefully from __________ to ________ (more likely the first part of this period), for signs of a slight cold, runny nose, loss of appetite, fever, listlessness, and/or irritability. Within a day or two, watch for a spot (or spots) resembling mosquito bites on which a small blister soon forms. Chickenpox is contagious 24–48 hours before the rash appears. Children who develop chickenpox may return when all pox are covered by a dry scab (about 5 or 6 days).

If you have any questions, please call the Center before bringing your child. We appreciate your cooperation in helping us keep incidences of illness to a minimum.

Reflective Thoughts

Outbreaks of communicable illnesses such as colds, flu, and head lice are common in group settings where there are young children. Explain why this occurs. Why is it important for teachers to understand the infectious process? What resources are available to teachers and families for improving their understanding of various childhood illnesses? Are you comfortable caring for a child who is ill?

increased risk of sustaining personal injury. Programs should maintain a list of substitute teachers so that staff members do not feel pressured to work when they are ill.

Administration of Medication The administration of medicine to young children is a responsibility that should always be taken seriously (Table 5–1). Policies and procedures for administering prescription and nonprescription medications, including ointments and creams; eye, ear, and nose drops; cough syrups; baby aspirin; inhalers; and nebulizer breathing treatments should be developed in accordance with state licensing or school district regulations to safeguard children as well as teaching staff. These policies and procedures should be in writing, familiar to all staff members, filed in an accessible location, and distributed to every family (Figure 5–5).

When children are enrolled in part-day programs, families may be able to alter medication schedules and administer prescribed doses at times when children are home. However, this may not be an option for children who are enrolled in full-day programs. In these cases, families will need to make prior arrangements with the child's teachers to have prescribed medications administered at the appropriate times.

Medication should never be given to a child without the family's written consent and written instructions from a licensed physician. The label on a prescription drug is considered an acceptable physician's directive. In the case of nonprescription medicines, families should obtain written instructions from the physician stating the child's name, the medication to be given, the dose, frequency it is to be administered, and any special precautions that may be necessary. There are risks associated with giving children over-the-counter medications that have not been authorized by

Table 5–1 Guidelines for Administering Medications to Children

1. Always wash your hands before handling medications and after administering them.
2. Be honest when giving children medication! Do not use force or attempt to trick children into believing that medicines are candy. Instead, use the opportunity to help children understand the relationship between taking a medication and recovering from an illness or infection. Also, acknowledge the fact that the taste of medicine may be disagreeable or a treatment may be somewhat unpleasant; offer a small sip of juice or cracker to eliminate an unpleasant taste or read a favorite story as a reward for their cooperation.
3. Designate one individual to accept medication from families and administer it to children; this could be the director or the head teacher. This step will help minimize the opportunity for errors, such as omitting a dose or giving a dose twice.
4. When medication is accepted from a family, it should be in the original container, labeled with the child's name, with the name of the drug, and include directions for the exact amount and frequency the medication is to be given.

⚠ **Caution: NEVER give medicine from a container that has been prescribed for another individual.**

5. Store all medicines in a locked cabinet. If it is necessary to refrigerate a medication, place it in a locked box and store it on a top shelf in the refrigerator.
6. Be sure to wash your hands before and after administering medication.
7. Concentrate on what you are doing and do not talk with anyone until you are finished.
   a. Read the label on the bottle or container three times:
      - when removing it from the locked cabinet
      - before pouring it from the container
      - after pouring it from the container
      - Administer medication on time, and give only the amount prescribed.
      - Be sure you have the correct child! If the child is old enough to talk, ask "What is your name?" and let the child state his/her name.
8. Record and maintain a permanent record of each dose of medicine that is administered (Figure 5–5). Include the:
   - date and time the medicine was given
   - name of the teacher administering the medication
   - dose of medication given
   - any unusual physical changes or behaviors observed after the medicine was administered
9. Inform the child's family of the dosage(s) and time medication was given, as well as any unusual reactions that may have occurred.
10. NOTE: Adults should never take any medication in front of children.

a physician. It is the physician's professional and legal responsibility to determine which medication and exact dosage is appropriate for an individual child. Teachers can protect themselves from potential liability by refusing to give medications without a doctor's order.

Immunization

Immunization offers permanent protection against all preventable childhood diseases, including diphtheria, tetanus, whooping cough, polio, measles, mumps, rubella, Haemophilus influenza, and chickenpox (Committee on Infectious Diseases, 2010; Stewart, 2008). Yet, despite several large-scale national, state, and local campaigns, many children still are not fully immunized. At present, it is estimated that only 76 percent of young children have received all of the recommended age-appropriate immunizations (CDC, 2009a). Consequently, efforts to improve the current rate of childhood immunization in the U.S. remain a priority objective of the Healthy People 2020 initiative (DHHS, 2010).

Figure 5–5 **Sample medication recording form.**

ADMINISTRATION OF MEDICATION FORM

Child's name ______________________________
Prescription number ______________________________
Date of prescription ______________________________
Doctor prescribing medicine ______________________________
Medication being given for ______________________________
Time medication is to be given by staff ______________________________
Time medication last given by parent ______________________________
Amount to be given at each time (dosage) ______________________________

I, ______________________ give my permission for the staff to administer the above prescription medication (according to the above guidelines) to ______________________ (child's name). I understand that the staff cannot be held responsible for allergic reactions or other complications resulting from administration of the above medication given according to the directions.

Signed ______________________ (parent or guardian)

Date ______________________

Staff Record
Name of staff accepting medication and form ______________________
Is medication in its original container? ______________________
Is original label intact? ______________________
Is there written permission from the doctor attached (or the original prescription)? __________

Signature of accepting staff ______________________

Administration Record

DATE	TIME	AMOUNT GIVEN	STAFF ADMINISTERING	INITIALS

Why are some families so seemingly complacent about having their children immunized? Perhaps they do not realize that some communicable illnesses are still life-threatening and continue to pose a threat to children who are not protected. Recent outbreaks of mumps, tuberculosis, and whooping cough, for example, have clearly demonstrated this potential (Barskey, Glasser, & Lebaron, 2009). Some families falsely believe that antibiotics are available to cure any infectious illness so they are willing to take a chance. Others have expressed concern about vaccine safety and the number of immunizations that children must receive (Gust et al., 2009). Some vaccines are now combined to help reduce this number. Manufacturers have also eliminated questionable substances, such as thimerosal, from vaccines to improve their safety (Child Health Alert, 2009; Gerber & Offit, 2009).

Immunizations protect children from many preventable childhood diseases.

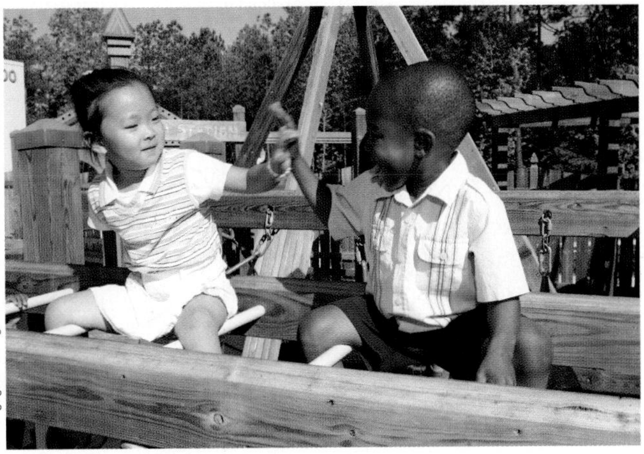

Most states require children's immunizations to be current when they enter school or enroll in early childhood programs. In states where immunization laws are lax, teachers must insist that every child be fully immunized unless families are opposed on religious or medical grounds (Silverman, 2009). Teachers should also be diligent in keeping their own immunizations up-to-date.

Vaccines work by triggering the body's immune system to produce protective substances, called antibodies. This process is similar to what occurs when a person becomes ill with certain

Issues To Consider — Childhood Immunizations

The number of young children who are not fully immunized against preventable communicable diseases remains relatively high (CDC, 2009a). Poverty, lack of accessibility to medical care, and failure to understand the importance of childhood immunization are reasons often cited for noncompliance. In addition, some families have expressed concern that vaccines can make children sick. Television programs, magazine articles, and word-of-mouth have attempted to link everything from SIDS, HIV/AIDS, arthritis, multiple sclerosis, and autism to childhood vaccines. However, to date, there has been no evidence to substantiate any of these associations (Child Health Alert, 2009; Gust et al., 2009; Gerber & Offit, 2009). Although minor discomforts, including mild fever, achiness, and pain at the injection site may occur, vaccines are considered safe (Pickering et al., 2009). To further improve the safety of immunizations, the American Academy of Pediatrics has urged physicians to administer the injectable form of polio vaccine (IPV), rather than the oral version (OPV), thus eliminating exposure to the live, but weakened, virus.

- As a teacher, how would you respond to families who were opposed to immunization because they felt they were unsafe?
- Where could you locate accurate information about the safety of vaccines?
- How would you handle situations where there is conflict between family beliefs and state regulation?
- On what basis does your state grant exceptions to immunization requirements for children?

infectious diseases. Infants are born with a limited supply of antibodies, acquired from their mothers, which will protect them against some communicable illnesses. However, this maternal protection is only temporary and, therefore, the immunization process must be initiated early in an infant's life. The immunization schedule jointly recommended by the Centers for Disease Control and Protection, the American Academy of Pediatrics (AAP), and the American Academy of Family Physicians (AAFP) appears in Figure 5–6. Similar recommendations are available for Canadians and children in other countries (CPS, 2009).

Infants and young children, especially those in group care, are encouraged to be immunized against Haemophilus influenza Type b (Hib), an upper respiratory infection and common cause of meningitis. (See Figure 5–6.) Vaccines for chickenpox (varicella) and hepatitis B, a viral infection spread through contact with body secretions and feces, are also required in some states and recommended in others (Pickering et al., 2009). Children who have special health problems often have a lowered resistance to communicable illnesses and are encouraged to be immunized against these diseases even though they may not be required. Immunizations can be obtained from most health care providers, neighborhood health clinics, or public health departments where the cost is often reduced or free.

Programs that employ more than one teacher (including aides and substitutes) are required to offer free hepatitis B immunizations to employees during the first 10 days of employment or within 24 hours following exposure to blood or body fluids containing blood (OSHA, 2001).

Figure 5–6 Recommended Childhood and Adolescent Immunization Schedule–United States 2010.

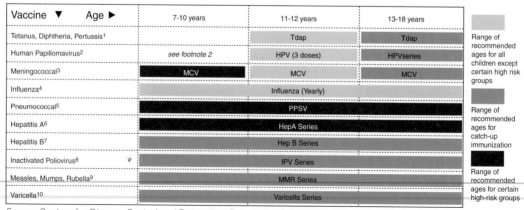

Vaccine ▼ Age ▶	Birth	1 month	2 months	4 months	6 months	12 months	15 months	18 months	19-23 months	2-3 years	4-6 years
Hepatitis B[1]	HepB	HepB				HepB					
Rotavirus[2]			RV	RV	RV[2]						
Diphtheria, Tetanus, Pertussis[3]			DTaP	DTaP	DTaP		DTaP				DTaP
Haemophiius influenzae type b[4]			Hib	Hib	Hib[4]	Hib					
Pneumococcal[5]			PCV	PCV	PCV	PCV				PPSV	
Inactivated Poliovirus[6]			IPV	IPV		IPV					IPV
Influenza[7]								Influenza (Yearly)			
Measles, Mumps, Rubella[8]						MMR			*see footnote*[8]		MMR
Varicella[9]						Varicella			*see footnote*[9]		Varicella
Hepatitis A[10]							HepA (2 doses)			HepA Series	
Meningococcal[11]										MCV	

Range of recommended ages for all children except certain high-risk groups

Range of recommended ages for certain high-risk groups

Vaccine ▼ Age ▶	7-10 years	11-12 years	13-18 years
Tetanus, Diphtheria, Pertussis[1]		Tdap	Tdap
Human Papillomavirus[2]	*see footnote 2*	HPV (3 doses)	HPVseries
Meningococcal[3]	MCV	MCV	MCV
Influenza[4]		Influenza (Yearly)	
Pneumococcal[5]		PPSV	
Hepatitis A[6]		HepA Series	
Hepatitis B[7]		Hep B Series	
Inactivated Poliovirus[8]		IPV Series	
Measles, Mumps, Rubella[9]		MMR Series	
Varicella[10]		Varicella Series	

Range of recommended ages for all children except certain high risk groups

Range of recommended ages for catch-up immunization

Range of recommended ages for certain high-risk groups

Source: Centers for Disease Control and Prevention. Recommended immunization schedules for persons aged 0 through18 years—United States, 2010. MMWR 2010; 58(51&52). Note: Additional information is available at www.cdc.gov.

Environmental Control

Communicable illnesses can also be controlled through a variety of environmental practices and modifications (Mink & Yeh, 2009; Mattern & Rotbart, 2008; AAP, 2002). Teachers should be familiar with these methods and understand how to implement them in their classrooms. Procedures should be written up, posted where they are visible, and reviewed periodically with all employees. Teachers must also take precautions, such as wearing gloves and frequent hand washing, to protect themselves from unnecessary exposure.

Because respiratory illnesses are common in group settings, special attention should be given to control measures that limit their spread. For example, children can be taught to cough and sneeze into their elbow or a tissue, dispose of the tissue properly, and then wash their hands. Children must also be reminded frequently to keep hands out of their mouth, nose, and eyes to prevent self-infection and the spread of infection to others.

Universal Infection Control Precautions The U.S. Department of Labor's Occupational Safety and Health Administration (OSHA) is responsible for protecting employees' safety by ensuring that workplace environments and practices meet federal guidelines. Regulations passed by OSHA require child care programs (except those without paid employees) to develop and practice **universal infection control precautions** for handling contaminated body fluids (Table 5–2). In addition, schools must also have a written plan for handling potentially infectious material, provide annual training for employees, and maintain records of any exposure (OSHA, 2001).

Universal precautions are designed to protect teachers from accidental exposure to blood-borne pathogens, including hepatitis B and HIV/AIDS. All body fluids are considered potentially infectious and, therefore, should be treated in the same manner. Any material that has been contaminated with blood or other body fluids that might possibly contain blood, such as urine, feces, saliva, and vomitus, must be handled with caution, regardless of whether or not a child is known to be ill.

Disposable latex gloves should always be accessible to teachers; non-latex gloves must be provided if a teacher or child has a latex sensitivity. They must always be worn whenever handling soiled objects or caring for children's injuries. Gloves should be removed by pulling them off inside out and carefully discarding them after use with an individual child. Thorough hand washing must follow to prevent any further spread of infection; wearing gloves does not eliminate the need for washing one's hands. Children's hands and skin should also be washed with soap and running water to remove any blood. Washable objects, such as rugs, pillows, or stuffed toys that have been contaminated with body fluids should be laundered separately from other items. Children's clothing

Table 5–2 Universal Precautions for Handling Body Fluids

Whenever handling body fluids or items contaminated with body fluids, be sure to:
• Wear disposable latex gloves when you are likely to have contact with blood or other body fluids, e.g., vomitus, urine, feces, or saliva. • Remove glove by grasping the cuff and pulling it off inside out. • Wash hands thoroughly. (Lather for at least 30 seconds.) • Dispose of contaminated materials properly. Seal soiled clothing in plastic bags to be laundered at home. Dispose of diapers by tying them securely in garbage bags. Place broken glass in a designated container. • Clean all surfaces with a disinfectant, such as a bleach solution (1 tablespoon bleach/1 cup water mixed fresh daily). • Subsidize the cost of hepatitis B immunizations for all employees.

universal infection control precautions – *special measures taken when handling bodily fluids, including careful hand washing, wearing latex gloves, disinfecting surfaces, and proper disposal of contaminated objects.*

should be rinsed out, sealed in a plastic bag, and sent home to be washed. Bloodstains on surfaces must be wiped up and disinfected with a commercial germicide or mixture of bleach and water (1 tablespoon bleach to 1 cup water).

Hand Washing Hand washing is perhaps the single most effective control measure against the spread of communicable and infectious illness in child care and school environments (see Table 5–3) (Rosen et al., 2009).

Infants and toddlers who are crawling on the floor, eating with their hands, or sucking their thumbs/fingers should have their hands washed frequently, and especially after diaper changes. Individual washcloths moistened with soap and water can be used for this purpose; however, infants and toddlers should also have their hands washed under running water several times a day. Preschoolers and adults should always wash with soap and running water. Children must be taught the correct procedure and supervised to make sure they continue to practice each step carefully. School-age children should be given several opportunities during the day to wash their hands. It is important that children wash their hands before and after eating or whenever they have blown their nose, used the bathroom, played outdoors or in sand, or touched animals. Although sanitizing hand gels are beneficial for limiting the spread of communicable illness, they are not considered a substitute for thorough hand washing and should be used only when running water is not available (CDC, 2009b; Kinnula et al., 2009; Vessey et al., 2007).

Cleaning Frequent cleaning of furniture, toys, and surfaces is also an effective method for limiting the spread of communicable illness (Bright, Boone & Gerba, 2010; Cosby et al., 2008). A solution of ¼ cup bleach to 1 gallon of water (or 1 tablespoon/1 quart) is inexpensive and effective for wiping off large

Table 5–3 When and How to Wash Hands

Following proper hand washing technique is critical for controlling the spread of infectious illnesses:

- Pull down paper towel.
- Turn on the water; wet hands and wrists under warm, running water.
- Apply soap and lather hands to loosen dirt and bacteria.
- Rub hands and wrists vigorously for a minimum of 30 seconds. Friction helps to remove microorganisms and dirt. (Have children sing the entire ABC song while rubbing their hands with soap.)
- Pay special attention to rubbing soap on the backs of hands, between fingers, and under nails.
- Rinse hands thoroughly under running water to remove dirt and soap. Keep hands lower than wrists to prevent recontamination. Leave the water running.
- Dry hand and arms carefully with paper towel.
- Use the paper towel to turn off water faucets. (This prevents hands from becoming contaminated again.)
- Open bathroom door with paper towel and discard it in an appropriate receptacle.

Correct hand washing technique should always be used:

- upon arrival or return to the classroom
- before handling food or food utensils
- before and after feeding children
- before and after administering medication
- after changing diapers or handling items contaminated with mucus, urine, feces, vomitus, or blood
- after personally using the restroom
- after cleaning up from snack or play activities, emptying garbage, or handling art materials such as clay and paint

play equipment, cribs, sleeping mats, and strollers. Note: *A new bleach solution must be prepared daily to maintain its disinfecting strength. Label spray bottles with the date and bleach/water ratio or purpose (e.g., general cleaning, disinfection of body fluid contamination).* Changing tables, mats, and potty chairs should be constructed of nonporous materials and free of any tears or cracks for ease of cleaning. They should be disinfected thoroughly after each use with a bleach solution that can be sprayed on and wiped off with paper towels. A stronger bleach solution (1 tablespoon bleach to 1 cup water) should be used to disinfect surfaces contaminated with blood or large amounts of urine, stool, or vomitus. Note: *You will be able to smell the bleach in this stronger solution.* Several non-bleach disinfecting solutions are also available commercially.

Frequent hand washing reduces the risk of communicable illness.

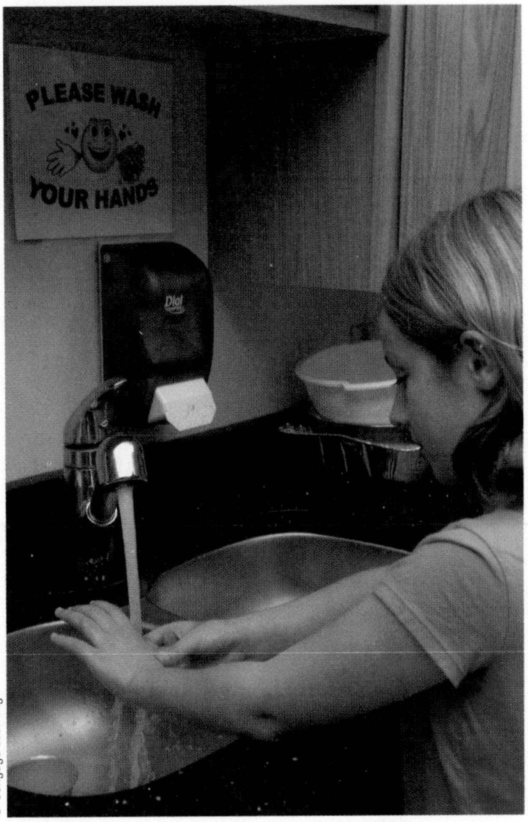

Toys that children have placed in their mouths should be removed for cleaning before they are used by another child. Items should be washed with soap and warm water, rinsed in a bleach solution, and allowed to air-dry. Some toys can also be sanitized in the dishwasher. Washable cloth and stuffed objects should be laundered between use by other children. Surfaces, such as tables, gate tops, car seats, and crib rails that children mouth or drool on should be scrubbed daily with soap and water and disinfected. Desktops and equipment in school-age classrooms should also be wiped off with a mild disinfectant at least once a week, or daily during the cold and flu season.

Diapering and Toileting Areas Children who are not toilet-trained can spread infectious illnesses through urine and feces (Gilbert et al., 2008; Lee & Greig, 2008). Maintaining separate diapering and toileting areas can significantly reduce contamination and the spread of infection from one child to another. Careful adherence to sanitary diapering procedures, disinfection of surfaces (free of cracks), and thorough hand washing will further reduce this risk (Table 5–4). Teachers may choose to wear disposable gloves when changing babies and/or handling soiled diapers, but this is not essential. Even if gloves are worn, meticulous hand washing must follow because they do not prevent contamination. Soiled diapers (disposable) should be placed in a covered waste container (lined with a plastic bag) that is not accessible to children. Cloth diapers must be sealed in a plastic bag and sent home for parents to launder. Infants' hands should be washed under running water following each diaper change.

Family preferences and cultural differences will influence when and how toilet training is initiated (Gonzalez-Mena & Eyer, 2009; Wald et al., 2009). When toddlers are ready to begin potty training, small, child-sized toilets should be made available (Table 5–5). Many states prohibit the use of shared potty-chairs in early childhood programs because they can spread infections if not properly sanitized. Families may wish to provide a chair for their child's sole use if the program's policy permits. However, teachers must still follow strict sanitizing procedures each time the chair is used. A mixture of ¼ cup bleach to 1 gallon water (or 1 tablespoon bleach to 1 quart water) mixed fresh daily can be used for most disinfecting purposes. Any soiled material should first be removed with soap and water before the surface is sprayed with a disinfecting solution. Bleach solutions should remain in contact with surfaces for at least 2 minutes (to allow adequate disinfection) before they are wiped off; allowing sprayed surfaces to air dry is preferable. Teachers should wash their hands carefully after completing cleaning procedures and also be sure that children have washed their hands!

Table 5-4 Sanitary Diapering Procedure

The consistent implementation of sanitary diapering procedures is important for reducing the spread of disease. Teachers should follow these steps:

- Organize and label all supplies.
- Have all items for diaper changing within reach.
- Place a disposable covering (paper towel, paper roll) over a firm changing surface. Do not change children on fabric chairs or sofas that could become soiled.
- If using gloves, put them on.
- Pick up the child, holding him/her away from your clothing to avoid contamination.
- Place the child on the paper surface; fasten security belt. Remove the child's clothing and/or shoes if necessary to prevent them from becoming soiled.
- Remove the soiled diaper and place in a covered, plastic-lined receptacle designated for this purpose.
- Clean the child's bottom with a disposable wipe and place in receptacle; pat skin dry.
- Remove the paper lining from beneath the child and discard.
- Wash your hands or wipe with a clean disposable wipe and discard. *Never leave the child alone.*
- Wash the child's hands under running water.
- Diaper and redress the child. Return the child to a play area.
- Disinfect the changing surface and any supplies or equipment that was touched with a bleach solution or other disinfectant.
- Remove gloves (if worn) and wash your hands again.

Table 5-5 Readiness Indicators for Toilet Training

Successful toilet training requires several things: Children's bodies must reach a certain point of physical maturation and they must have basic motor and cognitive skills that permit them to participate in this activity, including:

- an ability to understand the concepts of wet and dry
- a regularity to patterns of elimination (at least during daytime)
- language to express the need for elimination
- an ability to get clothing up and down

Room Arrangements Simple modifications in children's environments can also have a positive effect on the control of communicable illnesses. For example, room temperatures set at 68°–70°F are less favorable for the spread of infectious illnesses and are often more comfortable for children. Their smaller body surfaces make them less sensitive than adults to cooler temperatures.

Rooms should also be well ventilated to reduce the concentration of infectious organisms circulating within a given space. Doors and windows should be fitted with screens to prevent disease-carrying flies and mosquitoes from entering when they are opened, even briefly on cold days, to introduce fresh air. Mechanical ventilating systems should undergo routine cleaning and maintenance to improve the air quality in rooms. Taking children outdoors, even in winter, also improves their resistance to illness.

The humidity level in rooms should also be checked periodically, especially in winter when rooms are heated and there are fewer opportunities to let in fresh air. Extremely warm, dry air increases the chances of respiratory infection by causing the mucous lining of the mouth and nose to become dry and cracked. Moisture can be added to the air by installing a humidifier in the central heating system or using a cool-mist vaporizer in individual rooms. Cool-mist units eliminate the risk of burns, but they must be emptied, washed out with soap and water, disinfected, and refilled with fresh distilled water each day to prevent bacterial growth. Plants or small dishes of water placed around a room also provide added humidity, but they can encourage the growth of mold spores, which may aggravate children's allergies and asthma (Salo, Sever, & Zeldin, 2009).

The physical arrangement of a classroom also provides an effective method for controlling communicable and infectious illness. For example, separating infants and toddlers who are not toilet-trained from older children can significantly reduce the spread of intestinal illnesses. Surfaces such as floors, walls, counter tops, and furniture should be smooth and easy to clean. Laundry and food preparation areas should be separated from each other as well as from the classrooms. Pedal-operated sinks or faucets with infrared sensors are ideal for encouraging frequent hand washing and avoiding recontamination.

Activities can be rearranged to help reduce the spread of communicable illness.

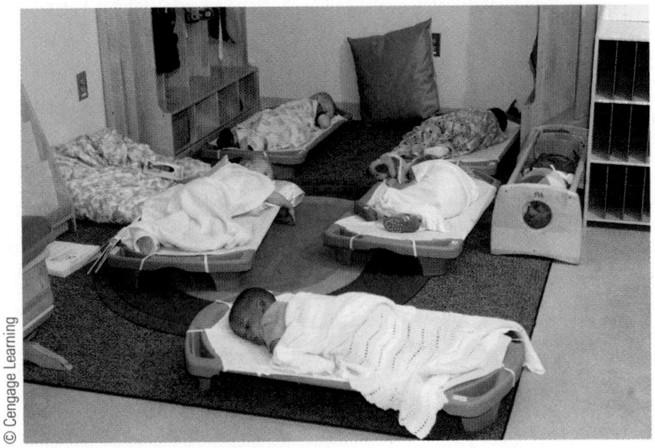

Measures taken to group children and limit close contact are also desirable. Crowding at tables or in play areas can be avoided by dividing children into smaller groups. During naptimes, children's rugs, cots, or cribs can be arranged in alternating directions, head to foot, to decrease talking, coughing, and breathing in each other's faces. Provisions should also be made for children to have individual lockers or storage space for personal items, such as blankets, coats, hats, toys, and toothbrushes to reduce potential contact and transfer of infectious organisms.

Several additional aspects of children's environments also deserve special attention. Sandboxes should be covered to prevent contamination from animal feces. Water tables and wading pools need to be emptied and washed out daily to prevent bacterial growth and the spread of communicable illness; a water pH of 7.2–8.2 and chlorine level of 0.4–3.0 parts per million should be maintained in swimming pools at all times (as specified in commercial test kits). Items that children put on their heads, such as hats, wigs, and beauty parlor items can spread head lice and, therefore, may not be appropriate to use as play items in group settings unless they can be washed or disinfected. Play clothes should be laundered often.

Education

Teachers also make a valuable contribution to the control of communicable illness through the health promotion lessons they design for children. Ongoing activities that address personal wellness, physical activity, and nutritious diet play an important role in improving children's resistance to illness and shortening the length of convalescence if they do become ill (Mink & Yeh, 2009). Topics of personal interest and value to young children include:

- appropriate technique and times for hand washing
- proper method for covering coughs, blowing noses, and disposing of tissues
- appropriate use of drinking fountains
- not sharing personal items, e.g., drinking cups, toothbrushes, shoes, hats, towels, eating utensils
- germs and how they spread
- dressing appropriately for the weather
- nutritious foods
- the importance of adequate rest and physical activity

Communicable illness outbreaks provide excellent opportunities for teachers to review important preventive health concepts and practices with children. Learning is more meaningful for children when it is associated with real-life experiences, such as when a classmate has chickenpox, a cold, or pinkeye. Teachers can use these opportunities to review correct hand washing procedures, reinforce the importance of eating healthy foods, conduct simple experiments to illustrate how germs spread, and model sound health practices for children to imitate. (Children are more likely to remember what they have seen than what they have been told.)

Families must be included in any educational program that is aimed at reducing the incidence of communicable illness. They should be informed of health practices and information being taught to the children. Teachers can also reinforce the importance of (1) serving nutritious meals and snacks, (2) making sure that children get sufficient rest and physical activity, (3) obtaining immunizations for infants, toddlers, and older children, and (4) scheduling routine medical and dental supervision. Successful control of communicable illness and the promotion of children's well-being depend on schools and families working together.

Reflective Thoughts

Teachers who work with young children are often exposed to communicable illness in the classroom. Sometimes families unknowingly bring sick children to school or child care. How do you feel about being exposed to contagious illness? Could you care for a child who was acutely ill knowing that you too might become sick? What precautions can you take to protect yourself from such illnesses? How could you help families address the problem of bringing sick children to school? What alternative care arrangements could you suggest for a working family?

Focus On Families — Giving Children Medication

Special precautions should be taken whenever administering medication to young children. Their bodies are more sensitive to many medications, and they may respond differently than an adult. It is also easy to give children too much of a medication because their dosages are typically quite small. Unattended medications must always be stored in a locked cabinet because they may attract a curious child's attention and lead to unintentional poisoning. Additional precautions for the safe administration of medication to children include:

- Always check with your child's physician before giving over-the-counter medications, especially to children under 2 years.
- Read the label carefully. Be sure you are giving the correct medication to the right child at the appropriate time interval. Also, double-check the dose that has been prescribed, and administer only that amount. Make sure the medication is approved for children; many drugs are not advised for children younger than 12 years.
- Ask your pharmacist about potential drug interactions—with other medications or food—that should be avoided. Also, learn about possible reactions that should be noted before giving your child any new medication.
- Always follow the instructions for administering a medication, and finish giving the full course that has been prescribed.
- Throw away any outdated medication. Old medications may lose their effectiveness or cause unexpected reactions. Always check with a pharmacist if in doubt.
- Store medications in their original container and according to instructions.
- Never tell children medicines are "candy," and avoid taking medication in front of children.

Classroom Corner **Teacher Activities**

Those Invisible Germs... (PreK–2, National Health Education Standard 1.2.3)

Concept: Germs are everywhere; germs are on the things we touch.

Learning Objectives

- Children will understand that germs are invisible and on most things we touch.
- Children will learn that correct hand washing removes germs.

Supplies

- baby powder or glitter; small spray bottle with water; paper towel; hand lotion

Learning Activities

- Read and discuss one of the following books:
  - *Germs Are Not for Sharing* by Elizabeth Verdick
  - *Those Mean Nasty Dirty Downright Disgusting but...Invisible Germs* by Judith Rice
  - *The Magic School Bus Inside Ralphie: A Book About Germs* (for older children) by Joanna Cole
- Ask children if they know what a germ is and if they can describe what they look like. Ask them where germs are found and what we can do to protect ourselves from them.
- Lightly spray water on the hands of half of the children; sprinkle with baby powder or glitter. Ask children to shake hands with one another and then examine their hands.
- Coat children's hands with a thin layer of hand cream (make sure no one has any allergies). Sprinkle their hands lightly with glitter. Have them attempt to brush the "germs" off by rubbing their hands together. Repeat this step using a paper towel. Finally, have children wash their hands with soap and warm water. After, ask the children which method was most effective for removing the "germs." Talk about why hand washing is important for keeping the germs away and staying healthy.
- Have children draw their own interpretations of what a germ looks like.

Evaluation

- Children can explain where germs are found and how they are spread.
- Children will demonstrate how to wash their hands correctly.

Additional lesson plans for grades 3–5 are available on this text's website.

Summary

- Communicable illnesses are common in group settings where there are young children. Reasons for this include children playing in close proximity, immature development of children's respiratory system, children's play and personal hygiene, adult carelessness, and poor hand washing practices.
- Communicable illnesses are passed from one person to another via airborne, fecal-oral, direct, or indirect methods.
- To be communicable, an illness requires a pathogen, a susceptible host, and a method for successful transmission.

- Practices that teachers can implement to control and manage communicable illness effectively in group settings include daily observations, health policies and sanitation procedures, enforcing immunization requirements, modifying the environment, working collaboratively with families, and educating children.

Terms to Know

antibodies *p. 114*
communicable *p. 115*
pathogen *p. 115*
susceptible host *p. 115*
respiratory tract *p. 115*
immunized *p. 115*
airborne transmission *p. 116*
fecal-oral transmission *p. 116*
incubation *p. 117*
contagious *p. 117*
prodromal *p. 117*
acute *p. 117*
convalescent *p. 118*
lymph glands *p. 118*
universal infection control precautions *p. 125*

Chapter Review

A. By Yourself:

1. Define each of the *Terms to Know* listed at the end of this chapter.
2. Describe two examples that illustrate how an illness can be spread via:
   a. airborne transmission
   b. indirect contact
3. What immunizations, and how many of each, are recommended for a 30-month-old child?
4. Where can families go to obtain immunizations for their children?
5. During what stage(s) of communicable illnesses are children most contagious?

B. As a Group:

1. Identify and discuss three factors that are required for an infection to be communicable.
2. What early signs would you be likely to observe in a child who was coming down with a respiratory virus?
3. Discuss specific practices that teachers can use in their classrooms to limit the spread of illnesses transmitted via:
   a. the respiratory tract
   b. the fecal-oral route
   c. skin conditions
   d. contaminated objects, e.g., toys, towels, changing mats
4. Discuss when and how universal precautions should be implemented in the classroom.
5. What special accommodations would be necessary if a program wanted to allow mildly ill children to remain onsite?

Case Study

Laura arrived at the child care center with a runny nose and cough. Her mother informed the teachers that it was probably "just allergies" and left before Laura could be checked in.

During their daily health check, the teachers discovered that Laura also had a fever, red throat, and swollen glands. Laura's mother is a single parent, a student at the local community college and works part time at an early childhood program in another part of town.

1. How should the teachers handle Laura's immediate situation? Should she be allowed to stay or should they try to contact Laura's mother?
2. If Laura is allowed to stay at the center, what measures can be taken to limit the risk of spreading illness to other children?
3. If this is a repeated occurrence, what steps can be taken to make sure Laura's mother complies with the center's policies?
4. How can the center help Laura's mother avoid similar situations in the future?

Application Activities

1. Obtain several agar growth medium plates. With sterile cotton applicators, culture one toy and the top of one table. Observe the "growth" after 24 hours and again after 48 hours. Wash the same item with a mild chlorine solution and repeat the experiment. Compare the results.
2. Contact the Office of Public Health in your state (province/territory). Obtain data on the percentage of children under 6 years of age who are currently immunized. How does this figure compare to national goals? What suggestions do you have for improving this rate? Conduct an Internet search to determine the immunization requirements for children enrolling in early childhood programs and kindergarten in your state.
3. Locate and read OSHA's regulations and guidelines for implementing a blood-borne pathogen workplace policy (document CFR 1910.1030) available on their website (http://www.osha.gov/SLTC/bloodbornepathogens/index.html). Develop a written compliance plan for an early childhood center or school building.
4. Discuss how you would handle the following situations:
   a. The father of a toddler in your center is upset because his child has frequent colds.
   b. You observe your teacher covering a cough with her hand and then continuing to prepare snacks for the children.
   c. Your toddler group has experienced frequent outbreaks of strep throat in the past 6 months.
   d. While reviewing immunization records, you discover that one child has received only one dose of DTaP, IPV, and Hib.
   e. Gabriel announces that he threw up all night. You notice that his eyes appear watery and his cheeks are flushed.
   f. You find that one of your aides has stored all of the children's toothbrushes together in a sealed, plastic container.
   g. Your classroom paraprofessional casually mentions that she has the stomach flu and has been throwing up all night.
5. Review and compare health care policies from an early childhood center, home-based program, Head Start program, and elementary school. How are they similar? How do they differ?

Helpful Web Resources

American Public Health Association	http://www.apha.org
Canadian Pediatric Society	http://www.cps.ca
Centers for Disease Control and Prevention (CDC)	http://www.cdc.gov
Maternal and Child Health Bureau	http://mchb.hrsa.gov
National Center for Health Statistics	http://www.cdc.gov
National Center for Preparedness, Detection, and Control of Infectious Diseases (NCPDCID)	http://www.cdc.gov/ncpdcid/
National Foundation for Infectious Diseases	http://www.nfid.org
National Institutes of Health	http://www.nih.gov

You are just a click away from additional health, safety, and nutrition resources! Go to www.CengageBrain.com to access this text's Education CourseMate website, where you'll find:

- a sample notification letter
- a medication administration form
- recommended immunization schedule
- glossary flashcards, activities, tutorial quizzes, videos, web links, and more

References

Alkon, A., To, K., Wolff, M., Mackie, J., & Bernzweig, J. (2008). Assessing health and safety in early care and education programs: Development of the CCHP health and safety checklist, *Journal of Pediatric Health Care*, 22(6), 368–377.

American Academy of Pediatrics (AAP). (2002). *Caring for our children: National health and safety performance standards: Guidelines for out-of-home care.* Washington, DC. Available online at http://nrc.uchsc.edu/CFOC/index.html.

Aronson, S. (2002). *Healthy young children: A manual for programs* (4th ed.). Washington, DC: NAEYC.

Barskey, A., Glasser, J., & Lebaron, C. (2009). Mumps resurgences in the United States: A historical perspective on unexpected elements, *Vaccine*, 27(44), 6186–6195.

Bright, K., Boone, S., & Gerba, C. (2010). Occurrence of bacteria and viruses on elementary classroom surfaces and the potential role of classroom hygiene in the spread of infectious diseases, *Journal of School Nursing*, 26(1), 33–41.

Canadian Paediatric Society (CPS). (2009). Routine childhood immunization schedule. Accessed on October 10, 2009, from http://www.cps.ca/caringforkids/immunization/VaccinationChild.htm.

Centers for Disease Control & Prevention (CDC). (2009a). Immunization rates remain stable at high levels among the nation's 19- through 35-month-old children. Accessed on October 11, 2009, from http://www.cdc.gov/media/pressrel/2009/r090827.htm.

Centers for Disease Control and Prevention (CDC). (2009b). Flu.gov. Accessed on April 29, 2010 from, http://www.flu.gov.

Child Health Alert. (2009). Court finds no link between vaccines and autism, *Child Health Alert*, 27, 4.

Committee on Infectious Diseases. (2010). Policy statement – Recommended childhood and adolescent immunization schedules—United States, 2010, *Pediatrics*, 125(1), 195–196.

Copeland, K., & Shope, T. (2005). Knowledge and beliefs about guidelines for exclusion of ill children from child care. *Ambulatory Pediatrics*, *5*(6), 365–371.

Cosby, C., Costello, C., Morris, W., Haughton, B., Devereaux, M., Harte, F., & Davidson, P. (2008). Microbiological analysis of food contact surfaces in child care centers, *Applied and Environmental Microbiology*, 74(22), 6918–6922.

Gerber, J., & Offit, P. (2009). Vaccines and autism: A tale of shifting hypotheses, *Clinical Infectious Diseases*, 48(4), 456–461.

Gilbert, M., Monk, C., Wang, H., Diplock, K., & Landry, L. (2008). Screening policies for daycare attendees: Lessons learned from an outbreak of E. coli 0157:H7 in a daycare in Waterloo, Ontario, *Canadian Journal of Public Health*, 99(4), 281–285.

Gonzalez-Mena, J., & Eyer, D. (2009). *Infants, toddlers, and caregivers*. NY: McGraw-Hill.

Gust, D., Kennedy, A., Weber, D., Evans, G., Kong, Y., & Salmon, D. (2009). Parents questioning immunization: Evaluation of an intervention, *American Journal of Health Behavior*, 33(3), 287–298.

Kinnula, S., Tapiainen, T., Renko, M., & Uhari, M. (2009). Safety of alcohol hand gel use among children and personnel at a child day care center, *American Journal of Infection Control*, 37(4), 318–321.

Lee, M., & Greig, J. (2008). A review of enteric outbreaks in child care centers: Effective infection control recommendations, *Journal of Environmental Health*, 71(3), 24–32, 46.

Mattern, C., & Rotbart, H. (2008). Germ proof your school, *School Nurse News*, 25(4), 31–34.

Mink, C., & Yeh, S. (2009). Infections in child-care facilities and schools, *Pediatrics in Review*, 30(7), 259–269.

Occupational Safety and Health Administration (OSHA). (2001). Revision to OSHA's blood borne pathogens standard. Accessed on October 11, 2009, from http://www.osha.gov/needlesticks/needlefact.html.

Pickering, L., Bake, C., Freed, G., Gall, S., Grogg, S., Poland, G., Rodewald, L., Schaffner, W., Stinchfield, P., Tan, L., Zimmerman, R., & Orenstein, W. (2009). Immunization programs for infants, children, adolescents, and adults: Clinical practice guidelines by the Infectious Diseases Society of America, *Clinical Infectious Diseases*, 49(6), 817–840.

Rosen, L., Zucker, D., Brody, D., Engelhard, D., & Manor, O. (2009). The effect of a hand washing intervention on preschool educator beliefs, attitudes, knowledge and self-efficacy, *Health Education Research*, 24(4), 686–698.

Salo, P., Sever, M., & Zeldin, D. (2009). Indoor allergens in school and day care environments, *Journal of Allergy and Clinical Immunology*, 124(2), 185–192.

Sandora, T., Shih, M., & Goldman, D. (2008). Reducing absenteeism from gastrointestinal and respiratory illness in elementary school students: A randomized, controlled trial of an infection-control intervention, *Pediatrics*, 121(6):e1555–e1562.

Silverman, R. (2009). Litigation, regulation, and education—protecting the public's health through childhood immunization, *New England Journal of Medicine*, 360(24), 2500–2501.

Stewart, A. (2008). Childhood vaccine and school entry laws: The case of HPV vaccine, *Public Health Reports*, 123(6), 801–803.

U.S. Department of Health & Human Services (DHHS). (2010). Healthy People 2020–Proposed objectives. Accessed on April 29. 2010 from http://www.healthypeople.gov/hp2020/Objectives/TopicAreas.aspx.

Vessey, J., Sherwood, J., Warner, D., & Clark, D. (2007). Comparing hand washing to hand sanitizers in reducing elementary school students' absenteeism, *Pediatric Nursing*, 33(4), 368–372.

Wald, E., Di Lorenzo, C., Cipriani, L., Colborn, D., Burgers, R., & Wald, A. (2009). Bowel habits and toilet training in a diverse population of children, *Journal of Pediatric Gastroenterology and Nutrition*, 48(3), 294–298.

CHAPTER

6

Communicable and Acute Illness: Identification and Management

NAEYC Standards *Chapter Links*

- **#1 a, b, and c:** Promoting child development and learning
- **#2 a, b, and c:** Building family and community relationships
- **#3 a, c, and d:** Observing, documenting, and assessing to support young children and families

Learning Objectives

After studying this chapter, you should be able to:

- Discuss why it is important for teachers to be knowledgeable about children's communicable and acute illnesses.
- Explain how communicable illnesses such as chickenpox, pinkeye, impetigo, and giardia are spread and identify appropriate control measures.
- Describe the teachers' role in addressing common acute childhood illnesses.

Because young children are especially vulnerable to a variety of communicable and acute illnesses, classroom teachers must be prepared to identify and implement policies and practices designed to limit their spread. Teachers can best prepare themselves for this role by becoming familiar with the signs and **symptoms** of common childhood illnesses and the precautionary measures appropriate for each. This knowledge can be useful for establishing program guidelines, creating meaningful lessons for children, and communicating important health information with families.

symptoms – *changes in the body or its functions that are experienced by the affected individual.*

Teachers should be able to identify the early signs of childhood illnesses.

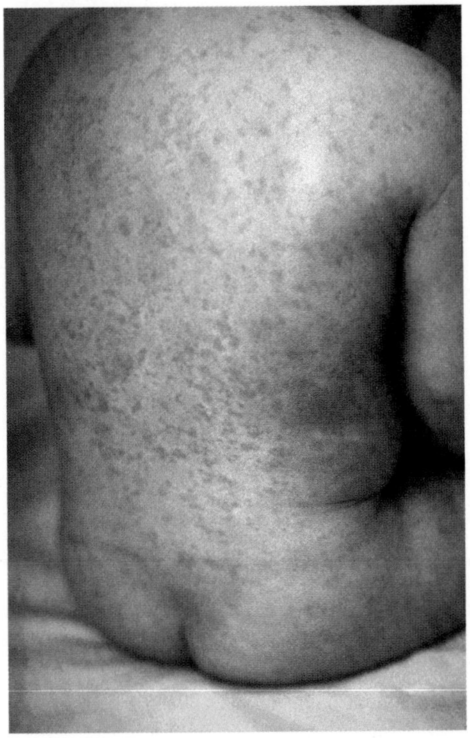

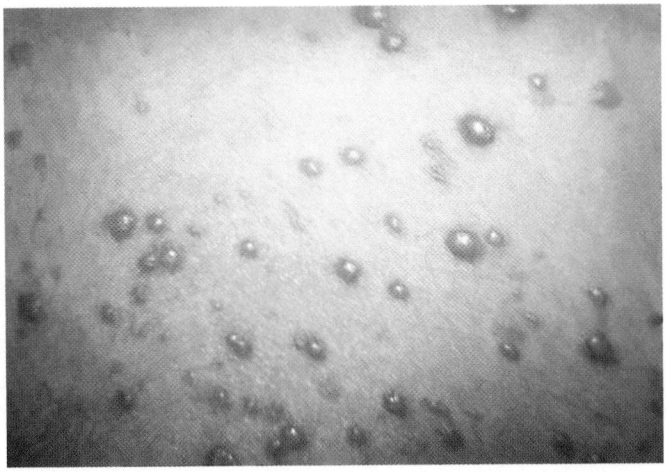

Communicable Childhood Illnesses

Protecting children's health in group settings requires teachers to have a sound understanding of common communicable illnesses—what causes them, how they are transmitted, and how they can be controlled. Their knowledge of childhood illnesses and ability to implement infection control procedures, including hand washing and disinfection, are important management skills. Table 6–1 provides brief descriptions of communicable illnesses that young children commonly experience.

Teachers should also be familiar with local public health policies that specify which communicable illnesses must be reported. Notifying health officials of existing cases enables them to monitor communities for potential outbreaks. They may also be able to provide additional information about an illness that teachers can share with families.

Reflective Thoughts

Teachers recognize the importance of addressing issues of diversity in their programs. However, little is often understood about how individuals from various backgrounds—cultures, recent immigrants, homeless families—view the concepts of health, illness, and traditional Western medicine. Notable differences between mainstream values, beliefs, and practices and those held by a particular group are common. Thus, teachers must make an effort to learn more about individual families and their unique beliefs and priorities in order to best serve children's health needs. Excellent resources are available on the National Center for Cultural Competence website (http://www11.georgetown.edu/research/gucchd/nccc). Take time to explore the information and self-assessment tools provided.

Table 6–1 Common Communicable Childhood Illnesses

Communicable Illness	Signs and Symptoms	Infectious Agent	Methods of Transmission	Incubation Period	Length of Communicability	Control Measures
Airborne Transmitted Illnesses						
Chickenpox	Slight fever, irritability, cold-like symptoms. Red rash that develops blister-like head, scabs later. Most abundant on covered parts of body, e.g., chest, back, neck, forearms.	Virus	Airborne through contact with secretions from the respiratory tract. Transmission from contact with blisters less common.	2–3 weeks after exposure	2–3 days prior to the onset of symptoms until 5–6 days after first eruptions. Scabs are not contagious.	Specific control measures: (1) Exclusion of sick children. (2) Practice good personal hygiene, especially careful hand washing. Children can return to group care when all blisters have formed a dry scab (approximately 1 week). Immunization is now available.
Common Cold	Highly contagious infection of the upper respiratory tract accompanied by slight fever, chills, runny nose, fatigue, muscle ache and headaches. Onset may be sudden.	Virus	Airborne through contact with secretions from the respiratory tract, e.g., coughs, sneezes, eating utensils, etc.	12–72 hours	About 1 day before onset of symptoms to 2–3 days after acute illness.	Prevention through education and good personal hygiene. Avoid exposure. Exclude first day or two. Antibiotics not effective against viruses. Avoid aspirin products (possible link to Reye's syndrome). Observe for complications, e.g., earaches, bronchitis, croup, pneumonia.
Fifth disease	Appearance of bright red rash on face, especially cheeks.	Virus	Airborne contact with secretions from the nose/mouth of infected person.	4–14 days	Prior to appearance of rash; probably not contagious after rash develops.	Children don't need to be excluded once rash appears. Frequent hand washing; frequent washing/disinfecting of toys/surfaces. Use care when handling tissues/nasal secretions.

Haemophilus influenza Type b (Hib)	An acute respiratory infection; frequently causes meningitis. Other complications include pneumonia, epiglottitis, arthritis, infections of the bloodstream, and conjunctivitis.	Bacteria	Airborne via secretions of the respiratory tract (nose, throat). Some children are carriers and may/may not have symptoms.	2–4 days	Throughout acute phase; as long as organism is present. Noncommunicable 36–48 hours after treatment with antibiotics.	Identify and exclude sick children. Treatment with antibiotics 3–4 days before returning to group care. Notify families of exposed children to contact their physician. Immunize children. Practice good hand washing techniques; sanitize contaminated objects.
Measles (Rubeola)	Fever, cough, runny nose, eyes sensitive to light. Dark red blotchy rash that often begins on the face and neck, then spreads over the entire body. Highly communicable.	Virus	Airborne through coughs, sneezes, and contact with contaminated articles.	8–13 days; rash develops approximately 14 days after exposure	From beginning of symptoms until 4 days after rash appears.	Most effective control method is immunization. Good personal hygiene, especially hand washing and covering coughs. Exclude child for at least 4 days after rash appears.
Meningitis	Sudden onset of fever, stiff neck, headache, irritability, and vomiting; gradual loss of consciousness, seizures, and death.	Bacteria	Airborne through coughs, nasal secretions; direct contact with saliva/nasal discharges.	Varies with the infecting organism; 2–4 days average	Throughout acute phase; noncommunicable after antibiotic treatment.	Encourage immunization. Exclude child from school until medical treatment is completed. Use universal precautions when handling saliva/nasal secretions, frequent hand washing, and disinfecting of toys/surfaces.
Mononucleosis	Characteristic symptoms include sore throat, intermittent fever, fatigue, and enlarged lymph glands in the neck. May also be accompanied by headache and enlarged liver or spleen.	Virus	Airborne; also direct contact with saliva of an infected person.	2–4 weeks for children; 4–6 weeks for adults	Unknown. Organisms may be present in oral secretions for as long as 1 year following illness.	None known. Child should be kept home until over the acute phase (6–10 days). Use frequent hand washing and careful disposal of tissues after coughing or blowing nose.

(*continued*)

Table 6–1 Common Communicable Childhood Illnesses *(continued)*

Communicable Illness	Signs and Symptoms	Infectious Agent	Methods of Transmission	Incubation Period	Length of Communicability	Control Measures
Airborne Transmitted Illnesses *(continued)*						
Mumps	Sudden onset of fever with swelling of the salivary glands.	Virus	Airborne through coughs and sneezes; direct contact with oral secretions of infected persons.	12–26 days	6–7 days prior to the onset of symptoms until swelling in the salivary glands is gone (7–9 days).	Immunization provides permanent protection. Peak incidence is in winter and spring. Exclude children from school or group settings until all symptoms have disappeared.
Roseola Infantum (6–24 mos.)	Most common in the spring and fall. Fever rises abruptly (102°–105°F) and lasts 3–4 days; loss of appetite, listlessness, runny nose, rash on trunk, arms, and neck lasting 1–2 days.	Virus	Person to person; method unknown.	10–15 days	1–2 days before onset to several days following fading of the rash.	Exclude from school or group care until rash and fever are gone.
Rubella (German Measles)	Mild fever; rash begins on face and neck and rarely lasts more than 3 days. May have arthritis-like discomfort and swelling in joints.	Virus	Airborne through contact with respiratory secretions, e.g., coughs, sneezes.	4–21 days	From one week prior to 5 days following onset of the rash.	Immunization offers permanent protection. Children must be excluded from school for at least 7 days after appearance of rash.
Streptococcal Infections (strep throat, scarlatina, rheumatic fever)	Sudden onset. High fever accompanied by sore, red throat; may also have nausea, vomiting, headache,	Bacteria	Airborne via droplets from coughs or sneezes. May also be transmitted by food and raw milk.	1–4 days	Throughout the illness and for approximately 10 days afterward, unless treated with antibiotics.	Exclude child with symptoms. Antibiotic treatment is essential. Avoid crowding in classrooms. Practice frequent hand washing,

	white patches on tonsils, and enlarged glands. Development of a rash depends on the infectious organism.				Medical treatment eliminates communicability within 36 hours. Can develop rheumatic fever or become a carrier if not treated.	educating children, and careful supervision of food handlers.
Tuberculosis	Many people have no symptoms. Active disease causes productive cough, weight loss, fatigue, loss of appetite, chills, night sweats.	Bacteria	Airborne via coughs or sneezes.	2–3 months	As long as disease is untreated; usually noncontagious after 2–3 weeks on medication.	TB skin testing, especially babies and young children if there has been contact with an infected person. Seek prompt diagnosis and treatment if experiencing symptoms; complete drug therapy. Cover coughs/sneezes. Practice good hand washing.
Blood-Borne Transmitted Illnesses						
Acquired Immuno-deficiency Syndrome (AIDS)	Flu-like symptoms, including fatigue, weight loss, enlarged lymph glands, persistent cough, fever, and diarrhea.	Virus	Children acquire virus when born to infected mothers, from contaminated blood transfusions, and possibly from breast milk of infected mothers. Adults acquire the virus via sexual transmission, contaminated drug needles, and blood transfusions.	6 weeks to 8 years	Lifetime	Exclude children 0–5 yrs. if they have open lesions, uncontrollable nosebleeds, bloody diarrhea, or are at high risk for exposing others to blood-contaminated body fluids. Use universal precautions when handling body fluids, including good hand washing techniques. Seal contaminated items, e.g., diapers, paper towels in plastic bags. Disinfect surfaces with bleach/ water solution (1:10) or other disinfectant.

(*continued*)

Table 6–1 Common Communicable Childhood Illnesses *(continued)*

Communicable Illness	Signs and Symptoms	Infectious Agent	Methods of Transmission	Incubation Period	Length of Communicability	Control Measures
Blood Borne Transmitted Illnesses *(continued)*						
Hepatitis B	Slow onset; loss of appetite, nausea, vomiting, abdominal pain, and jaundice. May also be **asymptomatic**.	Virus	Through contact with blood/body fluids containing blood.	45–180 days; average 60–80 days	Varies; some persons are lifetime carriers.	Immunization is preferable. Use universal precautions when handling any blood/body fluids; use frequent hand washing.
Contact (Direct and Indirect) Transmitted Illnesses						
Conjunctivitis (Pinkeye)	Redness of the white portion (conjunctiva) of the eye and inner eyelid, swelling of the lids, yellow discharge from eyes, and itching.	Bacteria or virus	Direct contact with discharge from eyes or upper respiratory tract of an infected person; through contaminated fingers and objects, e.g., tissues, washcloths, towels.	1–3 days	Throughout active infection; several days up to 2–3 weeks.	Antibiotic treatment. Exclude child for 24 hours after medication is started. Frequent hand washing and disinfection of toys/surfaces is necessary.
Cytomegalovirus (CMV)	Often no symptoms in children under 2 yrs.; sore throat, fever, fatigue in older children. High risk of fetal damage if mother is infected during pregnancy.	Virus	Person to person contact with body fluids, e.g., saliva, blood, urine, breast milk, in utero.	Unknown; may be 4–8 weeks	Virus present (in saliva, urine) for months following infection.	No need to exclude children. Always wash hands after changing diapers or contact with saliva. Avoid kissing children's mouths or sharing eating utensils. Practice careful hand washing with children; wash/disinfect toys and surfaces frequently.
Hand, Foot, and Mouth Disease	Affects children under 10 yrs. Onset of fever, followed by blistered sores in	Virus	Person to person through direct contact with saliva, nasal	3–6 days	7–10 days	Exclude sick children for several days. Practice frequent hand washing, especially after changing

asymptomatic – *having no symptoms.*

	the mouth/cheeks; 1–2 days later raised rash appears on palms of hands and soles of feet.		discharge, or feces.			diapers. Clean/disinfect surfaces.
Herpes simplex (cold sores)	Clear blisters develop on face, lips, and other body parts that crust and heal within a few days.	Virus	Direct contact with saliva, on hands, or sexual contact.	Up to 2 weeks	Virus remains in saliva for as long as 7 weeks following recovery.	No specific control. Frequent hand washing. Child does not have to be excluded from school.
Impetigo	Infection of the skin forming crusty, moist lesions usually on the face, ears, and around the nose. Highly contagious. Common among children.	Bacteria	Direct contact with discharge from sores; indirect contact with contaminated articles of clothing, tissues, etc.	2–5 days; may be as long as 10 days	Until treated with antibiotics and all lesions are healed.	Exclude from group settings until lesions have been treated with antibiotics for 24–48 hours. Cover areas with bandage until treated.
Lice (head)	Lice are seldom visible to the naked eye. White nits (eggs) are visible on hair shafts. The most obvious symptom is itching of the scalp, especially behind the ears and at the base of the neck.	Head louse	Direct contact with infected persons or with their personal articles, e.g., hats, hair brushes, combs, or clothing. Lice can survive for 2–3 weeks on bedding, carpet, furniture, car seats, clothing, etc.	Nits hatch in 1 week and reach maturity within 8–10 days	While lice remain alive on infested persons or clothing; until nits have been destroyed.	Infested children should be excluded from group settings until treated. Hair should be washed with a special medicated shampoo and rinsed with a vinegar/water solution (any concentration will work) to ease removal of all nits (using a fine-toothed comb). Heat from a hair dryer also helps to destroy eggs. All friends and family should be carefully checked. Thoroughly clean child's environment; vacuum carpets/upholstery, wash/dry or dry clean bedding, clothing, hairbrushes. Seal nonwashable items in plastic bag for 2 weeks.

(*continued*)

Table 6–1 Common Communicable Childhood Illnesses *(continued)*

Communicable Illness	Signs and Symptoms	Infectious Agent	Methods of Transmission	Incubation Period	Length of Communicability	Control Measures
Contact (Direct And Indirect) Transmitted Illnesses *(continued)*						
Ringworm	An infection of the scalp, skin, or nails. Causes flat, spreading, oval-shaped lesions that may become dry and scaly or moist and crusted. When it is present on the feet it is commonly called athlete's foot. Infected nails may become discolored, brittle, or chalky or they may disintegrate.	Fungus	Direct or indirect contact with infected persons, their personal items, showers, swimming pools, theater seats, etc. Dogs and cats may also be infected and transmit it to children or adults.	4–10 days (unknown for athlete's foot)	As long as lesions are present.	Exclude children from gyms, pools, or activities where they are likely to expose others. May return to group care following treatment with a fungicidal ointment. All shared areas, such as pools and showers, should be thoroughly cleansed with a fungicide.
Rocky Mountain Spotted Fever	Onset usually abrupt; fever (101°–104°F); joint and muscle pain, severe nausea and vomiting, and white coating on tongue. Rash appears on 2nd to 5th day over forehead, wrist, and ankles; later covers entire body. Can be fatal if untreated.	Bacteria	Indirect transmission: tick bite.	2–14 days; average 7 days	Not contagious from person to person.	Prompt removal of ticks; not all ticks cause illness. Administration of antibiotics. Use insect repellent on clothes when outdoors.

Scabies	Characteristic burrows or linear tunnels under the skin, especially between the fingers and around the wrists, elbows, waist, thighs, and buttocks. Causes intense itching.	Parasite	Direct contact with an infected person.	Several days to 2–4 weeks	Until all mites and eggs are destroyed.	Children should be excluded from school or group care until treated. Affected persons should bathe with prescribed soap and carefully launder all bedding and clothing. All contacts of the infected person should be notified.
Tetanus	Muscle spasms and stiffness, especially in the muscles around the neck and mouth. Can lead to convulsions, inability to breathe, and death.	Bacteria	Indirect: organisms live in soil and dust; enter body through wounds, especially puncture-type injuries, burns, and unnoticed cuts.	4 days to 2 weeks	Not contagious.	Immunization every 8–10 years affords complete protection.
Fecal/Oral Transmitted Illnesses						
Dysentery (Shigellosis)	Sudden onset of vomiting; diarrhea, may be accompanied by high fever, headache, abdominal pain. Stools may contain blood, pus, or mucus. Can be fatal in young children.	Bacteria	Fecal-oral transmission via contaminated objects or indirectly through ingestion of contaminated food or water and via flies.	1–7 days	Variable; may last up to 4 weeks or longer in the carrier state.	Exclude child during acute illness. Careful hand washing after bowel movements. Proper disposal of human feces; control of flies. Strict adherence to sanitary procedures for food preparation.
E. coli	Diarrhea, often bloody.	Bacteria	Spread through contaminated food, dirty hands.	3–4 days; can be as long as 10 days	For duration of diarrhea; usually several days.	Exclude infected children until no diarrhea; practice frequent hand washing, especially after toileting and before preparing food.

(continued)

Table 6–1 Common Communicable Childhood Illnesses *(continued)*

Communicable Illness	Signs and Symptoms	Infectious Agent	Methods of Transmission	Incubation Period	Length of Communicability	Control Measures
Fecal/Oral Transmitted Illnesses *(continued)*						
Encephalitis	Sudden onset of headache, high fever, convulsions, vomiting, confusion, neck and back stiffness, tremors, and coma.	Virus	Indirect spread by bites from disease-carrying mosquitoes; in some areas transmitted by tick bites.	5–15 days	Not contagious.	Spraying of mosquito breeding areas and use of insect repellents; public education.
Giardiasis	Many persons are asymptomatic. Typical symptoms include chronic diarrhea, abdominal cramping, bloating, pale and foul-smelling stools, weight loss, and fatigue.	Parasite (protozoa)	Fecal-oral transmission; through contact with infected stool (e.g., diaper changes, helping child with soiled underwear), poor hand washing, passed from hands to mouth (toys, food). Also transmitted through contaminated water sources.	7–10 days average; can be as long as 5–25 days	As long as parasite is present in the stool.	Exclude children until diarrhea ends. Scrupulous hand washing before eating, preparing food, and after using the bathroom. Maintain sanitary conditions in bathroom areas.
Hepatitis (Infectious; Type A)	Fever, fatigue, loss of appetite, nausea, abdominal pain (in region of liver). Illness may be accompanied by yellowing of the skin and eyeballs (jaundice) in adults, but not always in children. Acute onset.	Virus	Fecal-oral route. Also spread via contaminated food, water, milk, and objects.	10–50 days (average range 25–30 days)	7–10 days prior to onset of symptoms to not more than 7 days after onset of jaundice.	Exclude from group settings a minimum of 1 week following onset. Special attention to careful hand washing after going to the bathroom and before eating is critical following an outbreak. Report disease incidents to public health authorities. Immunoglobulin (IG) recommended for protection of close contacts.

Pinworms	Irritability, and itching of the rectal area. Common among young children. Some children have no symptoms.	Parasite; not contagious from animals.	Infectious eggs are transferred from person to person by contaminated hands (oral-fecal route). Indirectly spread by contaminated bedding, food, clothing, swimming pool.	Life cycle of the worm is 3–6 weeks; persons can also re-infect themselves.	2–8 weeks or as long as a source of infection remains present.	Infected children must be excluded from school until treated with medication; may return after initial dose. All infected and non-infected family members must be treated at one time. Frequent hand washing is essential; discourage nail biting or sucking of fingers. Daily baths and change of linen are necessary. Disinfect school toilet seats and sink handles at least once a day. Vacuum carpeted areas daily. Eggs are also destroyed when exposed to temperatures over 132°F. Education and good personal hygiene are vital to control.
Salmonellosis	Abdominal pain and cramping, sudden fever, severe diarrhea (may contain blood), nausea and vomiting lasts 5–7 days.	Bacteria	Fecal-oral transmission: via dirty hands. Also contaminated food (especially improperly cooked poultry, milk, eggs), water supplies, and infected animals.	12–36 hours	Throughout acute illness; may remain a carrier for months.	Attempt to identify source. Exclude children/adults with diarrhea; may return when symptoms end. Carriers should not handle or prepare food until stool cultures are negative. Practice good hand washing and sanitizing procedures.

Common Acute Childhood Illnesses

Children experience many forms of acute illness; however, not all of these are contagious (Bourgeois et al., 2009; Bradley, 2003). Teachers must be able to distinguish conditions that are contagious from those that are limited to an individual child. *However, teachers must never attempt to diagnose children's health problems.* Their primary responsibilities include identifying children who are ill, making them comfortable until parents arrive, and advising the family to contact their health care provider. The remainder of this chapter is devoted to several common childhood illnesses and acute health conditions.

Colds

Children may experience as many as seven to eight colds during a typical year. This number tends to decrease as children mature and their respiratory passageways increase in size, their immune systems become more effective at warding off illness, and they begin to develop healthy habits. Cold symptoms can range from frequent sneezing and runny nose to fever, sore throat, cough, headache, and muscle aches (Pappas et al., 2008).

Cause Most colds are caused by a viral **infection**, primarily rhinoviruses and coronoviruses. They spread rapidly and have a short incubation stage of 1 to 2 days.

Management Because colds are highly contagious during the first day or two, it is best to exclude children from group settings. Rest, and increased fluid intake (water, fruit juices, soups) are recommended. Non-aspirin, fever-reducing medication may help children feel more comfortable and is usually adequate treatment for a cold. (Note: Schools must obtain a physician's approval before administering any medication.)

Antibiotics are not effective against most viruses and are therefore of limited value for treating simple colds. However, a physician may prescribe antibiotics to treat complications or secondary infections, such as fever, red throat, white patches on their tonsils (one indication of strep throat), extreme fatigue, or yellow nasal drainage. Toddlers and preschool-age children are often more prone to these conditions and should be observed closely. Families should also be advised to seek immediate medical attention for children who do not improve after 4 to 5 days or if they develop any of these secondary complications.

Some children who have special needs, such as Down syndrome, leukemia, or allergies, may exhibit chronic cold-like symptoms including runny nose and a productive cough. It isn't necessary for these children to be excluded from school unless they develop signs of a secondary infection.

Diaper Rash (Diaper Dermatitis)

Diaper rash is an irritation of the skin in and around the buttocks and genital area. Infants who have sensitive skin or are formula-fed versus breastfed are more likely to experience periodic outbreaks of diaper rash (Hockenberry & Wilson, 2009).

Cause Prolonged contact with ammonia in urine and organic acids in stools can burn baby's skin, causing patches of red, raised areas or tiny pimples. In severe cases, open, weeping areas of the skin may become infected with yeast or bacteria. Reactions to fabric softeners, soaps, lotions, powders, antibiotics, foods, and certain brands of disposable diapers may also cause some infants and toddlers to develop diaper rash.

---

infection – *a condition that results when a pathogen invades and establishes itself within a susceptible host.*

Children typically experience many colds during the year.

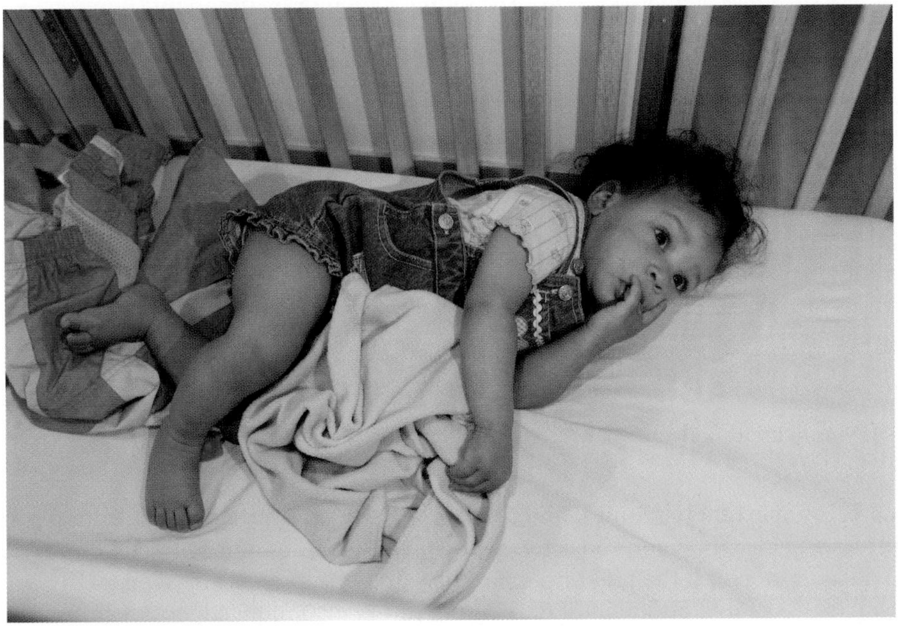

Management Prompt changing of wet and/or soiled diapers followed by a thorough cleansing of the skin is often sufficient to prevent and treat diaper rash. Baby products, such as powders and lotions, should be avoided because they can encourage bacterial growth when combined with urine and feces. In addition, infants are apt to inhale fine powder particles and many of these products contain phthalates which may have harmful effects on children's development and reproductive systems (Sathyanarayana et al., 2008). A thin layer of petroleum jelly or zinc oxide ointment can be applied to irritated areas to protect the skin. Allowing the infant to go without diapers (when at home) and exposing irritated skin to the air may also help speed the healing process. If the diaper rash does not improve in 2 or 3 days, parents should be encouraged to contact their health care provider.

Diarrhea

The term diarrhea refers to frequent watery or very soft bowel movements. They may be foul-smelling and also contain particles of blood or mucus. Young children's digestive systems tend to be more sensitive to foods and medications so that it is not uncommon for them to experience several episodes of diarrhea throughout the year.

Cause Diarrhea can either be infectious or noninfectious. Infectious forms of diarrhea include:

- viral or bacterial infections, such as rotavirus, hepatitis A, or salmonellosis
- parasitic, such as giardia

Causes of noninfectious diarrhea can include:

- fruit juices containing sorbitol (Orenstein, 2006)
- antibiotic therapy
- recent dietary changes
- food allergies, such as lactose or gluten intolerance
- food poisoning
- illnesses, such as earaches, colds, strep throat, or cystic fibrosis

Until new vaccines became available in 2006, approximately 55,000 -70,000 children were hospitalized each year for severe diarrhea caused by rotavirus (Cortese & Parashar, 2009). Because children under age three are the most frequent victims of this illness, infants are now being immunized at 2-, 4- and 6-months of age. Consequently, the numbers of children who experience rotavirus infections and hospitalizations have declined significantly.

Frequent or prolonged diarrhea can result in **dehydration**, especially in infants and toddlers. Dehydration involves a loss of body water and can occur quickly in young children due to their poor fluid regulation and small body size. Because excessive dehydration can be fatal in infants and young children, they should be observed closely for:

- dryness of the mouth
- **listlessness**
- sunken eyes
- absence of tears
- decreased or no urinary output
- rapid, weak pulse
- skin loses elasticity; dough-like

Management It is important to monitor and record the frequency (number) and amount (small, large) of bowel movements. The color, consistency, and presence of any blood, mucus, or pus should also be noted. Be sure to check the child's temperature and observe for any signs of discomfort. Prompt medical advice should be sought if diarrhea is severe or prolonged, or the child becomes lethargic or drowsy. Adults and children should practice meticulous hand washing to avoid infecting themselves and others.

Most cases of diarrhea can be treated by temporarily replacing solid foods in the child's diet with a commercially prepared electrolyte solution. This solution supplies important fluids and salts lost through diarrhea and helps to restore normal function. Liquids and soft foods can gradually be added back into the child's diet once the diarrhea has ended. Any complaint of pain that is continuous or located in the lower right side of the **abdomen** should be reported promptly to the child's family and checked by a physician.

Children who have experienced diarrhea during the past 24 hours should be excluded from group settings. Exceptions to this policy would include children whose diarrhea resulted from non-contagious conditions such as food allergies, changes in diet, or recent treatment with antibiotics. However, even these children may not feel well enough to attend school and participate in the day's activities. The problem and inconvenience of frequent accidental soiling may also be too time-consuming for teachers to manage.

Diarrhea lasting longer than a week should be cause for concern, especially if it is accompanied by bloating, change of appetite, or weight loss. The child should remain at home until a cause is determined, and conditions such as giardia, dysentery, or hepatitis A have been ruled out.

---

dehydration – *a state in which there is an excessive loss of body fluids or extremely limited fluid intake. Symptoms may include loss of skin tone, sunken eyes, and mental confusion.*

listlessness – *a state characterized by a lack of energy and/or interest in one's affairs.*

abdomen – *the portion of the body located between the diaphragm (located at the base of the lungs) and the pelvic or hip bones.*

Issues To Consider **Seasonal and H1N1 Flu**

Each year, seasonal flu and cold-like symptoms begin to make their appearance as the winter months approach. For the most part, these are relatively mild respiratory illnesses that affect 5 to 20 percent of the population annually. Only a small number of victims who are either very young, elderly, or have compromised immune systems die from the infection or develop serious complications that require hospitalization. However, recent events have drawn attention to the fact that communicable illnesses of pandemic proportions are not a thing of the past. Outbreaks of avian flu and SARS (severe acute respiratory syndrome) have raised international concerns about the potential for massive infection and significant numbers of deaths (Zimmer & Burke, 2009). Dense living conditions and modern travel methods have encouraged the rapid spread of newly emerging diseases, such as the H1N1 flu, to large numbers of people throughout the world. Children seem to be at particularly high risk for contracting the H1N1 flu and often experience a more severe form of the disease. Consequently, health care workers, employers, schools, and families have had to revisit their policies, practices, and understanding of communicable illness and containment methods (Child Health Alert, 2009; McFadden & Frelick, 2009). Many excellent planning resources and response guidelines are available online for families, schools, communities, health care organizations, businesses, and other professional groups: CDC (http://www.cdc.gov/h1n1flu); U.S. Department of Health & Human Services (www.flu.gov); and Public Health Agency of Canada (http://www.phac-aspc.gc.ca).

- What are the symptoms of H1N1 flu? How is it spread?
- What factors in your setting would increase children's risk of exposure?
- What community resources are available to help prepare your school or early childhood program in the event of an epidemic?
- What immediate precautionary measures could your program implement?
- Is H1N1 a reportable illness?

Dizziness

It is not unusual for children to complain of momentary dizziness or a spinning sensation after vigorous play. However, repeated complaints of dizziness should be noted and reported to the child's family. They should be advised to contact the child's physician to determine a possible underlying cause.

Cause Dizziness can be a symptom of other health conditions, including:

- ear infections
- fever
- headaches
- head injuries
- anemia
- nasal congestion and sinus infections
- brain tumor (rare)

Management Temporary episodes of dizziness usually respond to simple first aid measures. Have the child lie down quietly or sit with head resting on or between the knees until the sensation has passed. Quiet play can be resumed when the child no longer feels dizzy. Inform the child's family of this experience so they can continue to monitor the condition at home.

If dizziness is accompanied by any loss of balance or coordination, parents should be encouraged to check with the child's physician at once. Dizziness that results from an underlying health problem will usually not respond to most first aid measures.

Earaches

Earaches and ear infections are frequently a problem during the first 3 or so years of a child's life, affecting boys more often than girls (Bradley, 2003). More than half of all infants, especially those who are formula-fed versus breastfed, experience an ear infection before their first birthday (Hetzner et al., 2009). However, by age five, children usually begin to have fewer ear infections as structures in the ear, nose, and throat increase in size and resistance to infection (antibody formation) improves. Children of Native American and Eskimo ethnicity are known to experience a higher rate of ear infections, possibly related to structural differences in the ear canal (Singleton et al., 2009). Exposure to second-hand smoke has also been identified as a contributing factor. Additionally, studies have shown that children in group care tend to have a higher incidence of ear infections and of otitis media than those who stay at home (American Academy of Otolaryngology, 2009).

Cause A number of conditions can cause earache in children, including:

- upper respiratory infections, such as a cold
- allergies
- dental cavities and eruption of new teeth
- excessive ear wax
- foreign objects, such as plastic beads, food, small toy pieces, or stones
- bacterial infections, such as "swimmer's ear" or otitis media
- feeding infants in a reclining position

Earaches caused by an acute bacterial infection of the middle ear are known as *otitis media.* Children who have some forms of developmental disabilities, such as Williams syndrome, Turner's syndrome, Down syndrome, fragile X, autism, and cleft palate are at higher risk for developing this condition (Schieve et al., 2009). Otitis media causes an inflammation of the eustachian tube (passageway connecting the ear, nose, and throat), which can lead to a backup of fluid in the middle ear and result in pain, fever, and temporary or chronic hearing loss (Hockenberry & Wilson, 2009). Often, only one ear will be affected at a time, and the infection may or may not be accompanied by fluid accumulation behind the eardrum. Placing infants on their backs to sleep has been shown to be effective in decreasing the incidence of ear infection (Hunt et al., 2003). Children, especially infants and toddlers with limited language, should be observed carefully for signs of a possible ear infection, including:

- nausea, vomiting, and/or diarrhea
- tugging or rubbing of the affected ear
- refusal to eat or swallow
- redness of the outer ear

Reflective Thoughts

Sometimes families knowingly or unknowingly bring sick children to school or child care. Examine your feelings about being exposed to children's communicable illnesses. Do you feel differently depending on the illness? What steps can teachers take to improve their resistance to communicable illness? How would you respond to families who repeatedly ignore a program's exclusion policies? How might cultural differences influence what parents view as illness? What could you do to help families understand and respect a program's policies?

- fever
- dizziness or unsteady balance
- irritability
- discharge from the ear canal
- difficulty hearing
- crying when placed in a reclining position
- difficulty sleeping

Management Children who develop otitis media do not need to be excluded from group settings unless they are too ill to participate in daily activities or have other symptoms that are contagious. Teachers may be able to provide temporary relief from earache pain by having the child lie down with the affected ear on a soft blanket; the warmth helps to soothe discomfort. A small, dry cotton ball placed in the outer ear may also help reduce pain by keeping air out of the ear canal. If excess wax or a foreign object is causing the child's ear pain, it must be removed only by a physician.

Persistent complaints of ear pain or earache should not be ignored and need to be checked by the child's health care provider if symptoms last longer than 2 or 3 days. In most cases the fluid will clear up without treatment. However, chronic otitis media with fluid can interfere with children's speech and language development and may therefore require medical treatment (Proops & Archarya, 2009; Vernon-Feagons & Manlove, 2005).

Physicians now use several approaches to treat acute bacterial ear infections. Current guidelines recommend taking a wait-and-see approach and limiting the use of antibiotics to reduce the potential of drug resistance. If children are placed on oral antibiotics, it is important that all medication be taken; failure to finish medication can result in a recurrence of the infection. When children have taken all of the prescribed medication, they should be re-checked by a physician to make certain the infection is gone. In some cases, a second round of medication may be needed. Surgical insertion of small plastic tubes into the eardrum is sometimes recommended for children who have repeated infections and chronic fluid buildup to lessen the risk of permanent hearing loss (Singleton et al., 2009). Teachers should be alert to any children with tubes in their ears. Special precautions must be taken to avoid getting water in the outer ear canal during activities that involve water play, such as swimming, bathing, or playing in pools or sprinklers. Ear plugs or a special plastic putty are commonly used for this purpose.

The frequency of ear infections decreases as children get older.

Fainting

Fainting, a momentary loss of consciousness, occurs when blood supply to the brain is temporarily reduced.

Cause Possible causes for this condition in young children include:

- anemia
- breath-holding

- **hyperventilation**
- extreme stress, excitement, or hysteria
- drug reactions
- illness, infection, or extreme pain
- poisoning

Management Children may initially complain of feeling dizzy or weak. Their skin may appear pale, cool, and moist, and the child may collapse. If this occurs, lay the child down, elevate the legs 8 to 10 inches on a pillow or similar object, and observe breathing and pulse frequently. A light blanket can be placed over the child for extra warmth. Breathing is made easier if clothing is loosened from around the neck and waist. No attempt should be made to give the child anything to eat or drink until consciousness is regained. The child's family should be notified and encouraged to consult with their physician.

Fever

Activity, age, eating, sleeping, and the time of day cause normal fluctuations in children's temperatures. However, a persistent elevated **temperature** is usually an indication of illness or infection, especially if the child also complains of headache, coughing, nausea, or sore throat.

Cause Common causes of fever in children include:

- viral and bacterial illnesses, such as ear, skin, and upper respiratory infections
- urinary tract infections
- heat stroke and overheating

Changes in children's appearance and behavior may be an early indication of **fever**. Other indications may include:

- flushed or reddened face
- listlessness or desire to sleep
- "glassy" eyes
- loss of appetite
- complaints of not feeling well
- chills
- warm, dry skin; older children may have increased perspiration

Management Children's temperature should be checked if there is reason to believe that they may have a fever. Only digital and infrared **tympanic** thermometers are recommended for use in schools and group-care settings because of safety and liability concerns (Table 6–2). These thermometers are quick and efficient to use, especially with children who may be fussy or uncooperative, and they provide readings that are reasonably accurate (Table 6–3) (Devrim et al., 2007; Sganga et al., 2000). Infrared forehead thermometers are currently being marketed but studies have shown them to be unreliable. Glass mercury thermometers are considered unsafe to use with young children and also pose hazardous environmental concerns.

---

hyperventilation – *rapid breathing often with forced inhalation; can lead to sensations of dizziness, lightheadedness, and weakness.*

temperature – *a measurement of body heat; varies with the time of day, activity, and method of measurement.*

fever – *an elevation of body temperature above normal; a temperature over 99.4°F or 37.4°C orally is usually considered a fever.*

tympanic – *referring to the ear canal.*

Table 6–2 Preferred Methods for Checking Children's Temperature in Group Settings (in Rank Order)

infants and toddlers	axillary
2–5 years old	tympanic axillary oral
5 years and older	oral tympanic axillary

Children with an axillary temperature over 99.1°F (37.4°C) or a tympanic reading over 100.4°F (38°C) should be observed carefully for other symptoms of illness. Unless a program's exclusion policies require children with fevers to be sent home, they can be moved to a separate room or quiet area in the classroom and monitored. If there are no immediate indications of acute illness, children should be encouraged to rest. Lowering the room temperature, removing warm clothing, and offering extra fluids can also help make a child feel more comfortable. Fever-reducing medications should be administered only with a physician's approval. Families should also be notified so they can decide whether to take the child home or wait to see if any further symptoms develop.

Headaches

Headaches are not a common complaint of young children, but when they do occur they are usually a symptom of some other condition. Repeated complaints of headache should be brought to families' attention.

Cause Children may experience headaches as the result of several conditions, including:

- bacterial or viral infections
- allergies
- head injuries
- emotional tension or stress
- reaction to medication
- lead poisoning
- hunger
- eye strain
- nasal congestion
- brain tumor (rare)
- constipation
- carbon monoxide poisoning

Management In the absence of any fever, rash, vomiting, or **disorientation**, children who experience headaches can remain in care but should continue to be observed for other indications of illness or injury. Frequently, their headaches will disappear with rest. However, patterns of repeated or intense headaches should be noted and families encouraged to discuss the problem with the child's physician.

disorientation – *lack of awareness or ability to recognize familiar persons or objects.*

Table 6–3 A Comparison of Thermometer Options

Type	Advantages	Disadvantages	Normal Range	How to Use	How to Clean
Digital thermometer	Can be used to check oral and axillary temperatures	Takes 1–2 minutes to obtain a reading	(Axillary) 94.5°–99.0°F (34.7°–37.2°C)	Turn switch on; wait for beep to signal ready.	Remove disposable cover.
	Safe, unbreakable	Requires child to sit still	(Oral) 94.5°–99.5°F (34.7°–37.3°C)	Apply disposable sanitary cover (optional).	Wipe with alcohol or clean with soap and cool water.
	Numbers are easy to read	Axillary readings are less accurate than oral		Place under tongue (oral) or in crease of armpit; hold in place; wait for beep to signal reading	
	Beeps when ready	Must purchase batteries and disposable covers			
	Easy to clean				
Tympanic thermometer	Yields a quick reading	Thermometer is expensive to buy (approximately $40–60)	96.4°–100.4°F (35.8°–38°C)	Apply disposable earpiece.	Wipe instrument (probe) with alcohol.
	Easy to use	Accuracy of reading depends on correct positioning in child's ear canal (differs from child to child)		Turn on start button.	
	Can check child's temperature while asleep	Must purchase batteries and disposable ear piece coverings		Insert probe carefully into ear canal opening; reading appears in seconds.	
	Requires limited child cooperation				

Heat Rash

Heat rash is most commonly seen in infants and toddlers.

Cause Heat rash is caused by a blockage in the sweat glands and occurs more commonly during the summer months, although it may also develop when an infant or child is dressed too warmly. Some children have sensitive skin and may develop heat rash from clothing made of synthetic fabrics.

Management Heat rash is not contagious. However, several measures can be taken to make a child more comfortable. Affected areas can be washed with cool water, dried thoroughly, and dusted sparingly with cornstarch.

Lyme Disease

Lyme disease is a tick-borne infection most prevalent along the East Coast, although it has been identified in nearly every U.S. state and many provinces of Canada (Anderson & Chaney, 2009; Sockett & Artsob, 2009). The number of cases continues to increase. There were over 29,000 confirmed cases and 6200 probable cases reported in 2008, with children ages birth to 14 being the most common victims (CDC, 2009b).

Cause This bacterial illness is caused by the bite of a tiny, infected deer tick; however, not all deer ticks are infected, nor will everyone who is bitten develop Lyme disease. Many species of the deer tick are commonly found in grassy and wooded areas during the summer and fall months.

Management The most effective way to prevent Lyme disease is to take preventive measures whenever children will be spending time outdoors, especially in grassy or wooded areas (Table 6–4).

Because deer ticks are exceptionally small, they are easily overlooked. Development of any unusual symptoms following a tick bite should be reported immediately to a physician. Early symptoms of Lyme disease may be easily mistaken for other illnesses, which sometimes makes the condition difficult to diagnose. In the early weeks following a bite, a small red, flat, or raised area may develop at the site, followed by a localized rash that gradually disappears. Flu-like symptoms,

Table 6–4 Measures to Prevent Tick Bites

- Encourage children to wear long pants, a long-sleeved shirt, socks, shoes, and a hat; light-colored clothing makes it easier to spot small deer ticks.
- Apply insect/tick repellent containing DEET to clothing and exposed areas of the skin (Hansmann, 2009; Katz, Miller, & Hebert, 2008). Be sure to follow manufacturer's directions and avoid aerosol sprays that children might inhale.
- Discourage children from rolling in the grass or sitting on fallen logs.
- Remove clothing as soon as children come indoors and check all areas of the body (under arms, around waist, behind knees, in the groin, on neck) and hair.
- Bathe or shower to remove any ticks.
- Wash clothing in soapy water and dry in dryer. (Heat will destroy ticks.)
- Continue to check children for any sign of ticks that may have been overlooked on a previous inspection.
- Promptly remove any tick discovered on the skin and wash the area carefully. (See Chapter 9).

Lyme disease – *bacterial illness caused by the bite of infected deer ticks found in grassy or wooded areas.*

including fever, chills, fatigue, headache, and joint pain, may also be experienced during this stage. If the bacterial infection is not diagnosed early and treated with antibiotics, complications, including arthritis, heart, and/or neurological problems can develop within 2 years of the initial bite. A blood test is available for early detection.

Sore Throat

Sore throats are a relatively common complaint among young children, especially during the fall and winter seasons. Teachers must often rely on their observations to determine when infants and toddlers may be experiencing a sore throat because children of this age are unlikely to verbalize their discomfort. Fussiness, lack of interest in food or refusal to eat, difficulty swallowing, enlarged lymph glands, fever, and fatigue may be early indications that the child is not feeling well.

Cause Most sore throats are caused by a viral or bacterial infection. However, some children may experience a scratchy throat as the result of sinus drainage, mouth breathing, or allergies.

Management It is extremely important not to ignore a child's complaint of sore throat. A small percentage of sore throats are caused by a highly contagious streptococcal infection (Table 6–1). Although most children are quite ill with these infections, some may experience only mild symptoms, such as headache or stomachache and fever, or none at all. Unknowingly, they may become carriers of the infection and capable of spreading it to others. A routine throat culture is necessary to determine if a strep infection is present and which antibiotic will provide the most effective treatment. If left untreated, strep throat can lead to serious complications, including rheumatic fever, heart valve damage, and kidney disease (Hockenberry & Wilson, 2009).

Sore throats resulting from viral infections are not usually harmful, but they may cause the child considerable discomfort. Cool beverages (and popsicles) can soothe an irritated throat. Antibiotics are not effective against most viral infections and, therefore, seldom prescribed.

Stomachaches

Most children experience an occasional stomachache from time to time. However, children may use this term to describe a range of discomforts, from hunger or a full bladder to actual nausea, cramping, or emotional upset. Teachers can use their observation and questioning skills to determine a probable cause.

Cause Children's stomachaches are often a symptom of some other condition. There are many possible causes, including:

- food allergies or intolerance
- appendicitis
- **intestinal** infections, e.g., giardiasis, salmonella, E. coli
- urinary tract infections
- gas or constipation
- side effect to medication, especially antibiotics
- change in diet
- emotional stress or desire for attention
- hunger
- diarrhea and/or vomiting
- strep throat

intestinal – *pertaining to the intestinal tract or bowel.*

Management There are several ways to determine whether or not a child's stomach pain is serious. Is the discomfort continuous or a cramping-type pain that comes and goes? Does the child have a fever? Is the child able to continue playing? If no fever is present, the stomachache is probably not serious. Encourage the child to use the bathroom and see if **urination** or having a bowel movement relieves the pain. Have the child rest quietly to see if the discomfort goes away. Check with families to determine if the child is taking any new medication or has had a change of diet. Stomach pain or stomachaches should be considered serious if they:

- disrupt a child's activity, such as running, playing, eating, sleeping
- cause tenderness of the abdomen
- are accompanied by diarrhea, vomiting, or severe cramping
- last longer than 3 to 4 hours
- result in stools that are bloody or contain mucus

If any of these conditions occur while the child is attending school or group care, families should be notified and advised to seek prompt medical attention for the child.

Sudden Infant Death Syndrome (SIDS)

Sudden infant death syndrome (SIDS) refers to the unexplainable death of a seemingly healthy infant under 12 months of age. It is a leading cause of infant death, which tends to peak between the second and fourth months (National SIDS Resource Center, 2009). Deaths are more likely to occur during sleep (nighttime and naps), and especially during the fall and winter months. Despite aggressive awareness campaigns, approximately 2,000–3,000 infants continue to die each year (CDC, 2009a).

Cause Although no one single cause has yet been identified, several factors seem to place some babies at higher risk of dying from SIDS, including:

- premature birth
- weighing less than 3.5 pounds at birth
- being a male child
- being of African American or American Indian/Alaska Native ethnicity (MacDorman & Mathews, 2009)
- having a sibling who also died of SIDS
- family poverty
- prenatal exposure to alcohol and/or illicit drugs, such as cocaine, heroin, or methadone
- maternal smoking (during and after pregnancy) (Richardson, Walker, & Horne, 2009a)
- being born to a teenage mother

Children born into families with limited education and financial resources seem to experience the highest rate of SIDS deaths. Many of their mothers failed to obtain prenatal care or they engaged in unhealthy practices during and after their pregnancy. Infants who die of SIDS often experience repeated interruptions of breathing called **apnea.** Researchers continue to investigate possible connections between this breathing disturbance and other factors, including:

- toxic mattress fumes
- immunizations
- use of pacifiers
- air pollution
- bed sharing or co-sleeping with parents (Hauck et al., 2008)
- respiratory infections (such as colds and flu)
- swaddling (Richardson, Walker, & Horne, 2009b)

---

urination – *the act of emptying the bladder of urine.*
apnea – *momentary absence of breathing.*

To date there has been no scientific evidence linking toxic mattress fumes or immunizations to SIDS. In fact, babies who are immunized are less likely to die from SIDS (First Candle/SIDS Alliance, 2009). Evidence regarding bed-sharing practices as a risk factor remains controversial although most authorities encourage parents to place infants in their own crib (near parents) to sleep (Shapiro-Mendoza et al., 2009).

Recent studies have established a connection between low production of serotonin, a hormone that regulates breathing, and SIDS (Duncan et al., 2010). Other studies have identified a positive relationship between SIDS and air pollution (Richardson, Walker, & Horne, 2009a). These findings have led to recommendations that families avoid exposing babies to second-hand smoke and other forms of concentrated air pollution. The use of pacifiers has actually been shown to reduce SIDS deaths although questions remain about why this practice is beneficial (Mitchell, 2009; Sexton & Natale, 2009).

Management An infant's sleeping position has proven to be the strongest link to preventing SIDS (Kinney & Thach, 2009). This discovery led to a nationwide "Back to Sleep" campaign, which has been ongoing and credited with significantly reducing SIDS deaths (NICHD, 2009). Multiple child and maternal government and private agencies continue to educate parents about proper sleep positioning for infants—***that babies must always be placed on their backs for sleeping***— and have extended their efforts to include early childhood teachers and caregivers. Although fewer than 16 percent of SIDS fatalities occur in early childhood programs, teachers must take steps to avoid any preventable death (AAP, 2009; Moon, Calabrese, & Aird, 2008). Despite ongoing educational efforts, researchers have found that nearly one-quarter of early childhood teachers continue to place infants in unsafe conditions and sleeping positions. As a result, many states now address infant sleep position in their child care licensing regulations so that programs will no longer be able to ignore this critical safety measure.

Initial fears that babies would be more likely to choke when placed on their back for sleeping have not proven true. It isn't clear whether back-sleeping improves infants' oxygen intake or reduces their breathing in of carbon dioxide. However, the SIDS death rate has decreased by nearly 50 percent since this practice was initially recommended (CDC, 2009a).

Babies should not share a crib with another infant nor sleep in a bed with adults; both of these practices have been found to increase the risk of SIDS. However, researchers have found that placing an infant's crib in the same room with their parents can decrease this risk (Fu et al., 2008). Additional guidelines for reducing the risk of SIDS are outlined in Table 6–5.

Because infants spend many hours sleeping, it is important to change their position often during times when they are awake so they are not always on their backs. Weak neck muscles make

Table 6–5 Teacher Checklist: Practices to Reduce the Risk of Sudden Infant Death Syndrome (SIDS)

- Always put infants to sleep on their back unless a health condition prevents this.
- Use a firm mattress that fits snugly in a safety-approved crib. Never place infants on a waterbed, sheepskin, comforter, soft sofa cushions, or other soft bedding material.
- Remove pillows, thick or fluffy blankets, and soft toys from an infant's bed.
- Cover infants with a thin blanket, tucking the bottom half under the mattress (Figure 6–1).
- Dress infants in light sleepwear and do not raise room temperature to avoid overheating.
- Offer a pacifier to infants who use them.
- Avoid exposing infants to second-hand smoke, car exhaust, wood smoke, and other air pollutants.
- Limit infants' exposure to persons who have colds or other respiratory infections.
- Encourage mothers to obtain professional prenatal care for themselves *and* recommended well-child checkups for their infant.
- Encourage and support breastfeeding; this may help to protect infants against SIDS.
- Know how to respond to medical emergencies.

it difficult for infants to turn their head from side to side; flat spots may develop when they remain in the same position for extended periods. These can be prevented by changing infants' position and placing them on their tummies for brief periods while they are awake. Alternating an infant's position in the crib is also beneficial—one day the head should be placed at the head of the crib, the following day the head should be placed at the foot of the bed. This prevents the infant from consistently laying on the same side of his or her head every day.

Because there is often no identifiable cause for SIDS, families tend to blame themselves for having been negligent or using poor judgment. They may believe that somehow they could have prevented this tragedy. Consequently, families who have experienced the unexpected death of an infant from SIDS require special emotional support and counseling. Siblings may also be affected by an infant's death and should be included in counseling therapy. Local chapters of several national SIDS organizations offer information and support groups to help families cope with their grief, including:

- First Candle/SIDS Alliance (http://www.sidsalliance.org)
- National SIDS Resource Center (http://www.sidscenter.org)
- Association of SIDS and Infant Mortality Programs (http://www.asip1.org)
- Canadian Foundation for the Study of Infant Deaths (http://www.SIDSCanada.org)

Figure 6–1 Putting infants to sleep on their backs significantly reduces the risk of SIDS.

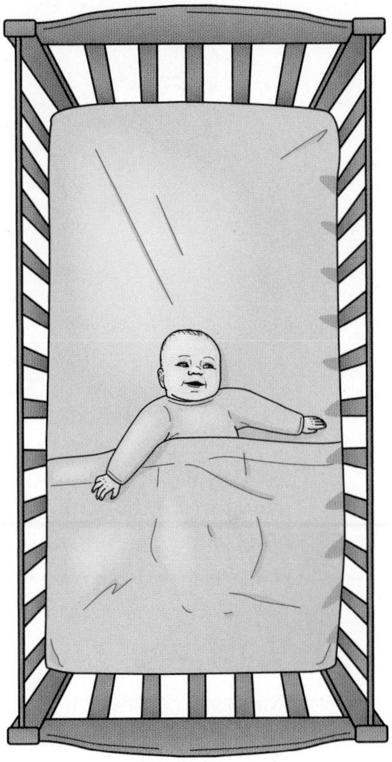

Teething

Teething is a natural process. Infants usually begin getting their first teeth around 4 to 7 months of age. Older children will begin the process of losing and replacing their baby teeth with a permanent set about the time they reach their fifth or sixth birthday.

Cause New teeth erupting through gum tissue can cause some children mild discomfort. However, most children move through this stage with relatively few problems.

Management An increase in drooling and chewing activity for several days or weeks may be the only indication that an infant is teething. Some infants become a bit more fussy, run a low-grade fever (under 100°F), and may not be interested in eating. However, high fevers, diarrhea, and vomiting are usually not caused by teething, but may be an indication of illness. Chilled teething rings and firm objects for children to chew often provide comfort and relief to swollen gums.

Toothache

Young children do not typically experience toothaches. Untreated oral health problems can cause pain and suffering, interfere with speech and language development, make eating difficult, affect school performance, and lead to early tooth loss. Preventive oral health care is an important component of wellness, and children should not have to forgo necessary dental treatment because of limited family income (Vargas & Arevalo, 2009; Malik-Kotru, Kirchner, & Kisby, 2009). Low-cost insurance (CHIP), Medicaid, and community resources, such as clinics and dental schools, are available to help families obtain essential dental care for children (National Maternal & Child Oral Health Resource Center, 2009).

Brushing teeth after eating helps to promote good oral health.

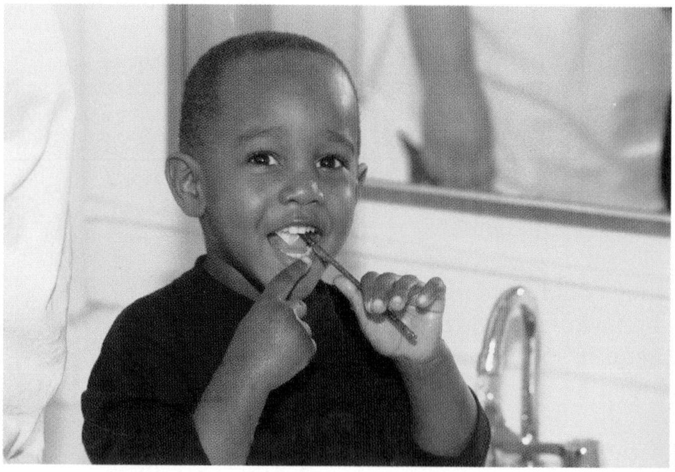
© Cengage Learning

Some infants and toddlers may experience temporary discomfort while teething. Older children may have similar discomfort when they begin losing baby teeth and their permanent teeth erupt.

Cause Although tooth decay is the most common cause of toothache, gum disease and injury can also be painful. Children may complain of a throbbing discomfort that sometimes radiates into the ear. Redness and swelling may also be observed around the gumline of the affected tooth. Foods that are hot or very sweet may intensify pain.

Management Complaints of toothache require prompt attention from the child's dentist. In the meantime, an icepack applied to the cheek on the affected side may make the child feel more comfortable. Aspirin-free products can also be administered by the child's family for pain relief. However, prevention, including proper brushing after eating and reduction of dietary sugars, is always the preferred approach for limiting tooth decay.

Vomiting

Vomiting can be a frightening and unpleasant experience for children. True vomiting is different from a baby who simply spits up after eating. Vomiting is a symptom often associated with an acute illness or other health problem (Hockenberry & Wilson 2009).

Cause A number of conditions can cause children to vomit, including:

- emotional upset
- viral or bacterial infection, such as stomach flu or strep throat
- drug reactions
- ear infections
- meningitis
- **salmonellosis**
- indigestion
- severe coughing
- head injury
- poisoning

Management The frequency, amount, and composition of vomited material is important to observe and record. Dehydration and disturbances of the body's chemical balance can occur with prolonged or excessive vomiting, especially in infants and toddlers. Children should be observed carefully for:

- high fever
- abdominal pain

salmonellosis – *a bacterial infection that is spread through contaminated drinking water, food, or milk or contact with other infected persons. Symptoms include diarrhea, fever, nausea, and vomiting.*

- signs of dehydration
- headache
- excessive drowsiness
- difficulty breathing
- sore throat
- exhaustion

Children who continue to vomit and show signs of a sore throat, fever, or stomach pains should be sent home as soon as possible. The teacher should also advise the child's family to contact their physician for further advice.

In the absence of any other symptoms, a single episode of vomiting may simply be due to an emotional upset, dislike of a particular food, excess mucus, or reaction to medication. Usually the child feels better immediately after vomiting and should be encouraged to rest quietly while remaining at school.

In addition to not feeling well, some children are upset by the act of vomiting itself. Extra reassurance and comforting can help make the experience less traumatic. Infants should be positioned on their stomachs, with their hips and legs slightly raised to allow vomited material to flow out of the mouth and prevent choking. Older children should also be watched closely so they don't choke or inhale vomitus.

West Nile Virus

Humans have long considered mosquitoes to simply be annoying insects that buzz in the ear, feast on exposed skin, and leave an itchy raised welt as their calling card. However, they are also capable of transmitting disease. The Centers for Disease Control and Protection (CDC) reported 1356 West Nile virus cases in the United States during 2008 (CDC, 2009c); a total of 2215 cases were reported in Canada for 2007 (Public Health Agency of Canada, 2008).

A majority of persons infected with the West Nile virus will have no symptoms of the illness. Some people will experience mild flu-like symptoms; a small percent will develop more serious symptoms, such as high fever, muscle weakness, rash, stiff neck, tremors, disorientation, coma, and even death. Young children and the elderly are at the greatest risk for developing the West Nile virus.

Cause West Nile virus is caused by the bite of an infected mosquito. The incidence is highest during the summer and fall seasons. However, there have also been limited reports of transmission via blood transfusion and the breast milk of an infected mother.

Management Prevention is the most important and effective strategy for avoiding this infectious illness (LaBeaud et al., 2009). Eliminating standing water found in flower pots, water fountains, bird baths, buckets, tire swings, small pools, and similar sources removes mosquito breeding sites. A number of products containing natural chemicals and bacteria are available to spray or to use in ponds that cannot be drained. Additional precautionary measures include applying mosquito repellents containing DEET whenever going outdoors, wearing protective clothing (long sleeves, long pants), staying indoors during early morning and evening hours when mosquitoes are at their peak activity, and making sure that screen doors and windows are in good repair. In most cases, persons with mild symptoms will recover without medical treatment. However, prompt medical attention should be sought for prolonged illness or if any serious complications develop.

Finally, rely on your intuition. Don't hesitate to call the doctor if you are unsure about the symptoms your child may be experiencing. Most physicians would rather be notified of a child's condition than to be called only when there is a crisis.

Focus On Families — When to Call the Doctor

Frequent bouts of illness are not uncommon among young children. With time, their bodies mature, they begin to build up resistance (immunity) to many illnesses, and their immunizations will have been completed. In the meantime, families often face the difficult task of deciding at what point their child is sick enough to warrant a call to the doctor. Although each child's symptoms and needs are different, there are guidelines that may be helpful in making this decision. Call the physician if your child:

- Experiences serious injury, bleeding that cannot be stopped, or excessive or prolonged pain.
- Is less than one month old and develops a fever, or is between 1 and 3 months of age and has a rectal temperature over 100.4°F.
- Has difficult, rapid, or noisy breathing.
- Experiences any loss of consciousness, including a seizure.
- Complains of unusual pain in an arm or leg. X-rays may be necessary to rule out a fracture.
- Has repeated episodes of vomiting or diarrhea and is unable to keep down liquids. Symptoms of dehydration include urination fewer than three times per day, dry lips or tongue, headache, lack of tears, and excessive drowsiness. A sunken fontanel (soft spot) is an additional symptom in infants. Young children can become dehydrated quickly.
- Develops an unusual skin rash, especially one that spreads.
- Has blood in his/her vomit, urine, or stool.
- Suffers an eye injury or develops an eye discharge. Children who have sustained an eye injury should always be seen by a physician.
- Develops stomach pain that is prolonged or interferes with appetite or activity.
- Becomes excessively sleepy and difficult to arouse.

Classroom Corner — Teacher Activities

Gear up for health...

Concept: Physical activity is important for staying healthy. (Grades 3–5; National Health Education Standards 1.5.1 and 6.5.1)

Learning Objectives

- Children will learn the importance of moving to stay healthy.
- Children will improve their aerobic condition.

Supplies

- worksheet for recording activities
- kick balls

(continued)

Classroom Corner **Teacher Activities** *(continued)*

- pedometers
- charts or graph paper
- Mylar balloons
- masking tape

Learning Activities

- Read and discuss any of the following books:
  - *Anna Banana: 101 Jump-Rope Rhymes* by Joanna Cole
  - *Norma Jean, Jumping Bean* by Joanna Cole
  - *Song and Dance Man* by Karen Ackerman
  - *Snow Dance* by Lezlie Evans
- As a group, discuss the benefits of physical activity in terms of improving the body's immune system to fight off germs and protect against illness. Encourage the children to brainstorm activities that will increase their respiratory and heart rates (jumping rope, running, riding bikes, going for a walk, playing soccer, etc.).
- Introduce the terms *aerobic* (activities that increase heart and breathing rates) and *anaerobic* (activities that improve muscle strength) and explain the differences. Prepare a worksheet with two columns: one headed "aerobic activities," the other "anaerobic activities." Have the children list as many activities as they can in each appropriate column. As a group, ask the children to share one activity listed on their sheet and compile a master class list. Challenge the children to engage in at least one of these activities each day.
- Set up a game of kick ball and give each child a pedometer to wear during the activity. At the end of 15 minutes, have each child record the number of steps he or she has taken. As an alternative, set up two cones and have children run laps; each week, increase the distance or number of laps children must run. Older children can graph their data (number of steps) while younger children might simply keep a daily tally. Varying the distance between cones, the number of laps run, or the length of playing time is an effective way to help children grasp the relationship between activity and health benefits. Children can also set weekly goals for themselves and gradually increase the number of steps they want to accumulate on their pedometer.
- Play balloon volleyball (great indoor activity). Group children into small teams, place a tape line on the floor, and instruct children to keep the balloon in motion by batting it back and forth. Have the children compare and describe how they felt before (heart beating slowly, easy to breathe) and after (breathing hard, heart beating fast, sweaty) the activity.

Evaluation

- Children will describe how physical activity improves health.
- Children will improve aerobic capacity by setting goals and recording their progress.

Additional lesson plans for grades PreK–2 are available on this text's website.

Summary

- Illness is common among young children in schools and group settings.
- Teachers can utilize multiple strategies to control the spread of illnesses:
  - careful observation and early identification of sick children
  - implementation of exclusion policies
  - thorough hand washing
  - environmental sanitation
  - ongoing health education
- Teachers should be familiar with the signs/symptoms, method of transmission, and control measures associated with common communicable and acute childhood illnesses.

Terms to Know

symptoms *p. 136*
asymptomatic *p. 142*
infection *p. 148*
dehydration *p. 150*
listlessness *p. 150*
abdomen *p. 150*
hyperventilation *p. 154*
temperature *p. 154*
fever *p. 154*
tympanic *p. 154*
disorientation *p. 155*
Lyme disease *p. 157*
intestinal *p. 158*
urination *p. 159*
apnea *p. 159*
salmonellosis *p. 162*

Chapter Review

A. By Yourself:

1. Define each of the *Terms to Know.*
2. Match each of the following signs/symptoms in column I with the correct communicable illness in column II.

Column I	Column II
1. swelling and redness of white portion of the eye	a. chickenpox
2. frequent itching of the scalp	b. strep throat
3. flat, oval-shaped lesions on the scalp, skin; infected nails become discolored, brittle, and chalky and may disintegrate	c. head lice
4. high fever; red, sore throat	d. shigellosis
5. mild fever and rash that lasts approximately 3 days	e. conjunctivitis
6. irritability and itching of the rectal area	f. ringworm
7. red rash with blister-like heads; cold-like symptoms	g. German measles
8. sudden onset of fever; swelling of salivary glands	h. scabies
9. burrows or linear tunnels under the skin; intense itching	i. pinworms
10. vomiting, abdominal pain, diarrhea that may be bloody	j. mumps
	k. Lyme disease

B. As a Group:

1. Discuss what a teacher should do in each of the following situations:
   a. You have just finished serving lunch to the children, when Kara begins to vomit.
   b. The class is involved in a game of keep-away. Theo suddenly complains of feeling dizzy.
   c. During check-in, a parent mentions that his son has been experiencing stomachaches every morning before coming to school.
   d. Lucy wakes up from her afternoon nap crying because her ear hurts.
   e. You have just changed a toddler's diaper for the third time in the last hour because of diarrhea.
   f. Christi enters the classroom, sneezing, and blowing his nose.
   g. While you are helping Jasmine put on her coat to go outdoors, you notice that her skin feels very warm.
   h. Randy refuses to eat his lunch because it makes his teeth hurt.
   i. While you are cleaning up the blocks, Sean tells you that his throat is sore and it hurts to swallow.
   j. You have just taken Monique's temperature (orally) and it is 102°F.

2. The concepts of illness and pain are often viewed differently by various cultural groups. Select two or three predominant cultures and research their beliefs about illness and pain. How might these differences in cultural values and beliefs influence your response in each of the situations described in Question #1?

Case Study

The teacher noticed that Carrie seemed quite restless today and was having difficulty concentrating on any task that she started. She continuously squirmed, whether in her chair or sitting on the floor. On a number of occasions the teacher also observed Carrie tugging at her underwear and scratching her bottom. She recalled that Carrie's mother had mentioned something about getting her younger brother tested for pinworms and wondered if this might be what she was observing.

1. What action should the teacher take in this situation?
2. What control measures should be implemented? At school? At home?
3. When can Carrie return to school?
4. If Carrie does have pinworms, for what length of time must the teacher carefully observe the other children for similar problems?
5. What special personal health measures should be emphasized with the other children?

Application Activities

1. With a partner, practice taking each other's axillary, oral, and tympanic temperatures. Follow steps for correct cleaning of the thermometer between each use.
2. Divide the class into groups of five to six students. Discuss how each member feels about caring for children who are ill. Could they hold or cuddle a child with a high fever or diarrhea? What are their feelings about being exposed to children's contagious illnesses? How might they react

if an infant just vomited on their new sweater? If they feel uncomfortable around sick children, what steps could they take to better cope with the situation?

3. Select another student as a partner and observe that person carefully for 20 seconds. Now look away. Write down everything you can remember about this person, such as eye color, hair color, scars or moles, approximate weight, height, color of skin, shape of teeth, clothing, and so on. What can you do to improve your observational skills?
4. Conduct an Internet search to learn more about avian (bird) flu. What is it? What steps are being taken at the national level to control its spread? What is your community doing?

Helpful Web Resources

Center for Disease Control	http://www.cdc.gov
Health Canada	http://www.hc-sc.gc.ca
Keep Kids Healthy	http://www.keepkidshealthy.com
Morbidity & Mortality Weekly	http://www.cdc.gov/mmwr
National Initiative for Children's Healthcare Quality (special needs)	http://www.nichq.org/
National Institutes of Health	http://www.nih.gov
Office of Minority Health	http://www.omhrc.gov/

You are just a click away from additional health, safety, and nutrition resources! Go to www.CengageBrain.com to access this text's Education CourseMate website, where you'll find:

- glossary flashcards, activities, tutorial quizzes, videos, web links, and more

References

American Academy of Otolaryngology — Head and Neck Surgery. (2009). *Fact sheet: Day care and ear, nose, and throat problems.* Accessed on October 19, 2009, from http://www.entnet.org/HealthInformation/dayCareENT.cfm.

American Academy of Pediatrics (AAP). (2009a). A child care provider's guide to safe sleep. Accessed October 20, 2009, from http://www.healthychildcare.org/pdf/SIDSchildcaresafesleep.pdf.

Anderson, A., & Chaney, A. (2009). Tick-associated diseases: Symptoms, treatment and prevention, *American Journal of Health Education*, 40(3), 183–189.

Bourgeois, F., Valim, C., McAdam, A., & Mandl, K. (2009). Relative impact of influenza and respiratory syncytial virus in young children, *Pediatrics*, 124(6), e1072–e1080.

Bradley, R. H. (2003). Child care and common communicable illnesses in children aged 37 to 54 months, *Archives of Pediatric & Adolescent Medicine,* 157(2), 196–200.

Centers for Disease Control & Prevention (CDC). (2009a). Sudden infant death syndrome (SIDS) and sudden unexpected infant death (SUID). Accessed on October 18, 2009, from http://www.cdc.gov/SIDS/index.htm.

CDC. (2009b). Reported cases of Lyme disease by year, United States, 1994–2008. Accessed on October 19, 2009, from http://www.cdc.gov/ncidod/dvbid/lyme/ld_UpClimbLymeDis.htm.

CDC. (2009c). *2008 West Nile virus activity in the United States.* Accessed on October 20, 2009 http://www.cdc.gov/ncidod/dvbid/westnile/surv&controlCaseCount08_detailed.htm.

Child Health Alert. (2009) Swine flu: What to expect? *Child Health Alert*, 27, 1–2.

Cortese, M., & Parashar, U. (2009). Prevention of rotavirus gastroenteritis among infants and children: Recommendations of the Advisory Committee on Immunization Practices (ACIP). *MMWR Recommendations & Reports,* 58(RR-2), 1–25.

Devrim, I., Kara, A., Ceyhan, M., Tezer, H., Uludağ, A., Cengiz, A.,Yiğitkanl, I., & Seçmeer, G. (2007). Measurement accuracy of fever by tympanic and axillary thermometry, *Pediatric Emergency Care*, 23(1), 16–19.

Duncan, J., Paterson, D., Hoffman, J., Mokler, D., Borenstein, N., Belliveau, R., Krous, H., Haas, E., Stanley, C., Nattie, E., Trachtenberg, R., & Kinnery, H. (2010). Brainstem serotonergic deficiency in sudden infant death syndrome, *JAMA*, 303(5), 430–437.

First Candle/SIDS Alliance. (2009). Immunizations and SIDS. Accessed on October 20, 2009, from www.firstcandle.org/media/Immunizations_And_SIDS.pdf.

Fu, L., Colson, E., Corwin, M., & Moon, R. (2008). Infant sleep location: Associated maternal and infant characteristics with sudden infant death syndrome prevention recommendations, *Journal of Pediatrics*, 153(4), 503–508.

Hansmann, Y. (2009). Treatment and prevention of Lyme disease, *Current Problems in Dermatology*, 37: 111–129.

Hauck, R., Signore, C., Fein, S., & Raju, T. (2008). Infant sleeping arrangements and practices during the first year or life, *Pediatrics*, 122(Suppl. 2), S113–120.

Hetzner, N., Razza, R., Malone, L., & Brooks-Gunn, J. (2009). Associations among feeding behaviors during infancy and child illness at two years, *Maternal & Child Health Journal*, 13(6), 795–805.

Hockenberry, M., & Wilson, D. (2009). *Wong's essentials of pediatric nursing.* (8th ed.). New York: Mosby.

Hunt, C. E., Lesko, S. M., Vezina, R. M., McCoy, R., Corwin, M. J., Mandell, F., Willinger, M., Hoffman, H., & Mitchell, A. A. (2003). Infant sleep position and associated health outcomes, *Archives of Pediatric & Adolescent Medicine,* 157(5), 469–474.

Katz, T., Miller, J., & Hebert, A. (2008). Insect repellents: Historical perspectives and new developments, *Journal of the American Academy of Dermatology*, 58(5), 865–871.

Kinney, H., & Thach, B. (2009). The sudden infant death syndrome, *New England Journal of Medicine,* 359(2), 119–129.

LaBeaud, A., Glinka, A., Kippes, C., & King, C. (2009). School-based health promotion for mosquito-borne disease prevention in children, *The Journal of Pediatrics*, 155(4), 590–592.

MacDorman, M., & Mathews, T. (2009). The challenge of infant mortality: Have we reached a plateau? *Public Health Report*, 124(5), 670–681.

Malik-Kotru, G., Kirchner, L., & Kisby, L. (2009). An analysis of the first dental visits in a federally qualified health center in a socioeconomically deprived area, *Journal of Clinical Pediatric Dentistry*, 33(3), 265–268.

McFadden, J., & Frelick, K. (2009). Managing risk around influenza A (H1N1) (swine flu)—What employers should know, *Health Law in Canada*, 29(4), 76–78.

Mitchell, E. (2009). What is the mechanism of SIDS? *Developmental Psychobiology*, 51(3), 215–222.

Moon, R., Calabrese, T., & Aird, L. (2008). Reducing the risk of sudden infant death syndrome in child care and changing provider practices: Lessons learned from a demonstration project, *Pediatrics*, 122(4), 788–798.

National Institute of Child Health & Human Development (NICHD). (2009). SIDS: "Back to Sleep" campaign. Accessed on October 20, 2009, from http://www.nichd.nih.gov/sids.

National Maternal and Child Oral Health Resource Center (2009). Accessed on October 20, 2009, from http://www.mchoralhealth.org/default.html.

National Sudden & Unexpected Infant/Child Death & Pregnancy Loss (SIDS) Resource Center. (2009). Accessed on October 18, 2009, from http://www.sidscenter.org/Statistics.html.

Orenstein, S. (2006). Fruit juice consumption and acute diarrhea in infants, Current Gastroenterology Reports, 8(3), e211–e213.

Pappas, D., Hendley, J., Hayden, F., & Winther, B. (2008). Symptom profile of common colds in school-aged children, *Pediatric Infectious Disease Journal*, 27(1), 8–11.

Proops, D., & Acharya, A. (2009). Diagnosing hearing problems, *Paediatrics and Child Health*, 19(10), 447–452.

Public Health Agency of Canada. *Human West Nile virus clinical cases and infections in Canada: 2008.* Accessed on October 20, 2009, from http://www.phac-aspc.gc.ca/wnv-vwn/mon-hmnsurv-2007_e.html.

Richardson, H., Walker, A., & Horne, R. (2009a). Maternal smoking impairs arousal patterns in sleeping infants, *Sleep*, 32(4), 515–521.

Richardson, H., Walker, A., & Horne, R. (2009b). Minimizing the risks of sudden infant death syndrome: To swaddle or not to swaddle? *Journal of Pediatrics*, 155(4), 475–481.

Sathyanarayana, S., Karr, C., Lozano, P., Brown, E., Calafat, A., Liu, F., & Swan, S. (2008). Baby care products: Possible sources of infant phthalate exposure, *Pediatrics*, 121(2), e260–e268.

Schieve, L., Boulet, S., Boyle, C., Rasmussen, S., & Schendel, D. (2009). Health of Children 3 to 17 years of age with Down syndrome in the 1997–2005 National Health Interview Survey, *Pediatrics*, 123(2), e253–e260.

Sexton, S., & Natale, R. (2009). Risks and benefits of pacifiers, *American Family Physician,* 79(8), 681–685.

Sganga, A., Wallace, R., Kiehl, E., Irving, T., & Witter, L. (2000). A comparison of four methods of normal newborn temperature measurement. *The American Journal of Maternal/Child Nursing*, 25(2), 76–79.

Shapiro-Mendoza, C., Kimball, M., Tomashek, K., Anderson, R., & Blanding, S. (2009). U.S. infant mortality trends attributable to accidental suffocation and strangulation in bed from 1984–2004: Are rates increasing?, *Pediatrics*, 123(2), 533–539.

Singleton, R., Holman, R., Plant, R., Yorita, K., Holve, S., Paisano, E., & Cheek, J. (2009). Trends in otitis media and myringotomy with tube placement among American Indian/Alaska native children and the U.S. general population of children, *Pediatric Infectious Diseases*, 28(2), 102–107.

Sockett, P., & Artsob, H. (2009). The emergence of Lyme disease in Canada, *Canadian Medical Association Journal*, 180(12), 1221–1224.

Vargas, C., & Arevalo, O. (2009). How dental care can preserve and improve oral health, *Dental Clinics of North America*, 53(3), 399–420.

Vernon-Feagans, L., & Manlove, E. (2005). Otitis media, the quality of child care, and the social/communicative behavior of toddlers: A replication and extension, *Early Childhood Research Quarterly*, 20(3), 306–328.

Zimmer, S., & Burke, D. (2009). Historical perspective – Emergence of influenza A (H1N1) viruses, *New England Journal of Medicine*, 361(3), 279–285.

UNIT 2

Keeping Children Safe

CHAPTER

7

Creating High-Quality Environments

NAEYC Standards *Chapter Links*

- **#1 a, b, and c:** Promoting child development and learning
- **#4 a, b, and d:** Using developmentally effective approaches to connect with children and families
- **#6 b, c, d, and e:** Becoming a professional

Learning Objectives

After studying this chapter, you should be able to:

- Discuss how to identify high-quality programs.
- Explain how licensure and registration of early childhood programs differ.
- Identify the features of high-quality programs and discuss how teachers' educational preparation affects children's development.
- Describe at least ten ways to make children's indoor and outdoor environments safe.

Children's growth and development are continually being shaped and influenced by their **environment**. Growth is enhanced through nurturing and responsive care giving, a healthy diet, homes and schools that are clean and safe, access to appropriate dental and health care, and communities that are free of drugs, violence, excessive traffic, and air pollution. Opportunities for learning, experiencing new challenges, and positive social interaction promote children's intellectual and psychological development. For these reasons, all aspects of children's environments must be given careful consideration so they provide physical, **cognitive**, and psychological conditions that have positive effects on children's growth and development.

environment – *the sum total of physical, cultural, and behavioral features that surround and affect an individual.*
cognitive – *the aspect of learning that refers to the development of skills and abilities based on knowledge and thought processes.*

Locating High-Quality Programs

Children's environments should support and promote their growth and development.

© Cengage Learning

Families have undergone many changes and, as a result, they often must rely on out-of-home arrangements for child care. Some families simply want their children to benefit from enrichment experiences and opportunities to socialize with their peers. Others may enroll children with special developmental needs in early intervention programs where they can receive individualized learning experiences and special services, such as speech or physical therapy (Allen & Cowdery, 2009). Older children may require a safe, educational place to stay before and after regular school hours. Regardless of their reason, families often find it challenging to locate high-quality and affordable programs. As a result, new programs are continuously being opened to meet increased demand, but quality is not always a priority.

Research continues to demonstrate that high-quality programs make a difference in children's development and family relationships (Stuhlman & Pianta, 2009; Rivera, 2008). Children enrolled in high-quality care show long-term gains in language and cognitive skills, improved readiness for school, and fewer problem behaviors (Adi-Japha & Klein, 2009; Dearing, McCartney, & Taylor, 2009). Although most families would prefer to have their child in an excellent program, the urgency and, at times, desperation of simply finding an available opening may force them to overlook this important issue. Cost and location considerations may understandably overshadow a family's concern about quality.

It is also true that many families simply do not know how to determine the quality of a program or even what features to look for. Some parents feel uncomfortable questioning teachers. Others may not be able to find a convenient high-quality program in their area even when they are dissatisfied with poor conditions in a current arrangement.

Educating Families

Advocacy groups and professional organizations have launched initiatives to help educate families about the characteristics associated with excellence in early childhood programs. Families can also retrieve similar information from professional websites.

Researchers have identified three characteristics common to high-quality early childhood programs (Neuman & Cunningham, 2009):

- small group size
- low teacher–child ratio (fewer children per teacher)
- teachers who have advanced educational training in early childhood

Families should always take time to observe any new program they are considering for their child and determine how the program measures up to these criteria. Additional areas that should also be noted include:

- physical facilities (clean, safe, spacious, licensed)
- program philosophy; developmentally appropriate goals and objectives
- nutritious meals and snacks
- opportunities for family involvement

- respectful of diversity
- toys and educational activities (developmentally appropriate, variety, adequate in number, organized learning experiences)
- health services

Educating families about how to recognize high quality in programs has obvious benefits for children. And, as demand for quality increases, programs that fail to improve their services may be forced out of business.

Resource and Referral Services

Many communities have resource and referral agencies devoted to helping families locate center- and home-based early childhood programs, as well as before- and after-school care. Families can request a list of available openings based on their specific child care needs, such as location, cost, preferred hours, philosophy, and child's age. Many independent agencies have been networked into state and national computerized databases; the National Association of Child Care Resource and Referral Agencies (NACCRRA) is one of the largest.

Child care resource and referral agencies do not necessarily restrict their listings to high-quality programs. Some agencies will include any program with available openings, while others screen programs carefully to ensure high standards. Consequently, families must spend time investigating individual programs to find one that best suits their needs and personal preferences. Resource and referral agencies in many areas play an active role in educating families about how to select an early childhood program. They are also vocal advocates for improved program quality and are committed to providing inservice training for early childhood teachers.

Professional Accreditation

A national system of voluntary **accreditation** for early childhood programs was established in 1985 by the National Association for the Education of Young Children (NAEYC). Its primary objective is aimed at promoting excellence and improving the quality of early education through a process of self-study (NAEYC, 2009a). The accreditation process identifies and recognizes outstanding early-education programs and provides an added credential that recognizes their commitment to quality. Programs are accredited for 3 years, at which time they must reapply. NAEYC recently completed an extensive revision of its standards and accreditation process for evaluating programs (http://www.naeyc.org/academy).

A number of organizations, including Head Start, the National Association for Family Child Care (NAFCC), and the National AfterSchool Association, have developed similar endorsement plans to recognize outstanding programs; a partial listing of national accrediting organizations is available at http://nccic.acf.hhs.gov/poptopics/nationalaccred.html. Several states have also begun to develop their own quality standards and voluntary accreditation systems.

Reflective Thoughts

Families are often faced with difficult choices when they try to locate child care options. Although efforts to improve the quality of early education programs continue, it is well known that not all programs reflect excellence. What does the literature suggest about how families select child care? What features distinguish high quality in early childhood programs? How can communities work together to improve the overall quality of care provided in their area? What efforts are needed to improve accessibility to high quality care for all children?

---

accreditation – *the process of certifying an individual or program as having met certain specified requirements.*

Licensing

Licensing standards help to assure the health and safety of children's environments.

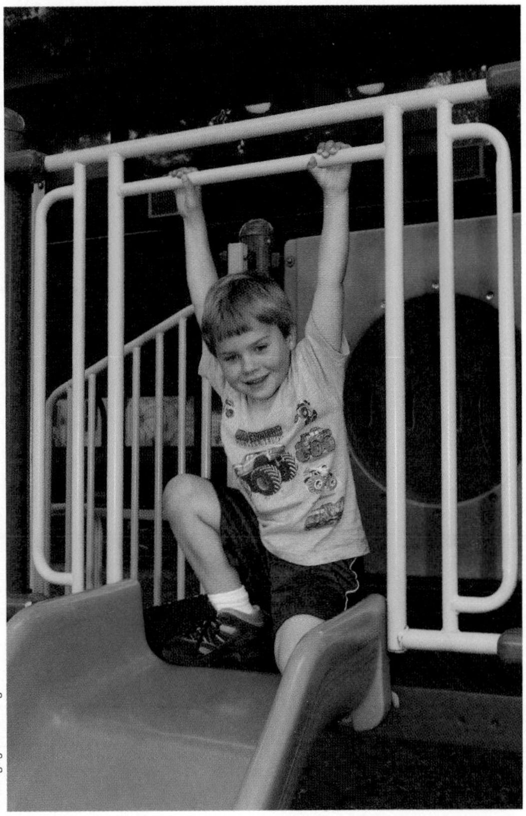

© Cengage Learning

Licensing standards are established by individual states. They reflect an attempt to ensure that early childhood environments are safe, appropriate, and healthful for young children. However, these regulations reflect only minimal health and safety requirements and also vary considerably from one state to another (Gupta et al., 2009). They in no way guarantee better conditions, programs, or child care. This is an issue of great concern, as programs are increasingly serving infants and children with special behavior, developmental, and medical needs.

Licensing requirements serve a twofold purpose. First, they are aimed at protecting children's physical and psychological well-being by regulating environmental and program safety. Second, licensing **regulations** afford minimal protection to the program and its personnel. By complying with licensing requirements, programs may be less likely to overlook situations that could result in negligence charges.

Early attempts to regulate child care programs dealt primarily with the sanitation and safety of physical settings. However, most current licensing regulations go beyond this narrow scope to also address teacher qualifications and the educational content of programs planned for children.

Each state has a designated agency that is authorized and responsible for conducting inspections and issuing or revoking licenses to operate. This agency also oversees the review and development of licensing standards and methods for enforcing **compliance**. Again, there are significant differences in licensing standards and levels of enforcement from one state to another. This fragmented approach also lacks a system for ensuring that individual states are actually carrying out their responsibilities.

In many states, home-based child care programs are governed by a separate set of regulations and often include an option of either becoming licensed or registered. Those choosing to be licensed are usually inspected by a licensing agent and are expected to meet certain standards. In contrast, the requirements for **registration** are often minimal. Teachers may simply be asked to place their name on a list, complete a self-administered checklist attesting to safe conditions, or attend a brief preservice informational program. An on-site home inspection is seldom conducted unless a complaint is registered. Child care programs based in churches and public schools and relative care are exempt from licensing regulation in many states.

Understandably, there is always controversy surrounding the issue of licensing for early childhood programs. Establishing licensing requirements that adequately protect young children's health and safety—yet are realistic for teachers and programs to achieve—can be challenging. In addition, some people believe that too much control or standards that are set too high will reduce the number of programs. The licensing process is also costly to administer and often difficult to

---

licensing – *the act of granting formal permission to conduct a business or profession.*
regulations – *standards or requirements that are set to ensure uniform and safe practices.*
compliance – *the act of obeying or cooperating with specific requests or requirements.*
registration – *the act of placing the name of a child care program on a list of active providers; usually does not require on-site inspection.*

enforce, so that lowering the standards may be a tempting option. On the other hand, many families and teachers favor stricter regulations to ensure higher-quality programs and improved respect for the early childhood profession.

Despite the ongoing controversy, licensing of early childhood programs is necessary. Ideally, licensing standards should adequately safeguard children, yet not be so overly restrictive that qualified individuals and programs are eliminated. The development of separate licensing requirements for in-home and center-based programs has been offered as one practical solution to this dilemma (Doherty et al., 2006).

Obtaining a License

A license permits an early childhood program to operate on a routine basis. As previously mentioned, the process for obtaining a license differs from state to state. However, the steps described here are generally representative of the procedure involved. In some cases, the process may require considerable time and effort, especially if major renovations must be made to the proposed facility. For others, approval may be obtained in a reasonably short time.

Persons interested in operating an early childhood or after-school program should first contact their state or local licensing agency. Questions regarding the applicant's qualifications and specific program requirements can usually be answered at this time.

In addition to complying with state licensing regulations, child care facilities must also be in accordance with local laws and ordinances. Zoning codes must be checked to determine whether or not the location permits a program to be operated in a given neighborhood. Often this requires meeting with local planning authorities and reviewing proposed floor plans.

Buildings that house early childhood programs must also pass a variety of inspections to be sure they meet fire, safety, and sanitation codes. These inspections are usually conducted by personnel from the local fire and public health departments. From these inspections, it is possible to determine what, if any, renovations may be necessary to comply with licensing regulations. In most cases, these are relatively simple; in other cases, the required changes may not be feasible or economical to make.

Application for a permanent license can be made once all these steps have been completed. Copies of the program's plans and policies may be requested by the licensing authorities for review. Final approval usually includes an on-site inspection of the facilities to ensure that all requirements and recommendations have been satisfied.

Federal Regulations

In addition to meeting state licensing requirements, early childhood programs that receive federal funds, such as Head Start, Early Head Start, and Even Start programs, must comply with an additional set of regulations. All schools and child care facilities, with the exception of religious-affiliated programs, built or remodeled after 1990 must also meet standards established by the Americans with Disabilities Act (ADA) (Child Care Law Center, 2007; U.S. Department of Justice, 1997).

Features of High-Quality Programs

Researchers are continually studying children in schools, home-, and center-based programs to determine what conditions and experiences are best for promoting learning and healthy development. Through the years, they have identified several key components that distinguish high-quality programs from those considered to be of mediocre or poor value (Buysse & Hollingsworth, 2009; Mashburn et al., 2008). The National Association for the Education of Young Children (NAEYC) (the largest organization representing early care and education in the United States) and other professional organizations have embraced these findings and incorporated them into their accreditation standards and recommended guidelines (APHA & AAP, 2002; Aronson, 2002).

Teacher Qualifications

Perhaps one of the weakest areas in many state licensing regulations pertains to staff qualifications. Emphasis is usually focused on the safety of physical settings, while staff requirements such as years of experience, educational preparation, and personal qualities are often lacking or poorly defined. Even when these issues are addressed in the licensing regulations, there is little consistency from one state to another.

Research has documented a positive correlation between a teacher's educational preparation and the ability to provide high-quality early childhood education (NAEYC, 2009b). Teachers who have a strong background in child development, value family involvement and communication, understand and respect diversity, and know how to create developmentally appropriate experiences are more effective in facilitating positive learning outcomes for children (Essa, 2010). As increasing numbers of children with behavior problems and developmental disabilities are enrolled in early childhood programs, teachers must also be prepared to meet their special needs (Buysse, Winton & Rous, 2009; Watson & McCathern, 2009). In addition, teachers must be able to work and communicate effectively with all children and families of diverse abilities and backgrounds.

Unfortunately, the licensing requirements in many states do not reflect what we currently know about the importance of employing teachers with formal training in early childhood education. Often, a person who is 18 years of age has a high school diploma, and passes a background check is qualified to be hired as an early childhood teacher. As a result, many of these individuals are not prepared to effectively handle the daily challenges involved in working with young children. This, combined with low salaries and long hours, often contributes to a high turnover rate, which also has a negative effect on children's development (Upshur, Wenz-Gross, & Reed, 2009). Initiatives to improve teacher preparation and salaries are being studied, funded, and incorporated into licensing regulations in an effort to improve the quality of care and education that young children receive (Miller & Bogatova, 2009). However, teachers must also take steps to continue their education and better prepare themselves to work with young children. Scholarship programs and professional opportunities are available to assist teachers in pursuing advanced education, including:

- on-the-job training/inservice training
- CDA (Child Development Associates credential)
- 1-year vocational training; child care or child development certificate
- 2-year associate degree (A.A.) (community college)
- 4-year bachelor degree (B.A.)
- advanced graduate training (M.A. and PH.D.)

Although many of these degree programs are offered on traditional campuses, an increasing number are now available online.

At a minimum, all directors and head teachers should have a 2-year associate degree with specialized training in early childhood (Vu, Hyun-Joo, & Howes, 2008). However, in many areas of the country, teachers and directors with advanced preparation are in short supply. Recently, individual states have begun to establish director credentialing programs in an effort to improve the quality of care and leadership in early childhood centers.

Some early childhood programs include paraprofessionals as part of their teaching team. These individuals may be aides who work for wages or are unpaid volunteers. Regardless of their position or previous experience, it is essential that paraprofessionals receive a thorough orientation to their job responsibilities and program procedures before working in the classrooms. This preparation enables paraprofessionals to be productive and effective when they begin working with the children and also improves employee retention.

Teachers who work in high-quality programs often have many special personal qualities and skills. They value communication and know how to develop meaningful relationships with children, families, and colleagues. They understand and respect diversity and make it a priority. They also possess qualities of warmth, patience, sensitivity to children's needs, respect for individual differences, and a positive attitude. They have the ability to plan, organize, make decisions, and resolve conflict. They also enjoy good personal health, which allows them to cope with the physical and emotional demands of long, action-packed days. Individuals with these qualities are not only better teachers, but they are also more likely to have a positive effect on young children's lives.

Staffing Ratios

Staff/child ratios are determined by individual states and typically reflect only the minimal number of adults considered necessary to protect children's well-being (Fiscella & Kitzman, 2009). However, the ability to provide positive learning experiences, individualized care, and conditions that safeguard children's health and safety requires more teachers than are generally mandated.

Ideally, high-quality early childhood programs provide one full-time teacher for every seven to eight children 3 to 6 years of age. Programs serving children with developmental disabilities should have one teacher for every four to five children, depending on the age group and severity of their needs. If children younger than 2 years are included, there should be at least one full-time teacher for every three to four children. A list of substitutes should also be available in the event of teacher illness or other absence.

Research suggests that small group size and low teacher/child ratios improve the quality of educational experiences that children receive. However, low ratios do not always guarantee that children will be safer (Gamble, Ewing, & Wilhelm, 2009). Much depends on the knowledge and supervisory skills of individual teachers.

Teachers who are part of high-quality programs practice life-long learning by attending professional meetings, inservice programs, workshops, and college classes. These experiences promote continued professional growth and competence by exposing teachers to new concepts, ideas, and approaches. They also provide teachers with opportunities to discuss common problems, share ideas, and discover unique solutions. This is especially important for teachers working in home-based programs, who may have limited interaction with other early childhood educators.

Group Size and Composition

When a license is issued to an early childhood program, specific conditions and restrictions under which it is allowed to operate are clearly defined. These conditions usually spell out:

- ages of children that can be enrolled
- group size per classroom
- maximum enrollment per program
- special populations of children to be served (e.g., children with behavior problems, children with developmental disabilities, infants, school-age, etc.)

For example, a program might be licensed to provide three half-day sessions for children 3 to 5 years of age, with a maximum enrollment of eighteen children per session. An in-home program might be licensed for at total of six children, ages birth to 4 years.

Group size is also recognized as an important indicator of high-quality programs (NAEYC, 2009a). For this reason, restrictions are typically placed on the number of children a program is permitted to enroll. This figure is determined by the amount of available space, children's ages, and any special needs children may have, as well as the number of teachers on site. However, it should be remembered that state regulations allow group sizes that are often much larger than is ideal for quality care.

A program's educational philosophy and range of services provided should be described in its admission policies. The age range, special needs, and total number of children that a program is licensed to serve must also be clearly stated to avoid parent misunderstandings.

Program Curriculum

The benefits children derive from participating in high-quality early childhood programs have been consistently documented (Dearing, McCartney & Taylor, 2009; Burchinal & Cryer, 2003). Because many children spend the majority of their waking hours in out-of-home early childhood programs, it is essential that **developmentally appropriate practices (DAP)**—learning environments and enriching opportunities—be provided. High-quality early education programs plan learning experiences that address children's needs across all developmental areas, including:

- physical
- cognitive
- emotional
- social
- language
- self-care
- motor

Curriculum delivery and content should be designed to address children's interests and to help them acquire new skills. Learning experiences should be planned and organized to take advantage of times when children are most likely to learn. Alternating activities that involve active and quiet play reduces the risk of children becoming overly fatigued and/or of losing interest. For example, a vigorous walk outdoors might be followed by a teacher-directed flannel board story or puppet

Small group size provides children with more individualized attention and is a feature of quality programs.

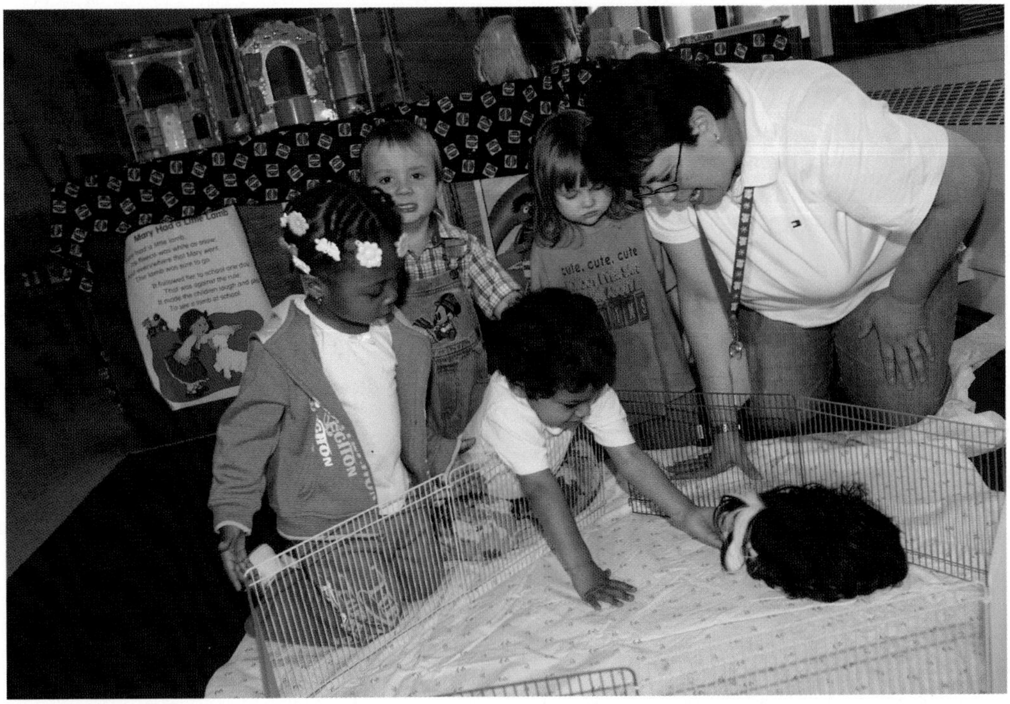

developmentally appropriate practices (DAP) – *learning experiences and environments that take into account children's individual abilities, interests, and diverse needs. DAP also reflects differences among families and values them as essential partners in children's education.*

show. It is also important to post daily activity schedules and lesson plans where families can see what children will be doing throughout the day.

Health Services

Safeguarding children's health and well-being is a fundamental responsibility of teachers and school administrators (Fiscella & Kitzman, 2009; APHA & AAP, 2002). Only when children are healthy can they fully benefit from everyday experiences and learning opportunities. High-quality programs take this role seriously and address children's health needs by:

- having written policies and procedures
- maintaining comprehensive health and safety records
- training personnel to administer first aid and emergency care
- developing emergency response plans
- planning for health, safety, and nutrition education

State child care licensing regulations generally determine the types of policies and records that programs are required to maintain. Similar guidelines are issued by state departments of education for public schools. Although states' requirements differ, quality programs may find it prudent to take a more comprehensive approach to recordkeeping for improved understanding and legal protection. Basic records that programs should maintain include:

- children's health assessments
- attendance
- emergency contact information
- developmental profiles
- adult health assessments
- fire and storm drills
- injuries
- daily health checks

Licensing authorities will review information in these records carefully during renewal visits.

Teachers in high-quality early childhood programs are trained to handle emergencies and provide first aid and emergency care to ill or injured children. They also have completed training in cardiopulmonary resuscitation (CPR). Programs choosing to meet only minimal standards should have at least one staff member who is trained in these techniques and can respond immediately to emergencies.

Notarized permission forms, similar to the one shown in Figure 7–1, listing the name, address, and telephone number of the child's physician should be completed by families when the child is first enrolled. This measure grants teachers authority to administer emergency care or secure emergency medical treatment. Emergency numbers for fire, police, ambulance, and poison control should be posted next to the telephone for quick reference.

Programs that provide care for mildly ill children should develop policies that address their special health needs. A quiet area should be provided in either a separate corner of the classroom or a room designated specifically for this purpose so that sick children can rest and also not expose others to their illnesses. Medical supplies, equipment, and hand washing facilities should be located nearby so they are easy to access.

Early childhood programs must develop emergency plans and procedures so they are prepared and able to respond to unexpected events in a prompt and organized manner (Table 7–1). These

---

notarized – *official acknowledgment of the authenticity of a signature or document by a notary public.*

Figure 7–1 Sample emergency contact information form.

EMERGENCY CONTACT INFORMATION

Child's Name ______________________ Date of Birth ______________
Address ______________________ Home Phone ______________
Mother's Name ______________________ Business Phone ______________
Father's Name ______________________ Business Phone ______________

Name of other person to be contacted in case of an emergency:

1. ______________________ Address ______________________
   Relationship (sitter, relative, friend, etc.) ______________ Phone ______________
2. ______________________ Address ______________________
   Relationship (sitter, relative, friend, etc.) ______________ Phone ______________

Authorization is hereby given for the Child Development Center Staff to release the above named child to the following persons, provided proper identification is first established (list all names of authorized persons, including immediate family):

1. ______________________ Relation: ______________
2. ______________________ Relation: ______________
3. ______________________ Relation: ______________

Physician to be called in an emergency:

1. ______________________ Phone ____________ or ____________
2. ______________________ Phone ____________ or ____________

Dentist to be called in an emergency:

1. ______________________ Phone ____________ or ____________

I, the undersigned, authorize the staff of the Child Development Center to take what emergency medical measures are deemed necessary for the care and protection of my child enrolled in the Child Development Center program.

______________________ ______________________
(Signature of Parent or Guardian/date) Signature witnessed by:
(Notary)

____
(Signature of Parent or Guardian/date) The above statement sworn before me on:

____

____

Download this form online at the text's Education CourseMate website.

Table 7–1 Principles of Emergency Preparedness

- Remain calm—do not panic.
- Be informed. Tune in a local station on your battery-powered radio.
- Get to a safe place. Develop and practice an appropriate disaster plan.
- Keep a first aid kit, bottled water, and flashlight handy.
- Take along children's health forms, emergency contact information, attendance records, and a cell phone.
- Learn basic emergency and first aid procedures.

plans should outline steps for protecting children's safety in the event of fire, severe storms such as tornadoes, major disasters such as earthquakes, floods, or hurricanes, and unauthorized intruders. Representatives from local fire and law enforcement departments, the Red Cross, and emergency preparedness groups are available to assist programs in developing their emergency plans. These plans should also be shared with families so they know what to expect in the event of an emergency and can also use them to model similar procedures at home.

Guidelines for Safe Environments

Nowhere is health and safety more important than in group programs serving young children. When families enroll children in a program, they expect that the teachers will safeguard their child's well-being. They assume the facilities, toys, and equipment will be safe for children's use, that teachers will carefully supervise their children's activities, that the environment is clean, and the food is healthy. These expectations require teachers to be well informed and knowledgeable about how to create and maintain environments that protect and promote children's health and safety.

As previously described, no uniform set of child care licensing standards exists in this country. However, several organizations have developed recommendations for out-of-home early childhood programs based on years of research data. The National Association for the Education of Young Children (NAEYC) has consistently defined and supported high standards for early-childhood programs. The American Academy of Pediatrics and the American Public Health Association have prepared a document entitled *Caring for Our Children: National Health and Safety Performance Standards Guidelines for Out-of-Home Child Care Programs,* which identifies approximately 180 regulation standards and safety practices. The remainder of this chapter addresses features of children's indoor and outdoor environments that require special attention. An indoor and outdoor safety checklist is provided in Table 7–4.

Indoor Safety

A great deal of thought and preparation is needed to create rooms that are safe for young children. Everything from the traffic flow, placement of furniture, and choice of floor coverings to the design of changing tables and proper storage requires careful study. Knowledge of children's abilities at each stage of development plays a key role in anticipating and eliminating potential safety hazards. (Refer to Table 8-2.) A safe environment encourages children to explore and learn through play, and is also less stressful for adults to work in (de Schipper et al., 2009).

Building and Site Location In a time of shrinking budgets and increasing demand for child care, the selection of an appropriate building often requires a creative approach. Although it would be ideal to plan and design a facility specifically for this purpose, few programs have sufficient funds for new construction. More often, existing buildings, such as unused classrooms in public schools, older houses, unoccupied stores, church basements, or places of business such as factories

Issues To Consider **Security in Early Childhood Programs**

Media reports of school shootings, child mistreatment, unauthorized visitors, and workplace violence have heightened concerns about security. Although many businesses have installed additional security devices in buildings and enhanced their security procedures, early childhood programs have been somewhat slower to respond (Addington, 2009; Lindle, 2008). Employee background checks, photo identification cards for teachers, and signed release forms authorizing child pickups are a few of the more common safety measures that programs utilize. Some centers have begun to install technology devices, such as touch keypads, Web cameras that allow families to view children on their computer screens at work, and electronic surveillance cameras to improve security in their buildings (Shelton, Owens, & Holim, 2009; Heinen et al., 2007). However, the cost of these systems is simply more than many programs can afford.

- What resources are available to schools and community-based early childhood programs for addressing basic security issues and improvement measures?
- What workplace policies and procedures are necessary to protect the safety of children and teachers?
- Are there any disadvantages to increasing security? What might they be?
- What does the need for increased security in schools and early childhood programs say about contemporary society?
- What newer technologies can be used to improve building security?

or hospitals are modified or remodeled to make them suitable for children. However, this type of work can be expensive and may not always be practical. In some instances, families and volunteers may be recruited to help complete a portion of the work and, thus, reduce the total cost.

With the exception of church-affiliated programs, home- and center-based programs are considered public facilities under the 1990 Americans with Disabilities Act (ADA) even if they are privately owned (Child Care Law Center, 2007). Consequently, they too must comply with guidelines set forth in this historical piece of legislation, which requires the removal of physical barriers that would otherwise deny access to individuals with disabilities. Early childhood programs cannot refuse to admit children on the basis of their disabilities. Program directors are expected to make reasonable adjustments in policies, practices, and facilities in order to accommodate all children. Admission can be denied in special circumstances only if the required modifications are unreasonably difficult or costly to complete, or if there is no alternative solution for meeting a child's special needs (U.S. Department of Justice, 1997). Consequently, this law has important implications throughout the site selection, building, and/or remodeling stages as more children with disabilities are enrolling in early childhood programs.

Location is always important to consider when selecting an appropriate site. Buildings chosen to house early childhood programs must meet local zoning requirements. These ordinances may make it difficult to locate programs in residential neighborhoods where they are often needed the most. Buildings should be located away from heavy traffic, excessive noise, air pollution, animals, exposure to chemicals, bodies of water, large equipment, and other similar hazards to protect children's health and safety. However, some of these conditions may be unavoidable for programs situated in inner city and rural areas. It then becomes even more essential that extra time and effort be devoted to safety awareness, policy development, and educational programs for children, teachers, and families.

Local fire codes also affect building selection. Older buildings and those not originally designed for infants and young children may require extensive changes before they pass inspection. Rooms that children occupy must have a minimum of two exits, one leading directly outdoors. All doors

Open spaces encourage infants' movement and play.

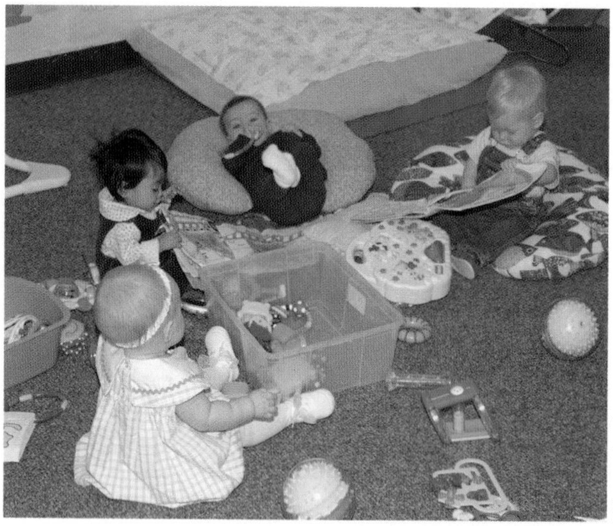

© Cengage Learning

should be hinged so they swing out of the room; this will prevent doors from slowing the evacuation process in the event of an emergency. Programs located on upper levels should have an enclosed stairwell for safe escape in the event of a fire.

How much space is needed depends to some extent on the type of program and services that will be offered. Per child, 35 square feet of usable floor space is considered an absolute minimum for adequate child care. However, teachers often find this amount of space crowded and difficult to work in. Ideally, high-quality programs should have 45 to 50 square feet of space per child for improved functionality and classroom safety. Additional space may be needed to accommodate large indoor play structures, special equipment for children with physical disabilities, or cribs for infants. However, it should also be kept in mind that large spaces may be difficult to supervise. Ground floor levels are always preferable for infants and preschool-aged children, although basement areas can be used for several hours at a time provided there are at least two exits.

Space The arrangement of space, or basic floor plan, should be examined carefully to determine the ease of conducting specific activities. For example, the traffic flow should allow ample room for children to arrive and depart without disturbing others who are playing. It should also accommodate separate areas for active/noisy play and quiet activities. Small rooms that lack storage space, adequate lighting, accessible bathrooms, or suitable outdoor play areas are inconvenient and frustrating for the staff and children.

Play spaces for infants and toddlers should be separated from those of older children to avoid injuries, confrontations, and the spread of illness. Large, open space that is free of obstacles encourages young children to move about and explore without hesitation.

Building Security Added precautions should be taken to protect children from unauthorized individuals while ensuring that families and legitimate visitors have safe access (Table 7–2). Buildings and outdoor play spaces should be evaluated carefully to determine if they are secure. Safety measures, such as locking outside doors and gates, installing key pads, or issuing card keys (used in hotels), can be implemented to control unauthorized visitors. Teachers and staff members should always be alert to persons entering the building and acknowledge their presence by making a point to greet them. Surveillance cameras can also be installed to monitor entrances and exits. Programs should develop and review plans for handling unauthorized visitors and summoning assistance in the event of an emergency. They may also want to establish a safe area of the building where children can be moved for added protection.

Reflective Thoughts

As adults, we often take great efforts to create environments and rules that will protect children from harm. Yet, it can be perplexing to understand why children continue to get themselves into situations that are unsafe. Why do you think this occurs? Are adults' and children's expectations and perceptions the same? (Try getting down on your hands and knees to understand how children view their environment.) How do cultural differences affect one's definition of a safe environment?

Table 7–2 Inventory Checklist: Planning for Program Security

Program administrators should work closely with local law enforcement, fire, and safety officials to assess a program's risk and to develop security plans that will protect children and staff members. Critical documents should be prepared and stored in a designated folder or box. All program staff should be familiar with its location and contents for quick retrieval in the event of an emergency, such as fire, earthquake, hurricane, or unauthorized intruders. Items that should be addressed include:

- Obtaining a copy of the building floor plan or blueprint
- Preparing a list of employees by name and room, and attaching their photograph
- Preparing a roster of the children by room and attaching their photograph; note any children who have special needs
- Knowing where all shut-off valves are located and how to turn them off
- Preparing an evacuation plan with alternate exit routes
- Posting evacuation plans in each classroom and reviewing them periodically with teachers
- Conducting monthly evacuation drills with children
- Maintaining hallways and exits that are clear of obstructions
- Making copies of parent authorization forms and emergency contact information
- Compiling a list of emergency personnel and telephone numbers
- Assigning specific emergency responsibilities to individual personnel and outlining each role on a master plan
- Informing families about the program's security plans and including the information in parent handbooks
- Keeping an emergency food supply on hand

Fire Safety Local fire officials can assist schools and in-home programs in the development and review of emergency procedures. They can be invited to tour the building layout and offer expert advice about planning efficient evacuation routes and notification procedures. Copies of the floor plans should be given to local fire authorities so they can familiarize themselves with the building layout and design. This will enable them to respond more efficiently in the event of a real emergency.

Smoke and carbon monoxide detectors should be present in rooms occupied by children, especially where infants and young children will be sleeping. Detectors should be tested each month to make sure they are functioning properly and batteries replaced annually (unless the system is wired). Additional fire safety precautions that can be taken include installing flame-retardant floor coverings and draperies and having at least one multipurpose fire extinguisher available. Staff should be familiar with the location of building exits and emergency evacuation procedures. Teachers should conduct monthly fire drills with the children so they will become familiar with the routine and not be frightened in the event of a real emergency (Table 7–3). Alternate evacuation routes should be planned and practiced so that teachers will know how to get out of a building if an area is blocked by fire. Plans for evacuating children with special needs should also be given careful attention.

Extension cords should not be used in classrooms. All electrical outlets should be covered with safety caps which can be purchased in most grocery or hardware stores. However, remember that caps are only a temporary solution. They are frequently removed by teachers and cleaning personnel, not always replaced, and also pose a choking hazard for young children if they are left laying around. An electrician can replace conventional outlets with childproof receptacles that do not require safety covers.

Bathroom Facilities Adequate bathroom facilities are also essential for convenience and health concerns. They should be accessible to both indoor and outdoor play areas. Installation of child-sized fixtures, including sinks, toilets, soap dispensers, and towel racks, allow children to care for their own needs. If only adult-sized fixtures are available, foot stools, large wooden blocks, or platforms securely anchored to the floor will facilitate children's independence. One toilet and sink should be available for every ten to twelve children. Programs serving children with disabilities should be designed to meet their special needs and comply with ADA standards (Child Care Law

Table 7–3 Teacher Checklist: How to Conduct a Fire Drill

Develop an Evacuation Plan
• Plan at least one alternate escape route from every room. • Post a written copy of the plan by the door of each room. • Review plans with new personnel.
Assign Specific Responsibilities
• Designate one person to call the fire department, preferably from a telephone outside of the building. Be sure to give the fire department complete information: name, address, approximate location of the fire inside the building, whether or not anyone is inside. Do not hang up until the fire department hangs up first. • Designate several adults to assemble children and lead them out of the building; assign extra adults, such as cooking or clerical staff, to assist with evacuation of younger children. • Designate one adult to bring a flashlight and the notarized emergency cards or class list. • Designate one person to turn off the lights and close the doors to the rooms.
Establish a Meeting Place
• Once outside, meet at a designated location so that everyone can be accounted for. • DO NOT GO BACK INTOTHE BUILDING!
Practice Fire Evacuation Drills
• Conduct drills at least once a month; plan some of these to be unannounced. • Practice alternate routes of escape. • Practice fire evacuation safety; for example, feel closed doors before opening them, select an alternate route if hallway or stairwells are filled with smoke, stay close to the floor (crawl) to avoid heat and poisonous gases, learn the stop-drop-roll technique. • Use a stopwatch to time each drill and record the results; strive for improvement.

Child-sized fixtures encourage independence.

Center, 2007). A separate bathroom area should also be available for adults and staff members.

Hand-washing facilities located near toilets and sleeping areas encourage children and teachers to wash their hands when needed. Hot water temperatures should be maintained between 105°F (40.5°C) and 120°F (48.8°C) to protect children from accidental burns (Smith, 2009). Liquid or foam soap dispensers placed near sinks encourage hand washing, are easy for children to use, and are less likely (than bar soap) to end up on the floor. The use of individual paper towels and cups improves sanitation and limits the spread of infectious illnesses. Smooth surfaces on walls and floors facilitate cleaning. Light-colored paint on walls makes dirty areas easy to notice and more likely to be cleaned.

Fixtures such as mirrors, light switches, and towel dispensers placed within children's reach, adequate lighting, and bright paint create a functional and pleasant atmosphere in which young children can manage self-care skills.

Surface and Furnishings Furniture and equipment should be selected to be comfortable and safe. Children are less likely to be injured if chairs and tables are appropriately proportioned and safely constructed. Furniture should meet federal safety standards and be sturdy enough to withstand frequent use. (See Chapter 8.) Items with sharp corners or edges should be avoided; many manufacturers now construct children's furniture with rounded corners. Bookcases, lockers, pianos, and other heavy objects should be anchored securely to the wall or floor to prevent children from tipping them over. Tall bookshelves should be replaced or cut in half to scale them down to child-size.

Materials such as tile, plastics, and vinyl are ideal for wall and floor coverings because they are easy to clean. However, floors covered with any of these materials can become quite slippery when wet. Injuries can be avoided by taking extra precautions such as positioning non-skid rugs or newspapers where liquids are likely to be spilled and wiping up any spills immediately. Providing a combination of carpeted and tiled areas addresses children's needs for soft, comfortable spaces and areas where they can engage in messy activities.

Each child should have an individual storage space, cubby, or locker where personal belongings can be kept. A child's private space is particularly important in group settings where most other things are shared. Individual cubbies also help to minimize the loss of prized possessions and aid in controlling infectious illnesses that can be transmitted through direct and indirect contact (such as head lice and pinkeye).

Additional safety features that improve the quality of children's classroom environments include having locked cabinets available for storing medicines and other potentially poisonous substances, such as cleaning products and paint. A telephone should also be located conveniently in the building and a list of emergency phone numbers, including the fire department, police, hospital, ambulance, and poison control center, posted directly nearby. A checklist for evaluating the safety of indoor and outdoor areas is illustrated in Table 7–4.

Children should have their own space for storing personal belongings.

Lighting and Ventilation Low windows and glass doors should be constructed of safety glass to prevent serious injuries if they are broken. Colorful pictures or decals placed at children's eye level also help to discourage them from accidentally walking into the glass. Doors and windows should be covered with screens to keep out unwanted insects; screens that can be locked also prevent children from falling out. Drapery and blind cords should hang freely (not be knotted or looped together) to prevent strangulation and also be fastened up high and out of children's reach.

Adequate lighting is essential in classrooms and hallways. Natural light from windows and glass doors creates rooms that are bright, attractive, and inviting to teachers and children.

Table 7–4 Teachers' Safety Checklist: Indoor and Outdoor Spaces

Indoor Areas	Date Checked	Pass/ Fail	Comments
1. A minimum of 35 square feet of usable space is available per child.			
2. Room temperature is between 68°–85°F (20°–29.4°C).			
3. Rooms have good ventilation:			
a. windows and doors have screens.			
b. mechanical ventilation systems are in working order.			
4. There are two exits in all rooms occupied by children.			
5. Carpets and draperies are fire-retardant.			
6. Rooms are well lighted.			
7. Glass doors and low windows are constructed of safety glass.			
8. Walls and floors of classrooms, bathrooms, and kitchen appear clean; floors are swept daily, bathroom fixtures are scrubbed at least every other day.			
9. Tables and chairs are child-sized and sturdy.			
10. Electrical outlets are covered with safety caps.			
11. Smoke detectors are located in appropriate places and in working order.			
12. Furniture, activities, and equipment are set up so that doorways and pathways are kept clear.			
13. Play equipment and materials are stored in designated areas; they are inspected frequently and are safe for children's use.			
14. Large pieces of equipment, e.g., lockers, piano, and bookshelves, are firmly anchored to the floor or wall.			
15. Cleaners, chemicals, and other poisonous substances are locked up.			
16. If stairways are used:			
a. Handrail is placed at children's height.			
b. Stairs are free of toys and clutter.			
c. Stairs are well-lighted.			
d. Stairs are covered with a nonslip surface.			
17. Bathroom areas:			
a. Toilets and washbasins are in working order.			
b. One toilet and washbasin are available for every 10–12 children; potty chairs are provided for children in toilet training.			
c. Water temperature is no higher than 120°F (48.8°C).			
d. Powdered or liquid soap is used for hand-washing.			
e. Individual or paper towels are used for each child.			
f. Diapering tables or mats are cleaned after each use.			
18. At least one fire extinguisher is available and located in a convenient place; extinguisher is checked annually by fire-testing specialists.			
19. Premises are free from rodents and/or undesirable insects.			
20. Food preparation areas are maintained according to strict sanitary standards.			

Table 7–4 Teachers' Safety Checklist: Indoor and Outdoor Spaces *(continued)*

Indoor Areas *(continued)*	**Date Checked**	**Pass/ Fail**	**Comments**
21. At least one individual on the premises is trained in emergency first aid and CPR; first aid supplies are readily available.			
22. All medications are stored in a locked cabinet or box.			
23. Fire and storm/disaster drills are conducted on a monthly basis.			
24. Security measures (plans, vigilant staff, key pads, locked doors, video cameras) are in place to protect children from unauthorized visitors.			
Outdoor Areas			
1. Play areas are located away from heavy traffic, loud noises, and sources of chemical contamination.			
2. Play areas are located adjacent to the premises or within safe walking distance.			
3. Play areas are well drained; if rubber tires are used for play equipment, holes have been drilled to prevent standing water.			
4. Bathroom facilities and a drinking fountain are easily accessible.			
5. A variety of play surfaces (e.g. grass, concrete, and sand) is available; shade is provided.			
6. Play equipment is in good condition (e.g. no broken or rusty parts, missing pieces, splinters, sharp edges, frayed rope, open "S" hooks, or protruding bolts)			
7. Selection of play equipment is appropriate for children's ages.			
8. Soft ground covers, approximately 12 inches in depth, are present under large climbing equipment; area is free of sharp debris (glass, sticks).			
9. Large pieces of equipment are stable and anchored securely in the ground; finishes are non-toxic and intact.			
10. Equipment is placed sufficiently far apart to allow a smooth flow of traffic and adequate supervision; an appropriate safety zone is provided around equipment.			
11. Play areas are enclosed by a fence at least four feet high, with a gate and workable lock for children's security and safety.			
12. There are no poisonous plants, shrubs, or trees in the area.			
13. Chemicals, insecticides, paints, and gasoline products are stored in a locked cabinet.			
14. Grounds are maintained on a regular basis and are free of debris; grass is mowed; broken equipment is removed.			
15. Wading or swimming pools are always supervised; water is drained when not in use.			

Sunlight is also a free, sustainable resource that is known to have a positive psychological effect on children's and adults' moods (Denissen et al., 2008).

Proper arrangement of artificial lighting is equally as important as the amount of brightness it produces. Areas of a room that are used for close activities, such as reading centers or art tables, require more lighting. Compact fluorescent lights are ideal for this purpose because they give off more light, create less glare, and cost less to operate.

Heating and cooling systems should be efficient and maintained annually. Room temperatures set between 68°F (20°C) and 85°F (29.4°C) year-round are ideal for children (Johnson et al., 2009). Hot radiators, exposed pipes, furnaces, fireplaces, portable heaters, or fans should not be accessible to children; if they cannot be removed, protective wire screening must be placed around them to prevent injuries.

Indoor Air Quality Every day, children are exposed to a variety of indoor air pollutants, including formaldehyde (in carpet and building materials), carbon monoxide, radon, asbestos, cigarette smoke, paint fumes, lead, numerous household chemicals, and pesticides. Studies continue to demonstrate a close relationship between these pollutants and an increased rate of respiratory illnesses, allergies, and asthma among children (Salo, Sever, & Zeldin, 2009). Because children's bodies are still growing and maturing, they are especially susceptible to the toxic chemicals found in these substances (Table 7–5).

Although it is impossible to avoid exposure to all toxic chemicals in an environment, increased awareness and understanding of control measures can be effective in reducing the health risks for children (Fuentes-Leonarte, Tenias, & Ballester, 2009; Muscato & Kennon, 2009). Labels on toys and art materials should always indicate that they are nontoxic. Indoor air quality can be significantly improved by simply increasing ventilation (opening doors and windows daily, turning on air conditioning), maintaining heating and ventilation systems, and avoiding the use of aerosol sprays around children. Many new alternative building materials and cleaning products, often labeled as "green products" or "building green," are being manufactured without toxic chemicals. Information about green school initiatives, alternative cleaning products, and safer cleaning practices

Table 7–5 Some Common Air Pollutants and Their Health Effects

Sources
• organic particles (e.g., dust mites) • molds • pollen • carbon monoxide • formaldehyde • insulation (e.g., asbestos, fiberglass) • ozone
Common Health Effects
• chronic cough • headache • dizziness • fatigue • eye irritation • sinus congestion • skin irritation • shortness of breath • nausea

Children's toys should always be made of nontoxic materials.

can be accessed on the Environmental Protection Agency's (EPA) website (www.epa.gov/sc3), the Children's Environmental Health Network website (http://www.cehn.org), and from several other organizations dedicated to maintaining healthy environments.

Outdoor Safety

The outdoors presents an exciting environment for children's imaginative play and learning (Bergen & Fromberg, 2009; Miller, Almon, & Miller, 2009; Staempfli, 2009). It also offers important health benefits by encouraging children to be active. Studies continue to link time spent in active outdoor play with reductions in childhood obesity, diabetes, and behavior problems (Barros, Silver, & Stein, 2009; Fadia et al., 2008). However, children's outdoor play areas are also a major source of unintentional injury and, therefore, require a heightened awareness of design, maintenance, and supervisory strategies (Vollman et al., 2009; Olsen, Hudson, & Thompson, 2008). Schools that use public parks for outdoor recreation should be particularly alert to safety hazards, such as animal waste, needles, glass, and poorly maintained play equipment (CPSC, 2008).

Space Safety must be a major consideration in the design of outdoor play areas. No less than 75–100 square feet of space per child (using the area at the same time) should be available to encourage active play and decrease the potential for unintentional injury. The National Health and Safety Performance Standards recommend that play areas for infants include a minimum of 33 square feet per child; 50 square feet per child is suggested for toddlers (APHA & AAP, 2002). Ideally, play areas should be located adjacent to the building so that bathrooms are readily accessible and children are not required to walk long distances. Traveling even a short distance to playgrounds with young children requires considerable time and effort, and often discourages spontaneous outdoor play.

A fence at least 4 feet in height should surround the play area and include two exits with latched gates to prevent children from wandering away. Railings or slats should be spaced less than 3½ inches or more than 9 inches apart to prevent children's heads or bodies from becoming entrapped. Sharp wire and picket-type fences are inappropriate and should not be used around young children.

An important design element in children's play areas involves how the space will be used (Dowda et al., 2009; Vollman et al., 2009). Play areas should be arranged so that children are clearly visible from all directions. Large open areas encourage activities such as running and tossing balls. Hard, flat surfaces allow children to use riding toys and to play outdoors during inclement weather, especially if these areas are covered. Flower beds provide children with space for gardening, while sand promotes imaginary play. Grassy areas and trees create a natural touch and offer protection from the sun. If trees are not available, large colorful canvas awnings can be purchased from play equipment companies or home improvement stores to provide shade. Separate areas designed for quiet and active play also help to reduce potential injuries. Always check with a local nursery or county extension office to be sure that flowers, trees, and other plantings are not poisonous to children. (See Figure 7–2 and Table 7–6 for a partial list.) Photographs and a comprehensive listing of poisonous plants are available at http://www.ansci.cornell.edu/plants. (Click on "Find - by common name.")

Figure 7–2 Examples of poisonous plants.

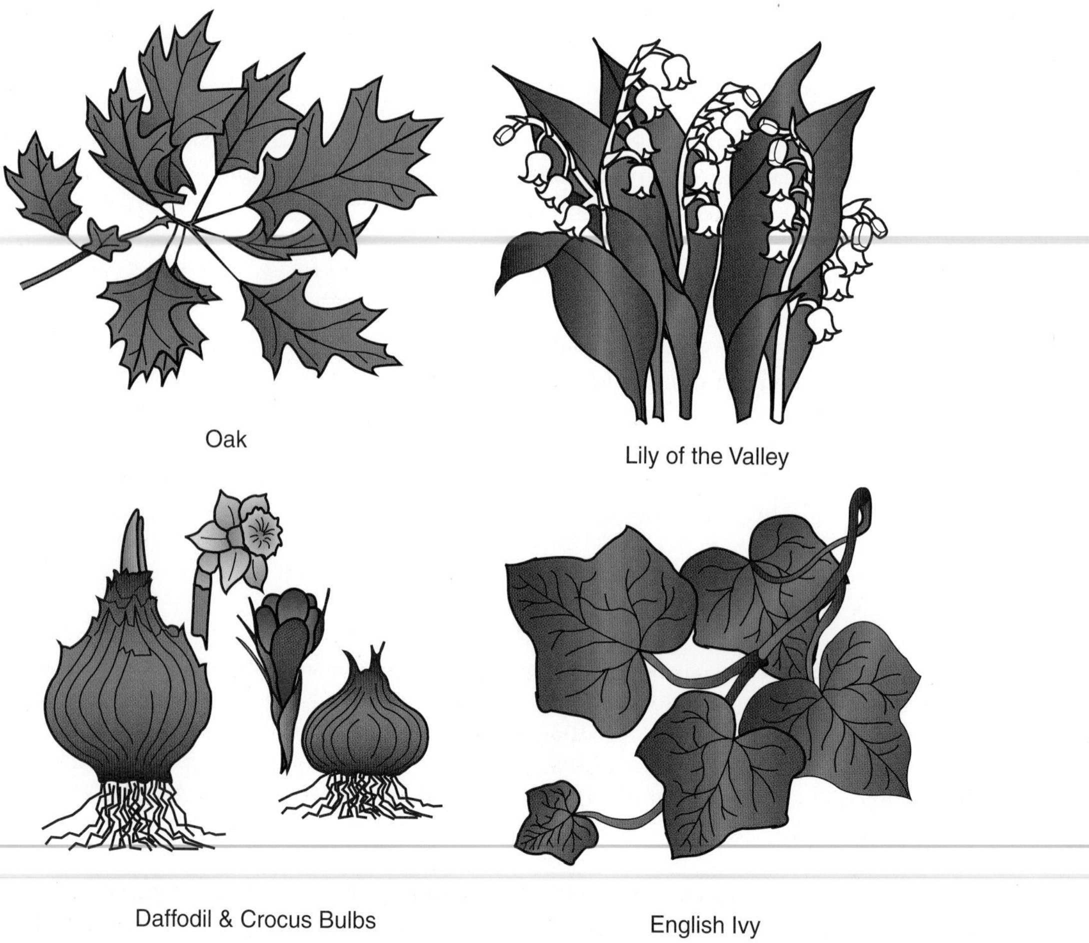

Table 7–6 Some Common Poisonous Vegetation

Vegetation	Poisonous Part	Complications
Bittersweet	Berries	Causes a burning sensation in the mouth. Nausea, vomiting, dizziness, and convulsions.
Buttercup	All parts	Irritating to the digestive tract. Causes nausea and vomiting.
Castor bean	Beanlike pod	Extremely toxic. May be fatal to both children and adults.
Daffodil, hyacinth, narcissus, jonquil, iris	Bulbs Underground roots	Nausea, vomiting, and diarrhea. Can be fatal.
Dieffenbachia	Leaves	Causes immediate burning and swelling around mouth.
English ivy	Leaves and berries	Ingestion results in extreme burning sensation.
Holly	Berries	Results in cramping, nausea, vomiting, and diarrhea.
Lily-of-the-valley	Leaves and flowers	Nausea, vomiting, dizziness, and mental confusion.
Mistletoe	Berries	Extremely toxic. Diarrhea and irregular pulse.
Oleander	Flowers and sap	Highly toxic; can be fatal. Causes nausea, vomiting, diarrhea, and heart irregularities.
Philodendron	Leaves	Ingestion causes intense irritation and swelling of the lips and mouth.
Rhubarb	Raw leaves	Can cause convulsions, coma, and rapid death.
Sweet pea	All parts, especially the seeds	Shallow respirations, possible convulsions, paralysis, and slow pulse.
Black locust tree	Bark, leaves, pods, and seeds	Causes nausea and weakness, especially in children.
Cherry tree	Leaves and twigs	Can be fatal. Causes shortness of breath, general weakness, and restlessness.
Golden chain tree	Beanlike seed pods	Can cause convulsions and coma.
Oak tree	Acorns and leaves	Eating large quantities may cause poisoning. Gradually causes kidney failure.
Rhododendron	All parts	Causes vomiting, convulsions, and paralysis.
Wisteria	Seed pods	Causes severe diarrhea and collapse.
Yews	Berries and foliage	Foliage is very poisonous and can be fatal. Causes nausea, diarrhea, and difficult breathing.

Designing outdoor playgrounds so they can be enjoyed by children of all abilities presents another unique challenge. Guidelines for ensuring that playgrounds comply with ADA standards are available at http://www.access-board.gov/play/guide/intro.htm. Solid, flat surfaces at least 3½ feet wide allow children to maneuver safely in their wheelchairs. Bright colors, textures, ramps, and handrails can easily be incorporated into play environments to improve their visibility and accessibility. Most manufacturers now offer a selection of modified outdoor play equipment that children with a range of abilities and special needs are able to use.

Equipment Each year approximately 200,000 children under the age of 12 are treated in emergency rooms as a result of playground injuries (CPSC, 2009a). Because most injuries involve play equipment, careful attention must be given to its selection, placement, and maintenance (Table 7–7; also see Chapter 8). Equipment choices should be based on:

- amount of available play space
- age and developmental appropriateness
- variety of learning experiences provided
- quality and safety of construction
- accessibility to all children (NCA, 2009)

Large pieces of equipment and portable climbing structures should be firmly anchored in the ground; posts should be sunk 12 to 18 inches below ground surface if anchored with metal pins or at least 6 inches if set in concrete. Play equipment for preschoolers should be no taller than 6 feet and located at least 9 feet from other equipment or hard surfaces such as concrete and asphalt to avoid injury in the event of a fall. This distance should be increased to 15 feet if the equipment has moving parts such as swings.

A safe fall zone must be established around play equipment.

© Cengage Learning

Because children are frequently injured on swings and teeter-totters, many states no longer permit programs to include them on newly constructed playgrounds (Vollman et al., 2009). The Consumer Product Safety Commission (CPSC) also discourages swings in public parks unless they meet strict safety standards (CPSC, 2008). Existing swing seats should be constructed of plastic or rubber to decrease the risk of impact injuries. If tires are used for swings, holes should be drilled to prevent water from collecting and allowing mosquitoes to breed. The size of any opening on equipment should also be carefully checked (openings must be less than 3½ inches or greater than 9 inches) to prevent children's heads from becoming entrapped.

Table 7–7 General Guidelines for Purchasing Outdoor Play Equipment

Consider:
• height of platforms and decks; these should be no higher than 4–5 feet for preschoolers and 6 feet for school-age children • railings present on all decks and platforms, especially those higher than 30 inches above ground • the size of all openings (including those between rungs and guardrails) should be less than 3½ inches or greater than 9 inches apart to prevent entrapment • hardware such as "S" hooks, protruding nuts and bolts, or moving pieces of rope that could injure fingers or catch on clothing; rope swings that could cause strangulation • materials used in construction (Wood/wood products require maintenance to avoid splintering and deterioration. Metal is strong, but becomes hot in sunlight and slippery when wet. Paints and chemicals used for wood treatment must be nontoxic.) • the type of surface material that will be needed under equipment • the amount of area required for safe installation (A clearance area of 9 feet is needed for stationary equipment; 15 feet is needed for equipment with moving parts such as swings.) • ladders that are set straight up and down (vs. on an angle) encourage children to hold onto rungs when climbing

Large trampolines have increased in popularity but are not appropriate in early childhood programs or school settings. The American Academy of Pediatrics discourages families from having trampolines in their backyards or schools from using them for physical education classes or athletic activities (Bond, 2008). Trampolines are also not recommended for children younger than 6 years due to an increasing number of serious injuries and deaths (Leonard & Joffe, 2009; Wootton & Harris, 2009).

For many years, decks and children's climbing structures were constructed with chromated copper arsenic (CCA)-treated lumber, which gave it a green tint. Studies have since shown that the arsenic compound could rub off on children's hands and potentially increase their risk of cancer (Barraj et al., 2009; CPSC, 2009b). CCA-treated lumber is no longer sold, but many play structures built with this material can still be found on playgrounds and in children's backyards. Subsequent studies have determined that applying an annual coat of oil-based sealant reduces children's exposure to the arsenic-based chemicals by 86–90 percent (CPSC, 2008). The chemicals can also leach into soil surrounding the base of treated timbers and should be removed periodically or covered with fresh surface material.

Sand boxes require special care to keep them safe for children (Table 7–8). Play sand, made specifically for children's sandboxes, can be purchased from local garden centers, building contractors, or cement suppliers. (**Note:** Sands used in construction may contain hazardous materials, such as asbestos, and should not be used for children.) Sandboxes should have good drainage and a tightly fitting cover to keep out animals and insects. If they cannot be covered, sand should be raked and inspected daily for animal feces, spiders, insects, sticks, stones, or other sharp debris before children play in it. Frequent sweeping of adjoining surfaces, especially sidewalks, reduces the potential for slipping and falling.

Wading or swimming pools can add interest to outdoor play areas. However, they require extra supervision, safety, and sanitation precautions. Every teacher should be familiar with water safety procedures and rescue breathing procedures and at least one adult on site should be CPR certified. Limiting the number of children participating in water activities at any given time improves teachers' ability to monitor and improve safety. Safety rules should be carefully explained to the children before an activity begins and then strictly enforced.

> ⚠ **Caution: Children must never be left unattended around any source of water, including sprinklers, wading pools, water tables, puddles, ditches, fountains, buckets, or toilets.**

It is essential that pool water be disinfected prior to use by each group of children to prevent the spread of disease, such as giardia and **cryptosporidiosis.** (See Table 6–1). Inexpensive water-quality test kits are available from pool supply stores. Permanent pools and natural bodies of water must be fenced (at least 5 feet in height; be sure to check local codes) and have self-closing gates. Gate alarms, pool safety covers, motion alarms, and the availability of proper flotation and rescue devices provide additional protection against accidental drownings.

Table 7–8 Teacher Checklist: Sandbox Care and Maintenance

Purchase only special play sand for children's sandboxes.

- Make sure there is adequate drainage to prevent water from pooling.
- Rake and check sand daily for spiders, stones, and sharp objects.
- Cover sand if at all possible; if not, be sure to check for animal feces before children play.
- Sweep adjoining surfaces to prevent slipping and falling.

---

cryptosporidiosis – *an infectious illness caused by an intestinal parasite. May be present in water (e.g., swimming pools, hot tubs, streams) contaminated with feces or from unwashed hands. Often causes severe diarrhea in children.*

Tricycles and other small riding toys are always children's favorites. However, they also are involved in many serious childhood injuries and are a common cause of head trauma (Mehan et al., 2009). Children should always wear bike helmets when they are riding, but it is also important that the helmets fit properly, are worn correctly, and meet safety standards established by the Consumer Product Safety Commission (Figure 7–3) (Lee et al., 2009; Keezer et al., 2007). ***Warning***: Children must not wear helmets while on play equipment to prevent entrapment and strangulation. A designated riding area away from where other children are playing can make riding less hazardous. It is also important to discuss rules for safe riding with children to avoid collisions and subsequent injury. Encouraging all children to ride in the same direction and allowing only one child on a bike at a time makes riding even safer.

Surface Materials Protective materials that are soft and resilient should be placed under all play equipment and extend approximately 4 feet out in all directions to create an adequate fall zone (Table 7–9). A minimum of 9–10 inches of sand, pea gravel, finely chopped rubber, or bark mulch

Figure 7–3 Helmets must fit and be worn properly to protect children from serious injury.

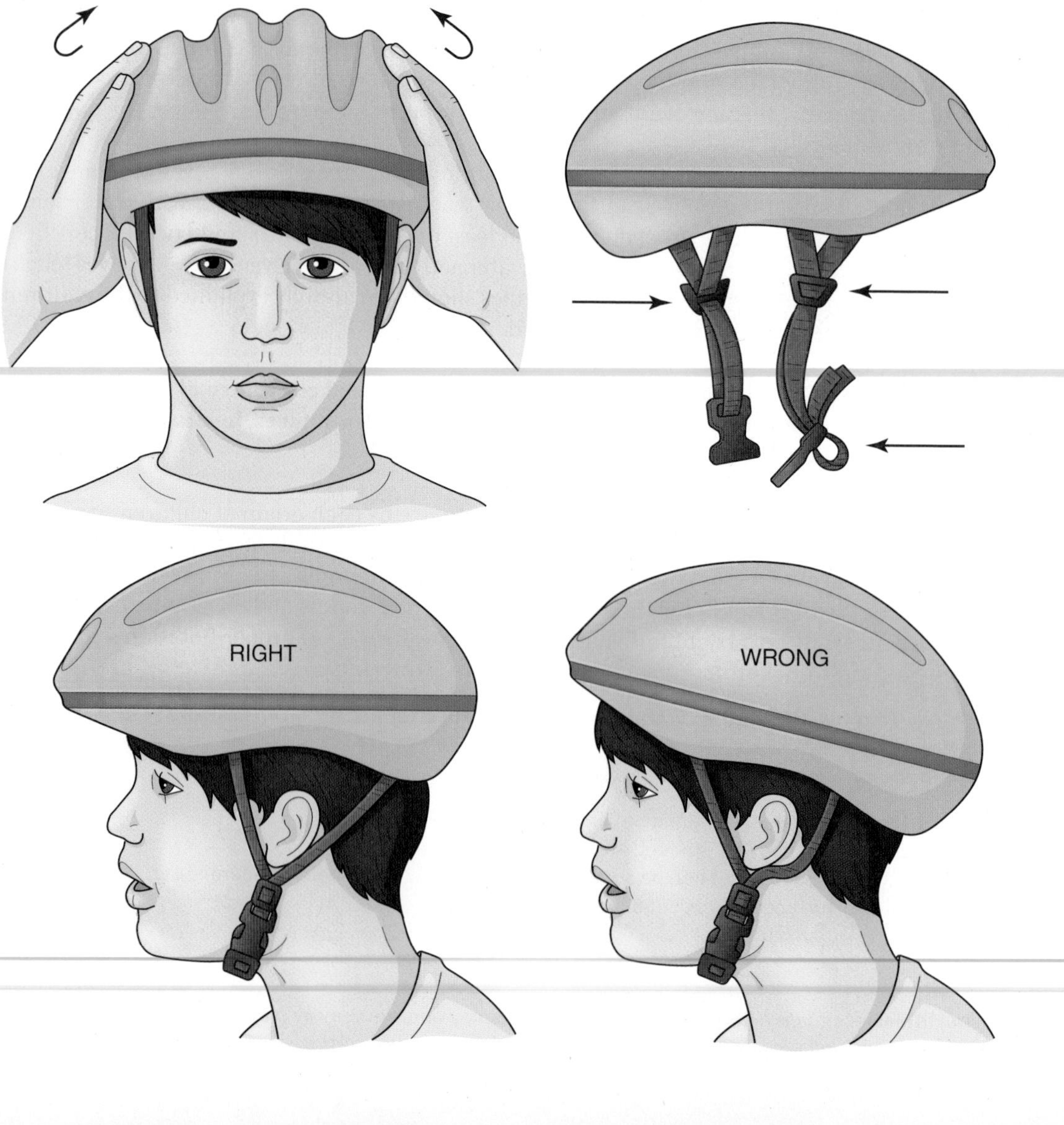

Table 7–9 Comparison of Surfacing Materials

Material	Advantages	Disadvantages
gravel, pea (3/8 inch diameter) (6–9 inches depth)	• relatively inexpensive • readily available • long-lasting; won't decompose • drains quickly • doesn't attract animals • easy to install	• requires a barrier for containment • becomes compact if wet and freezes • must be replenished periodically; may mix with soil below • not recommended with children under 5 years; small pebbles may be thrown or stuffed into noses, ears, or mouths • not wheelchair accessible; hazardous if gravel is scattered on hard surfaces nearby; can cause slipping and falls
gravel, medium (12 inches depth)	• qualities are similar to pea gravel	• disadvantages are similar to pea gravel • larger pieces tend to cause more superficial scrapes
bark mulch (6 inches depth)	• inexpensive • easy to install • drains quickly • readily available	• decomposes rapidly • must be contained with barriers; can wash away with heavy rains • absorbs moisture and freezes • compacts easily • difficult to find sharp objects (e.g. broken glass, sticks, nails, stones) in loose mulch • prone to microbial infestations
wood chips (6 inches)	• air trapped between chips promotes cushioning effect • low in cost • accessible to wheelchairs	• washes away with heavy rains • decomposes and must be replenished to maintain cushion-effect • may be thrown about by children but not likely to cause injury
sand (coarse or masonry sand) (12 inches)	• easy to obtain • inexpensive • does not deteriorate over time • easy to install • not as prone to microbial or insect infestation • accessible by wheelchairs	• must be replenished periodically to maintain cushioning effect • may be thrown about or eaten by children • gets into shoes and clothing • hazardous when spilled onto nearby hard surfaces such as cement and tile floors; can cause slipping and falls • causes slipping and falls on hard surfaces such as cement and tile floors • attractive to animals, especially cats if area not covered • must be raked and sifted frequently to check for undesirable objects (e.g. sticks, broken glass, stones) • requires good drainage beneath
shredded tires	• relatively low initial cost • requires good drainage system • doesn't deteriorate over time • not as likely to compact • less conducive to microbial and insect infestation • wheelchair accessible	• is flammable (10–12 inches) • may stain clothing if not treated • may contain metal particles from steel belted tires • easily thrown about by children but unlikely to cause injury

(*continued*)

Table 7–9 Comparison of Surfacing Materials

rubber tiles or mat systems (check manufacturer's recommendations)	• uniform cushioning effect • easy to clean and maintain • material remains in place • foreign objects are easily noticed • good accessibility to wheelchairs	• expensive to install • requires a flat surface; difficult to use on hills or uneven area • mat or tile edges may curl up and present a tripping hazard • some materials affected by frost

Note: Suggested material depths (noncompacted) are based on shock absorbency from falls of 6 feet.
Source: *Handbook for Public Playground Safety*, U.S. Consumer Product Safety Commission, 2008.

will provide adequate shock absorption (CPSC, 2008). These materials must be loosened frequently to prevent them from compacting and should be replaced periodically as they begin to deteriorate. Surface materials must also be checked daily for any sharp debris or animal waste. Special rubber matting has been developed as an alternative to natural fall zone materials and can be purchased through most outdoor equipment catalogues. Although the initial costs may be considerably greater, rubber matting tends to last longer under children's constant wear (Huang & Chang, 2009). Synthetic grasses, sprinkled with finely ground rubber tire particles for added cushioning, are being installed more often today in city parks and school playgrounds. Some questions have been raised about the safety of chemicals used in manufacturing these products and the potential for children inhaling or ingesting the fine, rubber particles (Claudio, 2008).

Maintenance Hazardous conditions can often be spotted if outdoor play areas are inspected carefully each day before children begin to play. Equipment with broken pieces, jagged or sharp edges, loose screws or bolts, or missing parts should be removed or made off-limits to children. Frequent inspections of play areas and removal of any poisonous vegetation, snakes, rodents or other small animals, sharp sticks, fallen branches, broken glass, or other harmful debris can also reduce unintentional injury. Wooden surfaces on play equipment should be sanded and repainted regularly.

Supervision Although individuals may go to great lengths to design attractive playgrounds and safe equipment, there is no substitution for first-rate supervision. Children must never be left unattended, and the younger they are the more closely adults need to supervise their play. Teacher supervision and safety management will be addressed in greater detail in Chapter 8.

Transportation

Some early childhood programs transport children to and from other school settings or on occasional field trips. Large passenger vans are often used for this purpose, but they are not considered safe and, in the event of an accident, may actually place occupants at increased risk for serious injury. Vans have a tendency to roll over and offer passengers limited structural protection. As a result, federal transportation officials currently recommend that early childhood programs replace existing passenger vans with small-scale school buses. These buses are designed with improved structural safety features (roof and fuel tanks) and, thus, offer greater protection.

Any vehicle used to transport children should be fitted with an appropriate safety restraint system (based on height, weight, and age) for each child:

- an infant-only carrier for infants (birth–1 year) weighing up to 20–22 pounds (9.1– 10.0 kg) (installed in the back seat, facing the rear of the car) with a three- or five-point harness.

A convertible safety seat for heavier infants should be purchased for babies under 1 year who weigh 20–35 pounds (9.1–15.9 kg).
- a child safety seat for children (1–4 years) weighing 20–40 pounds (9.1–18.2 kg) and who are able to sit up by themselves (installed in the back seat, facing forward)
- a booster seat, secured in the back seat, used in combination with a lap belt and shoulder harness for children (4–8 years) who have outgrown child safety seats and are under 4 foot 9 inches (57 inches; 142.5 cm) in height
- a vehicle lap belt and shoulder harness for children (age 8 years and older) who are at least 55–58 inches (137.5–145 cm) in height; children should always ride in the back seat.

It is also critical that safety seats and restraints be installed according to manufacturer's specifications and used correctly whenever children are in transit:

- They must be installed correctly (facing the front or back as is appropriate) and securely anchored in the vehicle.
- They must meet federal standards for manufacturing. (Safety ratings of children's car seats can be accessed online at http://www.nhtsa.dot.gov/CPS/CSSRating/index.cfm.)
- Children must always be buckled into the seat.

Children and adults must always be buckled in securely on every trip even though it may be a time-consuming process. Young children should always ride in the back seat of a vehicle to avoid injury from airbags.

The driver of any vehicle must be a responsible individual and possess a current license appropriate for the number of passengers to be transported. Families of children who are transported on a regular basis should become familiar with the driver so they feel comfortable with the arrangement. Written parental permission and special instructions should always be obtained from families before children are transported in any vehicle.

Motor vehicles used to transport children must be inspected and maintained on a regular basis to ensure their safe performance. Air conditioning and heating should be operational to protect children from temperature extremes. An ABC-type fire extinguisher should be secured in the front of the vehicle where it is accessible for emergencies. Liability insurance should be purchased to cover the vehicle, driver, and maximum number of intended passengers. Copies of children's health forms and emergency contact information should always be stored safely in the vehicle.

Special off-street areas should be designated for the sole purpose of loading and unloading children. If programs do not have space sufficient to accommodate this feature, they will need to concentrate more effort on safety education for

Children should always enter and exit from the curb-side of a car.

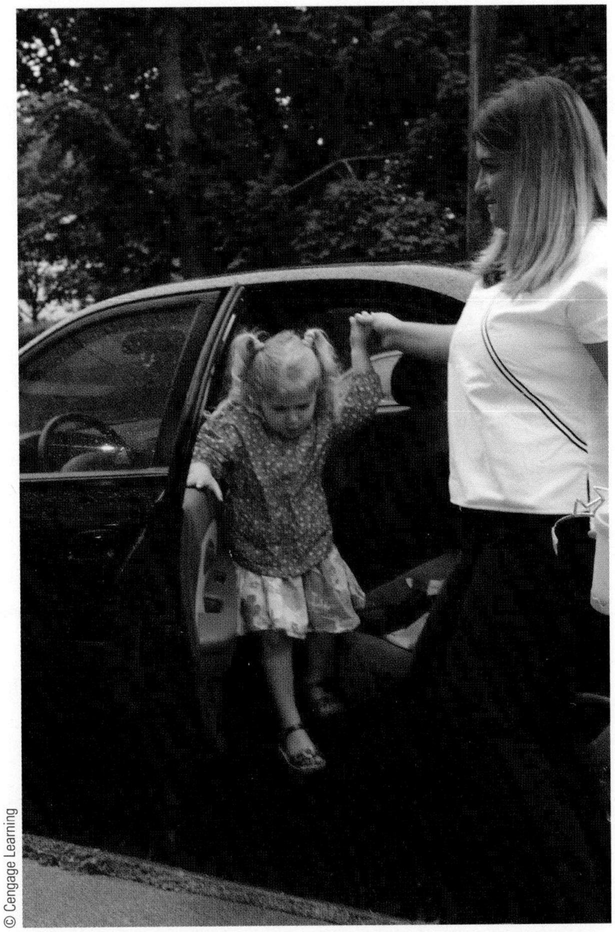

children and families. Children should always enter and exit vehicles from the curb-side rather than the street-side. Adequate parking should be available for families to reduce traffic congestion around school buildings and to improve children's safety. Families must also be reminded ***never*** to leave children alone in a vehicle, even for just a few minutes, in order to prevent abduction or overheating. (*Note: temperatures inside of a vehicle can become dangerously high in a short time even on mild days.*)

Families are sometimes asked to provide transportation for off-site field trips. However, this practice is risky and has the potential for creating serious legal problems in the event of an accident. Programs have no guarantee that privately owned vehicles or individual drivers meet the standards and qualifications previously discussed. As a result, programs may be even more vulnerable

Focus On Families — How to Choose High-Quality Child Care

All families want to find the best early childhood program placement for their children, but knowing what features to look for is often difficult. Small group size, a small ratio of adults to children, and teachers who have educational preparation in early childhood are three indicators commonly associated with excellent programs. Families should always take time to visit any program before enrolling their children and attempt to answer some of the following questions:

- Does the environment appear to be clean, safe, and appealing to children? For example, are electrical outlets covered, are sharp items stored out of children's reach, is the carpet intact and free of snags or stains, and do children wash their hands before eating?
- Is the program accredited or licensed?
- Do the children seem happy and under control? Are children encouraged in their efforts and allowed to express their feelings? Are teachers playing and talking with the children? Do they encourage children to help solve their own problems?
- Are children treated with respect and as individuals? Is the teacher's tone of voice warm and friendly versus harsh, demanding, or demeaning?
- Is there adequate adult supervision? Are there sufficient numbers of adults present who can respond to an injured child or classroom emergency while ensuring the safety of other children?
- Are there a sufficient number and variety of toys and materials for all children to use, or must children wait for others to finish? Are items easily accessible to children?
- Is the food served to children nutritious, age appropriate, and adequate in amount? If your child has food allergies, would his or her special needs be accommodated? Are weekly menus posted?
- Have the teachers been trained to work with young children? Do they appear to enjoy working with the children and take pride in their efforts? Are they knowledgeable about how to facilitate children's development and spot problems? Be sure to ask about their educational preparation and years of experience.
- Do you feel welcomed and encouraged to ask questions? Are there opportunities for you to become involved in your child's classroom?
- Are learning experiences planned for children, or are they left to wander or watch television?
- Is a daily schedule of the children's activities posted for you to read?
- Do you agree with the program's philosophy, and is it appropriate for your child's needs?
- Have the program's policies been explained clearly, and are they acceptable to you?

to lawsuits and charges of negligence. To avoid this risk, programs may want to use public transportation, such as a city bus, or contract with a private transportation company.

When private vehicles are used for transportation, several steps can be taken to protect children's safety. Travel routes should be planned in advance, reviewed with the director, and followed precisely by all drivers. Names of drivers, supervising adults, and children riding in each vehicle, as well as anticipated departure and arrival times, should also be left with a program administrator. Rules for safe traveling should be reviewed with all drivers and children before each excursion. Plans for handling an unplanned emergency, such as an ill child, flat tire, carjacking, or unusual weather, should also be discussed and reviewed routinely with drivers. At least one adult traveling with the group should have first aid and CPR training.

Classroom Corner | Teacher Activities

Recycle Everyday...

(PreK–2; National Health Education Standard 2.2.2)

Concept: You can recycle items instead of throwing them away in the trash.

Learning Objectives

- Children will learn that items can be recycled and then made into other products.
- Children will learn how to sort different items.

Supplies

- boxes (the size that reams of paper come in); newspapers, chipboard boxes, magazines/catalogs; milk jugs and plastic bottles; cans (emptied out and clean; make sure cans don't have a sharp ring)

Learning Activities

- Read and discuss the books:
  - *Recycle Every Day* by Nancy Elizabeth Wallace
  - *Recycle* by Gail Gibbons
- Decorate each box so children will know which items need to go in it (picture of a milk jug, a water or soda bottle, newspaper, etc.). Children can help decorate the boxes ahead of time.
- Spread items out on the floor to show how much space discarded items take up. Talk about how items can be sorted and recycled and not thrown away.
- Demonstrate how items need to be sorted according to the pictures on the box.
- Have children come up and pick an item to place in the correct box. Sort all items. If possible, plan a field trip to a recycling center.
- Discuss what happens to items that are tossed in the garbage. Talk about where all of the garbage is taken. Ask children for their ideas about ways that families can reduce the amount of garbage they throw away.

Evaluation

- Children can sort items.
- Children will explain that items can be recycled and made into other items instead of thrown away as trash.

Additional lesson plans for grades 3–5 are available on this text's premium website.

Summary

- Locating high-quality child care that is available, affordable, and convenient can be challenging for families.
- The environment affects all aspects of children's growth and development.
- Children's environments require thoughtful planning.
- Licensing regulations and procedures reflect minimal standards and vary from state to state. However, they provide some assurance that children's health and safety will be protected. Not everyone agrees about how much regulation is necessary.
- Adhering to licensing regulations can help to protect teachers from potential claims of negligence.
- Location, security, fire safety, plumbing, surfaces and furnishings, and air quality should be considered when planning children's indoor environments.
- Special attention should be given to space, play equipment, vegetation, surface materials, adult supervision, and transportation when planning outdoor play areas.

Terms to Know

environment *p. 172*
cognitive *p. 172*
accreditation *p. 174*
licensing *p. 175*
regulations *p. 175*
compliance *p. 175*
registration *p. 175*
developmentally appropriate practice (DAP) *p. 179*
notarized *p. 180*
cryptosporidiosis *p. 195*

Chapter Review

A. By Yourself

1. Match the definition in **Column I** with the term in **Column II**.

Column I	Column II
1. local ordinance that indicates what type of facility shall be in an area	a. regulation b. minimal
2. rule dealing with procedures	c. standards
3. method of action that determines current and future decisions	d. staff qualification
4. witnessed form that indicates the signature that appears on the form is really that of the person signing the form	e. notarized permissions f. policy
5. skills possessed by the people responsible for the operation of a business	g. zoning code
6. meeting the least possible requirements	

2. Identify and describe eight features of a high-quality early childhood program.
3. What steps are involved in obtaining a license to operate an early childhood program?
4. What type of car seat/restraint is appropriate for a 3-year-old? What about an 11-month-old infant who weighs 27 pounds?

B. As a Group

1. Locate and review the child care licensing regulations for your state posted online. Discuss the pros and cons of the following question: Should the quality of state child care licensing standards be raised?
2. In what ways does the environment influence a child's growth and development?
3. Describe several features that make an outdoor play yard safe for young children.
4. What steps can programs take to make their facilities secure from unwanted intrusions?
5. Discuss how a teacher's educational training affects the quality of a child's experiences in an early childhood program.
6. Brainstorm several ways that a school can "go green" and discuss what effect(s) this could potentially have on children's health.

Case Study

Linh Nam cares for several neighborhood children while their parents work at the local meatpacking factory. In the beginning, she agreed to take in one or two children on days when their parents were unable to find other child care arrangements. However, now Linh has seven children, 19 months to 6 years, who show up on a regular basis. Their parents are grateful and pleased with the nurturing care Linh provides. She fears that local licensing authorities will discover her activities, but is reluctant to contact them because she has no formal training in child care and isn't sure that her house will meet safety standards. She also knows that her friends depend on her for child care and could lose their jobs if they don't have anywhere to leave their children.

1. What are Linh's options?
2. What steps can Linh take to improve her chances of becoming licensed?
3. Should licensing (or registration) be mandatory for in-home child care?
4. Should programs that don't meet state licensing standards be closed down?
5. How can increasing demands for child care be balanced against a need to improve their quality?

Application Activities

1. Develop a safety checklist that teachers and families could use when inspecting children's outdoor play areas for hazardous conditions. Using your list, conduct an inspection of two different play yards (for example, public vs. private), or the same play area on two separate occasions and summarize your findings. Repeat the process for indoor areas.
2. Contact your local licensing agency. Make arrangements to accompany licensing personnel on an on-site visit of a center-based program; be sure to review the state licensing regulations beforehand. Observe how the licensing inspection is conducted. In several short paragraphs, describe your reactions to this experience.
3. Often licensing personnel are viewed as unfriendly or threatening authority figures. However, their major role is to offer guidance and help teachers create safe environments for children. Role-play how you would handle the following situations during a licensing visit. Keep in mind the positive role of licensing personnel (e.g. offering explanations, providing suggestions, and planning acceptable solutions and alternatives):
   - electrical outlets not covered
   - all children's toothbrushes found stored together in a large plastic bin

- open boxes of dry cereals and crackers in kitchen cabinets
- an adult-sized toilet and wash basin in the bathroom
- a swing set located next to a cement patio
- incomplete information on children's immunization records
- a teacher who prepares snacks without first washing his or her hands

4. Create a PowerPoint presentation to help families identify quality features in an early childhood program. Include photographs of actual programs to illustrate your points. Prepare a modified version for families in your community who may not speak English as their predominant language. Make presentations to several parent groups and have them evaluate the effectiveness of your program.
5. Prepare a brochure or simple checklist for families describing how to select high-quality early education programs.
6. Learn more about the CDA credential. Research this online (http://www.cdacouncil.org) or contact the Council for Professional Recognition, 2460 16th St., NW, Washington, DC, 20009-3575; (800) 424-4310. After reading the materials, prepare a brief summary describing the program and its requirements.
7. Invite a county extension agent or florist to bring in examples or cuttings of poisonous plants. Learn to identify at least five different plants.
8. Go to the U.S. Consumer Product Safety Commission website (http://www.cpsc.gov). Review and summarize the recommended safety standards for at least eight playground items. Prepare a parent handout that summarizes safety conditions that should be observed in public play areas.

Helpful Web Resources

Canadian Child Care Federation	http://www.cccf-fcsge.ca
Consumer Product Safety (Canada)	http://www.hc-sc.gc.ca
National Association for Family Child Care	http://www.nafcc.org
National Association for the Education of Young Children (NAEYC)	http://www.naeyc.org
National Association of Child Care Resource and Referral Agencies (NACCRRA)	http://www.naccrra.org
National Network for Child Care	http://www.nncc.org
National Program for Playground Safety	http://www.uni.edu/playground/
U.S. Product Safety Commission	http://www.cpsc.gov

You are just a click away from additional health, safety, and nutrition resources! Go to www.CengageBrain.com to access this text's Education CourseMate website, where you'll find:

- an emergency contact information form
- examples of common poisonous vegetation
- glossary flashcards, activities, tutorial quizzes, videos, web links, and more

References

Addington, L. (2009). "Cops and cameras": Public school security as a policy response to Columbine, *American Behavioral Scientist*, 52(10), 1426–1447.

Adi-Japha, E., & Klein, P. (2009). Relations between parenting quality and cognitive performance of children experiencing varying amounts of childcare, *Child Development*, 80(3), 893–906.

Allen, K. E., & Cowdery, G. (2009). *The exceptional child: Inclusion in early childhood education.* (6th ed.). Clifton Park, NY: Delmar Cengage Learning.

American Public Health Association (APHA) and American Academy of Pediatrics (AAP). (2002). *Caring for our children: National health and safety performance standards for out-of-home care.* Washington, DC.

Aronson, S. (2002). *Healthy young children: A manual for programs.* (4th ed.). Washington, DC: NAEYC.

Barraj, L., Scrafford, C., Eaton, W., Rogers, R., & Jeng, C. (2009). Arsenic levels in wipe samples collected from play structures constructed with CCA-treated wood: Impact on exposure estimates, *Science of the Total Environment*, 407(8), 2586–2592.

Barros, R., Silver, E., & Stein, R. (2009). School recess and group classroom behavior, *Pediatrics*, 123(2), 431–436.

Bergen, D., & Fromberg, D. (2009). Play and social interaction in middle childhood, *Phi Delta Kappan*, 90(6), 426–430.

Bond, A. (2008). Trampolines unsafe for children at any age, *AAP News,* 29(4), 29.

Burchinal, M., & Cryer, D. (2003). Diversity, child care quality, and developmental outcomes, *Early Childhood Research Quarterly,* 18(4), 401–426.

Buysse, V., & Hollingsworth, H. (2009). Program quality and early childhood inclusion, *Topics in Early Childhood Special Education*, 29(2), 119–128.

Buysse, V., Winton, P., & Rous, B. (2009). Reaching consensus on a definition of professional development for the early childhood field, *Topics in Early Childhood Special Education*, 28(4), 235–243.

Child Care Law Center. (2007). Questions & answers about the Americans with Disabilities Act: A quick reference (Information for child care providers). Accessed on November 5, 2009 from http://www.childcarelaw.org/docs/qanda-ada.pdf.

Claudio, L. (2008). Synthetic turf: Health debate takes root, *Environmental Health Perspectives*, 116(3), 117–122.

Consumer Product Safety Commission (CPSC). (2009a). Back to school safely. Accessed on November 4, 2009 from http://www.cpsc.gov/PR/tenenbaum090809.html.

CPSC. (2009b). Chromated copper arsenate (CCA) – Treated wood use in playground equipment. Accessed on November 4, 2009 from http://www.cpsc.gov/phth/ccafact.html.

CPSC. (2008). *Handbook of public playground safety.* Washington, DC.

de Schipper, E., Riksen-Walraven, J., Geurts, S., & Weerth, C. (2009). Cortisol levels of caregivers in child care centers as related to the quality of their caregiving, *Early Childhood Research Quarterly*, 24(1), 55–63.

Dearing, E., McCartney, K., & Taylor, B. (2009). Does higher quality early child care promote low-income children's math and reading achievement in middle childhood? *Child Development*, 80(5), 1329–1349.

Denissen, J., Butalid, L., Penke, L., & van Aken, M. (2008). The effects of weather on daily mood: A multilevel approach, *Emotion*, 8(5), 662–667.

Doherty, G., Forer, B., Lero, D., Goelman, H., & LaGrange, A. (2006). Predictors of quality in family child care, *Early Childhood Research Quarterly, 21*(3), 296–312.

Dowda, M., Brown, W., McIver, K., Pfeiffer, K., O'Neill, J., Addy, C., & Pate, R. (2009). Policies and characteristics of the preschool environment and physical activity of young children, *Pediatrics*, 123(2), e261–e266.

Essa, E. (2010). *Introduction to early childhood education.* 6th ed. Belmont, CA: Wadsworth.

Fadia, S., Flores, D., & Gbarayor, C. (2008). School-based obesity interventions: A literature review, *Journal of School Health*, 78(4), 189–196.

Fiscella, K., & Kitzman, H. (2009). Disparities in academic achievement and health: The intersection of child education and health policy, *Pediatrics*, 123(3), 1073–1080.

Fuentes-Leonarte, V., Tenías, J., & Ballester, F. (2009). Levels of pollutants in indoor air and respiratory health in preschool children: A systematic review, *Pediatric Pulmonology*, 44(3), 231–243.

Gamble, W., Ewing, A., & Wilhelm, M. (2009). Parental perceptions of characteristics of non-parental child care: Belief dimensions, family and child correlates, *Journal of Child & Family Studies,* 18(1), 70–82.

Gupta, R., Pascoe, J., Blanchard, T., Langkamp, D., Duncan, P., Gorski, P., & Southward, L. (2009). Child health in child care: A multi-state survey of Head Start and non-Head Start child care directors, *Journal of Pediatric Health Care*, 23(3), 143–149.

Heinen, E., Webb-Demsey, J., Moore, L., McClellan, C., & Friebel, C. (2007). Safety matters: How one district addressed safety concern, *Journal of School Violence*, 6(3), 113–130.

Huang, T., & Chang, L. (2009). Design and evaluation of shock-absorbing rubber tile for playground safety, *Materials & Design*, 30(9), 3819–3823.

Johnson, L., Ciaccio, C., Barnes, C., Kennedy, K., Forrest, E., Gard, L., Pacheco, F., Dowling, P., & Portnoy, J. (2009). Low-cost interventions improve indoor air quality and children's health, *Allergy & Asthma Proceedings*, 30(4), 377–385.

Keezer, M., Rughani, A., Carroll, M., & Haas, B. (2007). Head first: Bicycle-helmet use and our children's safety, *Canadian Family Physician*, 53(7), 1131–1136.

Lee, R., Hagel, B., Karkhaneh, M., & Rowe, B. (2009). A systematic review of correct bicycle helmet use: How varying definitions and study quality influence the results, *Injury Prevention*, 15(2),125–131.

Leonard, H., & Joffe, A. (2009). Children presenting to a Canadian hospital with trampoline-related cervical spine injuries, *Paediatric Child Health*, 14(2), 84–88.

Lindle, J. (2008). Real or imagined fear? *Educational Policy*, 22(1), 28–44.

Mashburn, A., Pianta, R., Hamre, B., Downer, J., Barbarin, O., Bryant, D., Burchinal, M., Early, D., & Howes, C. (2008). Measures of classroom quality in prekindergarten and children's development of academic, language, and social skills, *Child Development*, 79(2), 732–749.

Mehan, T., Gardner, R., Smith, G., & McKenzie, L. (2009). Bicycle-related injuries among children and adolescents in the United States, *Clinical Pediatrics*, 48(2), 166–173.

Miller, E., Almon, J., & Miller, E. (2009). Crises in the kindergarten: Why children need to play in school, *Education Digest*, 75(1), 42–45.

Miller, J., & Bogatova, T. (2009). Quality improvements in the early care and education workforce: Outcomes and impact of the T.E.A.C.H. Early Childhood *Project, *Evaluation & Program Planning*, 32(3), 257-277.

Muscato, L., & Kennon, T. (2009). School nurses champion cleaning for health, *NASN School Nurse*, 24(4), 148–149.

National Association for the Education of Young Children (NAEYC). (2009a). Accreditation of programs for young children. Accessed on November 4, 2009 from http://www.naeyc.org/academy.

NAEYC. (2009b). *Developmentally appropriate practice (in early childhood programs, serving children birth through age 8).* (C. Copple & S. Bredekamp, Eds.). Washington, DC: NAEYC.

National Center on Accessibility (NCA). (2009). A2R Webinar archive: Playgrounds. Accessed on November 4, 2009 from http://www.ncaonline.org/index.php?q=taxonomy/term/136/all.

National Highway Traffic Safety Commission. (2010). 4 Steps to Protect our Children. Accessed on June 23, 2010 from http://www.nhtsa.gov.

Neuman, S., & Cunningham, L. (2009). The impact of professional development and coaching on early language and literacy instructional practices, *American Educational Research Journal*, 46(2), 532–566.

Olsen, H., Hudson, S., & Thompson, D. (2008). Developing a playground injury prevention plan, *Journal of School Nursing*, 24(3), 131–137.

Rivera, M. (2008). The importance of quality early childhood education, *Education Digest*, 4(3), 61–65.

Salo, P., Sever, M., & Zeldin, D. (2009). Indoor allergens in school and day care environments, *Journal of Allergy and Clinical Immunology*, 124(2), 185–192.

Shelton, A., Owens, E., & Holim, S. (2009). An examination of public school safety measures across geographical settings, *Journal of School Health*, 79(1), 24–30.

Smith, C. (2009). Hot topic: Tap water not the only cause of scalds, *AAP News*, 30(10), 37.

Staempfli, M. (2009). Reintroducing adventure into children's outdoor play environments, *Environment & Behavior*, 41(2), 268–280.

Stuhlman, M., & Pianta, R. (2009). Profiles of educational quality in first grade, *Elementary School Journal*, 109(4), 323–342.

Upshur, C., Wenz-Gross, M., & Reed, G. (2009). A pilot study of early childhood mental health consultation for children with behavioral problems in preschool, *Early Childhood Research Quarterly*, 24(1), 29–45.

Vollman, D., Witsaman, R., Comstock, R., & Smith, G. (2009). Epidemiology of playground equipment-related injuries to children in the United States, 1996–2005, *Clinical Pediatrics* (Phila.), 48(1), 66–71.

Vu, J., Hyun-Joo, J., & Howes, C. (2008). Formal education, credential, or both: Early childhood program classroom practices, *Education & Development*, 19(3), 479–504.

Watson, A., & McCathern, R. (2009). Including children with special needs: Are you and your early childhood program ready? *Young Children*, 64(2), 20–26.

Wootton, M., & Harris, D. (2009). Trampolining injuries presenting to a children's emergency department, *Emergency Medical Journal*, 26(10), 728–731.

CHAPTER

8

Safety Management

NAEYC Standards *Chapter Links*

- **#1 a and c:** Promoting child development and learning
- **#2 a:** Building family and community relationships
- **#3 d:** Observing, documenting, and assessing to support young children and families
- **#4 b, and d:** Using developmentally effective approaches to connect with children and families
- **#5 a, b, and c:** Using content knowledge to build a meaningful curriculum
- **#6 b, c, d and e:** Becoming a professional

Learning Objectives

After studying this chapter, you should be able to:

- Define the term unintentional injury, and explain why the victims are most often young children.
- Describe the four basic principles of risk management.
- Discuss safety practices that teachers should implement in the classroom and outdoors to safeguard children.
- Identify two forms of negligence and discuss steps teachers can take to protect themselves from such charges.

Unintentional injuries are the leading cause of death and permanent disability among children under the age of 14 (Borse et al., 2009; CDC, 2008). They are also responsible for thousands of nonfatal injuries and are costly in terms of time, energy, suffering, and medical expense. Although children experience frequent mishaps, the most common causes of death (Table 8–1) due to unintentional injury include:

- motor vehicles—as pedestrians, riding a bicycle or wheeled toy
- drowning—in swimming pools, spas, bathtubs, ponds, toilets, buckets
- burns—from fireplaces, appliances, grills, chemicals, electrical outlets, residential fires, fireworks
- suffocation—from plastic bags, entrapment in chests or appliances, bedding, aspiration of small objects
- falls—from stairs, furniture, play equipment, windows
- poisoning—from pain relievers, vitamins with iron, carbon monoxide, cleaning products, insecticides, cosmetics

Table 8–1 Common Causes of Childhood Death Due to Unintentional Injury

Cause of Death	1- to 4-year-olds	5- to 9-year-olds
Motor vehicle/pedestrian	36.3%	51.4%
Drowning	28.4%	13.6%
Fire/burns	12.1%	11.3%
Suffocation	8.5%	4.8%
Falls	2.4%	1.6%
Poisoning	1.7%	1.7%
Total Deaths	1610	1044

Source: Centers for Disease Control and Prevention (CDC) Web-based Injury Statistics Query and Reporting System (WISQARS). (2006). Unintentional Injuries Deaths, Ages, 1–4 and 5–9.

Knowing that young children are especially vulnerable to unintentional injury makes it imperative that teachers and families understand how to organize environments, provide safe activities, and supervise children of all ages and developmental abilities.

What Is Unintentional Injury?

The term *unintentional injury* has replaced *accidents* when referring to injuries sustained by children. This is because in most instances, factors contributing to an accident are preventable. Childhood injuries are most often attributed to environmental hazards, lack of appropriate planning and adult supervision, or a child's immature development—conditions that are all manageable with improved knowledge and awareness.

Teachers have a professional and ethical responsibility to keep children safe.

Infants and toddlers are at highest risk for sustaining life-threatening injuries and medical emergencies. Their zealous interest and curiosity in learning about their surroundings, impulsive play, and immature development can unfortunately lead children into new and unexpected dangers. Likewise, older children continue to explore their environment with an even greater sense of enthusiasm, yet they still lack an adult's maturity, experience, and understanding necessary to anticipate the consequences of their behavior. Thus, adults must be continuously aware of children's developmental abilities and behavioral characteristics, as well as potential environmental hazards, in their efforts to protect children from injury (Table 8–2).

Teachers and administrators assume a major role and responsibility for protecting the safety of children in their care. This can be a particularly challenging task given the ages of children typically enrolled in early education programs, elementary schools and before-and-after school programs. However, teachers' unique training and experience enables them to implement safety measures that can eliminate needless childhood injuries.

Table 8–2 Developmental Characteristics and Injury Prevention

Age	Developmental Characteristics	Hazards	Preventive Measures
Birth to 4 months	Eats, sleeps, cries; rolls off flat surfaces	Burns	Set hot water heater to a maximum of 120°F.
			Always keep one hand on baby.
		Falls	Never turn back or walk away from a baby who is on a table or bed.
	Wriggles	Toys	Select toys that are too large to swallow, too tough to break, have no sharp points or edges, and have nontoxic finishes.
		Sharp objects	Keep pins and other sharp objects out of baby's reach.
		Suffocation	Filmy plastics, harnesses, zippered bags, and pillows can smother or strangle. A firm mattress and coverings that are tucked in are safest.
4–12 months	Grasps and moves about	Play areas	Keep baby in a safe place near an adult. The floor, full-sized bed, and yard are unsafe without supervision.
	Puts objects in mouth	Bath	Check temperature of bath water with elbow. Keep baby out of reach of faucets. *Never* leave alone in bath.
		Toys	Large beads on strong cord, unbreakable, rounded toys made of smooth wood or plastic (phthalate-free) are safe.
		Small objects	Keep buttons, beads, coins, and other small objects from baby's reach.
		Poisoning	Children of this age still need full-time protection.
		Falls	Don't turn your back or walk away when baby is on an elevated surface. Place gates in doorways and on stairways.
		Burns	Place guards around registers and floor furnaces. Keep hot liquids, hot foods, and electric cords on irons, toasters, and coffee pots out of baby's reach. Use sturdy and round-edged furniture. Avoid hot steam vaporizers.
1–2 years	Investigates, climbs, opens doors and drawers; takes things apart; likes to play	Gates, windows, doors	Securely fasten doors leading to stairways, driveways, and storage. Put gates on stairways and porches.
		Play areas	Keep screens locked or nailed. Fence the play yard. Provide sturdy toys with no small removable parts or with unbreakable materials. Keep electric cords to coffee pots, toasters, irons, and computers out of reach.

(continued)

Table 8–2 Developmental Characteristics and Injury Prevention (*continued*)

Age	Developmental Characteristics	Hazards	Preventive Measures
		Water	*Never* leave child alone in tub, wading pool, or around open or frozen water. Fence and gate pools; keep locked at all times.
		Poisons	Store all vitamins, medicines, and poisons in locked cabinets. Store cosmetics and household products, especially caustics and pesticides, out of child's reach. Store kerosene and gasoline in metal cans and out of children's reach.
		Burns	Provide guards for wall heaters, registers, and floor furnaces. Never leave children alone in the house. Supervise children closely to protect them from injuries.
2–3 years	Fascinated by fire; moves about constantly; tries to do things alone Imitates and explores; runs and is lightning fast; is impatient with restraint	Traffic	Keep child away from street and driveway with strong fence and consistent discipline. Use appropriate car seat restraints.
		Water	Eliminate water sources such as shallow wading pools and fountains unless carefully supervised.
		Toys	Provide large sturdy toys without sharp edges or small removable parts.
		Burns	Keep matches and cigarette lighters out of child's reach. Teach them about the danger of fire. Never leave children alone in the house. Keep hot liquids out of reach.
		Dangerous objects	Lock up medicine, household and garden poisons, dangerous tools, firearms, and garden equipment. Teach safe ways of handling appropriate tools and kitchen equipment.
		Playmates	Injuries happen more often when playmates are older—the 2-year-old may be easily hurt by bats, hard balls, bicycles, rough play.

3–6 years	Explores the neighborhood; climbs on objects; enjoys riding tricycles; plays and likes rough games	Tools and equipment	Store in a safe place, out of reach and locked. Teach safe use of tools and kitchen equipment.
	Frequently out of adult sight; likes to imitate adult actions	Poisons and burns	Keep medicines, household cleaning products, and matches locked up.
		Falls and injuries	Check play areas for attractive hazards such as old refrigerators, deep holes, trash heaps, construction, and old buildings.
		Drowning	Teach the danger of water and begin swimming instruction.
		Traffic	Help children learn rules and dangers of traffic. Insist on obedience where traffic is concerned. Use appropriate car seat restraints; always buckle children in.
6–12 years	Enjoys spending time away from home; participates in active sports, is part of a group, and will "try anything once" in traffic, on foot. or on a bicycle; teaching must gradually replace supervision	Traffic	Set a good example: drive safely, always wear seat belts. Teach pedestrian and bicycle safety rules. Don't allow play in streets or alleys.
		Personal	Teach self-protection skills: what to do if bullied; Internet and cell phone safety; resisting drugs and alcohol.
		Firearms	Store unloaded in a locked cabinet.
			Teach children to stay away from guns and tell an adult if they find one.
		Sports	Provide sound instruction, safe area, and equipment. Supervise any competition. Provide protective gear and insist that it be worn.
		Drowning	Teach swimming and boating safety.

Risk Management: Principles and Preventive Measures

Prevention of **unintentional injury** requires continuous awareness and implementation of **risk management** measures (Alkon et al., 2009; Children's Safety Network, 2009). Teachers and families must consider the element of safety in everything they do with young children (Table 8–2). This includes the rooms they organize, toys they purchase, and learning activities they plan. To new teachers or busy parents, this step may seem unnecessarily time-consuming. However, these are precisely the times when it is important to focus extra attention on children's safety. Any amount of preventive effort is worth the time if it spares one child from injury!

Knowledge of children's developmental skills is essential for protecting their safety (Berk, 2008). Understanding the differences in their cognitive, motor, social, and emotional abilities at various stages helps adults to anticipate children's actions and take steps to avoid unintentional injury. For example, knowing that infants put everything into their mouths should alert teachers to be extra vigilant of small items, such as a paper clip or pen cap, that might be dropped on the floor. Understanding that toddlers enjoy climbing should alert adults to the importance of fastening bookshelves and large pieces of play equipment securely to the wall or floor so they won't tip over. Recognizing that 4-year-olds' limited understanding of cause and effect makes them more vulnerable to hazardous situations in their environment is useful when designing a classroom or play yard. Or, knowing that boys are more likely to be involved in accidents than girls due to their preference for play that involves active, aggressive, and risk-taking behaviors can be used when planning large motor activities (Eberl et al., 2009; Rowe & Maughan, 2009). When adults are familiar with typical child development and also understand that children develop at different rates, they are able to use this information for:

- planning children's environments
- preparing learning activities
- selecting appropriate play equipment (indoor and outdoor)
- establishing safety guidelines
- supervising children's learning and play experiences
- developing safety education programs

It is important to recognize that circumstances, such as fatigue, change, or distraction increase the risk of unintentional injury (Table 8–3). It is also known that children in group-care settings

Table 8–3 Conditions That Contribute to Unintentional Injury

The risk of injury is greatest when:

- adults are not feeling well and suffering from symptoms of illness, discomfort, or fatigue
- adults are angry, emotionally upset, or faced with a difficult situation, such as an uncooperative child, an unpleasant conversation with a parent, a strained relationship with a staff member, or a personal problem
- new teachers, staff members, or visitors who are unfamiliar with the children and their routines are present
- conditions are rushed or planned late in the day
- there is a shortage of teachers; too few adults to provide adequate supervision
- children are not able to play outdoors due to inclement weather
- new children are included in a group and are unfamiliar with the environment, rules, and expectations
- rules have not been formulated or explained carefully to children

unintentional injury – *an unexpected or unplanned event that may result in physical harm or injury.*
risk management – *measures taken to avoid an event such as an injury or illness from occurring; implies the ability to anticipate circumstances and behaviors.*

Reflective Thoughts

Teachers are exposed to children's communicable illnesses on a daily basis. Calling in sick often creates a staff shortage since substitutes may be difficult to locate. How can a teacher determine if he/she is too sick to come to work? What are the risks involved in coming to work when you are sick? How might teacher illness contribute to children's unintentional injury?

are more likely to be injured while playing outdoors, especially on swings, climbing apparatus, and slides (Vollman et al., 2009; Loder, 2008). For this reason, some states no longer permit swings, teeter-totters, or large slides on new playgrounds. When children are at home, they are more likely to sustain injuries indoors, particularly in the kitchen and bathroom areas (Mao et al., 2009; U.S. CPSC, 2008b).

Environmental design and maintenance are also important considerations to address in the prevention of children's injuries. Local building codes, state child care licensing regulations, and Americans with Disabilities Act (ADA) architectural requirements provide guidelines for the construction of facilities that are safe and accessible (WBDG, 2009; U.S. Access Board, 2005). Consulting with licensing personnel during the planning phase of any new construction or remodeling project is also helpful for identifying safety features and ensuring that the facilities will comply with recommended standards.

Several organizations, including the National Association for the Education of Young Children (NAEYC) and the National Association of Child Care Resource and Referral Agencies (NACCRRA) have developed safety recommendations for children's environments. The American Academy of Pediatrics and the American Public Health Association have also collaborated to produce the National Health and Safety Performance Standards (guidelines for out-of-home child care programs, http://nrc.uchsc.edu/CFOC). The safety standards outlined in these documents are based on what is currently known about best practices and, when followed, can be helpful to schools in eliminating potentially hazardous conditions in children's environments.

Despite adults' best efforts, it is not possible to prevent every childhood injury. Regardless of how much care is exercised, some circumstances will be beyond a teacher's or parent's ability to control. For example, no amount of appropriate planning or supervision can prevent a toddler from suddenly bumping into a table edge or an older child unexpectedly losing his grip while climbing. However, the number and seriousness of injuries can be significantly reduced when basic risk management principles are followed:

- planning in advance
- establishing safety policies and guidelines
- maintaining good-quality supervision
- providing for safety education

Advanced Planning

Considerable thought and planning should go into the selection of equipment and activities that are appropriate for young children (Kuo, 2009; Walsh, 2008). Choices must take into account children's developmental abilities and also encourage the safe acquisition of new skills. Activities should be planned and equipment selected to stimulate children's curiosity, exploration, and sense of independence without endangering their safety (Staempfli, 2009; Frost, Wortham, & Reifel, 2004). When teachers invest time in planning, children are less likely to sustain injury because they will find the activities interesting, engaging, and appropriately suited to their abilities.

Organization is also fundamental to effective planning. Teachers must review each step of an activity and the materials that will be used before they are presented to children. Forgetting

Teachers must be able to anticipate children's unpredictable behaviors.

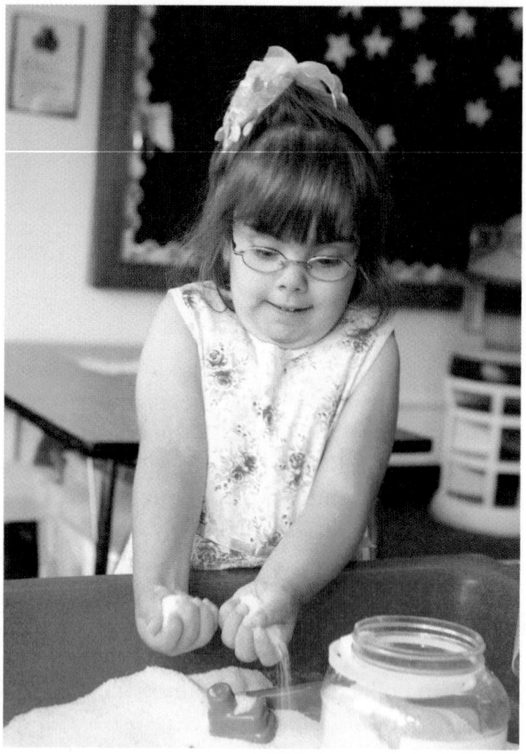

supplies or having any uncertainty about how to proceed greatly increases the risk of unintentional injury. Thinking a project through from start to finish allows the teacher to make adjustments and to substitute safer alternatives for those that may be potentially hazardous. Advanced planning also implies that a teacher is prepared for children's often unpredictable behaviors by developing appropriate safety guidelines. It also implies that adults always check the safety of play equipment (indoor and outdoor) before children begin to play.

An examination of accident records can also be useful during the planning stage. A pattern of similar injuries may suggest that teachers need to alter the way an activity is being conducted. For example, if it is noted that children are repeatedly hurt on the same piece of outdoor play equipment or during a similar classroom activity, a cause must be investigated immediately. Modifying safety guidelines, the amount of supervision, or the equipment itself may be necessary to protect children from any additional occurrences.

Establishing Safety Policies and Guidelines

Safety guidelines are statements about behavior that is considered acceptable as it relates to the welfare of an individual child, concern for group safety, and respect for shared property (Table 8–4). Too often, guidelines only inform children about what they should not be doing. They leave unclear what behaviors are valued or considered acceptable. However, when policies and guidelines are based on developmentally appropriate expectations, they can promote children's cooperative play and safe use of play equipment.

Teachers can encourage children's appropriate behavior by stating safety guidelines in positive terms, such as, "Slide down the slide on your bottom, feet first, so you can see where you are going." The only time the words "don't, "no" or "not" should be used is when a child's immediate safety is endangered. To be most effective, policies and guidelines should be stated clearly and in simple terms that young children are able to understand. When children are also given a brief explanation about why the guidelines are needed, they are more likely to comply.

There are no universal safety rules. Individual programs must develop their own policies and guidelines based on the:

- population of children being served
- type of program, equipment, and available space (indoor and outdoor)
- number of adults available for supervision
- nature of the activity involved

Programs serving very young children and children whose behavior is difficult to manage may need to establish limits that are more explicit and detailed. The type of equipment and whether it is being used in the classroom, outdoors, on large school playgrounds, or in home-based settings also influences how specific the guidelines must be to protect children from potential harm.

When safety guidelines are established, they must also be enforced consistently or children quickly learn that they have no meaning. However, a teacher must never threaten children or cause them to be afraid in order to gain compliance. Rather, children should be acknowledged when they

Table 8–4 Guidelines for the Safe Use of Play Equipment

Climbing Apparatus
Guidelines for Children
• Always hold on with both hands. • Keep hands to self. • Look carefully before jumping off equipment; be sure the area below is clear of objects and other children. • Be extra careful if equipment or shoes are wet from snow, rain or dew.
Guidelines for Adults
• Inspect equipment before children begin to play on it. Check for broken or worn parts and sharp edges; be sure the equipment is firmly anchored in the ground. • Be sure the depth of surface material under equipment is adequate and free of sharp stones, sticks, and toys. • Limit the number of children on climber at any one time. • Always have an adult in direct attendance when children are on the equipment. • Supervise children carefully if they are wearing slippery-soled shoes, sandals, long dresses or skirts, mittens, bulky coats, long scarves, or hooded jackets with drawstrings.
Swings
Guidelines for Children
• Wait until the swing comes to a full stop before getting on or off. • Always sit on the swing seat. • Only one child per swing at any time. • Only adults should push children. • Stay away from moving swings. • Hold on with both hands.
Guidelines for Adults
• Check equipment for safety, e.g., condition of chain/rope and seat, security of bolts or open-ended "S" rings (must be closed); also check ground beneath swings for sharp debris and adequate cushioning material. • Designate a "safe" area where children can wait their turn. • Plan for more than one adult to be in attendance at all times.

engage in appropriate safety behaviors. For example, a teacher might recognize a child's efforts by saying, "Carlos, I liked the way you rode your bike carefully around the other children who were playing," or "Tricia, you remembered to lay your scissors on the table before getting up to leave." Through repeated positive encouragement and adult modeling, children quickly learn to adopt appropriate safety behaviors.

Occasionally, a child will misuse play equipment or not follow directions. A gentle reminder is usually sufficient, but if this approach fails and the child continues to behave inappropriately the teacher must remove the child from the activity or area. A simple statement such as, "I cannot allow you to hit the other children," lets the child know this is not acceptable behavior. Permitting the child to return later to the same activity conveys confidence in the child's ability to follow expectations.

Rules never replace the need for adult supervision.

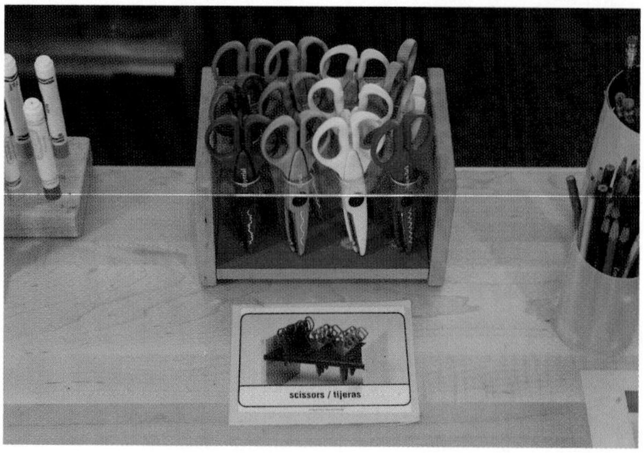

Safety policies and guidelines never replace the need for careful adult **supervision.** Young children tend to forget quickly and often need frequent reminders, especially when they are busy playing or excited about what they are doing. Guidelines should be realistic and allow children sufficient freedom to play within the boundaries of safety. If they are overly restrictive, children may be discouraged from exploring and experimenting. The need for extensive policies and guidelines can gradually be reduced as children become more dependable, aware of dangerous situations, and able to practice safe behaviors without reminders.

Quality Supervision

Although families and teachers have many responsibilities, their supervisory role is beyond question one of the most important (Morrongiello, Walpole, & McArthur, 2009; Petrass, Blitvich, & Finch, 2009). Children depend on responsible adult guidance for protection, as well as for learning appropriate safety behaviors. The younger children are, the more comprehensive and protective this supervision must be. As children gain additional motor coordination, cognitive skill, and experience in handling potentially dangerous situations, adult supervision can become less restrictive.

Quality supervision is also influenced by the nature of children's activities. For example, a cooking project that involves the use of a hot appliance must be supervised more carefully than painting at an easel or putting together a puzzle. Certain pieces of play equipment may also be more challenging for some children and, thus, require close teacher supervision at all times. The nature of an activity also affects the number of children a teacher can safely manage. One adult may be able to oversee several children building with hollow blocks or riding their bikes around a play yard, while a field trip to the fire station would require several adults to supervise.

⚠ **Caution: Never leave children unattended. If a teacher must leave an area, it should be supervised by another adult.**

Occasionally, there are children who are known to be physically aggressive or who engage in behaviors that could potentially bring harm to themselves or others (Berry & Schwebel, 2009). Teachers are legally and ethically obligated to supervise these children more closely and to protect the other children from harm. However, their responsibility goes beyond merely issuing a verbal warning for the child to stop—they must intervene and actually stop the child from continuing the dangerous activity even if it means physically removing the child from the area. Failure to intervene can result in legal action (Marotz, 2000). However, there are a number of additional approaches that teachers can use to effectively manage children's disruptive behaviors (Table 8–5).

An adequate number of adults must always be available to supervise children, especially in out-of-home programs. Minimal adult/child ratios for indoor and outdoor settings are generally established by individual state child care licensing regulations. NAEYC has recommended that there never be fewer than two adults present with any group of children. However, there are also considerable differences in adults' abilities to supervise and manage children's behavior. Some

supervision – *watching carefully over the behaviors and actions of children and others.*

Table 8–5 Teacher Checklist: Positive Strategies for Managing Children's Inappropriate Behavior

- Acknowledge and give attention for appropriate and desired behavior.
- Redirect the child's attention to some other activity.
- Provide the child with an opportunity for choices.
- Model the appropriate and desired behavior.
- Teach and encourage children to use problem-solving techniques.
- Ignore inappropriate behaviors, unless doing so is unsafe.
- Make changes in the environment to discourage inappropriate behavior.

teachers are less effective at controlling unruly or disruptive children. In these situations, it may be necessary to have more than the required number of adults available to safely monitor children's play.

Safety Education

One of the primary methods for avoiding unintentional injury is through safety education (Eichel & Goldman, 2009; Olsen, Hudson, & Thompson, 2008). Children can begin learning safe behaviors as soon as they understand the meanings of words. The earlier children learn about safety, the more naturally they will develop the attitudes and respect that lead to lifelong patterns of safe behavior.

A considerable amount of safety education occurs through **incidental learning** experiences and imitation of adult behaviors. Children who exhibit safe attitudes and practices can also serve as role models for other children. For example, several children may be jumping from the top of a platform instead of climbing down the ladder. Suddenly, one child yells, "You shouldn't be doing that. You could get hurt!" As a result, the children stop and begin using the ladder. Taking advantage of teachable moments can also prove to be an effective educational tool. For example, when children stand up on a swing or run with sharp objects in their hand, teachers can use these opportunities to explain why the behavior is not appropriate and help children to problem-solve safer alternatives. This form of learning is often most effective and meaningful for young children.

Safety education should also prepare children to cope with emergencies. Personal safety awareness and self-protection skills enable even young children to avoid potentially harmful situations, including being bullied on the playground. Children must know what to do in an emergency and how to get help. They should learn their home address and phone number as well as how to use the telephone. Older children can also begin to learn basic first aid skills.

Teachers should not overlook their own safety in their concern for children. It is easy for adults to be careless when they are under stress or have worked long, hard hours. Sometimes teachers take extraordinary risks in their zealous efforts to help children; however, it is at these times that even greater caution must be exercised. Planning scheduled breaks and maintaining healthful eating habits will improve a teacher's alertness and ability to make sound decisions.

Implementing Safety Practices

Much of the responsibility for maintaining a safe classroom environment belongs to teachers. Their knowledge of child development and daily contact with children gives them an advantageous position for identifying problem areas. However, safety must be a concern of all school personnel, including support staff such as classroom aides, cooks, receptionists, bus drivers, maintenance, and housekeeping personnel. Each person observes the environment differently, and may detect a safety hazard that had previously gone unnoticed.

---

incidental learning – *learning that occurs in addition to the primary intent or goals of instruction.*

Developmentally appropriate toys and learning materials are less likely to be a source of unintentional injury.

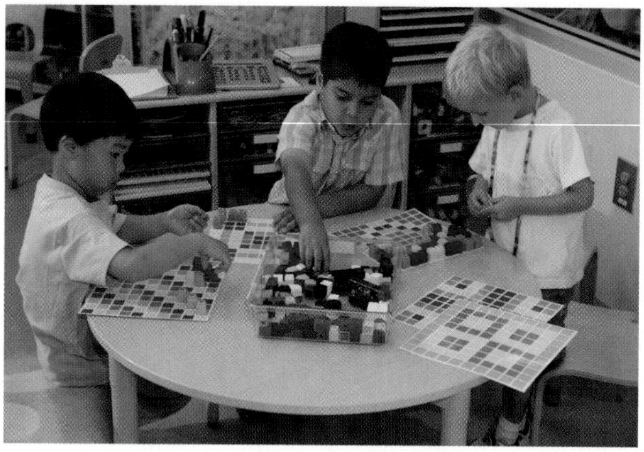

Safety must also be a continuous concern. Every time teachers rearrange the classroom, take children on a field trip or walk, add new play equipment, or plan a new activity, they must first stop to determine if there are any potential risks involved for the children or themselves. Differences in children's personalities and in group dynamics also make it necessary for teachers to continuously re-evaluate the safety guidelines currently in place. Extra precautions may be needed when children with special needs, chronic health problems, or behavior problems are present (Lee et al., 2008; Sinclair & Xiang, 2008). In these cases, it may be necessary for teachers to modify activities and/or equipment so they are safe and allow all children to participate.

Toys and Equipment

The majority of childhood deaths and injuries involving toys and play equipment are due to choking and improper use (Adu-Frimpong & Sorrell, 2009; U.S. CPSC, 2008c). Many of these injuries can be prevented by carefully selecting equipment and toys that are developmentally appropriate (Allen & Marotz, 2009; NAEYC, 2009). Children's interests, behavioral characteristics, and developmental abilities should serve as key considerations when choosing these items (Tables 8–6 and 8–7). Age warnings on product labels do not take into account children's individual differences and, therefore, are not always reliable. Some toys on the market meet only minimal U.S. safety standards and, thus, may pose a hazard for children whose skills are not as developmentally advanced. Injuries are also more likely to occur when children attempt to use educational materials and play equipment intended for older children, such as:

- toys that are too heavy for young children to lift
- rungs that are too large for small hands to grip securely
- steps that are too far apart
- climbing equipment and platforms that are too high above the ground
- balloons and small objects that can cause choking or suffocation (Figure 8–1)
- equipment that is unstable or not securely anchored

Table 8–6 Teacher Checklist: Guidelines for Selecting Safe Toys and Play Equipment

1. Consider children's age, interests, and developmental abilities (including problem-solving and reasoning skills); check manufacturers' labels carefully for recommendations and warnings.
2. Choose fabric items that are washable and labeled flame-retardant or nonflammable.
3. Look for high-quality construction; check durability, good design, stability, absence of sharp corners or wires, and strings shorter than 12 inches (30 cm).
4. Select toys that are made from nontoxic paints and materials.
5. Avoid toys and play materials with small pieces that a child could choke on.
6. Select toys and equipment that are appropriate for the amount of available play and storage space.
7. Avoid toys with electrical parts or those that are propelled through the air.
8. Choose play materials that children can use with minimal adult supervision.

Table 8–7 Examples of Appropriate Toy Choices for Infants, Toddlers, and Preschoolers

Infants	Toddlers	Preschoolers
nonbreakable mirrors	peg bench	puppets
cloth books	balls	dolls and doll houses
wooden cars	records	dress-up clothes
rattles	simple puzzles	simple art materials, e.g., crayons, markers, watercolors, play dough, blunt scissors
mobiles	large building blocks	
music boxes	wooden cars and trucks	
plastic telephone	dress-up clothes	
balls	bristle blocks	books, puzzles, lacing cards
toys that squeak	large wooden beads to string	simple musical instruments
blocks		cars, trucks, fire engines
nesting toys	cloth picture books	tricycle
teething ring	nesting cups	simple construction sets, e.g., Legos®, bristle blocks
washable, stuffed animals	pull and riding toys	play dishes, empty food containers
	plastic dishes, pots and pans	
	chunky crayons and paper	

The opposite may also occur. When play equipment has a singular purpose or is designed for younger children, older children may misuse it in their effort to create interest and challenge.

The amount of available classroom or play yard space will also influence choices. Equipment or toys that require a large area for their use will be a constant source of accidents if they are set up in spaces that are too small.

Quality is also very important to consider when purchasing toys. The materials and construction of toys and play equipment should be examined carefully and not purchased if they have:

- sharp wires, pins, or staples
- small pieces that could come loose, such as buttons, "eyes," screws, or magnets
- moving parts that can pinch fingers
- pieces that are smaller than 1.5 inches (3.75 cm) or balls less than 1.75 inches (4.4 cm) in diameter (for children under 3 years) (Figure 8–1)
- objects too heavy or large to be handled easily
- unstable bases or frames
- toxic paints or materials
- sharp metal edges or rough surfaces
- defective parts or construction that will not hold up under hard use
- strings or cords (longer than 12 inches) that could cause strangulation

Figure 8–1 Special devices can be purchased to determine the choking potential of small toys. Notice that the domino gets caught in the tube, but the die passes through the opening, which indicates a choking hazard.

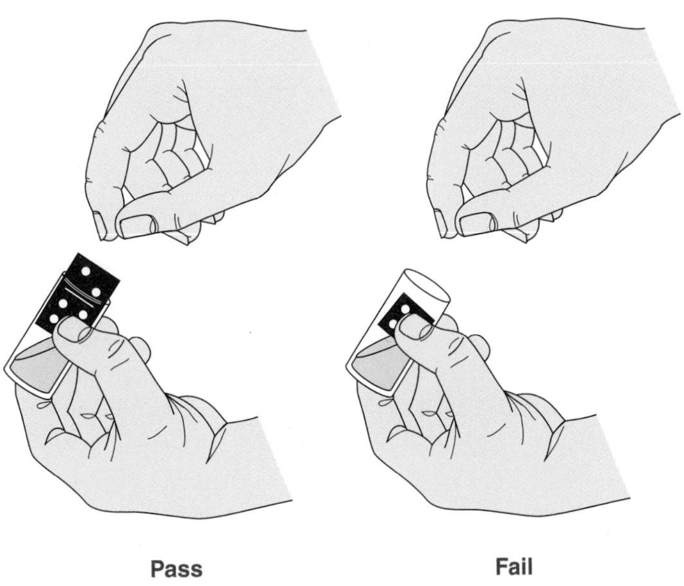

- parts that might cause electrical shock
- brittle plastic or glass parts that could easily break
- objects that become projectiles, such as darts, arrows, and air guns
- toys with small magnets that may become dislodged and swallowed

The amount of noise a toy produces should also be considered. Children's hearing is more sensitive than that of an adult's and can easily be damaged through repeated exposure to loud noises. Many children's toys emit sounds that exceed the 85- to 90-decibel threshold recommendation for safe hearing levels (ASHA, 2009). Adults should be cautious in purchasing toys that produce loud music and sounds in order to protect young children from early hearing loss.

Not all new toys and children's products are manufactured according to U.S. safety standards, especially those that are imported (Ofodile, 2009; Thibedeau, 2009). For this reason, extreme care should be taken when purchasing children's toys or equipment on the Internet. Hazard warnings and age recommendations may be absent, misrepresented, or not in compliance with statutory label requirements (U.S. Public Interest Research Groups, 2008). Occasionally, products that have been recalled because of hazardous features remain on store shelves, websites, and in garage sales. Families and teachers must take time to inspect items carefully and to make sure they meet all existing safety regulations.

Toys and play equipment should always be inspected on a daily basis, especially if they are used frequently by groups of children or are located outdoors where they are exposed to variable weather conditions. These items must be in good repair and free of splinters, rough edges, protruding bolts or nails, and broken or missing parts. Ropes on swings or ladders should be checked routinely and replaced if they begin to fray. Large equipment should be checked often to make sure it remains firmly anchored in the ground and that surface materials are of adequate depth and free of debris (see Chapter 7) (U.S. CPSC, 2008a).

Regularly scheduled maintenance ensures that toys and play equipment will remain in a safe condition. Equipment that is defective or otherwise unsafe for children to use should be removed promptly until it can be repaired. Items that cannot be repaired should be discarded.

Special precautions are necessary whenever large equipment or climbing structures are set up indoors. Positioning equipment in an open area away from furniture or other objects reduces children's risk for injury. Mats, foam pads, or large cushions placed around and under elevated structures will also help to protect children in the event of an unexpected fall. Guidelines for the safe use of indoor climbers should be demonstrated and explained carefully to children before they begin to play. The potential for injuries can be further reduced by positioning an adult next to the equipment so children's activities can be closely monitored.

Whenever new equipment, toys, or educational materials are introduced into a classroom or outdoor setting, safety is a prime concern. Policies and safety guidelines must be established and carefully explained to children. However, caution should be exercised not to establish too many restrictions that might otherwise dampen children's enthusiasm and interest. If several new items are being introduced into a classroom or outdoor environment, it is best to do this over a period of time so children are not overwhelmed by too many instructions.

Reflective Thoughts

Manufacturers are now labeling toys with age guidelines to help adults make safer choices. However, a child's chronological age does not necessarily reflect his/her developmental skills and abilities. What is meant by the term developmentally appropriate? How can a parent determine this? Why are age guidelines not always a reliable method for selecting children's toys and play equipment? Where can a parent or teacher locate information about product safety and recalls?

Children's furnishings, such as beds, cribs, playpens, strollers, carriers, and toys for infants and toddlers, must be selected with great care. As a consumer, it is important to remember that product design is most often responsible for childhood deaths. Strict manufacturing standards for children's furniture are continuously being updated by the U.S. Consumer Safety Product Commission (U.S. CSPC) and Canadian Consumer Corporate Affairs (Table 8–8). However, toys and furniture purchased at second-hand shops, garage sales, or on the Internet do not always meet these criteria and should be examined carefully. Information concerning children's toy and product recalls is available from the U.S. CSPC at (http://www.cpsc.gov) or from Safe Kids (http://www.safekids.org).

An adult should always be positioned in direct attendance when children are using playground equipment.

Classroom Activities

Safety must always be a priority when teachers select, plan, and implement children's learning activities. The potential for injury is present in nearly every activity, whether it is planned for indoor or outdoor settings (Obeng, 2009). Even small metal trucks or plastic golf clubs can cause harm when children use them incorrectly. Teachers should ask themselves the following questions when evaluating the safety of any activity:

- Is the activity age- and developmentally appropriate?
- What potential risks or hazards does this activity present?
- What special precautions do I need to take to make the activity safe?
- How should I respond if a child misuses the equipment or doesn't follow directions?
- What would I do in the event that a child is hurt while the activity is in progress?

After these questions have been given careful thought, teachers can begin to consider how to implement basic risk management principles—advanced planning, formulating safety guidelines, determining appropriate supervision, and providing safety education.

Materials selected for classroom activities should always be evaluated for safety risks before they are presented to children. Added safety precautions and more precise planning may be necessary whenever the following high-risk items are used as part of an activity:

- pointed or blunt objects such as scissors, knives, and woodworking tools (e.g., hammers, nails, saws)
- pipes, boards, blocks, or breakable objects
- electrical appliances (e.g., hot plates, radio, mixers)
- hot liquids (e.g., wax, syrup, oil, water)
- cosmetics or cleaning supplies

For added safety, projects that include any of these items should be set up in an area separated from other activities. Boundaries created with portable room dividers or a row of chairs improve a teacher's ability to closely monitor children's actions.

Restricting the number of children who can participate in an activity at any one time is another effective way to ensure safe conditions. Some activities may need to be limited to only one or two children so that a teacher can closely monitor their participation. Several methods can be used to control the number of children in a given area at any one time, including the use of color-coded necklaces or badges, or limiting the number of chairs at a table. These systems also help children determine if there is room to join the activity.

Table 8–8 Infant Equipment Safety Checklist

Back Carriers (not recommended for use before 4–5 months)	Yes	No
Carrier has restraining strap to secure child.		
Leg openings are small enough to prevent child from slipping out.		
Leg openings are large enough to prevent chafing.		
Frames have no pinch points in the folding mechanism.		
Carrier has padded covering over metal frame near baby's face.		
Bassinets and Cradles		
Bassinet/cradle has a sturdy bottom and a wide base for stability.		
Bassinet/cradle has smooth surfaces—no protruding staples or other hardware that could injure the baby.		
Legs have strong, effective locks to prevent folding while in use.		
Mattress is firm and fits snuggly against sides of bed.		
If cradle has slats, they must be spaced no more than 2 3/8 inches (6 cm) apart.		
Carrier Seats		
Carrier seat has a wide, sturdy base for stability.		
Carrier has nonskid feet to prevent slipping.		
Supporting devices lock securely.		
Carrier seat has crotch and waist strap.		
Buckle or strap is easy to use.		
Changing Tables		
Table has safety straps to prevent falls.		
Table has drawers or shelves that are easily accessible without leaving the baby unattended.		
Cribs		
Slats are spaced no more than 2 3/8 inches (6 cm) apart.		
No slats are missing or cracked.		
Mattress fits snugly—less than two fingers width between edge of mattress and crib side.		
Mattress support is securely attached to the head and footboards.		
Corner posts are no higher than 1/16 inch (1.0 mm) to prevent entanglement.		
There are no cutouts in head and footboards to allow head entrapment.		
Drop-side latches cannot be easily released by a baby.		
Drop-side latches securely hold sides in raised position.		
All screws or bolts that secure components of crib together are present and tight.		
Crib Toys		
Crib toys have no strings longer than 7 inches (178 cm) to prevent entanglement.		
Crib gym or other crib toy suspended over the crib must have devices that securely fasten to the crib to prevent it from being pulled into the crib.		
Components of toys are large enough not to be a choking hazard.		

Table 8–8 Infant Equipment Safety Checklist *(continued)*

Crib Toys *(continued)*	**Yes**	**No**
Crib mobiles should be removed when baby begins to get up on hands and knees or turns five months of age (whichever comes first).		
Gates and Enclosures		
Gate or enclosure has a straight top edge.		
Openings in gate are too small to entrap a child's head.		
Gate has a pressure bar or other fastener so it will resist forces exerted by a child.		
High Chairs		
High chair has restraining straps that are independent of the tray.		
High chair has a crotch strap; it must be used whenever baby sits in the high chair.		
Tray locks securely.		
Buckle on waist strap is easy to fasten and unfasten.		
High chair has a wide base for stability.		
High chair has caps or plugs on tubing that are firmly attached and cannot be pulled off and choke a child.		
If it is a folding high chair, it has an effective locking device.		
Hook-On Chairs		
Hook-on chair has a restraining strap to secure the child.		
Hook-on chair has a clamp that locks onto the table for added security.		
Hook-on chair has caps or plugs on tubing that are firmly attached and cannot be pulled off and become a choking hazard.		
Hook-on chair has a warning never to place chair where child can push off with feet.		
Pacifiers		
Pacifier has no ribbons, string, cord, or yarn attached.		
Shield is large enough and firm enough so it cannot fit in child's mouth.		
Guard or shield has ventilation holes so baby can breathe if shield does get into mouth.		
Pacifier nipple has no holes or tears that might cause it to break off in baby's mouth.		
Playpens		
Drop-side mesh playpen or mesh crib has warning label about never leaving a side in the down position.		
Playpens or travel cribs have top rails that automatically lock when lifted into the normal use position.		
There are no rotating hinges in the center of the top rail.		
Playpen mesh has small weave (less than 1/4–inch openings).		
Mesh has no tears or loose threads.		
Mesh is securely attached to top rail and floorplate.		
Wooden playpen has slats spaced no more than 2 3/8 inches (6 cm) apart.		
If staples are used in construction, they are firmly installed—none missing or loose.		

(continued)

Table 8–8 Infant Equipment Safety Checklist *(continued)*

Rattles/Squeeze Toys/Teethers	Yes	No
Rattles and teethers have handles too large to lodge in baby's throat.		
Rattles have sturdy construction that will not cause them to break apart in use.		
Squeeze toys do not contain a squeaker that could detach and choke a baby.		
Rattles with large, ball-like ends should not be given to babies.		
Strollers		
Stroller has a wide base to prevent tipping.		
Seat belt and crotch strap are securely attached to frame.		
Seat belt buckle is easy to fasten and unfasten.		
Brakes securely lock the wheel(s).		
Shopping basket low on the back and located directly over or in front of rear wheels.		
Leg holes can be closed when used in a carriage position.		
Toy Chests		
Toy chest has no latch to entrap child within the chest.		
Toy chest has a spring-loaded lid support that will not require periodic adjustment and will support the lid in any position to prevent lid slam.		
Chest has ventilation holes or spaces in front or sides, or under lid.		

Adapted from *The Safe Nursery*, U.S. Consumer Product Safety Commission (http://www.cpsc.gov/cpscpub/pubs/202.pdf).

When an activity involves the use of an electrical appliance, its condition should be inspected thoroughly and all safety guidelines be carefully explained to the children (Table 8–9). Equipment with frayed cords or plugs must never be used. Extension cords should also be avoided as they can cause children or adults to trip. Electrical appliances should always be placed on a table nearest the outlet and against the wall for safety. Never use appliances near a water source, including sinks, wet floors, or large pans of water, to avoid electrical shock.

Safety must also be a concern in the selection of children's art media and activities (OEHHA, 2009; U.S. CPSC, 1992). Children's art materials, such as paints, glue, crayons, and clay, must always be nontoxic. Liquids, such as paints and glue, should always be stored in plastic containers to prevent the danger of broken glass. Dried beans, peas, berries, or small beads, which children might stuff into their ears or nose or swallow, should not be used. Toothpicks and similar sharp objects are

Table 8–9 Teacher Checklist: Guidelines for the Safe Use of Electrical Appliances

Special precautions must be taken whenever an activity involves the use of an electrical appliance, including:

- placing the appliance on a low table or the floor so that children can easily reach.
- reminding children to stand back from appliances with moving parts to prevent their hair, fingers, or clothing from getting caught or burned.
- turning handles of pots and pans toward the back of the stove or hot plate.
- always detaching cords from the electrical outlet, never the appliance.
- promptly replacing safety caps in all electrical outlets when the project is finished.

also inappropriate. Fabric pieces, dried leaves or grasses, Styrofoam, packing materials, yarn, or ribbon provide safer alternatives for children's art creations. Additional safe substitutions for potentially hazardous art materials are provided in Table 8–10.

Special precautions should be taken in classrooms that have hard-surfaced or highly polished floors. Spilled water, paint, or other liquids and dry materials such as beans, rice, sawdust, flour, or cornmeal can cause floors to become extremely slippery and should be cleaned up promptly. Spreading newspapers or rugs out on the floor can help prevent children and adults from slipping and falling.

Children's art materials must be nontoxic.

Environments and activities that are safe for young children are also less stressful for adults. When classrooms and play yards are free of potential hazards, teachers can concentrate their attention on selecting safe activities, encouraging active play, and providing better supervision. Also, being familiar with a program's safety policies and procedures and having proper emergency training, such as first aid and CPR, can increase teacher confidence and lessen stress levels.

Table 8–10 Teacher Checklist: Safe Substitutes for Hazardous Art Materials

Avoid	Safe Substitutes
Powders—dry tempera paints, silica, pastels, chalk, dry clay, and cement can be inhaled. Use plaster of Paris only in well-ventilated area.	Use liquid tempera paints, water colors, crayons, and nontoxic markers.
Aerosol sprays—adhesives, fixatives, paints	Use brushes or spray bottles with water-based glues, paints, glue sticks, or paste.
Solvents and thinners—turpentine, rubber or epoxy cements, or those containing benzene, toluene, lacquers, or varnish. Avoid enamel-based paints that require solvents for cleanup.	Select water-based paints and glues, glue sticks, and inks.
Glitter (metal) can cause eye abrasion if rubbed.	Use salt crystals for a sparkling effect.
Permanent markers, dyes, and stains	Prepare natural vegetable dyes (e.g., beets, walnuts, onions) or commercial cold-water dyes.
Minerals and fibers—instant paper-maché (may contain lead and asbestos fibers); glazes, printing inks (colored newsprint, magazines), paints, especially enamels (may contain lead); builder's sand (may contain asbestos)	Use black-white newspaper and water-based glue to make paper-maché; choose water-based paints and inks; purchase special sandbox sand that has been cleaned.
Photographic chemicals	Use blueprint or colored paper set in the sun.

Additional precautions:

- Read ingredient labels carefully. Only choose materials that are labeled nontoxic. Older supplies may not comply with new federal labeling requirements and may contain harmful chemicals.
- Mix and prepare art materials (adults only) in a well-ventilated area away from children.
- Make sure children always wash their hands after working with art materials.
- Keep food and beverages away from areas where art activities are in progress.

Field Trips

Excursions away from a program's facilities can be an exciting part of children's educational experiences. However, field trips present added risks and liability concerns for schools and early education programs and, therefore, require that special precautions be taken.

Most importantly, programs should have written policies outlining procedures that must be followed when taking children on field trips. Families should be informed in advance of an outing and their written permission obtained for each excursion. On the day of the trip, a notice should be posted on the classroom door to remind families and staff of the children's destination and when they will be leaving and returning to the building. At least one adult accompanying the group should have first aid and CPR training. A first aid kit and cell phone should also be taken along. Tags can be pinned on children with the center's name and phone number. However, *do not* include the children's names: This enables strangers to call children by their name and makes it easier to lure them away from the group. A complete list of the children's emergency contact information, including families' telephone numbers, child's physician, and emergency service (e.g., ambulance, fire) numbers, should also be taken along. Procedures and safety policies should be carefully reviewed with the staff and children prior to the outing.

Special consideration should be given to the legal issues involved in conducting field trips (Child Care Law Center, 2005). Transporting children in the private vehicles of other families, staff, or volunteers, for example, can present serious liability concerns (see Chapter 7) (Marotz, 2000). There is almost no way of ensuring that a car is safe or an adult is a safe driver. Also, most states have laws that require appropriate safety restraints for each passenger, and not all vans and/or cars are properly equipped to provide these for multiple children (Thorenson et al., 2009). Therefore, it may be in a program's best interest not to use private vehicles for transporting children on field trips. Vehicles owned and operated by a program are usually required to carry liability insurance and are therefore preferable. However, neighborhood walks and public bus rides are always safe *alternatives.*

Pets

Pets can be a special classroom addition, but care must be taken so this is also a safe experience for both the children and animals. Children's allergies should be considered before pets visit or become permanent classroom residents. Also, precautions should be taken to be sure animals are free of disease and have current immunizations (if appropriate). Some animals, such as turtles, fish, and

Issues To Consider — Transportation Safety

Evening news anchors described the tragic death of a toddler forgotten in a child-care van. The child had been picked up from his home early that morning, placed in a car safety seat, and transported to a local child care center. However, personnel did not realize the child was missing from the center until the end of the day when it was time for the children to return home. The unconscious toddler was found still strapped in his car seat. Temperatures outside of the van had climbed into the 90s during the day. Despite emergency medical efforts, heat stroke claimed the child's life.

- What steps should have been taken to prevent this tragedy?
- What policies and procedures would keep this unfortunate event from being repeated?
- What measures should be taken to ensure children's safety during transportation? In private vehicles? In center vans? In school buses?

birds, are known carriers of illnesses that are communicable to humans, such as salmonella, and are therefore not appropriate to include in the classroom (Mink & Yeh, 2009). Instructions for the animal's care should be posted to serve as both a guideline and reminder to staff. Precautions must also be taken to protect pets from curious and overly exuberant children who may unknowingly cause harm or injury to the animal. Children must always wash their hands carefully after handling or petting animals in the classroom, zoo, or petting farm because animals are often carriers of infectious illnesses (MMWR, 2007).

Personal Safety

Not all teachers work in classrooms. Some organizations, such as Head Start and Parents as Teachers, employ educators and other professionals to work with children and families in their homes. Opportunities to work independently and one-on-one with clients are attractive options for many teachers. However, working alone and in neighborhoods that may be unfamiliar or are noted for high crime rates may present additional risks and concerns. Organizations should establish policies and procedures in advance to protect the safety of personnel who work in these conditions. Individuals can also take steps to ensure their own personal safety (Table 8–11).

Legal Implications

Safety issues have always generated a great deal of concern for teachers, school administrators, and program directors. However, recent lawsuits, legal decisions, and increased public awareness have contributed to a greater sense of uneasiness, scrutiny, and need for stricter regulation. Families want and have a right to be assured that facilities are safe. Families also expect schools and early education programs to safeguard their children's well-being during the hours they spend away from home.

Teachers should be familiar with the legal issues and responsibilities that affect their positions for several reasons. First, by law, teachers are expected to provide for children's safety. Second, the incidence of injury and accidents is known to be especially high among young children. Their

Table 8–11 Teacher Checklist: Personal Safety Practices for the Home Visitor

- Check with your organization to learn about policies and/or procedures that home visitors are expected to follow.
- Become familiar with the neighborhood; visit the area and address beforehand. Learn about the community and families living there.
- Talk with local police for information about the area and to determine if your concerns or fears are warranted.
- Let a supervisor know when you leave and where you are heading; give them your planned travel route and be sure to follow it.
- Take along a cell phone or pager; carry a whistle.
- Check in frequently with your supervisor; give them your location and share any immediate safety concerns.
- Schedule visits during the daytime. If evening visits are necessary, go in teams.
- Be alert and aware of your surroundings. Listen for unusual sounds, watch for suspicious people or activity, and leave if you feel uncomfortable.
- Know where to get help if something should happen.
- Complete a personal safety defense class to develop protective techniques and improve self-confidence.

immature developmental skills and unpredictable behavior always necessitates careful safety management.

The most important legal concerns for teachers center on the issues of liability (Moswela, 2008; Barrios, Jones, & Gallagher, 2007). Teachers are expected to have special training and to possess unique knowledge, skills, and experience. The term **liability** refers to the legal obligations and professional responsibilities, especially those related to safety, that are accepted by administrators and teachers when they agree to work with children. Failure to perform these duties in a reasonable and acceptable manner is considered **negligence**.

Negligence involves a teacher's failure to prevent an avoidable injury. For legal purposes, negligent acts are generally divided into two categories based on the circumstances and resulting damages or injuries. The first category involves situations in which a teacher does not take appropriate precautionary measures to protect children from harm. In this case, standards for establishing negligence would be based on whether a teacher with similar training and experience would have behaved in a similar manner in the same situation. If the teacher in question failed to uphold these standards, then his or her actions would be considered negligent. Examples of this form of negligence include a failure to provide appropriate or adequate supervision, permitting children to play on equipment known to be defective or in need of repair, or allowing children to engage in harmful activities such as throwing rocks or standing on top of elevated play equipment.

A second category of negligent acts includes situations in which the teacher's actions or decisions actually place children at risk. An example of this type of negligence might involve a teacher making arrangements to have children transported in private vehicles that are not insured, or planning classroom activities in which children are handling toxic chemicals or unsafe electrical equipment without proper protection or supervision.

Prevention is always the best method for ensuring children's safety and avoiding unpleasant legal problems and lawsuits. However, teachers, administrators, and programs can take additional measures to protect themselves (Marotz, 2000). It is advisable for teachers and administrators to obtain personal liability insurance unless they are already covered by their program's policy (Child Care Law Center, 2004). Liability insurance can be purchased from most private insurance companies and through the NAEYC. Accident insurance, purchased on individual children who are enrolled, also affords programs necessary protection.

Administrators and teachers should never hesitate to seek legal counsel on issues related to their roles and/or professional responsibilities. Programs may also want to seek legal counsel when developing policies to make certain they are consistent with the laws. Including a member of the legal profession on a board of directors or advisory council can provide a program with ready access to legal advice.

Teachers should always examine job descriptions carefully and be familiar with employer expectations before accepting a new position. This step helps to ensure that they have the appropriate qualifications and training necessary to perform all required duties. For example, if a teacher will be responsible for administering first aid to injured children, she or he should have completed basic first aid and CPR training prior to beginning employment. It is also imperative for administrators to screen potential candidates for teaching positions through careful interviewing and follow-up contacts with the individual's references. Background checks also help identify those with a history of criminal behavior. Although these steps may seem time-consuming, they will help to protect a program from hiring unqualified personnel.

Accurately maintained injury reports also provide added legal protection (Figure 8–2). Information included in these reports can be used in court as evidence in the event that a teacher or program is charged with negligence. An individual report should be completed each time a child

---

liability – *legal responsibility or obligation for one's actions owed to another individual.*
negligence – *failure to practice or perform one's duties according to certain standards; carelessness.*

Figure 8–2 **Sample Individual Injury Report Form.**

INDIVIDUAL INJURY REPORT FORM

Child's Name ______________________________ Date of Injury ______________

Parent ______________________________ Time ________ AM ___ PM ___

Address ______________________________ Parent notified ________ AM ___ PM ___

Description of injuries ____

____

First aid or emergency treatment administered: ______________________________

____

Was a doctor consulted? _____ Doctor's name and address ______________

Doctor's diagnosis ______________________________ ______

____

Number of days child was absent as a result of injury ______________________

Adult in charge when injury occurred ______________________________

Description of activity, location in facility and circumstances, immediately before and at the time of the injury

____

____

____

____

____

____

____

Report prepared by (full name): ______________________ Date ______________

is injured, regardless of how minor or unimportant the injury may seem at the time. This step is important because the outcome of some injuries may not be immediately apparent. Complications can sometimes develop months or years later, making it difficult for a teacher to recall a particular incident or injury in detail sufficient to defend themselves. Injury reports should be completed by the teacher who witnessed the incident and administered first aid treatment. The information should be recorded in clear, precise, and descriptive language. It should describe the nature and location of the injury in detail, how it occurred, the names of any witnesses, and what treatment was administered. Injury records provide a composite picture of the event and are also useful for detecting accident patterns. Because these records are considered legal documents, they should be kept on file for a minimum of 5 years.

Focus On Families — Sun Safety

Exposure to too much sun over a lifetime can have harmful health consequences, including skin cancer, premature aging of the skin, eye damage, and interference with the immune system's ability to function. Children's skin—even that of dark-skinned children—is especially sensitive to the sun's ultraviolet (UV) rays and tends to burn quickly and easily. Steps should always be taken to protect children's skin and minimize their sun exposure. Adults should also follow these same precautions.

- Avoid going outdoors between 10 a.m. and 4 p.m., when the sun's rays are the strongest and most damaging.
- Encourage children to play in the shade whenever possible. Rule of thumb—you shouldn't be able to see their shadow!
- Dress in protective clothing that is cool and loose fitting. Keep as much skin surface covered as possible. Children should be discouraged from wearing tank or halter tops. A hat with a brim provides shade protection for the face and eyes.
- Apply sunscreen with a sun protection factor (SPF) of at least 15 or higher 30 minutes before going outdoors. Reapply every 2 hours or more often if children are swimming, perspiring, or drying themselves with a towel. Sunburn occurs more quickly when the skin is wet.
- Wear sunglasses to protect eyes from UV radiation. Light-colored eyes (blue, gray) are particularly sensitive to sunlight and are more susceptible to damage.
- Become a "SunWise" school by registering at http://www.epa.gov/sunwise/becoming.html.

Classroom Corner — Teacher Activities

Fire Safety...

(Grades 3–5) (National Health Education Standards 1.5.3 and 1.5.4)

Concept: It is important that children know how to get out of a building in the event of a fire.

Learning Objectives

- Children will identify the three components of the fire triangle.
- Children will name potential fire safety hazards in homes.
- Children will conduct a home fire safety inspection.

Supplies

- A home fire safety checklist for each child. These can be downloaded from several online sites, including: http://www.sparky.org/PDF/SparkyChecklist.pdf

Learning Activities

- Have children read one of the following books and discuss it as a class.
  - *The Case of the Blazing Sun*, by John Erickson
  - *Fire Safety* by Lucia Raatma
  - *Firefighting Behind the Scenes* by Maria Ruth

(*continued*)

Classroom Corner **Teacher Activities** *(continued)*

- Introduce the fire triangle concept (heat, fuel, oxygen). Ask the children to provide examples for each component (ex., fuel/newspaper, heat/matches). Have the class develop a bulletin board display illustrating the fire triangle and the children's examples of common household sources.
- Provide each child with a copy of the home fire safety checklist. Instruct children to conduct a room-by-room inspection of their own home for potential fire hazards. Discuss the children's findings as a group.
- Have each child write a fire safety tip on a small piece of paper and place all suggestions in a container. Have the children take turns drawing a suggestion from the box and reading it aloud. Discuss each tip as a group. Alternatively, have the children take digital pictures of potential home fire hazards and upload them to a designated website. The teacher can then project individual photographs on a large screen, ask children to identify the potential hazards, and discuss a solution to correct each problem.

Evaluation

- Children will name the three fire triangle components and give an example of each.
- Children will conduct a home fire safety inspection.
- Children will identify at least three potential fire safety hazards in their homes.

Additional lesson plans for grades Pre K–2 are available on the premium website for this book.

Summary

- Unintentional injuries are the leading cause of death among young children.
- Limited motor, problem-solving, and anticipatory skills increase young children's risk of experiencing unintentional injury.
- The incidence of unintentional injury among children can be reduced when adults adhere to the principles of risk management; advanced planning; establishing safety policies and guidelines; providing appropriate supervision; and conducting safety education.
- Teachers must continuously be aware of safety in children's environments, from the toys and equipment presented to all planned activities including field trips.
- Teachers have a professional and moral obligation to take the precautionary measures necessary to protect children's well-being. Failure to uphold this responsibility could potentially result in negligence charges.

Terms to Know

unintentional injury *p. 212*
risk management *p. 212*
supervision *p. 216*
incidental learning *p. 217*
liability *p. 228*
negligence *p. 228*

Chapter Review

A. By Yourself

1. Match the item in **Column I** with those in **Column II.**

Column I	Column II
1. basic element of advanced planning	a. foresight
2. legal responsibility for children's safety	b. supervision
3. the ability to anticipate	c. education
4. limits that define safe behavior	d. planning
5. failure to protect children's safety	e. safety guidelines
6. watching over children's behavior	f. safe
7. environments free of hazards	g. negligence
8. the process of learning safe behavior	h. prevention
9. a key factor in injury prevention	i. liability
10. measures taken to ensure children's safety	j. organization

2. Fill in the blanks with one of the words listed below:

removed	unintentional injury	anticipate
legal	responsible	risk management principles
safety education	safety	inspected

A. The leading cause of death among young children is ____________.
B. Adults must be able to ____________ children's actions as part of advanced planning.
C. Families expect teachers to be ____________ for their child's safety.
D. Basic ____________ ____________ include advanced planning, establishing safety policies and guidelines, appropriate supervision, and safety education.
E. Injury records are considered ____________ documents.
F. Children's ______ must be a continuous teacher concern and responsibility.
G. Toys and play equipment should be ____________ daily.
H. A prime method for reducing the incidence of unintentional injuries can be achieved through ____________ ____________.

B. As a Group

1. Discuss why safety policies and guidelines must not be considered a replacement for adult supervision.
2. What actions must a teacher take if he or she notices that a piece of playground equipment is broken?
3. Discuss why infants and toddlers experience the highest rate of unintentional injury.
4. What preparations do teachers need to make before taking children on a field trip?
5. Divide into two groups and debate the advantages and disadvantages of taking children on field trips.

Case Study

Teachers at the Wee Ones Child Care Center, located in an inner-city neighborhood, know that field trips can be an important part of the curriculum. They have discussed organizing a trip to the local city zoo as part of a learning unit on animals. However, the teachers also realize the challenges involved in taking a group of twenty 3- and 4-year-olds on such an excursion, but believe the experience is especially valuable for these children. Since the zoo is located on the other side of town, the teachers have made arrangements to ride the city bus.

1. What criteria can teachers use to determine if a field trip is a worthwhile experience?
2. What types of planning are necessary to ensure a safe and successful field trip?
3. What are the advantages/disadvantages of using public transportation?
4. What safety precautions must teachers take before leaving the premises?
5. How might visiting a site ahead of time help teachers better plan for a field trip?
6. What problems should teachers anticipate when taking children on field trips?
7. What information should families be given?
8. Are off-premises field trips typically covered by school liability insurance policies?

Application Activities

1. Role-play how a teacher might handle a child who is not riding a tricycle in a safe manner.
2. Visit an early childhood program play yard or a public playground. Select one piece of play equipment and observe children playing on it for at least 15 minutes. Make a list of observed or anticipated dangers that could result from improper use. Prepare a set of developmentally appropriate guidelines for children's safe use of the equipment.
3. You have been asked to purchase outdoor play equipment for a new child development center. List the safety features you would look for when making your selections. Conduct an Internet search for companies that offer playground equipment and look over their options. Use this information to select basic outdoor equipment for the play yard of a small early childhood center that has three classes of twenty children each and a budget of $8,000. Be sure to include some pieces that are accessible to all children.
4. Prepare a room-by-room home safety checklist for families of (a) infants, (b) toddlers, and (c) preschool-age children.
5. Survey your own program, a nearby early childhood center, or an elementary school. Develop a building security plan based on the safety principles outlined in this chapter.

Helpful Web Resources

American Society for Testing and Materials	http://www.astm.org
Canadian Institute of Child Health	http://www.cich.ca
Canadian Safety Council	http://www.safety-council.org
Child Care Law Center	http://www.childcarelaw.org
Injury Control Resource Information Network	http://www.injurycontrol.com

National Center for Injury Prevention and Control	http://www.cdc.gov/ncipc
National Program for Playground Safety	http://www.uni.edu/playground
Safety Link	http://www.safetylink.com
U.S. Consumer Product Safety Commission	http://www.cpsc.gov

Videos

The following organizations offer health and safety videos appropriate for early childhood and elementary school programs. Some videos can be previewed online.

- Black Mountain Safety & Health
  - http://www.safety-video-bmsh.com/
  - 1-877-280-9447
- NAEYC
  - http://www.naeyc.org/store
  - 1-800-424-2460
- National Program for Playground Safety
  - http://www.uni.edu/playground
  - 1-800-554-PLAY
- OSHA School and Childcare Safety videos
  - http://www.oshasafetyvideos.com (click on Industry > Schools)
  - 1-888-443-1600

You are just a click away from additional health, safety, and nutrition resources! Go to www.CengageBrain.com to access this text's Education CourseMate website, where you'll find:

- classroom injury record form
- individual child injury report form
- glossary flashcards, activities, tutorial quizzes, videos, web links, and more

References

Adu-Frimpong, J., & Sorrell, J. (2009). Magnetic toys: The emerging problem in pediatric ingestions, *Pediatric Emergency Care*, 25(1), 42–43.

Allen, K. E., & Marotz, L. (2009). *Developmental profiles: Pre-birth through twelve*. Belmont, CA: Wadsworth.

Alkon, A., Bernzweig, J., To, K., Wolff, M., & Mackie, J. (2009). Child care health consultation improves health and safety policies and practices, *Academic Pediatrics*, 9(5), 366–370.

American Speech-Language-Hearing Association. (ASHA). (2009). *Noisy toys can damage your hearing*. Accessed on November 14, 2009, from http://www.asha.org/about/news/tipsheets/Watch-Out-for-Noisy-Toys.htm.

Barrios, L., Jones, S., & Gallagher, S. (2007). Legal liability: The consequences of school injury, *Journal of School Health*, 77(5), 273–279.

Berk, L. (2008). *Child development*. (8th ed.). Boston, MA: Allyn & Bacon.

Berry, J., & Schwebel, D. (2009). Configural approaches to temperament assessment: Implications for predicting risk of unintentional injury in children, *Journal of Personality*, 77(5), 1381–1410.

Borse, N., Gilchrist, J., Dellinger, A., Rudd, R., Ballesteros, M., & Sleet, D. (2009). Unintentional childhood injuries in the United States: Key findings from the CDC childhood injury report, *Journal of Safety Research*, 40(1), 71–74.

Centers for Disease Control and Prevention (CDC). (2008). *Childhood Injury Report*. Accessed on November 13, 2009 from http://www.cdc.gov/safechild/child_injury_data.htm.

CDC. (2006). Centers for Disease Control and Prevention Web-based Injury Statistics Query and Reporting System (WISQARS). Unintentional Injuries Deaths, Ages, 1–4 and 5–9. Accessed on November 15, 2009, from http://webappa.cdc.gov/cgi-bin/broker.exe.

Child Care Law Center. (2004). Liability insurance for family child care providers. Accessed on May 10, 2010 from, http://www.childcarelaw.org/docs/qanda-liabilityandinsurance.pdf.

Child Care Law Center. (2005). *Legal issues for family child care providers: Insuring your program: Vehicle and property insurance.* Accessed on May 10, 2010 from http://www.childcarelaw.org/docs/insuringyourprogramvehicleand-property.pdf.

Children's Safety Network. (2009). *Playground safety.* Accessed on May 10, 2010 from http://www.childrenssafetynet-work.org/topics/showtopic.asp?pkTopicID=32.

Eberl, R., Schalamon, J., Singer, G., Ainoedhofer, H., Petnehazy, T., & Hoellwarth, M. (2009). Analysis of 347 kindergarten-related injuries, *European Journal of Pediatrics*, 168(2), 163–166.

Eichel, J., & Goldman, L. (2009). Safety makes sense: A program to prevent unintentional injuries in New York City Public Schools, *Journal of School Health*, 71(5), 180–183.

Frost, J., Wortham, S., & Reifel, S. (2004). *Play and child development.* Upper Saddle River, NJ: Merrill Prentice Hall.

Kuo, C. (2009). The factors of design on playing equipment in young children schools, *Education*, 129(4), 755–769.

Lee, L., Harrington, R., Chang, J., & Connors, S. (2008). Increased risk of injury in children with developmental disabilities, *Research in Developmental Disabilities*, 29(3), 247–255.

Loder, R. (2008). The demographics of playground equipment injuries in children, *Journal of Pediatric Surgery*, 43(4), 691–699.

Mao, S., McKenzie, L., Xiang, H., & Smith, G. (2009). Injuries associated with bathtubs and showers among children in the United States, *Pediatrics,* 124(2), 541–547.

Marotz, L. R. (2000). Childhood and classroom injuries. (2000). In, J. L. Frost (Ed.), *Children and injuries.* Tucson, AZ: Lawyers & Judges Publishing Co.

Mink, C., & Yeh, S. (2009). Infections in child-care facilities and schools, *Pediatrics in Review*, 30(7), 259–269.

Morbidity and Mortality Weekly Report (MMWR). (2007). Guidelines for animals in school settings. Accessed on November 14, 2009, from http://www.cdc.gov/mmwr/preview/mmwrhtml/rr5605a5.htm.

Morrongiello, B., Walpole, B., & McArthur, B. (2009). Young children's risk of unintentional injury: A comparison of mothers' and fathers' supervision beliefs and reported practices, *Journal of Pediatric Psychology*, 34, 1063–1068.

Moswela, B. (2008). Knowledge of educational law: An imperative to the teacher's practice, *International Journal of Lifelong Education*, 27(1), 93–105.

National Association for the Education of Young Children (NAEYC). (2009). *Good toys for young children.* Accessed on November 14, 2009, from http://www.naeyc.org/files/naeyc/file/ecprofessional/Good%20Toys%20for%20Young%20Children.pdf.

National Institute of Building Sciences, Whole Building Design Guide (WBDG). (2009). Child care. Accessed on November 14, 2009, from http://www.wbdg.org/design/childcare.php.

Obeng, C. (2009). Injuries in preschool classrooms, *Health Education*, 109(5), 414–423.

Office of Environmental Health Hazard Assessment (OEHHA). (2009). *Guidelines for the safe use of art and craft materials* (updated October 2009). Accessed on November 14, 2009 from http://www.oehha.ca.gov/education/art/artguide.html.

Ofodile, U. (2009). Import (toy) safety, consumer protection, and the WTO agreement on technical barriers to trade: Prospects, progress and problems, *International Journal of Private Law*, 2(2), 163–184.

Olsen, H., Hudson, S., & Thompson, D. (2008). Developing a playground injury prevention plan, J*ournal of School Nursing*, 24(3), 131–137.

Petrass, L., Blitvich, J., & Finch, C. (2009). Parent/caregiver supervision and child injury: A systematic review of critical dimensions for understanding this relationship, *Family & Community Health*, 32(2), 123–135.

Rowe, R., & Maughan, B. (2009). The role of risk-taking and errors in children's liability to unintentional injury, *Accident Analysis & Prevention*, 41(4), 670–675.

Sinclair, S., & Xiang, H. (2008). Injuries among children with different types of disabilities, *American Journal of Public Health*, 98(8), 1510–1516.

Staempfli, M. (2009). Reintroducing adventure into children's outdoor play environments, *Environment & Behavior*, 41(2), 268–280.

Thibedeau, H. (2009). Safer toys coming, but not with Santa Claus, *Canadian Medical Association Journal*, 181(6-7), e111–e112.

Thorenson, S., Myers, L., Goss, C., & DiGuiseppi, C. (2009). Effects of a booster seat education and distribution program in child care centers on child restraint use among children aged 4 to 8 years, *Archives of Pediatric & Adolescent Medicine*, 163(3), 261– 267.

U.S. Access Board. (2005). *Guide to ADA accessibility guidelines for play areas.* Accessed on November 14, 2009, from http://www.access-board.gov/play/guide/intro.htm.

U.S. Consumer Product Safety Commission (CPSC). (2008a). *Handbook of public playground safety.* Accessed on May 10, 2010 from, www.cpsc.gov/cpscpub/pubs/325.pdf.

U.S. CPSC. (2008b). *Childproofing your home – 12 safety devices to protect your children.* Accessed on November 14, 2009, from http://www.cpsc.gov/CPSCPUB/PUBS/252.pdf.

U.S. CPSC. (2008c). *Voluntary standards.* Accessed on November 14, 2009, from http://www.cpsc.gov/volstd/toys/toys.html.

U.S. CPSC. (1992). Law requires review and labeling of art materials including children's art and drawing products. Accessed on November 14, 2009, from http://www.cpsc.gov/cpscpub/pubs/5016.html.

U.S. CPSC. *The safe nursery.* Accessed on November 14, 2009, from http://www.cpsc.gov/cpscpub/pubs/202.pdf.

U.S. Public Interest Research Groups. (2008). *Trouble in toyland: The 23rd annual survey of toy safety.* Accessed on November 14, 2009, from http://www.uspirg.org/issues/toy- safety.

Vollman, D., Witsaman, R., Comstock, D., & Smith, G. (2009). Epidemiology of playground equipment-related injuries to children in the United States, 1996-2005, *Clinical Pediatrics* (Phila.), 48(1), 66–71.

Walsh, P. (2008). Planning for play in a playground, *Exchange*, 30(5), 88–92.

CHAPTER

9

Management of Injuries and Acute Illness

NAEYC Standards *Chapter Links*

- **#1 a and b:** Promoting child development and learning
- **#2 a and b:** Building family and community relationships
- **#3 a, c and d:** Observing, documenting, and assessing to support young children and families
- **#3 c:** Knowing about and using observation, documentation, and other assessment tools and approaches.
- **#6 b:** Becoming a professional

Learning Objectives

After studying this chapter, you should be able to:

- Describe how emergency care and first aid differ.
- Name six life-threatening conditions and demonstrate the emergency treatment for each.
- Identify six non-life-threatening conditions and describe the first aid treatment for each.

Prevention of unintentional childhood injuries is a major responsibility of families and teachers (Pickett, Nichol, & Ehiri, 2010; Gaines & Schwebel, 2009). Schools can best achieve this goal by creating safe environments, providing health/safety education, and establishing proper procedures for handling emergencies (Marotz, 2000).

Programs often overlook the need to develop emergency policies and plans until an unexpected event occurs. This can result in unnecessary confusion, ineffective response, and ultimately place children and adults at risk. Advanced preparation and training ensures that staff will be ready to respond to emergencies in a prompt and knowledgeable manner (Figure 9–1). A school's comprehensive emergency response plan should address:

- training of personnel in infant/child CPR and basic first aid techniques
- designating staff who are responsible for administering emergency care
- obtaining contact information and notarized permission that authorizes emergency medical treatment from each child's parent/guardian. (Note: Most medical facilities will not treat minor children without the notarized consent of their legal parent or guardian.)
- having an accessible telephone

- posting emergency telephone numbers [e.g., families and their designated emergency contacts, hospital emergency room, fire department, emergency medical technicians (EMTs), law enforcement, local poison control] next to the telephone
- making arrangements for emergency transportation
- providing a fully equipped first aid kit that is stored in a central location (Table 9–1). Modified kits can be prepared for individual classrooms and for taking along on field trips (Table 9–2).

Copies of a program's emergency response plans should be made available to families and reviewed on a regular basis with staff members.

Figure 9–1 Planning guidelines for serious injury and emergency illness.

Serious Injury and Illness Plan

1. **Remain with the child at all times.** Keep calm and reassure the child that you are there to help. Your presence can be a comfort to the child, especially when faced with unfamiliar surroundings and discomfort. You can also provide valuable information about events preceding and following the injury/illness, symptoms the child exhibited, etc.
2. **Do not** move a child with serious injury unless there is immediate danger from additional harm, such as fire or electrical shock.
3. Begin appropriate emergency care procedures immediately. Meanwhile, send for help. Have another adult or child alert the person designated to handle such emergencies in your center.
4. **Do not** give food, fluids, or medications unless specifically ordered by the child's physician or Poison Control Center.
5. Call for emergency medical assistance if in doubt about the severity of the situation. Don't attempt to handle difficult situations by yourself. A delay in contacting emergency authorities could make the difference in saving a child's life. If you are alone, have a child dial the emergency number in your community (commonly 911).
6. If the child is transported to a medical facility before parents arrive, a teacher should accompany, and remain with the child until parents arrive.
7. Contact the child's family. Inform them of the nature of the illness/injury and the child's general condition. If the child's condition is not life-threatening, discuss plans for follow-up care, e.g., contacting the child's physician, transporting the child to a medical facility. If the family cannot be reached, call the child's emergency contact person or physician.
8. Record all information concerning serious injury/illness on appropriate forms within 24 hours; place in the child's folder and provide the family with a copy. If required, notify local licensing authorities.

Table 9–1 Basic First Aid Supplies for Schools

adhesive tape—1/2- and 1-inch widths	safety pins
antibacterial soap or cleanser	scissors—blunt tipped
bandages—assorted sizes	soap—preferably liquid
blanket	spirits of ammonia
bulb syringe	SAM rolled splints (small)
thermometers—2	cotton balls
flashlight and extra batteries	plastic bags (sealable)
gauze pads—sterile, 2×2s, 4×4s	tongue blades
instant cold packs or plastic bags for ice cubes	towels—large and small
needle—(sewing type)	triangular bandages for slings
roller gauze—1- and 2-inch widths; stretch	tweezers
latex or vinyl gloves	first aid book or reference cards
pen and small notepad	emergency telephone numbers
saline eye wash solution	

Table 9–2 Modified First Aid Kits

For in the Classroom	To Take on Field Trips
(Assemble in a child's plastic lunchbox.)	(Assemble in a "fanny pack.")
antibacterial soap	alcohol wipes or antibacterial soap
assorted gauze pads	adhesive bandages (non-latex)
adhesive bandages (non-latex)	cotton balls
cotton balls	latex or vinyl gloves
flashlight and batteries	plastic bags
instant ice packs	safety pins
non-allergenic tape	tweezers
plastic bags	emergency telephone numbers
safety pins	
saline contact solution	
scissors	
thermometer	
tweezers	
emergency telephone numbers	

Special attention must be given to addressing universal precautions when formulating a program's emergency policies and procedures. Universal precautions are special infection-control guidelines that have been developed to prevent the spread of diseases transmitted via blood and other body fluids, such as hepatitis B and C, and AIDS/HIV. (See Chapter 5.) These guidelines include several areas of precaution—barrier protection (including the use of latex/vinyl gloves and hand washing), environmental disinfection, and proper disposal of contaminated materials—that must be strictly followed when caring for children's injuries.

Teachers should know the fundamentals of emergency and first aid care.

Despite careful planning and supervision, childhood injuries and illnesses are inevitable. For this reason, it is important that teachers learn the fundamentals of emergency care and first aid (Table 9–3). Appropriate training and continued participation in refresher courses enable personnel to handle emergencies with skill and confidence (Obeng, 2009; Barrios, Jones, & Gallagher, 2007).

Teachers are responsible for administering initial and urgent care to children who are seriously injured or acutely ill. These measures are considered to be temporary and aimed at saving lives, reducing pain and discomfort, and preventing complications and additional injury. Once the child has been stabilized, responsibility for obtaining further medical treatment can then be transferred to the child's family (Marotz, 2000).

Table 9–3 The ABCs for Assessing Emergencies

A—Airway	Make sure the air passageway is open and clear. Roll the infant or child onto his/her back. Tilt the head back by placing your hand on the child's forehead and gently push downward (unless back or neck injuries are suspected). At the same time, place the fingers of your other hand under the child's chin and lift it upward.
B—Breathing	Watch for the child's chest to move up and down. Feel and listen for air to escape from the lungs with your ear.
C—Circulation	Note the child's skin color (especially around the lips and nail beds), and if the child is coughing or moving.

Emergency Care vs. First Aid

Emergency care refers to immediate treatment administered for life-threatening conditions. It includes a quick assessment of the emergency ABCs (Table 9–3). The victim should also be checked and treated for severe bleeding, shock, and signs of poisoning.

First aid refers to treatment administered for injuries and illnesses that are not considered life-threatening. Emergency care and first aid treatments are based on principles that should be familiar to anyone who works with young children:

1. Summon emergency medical assistance (911 in many areas) for any injury or illness that requires more than simple first aid.
2. Stay calm and in control of the situation.
3. Always remain with the child. If necessary, send another adult or child for help.
4. Don't move the child until the extent of injuries or illness can be determined. If in doubt, have the child stay in the same position and await emergency medical help.
5. Quickly evaluate the child's condition, paying special attention to an open airway, breathing, and circulation.
6. Carefully plan and administer appropriate emergency care. Improper treatment can lead to other injuries.
7. Don't give any medications unless they are prescribed for certain lifesaving conditions.
8. Don't offer diagnoses or medical advice. Refer the child's family to seek professional health care.
9. Always inform the child's family of the injury and any first aid care that has been administered.
10. Record all facts concerning the injury and treatments given on the appropriate forms; file in the child's permanent folder.

In all states, legal protection is granted to individuals who administer emergency treatment with reasonable care unless their actions are judged grossly negligent or harmful. This protection is commonly known as the **Good Samaritan Law**. Thus, teachers should not be reluctant to provide necessary care to an injured child for fear of being sued.

Life-Threatening Conditions

Situations that require emergency care to prevent death or serious disability are discussed in this section. The emergency techniques and suggestions included here are not intended as substitutes for certified first aid and cardiopulmonary resuscitation (CPR) training. Rather, they are included as a review of basic instruction and to enhance the teacher's ability to respond to children's emergencies. A course involving hands-on practice is necessary to master these skills. It is also important to complete a refresher course every few years.

Good Samaritan Law – *legal protection afforded to an individual who renders emergency or first aid care in a reasonable manner.*

Reflective Thoughts

When you place an emergency telephone call, it is important to remain calm and stay on the line. What information should you be prepared to give the dispatcher? Why shouldn't you hang up after making a report? What emergency telephone numbers should be posted in schools and child care facilities? Where should they be posted? What emergency numbers should children learn to dial?

Absence of Breathing

Breathing emergencies accompany many life-threatening conditions, such as asthma, drowning, electrical shock, convulsions, poisoning, severe injuries, suffocation, choking, and Sudden Infant Death Syndrome (SIDS). For this reason, adults who work with children should complete certified training in basic first aid and CPR. This training is available from most chapters of the American Red Cross and the American Heart Association (AHA) or from a local ambulance service, rescue squad, fire department, high school, or community parks and recreation department.

New guidelines for CPR were issued by the AHA in 2005. The changes simplified existing CPR procedures and recommended a single compression-to-ventilation rate of 30:2 for *persons of all ages* (with the exception of newborns) (Handley, 2009; AHA, 2006). A rescue breath is defined as being one second in length and sufficient to cause the chest to rise and fall. The AHA also initiated a new slogan, "push hard and push fast," to emphasize the critical importance of administering chest compressions (approximately 100 per minute) sufficient to maintain adequate blood flow. An adequate compression should depress the chest cavity by one-third to one-half of its depth.

It is important to remain calm while administering emergency lifesaving procedures and to perform them quickly and with confidence. Have someone call for an ambulance or emergency medical assistance while you begin mouth-to-mouth breathing. If you are alone, administer five cycles (30 chest compressions, 2 breaths,) before leaving the victim to call for help. The procedure for mouth-to-mouth breathing follows and is also illustrated in Figure 9–2.

1. Shake the child or infant and shout, "(Child's name), are you sleeping?" to determine if he/she is conscious or simply asleep. If there is no response, quickly assess the child's condition and immediately begin emergency breathing procedures.
2. Position the child on his/her back on a hard surface. Roll the injured victim as a unit, using extreme care to keep the spine straight.
3. Remove any vomitus, excess mucus, or foreign objects (only if they can be seen) by quickly sweeping a finger around the inside of the child's mouth.
4. To open the airway, gently tilt the child's head up and back by placing one hand on the forehead and the fingers (not thumb) of the other hand under the chin; push downward on the forehead and lift the chin upward (head tilt-chin lift).

⚠ **Caution: Do not tip the head back too far. Tipping the head too far can cause an obstruction of the airway. Keep your fingers on the jawbone, not on the tissue under the chin.**

5. Listen carefully for no more than 10 seconds to determine if the child is breathing: place your ear next to the child's nose and mouth and watch for a rise and fall of the chest and abdomen. If the victim is not breathing, begin CPR immediately.
6. ***For an infant*** (up to 1 year):
   a. Place your mouth over the infant's nose and mouth to create a tight seal.
   b. Gently give two small puffs of air (one second per breath with a short pause in between). Observe the chest (rise and fall) to be sure air is entering the lungs.

Figure 9–2 Cardiopulmonary resuscitation (CPR) for infants and children.

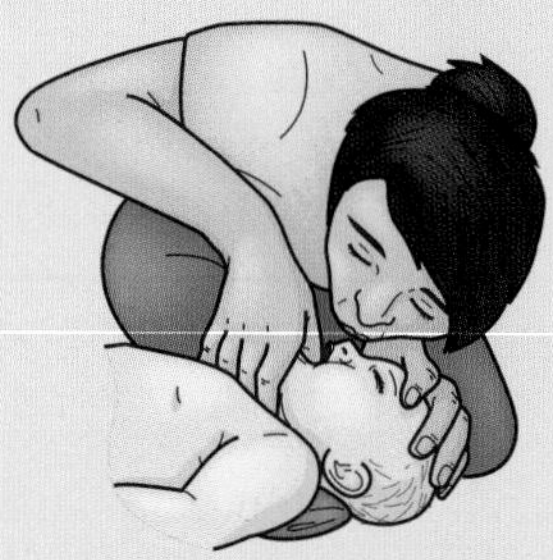

(A) Only if vomitus or foreign objects are clearly visible, use the tongue-jaw lift to open the mouth. Then use a finger to quickly check for the object. Remove only if visible.

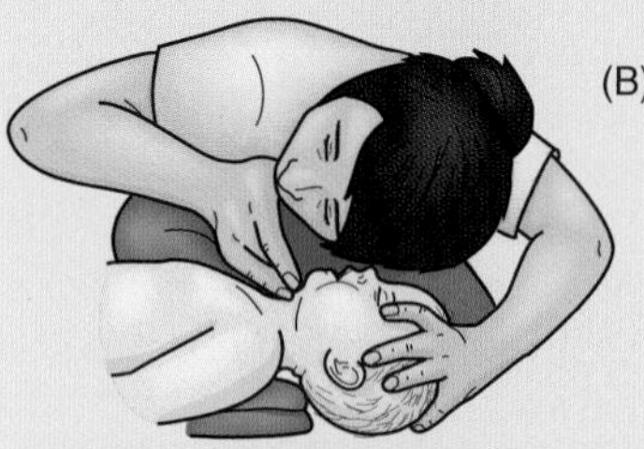

(B) Position child on his/her back. Gently tilt the head up and back by placing one hand on child's forehead and fingers of the other hand under the jawbone. Lift upwards (head tilt/chin lift). **Look** for the chest to rise/fall. **Listen** for breathing. **Feel** for breath on your cheek.

(C) *For an infant*: Place your mouth over the infant's nose and mouth creating a tight seal. Slowly and gently, give two small puffs of air (1–1 1/2 seconds), pausing between breaths. Check (look/listen) and administer 30 chest compressions. Repeat cycle of 2 breaths/30 chest compressions until the child begins to breathe. If air does not go in, reposition and try to breathe again.

(D) *For the child one year and older*: Place your mouth over the child's mouth forming a tight seal. Gently pinch the child's nostrils closed. Quickly give two small breaths of air (1-1 1/2 seconds per breath). If air does not go in reposition and try breathing again. Administer 30 chest compressions. Repeat cycle of 2 breaths/30 chest compressions until the child begins to breathe.

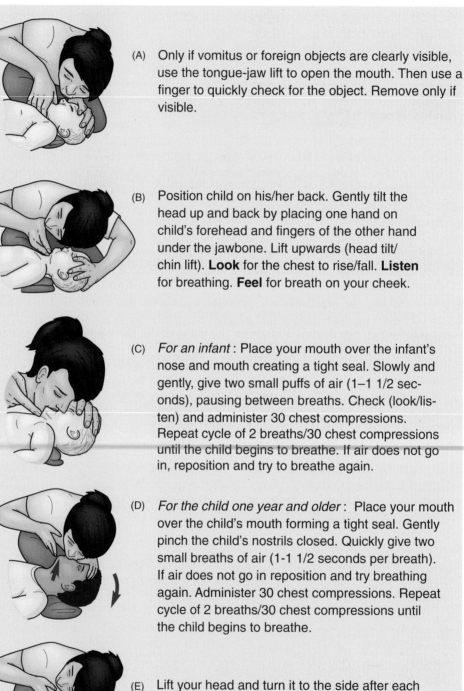

(E) Lift your head and turn it to the side after each breath. This allows time for air to escape from the child's lungs and also gives you time to take a breath and to observe if the child is breathing.

⚠ **Caution: Too much air forced into an infant's lungs may cause the stomach to fill with air (may cause vomiting and increased risk of aspiration). Always remember to use small, gentle puffs of air from your cheeks.**

  c. Immediately administer 30 quick chest compressions by placing two fingers just below the nipple line; each compression should depress the chest by one-third to one-half of its depth.
  d. Continue cycles of 30 chest compressions followed by 2 breaths (30:2) until the infant resumes breathing or emergency help arrives.

7. ***For a child*** (1 year and older):
   a. Gently pinch the nostrils closed and place your open mouth over the victim's open mouth, forming a tight seal.
   b. Give 2 small breaths of air (1 second per breath), pausing between breaths to make sure air is going into the child's lungs.
   c. Immediately administer 30 quick chest compressions by placing the heel of your hand over the nipple line; each compression should depress the chest by one-third to one-half of its depth.
   d. Continue cycles of 30 chest compressions followed by 2 breaths (30:2) until the child resumes breathing or emergency help arrives.
8. DO NOT STOP OR GIVE UP! Continue administering CPR (30 compressions, 2 breaths) until the child breathes alone or emergency medical assistance arrives.

If air does not appear to be entering the lungs or the chest does not rise and fall while administering CPR, check the mouth and airway for foreign objects. *Only* remove the object if it is clearly visible and easy to reach. (Refer to Airway Obstruction.) If the child resumes breathing, keep him/her lying down and roll (as a unit) onto one side; this is called the **recovery position** (Figure 9–3). Maintain body temperature by covering with a light blanket, and continue to monitor the child's breathing closely until medical help arrives.

Occasionally, families of children with special medical problems or life-threatening conditions make a decision not to have their child resuscitated and will obtain a Do Not Attempt to Resuscitate (DNAR) order from their physician. A copy of this document should be kept on file and honored in the event of a breathing emergency. School personnel should be made aware of the family's request.

Airway Obstruction

Children under 5 years of age account for nearly 90 percent of deaths due to airway obstruction (Cohen et al., 2009). More than 66 percent of the deaths occur in infants (Borse et al., 2008). Certain foods (Table 9–4) and small objects (Table 9–5) are common causes of aspiration and should not be accessible to children under age 5. However, children with some types of disabilities, and older children whose development is delayed, may also be more prone to choking and, thus, require continuous supervision.

Figure 9–3 The child should be placed in a recovery position to rest following emergency treatment.

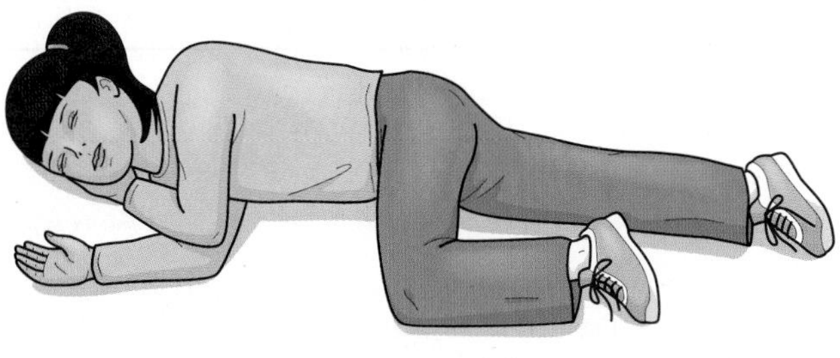

aspiration – *accidental inhalation of food, fluid, or an object into the respiratory tract.*
recovery position – *placing an individual in a side-lying position.*

Table 9–4 Teacher Checklist: Foods Commonly Linked to Childhood Choking

raw carrots	seeds (sunflower), peanuts, and other nuts
hot dogs	chewy cookies
pieces of raw apple	cough drops
grapes (whole)	raisins
fruit seeds and pits	pretzels
gummy or hard candies	popcorn
peanut butter sandwich	chewing gum

Table 9–5 Objects Commonly Linked to Childhood Choking

latex balloons (uninflated or pieces)
small batteries (calculator, hearing aid)
magnets
marker or pen caps
paper clips
small objects (less than 1.5 inches; 3.75 cm) in diameter
toys with small pieces
coins
marbles
small balls, blocks, beads, or vending machine toys

In most instances, children will be successful in coughing out an aspirated object without requiring emergency intervention. However, emergency lifesaving measures must be started immediately if:

- Breathing is labored or absent.
- Lips and nail beds turn blue.
- Cough is weak or ineffective.
- The child is unable to speak.
- The child becomes unresponsive.
- There is a high-pitched sound when the child inhales.

Respiratory infections can sometimes cause swelling and obstruction of children's airway. If this occurs, call immediately for emergency medical assistance. Time should not be wasted on attempting techniques for clearing an airway obstruction (foreign body). They are not effective and may actually cause the child more harm. Emergency techniques to relieve an airway obstruction should be attempted only if a child has been observed to be choking on an object or is unconscious and not breathing after attempts have been made to open the airway and to breathe for the child.

Different emergency techniques are used to treat infants, toddlers, and older children who are choking (AHA, 2006). Attempts to retrieve the object from the child's mouth should be made *only* if the object is clearly visible. Extreme care must be taken not to push the object further back into the airway.

For an infant: If the object cannot be removed easily and the infant is conscious, quickly:

- Have someone summon emergency medical assistance.
- Position the infant face down over the length of your arm, with the child's head lower than his/her chest and the head and neck supported in your hand (Figure 9–4). The infant can also be placed in your lap with the head lower than the chest.
- Use the heel of your hand to give five quick back blows between the infant's shoulder blades.

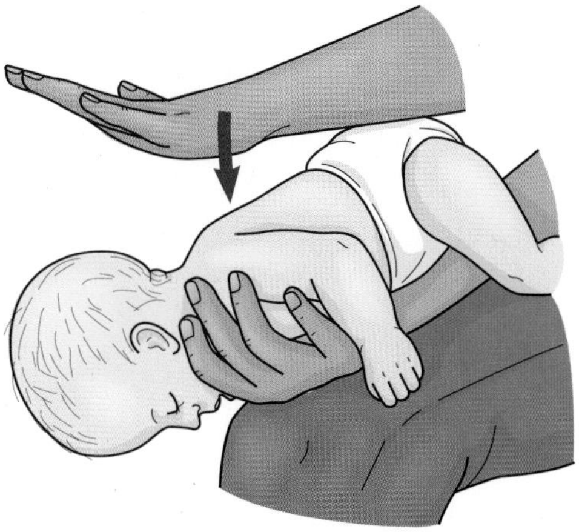

Figure 9–4 The infant's head should be positioned lower than the chest.

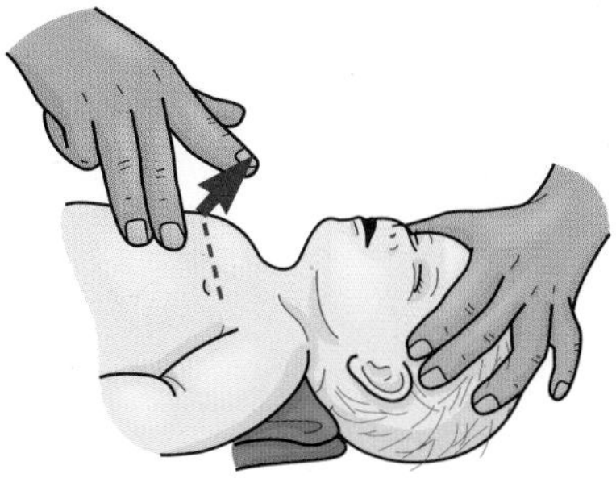

Figure 9–5 Location of fingers for chest compressions on an infant.

⚠ **Caution: Do not use excessive force as this could injure the infant.**

- Support and turn the infant over, face up, with the head held lower than the chest.
- Give five chest thrusts. Place two fingers just below the nipple line (Figure 9–5). Rapidly compress the infant's chest approximately 1/2–1 inch (1.3–2.5 cm); release pressure completely between thrusts, allowing the chest to return to its normal position.
- Look inside the child's mouth for the foreign object. If clearly visible and reachable, remove it.
- Repeat the steps, alternating five back blows and five chest thrusts until the object is dislodged and the infant begins to cry or lose consciousness.

For the child: If the object cannot be removed easily and the child is conscious, quickly:

- Summon emergency medical assistance.
- Administer the Heimlich maneuver. Stand or kneel behind the child with your arms around the child's waist (Figure 9–6).
- Make a fist with one hand, thumbs tucked in.
- Place the fisted hand (thumb-side) against the child's abdomen, midway between the base of the rib cage (xiphoid process) and the navel.
- Press your fisted hand into the child's abdomen with a quick, inward and upward thrust.
- Continue to repeat abdominal thrusts until the object is dislodged or the child regains consciousness.
- If the child loses consciousness and is still breathing, lower him/her to the floor and continue to administer abdominal thrusts until the object is dislodged (Figure 9–7).

If the infant or child **LOSES CONSCIOUSNESS AND IS NOT BREATHING**, stop and have someone call for an ambulance or emergency medical assistance if this has not already been done. Place the child flat on the floor or other hard surface (on back, face up) and begin CPR immediately (give two breaths, reposition if air is not going in; if the airway is open, give two breaths followed by abdominal thrusts). The AHA suggests that CPR chest compressions alone are sufficient to dislodge an object in the airway. Look inside of the child's mouth (for the foreign object) before each cycle of breaths is given and remove *only* if visible.

If the infant or child begins to breathe on his/her own, stop CPR and continue to monitor the child closely until medical help arrives. Roll the child (as a unit) onto his/her side (recovery position). Always be sure the child receives follow-up medical attention after the object has been dislodged and breathing is restored.

Figure 9–6 The Heimlich maneuver.

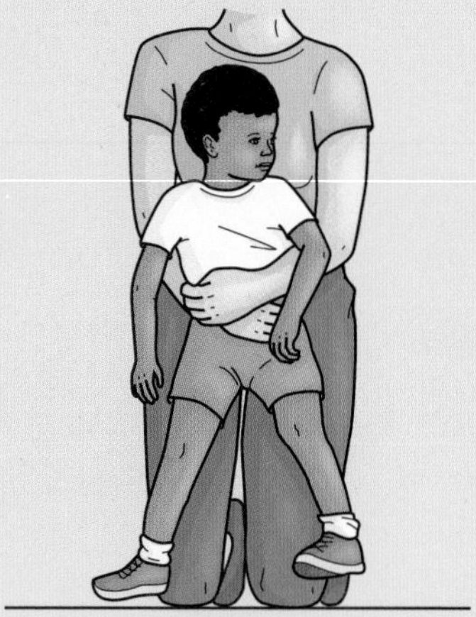

Stand or kneel behind the child with your arms around the child's waist.

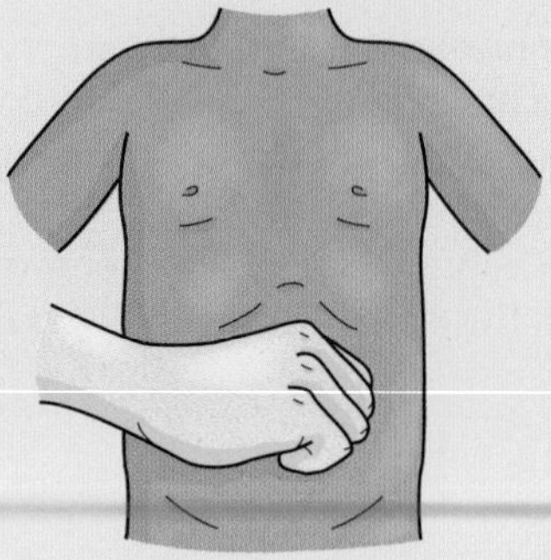

Make a fist with one hand. Place the fisted hand against the child's abdomen below the tip of the rib cage, slightly above the navel.

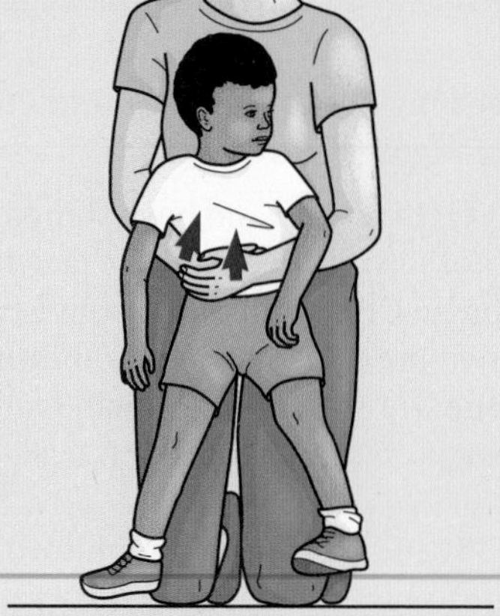

Grasp the fisted hand with your other hand. Press your fists into the child's abdomen with a quick upward thrust.

Shock

Shock frequently accompanies many types of injuries, especially those that are severe, and should therefore be anticipated. However, it can also result from extreme emotional upset and injuries, such as bleeding, pain, heat exhaustion, poisoning, burns, and fractures. Shock is considered a life-threatening condition that requires prompt emergency treatment. Early indicators of shock include:

- skin that is pale, cool, and clammy
- confusion, anxiety, restlessness
- increased perspiration
- weakness
- rapid, shallow breathing

Figure 9–7 Heimlich maneuver with child lying down.

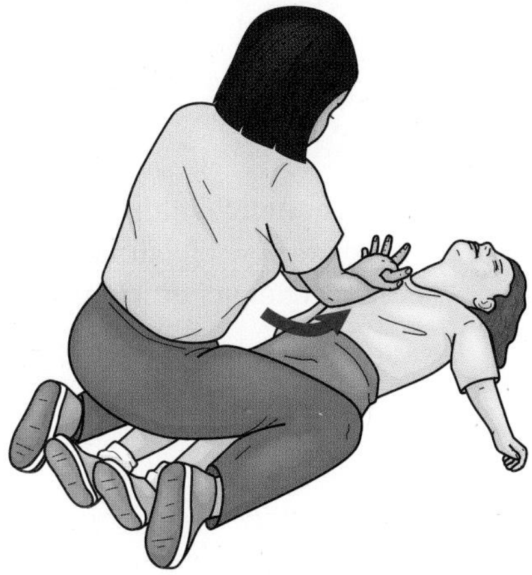

Signs of more serious shock may develop, and include:

- rapid, weak pulse
- bluish discoloration around lips, nails, and ear lobes
- dilated pupils
- extreme thirst
- nausea and vomiting
- unconsciousness

To treat a child in shock:

1. Have someone call for emergency medical assistance.
2. Quickly assess the ABCs. Try to identify what may have caused the shock (e.g., bleeding, poisoning) and treat the cause first.
3. Keep the child lying down.
4. Elevate the child's feet 8 to 10 inches, if there is no indication of back injuries or fractures to the legs or head.
5. Maintain body heat by covering the child lightly with a blanket.
6. Moisten a clean cloth and use it for wetting the lips and mouth if the child complains of thirst.
7. Stay calm and reassure the child until emergency medical help arrives.
8. Observe the child's breathing closely; give mouth-to-mouth resuscitation if necessary.

Asthma

Asthma is a chronic disorder of the respiratory system characterized by periods of wheezing, gasping, and labored breathing. Numerous factors are known to trigger an acute asthma attack, including allergic reactions, respiratory infections, emotional stress, air pollutants, and physical exertion (Salo, Sever, & Zeldin, 2009). Asthma attacks make breathing intensely difficult and, therefore, must be treated as a life-threatening event (Gilliland, 2009; Hockenberry, 2008). Schools should have an action plan in place for any child with a known history of asthma. (See Chapter 4).

Remaining calm and confident during a child's asthmatic attack is crucial. To treat a child who is having an asthma attack:

1. Summon emergency medical help immediately if the child shows signs of anxiety, wheezing, restlessness, loss of consciousness, or blue discoloration of the nail beds or lips. Fatigue, inability to recognize teachers, or loss of consciousness are dangerous signs of impending respiratory failure and/or cardiac arrest.
2. Reassure the child.
3. Administer any medications (such as an inhaler) prescribed for the child's acute asthmatic symptoms immediately.

4. Encourage the child to relax and breathe slowly and deeply. (Anxiety makes breathing more difficult.)
5. Have the child assume a position that is most comfortable. (Breathing is usually easier when sitting or standing up.)
6. Notify the child's family.

Bleeding

Occasionally, children receive injuries, such as a deep gash or head laceration, that will bleed profusely. Severe bleeding requires prompt emergency treatment. Again, it is extremely important that the teacher act quickly, yet remain calm. To stop bleeding:

1. Summon emergency medical assistance immediately if bleeding comes in spurts or is profuse and cannot be stopped.
2. Follow universal infection control precautions (wear disposable gloves, wash hands, dispose of contaminated items, clean and disinfect surfaces).
3. Place a pad of **sterile** gauze or clean material over the wound.
4. Apply firm pressure (5–10 minutes) directly over the site, using the flat parts of the fingers; do not let up, as bleeding may resume.
5. Place additional pads over the bandage next to the skin if blood soaks through; bleeding may restart if the wound is disturbed.
6. **Elevate** the bleeding part if there is no sign of a fracture.
7. Apply an ice pack, wrapped in a cloth or towel, to the site to help slow bleeding and decrease swelling.
8. Secure the bandage(s) in place when bleeding has stopped.
9. Locate the nearest pressure point above the injury and apply firm pressure if bleeding cannot be stopped with direct pressure and elevation (Figure 9–8).

⚠ **Caution: Tourniquets should be used only as a last resort and with the understanding that the extremity will probably need to be amputated.**

Save all blood-soaked dressings. Doctors will use them to estimate the amount of blood loss. Contact the child's family when bleeding is under control and advise them to seek prompt medical attention.

Diabetes

Two potentially life-threatening emergencies associated with diabetes are hypoglycemia and hyperglycemia. Teachers must be able to quickly distinguish between these two conditions in order to determine appropriate emergency measures (American Diabetes Association, 2009). The causes and symptoms of these complications are, in many respects, opposites of each other (Table 9–6).

Hypoglycemia, or insulin shock, is caused by low levels of sugar in the blood. It can occur whenever a diabetic child either receives an excessive dose of insulin or an insufficient amount of food. Other causes may include illness, delayed eating times, or increased activity. Similar symptoms are experienced by nondiabetic children when they become overly hungry. Hypoglycemia can often be quickly reversed by administering a sugar substance. Orange juice is ideal for this purpose because it is absorbed rapidly by the body. Concentrated glucose gel or tablets can also be purchased and used for emergency purposes. Hard candies, such as Life Savers™ or lollipops, **should not** be given because a child could easily choke.

---

sterile – *free from living microorganisms.*
elevate – *to raise to a higher position.*

Poisoning

Unintentional poisoning results when harmful substances have been inhaled, ingested, absorbed through the skin, or injected into the body. The majority of incidences occur in children under 6 and involve substances that have been ingested (Kanchan, Menezes, & Monteiro, 2009). Signs of poisoning may develop quickly or be delayed, and can include:

- nausea or vomiting
- abdominal cramps or diarrhea
- unusual odor to breath
- skin that feels cold and clammy
- burns or visible stains around the mouth, lips, or skin
- restlessness
- difficulty breathing
- convulsions
- confusion, disorientation, apathy, or listlessness
- loss of consciousness
- seizures

Emergency treatment of accidental poisoning is determined by the type of poison the child has **ingested** (McGregor, Parkar, & Rao, 2009; Madden, 2008). Poisons are divided into three basic categories: strong acids and **alkalis**, petroleum products, and all others. Examples of each type are included in Table 9–7.

If a child is suspected of swallowing a poisonous substance:

- Quickly check for redness or burns around the child's lips, mouth, and tongue. These are indications of a chemical burn, usually caused by strong acids or alkalis. **Do not give the child anything to drink; do not make the child vomit.**
- Smell the child's breath. If the poison is a petroleum product, then the odor of gasoline or kerosene will be present. **Do not give the child anything to drink; do not make the child vomit.**

If the child is ***conscious***:

- Quickly try to locate the container, which may provide clues about what the child has ingested. Also, try to estimate how much of the product the child may have swallowed.
- If you cannot find a container, do not delay in calling Poison Control.
- Call the nearest Poison Control Center (1-800-222-1222) or your city's emergency number (911 in many areas) and follow their instructions. Be sure to keep this number posted by the telephone.
- Observe the child closely for signs of shock and/or difficulty breathing.
- Do not give the child anything to eat or drink.

Table 9–7 Poisonous Substances

Strong Acid and Alkalis	Petroleum Products	All Others
bathroom, drain, and oven cleaners	charcoal lighter	medicines
battery acid	cigarette lighter fluid	plants
dishwasher soaps	furniture polish and wax	berries
lye	gasoline	cosmetics
wart and corn remover	kerosene	nail polish remover
ammonia	naphtha	insecticides
	turpentine	mothballs
	floor wax	weed killers
	lamp oil	

ingested – *the process of taking food or other substances into the body through the mouth.*
alkalis – *group of bases or caustic substances that are capable of neutralizing acids to form salts.*

If the child is ***unconscious***:

- Summon emergency medical assistance immediately.
- Monitor child's airway, breathing, and circulation; administer CPR if breathing stops.
- Do not give the child anything to eat or drink.
- Position the child in the recovery position (side-lying) to prevent choking on vomited material.
- Observe the child closely for signs of difficulty breathing.

Always check with the Poison Control Center and follow their instructions before attempting to treat childhood poisoning. If the child begins to vomit, keep his/her head lowered to prevent aspiration and choking. Contact the child's family as soon as possible.

Non-Life-Threatening Conditions

The majority of children's injuries and illnesses are not life-threatening but may require first aid care. Teachers who have received proper training can administer this type of care, but they are not qualified or expected to provide comprehensive medical treatment. Initial first aid treatment of children's injuries is important for reducing complications and making children feel more comfortable until their family arrives. The remainder of this chapter addresses conditions typically encountered by young children that may require first aid care.

Abrasions, Cuts, and Other Minor Skin Wounds

Minor cuts, scrapes, and abrasions are among the most common types of injury young children experience. First aid care is concerned primarily with the control of bleeding and the prevention of infection. To care for the child who has received a simple skin wound, do the following:

1. Follow universal infection control precautions, including the use of latex/vinyl gloves.
2. Apply direct pressure to the wound, using a clean cloth or sterile pad to stop any bleeding.
3. Wash the wound under running water for at least 5 minutes or until all foreign particles have been removed.
4. Cover the wound with a sterile bandage. A thin layer of antibiotic ointment can be applied to superficial abrasions if permitted.
5. Apply a cold pack, wrapped in a disposable paper towel or plastic bag, to the area; this can help to slow bleeding and reduce swelling.
6. Inform the child's family of the injury. Have them check to be sure the child's tetanus immunization is current.
7. Watch for signs of infection, such as warmth, redness, swelling, or drainage.

Puncture-type wounds and cuts that are deep or ragged require medical attention because of the increased risk of infection. Stitches may be needed to close a gash greater than 1/2 inch (1.2 cm), especially if it is located on the child's face, chest, or back.

Bites

Human and animal bites are painful and can lead to serious infection (Brook, 2009). The possibility of rabies should be considered with any animal bite that is unprovoked, unless the animal is known to be free of the virus. A suspected animal should be confined and observed by a veterinarian. In cases where the bite was provoked, the animal is not as likely to be rabid. First aid care for human and animal bites includes the following:

1. Follow universal infection control precautions, including the use of disposable gloves.
2. Allow the wound to bleed for a short while if the skin is broken (to remove any saliva) before applying direct pressure to stop bleeding.
3. Cleanse the wound thoroughly with soap and water or hydrogen peroxide and cover with a clean dressing.
4. Notify the child's family and advise them to have the wound checked by the child's physician.
5. Notify local law enforcement authorities immediately if the injury is due to an animal bite; provide a description of the animal and its location (unless it is a classroom pet).

An icepack reduces the pain and swelling of bumps and scrapes.

Most insect bites cause little more than local skin irritations. However, some children are extremely sensitive to certain insects, especially bees, hornets, wasps, and spiders. Signs of severe allergic reaction include:

- sudden difficulty breathing
- joint pain (delayed reaction)
- abdominal cramps
- vomiting
- fever
- red, swollen eyes
- hives or generalized itching
- shock
- weakness or unconsciousness
- swollen tongue

Allergic reactions to insect bites can be life-threatening and should be monitored closely. To treat a child for severe allergic reactions:

1. Call for emergency medical assistance (usually 911), especially if the child has never experienced this type of reaction before.
2. Encourage the child to rest quietly. Let the child assume a position that is most comfortable for breathing.
3. Administer any medication (such as an EpiPen®) immediately that the child may have at school for severe allergic reactions.

First aid measures for insect bites provide temporary relief from discomfort and prevent infection. If a stinger remains in the skin, an attempt should be made to remove it by scraping the area with the back of a flatware knife or clean credit card (removing with a tweezers may inject more venom into the skin). The area should then be washed and an ice/cold pack applied to decrease swelling and pain. Calamine lotion or a paste of baking soda and water can also be applied to the area to provide temporary pain relief.

Reflective Thoughts

Risk of exposure to blood-borne diseases, such as hepatitis B and C, and HIV/AIDS, is ever present when attending to injuries that involve blood or other body fluids. What steps can teachers take to protect themselves from exposure? What additional precautions can be taken? Where can teachers locate current information about these diseases? What is OSHA? What role does it play in establishing safe workplace conditions?

Blisters

A blister is a collection of fluid (white blood cells) that builds up beneath the skin's surface to protect the area against infection. Blisters most commonly develop from rubbing or friction, burns, or allergic reactions.

First aid care of blisters is aimed at protecting the affected skin from infection. If at all possible, blisters should not be broken. However, if they do break, wash the area with soap and water and cover with a bandage.

Bruises

Bruises result when small blood vessels rupture beneath the skin. They are often caused by falls, bumps, and blows. Fair-skinned children tend to bruise more easily. First aid care is aimed at controlling subsurface bleeding and swelling. Apply an ice or cold pack to the bruised area for 15 to 20 minutes and repeat three to four times during the next 24 hours. Later, warm moist packs can be applied several times daily to improve circulation and healing. Alert the child's family to watch for signs of infection or unusual bleeding if the bruising is extensive or severe.

Burns

Burns occur when body surfaces come in contact with heat, electrical current, or chemicals. Several factors affect the severity of an accidental burn and the need to call for emergency medical assistance, including the source, temperature of the source, affected body part or area, length of exposure, and victim's age and size (Table 9–8).

Burns sustained by children are always considered more serious because of their smaller body surface (Dissanaike & Rahimi, 2009; Hockenberry, 2008). Burns caused by heat are classified according to the degree (depth and extent) of tissue damage:

- first degree—surface skin is red with some pain and swelling
- second degree—surface skin is red and blistered with swelling and severe pain
- third degree—burn is deep; skin and underlying tissues may be brown, white, and/or charred. Pain is often minimal, but these burns require emergency medical attention—call for help immediately.

Table 9–8 Teacher Checklist: Burns—When to Call for Emergency Medical Assistance

Always call for emergency medical assistance if:
- a child or elderly person is involved
- the victim experiences any difficulty breathing
- burned areas are located on the face, head, neck, feet, hands, or genitalia
- multiple areas of the body have been burned
- burned area is larger than 2 to 3 inches (5 to 7.5 cm)
- chemicals, electrical current, smoke, or an explosion has caused the burn

First aid care of minor burns (first and second degree) that are no larger than 3 inches (7.5 cm) includes the following:

1. Use caution to protect yourself from the heat source.
2. Quickly **submerge** the burned areas in cool water, hold under running water, or cover with a cool, wet towel for 5 to 10 minutes. Cool water temperatures reduce the depth of a burn as well as lessen swelling and pain.
3. Cover the burn with a sterile gauze dressing and tape in place. Do not use greasy ointments because dirt and bacteria can collect in these creams and increase the risk of infection.
4. Elevate the burned body part to relieve discomfort.
5. Burns that involve feet, face, hands, or genitals, cover a large area (greater than 2 to 3 inches/5 to 7.5 cm) or cause moderate blistering are critical and require immediate medical attention. Families should be advised to contact the child's health care provider.

In the case of third degree burns, stop the burning process but do not attempt to cool the burn or to remove burnt clothing. Cover any open areas with a dry, sterile dressing and call immediately for emergency medical assistance.

Chemical burns should be rinsed for 10 to 15 minutes under cool, running water. Remove any clothing that may still have the chemical on it. Call for emergency medical assistance or the nearest Poison Control Center for further instructions. The child's family should also be advised to contact their physician.

Burns caused by smoke or electrical current should not be cooled with water and require immediate medical attention.

Eye Injuries

Most eye injuries are not serious and can be treated by teachers. However, because eyes are delicate structures, it is important to know how to properly care for different types of injuries. Families should always be informed of any injury to their child's eye(s) so they can continue to observe and consult with a physician if they have concerns.

A sudden blow to the eye from a snowball, wooden block, or other hard object is usually quite painful. First aid treatment includes the following:

1. Keep the child quiet.
2. Apply an ice pack to the eye for 15 minutes if there is no bleeding.
3. Use direct pressure to control any bleeding around the eye. Do not apply pressure to the eyeball itself. Cleanse and cover skin wounds with a sterile gauze pad.
4. Summon emergency medical assistance at once if the child complains of inability to see or is seeing spots or flashes of light.
5. Inform the child's family about any blow to the eye so they can continue to monitor the child's condition.

Foreign particles such as sand, cornmeal, or specks of dust frequently find their way into children's eyes. Although it is natural for children to want to rub their eyes, this must be discouraged to prevent further injury to the eyeball. Spontaneous tearing is often sufficient to wash the object out of the eye. If the particle is visible, it can also be removed with the corner of a clean cloth or by flushing the eye with saline eye wash solution or lukewarm water. If the particle cannot be removed easily, the eye should be covered and medical attention sought.

An object that penetrates the eyeball *must never be removed* (Podbielski et al., 2009). Place a paper cup, funnel, or small cardboard box over *both* the object and the eye. Cover the uninjured eye with a gauze pad and secure both dressings (cup and gauze pad) in place by wrapping an elastic

---

submerge *–to place in water.*

roller bandage around the head. Movement of the injured eyeball should be kept to a minimum and can be achieved by covering both eyes. Seek immediate medical treatment.

A thin cut on the eye's surface can result from a piece of paper, toy, or child's fingernail. Injuries of this type cause severe pain and tearing. The teacher should cover *both* of the child's eyes with a gauze dressing and notify the child's family to seek *immediate* medical attention.

Chemical burns to a child's eye are very serious. Ask another staff member to call immediately for emergency medical assistance so the child can be transported to the nearest medical facility. Begin immediately to flush the child's eye with lukewarm water or saline eye wash solution. Tip the child's head toward the affected eye and use a small bulb syringe or bottle to rinse the eye for at least 15 minutes. Meanwhile, contact the child's family.

Fractures

A fracture is a break or crack in a bone. A teacher can check for possible fractures by observing the child for:

- particular areas of extreme pain or tenderness
- an unusual shape or deformity of the bone
- a break in the skin with visible bone edges protruding
- swelling
- a change in skin color around the injury site
- numbness or a tingling sensation

Families should always be informed of any injury to a child's eye.

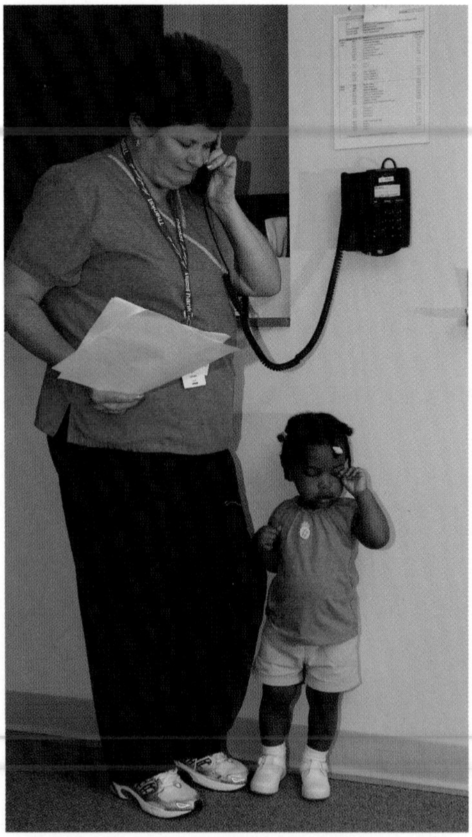

A child who complains of pain after falling should not be moved, especially if a back or neck injury is suspected. Have someone call immediately for an ambulance or emergency medical assistance. Keep the child warm and observe carefully for signs of shock. Avoid giving the child anything to eat or drink in the event that surgery is necessary. Stop any bleeding by applying direct pressure.

If no emergency medical help is available, only persons with prior first aid training should attempt to splint a fracture. Splinting should be completed before the child is moved. Splints can be purchased from medical supply stores or improvised from items such as a rolled-up magazine, pillow or blanket, a ruler, or a piece of board. Never attempt to straighten a fractured bone. Cover open wounds with a sterile pad but do not attempt to clean the wound. Elevate the splinted part on a pillow and apply an ice pack to reduce swelling and pain. Observe the child closely for signs of shock and contact the child's family immediately so they can notify their physician.

Frostbite and Hypothermia

Frostbite results when body tissues freeze from exposure to extremely cold temperatures. Certain parts of the body are especially prone to frostbite, including the ears, nose, fingers, and toes, especially if clothing or shoes become wet. Frostbite can develop within minutes, causing the skin to take on a hard, waxy, gray-white appearance with or without blisters. For this reason, infants and young children should be monitored closely during extremely cold weather so they don't remove hats, boots, or mittens. Initially, the child may experience considerable pain or have no discomfort. However, when tissues begin to warm, there is often a tingling and painful sensation. First aid treatment for frostbite consists of the following:

- Bring the child indoors and into a warm room.
- Remove wet clothing; replace with dry clothing or wrap the child in blankets for warmth.
- Contact the child's family; have them take the child to the nearest medical facility.
- *Do not* rewarm the affected part(s) unless no medical care is available.
- Handle the frostbitten part(s) with care; avoid rubbing or massaging the area as this could further damage frozen tissue.
- Elevate the affected area(s) to ease pain and prevent swelling.

Exposure to cold temperatures can also cause **hypothermia**, a drop in body temperature that slows heart rate, respirations, and metabolism. This slowing of body functions reduces the amount of available oxygen and can lead to shivering, drowsiness, loss of consciousness, and cardiac arrest (begin CPR). Emergency medical personnel should be summoned at once.

Heat Exhaustion and Heat Stroke

First aid treatment of heat-related illness depends on distinguishing heat exhaustion from heat stroke. A child who has lost considerable fluid through sweating and is overheated may be suffering from **heat exhaustion**. The following symptoms would be observed:

- skin is pale, cool, and moist with perspiration
- weakness or fainting
- thirst
- nausea
- abdominal and/or muscle cramps
- headache
- normal or below-normal body temperature

Heat exhaustion is not considered life-threatening. It usually occurs when a child has been playing vigorously in extreme heat or humidity. First aid treatment for heat exhaustion is similar to that for shock:

1. Have the child lie down in a cool place.
2. Elevate the child's feet 8–10 inches (20–25 cm).
3. Loosen or remove the child's clothing.
4. Sponge the child's face and body with tepid (lukewarm) water.
5. Offer frequent sips of cool water.

Heat stroke is a life-threatening condition that requires immediate treatment. The child's temperature begins to rise quickly and dangerously as perspiration stops and the body's temperature-regulating mechanism fails (Holcomb, 2009; Wagner & Boyd, 2009). For example, children left in a parked car with the windows rolled up on a warm day (70 degrees and over) can quickly develop heat stroke and die. Symptoms of heat stroke include:

- high body temperature (102°–106°F; 38.8°–41.1°C)
- dry, flushed skin
- headache or confusion
- seizures
- diarrhea, abdominal cramps
- loss of consciousness
- shock

---

hypothermia – *below-normal body temperature caused by overexposure to cold conditions.*
heat exhaustion – *above-normal body temperature caused by exposure to too much sun.*
heat stroke – *failure of the body's sweating reflex during exposure to high temperatures; causes body temperature to rise.*

Emergency treatment for heat stroke is aimed at cooling the child as quickly as possible:

1. Summon emergency medical assistance at once.
2. Move the child to a cool place and remove outer clothing.
3. Sponge the child's body with cool (not cold) water. The child can also be placed in a shallow tub of cool water or gently sprayed with a garden hose. Do not leave child unattended!
4. Elevate the child's legs to decrease the possibility of shock.
5. Offer small sips of cool water only if the child is fully conscious.
6. Notify the child's family.

Nosebleeds

Accidental bumps, allergies, nose picking, or sinus congestion can all cause a child's nose to bleed. Most nosebleeds are not serious and can be stopped quickly. If a nosebleed continues for more than 30 minutes, get medical help. To stop a nosebleed, do the following:

1. Place the child in a sitting position, with head tilted slightly forward, to prevent any swallowing of blood.
2. Have the child breath through his/her mouth.
3. Follow universal infection control precautions, including the use of latex/vinyl gloves.
4. Firmly grasp the child's nostrils (lower half) and squeeze together for at least 5 minutes before releasing the pressure.
5. If bleeding continues, pinch the nostrils together for another 10 minutes.
6. Have the child play quietly for the hour or so afterward to prevent bleeding from resuming.
7. Encourage parents to discuss the problem with the child's physician if nosebleeds occur repeatedly.

Seizures

Infants and young children experience seizures for a variety of reasons. Simple precautionary measures can be taken during and immediately after a seizure to protect a child from injury and should include the following:

Firmly grasp and squeeze the child's nostrils to stop a nosebleed.

1. Call for emergency medical assistance if this is the first time a child has experienced a seizure. If the child has a known seizure disorder, call for emergency help if the seizure lasts longer than 3 to 4 minutes or the child experiences severe difficulty breathing or stops breathing.
2. Encourage everyone to remain calm.
3. Carefully lower the child to the floor. Protect the child's head from striking the floor or nearby objects by placing a small pillow or item of soft clothing under the child's head.
4. Move furniture and other objects out of the way.
5. Do not hold the child down.
6. Do not attempt to force any protective device into the child's mouth.
7. Loosen tight clothing around the child's neck and waist to make breathing easier.
8. Watch carefully to make sure the child is breathing.

9. Place the child in the recovery position (on one side) with head slightly elevated when the seizure ends. This prevents choking by allowing oral secretions to drain out of the mouth.

When the seizure has ended, the child can be moved to a quiet area and encouraged to rest or sleep. An adult should continue to monitor the child closely and always notify the child's family.

Splinters

Most splinters under the skin's surface can be easily removed with a sterilized needle and tweezers (only bleach or alcohol should be used for this purpose). Clean the skin around the splinter with soap and water or alcohol before starting and after it has been removed. Cover the area with a bandage. If the splinter is very deep, do not attempt to remove it, and inform the child's family to seek medical attention. Also, make sure the child's tetanus immunization is current.

Sprains

A sprain is caused by injury to the ligaments and tissue surrounding a joint and often results in pain and considerable swelling. In most cases, only an X-ray can confirm whether an injury is a sprain or fracture. If there is any doubt, it is always best to splint the injury and treat it as if it were broken. Elevate the injured part and apply ice packs intermittently for 15 to 20 minutes at a time for several hours. Notify the child's family and encourage them to have the child examined by a physician.

Tick Bites

Ticks are small, oval-shaped insects that generally live in wooded areas and on dogs. On humans, ticks frequently attach themselves to the scalp or base of the neck. However, the child is seldom aware of the tick's presence. Diseases, such as Rocky Mountain Spotted Fever and Lyme disease, are rare but serious complications of a tick bite. If a child develops chills, fever, or rash following a known tick bite, medical treatment should be sought at once.

Ticks should be removed carefully. Grasp the tick closely to the skin with tweezers, pulling steadily and straight out to remove all body parts; do not squeeze or twist. Wash the area thoroughly with soap and water and apply a disinfectant such as alcohol. Observe the site closely for several days and contact a physician if any signs of infection and/or rash develop.

Tooth Emergencies

The most common injuries to children's teeth involve chipping or loosening of a tooth. Blood may be involved so universal infection control precautions must be followed when caring for the child or handling the tooth. A tooth that has been knocked loose by a blow or fall will often retighten itself within several days. Care should be taken to keep the tooth and gum tissue clean, avoid chewing on hard foods, and watch for signs of infection (redness, swelling).

If a tooth has been completely dislodged, the child should be seen by a dentist and monitored for signs of infection. Although dentists will seldom attempt to replace a baby tooth, it is important to save the tooth and send it home with the child. Dentists are more apt to try re-implanting children's permanent teeth, but this process requires prompt emergency treatment to be successful.

- Rinse out the tooth socket (hole remaining in the gum); apply direct pressure to stop bleeding.
- Handle the tooth with care; do not to touch the root-end.
- Place the tooth in a small cup of milk or water; if this isn't available, wrap the tooth in a damp cloth.
- Get the child to a dentist within an hour of the injury (Glendor, 2009).

⚠ **Caution: To avoid accidental choking, do not attempt to reinsert the tooth into the socket or have a child hold the tooth in place.**

Focus On Families — Poison Prevention in the Home

Children under the age of 6 are the most frequent victims of unintentional poisonings.

Their curiosity and limited understanding often lead them unknowingly into risky situations. In many households, items such as cleaning products, garden chemicals, automobile waxes, charcoal lighter, lamp oil, and medications are commonly left in places accessible to young children. Often, simple precautions can be taken to make children's environments safe.

- Always place potentially dangerous substances in a locked cabinet. Don't rely on your child's ability to "know better."
- Supervise children closely whenever using harmful products. Take them with you if the doorbell rings or if you must leave the room.
- Teach children not to put anything into their mouths unless it is given to them by an adult.
- Test the paint on your house, walls, children's furniture, and toys to be sure it doesn't contain lead. Contact the National Lead Information Center for information (1-800-424-LEAD).
- Check before purchasing plants and flowers (indoor and outdoor) to make certain they are not poisonous.
- Insist that vitamins and medications, including those purchased over-the-counter, are in child-resistant containers.
- Post the number of the nearest Poison Control Center near the telephone.
- Caution visitors to keep purses, suitcases, and backpacks out of children's reach.

Classroom Corner — Teacher Activities

Preventing Burns

(PreK–2; National Health Education Standards 5.2.1 and 5.2.2))

Concept: There are things that are safe to touch and play with and other things that can hurt you.

Learning Objectives

- Children will be able to identify items that are safe to touch and other items that are not safe.
- Children will explain what to do if they aren't sure that an item is safe to touch.

Supplies

- pictures of a stove, lighter, matches, campfire, candle, barbeque grill, ball, car, apple, crayons, a stuffed toy, and a block
- two pieces of string (long enough to make two big circles to sort the cards in)
- picture of a smiling face and a frowning face

Learning Activities

- Read and discuss one of the following books:
  - *Firefighters* by Robert Maass
  - *Tonka Fire Truck to the Rescue* by Ann Martin

(*continued*)

Classroom Corner **Teacher Activities** *(continued)*

- Tell the children you are going to talk about some items that are safe to touch and play with and others that aren't safe and can hurt them.
- Hold up the picture cards and talk about each item.
- Tell the children you are going to sort the picture cards by items that are safe to touch and those that are not. Put the smiling face in the middle of one of the circles and the frowning face in the middle of the other.
- Call a child to come up and pick a card and tell the other children if it is a safe item to touch and play with or an unsafe item. Continue until all cards have been sorted.
- Tell the children if they are not sure an item is safe or not to ask a grownup.

Evaluation

- Children will name at least two items safe to touch and two items they should not touch.
- Children will state what to do when they aren't sure if an object is safe to touch.

Additional lesson plans for grades 3–5 are available on this text's premium website.

Summary

- Schools and early childhood programs should have policies and procedures in place for managing childhood emergencies, including:
  - personnel who are trained in first aid and CPR
  - emergency contact information and telephone numbers
  - first aid supplies
- Emergency care is administered for life-threatening conditions.
  - The ABCs are used to assess a victim's condition: airway, breathing, and circulation.
  - Teachers never offer a diagnosis or medical advice.
  - Families are responsible for obtaining follow-up medical treatment after teachers have provided initial emergency or first aid care.
- First aid treatment is given for conditions that are not life-threatening.

Terms to Know

Good Samaritan Law *p. 240*
aspiration *p. 243*
recovery position *p. 243*
sterile *p. 248*
elevate *p. 248*
resuscitation *p. 250*
paralysis *p. 252*
ingested *p. 253*
alkalis *p. 253*
submerge *p. 257*
hypothermia *p. 259*
heat exhaustion *p. 259*
heat stroke *p. 259*

Chapter Review

A. By Yourself

1. Complete each of the given statements with a word selected from the following list. Take the first letter from each answer and place it in the appropriate space following question "j" to spell out one of the basic principles of first aid.

airway	evaluate
breathing	plans
diagnose	pressure
elevating	responsible
emergency	resuscitation

a. Always check to be sure the child is ____________.
b. The immediate care given for life-threatening conditions is ____________ care.
c. Schools and early childhood programs should develop ____________ for handling emergencies.
d. If an infant is found unconscious and not breathing, begin mouth-to-nose/mouth ____________ immediately.
e. The first step in providing emergency care is to quickly the ____________ child's condition.
f. Bleeding can be stopped by applying direct ____________.
g. When evaluating a child for life-threatening injuries, be sure to check for a clear ____________, breathing, and circulation.
h. Families are ____________ for any additional medical treatment of a child's injuries.
i. Treatment of shock includes ____________ the child's legs 8 to 10 inches.
j. Teachers never ____________ or give medical advice.

A basic principle of first aid is _ _ _ _ _ _ _ _ _ _.

2. Describe what each letter of the emergency ABCs stands for and explain how you would assess a victim.
3. Explain the Good Samaritan Law and the purpose it serves.
4. Describe the classification of burns and how each level should be treated.

B. As a Group

1. Explain why a child who has fallen and bumped his head must be closely monitored for the next 48 hours despite the fact that he appears to be okay.
2. Assume that you are the teacher in the following scenarios. Role-play how you would respond:
   a. Child is having a nose bleed.
   b. Child appears to be experiencing a seizure.
   c. Toddler is choking on a bead that she found on the floor.
   d. Child is having an acute asthma attack.
   e. Child was pushed off of a piece of playground equipment and fell several feet to the ground; child appears disoriented, is pale, and has cool, clammy skin.
3. Discuss why you wouldn't begin the Heimlich maneuver immediately on a child who was choking but still able to cough. At what point would you initiate this emergency measure?
4. Describe how a teacher would determine if a child with diabetes was experiencing hypoglycemia or hyperglycemia. How does the treatment of each differ?

Case Study

The assistant director of the Cactus Kids Child Care Center was surprised one morning when a child care licensing surveyor from the local public health department paid an unannounced visit. She was confident that her center was in tip-top shape and would have no problem passing its annual safety inspection. As the surveyor entered one of the classrooms, she observed teachers attending to a child who appeared to be having a seizure. The director thought the child had a history of seizures, but ran back to the office to check her file.

1. What first aid measures should the teachers be administering?
2. How would their management strategies differ if the child has had no previous history of seizures?
3. Should the child's family be called? Why?
4. What conditions in the classroom could potentially trigger a seizure?
5. If the child's seizure continues longer than 5 minutes, what should the teachers do?
6. What information should be recorded during and following the seizure?

Application Activities

1. Complete basic CPR and first aid courses.
2. Design a poster or bulletin board illustrating emergency first aid for a young child who is choking. Offer your project to a local school or early childhood program where it can be displayed for families to read.
3. Divide the students into small groups. Discuss and demonstrate the emergency care or first aid treatment for each of the following situations. A child who:
   - burned several fingers on a hot plate
   - ate de-icing pellets
   - splashed turpentine in his/her eyes
   - fell from a climbing gym
   - is choking on popcorn
   - slammed fingers in a door
   - is found chewing on an extension cord
4. As a class project, prepare listings of emergency services and telephone numbers in your community. Distribute them to local early childhood centers or family day care homes.

Helpful Web Resources

Canadian Health Network	http://www.canadian-health-network.ca
Children's Safety Network	http://www.childrenssafetynetwork.org/
International Bicycle Fund (bicycle safety materials)	http://www.ibike.org/education/
Learn CPR (child) (online video clip)	http://depts.washington.edu/learncpr/childrencpr.html
Learn CPR (infant) (online video clip)	http://depts.washington.edu/learncpr/infantcpr.html
National Safe Kids Campaign	http://www.safekids.org
National Safety Council	http://www.nsc.org
Poison Prevention.Org	http://www.poisonprevention.org

You are just a click away from additional health, safety, and nutrition resources! Go to www.CengageBrain.com to access this text's Education CourseMate website, where you'll find:

- emergency contact information and medical authorization form
- individual injury report form
- glossary flashcards, activities, tutorial quizzes, videos, web links, and more

References

American Diabetes Association (ADA). (2009). Diabetes care in the school and day care setting, *Diabetes Care,* 32(10), S68–S72.

American Heart Association (AHA). (2006, Winter). Highlights of the 2005 American Heart Association Guidelines for cardiopulmonary resuscitation and emergency cardiovascular care, *Currents*, 16(4), 2–28.

Barrios, L., Jones, S., & Gallagher, S. (2007). Legal liability: The consequences of school injury, *Journal of School Health*, 77(5), 273–280.

Borse, N., Gilchrist, J., Dellinger, A., Rudd, R., Ballesteros, M., & Sleet, D. (2008). *CDC Childhood injury report: Patterns of unintentional injuries among 0–19 year olds in the United States, 2000–2006.* Atlanta (GA): Centers for Disease Control and Prevention, National Center for Injury Prevention and Control.

Brook, I. (2009). Management of human and animal bite wound infection: An overview, *Current Infectious Disease Reports*, 11(5), 389–395.

Cohen, S., Avital, A., Godfrey, S., Gross, M., & Kerem, E. (2009). Suspected foreign body inhalation in children: What are the indications for bronchoscopy?, *The Journal of Pediatrics*, 155(2), 276–280.

Dissanaike, S., & Rahimi, M. (2009). Epidemiology of burn injuries: Highlighting cultural and socio-demographic aspects, *International Review of Psychiatry*, 21(6), 505–511.

Gaines, J., & Schwebel, D. (2009). Recognition of home injury risks by novice parents of toddlers, *Accident Analysis & Prevention*, 41(5), 1070–1074.

Gilliland, F. (2009). Outdoor air pollution, genetic susceptibility, and asthma management: Opportunities for intervention to reduce the burden of asthma, *Pediatrics*, 123, Suppl. March 2009, S168–S173.

Glendor, U. (2009). Has the education of professional caregivers and lay people in dental trauma failed? *Dental Traumatology*, 25(1), 12–18.

Handley, A. (2009). Compression-only CPR—To teach or not to teach?, *Resuscitation*, 80(7), 752–754.

Hockenberry, M. (2008). *Wong's essentials of pediatric nursing.* (8th ed.). New York: Mosby.

Holcomb, S. (2009). Pediatric heatstroke, *Nursing*, 39(9), 64–68.

Kanchan, T., Menezes, R., & Monteiro, F. (2009). Fatal unintentional injuries among young children – A hospital based retrospective analysis, *Journal of Forensic and Legal Medicine*, 16(6), 307–311.

Kroncke, E., Niedfeldt, M., & Young, C. (2008). Use of protective equipment by adolescents in inline skating, skateboarding, and snowboarding, *Clinical Journal of Sport Medicine*, 18(1), 38–43.

Madden, M. (2008). Responding to pediatric poisoning, *Nursing*, 38(8), 52–55.

Marotz, L. (2000). Childhood and classroom injuries. In J. L. Frost (ed.), *Children and injuries.* Tuscon, AZ: Lawyers & Judges Publishing Co.

McGregor, T., Parkar, M., & Rao, S. (2009). Evaluation and management of common childhood poisonings, *American Family Physician*, 79(5), 397–403.

Melo, J., Di Rocco, F., Lemos-Júnior, L., Roujeau, T., Thélot, B., Sainte-Rose, C., Meye, P., & Zerah, M. (2009). Defenestration in children younger than 6 years old: Mortality predictors in severe head trauma, *Journal of Child's Nervous System*, 25(9), 1077–1083.

Obeng, C., (2009). Injuries in preschool classrooms, *Health Education*, 109(5), 414–423.

Pickett, W., Nichol, M., & Ehiri, J. (2010). Unintentional injuries in children. In J. Ehiri, (ed.), *Maternal & Child Health.* New York: Springer.

Podbielski, D., Surkont, M., Tehrani, N., & Ratnapalan, S. (2009). Pediatric eye injuries in a Canadian emergency department, *Canadian Journal of Ophthalmology*, 44(5), 519– 522.

Salo, P., Sever, M., & Zeldin, D. (2009). Indoor allergens in school and day care environments, *Journal of Allergy and Clinical Immunology*, 124(2), 185–192.

Wagner, C., & Boyd, K. (2009). Pediatric heatstroke, *Air Medical Journal*, 27(3), 118–122.

CHAPTER 10

Maltreatment of Children: Abuse and Neglect

NAEYC Standards *Chapter Links*

- **#1 a, b, and c:** Promoting child development and learning
- **#2 a, b, and c:** Building family and community relationships
- **#3 a, c, and d:** Observing, documenting, and assessing to support young children and families
- **#4 a and c:** Using developmentally effective approaches to connect with children and families
- **#5 c:** Using content knowledge to build meaningful curriculum
- **#6 a, b, c, and e:** Becoming a professional

Learning Objectives

After studying this chapter, you should be able to:

- Explain the significance of Public Law 93-247.
- Describe how discipline and punishment differ.
- Provide an example of each form of abuse (physical, emotional/verbal, sexual) and neglect (physical and emotional/psychological).
- Describe factors that may perpetuate abusive and/or neglectful acts.
- Discuss the protective steps programs can take to avoid accusations of abuse.
- Identify individuals who are mandated by law to report abuse and neglect.
- Explain how teachers can help children who may be abused or neglected.

For many reasons, the true extent of **abuse** and **neglect** may be difficult to determine with any degree of accuracy. Although an estimated three million cases are reported to investigative authorities in the United States each year, many incidences are unreported (U.S. Department of Health & Human Services, 2007). In 2007, more than 1,700 children died from maltreatment, but the actual number may be considerably more than the data reveal (CDC, 2009). In addition, thousands of children are known to suffer serious and sometimes permanent physical and emotional injuries that are also never reported (Neigh, Gillespie, & Nemeroff, 2009).

---

abuse – *to mistreat, attack, or cause harm to another individual.*
neglect – *failure of a parent or legal guardian to properly care for and meet the basic needs of a child under 18 years of age.*

Historical Developments

Accounts of child abuse date from ancient times to the present. Throughout history, young children, especially those with developmental disabilities, have suffered abusive and neglectful treatment. They have also been subjected to cultural practices that by today's standards would be considered inhumane. In many societies, children had no rights or privileges whatsoever, including the right to live.

One of the first child abuse cases in this country to attract widespread public attention involved a young girl named Mary Ellen. Friends and neighbors were concerned about the regular beatings Mary Ellen received from her adoptive parents. However, in 1874 there were no organizations responsible for dealing with the problems of child abuse and neglect. Consequently, Mary Ellen's friends contacted the New York Society for the Prevention of Cruelty to Animals on the basis that she was a human being and, therefore, also a member of the animal kingdom. Her parents were found guilty of cruelty to animals and eventually Mary Ellen was removed from their home. This incident brought gradual recognition to the fact that some form of care and protection was needed for the many maltreated and abandoned children in this country.

Although child abuse continued to be a major problem, it wasn't until 1961 that the subject once again received national attention. For a period of years, Dr. C. Henry Kempe studied various aspects of child abuse and was concerned about children whose lives were endangered. He first introduced the phrase "battered child syndrome" in 1961 during a national conference that he organized to address problems related to the harsh treatment of children (Kempe & Helfer, 1982).

The passage of Public Law (PL) 93–247, the Child Abuse Prevention and Treatment Act (CAPTA) on January 31, 1974, signified a turning point in the history of child abuse and neglect. For the first time, national attention was drawn to the issue of childhood maltreatment. This law also created the National Center on Child Abuse and Neglect, and required individual states to establish a central agency with legal authority to investigate and prosecute incidences of abuse and neglect. PL 93–247 also mandated states to develop policies, procedures, definitions, and laws that addressed these problems. In October 1996, CAPTA was reauthorized and amended to more clearly define circumstances related to the withholding of medical treatment in life-threatening situations. Changes in the 2003 reauthorization required states to expand their services to include adoption, foster care, abandoned infants, and family violence prevention. Additional funding was also appropriated for child protective worker training and efforts to strengthen collaboration among community agencies (Child Welfare Information Gateway, 2009).

Although child abuse and neglect have occurred throughout history, it is only recently that public attention has recognized the magnitude of this problem. And, only now are professionals realizing the full impact and prolonged effects that maltreatment has on children's development.

Discipline Vs. Punishment

The term **discipline** is derived from the word disciple and refers to the act of teaching or guiding. When used appropriately, discipline can be effective for helping children learn socially acceptable behavior. However, when it is used improperly or involves threats, fear, or harsh physical **punishment**, it teaches children only anger and violence.

For decades, the right to punish or discipline children as families saw fit was considered a parental privilege. Consequently, outsiders often overlooked or ignored incidences of cruelty to children so as not to interfere in a family's personal affairs. However, public attitudes regarding family privacy and the rights of families to discipline children as they wished began to change.

discipline – *training or enforced obedience that corrects, shapes, or develops acceptable patterns of behavior.*

punishment – *a negative response to what the observer considers to be wrong or inappropriate behavior; may involve physical or harsh treatment.*

Educators, health and law enforcement professionals, neighbors, and concerned friends grew intolerant of the abusive and neglectful treatment of young children. They began to speak out against such behavior and to serve as advocates for innocent children who were being victimized by adults.

One of the most difficult aspects of this problem is deciding at what point discipline or punishment becomes maltreatment. For example, when does a spanking or verbal **reprimand** constitute abuse? Is sending a child to his room without dinner neglect? In an attempt to establish clear guidelines, federal legislation forced states to define abuse and neglect and to establish policies and procedures for addressing individual cases.

Abuse and Neglect

Child maltreatment refers to any situation or environment in which a child is not safe due to inadequate protection, exposure to hazardous conditions, exploitation, mistreatment, or harm intentionally inflicted by adults. For legal purposes, a child is defined as an individual under 18 years of age. The most commonly recognized categories of maltreatment include:

- physical abuse
- emotional or verbal abuse
- sexual abuse
- physical neglect
- emotional or psychological neglect

Physical abuse is the most common form of abuse and is characterized by a range of visible, non-accidental injuries, such as cuts, burns, welts, fractures, scratches, and missing hair (Figure 10–1). The explanations families provide for these injuries are often inconsistent or unreasonable based on the child's age and/or developmental stage (Pierce et al., 2010). A combination of new and older or untreated injuries may suggest repeated abuse. In almost every instance, observable changes in the child's behavior, including shyness, fearfulness, passiveness, anger, aggression, or apprehension will accompany physical injuries (Table 10–1).

The **shaken baby syndrome**, another form of physical abuse, is typically seen in infants and young children. It is caused by vigorously shaking or tossing a child into the air, often because of persistent crying (Figure 10–2). The whiplash motion causes internal bleeding and bruising in the infant's brain that can result in blindness, deafness,

A child is legally defined as an individual under the age of 18 years.

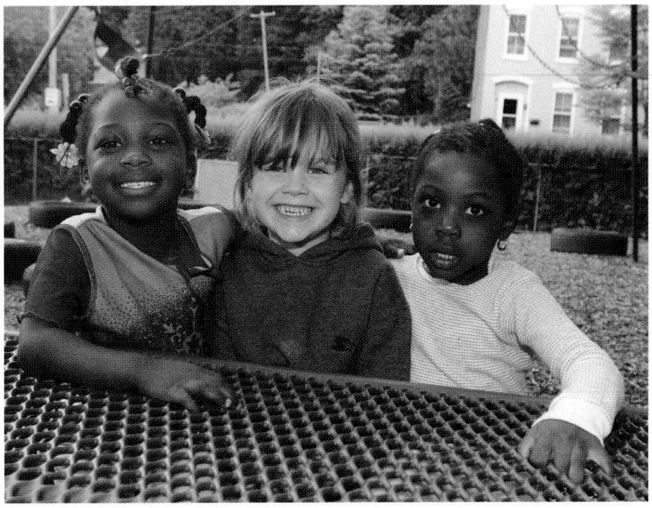

Figure 10–1 Percent of reported abuse and neglect by category.

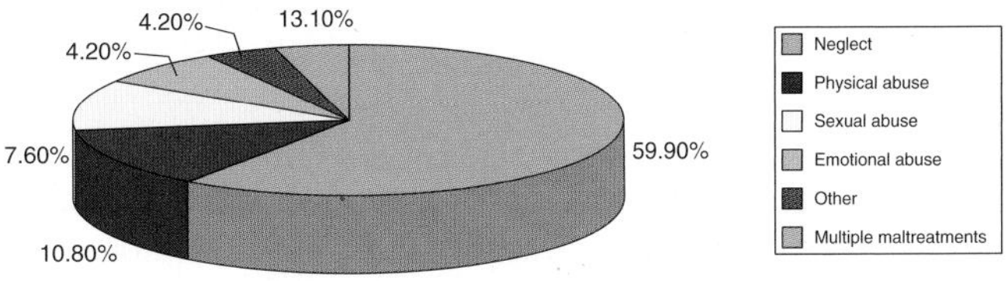

Source: U.S. Department of Health & Human Services, Administration for Children & Families. Child Maltreatment 2007. Retrieved February 17, 2010 at http://www.acf.hhs.gov/programs/cb/pubs/cm07/chapter3.htm#types.

reprimand – *to scold or discipline for unacceptable behavior.*
physical abuse – *injuries, such as welts, burns, bruises, or broken bones, that are caused intentionally.*
shaken baby syndrome – *forceful shaking of a baby that causes head trauma, internal bleeding, and sometimes death.*

Table 10–1 Teacher Checklist: Identifying Signs of Abuse and Neglect

Physical Abuse

- has frequent or unexplained injuries, e.g., burns, fractures, bruises, bites, eye or head injuries
- complains frequently of pain
- wears clothing to hide injuries; clothing may be inappropriate for weather conditions
- reports harsh treatment
- is often late or absent; arrives too early or stays after dismissal from school
- seems unusually fearful of adults, especially parents
- appears malnourished or dehydrated
- avoids logical explanations for injuries
- is withdrawn, anxious, or uncommunicative or may be outspoken, disruptive, and aggressive
- lacks affection, both giving and seeking
- is given inappropriate food, beverages, or drugs

Emotional/Verbal Abuse

- seems generally unhappy; seldom smiles or laughs
- is aggressive and disruptive or unusually shy and withdrawn
- reacts without emotion to unpleasant statements and actions
- displays behaviors that are unusually adult-like or child-like
- has delayed growth and/or emotional and intellectual development

Sexual Abuse

- wears underclothing that may be torn, stained, or bloody
- complains of pain or itching in the genital area
- has symptoms of venereal disease
- has difficulty getting along with other children, e.g., withdrawn, baby-like, anxious
- has rapid weight loss or gain
- experiences sudden decline in school performance
- becomes involved in delinquency, including prostitution, running away, alcoholism, or drug abuse
- is fascinated with body parts, uses sexual terms and talks about sexual activities that are unfamiliar to children of this age

Physical Neglect

- has a bad odor from dirty clothing or hair; repeatedly arrives unclean
- is in need of medical or dental care; may have untreated injuries or illness
- is often hungry; begs or steals food while at school
- dresses inappropriately for weather conditions; shoes and clothing often sized too small or too large
- is chronically tired; falls asleep at school, lacks the energy to play with other children
- has difficulty getting along with other children; spends much time alone

Emotional/Psychological Neglect

- performs poorly in school
- appears apathetic, withdrawn, and inattentive
- is frequently absent or late to school
- uses any means to gain teacher's attention and approval
- seldom participates in extracurricular activities
- engages in delinquent behaviors, e.g., stealing, vandalism, sexual misconduct, abuse of drugs or alcohol

fractures, learning disabilities, seizures, and death (Togioka et al., 2009). Prevention of this senseless tragedy requires adults to understand that shaking a child can have devastating effects and that crying is normal because it is an infant's primary mode of communication.

Figure 10–2 Tossing or shaking young children can result in permanent brain injuries.

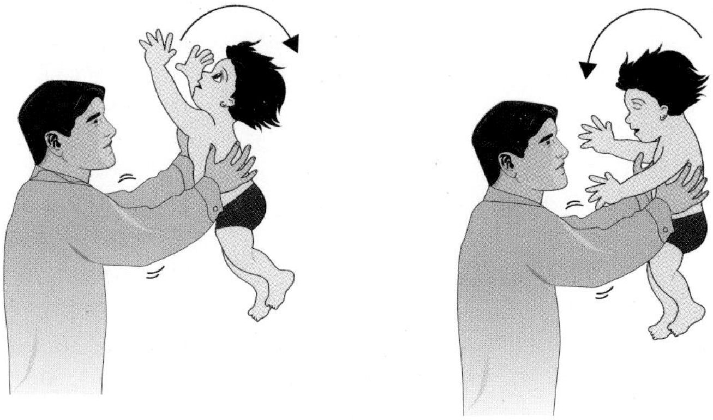

Physical abuse frequently begins as an innocent act of frustration or punishment. In other words, most adults do not set out to intentionally harm a child. However, in the process of disciplining the child, quick tempers and uncontrollable anger may lead to punishment that is severe and sufficiently violent to cause injuries and sometimes even death. In some cases, this outburst represents a one-time, regrettable incidence of poor judgment, while in others maltreatment may be a repetitive pattern (Mersky et al., 2009). Regardless of the circumstances, the hurtful treatment of children is never considered acceptable.

Emotional or **verbal abuse** occurs when caregivers repeatedly and unpredictably criticize, verbally assault, ignore, or belittle a child's behavior and/or achievements (Ferguson, 2009; Reinert & Edwards, 2009). Their demands and expectations are often unrealistic given the child's age and developmental abilities. Chronic exposure to negative statements, such as "Why can't you ever do things right?" or "I knew you were too stupid" have lifelong effects on children's emotional and intellectual development. In many cases, verbal assaults turn into physical abuse over time. Toddlers and preschoolers are the most frequent victims of this form of abuse because they are often defenseless.

Notable changes in a child's behavior are often an early indicator of verbal abuse (Table 10–1). Careful observation and documentation of adult–child interactions can be useful for identifying the potential signs of emotional abuse. Unlike the immediate harm caused by an act of physical abuse, the effects of verbal abuse may not appear until years later. This fact makes it difficult to identify and treat the problem before the abuse has left permanent scars on the child's personality and development. Sadly, many children will go on to engage in antisocial behaviors and to experience serious psychiatric disorders later in life (Shipman & Taussig, 2009; Wilson & Widom, 2009).

Sexual abuse involves any sexual involvement between an adult and a child, including fondling, exhibitionism, rape, incest, child pornography, and prostitution. Such acts are considered abusive regardless of whether or not the child agreed to participate (Peter, 2009). This belief is based on the assumption that children are incapable of making a rational decision or may not be able to refuse because of adult pressure. For this reason, the incidence of sexual abuse is probably much greater than reported and often not discovered until years later. Girls are sexually abused at a rate nearly twice that of boys (Maikovich, Koenen, & Jaffee, 2009). More often, the perpetrator is male and not a stranger to the child, but rather someone the child knows and trusts, such as a babysitter, relative, caretaker, stepparent, or teacher. Victims may be exposed to sexually transmitted diseases (STDs) and should be observed for characteristic symptoms (Table 10–2). Children who have been sexually abused also suffer a high rate of adult-onset mental health disorders (Neigh, Gillespie, & Nemeroff, 2009; Runyon, Steer, & Deblinger, 2009). Many sexually abused adolescents become runaways or prostitutes, or engage in a range of violent or dependency behaviors (Kim et al., 2009; Wilson & Widom, 2009).

---

emotional abuse – *repeated humiliation, ridicule, or threats directed toward another individual.*
verbal abuse – *to attack another individual with words.*
sexual abuse – *any sexual involvement between an adult and child.*

Table 10–2 Teacher Checklist: Identifying Symptoms of Common Sexually Transmitted Diseases (STDs)

Gonorrhea	May cause painful or burning discomfort when urinating, increased vaginal discharge (yellow, green), or vaginal bleeding. Discharge, anal itching, soreness, bleeding, or painful bowel movements are characteristic of rectal infections. May cause sore throat (oral sex). Many victims have no symptoms, but are still contagious; serious complications can develop if left untreated.
Chlamydia trachomatis	May cause abnormal vaginal discharge or burning discomfort when urinating 5 to 7 days following infection. Victims may not have any immediate symptoms; however, if left untreated infection can damage a woman's reproductive organs.
Syphilis	Symptoms appear in stages following infection. Initial stage: within 10 days to 3 months a chancre (painless sore) appears at the point of contact (vagina, rectum, mouth, penis) and heals. Second stage: 6 weeks to 6 months after sore heals a generalized rash appears along with fever and enlarged lymph glands. Curable with antibiotics.
Trichomoniasis	The most common and curable STD. Symptoms appear within 5 to 28 days and typically include a frothy, yellow-green, foul-smelling vaginal discharge, burning during urination, irritation, and itching around the genital area.
Genital herpes	Many victims have no symptoms. Others may develop painful blister-like sores (around vagina, rectum, penis, mouth), fever, flu-like symptoms, and swollen glands several days following infection; sores heal in 2 to 4 weeks. Re-occurrence of sores is common.
Condyloma (genital warts)	Caused by the human papilloma virus (HPV); single or clusters of warts may develop around the genital area within weeks or months following infection. Not everyone will develop symptoms. A vaccine is currently available.
AIDS	Infected persons usually have no initial symptoms. Blood tests can detect the HIV virus 6 weeks after exposure.

Physical neglect is defined as a family's abandonment of a child or their failure to provide for the child's basic needs and care (Dubowitz, 2009). More than half of all substantiated cases of maltreatment involve some form of neglect, including inadequate or inappropriate food, shelter, clothing, and/or cleanliness. Parents may be charged with medical neglect if they fail to obtain appropriate medical treatment, including immunizations, or refuse to give medications that are necessary to address children's health and dental needs (failing to do so may place the child at risk of disability or death) (CDC, 2008). Families are also being prosecuted for educational neglect if they fail to enroll children in school, allow them to drop out prematurely, or permit children to be truant from school. The courts are also charging adults with neglect if they supply drugs or alcohol to underage children or knowingly permit children to have access to, or use, illegal substances.

Parents who leave children alone and unsupervised may be charged with physical neglect. The term **latch-key** has been used to describe the significant numbers of school-aged children who are consistently left home alone during the hours before and after school (Flynn & Rodman, 2008). A shortage of programs, lack of trained personnel, and cost have made it difficult for many

---

physical neglect – *failure to meet children's fundamental needs for food, shelter, medical care, and education, including abandonment.*

latch-key – *a term that refers to school-age children who care for themselves without adult supervision before and after school hours.*

working families to secure adequate before- and after-school care for school-aged children. Many unanswered questions continue to be raised about whether these children are at greater risk for accidental injury and/or emotional distress as a result of being left alone (Ruiz-Casares & Heyman, 2009). In the meantime, teachers can share information with families to help them decide when it is appropriate and safe for children to stay home by themselves (Table 10–3).

Emotional or psychological neglect is perhaps the most difficult form of maltreatment to recognize and document. For this reason, many states do not include it in their reporting laws. Emotional neglect reflects a basic lack of parental interest and/or responsiveness to a child's psychological needs and development (Egeland, 2009; Schmalz et al., 2009) (Table 10–1).

Parents fail to see the need, or do not know how, to show affection or converse appropriately with their child. The absence of any emotional connection, such as hugging, kissing, touching, conversation, or facial expressions revealing pleasure or displeasure, can lead to developmental delays and stunted growth. The term **failure to thrive** is used to describe this condition when it occurs in infants and young children. A lack of measurable gains in weight and/or height is often one of the first indications of psychological neglect (Legano, McHugh, & Palusci, 2009).

Table 10–3 Tips for Determining If Children Are Ready to Be Left Home Alone

- Has your child expressed interest in staying home alone?
- Does your child typically understand and abide by family rules?
- Is your child reliable and able to handle responsibility in a mature manner?
- Does your child handle unexpected events in a positive way?
- Is your child able to entertain her/himself for long periods of time or does she/he require constant supervision?
- Have you rehearsed safety and emergency procedures so your child knows how to respond in the event of a fire, an unwanted telephone call, or someone knocking at the front door?
- Does your child know how to reach you if necessary? Is there another adult your child can contact if you are not available?
- Has your child experienced being left home alone for short periods?
- Does your child have any fears that would be a problem if he/she were left alone?

Issues To Consider — Cultural Practices and Child Abuse

Members of a local Vietnamese community were irate following the arrest of a boy's 23-year-old parents for child abuse. Teachers had noted purple "bruises" on the little boy's back and chest when he arrived at school one day. The couple denied any wrongdoing, insisting they were merely performing "cao gio," a traditional Vietnamese practice used to cure fever. Following the application of medicated oil to the skin, a warm coin or spoon is scraped along the spine and chest until reddened patches appear. The boy's parents believed this would eliminate "bad winds" that had caused his fever.

- Is this abuse?
- How do cultural differences affect parental practices and values?
- Should families be expected to give up traditional cultural practices related to healing and medicine when they immigrate to this country?
- Why is it important for teachers to acquire an understanding of cultural differences?

---

emotional or psychological neglect – *failure to meet a child's psychological needs for love and attention.*

failure to thrive – *a term used to describe an infant whose growth and mental development are severely slowed due to lack of nurturing or mental stimulation.*

Understanding the Dynamics of Abuse and Neglect

Abusive adults come from all levels of social, economic, educational, ethnic, religious, and occupational backgrounds (Barth, 2009). They live in rural areas, as well as small towns and large cities. It is a common misconception that child maltreatment is committed only by adults who are uneducated, alcoholics, drug abusers, or from poor neighborhoods. Although the incidence is significantly higher among these groups, such generalizations may be overly simplistic where such complex social and economic issues are involved.

One explanation for why the incidence of child abuse or neglect appears to be greater among disadvantaged families may relate to their increased reliance on public and social service programs. Frequent communication and visits with these families allow agency personnel to more closely monitor their actions. Furthermore, disadvantaged families often face circumstances that make daily living more stressful and limit their options. Simply finding adequate food, clothing, housing, and transportation can become overwhelming demands (Guterman et al., 2009). In contrast, families with greater financial resources may have more choices available to them and can afford private medical care, move from doctor to doctor, and even seek treatment in neighboring cities. This flexibility limits their contact with a single health care provider and makes it easier for families to avoid immediate suspicion.

Researchers continue to study childhood maltreatment in an effort to better understand the complex nature of this problem. To date, they have identified three major risk factors:

- characteristics of adults with a potential for committing abuse/neglect
- presence of a child who is viewed as "special"
- family and environmental stressors

It is believed that for abuse and neglect to take place, all three risk factors must occur at approximately the same time.

Characteristics of Abusive/Neglectful Adults

Certain adult behaviors and predispositions are commonly associated with abusive tendencies, including:

- a history of repeated fear, anger, and rejection
- low self-esteem
- difficulty in forming long-term relationships (e.g., friendships, marriage) that leads to social isolation and loneliness; looks to the child for love
- lack of trust
- early marriage and pregnancy
- maternal depression (Conron et al., 2009)
- use of harsh punishment to "discipline" children
- impulsive tendencies
- low tolerance for stress (Guterman et al., 2009)
- drug and alcohol addictions
- poor problem-solving abilities

Although not every adult who exhibits these characteristics is abusive or neglectful, likewise not every abusive or neglectful caregiver will necessarily display all of these behaviors (Barth, 2009). In many cases, adults simply lack the knowledge and skills needed to be a successful parent. Their ignorance about children's development can lead to expectations that may be unrealistic and developmentally inappropriate based on the child's age and abilities (Bugental & Schwartz, 2009). For example, a parent may become upset because a 15-month-old wets the bed, a toddler spills milk, or a 7-year-old loses a mitten. Intolerance, frustration, and uncontrolled anger can, in turn, lead to a subsequent outlash of abusive behavior. Drugs and alcohol addictions may further reduce an adult's ability to be nurturing or to respond appropriately to children's needs. Evidence also suggests that adults who grew up in abusive families are more likely to treat their own children in a similar manner (Manders & Stoneman, 2009; Whiting et al., 2009).

A Child Who Is Viewed as "Special"

Occasionally an abusive or neglectful caregiver will single out a child whom they consider to differ in some way from their expectations. These differences may be real or imagined; in either case, the adult is convinced that they truly exist. Some characteristics commonly cited by abusive or neglectful adults include a child who is:

- developmentally delayed
- disobedient or uncooperative
- physically unattractive
- unintelligent
- hyperactive
- fussy
- clumsy
- frequently ill
- very timid or weak
- resembles someone the adult dislikes

Children who have developmental disabilities are at greater risk for abusive and neglectful treatment.

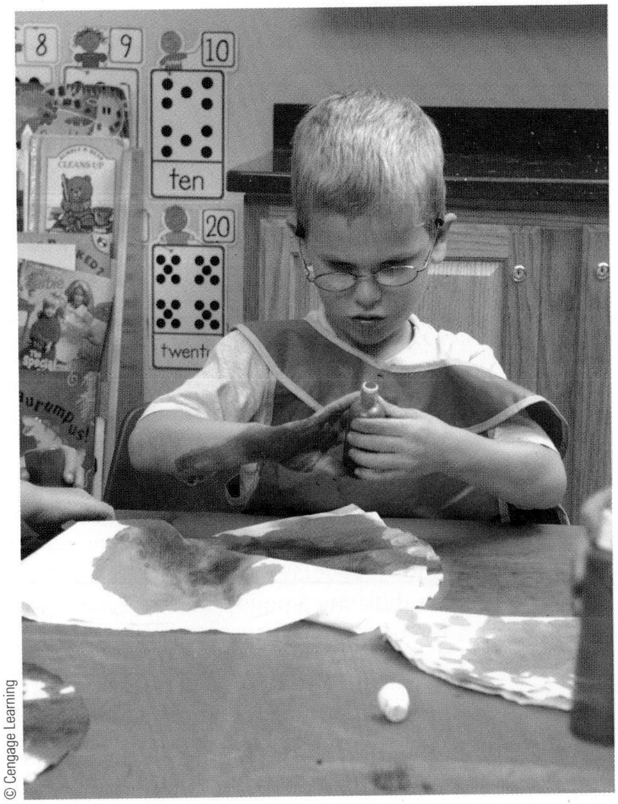

Victims of child maltreatment include an almost equal number of boys and girls. Children under age 4 years and those who have developmental disabilities, especially autism, are at highest risk for physical abuse (Manders & Stoneman, 2009). Infants under 12 months and children over the age of 6 years are more likely to suffer from neglect. The risk of maltreatment is also greater for children who are born outside of marriage, from unwanted or unplanned pregnancies, stepchildren, living in foster homes, or living in families where domestic violence is also occurring.

Family and Environmental Stresses

All individuals and families face conflict and crises from time to time. However, some are better able than others to cope with stressful events. In many maltreatment cases, stress is the **precipitating** factor. That is, conflict is sufficient to push an adult to action (abuse) or withdrawal (neglect) as a caretaker (Guterman et al., 2009; McPherson et al., 2009).

Adults who mistreat children often have difficulty discriminating between events that are

precipitating – *factors that trigger or initiate a reaction or response.*

Reflective Thoughts

Teachers (including assistants, aides, and students) are required to report suspected incidences of child abuse and/or neglect. How do you determine what to report? Should the family be informed when a report has been filed? What are your feelings about making a report when it is likely the family will know who filed the complaint? What professional responsibilities do you have to the child and family?

significantly stressful and those that are not. Instead, they find all crises equally threatening, overwhelming, and difficult to manage. The following examples illustrate the range of personal and environmental stressors that could potentially lead to a loss of control, especially when they occur in combination with other events that are also perceived as stressful:

- flat tire
- clogged sink
- broken window
- lost keys
- job loss
- illness, injury, or death
- financial pressures
- divorce or other marital problems
- moving
- birth of another child

Some events may seem trivial in comparison to others. Yet, any one may become the "straw that breaks the camel's back" and trigger abusive behavior. The level of an adult's anger may also be inappropriate and out of proportion to the actual event and ultimately taken out on the child.

Protective Measures for Programs and Teachers

It is essential that early childhood programs and school personnel take steps to protect themselves from potential accusations of child maltreatment. Special attention should be given to careful hiring practices, policy development, and ongoing training of personnel, including:

- conducting background checks on new employees for any prior record of child abuse or felony convictions. (These are mandated in most states and conducted by state law enforcement agencies.)
- hiring individuals with formal training in early education and child development
- contacting an applicant's references (nonrelative) and requesting information about the applicant's prior performance
- reviewing an employee's past employment record, including reasons for leaving previous jobs
- establishing a code of conduct regarding appropriate child–teacher behavior
- providing continued inservice training, especially on topics related to identification of abuse/neglect, effective behavior management strategies, and teaching children self-protection skills (Table 10–4)
- establishing a policy of nontolerance toward any form of abusive behavior, including harassment and harsh discipline

Teachers can take additional measures to protect themselves against the possibility of false accusations (Stover, 2000). Conducting daily health checks upon a child's arrival and recording all findings can protect teachers from being blamed for a bruise or scratch that may have occurred elsewhere. Teachers should also maintain thorough records of children's injuries so there is factual evidence that describes the circumstances and treatment administered. It is also preferable not to leave a teacher alone with children. A second teacher who serves as an eyewitness can eliminate any suspicions of wrongdoing. Teachers should also participate in inservice training opportunities to improve their understanding of child maltreatment and their role in successful intervention.

Table 10–4 Teacher Checklist: Strategies for Positive Behavior Management

- ***Reinforce*** desirable behaviors. Give lots of hugs and pats, adult attention, and verbal acknowledgment for things the child is doing appropriately; reinforcement should be given often and immediately following the appropriate behavior. "I really like the way you are sharing your toys" or "That was nice of you to let Mat have a turn on the bike."
- ***Redirect*** the child to another activity or area when he/she is behaving inappropriately; don't comment on the inappropriate behavior. "Juan, could you come and help me set the table?" or "Let's go to the block area and build a zoo together."
- ***Consistent expectations*** help children understand their limits and the way in which adults expect them to behave. Expectations should be realistic and state behavior that is considered appropriate. Keep explanations simple and brief. "Mika, you need to sit on the sofa; feet go on the floor" or "We need to walk in the halls."
- ***Consequences*** can be used together with other management strategies. Most children understand consequences from an early age on. "When your hands are washed we can eat" or "I will have to take the ball away if you throw it at the window again."
- ***Ignoring*** undesirable behaviors, such as tantrums or throwing things can be effective for decreasing the attention-getting response children may be looking for. Don't look at the child or discuss the behavior with the child.
- ***Practice*** desirable behaviors when the child behaves inappropriately. For example, if the child scatters crayons across the floor, he/she needs to pick them up and then be acknowledged for doing what was asked. An adult may also model the desired behavior by helping the child to pick up the crayons.

Finally, teachers may want to purchase their own professional liability insurance unless they are covered by their employer's policy.

Inservice Training

Teachers are morally and legally responsible for identifying the early signs of child maltreatment. However, to be effective, they must also be well informed. Teachers can acquire the knowledge and skills they need to fulfill this responsibility by participating in ongoing inservice training. Topics that teachers will find beneficial include:

- an explanation of relevant state laws
- teachers' rights and responsibilities
- how to identify child abuse and neglect
- development of school policies and procedures for handling suspected cases
- exploration of teacher and staff reactions to abuse and neglect
- identifying community resources and services
- classroom strategies for helping abused and neglected children
- stress reduction and time management.

Teachers also play a valuable role advocating for laws, policies, and programs that protect children's rights and well-being.

Reporting Laws

Reporting laws support the philosophy that parenthood carries with it certain obligations and responsibilities toward children. Therefore, punishment of abusive adults is not the primary objective. Rather, the purpose of these laws is to protect children from maltreatment and exploitation. Every attempt is made to maintain family unity by helping families find solutions to problems that may be contributing to the abuse or neglect. Contrary to common belief, removing children from their homes is not always the best solution. Alternative placements and frequent moves may not improve the stability or quality of a child's life. Criminal action against parents is usually reserved for cases in which the adults are unwilling or unable to cooperate with prescribed educational and treatment programs.

Each case of maltreatment involves a unique and complex set of conditions, including home environments, economic pressures, individual temperaments, cultural differences, along with many other factors. For this reason, most child abuse laws and definitions are purposely written in general terms. This practice allows the legal system and social agencies greater flexibility in determining whether or not an adult has acted irresponsibly.

Laws in every state identify certain groups and professionals who are required to report suspected incidences of abuse or neglect, including:

- teachers, including assistants and student teachers
- center directors and principals
- health care providers (e.g., doctors, nurses, dentists, pharmacists, psychologists, mental health counselors)
- law enforcement personnel
- social workers
- clergy

Program Policy

Every school and early childhood program should have a written action plan for addressing suspected incidences of abuse and neglect (Hinkelman & Bruno, 2008). Policies and procedures should be reviewed frequently with staff to ensure their understanding and compliance. In larger programs teachers may report directly to the director, principal, head administrator, or health consultant who, in turn, contacts appropriate local authorities and files a report. However, if at any time teachers are not satisfied that their concerns have been properly reported, they are obligated by law to personally report the incidence. In home-based programs or smaller centers, an individual staff member may be responsible for initiating the report. Failure to do so may prolong a potentially harmful situation for the child, and result in criminal prosecution and monetary fines for the teacher.

Initial reports are usually made by telephone and followed up with a written report that is completed several days later (Table 10–5). All information is kept strictly confidential, including the identity of the person making the report. Protection against liability and criminal charges is afforded by most reporting laws to anyone who reports abuse or neglect without deliberate intent to harm another individual.

Parenthood implies that an adult is willing to assume certain obligations and responsibilities for children.

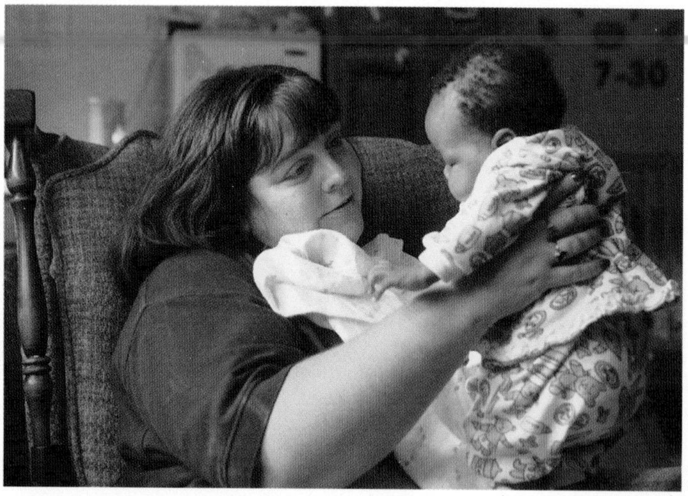

© Cengage Learning

Reflective Thoughts

In many families, economic pressures contribute to the problem of child abuse and neglect. How does poverty increase the probability of child abuse? How might cultural values affect this association? What resources are available to families living in poverty to help with everyday living expenses? What potential effects might poverty and an abusive childhood have on a child's self-concept?

Table 10–5 Teacher Checklist: What to Include in a Written Child Abuse/Neglect Report

1. The name and address of the child and the parents or caretakers (if known).
2. The child's age.
3. The nature and extent of the child's injuries or description of neglect including any evidence of previous injuries or deprivation.
4. The identity of the offending adult (if known).
5. Other information that the reporting person believes may be helpful in establishing the cause of injuries or neglect.
6. The name, address, telephone number, and professional title of the individual making the report.

It is not the teacher's role to prove suspicions of abuse and neglect before making a report (Goebbels, Nicholson, & Walsh, 2008). If there is any reason to believe that a child is being mistreated or inadequately cared for, local child protective services or the National Child Abuse Hotline (800-422-4453) should be contacted immediately. As long as a report is made in good faith, the teacher is merely indicating that a family may be in need of help. The law does not require the family or adult in question to be notified when a report is filed. In some cases, doing so could place the child in additional danger, especially if sexual or harsh physical abuse is involved. Other families may experience relief when their problems are finally recognized. Therefore, the decision of whether or not to inform the family or adult in question may depend on the particular circumstances.

Reporting a family, colleague, or acquaintance can be difficult. However, as advocates for children's rights, teachers must always be concerned about children's safety and welfare. Unless the child is in immediate danger, trained personnel will generally meet with the family or caregiver within a few days to evaluate circumstances surrounding the incident. Legal action may be taken depending on the seriousness of the situation or arrangements may be made to provide family-centered support services.

The Role of the Teacher

Teachers may be one of the few advocates children can turn to when they are being mistreated. They play an important role in addressing the issue of abuse and neglect through their ability to establish effective communication with children, provide emotionally supportive and accepting environments, identify and report suspicions of abuse and/or neglect, and help children learn socially appropriate behaviors.

Early Identification and Reporting

Teachers are in an ideal position to identify and help children who are being mistreated (Egeland, 2009; Goebbels, Nicholson, & Walsh, 2008). Daily health checks and frequent interactions with children enable teachers to recognize early changes in children's behavior and/or appearance (see Chapter 2). Because maltreatment is often a pattern of behavior, written documentation of each incident is important and should include:

- a precise description of the type, location, size, and severity of any suspected injury (Figure 10–3)
- the child's explanation of how the injury occurred
- any explanation provided by the family or caretakers describing how the injury occurred
- obvious signs of neglect (e.g., malnutrition, uncleanliness, inappropriate dress, excessive fatigue, lack of medical or dental care)
- recent or significant changes in the child's behavior
- nature of parent/child interactions

Figure 10–3 Form for illustrating the location, size, and nature of suspected abusive injuries.

Child's Name: ______________________
Date: ______________________
Comments: ______________________
Description of Injury: ______________________
Location and Size of Injury: ______________________
Color of Injury: ______________________
Desciption of Child's Behavior: ______________________
Additional Comments/Concerns: ______________________
Reported by: ______________________

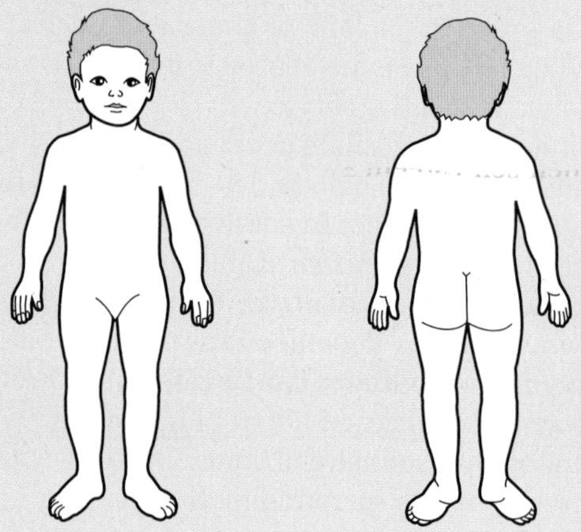

This information provides child protective authorities with additional supporting evidence and may also be helpful for determining the types of services and intervention programs most appropriate for the children and their families.

Teachers must not ignore their professional and legal responsibilities to protect children's safety. In many cases, a teacher may be the only adult whom a child trusts enough to reveal maltreatment. Teachers must be able to identify the signs of abuse and neglect and know when and how to report suspected cases to the appropriate authorities. They must also be aware of cultural differences in parenting skills and expectations so as not to misinterpret what they may witness (Zhai & Gao, 2009).

Providing a Supportive Environment for Children

Teachers also play an important role in helping children understand and cope with the effects of abusive and neglectful treatment (Gabalda et al., 2009). They must be positive role models and accept children for who they are, listen to their concerns without judgment, encourage their efforts, and praise their successes. For many children, teachers may be the only adult in their lives who accepts them unconditionally and shows a sincere interest in their well-being without threatening or causing them harm.

As children develop a trusting relationship, they may begin to open up and to verbalize their personal feelings. Play therapy can be especially effective with young children by providing opportunities where they can act out anger, fears, and anxieties related to abusive treatment (Bowers, 2009). Housekeeping activities, puppets, and doll play are ideal activities for this purpose. For example, talking about how the puppet or doll (child) feels when it is mistreated may help to draw out a child's true feelings. At the same time, teachers can model effective parenting skills for children, such as appropriate ways of talking to, treating, and caring for the puppets or dolls.

Artwork can also be an effective means for encouraging children's expressions of feelings and concerns. For example, self-portraits may reveal an exaggeration of certain body parts or circumstances that children have experienced. Pictures may also depict unusual practices that children have been subjected to, such as being tied up, locked in a closet, or struck with an object. However, extreme caution must always be exercised when attempting to interpret children's artwork. A child's immature drawing skills and lack of perspective can easily cause an inexperienced observer to misinterpret or reach false conclusions. Therefore, it is best to view unusual items in children's drawings as additional clues, rather than as absolute indicators of abusive or neglectful treatment.

Teachers can be instrumental in helping children learn how to manage their own anger and to express emotions in ways that are both appropriate and socially acceptable (Shipman & Taussig, 2009). For example, a teacher might say, "Rosa, if you want another cracker, you need to say 'Please can I have another cracker.' No one can understand when you whine or cry." Or, "I can't let you hit Rodney. You need to ask him, 'May I please have a turn on the bike?'"

Teachers can also help children develop skills that will improve their resiliency to maltreatment (see Chapter 1) (Schultz et al., 2009). Building trusting and respectful relationships with children is an important step in boosting their self-esteem and self-concept. Teachers can accomplish this by:

- responding to children in a consistent and supportive manner
- setting aside a private space that children can call their own
- establishing gradual limits for acceptable behavior; setting routines and schedules that provide order in children's lives that often have been dominated by turmoil
- letting children know they are available whenever they need someone, whether it be for companionship, extra attention, or reassurance
- taking time to prepare children for new experiences; informing children of expectations in advance enhances the "safeness" of their environment
- encouraging children to talk about their feelings, fears, and concerns

A number of educational programs and materials have been developed to help improve children's awareness and ability to respond to maltreatment (Table 10–6). Many good resources are available on the Internet or through local public libraries, schools, and pediatric and mental health offices.

Table 10–6 Teachers Checklist: Children's Books about Maltreatment

Bernstein, S., & Ritz, K. (1991). *A family that fights.* Morton Grove, IL: Albert Whitman & Co.

Federico, J. (2009). *Some parts are not for sharing.* Mustang, OK: Tate Publishing & Enterprises. (also available in Spanish)

Fitts, S., & Asay, D. (1999). *A stranger in the park.* Scottsdale, AZ: Agreka Books.

Foltz, L. (2003). *Kids helping kids break the silence of sexual abuse.* Lighthouse Point, FL: Lighthouse Point Press (for older children).

Girard, L. (1992). *My body is private.* Morton Grove, IL: Albert Whitman & Co.

Girard, L. (1993). *Who is a stranger and what should I do?* New York: Concept Books.

Gross, P. (1996). *Stranger safety.* Southfield, MI: Roo Publishing.

Holmes, M., Mudlaff, S., & Pillo, C. (2000). *A terrible thing happened: A story for children who have witnessed violence or trauma.* Washington, DC: Magination Books.

Joyce, I. (2000). *Never talk to strangers: A book about personal safety.* Racine, WI: Golden Books.

Kehoe, P. (1987). *Something happened and I'm scared to tell: A book for young victims of abuse.* Seattle, WA: Parenting Press.

Kleven, S., & Bergsma, J. (1998). *The right touch.* Bellevue, WA: Illumination Arts.

Kraizer, S. (1996). *The safe child book: A commonsense approach to protecting children and teaching children to protect themselves.* NY: Fireside Press.

Loftis, C. (1997). *The words hurt: Helping children cope with verbal abuse.* New York: Horizon Press.

Pendziwol, J. (2006). *Once upon a dragon: Stranger safety for kids (and dragons).* Tonawanda, NY: Kids Can Press.

(*continued*)

Table 10–6 Teachers Checklist: Children's Books about Maltreatment *(continued)*

Schor, H. (2002). *A place for Starr: A story of hope for children experiencing family violence.* Charlotte, NC: Kidsrights Press.
Spelman, C., & Weidner, T. (2000). *Your body belongs to you.* Morton Grove, IL: Albert Whitman & Co.
Stowell, J., & Dietzel, M. (2000). *My very own book about me: A personal safety book.* Spokane, WA: ACT for Kids.
Wachter, O. (2002). *No more secrets for me.* London: Little Brown & Co.

Caution should be used when selecting materials so they are developmentally appropriate, instructive, and not frightening to young children (Topping & Barron, 2009). Social workers, nurses, doctors, mental health specialists, teachers, and public service groups can often be called upon to provide educational programs for children and families.

Caring adults provide children with much needed companionship, reassurance, and individualized attention.

© Cengage Learning

It is also important to help children develop effective communication and self-protection skills. Although children may not fully understand the complexity of abuse or neglect, these skills enhance resilience and improve children's ability to recognize "uncomfortable" situations, how and when to tell a trusted adult, and how to assert themselves by saying no when someone attempts an inappropriate behavior. Informed children can be the first line of defense against abuse and neglect if they know that being beaten, forced to engage in sexual activity, or left alone for long periods is not normal or the type of treatment they deserve.

Educating Families

Raising young children is a challenging and demanding task. Many adults today have not had the same opportunities to learn parenting skills that past generations once had. They have often grown up in smaller families and had fewer opportunities to practice parenting firsthand until their own children arrive. Employment opportunities may require relocation to distant cities and result in the loss of extended family contact and support. And, more often than not, today's parents are holding down full-time jobs in addition to raising children. As a result, daily stress levels may challenge some parents' ability to be patient, nurturing, and responsive to children's developmental needs. However, these circumstances in no way excuse harsh or neglectful treatment of children. They may signal the importance of early recognition and intervention.

There are many ways teachers can help families in these situations (Draper et al., 2009; Stagner & Lansing, 2009). Daily contacts provide opportunities for identifying families in crises and directing them to appropriate community services and programs, such as:

- child protective services
- day care and "crisis" centers
- family counseling
- help or "hot" lines
- temporary foster homes
- homemaker services
- transportation
- financial assistance
- parenting classes
- employment assistance
- home visitors
- self-help or support groups

Focus On Families — Anger Management

Being a parent has many positive rewards, but it can also be a challenging and stressful role to fulfill. At times, children are likely to behave in ways that we find upsetting and cause us to react in anger. Although this behavior is understandable, it does not teach children how to handle their feelings of frustration or disappointment in a positive manner. Instead, our actions may teach children how to shout, say hurtful words, and respond in an emotional or physical fashion, rather than in a thoughtful and constructive way. When adults practice effective anger management strategies, they become positive role models for children. The next time your child makes you angry, try several of the following techniques:

- Take a deep breath. Thoroughly assess the situation before you react.
- Leave the room. Take a brief "time out" and regain control of your emotions.
- Consider whether the situation or the child's behavior is actually worth your becoming upset. Could the outcome affect the long-term relationship you have with your child?
- Tell children what has upset you and why.
- Avoid lengthy explanations and arguments with your child. Children are more likely to understand statements when they are brief and to the point.
- Learn to recognize your tolerance limits and what behaviors are most likely to make you upset.
- Always find something good to say about your child soon afterward. This helps children to understand that you still love them despite their unacceptable behavior.

Classroom Corner — Teacher Activities

We Have Many Kinds of Feelings (PreK–2). (National Health Education Standards 4.2.1)

Concept: We all have feelings and it is important to talk about our feelings

Learning Objectives

- Children will learn that there are many different types of feelings.
- Children will learn that it is important to talk about their feelings.

Supplies

- large piece of paper to write down comments from the children
- marking pen
- two puppets (any kind)
- small pile of blocks
- three small cars
- box of crayons
- two pieces of paper

(continued)

Classroom Corner **Teacher Activities** *(continued)*

Learning Activities

- Read and discuss the following books (see Appendix D for additional titles):
  - *The Way I Feel* by Janan Cain
  - *Big Feelings* by Talaris Institute
- Ask children if they have felt the same as the children in the story. Ask children to talk about what makes them feel scared, happy, angry, and so on.
- Next, role-play with the puppets. Have puppet one playing with three cars and have puppet two come over to play. Have puppet one ask puppet two if she would like to play with a car. Ask the children how they think puppet two feels when she got to play with a car.
- Next, have puppet one stacking and playing with blocks. Then have puppet two come over and knock down his blocks. Ask children how they think puppet one is feeling after his block building was knocked down. Talk about what puppet two should have done differently (asked to play, asked a teacher for other blocks, and so on).
- Finally, have puppet one drawing with paper and crayons. Have puppet two come over and ask puppet one if she can play. Have puppet one say, "No, I am playing with these." Ask children how puppet two is feeling, and talk about what puppet two can do to get some crayons and paper (grab them—not appropriate; ask a teacher to get them some crayons and paper—appropriate).

Evaluation

- Children will name several different kinds of feelings.
- Children will describe behaviors that evoke specific feelings.

Additional lesson plans for grades 3–5 are available on the premium website for this book.

Teachers also play an important role in educating families about critical topics such as child development, effective discipline, nutritious foods, activities that promote learning, and healthy lifestyle behaviors that will strengthen their child-rearing skills. Teachers must, however, be sensitive to cultural differences in parenting practices that could be misinterpreted as abusive (Dettlaff, Earner, & Phillips, 2009; Zhai & Gao, 2009). Supportive partnerships and open lines of communication can be established with families for both prevention and intervention purposes. Teachers can also be proactive and offer workshops through their local schools, child development centers, after-school programs, or community agencies on a variety of topics that will benefit families, such as:

- child growth and development
- identification and management of behavior problems
- principles of good nutrition; feeding problems
- how to meet children's social and emotional needs at different stages
- preventive health care for children
- locating and utilizing community resources
- stress and tension relievers for parents
- safe environments and injury prevention
- financial planning
- organizing a family support group

Summary

- Public Law 93-247, the Child Abuse Prevention and Treatment Act:
  - was the first national law that addressed the problems of child abuse and neglect
  - provides legal protection to children who are maltreated
  - requires states to pass laws, designate an investigative agency, and establish policies
  - reauthorizations of this act reflect concern about contemporary maltreatment issues, including adoption, foster care, abandoned infants, family violence, and improved interagency collaboration
- Discipline involves guiding or teaching children how they should behave.
  - Punishment teaches children negative behaviors, including anger and violence.
- Children under 18 years are protected by law from harm, exploitation, and inadequate care.
  - Most states recognize four categories of abuse/neglect, including physical abuse, sexual abuse, emotional abuse, and physical neglect; emotional/psychological neglect is recognized in some states.
- The potential for abuse and/or neglect is thought to be greatest when three factors exist at approximately the same time: an adult who has abusive tendencies, a child who is viewed as being "special," and environmental stressors.
- Programs and schools must take steps to protect themselves against possible claims of abuse or neglect through careful hiring practices and inservice training.
- Teachers are required to report suspected incidences of abuse or neglect and are protected by the law if reports are made in good faith.
  - Programs should have a procedure in place for handling incidences of abuse and neglect.
- Teachers play an important role in the prevention and treatment of child abuse/neglect through early identification and reporting, providing emotional support to children, educating families, helping children learn socially acceptable behaviors, and advocating on behalf of children.

Terms to Know

abuse *p. 267*
neglect *p. 267*
discipline *p. 268*
punishment *p. 268*
reprimand *p. 269*
physical abuse *p. 269*
shaken baby syndrome *p. 269*
emotional abuse *p. 271*
verbal abuse *p. 271*
sexual abuse *p. 271*
physical neglect *p. 272*
latch-key *p. 272*
emotional/psychological neglect *p. 273*
failure to thrive *p. 273*
precipitating *p. 275*

Chapter Review

A. By Yourself:

1. Define each of the Terms to Know.
2. Select a word from the list below to complete each of the following statements.

teachers	definition
trust	expectations
physical	neglect
psychological	identify
sexual	confidential
childhood	reported

   1. A child's excessive fascination with body parts and talk about sexual activities may be an indication of _____________ abuse.
   2. Public Law 93-247 requires states to write a legal _____________ of child abuse and neglect.

3. Injury that is intentionally inflicted on a child is called ___________ abuse.
4. Malnutrition, lack of proper clothing, or inadequate adult supervision are examples of physical ___________.
5. Verbal abuse sometimes results because of unrealistic parent demands and ________.
6. Emotional or ___________ neglect is one of the most difficult forms of neglect to identify.
7. Reporting laws usually require ___________ to report suspected cases of child abuse and neglect.
8. Information contained in reports of child abuse or neglect is kept ___________.
9. Many abusive adults were abused during their own ___________.
10. Lack of ___________ makes it difficult for many abusive and neglectful adults to form friendships.
11. Daily contact with children helps teachers to ___________ children who are maltreated.
12. Suspected abuse or neglect does not have to be proven before it should be ________.

B. As a Group:

1. Describe five observable clues that might suggest a child is being maltreated.
2. Discuss what teachers should do if they suspect that a child is being abused or neglected.
3. Describe what information should be included in both an oral and written report.
4. Discuss four ways that teachers can help abused and neglected children in the classroom.
5. Compile a list of services available in your community to help abusive or neglectful families; include contact information and a brief description for each.
6. Why does the incidence of child abuse and neglect appear to be higher among disadvantaged families?

Case Study

When it was time for snacks, 4-year-old Jimmy said he wasn't hungry and refused to come over and sit down. At the teacher's gentle insistence, Jimmy reluctantly joined the other children at the table. Tears began to roll down his cheeks as he tried to sit in his chair. Jimmy's teacher watched for a few moments and then walked over to talk with him. Initially, he denied that anything was wrong, but later told the teacher that he "had fallen the night before and hurt his bottom."

The teacher took Jimmy aside and comforted him. She asked Jimmy if he would show her where he had been hurt. When Jimmy loosened his jeans, the teacher observed what appeared to be a large burn with some blistering approximately 2 inches in length by 1 inch in width on his left buttock. Several small bruises were also evident along one side of the burn. Again, the teacher asked Jimmy how he had been hurt, and again he replied that he "had fallen."

1. What actions should Jimmy's teacher take? Should she tell anyone else?
2. Would you recommend that Jimmy's teacher report the incident right away or wait until she has gathered more evidence? Why?
3. To whom should the teacher report what she has observed?
4. Using the information provided, write up a complete description of Jimmy's injury.
5. If you were Jimmy's teacher, would your feelings and responses be any different if this was a first-time versus a repeated occurrence?
6. Is it necessary for the teacher to notify Jimmy's family before making a report?
7. In what ways can the teacher be of immediate help to Jimmy?
8. What should the teacher do if this happens again?

Application Activities

1. Gather statistics on the incidence of child abuse and neglect for your city, county, and state. Compare your numbers to the national rates.
2. Write a 2-minute public service announcement for radio and television alerting the community to the problems of child abuse and neglect.
3. Locate at least five agencies or services in your community that provide assistance to abusive or neglectful families. Collect materials from these agencies and prepare a written description of their services.
4. Develop a pamphlet that illustrates self-protection skills for young children. Use it with a group of 3- to 4-year-olds. Evaluate their response.
5. Identify organizations in your community that work with families of sexually abused children. Do they also offer similar programs for children?
6. Develop a bibliography of resources on various parenting issues.
7. Conduct an Internet search to learn about the CASA (Court Appointed Special Advocates) program. What role do they play in helping abused and neglected children? Is there a CASA program in your area? What qualifications are required of volunteer participants?

Helpful Web Resources

American Professional Society on Abuse of Children	http://www.apsac.org
Boys and Girls Clubs of America	http://www.bgca.org
Child Welfare Information Gateway	http://www.childwelfare.gov
Child Welfare League of America (CWLA)	http://www.cwla.org
Family Violence Prevention Fund	http://www.endabuse.org
Prevent Child Abuse America	http://www.preventchildabuse.org
Shaken Baby Alliance	http://www.shakenbaby.com

You are just a click away from additional health, safety, and nutrition resources! Go to www.CengageBrain.com to access this text's Education CourseMate website, where you'll find:

- form for recording suspected child abuse
- glossary flashcards, activities, tutorial quizzes, videos, web links, and more

References

Barth, R. (2009). Preventing child abuse and neglect with parent training: Evidence and opportunities, *The Future of Children*, 19(2), 95–118.

Bowers, N. (2009). A naturalistic study of the early relationship development process of nondirective play therapy, *International Journal of Play Therapy*, 18(3), 176–189.

Bugental, D., & Schwartz, A. (2009). A cognitive approach to child mistreatment prevention among medically at-risk infants, *Developmental Psychology*, 45(1), 284–288.

Centers for Disease Control & Prevention (CDC). (2009). Child maltreatment. Accessed on December 10, 2009 from http://www.cdc.gov/violenceprevention/pdf/CM-DataSheet-a.pdf.

CDC. (2008). Child maltreatment surveillance: Uniform definitions for public health and recommended data elements. Accessed on March 2, 2010 from http://www.cdc.gov/violenceprevention/pdf/CM_Surveillance-a.pdf.

Child Welfare Information Gateway. (2009). *Major federal legislation concerned with child protection, child welfare, and adoption.* Accessed on December 15, 2009 from http://www.childwelfare.gov/pubs/otherpubs/majorfedlegis.cfm.

Conron, K., Beardslee, W., Koenen, K., Buka, S., & Gortmaker, S. (2009). A longitudinal study of maternal depression and child maltreatment in a national sample of families investigated by child protective services, *Archives of Pediatric & Adolescent Medicine*, 163(10), 922–930.

Dettlaff, A., Earner, I., & Phillips, S. (2009). Latino children of immigrants in the child welfare system: Prevalence, characteristics, and risk, *Child & Youth Services Review*, 31(7), 775–783.

Draper, K., Siegel, C., White, J., Solis, C., & Mishna, F. (2009). Preschoolers, parents, and teachers (PPT): A preventive intervention with an at risk population, *International Journal of Group Psychotherapy*, 59(2), 221–242.

Dubowitz, H. (2009). Tackling child neglect: A role for pediatricians, *Pediatric Clinics of North America*, 56(2), 363–378.

Egeland, B. (2009). Taking stock: Childhood emotional maltreatment and developmental psychopathology, *Child Abuse & Neglect*, 33(1), 22–26.

Ferguson, K. (2009). Exploring family environment characteristics and multiple abuse experiences among homeless youth, *Journal of Interpersonal Violence*, 24(11), 1875–1891.

Flynn, C., & Rodman, H. (2008). Latch-key children and after-school care: A feminist dilemma, *Review of Policy Research*, 8(3), 663–673.

Gabalda, M., Broth, M., Thompson, M., & Kaslow, N. (2009). Children's emotional abuse and relational functioning: Social support and internalizing symptoms as moderators, *Journal of Child & Adolescent Trauma*, 2(3), 179–197.

Goebbels, A., Nicholson, J., & Walsh, K. (2008). Teachers' reporting of suspected child abuse and neglect: Behaviour and determinants, *Health Education & Research*, 23(6), 941–951.

Guterman, N., Lee, S., Taylor, C., & Rathouz, P. (2009). Parental perceptions of neighborhood processes, stress, personal control, and risk for physical child abuse and neglect, *Child Abuse & Neglect*, 33(12), 897–906.

Hinkelman, L., & Bruno, M. (2008). Identification and reporting of child sexual abuse: The role of elementary school professionals, *The Elementary School Journal*, 108(5), 376–398.

Kempe, C. H., & Helfer, R. (Eds.). (1982). *The battered child.* Chicago: University of Chicago Press.

Kim, M., Tajima, E., Herrenkohl, T., & Huang, B. (2009). Early child maltreatment, run- away youths, and risk of delinquency and victimization in adolescence: A meditational model, *Social Work Research*, 33(1), 19–28.

Legano, L., McHugh, M., & Palusci, V. (2009). Child abuse and neglect, *Current Problems in Pediatric & Adolescent Health Care*, 39(2), e1–e31.

Maikovich, A., Koenen, K., & Jaffee, S. (2009). Posttraumatic stress symptoms and trajectories in child sexual abuse victims: An analysis of sex differences using the National Survey of Child & Adolescent Well-being, *Journal of Abnormal Child Psychology*, 37(5), 727–737.

Manders, J., & Stoneman, Z. (2009). Children with disabilities in the child protective services system: An analog study of investigation and case management, *Child Abuse & Neglect*, 33(4), 229–237.

McPherson, A., Lewis, K., Lynn, A., Haskett, M., & Behrend, T. (2009). Predictors of parenting stress for abusive and nonabusive mothers, *Journal of Child & Family Studies*, 18(1), 61–69.

Mersky, J., Berger, L., Reynolds, A., & Gromoske, A. (2009). Risk factors for child and adolescent maltreatment, *Child Maltreatment*, 14(1), 73–88.

Neigh, G., Gillespie, C., &Nemeroff, C. (2009). The neurobiological toll of child abuse and neglect, *Trauma, Violence & Abuse*, 10(4), 389–410.

Peter, T. (2009). Exploring taboos: Comparing male- and female-perpetrated sexual abuse, *Journal of Interpersonal Violence*, 24(7), 1111–1128.

Pierce, M., Kaczor, K., Aldridge, S., O'Flynn, J., & Lorenz, D. (2010). Bruising characteristics discriminating physical child abuse from accidental trauma, *Pediatrics*, 125(1), 67–74.

Reinert, D., & Edwards, C. (2009). Childhood physical and verbal mistreatment, psychological symptoms, and substance use: Sex differences and the moderating role of attachment, *Journal of Family Violence*, 24(8), 589–596.

Ruiz-Casares, M., & Heyman, J. (2009). Children home alone unsupervised: Modeling parental decisions and associated factors in Botswana, Mexico, and Vietnam, *Child Abuse & Neglect*, 33(5), 312–323.

Runyon, M., Steer, R., & Deblinger, E. (2009). Psychometric characteristics of the Beck Self-Concept Inventory for Youth with adolescents who have experienced sexual abuse, *Journal of Psychopathology and Behavioral Assessment*, 31(2), 129–136.

Schmalz, M., Boos, K., Schmalz, G., & Huntington, M. (2009). Failure to thrive, *Journal of Family Practice*, 58(10), 530–544.

Schultz, D., Tharp-Taylor, S., Haviland, A., & Jaycox, L. (2009). The relationship between protective factors and outcomes for children investigated for maltreatment, *Child Abuse & Neglect*, 33(10), 684–698.

Shipman, K., & Taussig, H. (2009). Mental health treatment of child abuse and neglect: The promise of evidence-based practice, *Pediatric Clinics of North America*, 56(2), 417–428.

Stagner, M., & Lansing, J. (2009). Progress toward a prevention perspective, *The Future of Children*, 19(2), 19–38.

Stover, D. (2000). Fairness for teachers charged with harassment, *The Educational Digest*, 66(3), 29–33.

Togioka, B., Arnold, M., Bathurst, M., Ziegfeld, S., Nabaweesi, R., Colombani, P., Chang, D., & Abdullah, F. (2009). Retinal hemorrhages and shaken baby syndrome: An evidence-based review, *Journal of Emergency Medicine*, 37(1), 98–106.

Topping, K., & Barron, I. (2009). School-based child sexual abuse prevention programs: A review of effectiveness, *Review of Educational Research*, 79(1), 431–436.

U.S. Department of Health & Human Services. (2007). Child maltreatment 2007. Accessed on December 12, 2009 from http://www.acf.hhs.gov/programs/cb/pubs/cm07/chapter2.htm.

Whiting, J., Simmons, L., Havens, J., Smith, D., & Oka, M. (2009). Intergenerational transmission of violence: The influence of self-appraisals, mental disorders and substance abuse, *Journal of Family Violence*, 24(8), 639–648.

Wilson, H., & Widom, C. (2009). A prospective examination of the path from child abuse and neglect to illicit drug use in middle adulthood: The potential mediating role of four risk factors, *Journal of Youth & Adolescence*, 38(3), 340–354.

Zhai, F., & Gao, Q. (2009). Child maltreatment among Asian Americans: Characteristics and explanatory framework, *Child Maltreatment*, 14(2), 207–224.

CHAPTER

11

Planning for Children's Health and Safety Education

NAEYC Standards *Chapter Links*

- **#1 a, b, and c:** Promoting child development and learning
- **#2 a, b, and c:** Building family and community relationships
- **#3 a, b, c, and d:** Observing, documenting, and assessing to support young children and families
- **#4 a, b, c, and d:** Using developmentally effective approaches to connect with children and families
- **#5 a, b, and c:** Using content knowledge to build meaningful curriculum
- **#6 b, c, and d:** Becoming a professional

Learning Objectives

After studying this chapter, you should be able to:

- Explain why it is important to include families in children's learning experiences.
- Discuss the role of teacher inservice training as it relates to children's health and safety education.
- Identify and describe the four basic elements of instructional design.
- Develop health and safety activity plans based on the format outlined in this chapter.

Many of today's health problems result from a combination of environmental and self-imposed factors (CDC, 2009). Unhealthy eating habits, inactivity, pollution, increased stress, inadequate medical or dental care, poverty, violence, and substance abuse (alcohol, drugs, and tobacco) continue to challenge the quality of children's health (Guyer et al., 2009; Palloni et al., 2009). They also pose a threat to children's academic success and to their potential to become healthy, productive adults (Ding et al., 2009; Fiscella & Kitzman, 2009).

The early years are an important time when lifelong health behaviors, **attitudes**, and **values** are being formed. It is also a time when children are open and receptive to new ideas, changes,

attitudes – *beliefs or feelings one has toward certain facts or situations.*
values – *the beliefs, traditions, and customs an individual incorporates and utilizes to guide behavior and judgments.*

and suggestions. For these reasons, it is important to design developmentally appropriate learning experiences that provide children and their families with sound information that promotes a healthy lifestyle. This includes improving their understanding of factors that influence health outcomes, encouraging positive decision-making, and motivating children and adults to assume an active role in achieving personal well-being.

Family Involvement in Health and Safety Education

Families are children's first and most important teachers. They shape children's early attitudes and health/safety practices through an ongoing combination of direct instruction, **incidental learning**, and modeling of adult behaviors (Lawson & Flocke, 2009). Daily activities often become important teachable moments. For example, a parent may discuss the benefits of eating fruits and vegetables while the child washes (and samples) the broccoli for tonight's dinner or helps to plant tomatoes in a vegetable garden.

Successful health and safety education programs are built on a strong foundation of family involvement (McBride et al., 2009; Rogers et al., 2009). When teachers collaborate with children's families, they are able to discover their goals and priorities, and thus design instruction that is responsive to children's needs (Huntsinger & Jose, 2009). There are many resourceful ways that teachers can involve families in children's health/safety education, including inviting them to:

- prepare and contribute to newsletters
- accompany children on field trips
- share special talents, skills, or cultural traditions
- serve as a guest speaker
- help with class projects, demonstrations, films, discussions
- assist with health assessments and policy development

Family involvement also provides unique opportunities for sharing health information and improving the likelihood that learning experiences will be reinforced in the child's home. It also reduces the potential frustration that children may sense if they receive information at school that is inconsistent with family values and practices. Family members may also benefit indirectly by learning how to make positive changes in their own health practices. Additional advantages of family involvement include:

- better understanding of children's developmental needs
- improved parental esteem
- increased ability to foster and reinforce children's learning
- enhanced parenting skills
- improved communication between home and school

The combined resources and efforts of families, children, and teachers can bring about meaningful improvements in health and safety behaviors for everyone.

Successful health and safety education is built on family involvement.

incidental learning – *learning that occurs in addition to the primary intent or goals of instruction.*

The Role of Teacher Inservice in Health and Safety Education

Learning experiences that address health and safety issues are essential in children's educational programs. Yet most teachers have had only limited preservice training in health education and may not be adequately prepared to assume this responsibility. However, teachers can acquire valuable information about developmentally appropriate content and effective instructional techniques for teaching health and safety through continued **inservice** opportunities.

Inservice education that is ongoing and focused on enriching teacher's knowledge and skills is a characteristic feature of high-quality programs. It can be delivered in a number of ways, such as giving teachers access to professional journals or providing financial incentives so they can attend educational conferences. Arrangements can also be made for guest speakers to present training sessions on a variety of important topics, such as:

- schools, early childhood programs, and the law
- emergency preparedness
- identifying child abuse
- advances in health screening
- review of sanitation procedures
- stress and anger management
- working with diverse families
- infectious disease updates
- current information on specific health problems (e.g., epilepsy, autism, diabetes, HIV/AIDS, allergies)
- review of first aid techniques and CPR training
- health promotion practices, including children's mental health
- nutrition education
- cultural awareness and sensitivity
- violence and bullying prevention

It is important that all teaching and support staff be included in inservice training opportunities. However, care must be taken to ensure that information and materials are meaningful to all participants whose educational backgrounds and professional roles may differ.

Effective Instructional Design

Opportunities to promote children's health awareness and to bring about desired behavioral changes present exciting challenges for teachers. To successfully achieve this goal, teachers must create learning experiences that systematically build children's knowledge base and health-promoting

Reflective Thoughts

Historically, it was considered a family's right and responsibility to teach children values and attitudes associated with health and safety. Teachers were expected to focus their efforts on academic instruction. Is this assumption true today? What factors may be contributing to this change? How does a teacher determine what values and attitudes are important to teach children? What steps can a teacher take to be sure that learning experiences are bias-free? What can teachers do to make sure these experiences respect a family's cultural values?

---

inservice – *educational training provided by an employer.*

Table 11–1 HECAT Instructional Modules

Resource lesson modules are available for the following topics:
• Alcohol and other drugs • Healthy eating • Mental and emotional health • Personal health and wellness • Physical activity • Safety • Sexual health • Tobacco • Violence prevention

Source: Centers for Disease Control & Prevention (CDC). (2007). *Health Education Curriculum Analysis Tool (HECAT)*. Atlanta, GA: CDC.

skills. Effective instructional design requires that four basic elements be addressed: topic selection, behavioral objectives, content presentation, and evaluation.

Topic Selection

The ability to select and prepare meaningful learning activities requires an understanding of children's developmental needs. Too frequently, instruction is approached in a haphazard fashion with topics selected at random rather than according to any long-range plan. Several tools are now available to assist teachers and schools in planning a curriculum that advances children's knowledge of health and safety along an increasingly complex continuum. The *National Health Education Standards* for grades PreK–12 provides such a framework and ensures that comprehensive health education is also developmentally appropriate (Appendix A) (Tappe, Wilbur, & Telljohann, 2009). The Centers for Disease Control & Prevention (CDC) have also developed an evidence-based instrument, the *Health Education Curriculum Analysis Tool* (HECAT), that can be accessed from their website (http://www.cdc.gov/HealthyYouth) (Table 11–1). Here you will also find lesson plans, student materials, and teacher resources by topic and grade level, and in multiple languages. This content is consistently aligned with the National Health Education Standards.

Thoughtful planning helps to ensure that topics and learning activities will attract and hold children's attention. Lessons that focus on isolated facts or address topics on a one-time only basis are quickly forgotten (Essa, 2010). Teachers must also consider the diversity of children's backgrounds and abilities and prepare learning experiences that are free of any gender, cultural, and/or ethnic bias.

When teachers plan health and safety learning experiences that are meaningful and integrated across the entire curriculum (e.g., dramatic play, language arts, science, math, outdoor play), children's understanding, retention, and motivation are significantly improved (Copple & Bradekamp, 2009). This approach also helps children to establish important connections between

Educational activities should reflect children's needs and interests.

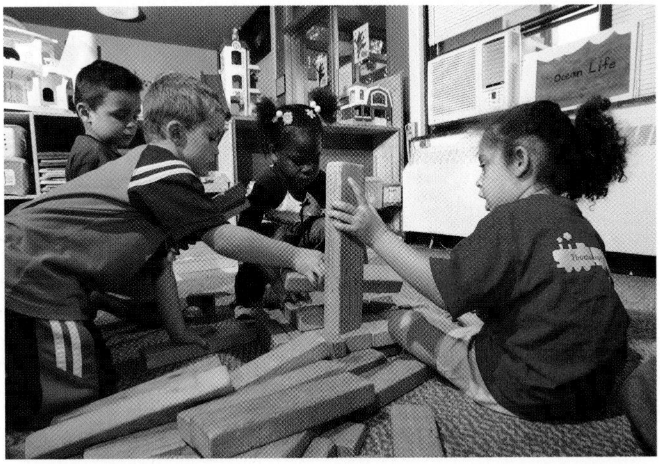

what they learn in the classroom and their personal lives. A simple explanation is often effective in helping children to understand the value of making healthy decisions, such as "Washing your hands gets rid of germs that can make you sick. When you are well, you can take part in the fun things we do at school."

There are many developmentally appropriate health/safety **concepts** that can be introduced throughout the early curriculum. For example, toddlers enjoy learning about:

- body parts
- growth and development
- nutritious food
- social skills/positive interaction—getting along with others
- the five senses
- personal care skills—brushing teeth, hand washing, bathing, toilet routines, dressing
- friendship
- developing self-esteem and positive self-concepts
- cooperation
- exercise/movement routines
- safe behaviors

Topics of interest to preschool children include:

- growth and development
- oral health
- safety and injury prevention—home, playground, water, firearms, traffic, poison, fire
- community helpers
- poison prevention
- emotional health—fostering positive self-image, feelings, responsibility, treating others with respect, dealing with stress, anger management
- personal cleanliness and grooming
- correct posture
- food and healthful nutrition
- the importance of sleep
- families
- the importance of physical activity
- control and prevention of illness
- manners
- environmental health and safety
- personal protection skills

School-aged children are eager to explore topics in greater detail, including:

- personal appearance
- oral health
- dietary nutrients and food and nutrition
- consumer health—taking medicines, understanding advertisements, reading labels, quackery, when to seek assistance
- factors affecting growth
- emotional health—personal feelings, making friends, family interactions, getting along with others, problem-solving, bullying, and harassment
- roles of health professionals
- communicable illnesses and prevention measures

---

concepts – *combinations of basic and related factual information that represent a more generalized statement or idea.*

- personal safety and injury prevention—bicycle, pedestrian, water, playground, firearm, and home safety
- first aid techniques
- coping with stress—anger management, conflict resolution
- physical fitness

Behavioral Objectives

The ultimate goal of health and safety education is the development and maintenance of positive knowledge, attitudes, and behaviors. Learning is demonstrated when children are able to make sound decisions and carry out health and safety practices that preserve or improve their present state of health. **Objectives** describe the desired changes in an individual's knowledge, behaviors, attitudes, and/or values that can be observed and measured upon completion of the learning experience (Orlich et al., 2010; Meeks, Heit, & Page, 2008).

Objectives serve several purposes:

- as a guide in the selection of content material
- as a means for identifying precise changes in learner knowledge or behavior
- as an aid in the selection of appropriate learning experiences
- as an evaluation or measurement tool

To be useful, objectives must be written in terms that are clear and meaningful; for example, "The child will select appropriate clothing to wear on a rainy day." The key word in this objective is "select." It is a specific behavioral change that can be evaluated and measured. In contrast, the statement, "The child will know how to dress for the weather," is vague and cannot be accurately determined. Additional examples of precise and measurable terms include to:

- draw
- list
- discuss
- explain
- select
- write
- recognize
- describe
- identify
- answer
- demonstrate
- match
- compare

Measurable objectives are more difficult to develop for learning experiences that involve values, feelings, and/or attitudes. Behavioral changes associated with this type of learning may not be immediately observable. Rather, it must be assumed that at some later point, children's behaviors will reflect what they have previously learned.

Content Presentation

Teachers serve as facilitators in the educational process, selecting instructional methods that are developmentally appropriate for children and support the stated objectives (Gordon & Browne, 2010). This is an important element in designing effective learning experiences for children and one that allows teachers to express their creativity. When deciding on a method, teachers should consider:

- presenting only a few, simple concepts during each session
- limiting presentations to a maximum of 5–10 minutes for toddlers, 10–15 minutes for preschoolers, and 15–25 minutes for school-aged children
- tailoring content presentation to address children's diverse needs, abilities, and interest levels

---

objectives – *clear, meaningful descriptions of specific behavioral outcomes; can be observed and measured.*

- taking into account class size, children's ages, the nature of content to be presented, and the available resources
- emphasizing the positive aspects of concepts; avoid confusing combinations of do's and don'ts, good and bad comparisons
- creating learning experiences that involve children in hands-on activities with real-life materials
- explaining ideas in terms that are simple and familiar to children
- building in repetition to reinforce children's understanding and retention
- providing encouragement and positive reinforcement to acknowledge children's accomplishments

A variety of effective instructional methods can be used to present health/safety content, including:

- group discussion
- media (e.g., filmstrips, records, models, specimens, videos, audio tapes)
- demonstrations, experiments, and role play
- teacher-made displays (e.g., posters, bulletin boards, booklets, flannel boards)
- art activities
- printed resource material (e.g., pamphlets, posters, charts) (See Table 11–2 for ways to evaluate printed resource material.)
- puppet shows
- books and stories
- guest speakers
- personal example

Methods that actively involve young children in learning experiences are always the most desirable and effective (Bajracharya, 2009). When learning activities involve participation, they hold children's attention longer and improve **retention**. Examples of instructional methods that actively engage children in learning include:

- dramatic play (e.g., dressing up, hospital, dentist office, restaurant, traffic safety, supermarket)
- field trips (e.g., visits to a hospital, dental office, exercise class, supermarket, farm)
- art activities (e.g., posters, bulletin boards, displays, pictures, flannel boards created by children)
- hands-on experiences (e.g., hand washing, brushing teeth, grocery shopping, cooking projects, growing seeds, animal care, conducting simple science experiments)
- puppet shows (e.g., care when you are sick, protection from strangers, health checkups, good grooming practices)
- games and songs
- guest speakers (e.g., firefighter, dental hygienist, nurse, aerobics, dance instructor, nutritionist, poison control staff, mental health professional)

Children learn best when they are involved in the activity.

When several sessions are planned on a similar topic or theme, a combination of instructional methods can be used to

retention – *the ability to remember or recall previously learned material.*

Table 11–2 Teacher Checklist: How to Evaluate Printed Resource Material

Look for materials that:

- are prepared by reputable authorities in the field or by a reliable source
- contain unbiased information; avoid promotion or advertisement of products
- present accurate, up-to-date facts and information
- involve the learner
- are thought-provoking or raise questions and answers
- are attractive
- enhance the quality of the learning experience
- are worth the costs involved
- support your program's philosophy

maintain children's interest, reinforce key concepts, and ensure an integrated approach. For example, a teacher might arrange an obstacle course or take the children on a long walk outdoors following a lesson on the importance of physical activity.

Many governmental and commercial agencies offer excellent educational resource materials and lesson plans on health, safety, and nutrition topics that are appropriate for young children. A number of these websites are identified throughout the book.

Evaluation

Effective instructional design also requires that an **evaluation** be conducted throughout the development and presentation stages. Evaluation provides feedback concerning the quality of instruction and reveals whether or not students have learned what a teacher initially set out to teach. Evaluation procedures also help teachers to determine the strengths, weaknesses, and areas of instruction that require improvement (Stuhlman & Pianta, 2009; Hubbard & Rainey, 2007)

Evaluation is accomplished by measuring positive changes in children's behavior. Goals and objectives established at the onset of instructional design are used to determine whether or not the desired behavioral changes have been achieved. Do children remember to wash their hands after using the bathroom without having to be reminded? Do children check for traffic before dashing out into the street after a runaway ball? Do children brush their teeth at least once daily? Are safety rules followed by the children when an adult is not there to remind them? In other words, evaluation is based on demonstrations of persistent change in children's observable behaviors.

Evaluation must not be looked upon as a final step. Rather, it should add a dimension of quality throughout the entire instructional program. The following criteria may be used for the evaluation process:

- Do the objectives identify important areas where learning should occur?
- Are the objectives clearly stated, realistic, and measurable?
- Were children able to achieve the desired outcomes?
- Was the instructional method effective? Were children interested and engaged in the learning experiences?
- How could the lesson be improved?

Evaluation must not be viewed as a self-critical process even if the findings suggest that the intended learner outcomes were not achieved. Rather, the evaluation process helps to identify weaknesses in content, activity design, and/or presentation that teachers can use to improve future instruction.

---

evaluation – *a measurement of effectiveness for determining whether or not educational objectives have been achieved.*

Reflective Thoughts

Planning effective learning experiences for children requires time and effort. The Internet now offers easy access to a wealth of information, particularly in the areas of health, safety, and nutrition. Should all of this information be trusted? What criteria can you use to evaluate the accuracy of information found on websites? What additional steps can you take to ensure that material you use for developing learning experiences is reliable?

Issues To Consider Fire Safety

The headlines read, "Three young children found dead after fire guts basement apartment." Firefighters had worked frantically, but intense flames forced them out of the burning building before the children could be located. The children had been playing with matches in their mother's closet when flames spread to nearby clothing. Smoke inhalation claimed the lives of all three children.

- What developmental characteristics might have contributed to this incident?
- What skills must young children learn to avoid a similar tragedy?
- What do families need to know?
- What classroom safety lessons can teachers introduce to help children learn the appropriate ways to respond in the event of a house fire?
- Describe how these learning experiences can be integrated across the curriculum.

Activity Plans

A teacher's day can be filled with many unexpected events. Activity plans encourage advanced planning and organization. Time spent on advanced planning enables a teacher to be better organized, prepared, and able to focus on presenting the learning activity.

A written format for activity plans is often as individualized as are teachers. However, activity plans for health/safety instruction should include several basic features:

- subject title or concept to be presented
- specific objectives
- materials list
- step-by-step learning activities
- evaluation and suggestions for improvement

Activity plans should contain enough information so they can be used by anyone, including a substitute teacher, classroom aide, or volunteer. Objectives should clearly indicate what children are expected to learn so that activities can be modified to meet the needs of a particular group. A description of materials, how they are to be used, and necessary safety precautions should also be addressed. Examples of several activity plans follow.

Planning is a key component of effective health and safety instruction.

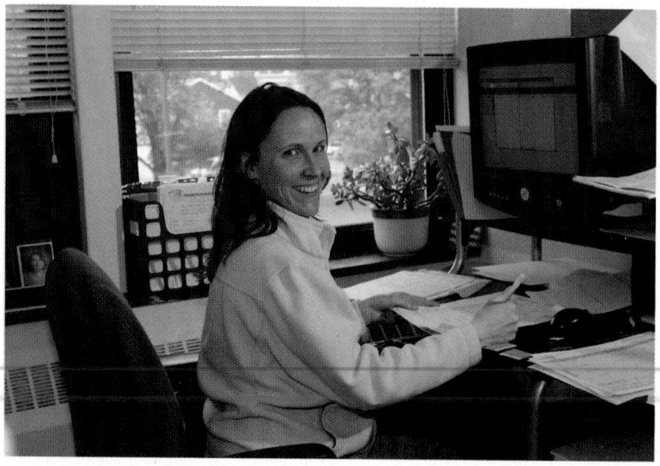

Activity Plan #1: Germs and Illness Prevention

CONCEPT Sneezing and coughing release germs that can cause illness.

OBJECTIVES

- Children will be able to discuss why it is important to cover coughs and sneezes.
- Children will be able to identify the mouth and nose as major sources of germs.
- Children will cover their coughs and sneezes without being reminded.

MATERIALS LIST

- Two large balloons and a small amount of confetti
- Dolls or stuffed animals
- Doctor kit
- Stethoscopes
- Old lab coats or men's shirt to wear as uniforms

(Note: Check before conducting this activity to be sure no one has a latex allergy.)

LEARNING ACTIVITIES

A. Fill both balloons with a small amount of confetti. When the activity is ready to be presented to children, carefully inflate one of the balloons by blowing into the balloon.

⚠ **Caution: Remove your mouth from the balloon each time before inhaling.**

When it is inflated, quickly release pressure on the neck of the balloon, but do not let go of the balloon itself. Confetti will escape as air leaves the balloon, imitating germs as they leave the nose and mouth during coughs and sneezes. Repeat the procedure. This time, place your hand over the mouth of the balloon as the air escapes (as if to cover a cough or sneeze). Your hand will prevent most of the confetti from escaping into the air.

B. Discuss the differences between the two demonstrations with the children: "What happens when someone doesn't cover their mouth when they cough?" "How does covering your mouth help when you cough or sneeze?"

C. Include a discussion of why it is important to stay home when you are sick or have a cold.

D. Help children set up a pretend hospital where they can care for "sick" dolls or animals. Encourage children to talk about how it feels to be sick or when they must take medicine. Reinforce the importance of covering coughs and washing hands to keep from becoming sick.

E. Have several books available for children to look at and discuss:

Berger, M. (1995). *Germs make me sick.* New York: HarperCollins.
Capeci, A. (2001). *The giant germ (Magic School Bus Chapter Book 6).* New York: Scholastic.
Rice, J. (1997). *Those mean, nasty, dirty, downright disgusting but invisible germs.* St. Paul, MN: Redleaf Press.
Romanek, T. (2003). *Achoo: The most interesting book you'll read about germs.* Toronto, ON: Kids Can Press.
Verdick, E. & Heinlen, M., (2006). *Germs are not for sharing.* Minneapolis, MN: Free Spirit Press.
Wilson, K. & Chapman, J. (2007). *Bear feels sick.* New York: Margaret K. McElderry Books.

EVALUATION

- Children can describe the relationship between germs and illness.
- Children identify coughs and sneezes as a major source of germs.
- Children voluntarily cover their own coughs and sneezes.

Activity Plan #2: Hand Washing

CONCEPT Germs on our hands can make us sick and/or spread illness to others.

OBJECTIVES

- Children can describe when it is important to wash their hands.
- Children can demonstrate the hand-washing procedure without assistance.
- Children will value the concept of cleanliness as demonstrated by voluntarily washing their hands at appropriate times.

MATERIALS LIST

- Liquid or bar soap
- Paper towel
- Sink with running water

LEARNING ACTIVITIES

A. Present the finger play "Bobby Bear and Leo Lion." Have children gather around a sink to observe a demonstration of the hand washing procedures as the story is read.

One bright, sunny morning, Bobby Bear and Leo Lion (make a fist with each hand, thumbs up straight), who were very good friends, decided to go for a long walk in the woods (move fists in walking motion). They walked and walked, over hills (imitate walking motion raising fists) and under trees (imitate walking motion lowering fists) until they came to a stream where they decided to cool off.

Bobby Bear sat down on a log (press palm of hand on faucet with adequate pressure to release water or turn on the faucet) and poured water on Leo Lion. Leo Lion danced and danced under the water (move hand and fingers all around underneath the water) until he was all wet. Then it was Bobby Bear's turn to get wet, so Leo Lion (hold up other fist with thumb up) sat down on a log (press palm of hand on faucet with adequate pressure to release water), and Bobby Bear danced and danced under the water until he was all wet (move other hand under water).

Correct hand washing is an important skill for children to learn.

This was so much fun that they decided to take a bath together. They found some soap, picked it up (pick up bar of soap), put a little on their hands (rub a little soap on hands), then laid it back down on the bank (place soap in dish on side of sink). Then they rubbed the soap on their fronts and backs (rub hands together for 30 seconds) until they were all soapy.

After that, Bobby Bear jumped back on his log (press faucet) and poured water on Leo Lion until all his soap was gone (move hand under water). Then Leo Lion jumped back on his log (press other faucet), poured water on Bobby Bear, and rinsed him until all his soap was gone (move other hand under water).

Soon the wind began to blow and Bobby Bear and Leo Lion were getting very cold. They reached up and picked a leaf from the tree above (reach up and take a paper towel from the dispenser) and used it to dry themselves off (use paper towel to dry both hands). When they were all dry, Bobby Bear and Leo Lion carefully dropped their leaves into the trash can (drop paper towel into wastebasket). They joined hands (use fists, thumbs up and joined; walking motion, rapidly) and ran merrily back through the woods.[1]

B. Discuss the proper hand-washing procedure with small groups of children. Ask simple questions and encourage all children to contribute to the discussion.

- "When is it important to wash our hands?"
- "What do we do first? Let's list the steps together."
- "Why do we use soap?"
- "Why is it important to dry our hands carefully after washing them?"

C. Talk with children about the importance of washing hands after blowing their nose, coughing into their hands, playing outdoors, using the bathroom, and before eating. Model these behaviors and set a good example for children.

D. Set up a messy art activity, such as finger paint, clay, glue, or gardening. Practice hand washing. Have children look at their hands before and after washing them. Point out the value of washing hands carefully.

E. Have children practice washing their hands for as long as it takes them to sing the complete ABC song.

F. Read and discuss with the children several of the following books:

Boynton, S. (2007). *Bath time!* New York: Workman Publishing Company.
Brown, R. (2005). *All dirty! All clean!* Brentwood, TN: Sterling Publications.
Edwards, F. B. (2000). *Mortimer Mooner stopped taking a bath.* Kingston, ON: Pokeweed Press.
Gerver, J. (2005). *Bath time.* New York: Children's Press.
Katz, A. (2001). *Take me out of the bathtub, and other silly dilly songs.* New York: Scholastic.
Ross, R. (2000). *Wash your hands!* LaJolla, CA: Kane/Miller Book Publishers.
Showers, P. (1991). *Your skin and mine.* New York: HarperCollins Juvenile Books.
Woodruff, E. (1990). *Tubtime.* New York: Holiday House, Inc.

G. Observe children washing their hands from time to time to make sure they continue to follow good procedures.

H. Observe children at different times throughout the day to determine if they are using correct technique and washing hands at appropriate times.

EVALUATION

- Was the finger play effective for demonstrating the hand-washing technique?
- Do the children wash their hands correctly without assistance?
- Do the children wash their hands at the appropriate times without being reminded?

[1] The author would like to acknowledge Rhonda McMullen, a former student and graduate of the Early Childhood Program, University of Kansas, for sharing her delightful story and creative ways with young children.

Activity Plan #3: Dressing Appropriately for the Weather

CONCEPT Clothing helps to keep us healthy.

OBJECTIVES

- When given a choice, children will match appropriate items of clothing with different types of weather (e.g., rainy, sunny, snowy, hot, cold).
- Children will be able to perform two of the following dressing skills: button a button, snap a snap, or zip up a zipper.
- Children will demonstrate proper care and storage of clothing by hanging up their coats, sweaters, hats, and so on, at least two out of three days.

MATERIALS LIST

- Items for a clothing store, such as clothing, cash register, play money, mirror
- Old magazines and catalogues containing pictures of children's clothing
- Paste
- Paper or newspaper
- Buttons, snaps, and zippers sewn on pieces of cloth
- Dolls and doll clothes
- Books and pictures

LEARNING ACTIVITIES

A. Read and discuss with the children several of the following books:

Andersen, H. C. (2002). *The emperor's new clothes.* New York: North South Winds Press.
Jennings, P. (1996). *What should I wear?* New York: Random House.
Kondrchek, J. & de la Vega, E. (2009). *What should I wear today*? Hockessin, DE: Mitchell Lane Publishers.
Neitzel, S. (1994). *The jacket I wear in the snow.* New York: Morrow Books.
Scarry, R. (2002). *Richard Scarry's what will I wear?* New York: Random House.
Watanabe, S. (1992). *How do I put it on?* New York: Collins.

B. Help children set up a clothing store. Provide clothing appropriate for boys and girls. Include items that could be worn for different types of weather conditions. Talk about the purpose of clothing and how it helps to protect our bodies. Help children identify qualities in clothing that differ with weather conditions (e.g., short sleeves vs. long sleeves, light colors vs. dark colors, lightweight fabrics vs. heavyweight fabrics, etc.).

C. Have children select two different seasons or weather conditions. Give children old magazines or catalogues from which they can choose pictures of appropriate clothing. Display completed pictures where families will see them. Younger children can point to and name various items of clothing.

D. Provide children with pieces of cloth on which a button, zipper, and snap have been sewn. Working with a few children at a time, help each child master these skills. Have several items of real clothing available for children to practice putting on and taking off.

EVALUATION

- Children select at least two appropriate items of clothing for three different types of weather.
- Children are able to complete two of the following skills—buttoning a button, snapping a snap, zipping a zipper.
- Children hang up their personal clothing (e.g., hats, coats, sweaters, raincoats) at least two out of three days.

Activity Plan #4: Dental Health

CONCEPT Proper dental hygiene helps to keep teeth healthy.

OBJECTIVES

- Children will be able to identify at least two purposes that teeth serve.
- Children can name at least three foods that are good for healthy teeth.
- Children can describe three ways to promote dental health.

MATERIALS LIST

- Men's old shirts (preferably white) to use as dental uniforms
- Stuffed animals
- Tongue blades
- Children's books on dental health
- Old magazines
- Plastic fruits and vegetables
- Gardening tools

LEARNING ACTIVITIES

A. Locate learning and resource materials about children's dental care on the following websites:

American Dental Association (http://www.ada.org); American Academy of Pediatric Dentistry (http://www.aapd.org); National Head Start Oral Health Resource Center (http://www.mchoralhealth.org/HeadStart/index.html); CDC: Children's Oral Health (http://www.cdc.gov/oralhealth/topics/child.htm).

B. Read one or more of the following books during group time. Talk with the children about the role teeth play (e.g., for chewing, speech, smiling, a place for permanent teeth) and why it is important to take good care of them.

Bagley, K. (2000). *Brush well!* Mankato, MN: Capstone Press.
Frost, H. (1999). *Going to the dentist.* Mankato, MN: Pebble Books.
Mercer, M. (2001). *Just going to the dentist.* New York: Golden Books.
Palatini, M. (2004). *Sweet tooth.* New York: Simon & Schuster Children's Publishing.
Schoberle, C. (2000). *Open wide! A visit to the dentist.* New York: Simon Spotlight.
Smee, N. (2000). *Freddie visits the dentist.* Hauppauge, NY: Barrons Educational Series.

C. Set up a "dentist" office for dramatic play. Have old white shirts available for children to wear as uniforms. Place stuffed animals in chairs so children can practice their "dentistry" skills using wooden tongue blades and cotton balls.
D. Spread out plastic fruits, vegetables, child-sized gardening tools, and baskets on the floor. Have children plant a garden with foods that are healthy for their teeth.
E. Discuss ways children can help to keep their teeth healthy (e.g., daily brushing with a fluoride toothpaste; regular dental checkups; eating nutritious foods/snacks (especially raw fruits, vegetables); avoiding chewing on nonfood items such as pencils, spoons, and keys; limiting sweets).
F. Help children construct "healthy food" mobiles. Use old magazines to cut out pictures of foods that promote healthy teeth. Paste pictures on paper, attach with string or yarn, and tie to a piece of cardboard cut in the shape of a smile.
G. Have children help plan snacks for several days; include foods that are nutritious and important for healthy teeth.

EVALUATION

- Children name at least two functions that teeth serve.
- Children identify at least three foods that are important for healthy teeth.
- Children describe three oral health practices that help to keep teeth healthy.

Activity Plan #5: Tooth-brushing

CONCEPT Teeth should be brushed after meals and snacks to stay white and healthy.

OBJECTIVES

- Children can state appropriate times when teeth should be brushed.
- Children can demonstrate proper tooth-brushing technique.
- Children can describe one alternate method for cleaning teeth after eating.

MATERIALS LIST

- One white egg carton per child
- Cardboard
- Pink construction paper
- Several old toothbrushes
- Cloth
- Grease pencil
- Toothpaste and toothbrushes (donated)

LEARNING ACTIVITIES

A. Invite a dentist or dental hygienist to demonstrate proper tooth brushing to the children. Ask the speaker to discuss how often to brush, when to brush, how to brush, alternate ways of cleaning teeth after eating, what type of toothpaste to use, and correct care of toothbrushes. This may also be an ideal opportunity to invite families to visit so they can reinforce tooth-brushing skills at home.

B. Help children construct a set of model teeth from egg cartons (Figure 11–1). Cut an oval approximately 14 inches in length from lightweight cardboard; crease oval gently along the

Figure 11–1 A set of egg carton "teeth."

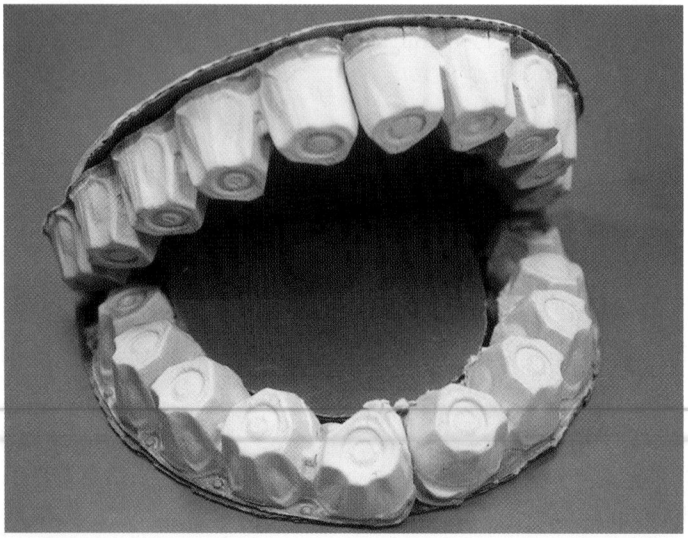

center. Cut the bottom portion of an egg carton lengthwise into two strips. Staple egg carton "teeth" along the small ends of the oval. Glue pink construction paper along the edges where "teeth" are fastened to form "gums." Also cover the backside of the oval with pink construction paper. Use a grease pencil to mark areas of plaque on the teeth. Cover the head of an old toothbrush with cloth and fasten. With the toothbrush, have children demonstrate correct tooth-brushing technique to remove areas of plaque (grease pencil markings).

C. Obtain pamphlets about children's dental health from your local dental health association or download information from reliable dental websites. Prepare a parent newsletter article reinforcing the concepts children have been learning.

D. Send a note home to families and request that children bring a clean toothbrush to school. (Local dentists and dental associations may be willing to donate brushes.) Practice step-by-step tooth brushing with small groups of children.

E. Older children will enjoy designing posters or bulletin board displays that reinforce proper dental hygiene.

F. Read and discuss with children several of the following books:

Beeler, S. (2001). *Throw your tooth from the roof: Tooth traditions from around the world*, Queensland, AU: Sandpiper Publishing.
Keller, L. (2000). *Open wide: Tooth school inside.* New York: Henry Holt & Co.
Miller, E. (2009). *The tooth book: A guide to healthy teeth and gums.* New York: Holiday House.
Schuh, M. (2008). *Brushing teeth.* Mankato, MN: Capstone Press.
Simms, L. & Catrow, D. (2002). *Rotten teeth.* Queensland, AU: Sandpiper Publishing.
Vrombaut, A. (2003). *Clarabella's teeth.* Boston, MA: Houghton Mifflin Harcourt.
West, C. (1990). *The king's toothache.* New York: HarperCollins.

EVALUATION

- Children identify times when teeth should be brushed.
- Children demonstrate correct tooth-brushing technique.
- Children correctly describe at least one alternate method for cleaning their teeth after eating.

Activity Plan #6: Understanding Feelings (Emotional Health)

CONCEPT Feelings affect the state of one's mental as well as physical well-being.

OBJECTIVES

- Children will be able to name at least four feelings or emotions.
- Children will begin to express their feelings in words.

MATERIALS LIST

- Old magazines, glue, paper
- Large, unbreakable mirror
- Shoe boxes

LEARNING ACTIVITIES

A. Read and discuss with the children several of the following books:

Appelt, K. (2003). *Incredible me!* New York: Harper Collins.
Bang, M. (1999). *When Sophie gets angry—Really, really, angry.* New York: Scholastic.
Blumenthal, D. (1999). *The chocolate-covered-cookie tantrum.* New York: Clarion Books.
Cain, J. (2000). *The way I feel.* Seattle, WA: Parenting Press.
Carle, E. (2000). *The grouchy ladybug.* New York: Scholastic.
Carle, E. (2000). *The very lonely firefly.* New York: Scholastic.

Carlson, N. (1998). *I like me.* New York: Scholastic.
Crary, E. (1996). *I'm scared.* Seattle, WA: Parenting Press.
Crary, E. (1996). *I'm mad.* Seattle, WA: Parenting Press.
Gainer, C. (1998). *I'm like you, you're like me: A child's book about understanding and celebrating each other.* Minneapolis, MN: Free Spirit Publishing.
Lewis, P. (2002). *I'll always love you.* Wilton, CT: Tiger Tales.
Milford, S. (2008). *Happy school year!* New York: Scholastic.
Nolan, A. (2009). *What I like about me.* New York: Reader's Digest.
Shuman, C. (2003). *Jenny is scared! When sad things happen in the world.* Washington, DC: Magination Press.
Snow, T. & Snow, P. (2007). *Feelings to share from A to Z.* Oak Park Heights, MN: Maren Green Publishing.
Spelman, C. M. (2000). *When I feel angry.* Morton Grove, IL: Albert Whitman & Co.
Thomas, P. (2000). *Stop picking on me.* Hauppauge, NY: Barron's Juveniles.

B. During large or small group time, encourage children to talk about different feelings people experience. Stress that many of these feelings are normal and that it is important to learn acceptable and healthy ways of expressing them. Ask children, one at a time, to name a feeling (e.g., happy, sad, tired, bored, special, excitement, surprise, fear, lonely, embarrassed, proud, or angry). Have children act out the feeling. Encourage children to observe the expressions of one another. Help children learn to recognize these feelings. "Have you ever seen someone look like this?" "Have you ever felt like this?" "What made you feel like this?" Discuss and role-play healthy ways to cope with these feelings.
C. Place an unbreakable mirror where children can see themselves. Encourage them to imitate some of the feelings they have identified and observe their own facial expressions.
D. Make a collage of feelings using pictures of people from old magazines. Help children identify the feelings portrayed in each picture.
E. Construct "I Am Special" boxes. Have children decorate old shoe boxes with pictures of things that reflect their individuality, such as favorite foods, activities, toys, and so on. Have children fill their boxes with items that tell something special about themselves; for example, a hobby, favorite toy, photograph, souvenir from a trip, pet, or picture of their family. Children can share their boxes and tell something special about themselves during "Show and Tell" or large group time.

Have children role play different emotions.

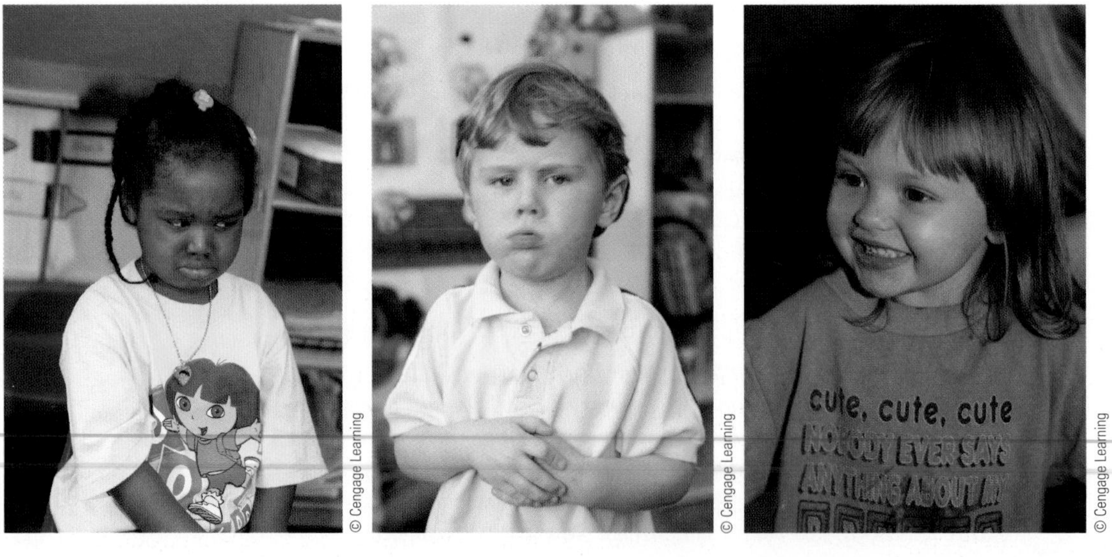

F. Older children can be involved in role play. Write out problem situations on small cards; for example, "You and another child want the same toy," "Someone knocks down the block structure you just finished building," "Another child pushes you," "A friend says he/she doesn't like you anymore." Have pairs of children select a card and act out acceptable ways of handling their feelings in each situation. Discuss their solutions.

EVALUATION

- Children name at least four different feelings or emotions.
- Children use words rather than physical aggression to handle emotional situations.

Activity Plan #7: Safety in Cars

CONCEPT Safety rules are important to follow in and around vehicles.

OBJECTIVES

- Children will understand the purpose and importance of wearing seat belts or sitting in an appropriate safety car seat.
- Children can name at least one important safety rule to follow in and around cars.

MATERIALS LIST

Educational materials on child passenger safety can be downloaded from many websites, including the Children's Safety Network (www.childrenssafetynetwork.org) and the National Highway Traffic Safety Administration (www.nhtsa.dot.gov). Take photographs of children demonstrating the following safety rules:

a. Always hold an adult's hand when going to and from the car; never dash ahead.
b. Always get in and out of a car on the curbside.
c. Open and close car doors properly. Place both hands on the door handle to reduce the possibility of getting fingers caught in the door.
d. Sit in the car seat; never ride standing.
e. Put on seat belt or use safety car seat.
f. Lock all car doors before starting out.
g. Ride with arms, legs, head, and other body parts inside the car.
h. Don't play with controls inside of the car.
i. Ride quietly so as not to disturb the driver.

LEARNING ACTIVITIES

A. Discuss with the children information found in the pamphlets. Stress the importance of wearing seat belts or riding in an appropriate car seat restraint. Later, have children take the pamphlets home to share with families.
B. Mount photographs of children demonstrating safety rules on posterboard or display them on a table. Encourage children to identify the safe behavior demonstrated in each picture.
C. Use large group time to discuss with the children the importance of the safety rule illustrated in each of the photographs.
D. For dramatic play, use large wooden blocks, cardboard boxes or chairs, and a "steering wheel" to build a pretend car. Have children demonstrate the car safety rules as they play.
E. Prepare a chart with all of the children's names. Each day, have children place a checkmark next to their name if they rode in a car seat and wore their seat belt on the way to school.
F. Establish a parent committee to plan a "Safe Riding" campaign. On randomly selected days, observe families and children as they arrive and depart from the center; record whether or not they were wearing seat belt restraints. Enlist children's artistic abilities to design and make awards to be given to families who ride safely. Repeat the campaign again in several months.

Children can begin to identify safety signs.

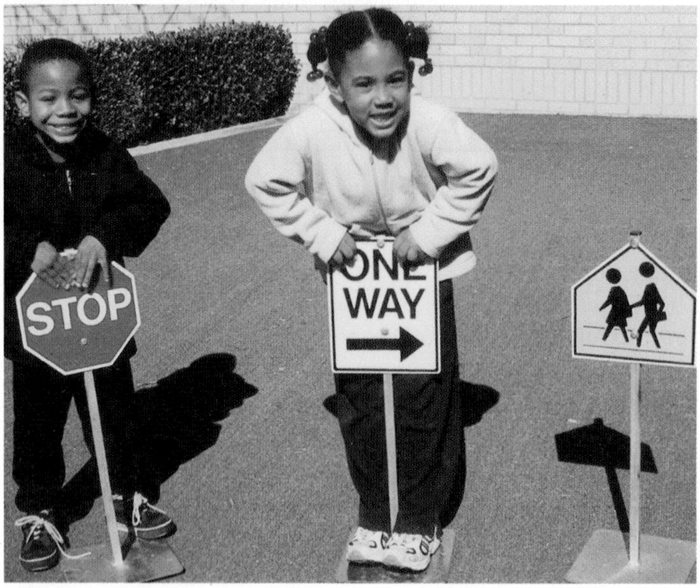

EVALUATION

- Children are observed wearing seat belts or sitting in a proper safety car seat.
- Children name one safety rule to observe when riding in a car.

Activity Plan #8: Pedestrian Safety

CONCEPT Children can begin to learn safe behaviors to follow in and around traffic and develop a respect for moving vehicles.

OBJECTIVES

- Children will be able to identify the stop, go, and walk signals.
- Children will describe two rules for safely crossing streets.
- Children will begin to develop respect for moving vehicles.

MATERIALS LIST

- Flannel board and characters
- Cardboard pieces, poster paint, wooden stakes
- Masking tape, yarn or string
- 6-inch paper plates
- Red, green, and yellow poster paint
- Black marker

LEARNING ACTIVITIES

A. Read and discuss with the children several of the following books:

Berenstain, S., & Berenstain, J. (1999). *My trusty car seat: Buckling up for safety*. New York: Random House.

Committee, C. B. (2000). *Buckles buckles everywhere.* Columbia, SC: Palmetto Bookworks.

Llewellyn, C. (2006). *Watch out! On the road.* Hauppauge, NY: Barron Education Series.

Mattern, J. (2007). *Staying safe in the car.* New York: Weekly Reader Early Learning.
Rathmann, P. (1995). *Officer Buckle and Gloria.* New York: Putnam Publishing Group.
Thomas, P. (2003). *I can be safe.* Hauppauge, NY: Barron Education Series.

B. Discuss rules for safely crossing streets:
   a. Always have an adult cross streets with you. (This is a must for preschool children.)
   b. Cross streets only at intersections.
   c. Always look both ways before stepping out into the street.
   d. Use your ears to listen for oncoming cars.
   g. Don't walk out into the street from between parked cars or in the middle of a block.
   h. Ask an adult to retrieve balls and toys from streets.
   i. Always obey traffic signs.
C. Introduce basic traffic signs (only those that have meaning to young pedestrians) such as stop, go, walk, pedestrian crossing, one-way traffic, bike path, and railroad crossing. Help children learn to recognize each sign by identifying distinguishing features such as color, shape, and location.
D. Help children to construct the basic traffic signs using cardboard and poster paint. Attach signs to wooden stakes. Set up a series of "streets" in the outdoor play yard using string, yarn, or pieces of cardboard to mark paths; place traffic signs in appropriate places. Select children to ride tricycles along designated "streets" while other children practice pedestrian safety.
E. Prepare a flannel board story and characters to help children visualize pedestrian safety rules.
F. Help children construct a set of stop-go-walk signs. Have each child paint three paper plates—one red, one green, one yellow. On a plain white plate, write the word WALK. Fasten all four plates together with tape or glue to form a traffic signal.

EVALUATION

- Children respond correctly to traffic signals: stop, go, walk.
- Children state two rules for safely crossing streets. (Puppets can be used to ask children questions.)
- Children demonstrate caution in the play yard while riding tricycles and other wheeled toys and also as pedestrians.

Activity Plan #9: Poisonous Substances—Poison Prevention

CONCEPT Identification and avoidance of known and potentially poisonous substances.

OBJECTIVES

- Children will name at least three poisonous substances.
- Children can identify at least one safety rule that will help prevent accidental poisoning.

MATERIALS LIST

- Old magazines
- Large sheet of paper
- Glue
- Small squares of paper or self-adhesive labels
- Marking pens

LEARNING ACTIVITIES

A. Invite a guest speaker from your local hospital emergency room or Public Health Department to talk with the children about poison prevention.

B. Show children pictures and/or real labels of poisonous substances. Include samples of cleaning items, personal grooming supplies, medicines, perfumes, plants, and berries.

C. Discuss rules of poison prevention:

   a. Only food should be put into the mouth.
   b. Medicine is not candy and should only be given by an adult.
   c. An adult should always inform children that they are taking medicine, not candy.
   d. Never eat berries, flowers, leaves, or mushrooms before checking with an adult.

D. Make a wall mural for the classroom displaying pictures of poisonous substances. Be sure to include a sampling of cleaning products, personal grooming supplies, medicines, plants; products commonly found in garages, such as insecticides, fertilizers, gasoline, and automotive fluids. Glue pictures of these products on a large sheet of paper. Display the mural where parents and children can look at it.

EVALUATION

- Children point to or name at least three poisonous substances.
- Children state and role-play at least one safety rule that can help to prevent accidental poisoning.

TEACHER RESOURCES

Handbook of Poisonous and Injurious Plants, by Nelson, L., Shih, R., & Balick, M. (2007), Warren, MI: Springer.

Learn about chemicals around your house. U.S. Environmental Protection Agency. (A virtual room-by-room tour, available online at http://www.epa.gov/kidshometour).

Preventing poisonings at home. American Association of Poison Control Centers. (Available online at: http://www.aaocc.org/dnn/Portals/0/PreschoolEducation/takeHomeColor.pdf).

Quills up – Stay away! National Capital Poison Center. (Teacher guide and resource materials available online at: http://www.poison.org/prevent/preschool.asp.)

Learning about fire safety is important for young children.

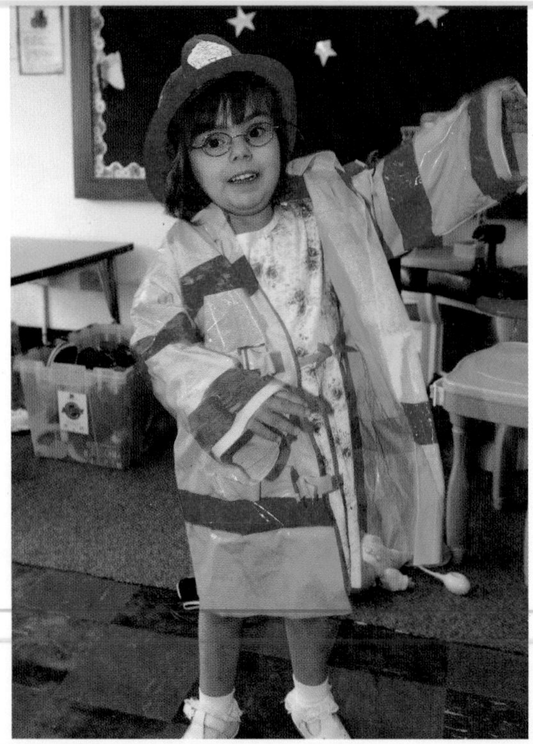

Activity Plan #10: Fire Safety

CONCEPT Fire safety rules are important to know in the event of a fire.

OBJECTIVES

- Children can describe what they would do if there was a fire at their house or school.
- Children can demonstrate stop, drop, and roll.
- Children can state what firefighters do and how they put out fires.

MATERIALS LIST

- Large cardboard boxes
- Poster board
- Photograph of each child
- Chalk and paint in fire colors (red, orange, and yellow)
- Small spray bottles

- Paper and plastic wrap
- Rolling pin
- Tape

LEARNING ACTIVITIES

A. Read and discuss with the children several of the following books:
   Cuyler, M. (2001). *Stop, drop & roll.* New York: Simon & Schuster Children's Publishing.
   Demarest, C. (2003). *Firefighters A to Z.* New York: Margaret K. McElderry Books.
   Gibbons, G. (1987). *Fire fire.* New York: Harper Collins.
   MacLean, C. (2004). *Even firefighters hug their moms.* New York: Puffin.
   Pendziwol, J. (1999). *No dragons for tea: Fire safety for kids (and dragons).* Tonawanda, NY: Kids Can Press.

B. Invite a firefighter to speak about important safety skills, such as stop, drop, and roll; crawling low on the floor to stay away from smoke and heat; and planning alternative evacuation routes.

C. Construct a fire obstacle course. Build a tunnel out of cardboard boxes. Establish a "designated meeting place" at the end of the tunnel by displaying a poster with children's photographs. Have children begin the obstacle course by demonstrating the correct stop, drop, and roll technique. Next, have children crawl through the tunnel on their hands and knees; this shows children the appropriate way for navigating through a smoke-filled room before arriving at the designated safe area. Be sure to encourage and reinforce children's efforts.

D. Take cardboard boxes outside and have the children decorate them to look like buildings. Have children draw fire on the buildings using red, yellow, and orange chalk. Children can then use small spray bottles filled with water to put out the fire.

E. Add firefighter figures, ladders, fire trucks, and other fire-related materials to the block area.

F. Create a fire painting. Have the children paint a picture with thick red and yellow tempera paint. While the paint is still wet, cover with plastic wrap and secure to the back of the painting with tape. Have the child use a rolling pin to roll back and forth over their painting (colors will merge)

EVALUATION

- Children describe how they would get out of their house or school safely during a fire and where they would go once outside the building.
- Children demonstrate how to stop, drop, and roll.
- Children explain what firefighters do and how they put out fires.[2]

Focus On Families — Evaluating Health-Safety Information on the Internet

The Internet has substantially increased consumer access to health and safety information. As a result, we are often more aware of current developments and better able to make informed decisions. However, the lack of any regulatory control has also allowed considerable misinformation to be posted on websites, particularly in the areas of health and safety. Thus, consumers must approach such information with caution. Consider:

- What individual or group is responsible for this site? Check the URL (Web address): information on sites maintained by the government (.gov) and educational institutions (.edu) is generally considered more reliable.

(continued)

[2] The author would like to thank Allison Moore, a former student and graduate of the Early Childhood program, Department of Human Development and Family Life, University of Kansas, for her innovative lesson plan.

Focus On Families **Evaluating Health-Safety Information** *(continued)*

- Are the individuals who prepared and run the site qualified? (Often the credentials of advisory board members or the webmaster will be included.)
- Who is the intended audience? Is the purpose to entertain, inform, or educate?
- Is the site current? How recently was the information updated? It may be difficult to know if the date posted on a Web page refers to when the information was originally written, last revised, or actually posted.
- Does the information appear to be objective and free of bias? Sites run by private individuals or commercial groups may reflect personal opinion or an attempt to sell a product. Facts and figures should include a reference to the original source of information.
- What links are included? Anyone can establish a link to another web page, so this may not prove to be a valid strategy for evaluating a site's credibility.
- Does the site include a way to contact the owner if you have questions or wish to obtain additional information?

Summary

- Unhealthy lifestyle practices and attitudes are responsible for many contemporary health problems. They are also known to interfere with children's ability to learn.
- Including families in children's health and safety education encourages consistency between school and home.
  - When families are informed about what children are learning at school, they can reinforce the same information, practices, and values at home.
  - When teachers are aware of differences (e.g., cultural, linguistic, ethnic) in families' values regarding health, they will be able to create learning experiences that are more responsive to children's needs.
- Ongoing inservice opportunities help teachers stay current, especially in the areas of health and safety, where new developments and information are always emerging.
  - Education is a key element in reducing health problems.
  - It raises children's awareness and ability to make informed decisions.
  - It encourages children's early efforts to assume some responsibility for their personal health.
  - It contributes to improved health and safety behaviors and quality of life.
- Effective health and safety instruction is based on four key design elements:
  - Topics should be selected to address children's interests and developmental needs; they must also be free of bias.
  - Learning objectives describe changes in an individual's behavior that can be expected as the result of instruction.
  - A variety of instructional methods can be used when presenting health and safety content; they should inspire creativity and hold children's attention.
  - Evaluation should be a continuous process and assess all aspects of the instructional process.
- Preparing lesson plans in advance improves the ability to be organized, safe, creative, and focused on the learning activity.

Terms to Know

attitudes *p. 290*
values *p. 290*
incidental learning *p. 291*
inservice *p. 292*
concepts *p. 294*
objectives *p. 295*
retention *p. 296*
evaluation *p. 297*

Chapter Review

A. By Yourself:

1. Match each of the following definitions in **column I** with the correct term in **column II**.

Column I	Column II
1. to assess the effectiveness of instruction	a. education
2. favorable changes in attitudes, knowledge, and/or practices	b. outcome
3. a sharing of knowledge or skills	c. positive behavior changes
4. ideas and values meaningful to a child	d. attitude
5. subject or theme	e. relevance
6. feeling or strong belief	f. topic
7. occurs in conjunction with daily activities and routines	g. incidental learning
8. the end product of learning	h. evaluation
	i. retention

2. The following is a list of suggested health/safety topics. Place an A (appropriate) or NA (not appropriate) next to each of the statements. Base your decision on whether the topic is/is not suitable for preschool-aged children.
   ______ dental health
   ______ feelings and how to get along with others
   ______ primary causes of suicide
   ______ consumer health (e.g., understanding advertisements, choosing a doctor, medical quackery)
   ______ eye safety
   ______ the hazards of smoking
   ______ how to safely light matches
   ______ physical fitness for health
   ______ cardiopulmonary resuscitation
   ______ the importance of rest and sleep
   ______ safety at home
   ______ animal families

B. As a Group:

1. Discuss why it is essential to provide health and safety learning experiences during a child's early years.
2. Explain why evaluation of learning experiences must be a continuous process and not simply an assessment of outcomes. How can this information be used to improve future lessons?
3. Debate the pros and cons of including families in children's health and safety education.
4. Explain how programs benefit from investing in inservice training for teachers.
5. Discuss how teachers can determine if health and safety resource materials are reliable.

Case Study

Eduardo, a new assistant, was asked by his head teacher to develop a lesson on "Healthy Eating Helps Us Grow." Although eager to be given this assignment, Eduardo was also apprehensive about planning something that 4-year-olds would enjoy. He arrived early that morning and set up a grocery store for dramatic play, books about food for the children to read, and magazine pictures of foods for the children to sort into categories using the Food Pyramid. The children played "grocery shopping" for a while, looked at several of the books, but weren't interested in the sorting activity.

1. Were the activities Eduardo planned appropriate for 4-year-olds?
2. How effective was this lesson for teaching children about healthy eating habits?
3. What are some realistic learning objectives that Eduardo might have established in preparation for this lesson?
4. How would Eduardo evaluate what the children may have learned from these activities?
5. What changes would you make in Eduardo's instructional strategies?

Application Activities

1. Interview a toddler, preschool, and a first- or second-grade teacher. Ask each to describe the basic health and safety concepts they emphasize in their classrooms. Arrange to observe one of the teachers conducting a health/safety learning activity with children. What were the teacher's objectives? Was the instructional method effective? Did the teacher involve children in the learning activities? Were the children attentive? Were the objectives met?
2. Visit several websites that provide information about appropriate child seat-belt restraints and car safety seats. Read and compare the information. Do all statements agree? If not, in what ways does the information differ? For what audience is the material written (e.g., families, children, teachers and other professionals)?
3. Develop a lesson plan for a unit on "What Makes Us Grow?" Include objectives, length of time, materials, learning activities, measures for evaluation, and any teacher resource information. Exchange lesson plans with another student; critique each other's plan for clarity of ideas, thoroughness, organization and creativity.
4. Select, read, summarize, and evaluate six children's books listed in the activity plans included in this chapter.

Helpful Web Resources

American Dental Association	http://www.ada.org
American Heart Association	http://www.americanheart.org
Awesome Library	http://www.neat-schoolhouse.org
Canadian Childcare Resource & Research Unit	http://www.childcarecanada.org
Center for Disease Control & Protection	http://www.cdc.gov
Children, Stress, & Natural Disasters; University of Illinois	http://web.extension.uiuc.edu/disaster/teacher/teacher.html
Children's Safety Network	http://www.childrenssafetynetwork.org/
Consumer Product Safety Commission	http://www.cpsc.gov

Dole Food Company	http://www.dole.com
Environmental Protection Agency	http://www.epa.gov
KidSource Online	http://www.kidsource.com
National Dairy Council	http://www.nationaldairycouncil.org
National Fire Protection Association	http://www.nfpa.org
National Highway Traffic Safety Administration	http://www.nhtsa.dot.gov
National Institutes of Health	http://www.nih.gov
PE (physical education) Central	http://www.pecentral.org
The Weather Channel on the Web	http://www.weatherclassroom.com

You are just a click away from additional health, safety, and nutrition resources! Go to www.CengageBrain.com to access this text's Education CourseMate website, where you'll find:

- glossary flashcards, activities, tutorial quizzes, videos, web links, and more

References

Bajracharya, S. (2009). Emphasizing sustainable health and wellness in a health education curriculum, *American Journal of Health Education*, 40(1), 56–64.

Centers for Disease Control & Prevention (CDC). (2009). Chronic disease prevention. Accessed on December 2, 2009, from http://www.cdc.gov/nccdphp/.

CDC. (2007). *Health education curriculum analysis tool (HECAT).* Accessed on February 18, 2010, from http://www.cdc.gov/HealthyYouth/HECAT/index.htm.

Copple, C., & Bradekamp, S. (Eds.). (2009). *Developmentally appropriate practice (in early childhood programs, serving children birth through age 8).* Washington, DC: National Association for the Education of Young Children (NAEYC).

Ding, W., Lehrer, S., Rosenquist, J., & Audrain-McGovern, J. (2009). The impact of poor health on academic performance: New evidence using genetic markers, *Journal of Health Economics*, 28(1), 578–597.

Essa, E. (2010). *Introduction to early childhood education.* (6th ed.). Belmont, CA: Wadsworth Cengage Learning.

Fiscella, K., & Kitzman, H. (2009). Disparities in academic achievement and health: The intersection of child education and health policy, *Pediatrics*, 123(3), 1073–1080.

Gordon, A., & Browne, K. (2010). *Beginnings and beyond.* (8th ed.). Belmont, CA: Wadsworth Cengage Learning.

Guyer, B., Ma, S., Grason, H., Frick, K., Perry, D., Sharkey, A., & McIntosh, J (2009). Early childhood health promotion and its life course health consequences, *Academic Pediatrics*, 9(3), 142–149.

Hubbard, B., & Rainey, J. (2007). Health literacy instruction and evaluation among secondary students, *American Journal of Health Education*, 77(8), 408–434.

Huntsinger, C., & Jose, P. (2009). Parental involvement in children's schooling: Different meanings in different cultures, *Early Childhood Research Quarterly*, 24(4), 398–410.

Lawson, P. & Flocke, S. (2009). Teachable moments for health behavior change: A concept analysis, *Patient Education and Counseling*, 76(1), 25–30.

McBride, B., Dyer, W., Liu, Y., Brown, G., & Hong, S. (2009). The differential impact of early father and mother involvement on later student achievement, *Journal of Educational Psychology*, 101(2), 498–508.

Meeks, L., Heit, P., & Page, R. (2008). (6th ed.). *Comprehensive school health education.* New York: McGraw-Hill.

Orlich, D., Harder, R., Callahan, R., Trevisan, M., & Brown, A. (2010). *Teaching strategies.* (9th ed.). Belmont, CA: Wadsworth Cengage Learning.

Palloni, A., Milesi, C., White, R., & Turner, A. (2009). Early childhood health, reproduction of economic inequalities and the persistence of health and mortality differentials, *Social Science & Medicine*, 68(9), 1574–1582.

Rogers, M., Theule, J., Ryan, B., Adams, G., & Keating, L. (2009). Parental involvement and children's school achievement, *Canadian Journal of School Psychology*, 24(1), 34–57.

Stuhlman, M., & Pianta, R. (2009). Profiles of educational quality in first grade, *The Elementary School Journal*, 109(4), 323–342.

Tappe, M., Wilbur, K., & Telljohann, S. (2009). Articulation of the National Health Education Standards to support learning and healthy behaviors among students, *American Journal of Health Education*, 40(4), 245–253.

UNIT

3

Foods and Nutrients: Basic Concepts

CHAPTER

12

Nutritional Guidelines

NAEYC Standards *Chapter Links*

- **#1 a, b, and c:** Promoting child development and learning
- **#2 a and c:** Building family and community relationships
- **#3 a, b, c, and d:** Observing, documenting, and assessing to support young children and families
- **#6 b, c, and e:** Becoming a professional

Learning Objectives

After studying this chapter, you should be able to:

- Outline the steps for evaluating the nutrient content of a meal or meals.
- Use the *Dietary Guidelines for Americans* to achieve your personal nutritional goals.
- Classify foods according to the Food Guide Pyramid and identify the nutrient strengths of each major food group.
- Evaluate the nutritional quality of a food item from its package label.

Diet has a direct effect on the quality of a person's health and well-being. It is also important to note that all persons throughout life require the same nutrients, but in varying amounts. Young children have a significant need for nutrients that support growth and provide energy; older children and adults require nutrients to maintain and repair body tissue and to provide energy.

To teach healthy food habits, teachers and families must first set a good example. Children typically model the eating behaviors of adults they love and admire. To set a positive example, adults must be knowledgeable about basic nutrition and understand how to maintain healthy eating habits. The ability to apply this knowledge to the care of children will, it is hoped, follow.

Nutrition is the study of food and how it is used by the body. Nutritionists study foods because foods contain **nutrients**, which are chemical substances that serve specific purposes. Nutrients meet the body's need for:

- sources of energy
- materials for growth and maintenance of body tissue
- regulation of body processes

nutrition – *the study of food and how it is used by the body.*
nutrients – *the components or substances that are found in food.*

Table 12–1 Nutrients and Their Roles

	Calories per Gram	Energy	Build/Maintain Body Tissues	Regulators
Carbohydrates	4	X		
Fats	9	X		
Proteins (needed for every function)	4	X	X	X
Minerals			X	X
Water			X	X
Vitamins				X*

* required in a regulatory role only.

Table 12–1 shows the relationship between nutrients and their functions. Note that most nutrients serve one or two primary functions; however, protein plays a critical role in all three.

Nutrients are needed in adequate amounts for normal body function to take place. An inadequate supply or poor utilization of nutrients may lead to **malnutrition** or **undernutrition** and result in abnormal body function and poor general health. Malnutrition may also result from excessive intake of one or more nutrients to the exclusion of others. This, too, may interfere with normal body functions and contribute to health problems. For example, there is currently much concern about excessive consumption of dietary fats and cholesterol and of self-supplementation with specific minerals and vitamins.

Approximately 50 nutrients are known to be essential for humans. An **essential nutrient** is one that must be provided by food substances, as the body is unable to manufacture it in adequate amounts. Persons of all ages require the same essential nutrients, only in different amounts. Factors such as age, activity, gender, health status, and lifestyle determine how much of a particular nutrient is required. Information regarding the amounts of nutrients found in specific foods can be found online (http://www.nal.usda.gov/fnic/foodcomp/search) and in many books.

A healthful diet is based on a daily intake of nutritious foods and meals. What should we eat? What should we not eat? How much should we eat? The answers to these important questions have led to the development of a number of nutritional tools and guidelines. Each provides information that will promote healthful eating habits; the choice lies with the individual and may depend on the time available, the ease of use, and personal interest.

Regardless of the guideline selected, the common factor necessary for optimum nutrition is the inclusion of a wide variety of foods. Some foods contain many nutrients, while others yield only a few. No single food includes enough of all nutrients to support life. Thus, consuming a diet that includes a variety of foods improves the likelihood that all essential nutrients will be obtained.

Dietary Reference Intakes (DRIs)

The "master guideline" for nutrition planning in the United States and Canada is the **Dietary Reference Intakes (DRIs)**. The latest revision of this plan reflects major changes in the format and philosophy of the original 1941 document known as the Recommended Daily Dietary Allowances

---

malnutrition – *prolonged inadequate or excessive intake of nutrients and/or calories required by the body.*
undernutrition – *an inadequate intake of one or more required or essential nutrients.*
essential nutrient – *nutrient that must be provided in food because it cannot be synthesized by the body at a rate sufficient to meet the body's needs.*
Dietary Reference Intake (DRI) – *a plan that presents the recommended goals of nutrient intakes for various age and gender groups.*

(RDAs). Emphasis is now placed on the relationship between dietary intake, health, and the reduced risk of chronic disease. The updated guideline, released over a period of several years, is presented as four components. Table 12–2 illustrates the first two portions of the document. The DRIs consist of:

- Recommended Daily Allowance (RDA)—goals for nutrient intake by individuals.
- Adequate Intake (AI)—goals for nutrient intake when an RDA has not been determined.
- Estimated Average Requirement (EAR)—amount of a nutrient that is estimated to meet the requirements of 50 percent of the individuals in a given life-stage or gender group; this number is used to establish the RDAs.
- Tolerable Upper Intake Level (UL)—the highest intake level that is likely to pose no health risk; exceeding this limit could cause potential toxicity and health risks.

The DRIs are used to set national nutritional policy as well as for *assessing* the nutrient intakes of individuals/groups and *planning* diets for individuals/groups (Wiener et al., 2009). They are also used for determining the nutrient information present on food labels (Miller et al., 2009; Taylor, 2009). It is suggested that RDAs, AIs, and ULs be used in planning diets for individuals, while the EAR is more useful in planning for groups. EARs are believed to be important in the nutrient intake assessment of individuals and groups (Clark & Fox, 2009).

For the Dietary Reference Intake guidelines to be meaningful, the nutrient content of foods must be known (see *www.nal.usda.gov/fnic/foodcomp/search*). To evaluate a diet by means of the Dietary Reference Intake guidelines, the following steps are required:

1. List the amounts of all foods and beverages consumed during one 24-hour period.
2. Use nutrient value tables or a computer software program to determine the nutrient content of each food and beverage consumed.
3. Total the amount of each nutrient consumed during the day.
4. Determine if the amount of nutrients consumed is sufficient by comparing the total amount of each nutrient consumed with the Dietary Reference Intake for the appropriate age and gender group (Table 12–2).

Dietary Guidelines for Americans

The National Nutrition Monitoring and Related Research Act of 1990 requires the Secretaries of Health and Human Services (HHS) and the U.S. Department of Agriculture (USDA) to issue a joint report, called the ***Dietary Guidelines for Americans***, at least every 5 years. The new 2010 Dietary Guidelines for Americans reflect the Advisory Committee's efforts to establish recommendations based on current scientific evidence regarding nutrition's role in health maintenance and disease prevention. This document is available online (http://www.dietaryguidelines.gov).

The *Dietary Guidelines* have come to serve as the basis for nearly all nutrition information in the United States (USDA, 2010). While the Dietary Reference Intakes (DRIs) address only specific nutrients, the Dietary Guidelines focus on eating and activity behaviors and their impact on the health of persons 2 years of age and older. Key recommendations include:

- **Adequate nutrients within calorie needs**—including a wide variety of nutrient-dense foods in one's diet while limiting fats, cholesterol, sugars, salt, and alcohol.
- **Weight management**—maintaining a healthy balance of calories consumed (food and beverages) with calories burned through physical activity to lower the risk of becoming overweight or obese.

Dietary Guidelines for Americans – *a report that provides recommendations for daily food choices, to be balanced with physical activity, to promote good health and reduce certain disease risks.*

Table 12–2 Dietary Reference Intakes (DRIs): Recommended Intakes for Individuals

Life Stage Group	Vit A (µg/d)[a]	Vit C (mg/d)	Vit D (µg/d)[b, c]	Vit E (mg/d)[d]	Vit K (µg/d)	Thiamin (mg/d)	Riboflavin (mg/d)	Niacin (mg/d)[e]	Vit B_6 (mg/d)	Folate (µg/d)[f]	Vit B_{12} (µg/d)	Panto-thenic Acid (mg/d)	Biotin (µg/d)	Choline[g] (mg/d)
Infants														
0–6 mo	400*	40*	5*	4*	2.0*	0.2*	0.3*	2*	0.1*	65*	0.4*	1.7*	5*	125*
7–12 mo	500*	50*	5*	5*	2.5*	0.3*	0.4*	4*	0.3*	80*	0.5*	1.8*	6*	150*
Children														
1–3 y	**300**	**15**	5*	**6**	30*	**0.5**	**0.5**	**6**	**0.5**	**150**	**0.9**	2*	8*	200*
4–8 y	**400**	**25**	5*	**7**	55*	**0.6**	**0.6**	**8**	**0.6**	**200**	**1.2**	3*	12*	250*
Males														
9–13 y	**600**	**45**	5*	**11**	60*	**0.9**	**0.9**	**12**	**1.0**	**300**	**1.8**	4*	20*	375*
14–18 y	**900**	**75**	5*	**15**	75*	**1.2**	**1.3**	**16**	**1.3**	**400**	**2.4**	5*	25*	550*
19–30 y	**900**	**90**	5*	**15**	120*	**1.2**	**1.3**	**16**	**1.3**	**400**	**2.4**	5*	30*	550*
31–50 y	**900**	**90**	5*	**15**	120*	**1.2**	**1.3**	**16**	**1.3**	**400**	**2.4**	5*	30*	550*
51–70 y	**900**	**90**	10*	**15**	120*	**1.2**	**1.3**	**16**	**1.7**	**400**	**2.4**[i]	5*	30*	550*
70 y	**900**	**90**	15*	**15**	120*	**1.2**	**1.3**	**16**	**1.7**	**400**	**2.4**[i]	5*	30*	550*
Females														
9–13 y	**600**	**45**	5*	**11**	60*	**0.9**	**0.9**	**12**	**1.0**	**300**	**1.8**	4*	20*	375*
14–18 y	**700**	**65**	5*	**15**	75*	**1.0**	**1.0**	**14**	**1.2**	**400**[i]	**2.4**	5*	25*	400*
19–30 y	**700**	**75**	5*	**15**	90*	**1.1**	**1.1**	**14**	**1.3**	**400**[i]	**2.4**	5*	30*	425*
31–50 y	**700**	**75**	5*	**15**	90*	**1.1**	**1.1**	**14**	**1.3**	**400**[i]	**2.4**	5*	30*	425*
51–70 y	**700**	**75**	10*	**15**	90*	**1.1**	**1.1**	**14**	**1.5**	**400**	**2.4**[h]	5*	30*	425*
70 y	**700**	**75**	15*	**15**	90*	**1.1**	**1.1**	**14**	**1.5**	**400**	**2.4**[h]	5*	30*	425*

(continued)

Table 12-2 Dietary Reference Intakes (DRIs): Recommended Intakes for Individuals *(continued)*

Life Stage Group	Vit A (μg/d)[a]	Vit C (mg/d)	Vit D (μg/d)[b, c]	Vit E (mg/d)[d]	Vit K (μg/d)	Thiamin (mg/d)	Riboflavin (mg/d)	Niacin (mg/d)[e]	Vit B_6 (mg/d)	Folate (μg/d)[f]	Vit B_{12} (μg/d)	Pantothenic Acid (mg/d)	Biotin (μg/d)	Choline[g] (mg/d)
Pregnancy														
14–18 y	**750**	**80**	5*	**15**	75*	**1.4**	**1.4**	**18**	**1.9**	**600**[j]	**2.6**	6*	30*	450*
19–30 y	**770**	**85**	5*	**15**	90*	**1.4**	**1.4**	**18**	**1.9**	**600**[j]	**2.6**	6*	30*	450*
31–50 y	**770**	**85**	5*	**15**	90*	**1.4**	**1.4**	**18**	**1.9**	**600**[j]	**2.6**	6*	30*	450*
Lactation														
14–18 y	**1,200**	**115**	5*	**19**	75*	**1.4**	**1.6**	**17**	**2.0**	**500**	**2.8**	7*	35*	550*
19–30 y	**1,300**	**120**	5*	**19**	90*	**1.4**	**1.6**	**17**	**2.0**	**500**	**2.8**	7*	35*	550*
31–50 y	**1,300**	**120**	5*	**19**	90*	**1.4**	**1.6**	**17**	**2.0**	**500**	**2.8**	7*	35*	550*

Note: This table (taken from the DRI reports, see www.nap.edu) presents Recommended Dietary Allowances (RDAs) in bold type and Adequate Intakes (AIs) in ordinary type followed by an asterisk(*). RDAs and AIs may both be used as goals for individual intake. RDAs are set to meet the needs of almost all (97 to 98 percent) individuals in a group. For healthy breastfed infants, the AI is the mean intake. The AI for other life stage and gender groups is believed to cover needs of all individuals in the group, but lack of data or uncertainty in the data prevent being able to specify with confidence the percentage of individuals covered by this intake.

[a] As retinol activity equivalents (RAEs). 1 RAE=1 μg retinol, 12 μg β-carotene, 24 μg α-carotene, or 24 μg β-cryptoxanthin. The RAE for dietary provitamin A carotenoids is twofold greater than retinol equivalents (RE), whereas the RAE for performed vitamin A is the same as RE.

[b] As cholecalciferol, 1 μg cholecalciferol = 40 IU vitamin D.

[c] In the absence of adequate exposure to sunlight.

[d] As α-tocopherol. α-Tocopherol includes *RRR*-α-tocopherol, the only form of α-tocopherol that occurs naturally in foods, and the *2R*-stereoisomeric forms of α-tocopherol (*RRR-, RSR-, RRS*-α-tocopherol) that occur in fortified foods and supplements. It does not include the 2S-stereoisomeric forms of α-tocopherol (*SRR-, SSR-, SRS-*, and *SSS*-α-tocopherol), also found in fortified foods and supplements.

[e] As niacin equivalents (NE). 1 mg of niacin = 60 mg of tryptophan; 0–6 months = performed niacin (not NE).

[f] As dietary folate equivalents (DFE). 1 DFE = 1 μg food folate = 0.6 μg of folic acid from fortified food or as a supplement consumed with food = 0.5 μg of a supplement taken on an empty stomach.

[g] Although AIs have been set for choline, there are few data to assess whether a dietary supply of choline is needed at all stages of the life cycle, and it may be that the choline requirement can be met by endogenous synthesis at some of these stages.

[h] Because 10 to 30 percent of older people may malabsorb food-bound B12, it is advisable for those older than 50 years to meet their RDA mainly by consuming foods fortified with B_{12} or a supplement containing B_{12}.

[i] In view of evidence linking folate intake with neural tube defects in the fetus, it is recommended that all women capable of becoming pregnant consume 400 μg from supplements or fortified foods in addition to intake of food folate from a varied diet.

[j] It is assumed that women will continue consuming 400 μg from supplements or fortified food until their pregnancy is confirmed and they enter prenatal care, which ordinarily occurs after the end of the periconceptional period—the critical time for formation of the neural tube.

Source: Dietary Reference Intakes (DRIs): Recommended Intakes for Individual Vitamins, Food and Nutrition, 2006. Reprinted with permission of the National Academy of Sciences, courtesy of the National Academies Press, Washington, D.C.

Figure 12–1 Physical activity recommendations for children.

The American Academy of Pediatrics (AAP), National Association for Sport & Physical Education (NASPE), and Canadian Academy of Sport Medicine (CASM) encourage daily physical activity for children of all ages:

- *infants* should have ample opportunities to explore their environment and should not be confined to a stroller or carrier for longer than 60 minutes/day.
- *toddlers* should accumulate at least 30 minutes of structured, vigorous physical activity and at least 60 minutes or more of free play.
- *preschoolers and school-age children* should participate in at least 60 minutes of structured physical activity during the day. They should also be given opportunities to engage in several hours of unstructured physical activity.

- **Physical activity**—participating in some form of physical activity each day. The American Academy of Pediatrics (AAP), National Association for Sport & Physical Education (NASPE), and Canadian Academy of Sport Medicine (CASM) support this recommendation and encourage children of all ages to engage in moderate to vigorous activity daily (AHA, 2009; NASPE, 2009; CDC, 2008) (Figure 12–1). Excess weight and a sedentary lifestyle have been linked to many chronic diseases. Teachers have a responsibility to plan appropriate physical activities for children and to model their own enjoyment and participation in these activities.
- **Food groups to encourage**—consuming more fruits, vegetables, whole grain products, and low-fat dairy products is strongly encouraged. Many children's diets fail to include adequate servings of these foods, which can result in deficiencies of vitamins, minerals, and other nutrients essential for healthy growth and development (Dave et al., 2009; Horodynski et al., 2009). Adults are also encouraged to increase their consumption of fruits, vegetables, whole-grain products and to select fat-free or low-fat dairy products. Whole grains are an excellent source of fiber and other nutrients essential to a balanced diet and are also low in fat. Fruits and vegetables are rich sources of many vitamins and minerals and are also naturally high in fiber.
- **Fats**—high fat intake is associated with the development of some chronic diseases and, when combined with minimal physical activity, can promote obesity. Total fat intake should be limited to no more than 20–30 percent of one's daily calories. Less than 10 percent of these calories should come from saturated (animal) fats. Cholesterol intake should be limited to less than 300 mg per day. Meat and dairy products should be low-fat and trans-fats avoided in all processed foods.
- **Carbohydrates**—are an important source of energy and fiber. However, foods high in added refined sugar should be limited. Adequate servings of fruits, vegetables, and whole grain products should be included each day.
- **Sodium and potassium**—reducing high sodium (salt) and low potassium intake to address the increasing incidence of high blood pressure in this country. Although sodium is essential for life, most people obtain enough from their food without adding extra salt. Sodium intake should be limited to no more than 1500-2000 mg (approximately 3/4 teaspoon) or less each day. Fruits, vegetables, and whole grains in their simplest forms contain little sodium and are ideal for including in one's diet; many are also rich sources of potassium. Most processed foods, canned and fast foods are quite high in sodium and salt and, thus, their consumption should be limited.
- **Alcoholic beverages**—persons who choose to consume alcohol should do so in moderation (one drink/day for women, two drinks/day for men). Women who are pregnant or breast-feeding should avoid alcohol.

- **Food safety**—young children are at a higher risk for food-borne illnesses. Washing hands, keeping food preparation areas clean, cooking food to proper temperatures, storing foods in proper refrigeration, and following instructions on food labels are important steps for reducing the risk of food-borne illness.

Canada has developed similar guidelines, entitled *Canada's Food Guide*. The newest version of this document was released in 2007 and encourages citizens to follow healthy eating patterns. A companion document, *Canada's Physical Activity Guide to Healthy Active Living*, stresses the importance of establishing daily activity practices.

Other Nutrition Guidelines

The U.S. Public Health Service continues to update the original *Healthy People* guidelines. Several statements in the *Healthy People 2020* document that specifically address children's nutritional needs are:

- eliminating very low food insecurity among children in U.S. households
- reducing the proportion of children who are overweight or obese
- increasing the contribution of fruits, vegetables, whole grains, and calcium to the diets of children 2 years and older
- reducing the consumption of calories from solid fats and added sugars in the population aged 2 years and older
- increasing the proportion of States and school districts that require regularly scheduled elementary school recess
- increasing the proportion of consumers who follow key food safety practices

Several non-profit organizations, including the American Heart Association and the National Cancer Institute, also advise similar healthy eating and physical activity behaviors. Their guidelines call for reducing fat, cholesterol, sodium, and alcohol in the diet and increasing vegetable, fruit, and whole grain consumption.

The Food Guide Pyramid

The Food Guide Pyramid provides a graphic illustration of the Dietary Guidelines for Americans (Figure 12–2). It emphasizes the importance of consuming a wide variety of foods from each food group and recommends intakes that are flexible for individuals of different ages, gender, and activity levels. The vertical stripes represent each of the essential food groups:

Figure 12–2 MyPyramid is an interactive, web-based tool designed to promote healthy eating and activity habits.

- orange for grains
- green for vegetables
- red for fruits
- yellow for oils
- blue for milk
- purple for meats and beans

The Pyramid conveys the importance of consuming a meal pattern that includes a wide variety of foods (represented by the various color bands) and moderation of eating that is balanced with physical activity. The varying widths of the Pyramid's stripes indicate the

Table 12–5 Good to Excellent Vitamin C Sources

orange*	tomatoes*
orange juice*	grapefruit*
strawberries*	mustard greens
cauliflower	spinach
broccoli	cabbage
sweet peppers, red or green	tangerine*

*May cause allergic reactions.

sunflower) used in cooking, as well as the oils from fish. Plant oils contain no cholesterol and are considered beneficial. Foods such as nuts, olives, and avocados also have a naturally high oil content that has many health benefits. Some oils are used mainly as flavorings, such as walnut oil and sesame oil. Mayonnaise, certain salad dressings, and soft (tub or squeeze) margarine with no trans-fats are considered oils. Solid fats are also included in the Oils group. Some food products are made from animal sources (butter) while others (stick and soft margarine) are converted from a liquid to a solid form by a process called hydrogenation. In general, the nutrient contribution of this group is low and the calorie content is high.

Milk

This group includes milk and milk-based foods that retain their calcium content, such as homemade puddings, frozen yogurts, and ice creams; hard cheeses such as Swiss and cheddar; soft cheeses such as ricotta and cottage cheese; and all yogurts. Dairy products that provide little or no calcium include butter, cream cheese, and cream and, thus, they are not considered part of the Milk group. Foods that provide **calcium** equal to that in one cup of milk are:

1 1/2 ounces cheddar cheese	1 2/3 cup cottage cheese
1 cup pudding	1 1/4 ounces mozzarella cheese
1 3/4 cups ice cream	1 cup plain yogurt

The Milk group is a major source of dietary calcium but a poor source of iron and vitamins A and C. Children should consume a daily total of 2 cups of milk or the equivalent from this group; adults should have 3 cups. Servings may be divided into 1/2-cup portions in consideration of children's smaller appetites and stomach capacity. Because foods in the Milk group tend to be high in fat and cholesterol, reduced- and low-fat products are preferred choices. However, children should not be given low-fat milk and dairy products prior to the age of 2. Infants and toddlers require the additional fats and fat-calories for energy and healthy nervous system development.

Meat and Beans

Beef, veal, pork, lamb, fish, and poultry are included in the Meat and Beans group. Other foods included in this group are eggs, legumes such as dry peas and beans, nuts, and nut butters such as peanut butter. Cheese may also be substituted for meats; however, it should be remembered that cheeses are high in cholesterol and do not contain iron, which is a nutrient strength of this food group. The Meat and Beans group is also a major source of dietary protein and B-vitamins.

---

calcium – *mineral nutrient; a major component of bones and teeth.*

The recommended daily intake from the Meat and Beans group, as with the other groups, varies by individual, based on age, gender, and physical activity. Children 2 to 3 years old require approximately 2-ounce equivalents daily; children 4 and older require 3- to 4-ounce equivalents. The following foods contain **protein** that is approximately equal to that in one ounce of meat, poultry, or fish:

1 egg
1 ounce of cheese
1/4 cup cottage cheese
1/4 cup cooked dried peas or beans
2 tablespoons peanut butter

Children's nutrient needs are influenced by age, gender and activity level.

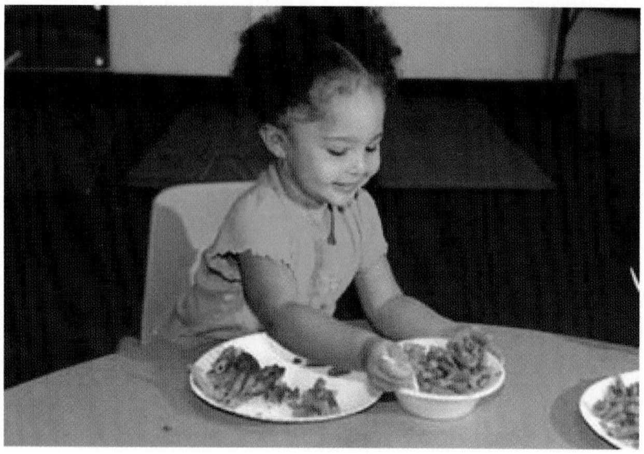

© Cengage Learning

Discretionary Calories

Foods consumed from each of the Pyramid groups provide calories for energy. How many calories an individual needs to take in varies according to age, gender, and level of physical activity. The interactive Food Pyramid offers tools that help a person determine how many calories are needed each day (http://www.mypyramid.gov).

Discretionary calories represent the difference between the number of calories a person takes in from the recommended servings in each food group and one's ideal or target caloric goal. They can be compared to discretionary income: Just as your budget contains discretionary or extra income to cover special expenses like vacation trips or DVDs, your diet may contain a small number of discretionary calories that can be "spent" on foods that may be higher in fats, added sugar, and/or alcohol. Persons who are relatively sedentary will have, on the average, between 100–300 discretionary calories each day depending on the foods they have chosen to consume from each of the food groups.

Adding a large number of foods that contain discretionary calories can dilute the healthful quality of a person's diet (Story, 2009; Bachman et al., 2008). For example, the vitamin C and calorie contribution of an apple is altered significantly when sugars, fats, and flour are added, such as when making an apple pie (Table 12–6).

Table 12–6 How Added Sugar and Fats Alter a Food's Calories and Nutrient Contribution

	Calories	Potassium	Vitamin C
Banana, 1/2 cup sliced	67	268 mg	6.5 mg
Banana chips, 1 ounce	147	152 mg	1.8 mg
Banana pudding, 1/2 cup	72	62 mg	0.3 mg
Banana bread, 1 slice	196	80 mg	1.0 mg
Banana cream pie, 1/8 pie	387	238 mg	2.3 mg
Banana waffle, 1 small round	212	140 mg	1.1 mg

protein – *class of nutrients used primarily for structural and regulatory functions.*

Reflective Thoughts

The use of the Pyramid as a guide for making healthy food choices requires an understanding that individual foods within a food group can vary greatly in nutrient content relative to sugar, fat, and calories. Choose different foods within a given Pyramid food group and assign them to one of the following categories:

a. unrestricted—eat any amount every day (high nutrient content but low in fat and sugar)

b. moderately restricted—eat only one to three times per day (moderately high in fat and/or sugar)

c. very restricted—eat only two to three times per week (high in fat and/or sugar and calories)

Food Labels

The Nutritional Labeling and Education Act, passed in 1990, resulted in significant changes in food product labeling. The food label, regulated by the Food and Drug Administration (FDA) and the U.S. Department of Agriculture (USDA), underwent further revision in 1994 (Figure 12–3), which resulted in the current label format that provides:

- Easy-to-read nutrition information on packaged foods.
- Serving sizes in commonly consumed amounts. This prevents using small serving sizes to make food products that are high in fat, cholesterol, sodium, or calories look better than they are.
- A list of all ingredients (in decreasing order relative to the total amount) on their label.
- **Percent Daily Values (%DV)** that show how a serving of food fits into a total day's diet.
- **Nutrition claims** that mean the same on every product (Figure 12–4).
- Voluntary information for the most commonly eaten fresh fruits and vegetables, raw fish, and cuts of meat. This information may appear on posters or in brochures in the same area as the food is sold.

Food manufacturers are required to list trans-fats (liquid oils that have been converted into solid fats, such as margarine) as well as saturated fats and cholesterol on their labels. Food allergens (milk, eggs, tree nuts [such as almonds, walnuts], peanuts, shellfish [such as shrimp, crab, lobster], fish, wheat, and soy) that could potentially cause life-threatening reactions must also be identified on food labels (U.S. Food & Drug Administration, 2006). Manufacturers are allowed to list health claims on their labels, such as "may reduce the risk of heart disease," as long as there is scientific evidence to back up the statement.

Calories from Fat

Labels must also disclose the amounts of fat, saturated fat, trans-fats, and the number of calories from fat. With this information present (amount of fat and calories from fat), the percent of calories from fat can easily be determined:

$$\text{Percent of calories from fat} = \frac{\text{fat calories/serving}}{\text{total calories/serving}} \times 100$$

To calculate the number of calories from fat, use this formula:

$$\text{calories from fat} = \text{grams (g) of fat/serving} \times 9 \text{ (cal/g)}$$

Percent Daily Values (%DV) – *measures of the nutritional values of food; used in nutrition labeling.*
nutrition claims – *statements of reduced calories, fat, or salt on the food labels.*

Figure 12–3 A typical food label.

Nutrition Facts

Serving Size 3/4 cup (30g)
Servings Per Container about 15

Amount Per Serving	Cereal	Cereal with 1/2 cup Skim Milk
Calories	100	140
Calories from Fat	5	5
	% Daily Value**	
Total Fat 0.5g*	1%	1%
Saturated Fat 0g	0%	0%
Polyunsaturated Fat 0g		
Monounsaturated Fat 0g		
Cholesterol 0mg	0%	0%
Sodium 220mg	9%	12%
Potassium 190mg	5%	11%
Total Carbohydrate 24g	8%	10%
Dietary Fiber 5g	21%	21%
Soluble Fiber 1g		
Insoluble Fiber 4g		
Sugars 6g		
Other Carbohydrate 13g		
Protein 3g		
Vitamin A	15%	20%
Vitamin C	0%	2%
Calcium	0%	15%
Iron	45%	45%
Vitamin D	10%	25%
Thiamin	25%	30%
Riboflavin	25%	35%
Niacin	25%	25%
Vitamin B_6	25%	25%
Folate	25%	25%
Vitamin B_{12}	25%	35%
Phosphorus	15%	25%
Magnesium	15%	20%
Zinc	10%	15%
Copper	10%	10%

*Amount in Cereal. One half cup skim milk contributes an additional 40 calories, 65mg sodium, 200mg potassium, 6g total carbohydrate (6g sugars), and 4g protein

**Percent Daily Values are based on a 2,000 calorie diet. Your daily values may be higher or lower depending on your calorie needs:

		Calories: 2,000	2,500
Total Fat	Less than	65g	80g
Saturated Fat	Less than	20g	25g
Cholesterol	Less than	300mg	300mg
Sodium	Less than	2,400mg	2,400mg
Potassium		3,500mg	3,500mg
Total Carbohydrate		300g	375g
Dietary Fiber		25g	30g

Figure 12–4 Commonly used labeling terms defined.

WHAT SOME CLAIMS MEAN

high-protein: at least 10 grams (g) high-quality protein per serving

good source of calcium: at least 100 milligrams (mg) calcium per serving

more iron: at least 1.8 mg more iron per serving than reference food. (Label will say 10 percent more of the Daily Value for iron.)

fat-free: less than 0.5 g fat per serving

low-fat: 3 g or less fat per serving. (If the serving size is 30 g or less or 2 tablespoons or less, 3 g or less fat per 50 g of the food.)

reduced or fewer calories: at least 25 percent fewer calories per serving than the reference food

sugar-free: less than 0.5 g sugar per serving

reduced sugar: reduced sugar: at least 25% less sugar per serving when compared with a similar food

sodium-free: less than 5 mg. of sodium per serving

light or lite (two meanings):

- one-third fewer calories or 50% less fat per serving than the reference food. (If more than half of the food's calories are from fat, the fat must be reduced by 50 percent)
- a "low-calorie" or "low-fat" food whose sodium content has been reduced by 50 percent of the reference food

low cholesterol: 20 mg. or less of cholesterol and 2 gm. or less of saturated fat per serving

The following calculations (percent of calories from fat) for some selected foods will show how the fat content reported on labels may sometimes be misleading:

Cheddar cheese—1 ounce = 115 calories and 9 g of fat:

Calories from fat = $9 \times 9 = 81$

Percent calories from fat = $81/115 \times 100 = 70\%$

Eggs—one egg = 75 calories and 6 g of fat:

Calories from fat = $6 \times 9 = 54$

Percent calories from fat = $54/75 \times 100 = 72\%$

90% fat-free ground beef—3 ounces = 185 calories and 10 g of fat:

Calories from fat = $10 \times 9 = 90$

Percent calories from fat = $90/185 \times 100 = 49\%$

For all of these examples, the grams of fat (9, 6, and 10) are low, yet they all presented more than 30 percent of calories from fat.

The recommendation that no more than 30 percent of calories should come from fat does not mean that all healthy food choices must derive less than 30 percent of their calories from fat. This would virtually eliminate all red meat and most dairy products. However, it does mean that if you eat a lean hamburger with 49 percent fat-calories, it might be better to skip the French fries at 47 percent fat-calories and substitute an apple, banana, or orange with less than 10 percent of calories from fat.

The procedure for calculating the percent of fat-calories may seem somewhat tedious at first. However, after completing several of these calculations you will be able to quickly skim a label and estimate a food item's nutrient density or fat-calorie ratio.

Focus On Families — Dietary Guidelines for Americans

- The *Dietary Guidelines for Americans* encourages a diet that is moderate in sugar consumption. Many foods such as milk/dairy products and fruit have naturally occurring sugars. Foods that have sugars added during processing or preparation contribute unnecessary calories and are often low in many vitamins and minerals. Although sugar is not harmful when consumed in limited amounts, it provides no beneficial dietary nutrients.
- Know your food labels: A *reduced sugar* food item contains at least 25 percent less sugar than the reference food. *No added sugar* or *without added sugar* foods indicate that no sugars were added during processing or packaging. *Sugar-free* foods contain less than 0.5 grams sugar per serving.
- The following terms, if listed as the first or second ingredient of a food label, indicate the food is likely high in sugar: Brown sugar, corn sweetener or corn syrup, fructose, fruit juice concentrate, glucose, dextrose, high-fructose corn syrup, honey, lactose, maltose, molasses, raw sugar, table sugar (sucrose), syrup.
- Major food sources of sugar in the United States include sodas, cakes, candy, cookies, pies, fruit drinks and punches, and dairy desserts such as ice cream. Healthy foods that contain added sugar should be limited in the diet: chocolate milk, presweetened cereals, and fruits packed in syrup. If these foods are eaten, do so in moderation and choose smaller serving sizes. (A serving of soda in the 1950s was 6.5 ounces compared to a 20-ounce serving today!)

Classroom Corner — Teacher Activities

Tasting a Rainbow... (PreK–2; National Health Education Standards 1.2.1 and 8.2.1)

Concept: Fruits and vegetables are healthy foods to eat and we should eat a variety of them.

Learning Objectives

- Children will learn that fruits and vegetables are healthy foods to eat.
- Children will experience tasting a variety of fruits and vegetables.

Supplies

- one red fruit and vegetable (apple, strawberry, tomato, watermelon, red pepper)
- one orange fruit and vegetable (orange, acorn squash, orange pepper, cantaloupe, yam, carrot)
- one green fruit and vegetable (grape, lime, spinach, honeydew, green pepper, apple, pear, broccoli, bean, pea, kiwi)
- one yellow fruit and vegetable (banana, pineapple, lemon, yellow squash, corn)
- one purple fruit and vegetable (purple grape, purple cabbage)
- one blue fruit (blueberry)
- hand wipes, plates, forks

Learning Activities

- Read and discuss one of the following books:
  - *Give Me 5 a Day* by Kathy Reeves, Brenda Crosby, Jennifer Hemphill, and Elizabeth Hoffman
  - *I Will Never Not Ever Eat a Tomato* by Lauren Child
- Tell children that bodies need healthy foods, like fruits and vegetables, to stay healthy and help us grow. Show children a picture of a rainbow; explain that fruits and vegetables come in many colors like a rainbow.
- Have all children wash their hands with wipes. Hand each child a plate with fruit, a plate with vegetables, and a fork. Make sure all the fruits and vegetables are cut into bite-sized pieces to prevent choking. Talk about how the colors of the food on their plates are the same colors that make up a rainbow.
- Give children an opportunity to taste each item and talk about how each tastes. Focus the activity on the importance of tasting a variety of fruits and vegetables instead of on children's likes and dislikes.

Evaluation

- Children will name several kinds of fruits and vegetables.
- Children will taste a variety of fruits and vegetables.

Additional lesson plans for grades 3–5 are available on this text's Education CourseMate website.

Summary

- The dietary reference intakes (DRI) are nutrient goals based on gender and age that are considered essential for maintaining health. They are used for policy development, dietary assessment, meal planning, and appear on food labels.
- The *Dietary Guidelines for Americans* are a set of recommendations that encourage food selections which meet nutrient needs, reduce the known harmful effects of over consumption of some nutrient groups, promote physical activity, and stress food safety.
- The Food Guide Pyramid is the most practical guide for making healthful food choices; foods are grouped by similar characteristics and nutrient strengths. A health-promoting diet is ensured by consuming a variety of foods from all food groups in the amounts recommended.
- Food labels must include a list of all ingredients in a product; nutrient values, fat, and calories present in the item based on serving size; known allergens; and, manufacturer's contact information.
- Determining the percent of calories from fat in a given food serving is useful for limiting excessive dietary fat intake.

Terms to Know

nutrition *p. 318*
nutrients *p. 318*
malnutrition *p. 319*
undernutrition *p. 319*
essential nutrient *p. 319*
Dietary Reference Intake (DRI) *p. 319*
Dietary Guidelines for Americans *p. 320*
calcium *p. 327*
protein *p. 328*
Percent Daily Values (%DV) *p. 329*
nutrition claims *p. 329*

Chapter Review

A. By Yourself:

1. Match the foods in **column I** to the appropriate food group in **column II**. Some foods may include more than one food group.

Column I	Column II
1. Navy beans	a. Milk group
2. Rice	b. Meat and Beans group
3. Spaghetti	c. Grain group
4. Hamburger pizza	d. Vegetable group
5. Macaroni and cheese	e. Fruit group
6. Peanut butter sandwich	f. Oils group
7. French fries	g. Discretionary calories
8. Ice cream	
9. Popcorn	
10. Carbonated beverages	

B. As a Group:

1. Describe the energy sources in food. What nutrients yield energy?
2. Discuss how an individual might use the Dietary Guidelines for Americans to improve their personal well-being.
3. Explain what dietary reference intakes are and how they can be used for planning a child's daily diet.
4. Debate the merits and limitations of the current Food Guide Pyramid.
5. Explain how foods labeled *low-fat, fat-free,* and *reduced calories* differ.

Case Study

1. Betsy, age 3½ , drinks milk to the exclusion of adequate amounts of foods from other food groups. What nutrient is Betsy receiving in excess? What two nutrients are most likely to be deficient?
2. Jason, age 4, refuses to eat fruit. He will occasionally accept a small serving of applesauce and a few bites of banana but little else. What two nutrients are probably deficient in Jason's diet?
3. Jeremy, age 3, is allergic to milk and dairy products. What nutrient is deficient in Jeremy's diet?
4. Tommy, age 2, by choice will eat only high carbohydrate foods, preferably those that are sweet. He rejects high-protein, high-fat foods such as meats and cheese. How would you change his diet to provide adequate protein and fat for normal growth and nerve development without increasing his carbohydrate intake with high-fat pastries, cakes, and so on?
5. Mary, age 4, refuses milk and all milk products; she likes to drink a variety of juices. How would you adjust her diet to ensure that she meets her calcium requirement?

Application Activities

1. Record your personal food intake for the past 24 hours. Go to *www.MyPyramid.gov* and generate "My Pyramid Plan" by entering your age, gender, and activity level. Analyze the results of your 24-hour food intake by comparing it with the Pyramid Plan recommendations.
2. Plan a day's menu for a 4-year-old girl who does an extra 45 minutes of activity each day. Include the recommended amounts from each food group, the calorie pattern on which the recommendations are based, and the number of oils/discretionary calories recommended per day from My Pyramid Plan.
3. Assume that a child is allergic to citrus fruit and strawberries (common food allergies).What fruit and/or vegetable choices could be substituted to provide adequate vitamin C?
4. The next time you eat pizza, note the amount that you consumed. Use the Pyramid as a guide to evaluate the number of servings you received from each of the different food groups. If you had a green salad with your pizza, what nutrients did it add? Estimate how many 1-cup servings the salad would have yielded.

Helpful Web Resources

Canada's Food Guide	http://www.hc-sc.gc.ca/fn-an/food-guide-aliment/index-eng.php
Federal Citizen Information Center	http://www.pueblo.gsa.gov
Food and Drug Administration (FDA) (Food labels)	http://www.fda.gov/Food/default.htm
Food Guide Pyramid for Kids	http://www.mypyramid.gov/kids
Tufts University Center on Nutrition Science and Policy	http://nutrition.tufts.edu
United States Department of Agriculture (USDA) News Site	http://www.usda.gov
United States Department of Agriculture MyPyramid.gov	http://www.mypryamid.gov

You are just a click away from additional health, safety, and nutrition resources! Go to www. CengageBrain.com to access this text's Education CourseMate website, where you'll find:

- glossary flashcards, activities, tutorial quizzes, videos, web links, and more

References

American Heart Association (AHA). (2009). Exercise (physical activity) and children. Accessed on December 18, 2009 from http://www.americanheart.org/presenter.jhtml?identifier=4596.

Anderson, J., Baird, P., Davis, R., Ferreri, S., Knudtson, M., Koraym, A., Waters, V., & Williams, C. (2009). Health benefits of dietary fiber, *Nutrition Reviews*, 67(4), 188–205.

Bachman, J., Reedy, J., Subar, A., & Krebs-Smith, S. (2008). Sources of food group intakes among the US population, 2001–2002, *Journal of the American Dietetic Association*, 108(5), 804–814.

Centers for Disease Control & Prevention (CDC). (2008). How much physical activity do children need? Accessed on December 18, 2009 from http://www.cdc.gov/physicalactivity/everyone/guidelines/children.html.

Clark, M., & Fox, M. (2009). Nutritional quality of the diets of US public school children and the role of the school meal programs, *Journal of the American Dietetic Association*, 109(2), S44–S56.

Dave, J., Evans, A., Saunders, R., Watkins, K., & Pfeiffer, K. (2009). Associations among food insecurity, acculturation, demographic factors, and fruit and vegetable intake at home in Hispanic children, *Journal of the American Dietetic Association*, 109(4), 697–701.

Horodynski, M., Brophy-Herb, H., Chen, C., Stommel, M., & Weatherspoon, L. (2009). Mother's self-efficacy, "picky eater" perception, food choices and toddler's fruit and vegetable consumption in low-income African American and Caucasian mothers, *Journal of Nutrition Education and Behavior*, 41(4), S13–S19.

Massi, L., Silk, K., Von Friederichs-Fitzwater, M., Hamner, H., Prue, C., & Boster, F. (2009). Developing effective campaign messages to prevent neural tube defects: A qualitative assessment of women's reactions to advertising concepts, *Journal of Health Communication*, 14(2), 131–159.

Miller, G., Drewnowski, A., Fulgoni, V., Heaney, R., King, J., & Kennedy, E. (2009). It is time for a positive approach to dietary guidance using nutrient density as a basic principle, *Journal of Nutrition*, 139(6), 1198–1202.

Mitka, M. (2005). Government unveils new food pyramid: Critics say nutrition tool is flawed. *Journal of the American Medical Association*, 1(293), 2581–2582.

National Association for Sport and Physical Education (NASPE). (2009). Physical activity for children: A statement of guidelines for children ages 5–12, (2nd ed.). Accessed on December 18, 2009 from http://www.aahperd.org/naspe/standards/nationalGuidelines/PA-Children-5-12.cfm.

Renda, M., & Fischer, P. (2009). Vegetarian diets in children and adolescents, *Pediatrics in Review*, 30(1), e1–8.

Story, M. (2009). The third School Nutrition Dietary Assessment study: Findings and policy implications for improving the health of US children, *Journal of the American Dietetic Association*, 109(2), S7–S13.

Taylor, C. (2009). How the nutrition food label was developed, Part 1: The Nutrition Facts Panel, *Journal of the American Dietetic Association*, 108(3), 437–442.

Thompson, M., Cole, D., & Ray, J. (2009). Vitamin B-12 and neural tube defects: The Canadian experience, *American Journal of Clinical Nutrition*, 89(2), 697S–701S.

USDA. (2005). MyPyramid.gov. Accessed on December 18, 2009 from http://www.mypyramid.gov.

USDA. (2010). *Dietary Guidelines for Americans.* Accessed on June 3, 2010 from http://www.cnpp.usda.gov/dietaryguidelines.htm.

U.S. Food & Drug Administration. (2006). Food Allergen Labeling and Consumer Protection Act of 2004. Accessed on December 18, 2009 from http://www.cfsan.fda.gov/~dms/alrgact.html.

Wiener, F., Schmidt, M., Munson, K., Khoury, P., Kalkwarf, H., & Daniels, S. (2009). Dietary intake of 3 year old children: Do they meet recommended intake? *Current Pediatric Reviews*, 5(2), 128–134.

CHAPTER 13

Nutrients That Provide Energy (Carbohydrates, Fats, and Proteins)

NAEYC Standards *Chapter Links*

- **#1 a, b, and c:** Promoting child development and learning
- **#2 a and c:** Building family and community relationships
- **#3 b, c, and d:** Observing, documenting, and assessing to support young children and families
- **#4 a:** Using developmentally effective approaches to connect with children and families
- **#6 c:** Becoming a professional

Learning Objectives

After studying this chapter, you should be able to:

- Identify the three nutrient classes and the amount of energy each yields.
- Explain the differences between simple, compound, and complex carbohydrates.
- Plan a day's diet that meets the recommended 30 percent of calories from fat and is low in saturated fatty acids and cholesterol.
- Discuss why proteins are not an ideal energy source.

Energy is generally defined as the ability to do work. Examples of work performed by the body are (1) locomotion and movement, (2) building new tissues, (3) maintaining body temperature, and (4) digesting, absorbing, and metabolizing food. In other words, energy is required for the performance of all body functions. In terms of survival, the need for energy is second only to the need for oxygen and water.

---

energy – *power to perform work.*

Food as an Energy Source

The amount of potential energy in a food is expressed in **calories**; for example, a 1-cup serving of ice cream supplies 185 calories, a large apple provides 116 calories. The energy cost of a given activity is also measured and expressed in calories; for example, swimming for 30 minutes expends about 150 calories and skipping for 10 minutes burns about 70 calories.

The carbohydrates, fats, and proteins derived from foods supply energy for the body's activities. Vitamins, minerals, and water do not yield calories but they are essential for the functioning of **enzymes**, **coenzymes**, and **hormones**. Enzymes and coenzymes are vitamin-containing substances that initiate and participate in the many metabolic reactions involved in the release of energy from carbohydrates, fats, and proteins. Hormones, such as thyroxin and insulin, while not directly involved in energy-releasing reactions, regulate many of these reactions. For example, several hormones are required to maintain a blood sugar level that provides energy sufficient to meet all body needs. The caloric value of any given food is determined by its carbohydrate, fat, and protein content. The relative numbers of calories contained in carbohydrates, fats, and proteins are:

- carbohydrates—4 calories per gram
- fat—9 calories per gram
- proteins—4 calories per gram

A **gram** is a metric unit of measurement for weight. The symbol for gram is "g." There are 28 grams in one ounce, and 454 grams in one pound. A metal paper clip weighs about one gram. A **milligram** is a metric unit of weight that is equal to one-thousandth of a gram: There are 1,000 milligrams in a gram. The symbol for milligram is "mg."

Every individual has different energy requirements. These requirements vary slightly on a day-to-day basis and are determined by a combination of:

- basal metabolic rate (BMR)
- physical activity
- energy spent to release energy from food (thermic energy of food)

Energy Utilization

The term **basal metabolic rate (BMR)** describes the energy needed just to carry on vital involuntary body processes, such as blood circulation, breathing, cell activity, body temperature maintenance, and heartbeat. The BMR varies little from day to day. A child's BMR will be higher than an adult's due to a faster heartbeat, respiratory rate, and the additional energy required for growth. BMR does not reflect voluntary activity, although physical activity taken to the aerobic level will increase heartbeat and breathing rates, which will temporarily increase BMR. For most children and adults, the energy required to meet basal metabolic needs is greater than energy expended for voluntary physical activity.

Physical activity is the aspect of an individual's energy need that is subject to the greatest conscious control. For instance, participation in tennis or swimming as a recreational activity requires far more energy than reading or watching television. Although children seem to be on-the-go most of the time, they should also engage in periods of vigorous physical activity on a daily basis. The

---

calories – *units used to measure the energy value of foods.*
enzymes – *proteins that catalyze body functions.*
coenzymes – *a vitamin-containing substance required by certain enzymes before they can perform their prescribed function.*
hormones – *special chemical substances produced by endocrine glands that influence and regulate specific body functions.*
gram – *a metric unit of weight (g); approximately 1/28 of an ounce.*
milligram – *a metric unit of weight (mg); approximately 1/1000 of a gram.*
basal metabolic rate (BMR) – *minimum amount of energy needed to carry on the body processes vital to life.*

benefits of physical activity include improved cognitive and motor development, opportunities for socialization, a sense of personal accomplishment, improved physical and mental health, and increased fitness. The additional calories used during vigorous physical activity provide an opportunity to increase children's food intake and, thus, make it easier to meet their nutrient requirements.

Thermic energy of food refers to the energy required to **digest**, **absorb**, transport, and **metabolize** nutrients in food. This factor accounts for approximately 10 percent of an individual's total energy requirement.

Children require more energy per unit of body weight than do adults due to rapid growth (Kirby & Danner, 2009). In turn, the rate of growth (cell division and/or enlargement of existing cells) is determined by the availability of an adequate energy supply (Bier, 2008). Physical activity and body mass also affect the amount of energy an individual child needs. In general, a child's daily caloric requirement is calculated solely on the basis of normal body weight. For example, a 4-year-old child needs approximately 40 calories per pound of body weight. (The energy needs of infants are detailed in Chapter 16.) For comparison, a moderately active adult female requires approximately 18 calories per pound; a moderately active adult male needs approximately 21 calories per pound. (Moderately active has been described as equal time "on the feet and on the seat.") Males have a higher BMR than do females due to their greater muscle-to-fat ratio; muscle tissue requires BMR energy, while fat needs zero energy for storage or retrieval.

The energy needs of active, growing children are considerably greater than those of an adult.

Balancing the number of calories eaten with the number of calories expended results in a stable body weight. (See *Dietary Guidelines for Americans* in Chapter 12.) Consuming fewer calories than are needed leads to weight loss and can slow children's growth rate because body tissue must be utilized to meet energy demands. When children's diets provide adequate calories from carbohydrates and fat, proteins can be used to support growth. Carbohydrates should supply at least half of children's and adult's daily calories, with starches being the preferred carbohydrate because they contribute important vitamins, minerals, and fiber as well as energy.

Excess Energy

Consuming an excess of calories over a period of time can lead to obesity. Children who are overweight are often less active than their slimmer playmates and may require fewer calories due to their reduced activity level. Their bulkier body mass can make coordinated movements difficult

thermic energy of food – *energy required to digest, absorb, transport, and metabolize nutrients in food.*

digestion – *the process by which complex nutrients in foods are changed into smaller units that can be absorbed and used by the body.*

absorption – *the process by which the products of digestion are transferred from the intestinal tract into the blood or lymph or by which substances are taken up by the cells.*

metabolism – *all chemical changes that occur from the time nutrients are absorbed until they are built into body tissue or are excreted.*

Quiet activities burn fewer calories than active play.

and, thus, increase the risk of accidental injury (McHugh, 2010; Pollack, 2009). This may also contribute to the obese child's reluctance to engage in active play, which can lead to additional weight gain. Thus, it is important to stop this vicious cycle during the child's early years because there is strong evidence that child obesity results in adult obesity (Harris, Perreira, & Lee, 2009). There are also many known health risks associated with childhood obesity, including breathing disturbances during sleep, asthma, muscle and joint problems, diabetes, and heart disease (Krul et al., 2009; Rundle et al., 2009; Spicuzza, Leonardi, & La Rosa, 2009). Children who are significantly overweight may be subjected to teasing from their peers and excluded from play activities. This can foster additional problems for the child, including negative self-image, decreased fitness level, and fewer opportunities for socialization (Duarte et al., 2009).

Increasing children's participation in physical activity and providing them with a healthful diet based on nutrient-dense foods can have positive outcomes, especially if they are overweight (Table 13–1) (Donnelly et al., 2009; Janz et al., 2009). Children's calories should never be drastically reduced, as this can cause a deficiency of essential energy and nutrients and potentially contribute to eating disorders (Brown & Summerbell, 2009). A safer approach is to adjust calorie intake to keep body weight stable while the child continues to grow taller. Over time, this will bring the weight-height ratio (also known as body mass index, or BMI) back into a normal range. Any time children are placed on a weight-reduction program, they must be closely monitored by a physician to ensure that all nutritional needs are being met adequately.

Carbohydrates as Energy Sources

Carbohydrates yield 4 calories per gram and should be a child's primary source of energy (Figure 13–1). At least half of a child's caloric requirement should be derived from carbohydrates, especially complex (starch) sources; refined sugars should make up no more than 10 percent of the

Table 13–1 Health Improvement Tips for Children Who Are Overweight

- Increase the amount of physical activity in which a child participates. This is often the most effective approach to weight control
- Make slight changes in a child's meals and snacks to help a child control weight. For example, offer fat-free animal crackers or fresh fruit rather than a chocolate cookie or chips.
- Serve foods in the proper portion sizes to avoid overeating.
- Encourage water consumption and reduce a child's intake of sweetened beverages.
- Avoid clean plate requirements.
- Substitute fresh fruit or low-fat, low-sugar, dairy-based desserts for high-calorie desserts. Do not exclude desserts; this only increases their importance for the child.
- Be a good role model for children and follow healthy eating and physical activity habits

daily calories. For example, a child who requires 1,600 calories should get at least 800 calories from carbohydrates; 800 calories are supplied by 200 grams of carbohydrates. Many experts recommend that adults consume a minimum of 125 grams (500 calories) of carbohydrates daily. Children require a greater percentage, but the exact minimum amount needed is unknown.

Foods that contain complex and unprocessed carbohydrates are ideal choices for children's snacks. Fresh fruits and vegetables, fruit and vegetable juices, and whole grain products such as breads, cereals, and crackers are nutritious and usually readily accepted.

Consumption of refined sugar has steadily increased since 1900, while the intake of complex carbohydrates, such as starches, has dropped during the same period. Current recommendations suggest that people include more complex carbohydrates in their diet and decrease the amounts of refined sugars. This simply means that a person should consume less sugar and more starch and fiber from the grain, vegetable, and fruit groups. Three general classes of carbohydrates are found in foods: simple sugars, compound sugars, and complex carbohydrates.

Figure 13–1 **Carbohydrates = 4 calories/gram.**

Simple Sugars

Simple sugars consist of one sugar unit that requires no further digestion prior to absorption. Examples of simple sugars are:

- glucose
- fructose
- galactose

At least half of a child's calories should come from carbohydrates

Issues To Consider **Are We Having an Obesity Epidemic?**

The media tell us almost daily that we are fat and getting fatter. Depending upon the source, the story will be that "30–50 percent of all Americans are obese," or 20 percent above their normal body weight. The message will then proceed to tell us that obesity increases our risk for several diseases.

- Why do Americans not take these warnings seriously enough to really try to achieve and maintain body weight and thus reduce risk of disease?
- How much attention is or should be given to helping children balance energy input with energy output so they will not be as likely to experience an obesity problem?
- Discuss the importance of including physical activity as routine programming in early childhood and school-based programs.

It is reported that families with young children are eating away from home and at fast-food restaurants more often.

- What are the common menu choices for children and adults in these restaurants?
- Consider the amount of high fat foods available, the lack of fruit, vegetables, and milk as menu items, and the average total calorie count of fast-food offerings.
- Could the accelerated use of fast-food offerings be contributing to the increase of obesity in children and adults? Explain.
- What healthier food options could restaurants offer on children's menus?

Glucose is the only form of sugar that body cells are able to utilize. However, most glucose that circulates in the blood results from the digestion of more complex carbohydrates (starches).

Fructose is present in honey and high-fructose corn syrup and is the sweetest of all other sugars. In some cases, smaller amounts of fructose may be used to achieve a desired degree of sweetness.

Galactose is not found freely in foods but results from the digestion of sugars present in milk.

Compound Sugars

Compound sugars consist of two simple sugars that are joined together. Consequently, compound sugars must be digested to their component simple sugars before they can be absorbed and utilized by body cells. Two important examples of compound sugars are:

- sucrose
- lactose

In its refined form, sucrose is commonly known as table sugar and is found in sugar beets, sugar cane, fruits, vegetables, and honey. When sucrose occurs in fruits and vegetables, it is accompanied by other essential nutrients such as vitamins, minerals, and water. However, refined table sugar contributes no nutrients—only calories. For this reason, calories from table sugar are frequently called "empty calories." Consuming too many empty calories can lead to obesity accompanied by a deficiency of some essential nutrients. Children who are allowed to eat too many foods containing refined sugar may not be hungry for more healthful foods that contain the essential nutrients required for normal growth and development.

Refined sucrose, or table sugar has also been linked to a number of health concerns, including tooth decay in children. Additional factors that increase the risk of tooth decay include the stickiness of the food containing sugar, the frequency and timing of eating, the frequency of tooth brushing, whether the sugar is contained in a meal with other foods or in a stand-alone snack, and whether the sugar-containing food is accompanied by a beverage.

Lactose, commonly referred to as "milk sugar," is found in milk and dairy products including many processed foods. It is the only carbohydrate found in an animal-source food. Lactose occurs in the milk of mammals, including human breast milk. It is the least sweet of all common sugars, which explains why 1 cup of 2-percent milk with the equivalent of 1 tablespoon of sugar in the form of lactose does not taste sweet. It has advantages over other sugars in that lactose aids in establishing and maintaining beneficial intestinal bacteria. Calcium is also used more efficiently by the body if lactose is present. Fortunately, calcium and lactose occur in the same food—milk.

Although lactose is usually a beneficial sugar, it can present problems for some individuals. Some people do not produce the enzyme lactase, which is needed to break lactose down to its component simple sugars so that it can be absorbed. This condition is commonly referred to as lactose intolerance, and may cause considerable intestinal discomfort, cramping, gas, and diarrhea. Some individuals can tolerate small amounts of milk (1 to 2 cups a day) and other dairy products if they are consumed in several smaller servings. Dairy products such as yogurt and buttermilk are often better tolerated than milk. Lactose intolerance is more common among certain racial and ethnic populations, including persons of Native American, Asian American, Mexican American, African American, and Jewish descent (Nicklas et al., 2009). Adults are more likely to develop this condition and to experience its troublesome symptoms.

Complex Carbohydrates

Complex carbohydrates are composed of multiple units of simple sugars joined together. Complex carbohydrates must be broken down into their component simple sugars before the body can absorb, use, and store them. The digestion of only one complex carbohydrate often results in thousands of simple sugars units. Complex carbohydrates that are important to human nutrition are:

- starch
- cellulose
- glycogen

Starches are the only digestible form of complex carbohydrates found in foods. They are available in large amounts in grains, legumes (peas, peanuts), dried beans, and root vegetables such as potatoes, sweet potatoes, and carrots. The starches in these foods are usually accompanied by a host of vitamins and minerals that the body requires and are, therefore, desirable components of a healthful diet.

Cellulose is an indigestible complex carbohydrate found in whole grains, nuts, fruits, and vegetables. Because humans are unable to digest cellulose, it cannot be absorbed and used by body cells and, therefore, does not contribute any calories. Although it cannot be absorbed, cellulose is a primary source of insoluble fiber that increases the rate of food transit through the intestinal tract. It increases the frequency of intestinal waste elimination by decreasing time for digestion, the absorption of food components, and cholesterol uptake. Rapid transit of materials through the gastrointestinal tract has also been shown to reduce absorption of substances that may increase the risk of some cancerous formations (Tan & Seow-Choen, 2007). Cellulose is also thought to provide some detergent effect to teeth, thus promoting dental health.

Another complex carbohydrate of physiological importance is glycogen. Glycogen is often referred to as animal starch and is the only form in which carbohydrate is stored in the body for future conversion into sugar and subsequent energy.

The use of artificial sweeteners to replace sugar as a means of reducing calorie intake has become a common practice. FDA-approved artificial sweeteners include saccharin, aspartame (Nutrasweet), acesulfame potassium (Sunett), sucralose (Splenda), Neotame, and stevia (National Cancer Institute, 2009). Used in moderation, these sweeteners are accepted as safe for adult consumption. However, their use in children's diets is questionable because foods that typically include them are usually poor sources of essential nutrients to begin with. Also, most children have from birth a strong preference for a sweet taste that does not need to be enhanced by "fake" sweeteners. Children who are born with a condition known as phenylketonuria (PKU), a genetic disease characterized by an inability to properly metabolize the essential amino acid phenylalanine, must not use aspartame because it contains this compound. Accumulation of this toxic substance may cause severe and irreversible brain damage.

Figure 13–2 **Fats = 9 calories/gram.**

Fats as Energy Sources

For the past several decades, fats have been the target of much negative press and, as a result, the food industry has responded with a deluge of low-fat and fat-free foods. However, fat is an essential nutrient for young children and is required for normal growth, development, and the production of body regulators. It also provides the most concentrated source of dietary energy, which is an important consideration when feeding young children whose stomach capacity is relatively small (Figure 13–2).

Each gram of fat consumed supplies approximately 9 calories. Foods in which fats are readily identified include butter, margarine, cheese, shortening, oils, and salad dressings. Less obvious sources of fats are found in meats, whole milk, egg yolks, nuts, and nut butters. Fruits and vegetables contain little fat, with the exception of the avocado, which is quite rich in healthy fats. Most bread and cereal products are naturally low in fat. However, baked products such as cakes, pies, doughnuts, and cookies are usually high in added fats. Although some dietary fat is

Reflective Thoughts

Fat intake seems to be a prime dietary concern of most Americans, and yet many U.S. children have higher blood cholesterol levels, body fat percentages, and BMIs than children in other countries (Bingham et al., 2009). How can we reduce children's intake of cholesterol, a fat-like substance found only with animal-source foods, without limiting the essential fats children require for normal growth and brain development?

The American Academy of Pediatrics (AAP) and the American Heart Association (AHA, 2010b) recommend that fat intake not be reduced before 2 years of age because infants and young children need 50 percent of their energy from fat to ensure normal growth and brain development. However, after the child has reached age 2, the AAP recommends a gradual decrease in fat to result in 30 percent of energy from fat by age 4 or 5 years. This fat reduction is particularly important for children in families with a history of early heart disease.

- Which of the Pyramid food groups would contribute the most animal fat and cholesterol?
- Which three food groups contribute little fat and no cholesterol?
- How could a green vegetable or piece of fruit become a source of fat and cholesterol?

required for good health, recommendations have been made to reduce average fat intake to about 30 percent of total daily calories. However, the American Academy of Pediatrics and the American Heart Association recommend that there should be no dietary fat restriction for children under 2 years of age unless they have a family history of obesity, heart disease, or diabetes (AHA, 2010a; Barlow & the Expert Committee, 2007). The 2010 *Dietary Guidelines for Americans* advises that total fat intake be maintained "between 30 to 35 percent of calories for children 2 to 3 years of age and between 25 to 30 percent of calories for children and adolescents 4 to 18 years of age," with most fats coming from fish, nuts, and vegetable oils. Thus, if a child requires 1,600 calories, his or her diet should include 50–55 grams of fat or approximately 480 calories from fat. This amount is equivalent to approximately 4 tablespoons of butter, margarine, or vegetable oil.

Although they provide more than twice as much energy per gram as do carbohydrates, fats are a less desirable energy source for children. They are more difficult for children to digest than carbohydrates and are accompanied by fewer essential nutrients. However, fats should not be reduced below 30 percent of a child's daily calories because they perform important functions for the child:

- allow normal growth and development of brain and nerve tissues
- contribute the essential fatty acids (**linoleic** and **linolenic**)
- are carriers of important fat-soluble vitamins
- provide a concentrated energy source to meet the child's calorie needs

The practice of lowering a very young child's fat intake through the use of fat free or skim milk is not a safe or an acceptable option. Most authorities believe this practice may lead to insufficient calorie intake and essential fatty acid (EFA) deficiency. In addition, infants and young children (under 2 years of age) who consume the same amount or more of skim milk as they previously consumed of breast milk or formula will receive a higher and possibly excessive amount of protein and minerals. These excesses require the body to excrete greater amounts of waste and minerals, which the child's kidneys may not be mature enough to handle (Whitney & Rolfes, 2010). Low fat (2 percent) milk may be given to children older than 2 years and may be advised if there is a strong family history of cardiovascular disease (CVD).

Fats must undergo digestion and absorption into the body before their energy can be released. Digestion of dietary fats produces:

- fatty acids
- glycerol

The resulting fatty acids and glycerol are in forms that the body can readily absorb and utilize.

The fatty acids in foods are either saturated or unsaturated. Those found in animal-source foods such as meat, milk, cheese, and eggs yield fatty acids that are primarily saturated (Table 13–2). Fats containing predominantly saturated fatty acids are usually solid at room temperature and are often accompanied by cholesterol. Cholesterol and saturated fats have been extensively investigated as undesirable dietary components that should be limited in a person's diet. However, after years of study, few definitive conclusions have been reached regarding dietary cholesterol's role in cardiovascular disease or the advisability of lowering children's intake of saturated fatty acids and cholesterol. However, the American Heart Association (AHA) does recommend that dietary intake of saturated and **trans-fats** be limited (AHA, 2010b). It is important to remember that cholesterol is found only in animal-source food fats. However, do not equate high fat with high cholesterol. For example, coconut derives 83 percent of its calories from fat, and 89 percent of its fatty acids are saturated, but it has no cholesterol.

---

linoleic acid – *a polyunsaturated fatty acid, which is essential (must be provided in food) for humans; also known as omega-6 fatty acid.*

linolenic acid – *one of the two polyunsaturated fatty acids that are recognized as essential for humans; also known as omega-3 fatty acid.*

trans-fats – *unsaturated fats that have been converted to a solid by a process called hydrogenation.*

Table 13–2 Comparison of Saturated Fat Values in Foods

Food Category	Portion	Saturated Fat Content (grams)	Calories
Cheese			
• Regular cheddar cheese	1 oz	6.0	114
• Low-fat cheddar cheese	1 oz	1.2	49
Ground beef			
• Regular ground beef (25% fat)	3 oz (cooked)	6.1	236
• Extra lean ground beef (5% fat)	3 oz (cooked)	2.6	148
Milk			
• Whole milk (3.25%)	1 cup	4.6	146
• Low-fat (1%) milk	1 cup	1.5	102
Breads			
• Croissant (med)	1 medium	6.6	231
• Bagel, oat bran (4")	1 medium	0.2	227
Frozen desserts			
• Regular ice cream	½ cup	4.9	145
• Frozen yogurt, low-fat	½ cup	2.0	110
Table spreads			
• Butter	1 tsp	2.4	34
• Soft margarine with zero *trans fats*	1 tsp	0.7	25
Chicken			
• Fried chicken (leg with skin)	3 oz (cooked)	3.3	212
• Roasted chicken (breast no skin)	3 oz (cooked)	0.9	140
Fish			
• Fried fish	3 oz	2.8	195
• Baked fish	3 oz	1.5	129

Unsaturated fats are usually soft at room temperature or are in oil form. Monounsaturated fatty acids (**MUFAs**), which have only one point of unsaturation, are currently being reported to be most effective in controlling the type and amount of fat and cholesterol circulating in the blood. Thus, olive oil and canola oil, both high in MUFAs, are recommended for use by persons prone to cardiovascular disease (CVD).

Fats found in plant-source foods such as corn oil or sunflower oil contain mostly unsaturated fatty acids. Many plant oils are polyunsaturated, which means the fatty acids contain numerous unfilled attachment sites. Polyunsaturated fatty acids are often called **PUFAs**. Linoleic and linolenic acids are polyunsaturated fatty acids that are essential for all humans, but are needed in greater amounts for infants and children than for adults. They play a critical role in visual and neural system development, and must be obtained from food sources because the human body is unable to produce them. Plant-based foods are ideal choices as they do not contain cholesterol. Protein links with fat to produce lipoproteins, which are involved in the transport of fat and cholesterol in the blood. A high blood level of high density lipoproteins (HDLs), which have a greater ratio of protein

MUFAs – *monounsaturated fatty acids; fatty acids that have one double hydrogen bond; nuts, avocados, and olive oil are high in this form of fat.*

PUFAs – *polyunsaturated fatty acids; fatty acids that contain more than one bond that is not fully saturated with hydrogen.*

to fat, is currently thought to reduce the risk of cardiovascular disease. Physical activity has been identified as the most effective way to increase HDL (good cholesterol) levels in blood.

Proteins as Energy Sources

Proteins are the third class of nutrients that the body can use as an energy source. Proteins supply 4 calories per gram; the same amount of energy that is derived from carbohydrates (Figure 13–3). Although they both yield the same number of calories per gram, proteins such as meats, seafood, and cheeses generally cost more to purchase than do carbohydrates. Thus, relying on protein to supply energy is like filling your car's gas tank with premium fuel when a less expensive grade would work as well.

Proteins must be digested into their component amino acids prior to absorption and utilization by the body. Each protein is unique in the number, arrangement, and specific amino acids from which it is built. Because proteins (amino acids) function as materials to build body tissues and as regulators of body functions, they will be discussed in greater detail in subsequent chapters.

Figure 13–3 **Proteins = 4 calories/gram.**

Focus On Families **Healthy Families**

Calculate and graph your child's body mass index (BMI) using the following method. (Teachers can provide families with a BMI table from the CDC website: http://www.cdc.gov.)

Example: Height - 4 ft. 0 in. Weight - 75 lbs.

1. Multiply weight (pounds) by 703: $75 \times 703 = 52{,}725$
2. Multiply height (inches) by 48 (inches): $48 \times 48 = 2{,}304$
3. Divide the answer in step 1 by the answer in step 2: $52{,}725/2{,}304 = 23$

The higher a child's BMI, the greater the risk for certain health-related diseases. Regardless of where a child's BMI appears on the graph, all families should consider adopting the following lifestyle changes.

- Sit as a family at mealtime. All distractions such as televisions, video games, and computers should be turned off. Mealtime is the time to begin healthy, non-stressful conversations with your family.
- Use the Food Guide Pyramid to guide your food choices and to incorporate a wide variety of foods into your family's diet. Choose the majority of foods from the fruits, vegetables, and grains groups. Use My Pyramid Plan to choose the right foods and serving sizes for each family member.
- Encourage healthy snacking at planned times. Empty-calorie snacking throughout the day will cause a child to eat poorly at meals.
- Shop sensibly and avoid purchasing "junk" food. If those foods are readily available, it is difficult to encourage healthy snacking.

Classroom Corner — Teacher Activities

Roll the Cube and Move... (PreK-2, National Health Education Standard 1.2.1, 7.2.1)

Concept: Food gives us energy and energy is what helps us move.

Learning Objectives

- Children will learn that eating food provides the body with energy to move.
- Children will practice different movement activities: clapping, jumping, stomping, running, touching their toes, and tossing a bean bag.

Supplies

- Cube or small box with pictures representing each of the above actions
- Bean bags (one per child)

Learning Activities

- Talk about the importance of eating healthy foods such as fruits, vegetables, whole grains, meats, dairy, and proteins to give our body energy. Explain that energy is what enables the body to move.
- Explain the movement cube. Demonstrate the actions represented by each picture on the cube (hands together—clapping; toes—touch your toes, and so on).
- Have children take turns rolling the cube and performing the appropriate action.

Evaluation

- Children will name several foods that give them energy.
- Children will perform a variety of movement activities.

Additional lesson plans for grades 3–5 are available on the premium website for this book.

Summary

- The body requires energy to perform its work, including internal involuntary activity and voluntary physical activity.
- A person's total energy requirement is a composite of (a) basal metabolic need, (b) voluntary physical activity, and (c) metabolism to release energy for both of these activities (a and b).
- The nutrient classes that yield energy are carbohydrates (4 calories/gram), proteins (4 calories/gram), and fats (9 calories/gram).
- Carbohydrates come in different forms: simple sugars (glucose and fructose), compound sugars (sucrose and lactose), and complex carbohydrates (starch). Cellulose is a carbohydrate that does not yield energy but is important as a source of fiber.
- The fatty acids of different fats may be saturated or unsaturated and all yield nine calories per gram. Two unsaturated fatty acids (linoleic and linolenic) are essential for children's growth.
- Proteins are inefficient sources of energy and are not usually burned for energy unless there are not enough carbohydrates and fats available to meet energy needs.

Terms to Know

energy *p. 337*
calories *p. 338*
enzymes *p. 338*
coenzymes *p. 338*
hormones *p. 338*
gram *p. 338*
milligram *p. 338*
basal metabolic rate (BMR) *p. 338*
thermic energy of food *p. 339*
digest (digestion) *p. 339*
absorb (absorption) *p. 339*
metabolize (metabolism) *p. 339*
linoleic acid *p. 345*
linolenic acid *p. 345*
trans-fats *p. 345*
MUFAs *p. 346*
PUFAs *p. 346*

Chapter Review

A. By Yourself:

1. Match the terms in **column II** to the correct phrase in **column I.**

Column I	Column II
1. a simple sugar	a. amino acids
2. digestible complex carbohydrate	b. cellulose
3. found in meats, dairy products, legumes, and eggs	c. protein
4. building blocks of proteins	d. carbohydrate
5. found in grains, fruits, vegetables, and milk products	e. glucose f. fats
6. richest source of energy	g. starch
7. indigestible complex carbohydrate	h. sucrose
8. table sugar (complex sugar)	i. trans-fats

2. Explain why fat intake must not be restricted for children younger than 2 years.
3. Give two examples of saturated and unsaturated fats.
4. Discuss the factors that determine how many calories an individual requires.

B. As a Group:

1. Conduct an online search of scholarly articles on childhood obesity. Why are more children overweight or obese today? In what ways can teachers begin to address this problem in their programs?
2. Discuss the cause of lactose intolerance, which groups of children are more likely to experience this condition, and what dietary modifications would need to be made.
3. Prepare a convincing argument to counter the statement, "Carbohydrates are bad for you."
4. Discuss whether all fats are unhealthy and should thus be eliminated from one's diet.
5. Go to the National Institutes of Health website (http://hp2010.nhlbihin.net/portion) and take the "Portion Distortion" quiz. Make up your own set of slides illustrating additional examples of food items with their correct portion sizes and activity equivalents.

Case Study

Terry, age 5, has several decayed teeth. His dentist has suggested a program of proper dental hygiene plus limiting his intake of refined sucrose.

Plan a day's menu for Terry that contains at least 150 grams of carbohydrates without any refined sucrose (table sugar). Use the following average amounts of carbohydrates:

bread, cereals, pastas	15 grams/slice or ounce
fruits and juices	10 grams/$\frac{1}{2}$ adult serving
starchy vegetables	10 grams/$\frac{1}{2}$ adult serving
milk	6 grams/$\frac{1}{2}$ cup

Application Activities

1. Using the cereal label in Figure 13–4 determine the following: (a) the number of calories derived from carbohydrates; (b) the approximate percentage of total calories derived from sucrose and other sugars.

Figure 13–4 Cereal label.

Nutrition Facts

Serving Size 3/4 cup (30g)
Servings Per Container about 15

Amount Per Serving	Cereal	Cereal with 1/2 cup Skim Milk
Calories	100	140
Calories from Fat	5	5
		% Daily Value**
Total Fat 0.5g*	1%	1%
Saturated Fat 0g	0%	0%
Polyunsaturated Fat 0g		
Monounsaturated Fat 0g		
Cholesterol 0mg	0%	0%
Sodium 220mg	9%	12%
Potassium 190mg	5%	11%
Total Carbohydrate 24g	8%	10%
Dietary Fiber 5g	21%	21%
Soluble Fiber 1g		
Insoluble Fiber 4g		
Sugars 6g		
Other Carbohydrate 13g		
Protein 3g		
Vitamin A	15%	20%
Vitamin C	0%	2%
Calcium	0%	15%
Iron	45%	45%
Vitamin D	10%	25%
Thiamin	25%	30%
Riboflavin	25%	35%
Niacin	25%	25%
Vitamin B_6	25%	25%
Folate	25%	25%
Vitamin B_{12}	25%	35%
Phosphorus	15%	25%
Magnesium	15%	20%
Zinc	10%	15%
Copper	10%	10%

*Amount in Cereal. One half cup skim milk contributes an additional 40 calories, 65mg sodium, 200mg potassium, 6g total carbohydrate (6g sugars), and 4g protein.

**Percent Daily Values are based on a 2,000 calorie diet. Your daily values may be higher or lower depending on your calorie needs:

	Calories:	2,000	2,500
Total Fat	Less than	65g	80g
Saturated Fat	Less than	20g	25g
Cholesterol	Less than	300mg	300mg
Sodium	Less than	2,400mg	2,400mg
Potassium		3,500mg	3,500mg
Total Carbohydrate		300g	375g
Dietary Fiber		25g	30g

2. Which of the nutrient contributions of this cereal are increased by the addition of milk?
3. Explain why cereal with milk has a higher carbohydrate value than cereal alone.
   a. Is this cereal predominantly starch or sucrose?
   b. Do starches and complex carbohydrates increase with the addition of milk?
4. Calculate the caloric requirement of a 4-year-old child who weighs 42 pounds.
5. Determine the number of calories in a serving of food that contributes the following: arbohydrate—12 grams; protein—8 grams; fat—10 grams.

Helpful Web Resources

Canadian Council of Food & Nutrition	http://www.ccfn.ca
Center for Science in Public Interest (CSPI)	http://www.cspinet.org
Health-Kids.gov	http://www.kids.gov
Women, Infants, and Children (WIC)	http://www.fns.usda.gov
WebMD	http://www.webmd.com
United States Department of Agriculture, MyPyramid.gov	http://www.mypyramid.gov

You are just a click away from additional health, safety, and nutrition resources! Go to www.CengageBrain.com to access this text's premium website, where you'll find:

- glossary flashcards, activities, tutorial quizzes, videos, web links, and more

References

American Heart Association (AHA). (2010a). *Dietary recommendations for children.* Accessed on January 5, 2010 from http://www.americanheart.org/presenter.jhtml?identifier=3033999.

American Heart Association (AHA). (2010b). Fat. Accessed on January 5, 2010 from http://www.americanheart.org/presenter.jhtml?identifier=4582.

Barlow, S., and the Expert Committee. (2007). Expert Committee recommendations regarding the prevention, assessment, and treatment of child and adolescent overweight and obesity: Summary report, *Pediatrics*, 120, S229–S253.

Bier, D. (2008). Growth in the first two years of life, *Nestle Nutrition Workshop Series*, 61, 135–144.

Bingham, M., Harrell, J., Takada, H., Washino, K., Bradley, C., Berry, D., Park, H., & Charles, M. (2009). Obesity and cholesterol in Japanese, French, and U.S. children, *Journal of Pediatric Nursing*, 24(4), 314–322.

Brown, T., & Summerbell, C. (2009). Systematic review of school-based interventions that focus on changing dietary intake and physical activity levels to prevent childhood obesity: An update to the obesity guidance produced by the National Institute for Health and Clinical Excellence, *Obesity Reviews*, 10(1), 110–141.

Donnelly, J., Greene, J., Gibson, C., Smith, B., Washburn, R., Sullivan, D., DuBose, K., Mayo, M., Schmelzle, K., Ryan, J., Jacobsen, D., & Williams, S. (2009). Physical activity across the curriculum (PAAC): A randomized controlled trial to promote physical activity and diminish overweight and obesity in elementary school children, *Preventive Medicine*, 49(4), 336–341.

Duarte, C., Sourander, A., Nikolakaros, G., Pihlajamaki, H., Helenius, H., Piha, J., Kumpulainen, K., Moilanen, I., Tamminen, T., Almqvist, F., & Must, A. (2009). Child mental health problems and obesity in early adulthood, *Journal of Pediatrics*, 156(1), 93–97.

Harris, K., Perreira, K., & Lee, D. (2009). Obesity in the transition to adulthood: Predictions across race/ethnicity, immigrant generation, and sex, *Archives of Pediatrics & Adolescent Medicine*, 163(11),1022–1028.

Janz, K., Kwon, S., Letuchy, E., Eichenberger Gilmore, J., Burns, T., Torner, J., Willing, M., & Levy, S. (2009). Sustained effect of early physical activity on body fat mass in older children, *American Journal of Preventive Medicine*, 37(1), 35–40.

Kirby, M., & Danner, E. (2009). Nutritional deficiencies in children on restricted diets, *Pediatric Clinics of North America*, 56(5), 1085–1103.

Krul, M., van der Wouden, J., Schellevis, F., van Suijlekom-Smit, L., & Koes, B. (2009). Musculoskeletal problems in overweight and obese children, *Annuals of Family Medicine*, 7(4), 352–356.

McHugh, M. (2010). Oversized young athletes: A weighty concern, *British Journal of Sports Medicine*, 44(1), 45–49.

National Cancer Institute. (2009). Artificial sweeteners and cancer. Accessed on January 4, 2010 from http://www.cancer.gov/cancertopics/factsheet/Risk/artificial-sweeteners.

Nicklas, T., Qu, H., Hughes, S., Wagner, S., Foushee, H., Russell, H., & Shewchuk, R. (2009). Prevalence of self-reported lactose intolerance in a multiethnic sample of adults, *Nutrition Today*, 44(5), 222–227.

Pollack, K. (2009). An injury prevention perspective on the childhood obesity epidemic, *Preventing Chronic Disease*, 6(3), A107–114.

Rundle, A., Goldstein, I., Mellins, R., Ashby-Thompson, M., Hoepner, L., & Jacobson, J. (2009). Physical activity and asthma symptoms among New York City Head Start children, *Journal of Asthma*, 46(8), 803–809.

Spicuzza, L., Leonardi, S., & La Rosa, M. (2009). Pediatric sleep apnea: Early onset of the 'syndrome'?, *Sleep Medicine Reviews*, 13(2), 111–122.

Tan, K., & Seow-Choen, F. (2007). Fiber and colorectal diseases: Separating fact from fiction, *World Journal of Gastroenterology*, 13(31), 4161–4167.

Whitney, E., & Rolfes, S. (2010). *Understanding nutrition.* (11th ed.). Belmont, CA: Wadsworth.

CHAPTER 14

Nutrients That Promote Growth of Body Tissues (Proteins, Minerals, and Water)

NAEYC Standards *Chapter Links:*

- **#1 a, b, and c:** Promoting child development and learning
- **#2 a and c:** Building family and community relationships
- **#3 b, c, and d:** Observing, documenting, and assessing to support young children and families
- **#4 a:** Using developmentally effective approaches to connect with children and families
- **#6 c:** Becoming a professional

Learning Objectives

After studying this chapter, you should be able to:

- Describe how growth occurs.
- Differentiate between non-essential and essential amino acids.
- Identify food sources that are complete and incomplete proteins.
- Describe the essential roles that minerals play in the growth process.
- Explain why children's need for water is greater than an adult's.
- Identify how vitamins contribute to growth.

Infancy and early childhood are periods of rapid growth. During the first 6 months of life, infants will typically double their birth weight and triple it by the end of the first year. Their birth length increases by approximately 50 percent during this same period. Together, birth weight and length are considered reliable measures of healthy growth. A lack of gain in either dimension is cause for concern. Head circumference is another indicator used to monitor a child's growth and development, especially of the brain.

Infancy is a period of rapid growth.

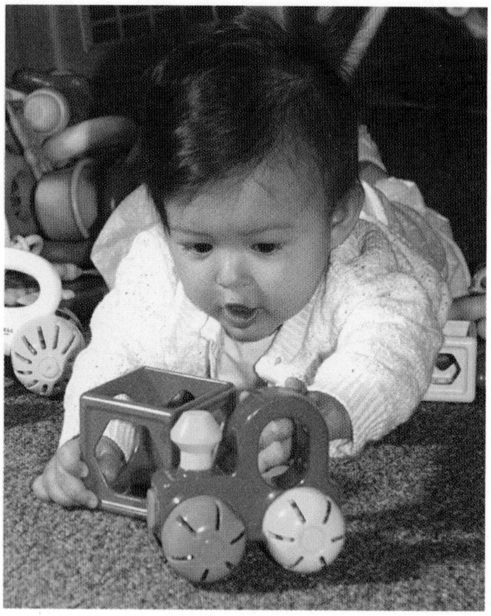

Children's Growth

Growth may be defined as an increase in physical size of either the entire body or of any body part. Growth occurs by (1) an increase in the number of cells, or by (2) an increase in the size of individual cells. At various stages of the child's life, either or both types of growth may be occurring. Although young children are continually growing, the rate is often irregular. Periods of linear growth (height) are followed by a brief plateau and then by a period of weight gain. Children's appetite and nutrient needs are greatest during the linear growth phase. Failure to meet nutrient needs for growth may result in a small-for-age child who also experiences decreased resistance to disease, poor utilization of food eaten, lack of energy, and delays in expected physical and mental development.

Proteins for Growth

Proteins play an important role in growth by supplying the material from which all body cells (tissues and fluids, such as hormones and antibodies) are built. Approximately 15 percent of body weight consists of protein, which is concentrated in muscles, glands, organs, bones, blood, and skin (Figure 14–1).

Proteins are composed of hundreds of individual units called **amino acids**. The human body is able to manufacture some of the amino acids needed to build proteins; these amino acids are termed **non-essential amino acids**. Amino acids that the body cannot manufacture in the required amounts must be supplied by proteins in foods; these amino acids are called **essential amino acids**.

When all essential amino acids occur in adequate amounts in food protein, that protein is said to be a **complete protein**. Complete proteins typically occur in animal-source foods such as meats, milk, eggs, and cheese.

Figure 14–1 How protein is distributed in the body.

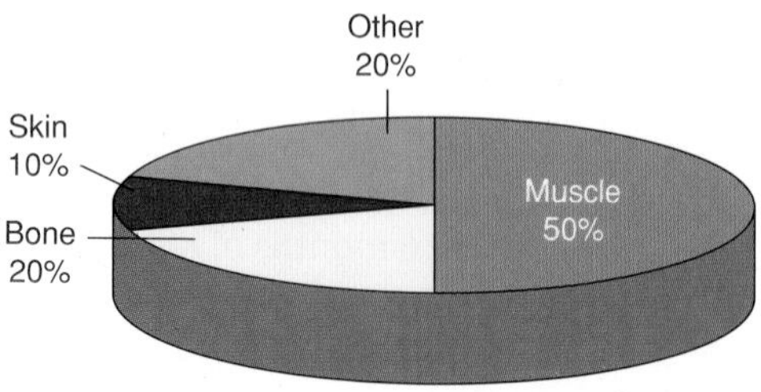

Incomplete proteins are those that lack adequate amounts of one or more essential amino acids. Proteins from plant sources such as grains, legumes (peas, peanuts), dried beans, and vegetables (such as corn) are incomplete proteins. One exception is the soybean (from which tofu is made), which supplies adequate amino acids to support growth in young children. However, soybean consumption can interfere with iron absorption when consumed in large amounts. Gelatin, an animal-source food, is also an incomplete protein.

amino acids – *the organic building blocks from which proteins are made.*
non-essential amino acids – *amino acids that are produced in the body.*
essential amino acids – *amino acids that can only be obtained from protein food sources.*
complete protein – *protein that contains all essential amino acids in amounts relative to the amounts needed to support growth.*
incomplete proteins – *proteins that lack required amounts of one or more essential amino acids.*

Complete protein intake may be achieved by combining two or more incomplete proteins that are complementary. A food that supplies an amino acid that is absent or in low quantities in another food is said to complement that food. For example, wheat, which is deficient in lysine, may be combined with peanuts, which contain adequate amounts of lysine but lack another essential amino acid provided by wheat (Insel, Turner, & Ross, 2009). The resulting combination of wheat and peanuts contains all the essential amino acids and is equivalent to a complete protein. For example, the wheat-peanut combination could be served as a peanut butter sandwich or a peanut sauce on pasta. Plant proteins are lower in fat and typically less expensive to purchase than animal-based proteins. However, incomplete proteins must be consumed in larger amounts to achieve the equivalent of a complete protein. For instance, 1 cup of beans will complement 2⅔ cups of rice to form a complete protein.

Essential amino acids resulting from the digestion of food protein must be supplied and used within a relatively short time (approximately 24 hours), as they are not stored for future use. All essential amino acids must be available several times each day to form the complete proteins needed to support rapid growth.

Young children who follow a diet that consists primarily of incomplete proteins may have difficulty consuming the larger quantities of food (incomplete proteins) necessary to meet protein requirements given their smaller stomach capacity. However, most children are able to achieve normal growth and development as long as careful attention is paid to planning a well-balanced diet (Craig & Mangels, 2009). Children who follow this type of diet often have a BMI that is closer to normal (Renda & Fischer, 2009).

Many favorite dishes are good examples of incomplete protein combinations that result in a complete protein equivalent. Foods may be combined in either of two ways to obtain adequate protein for a lower cost than most animal-based proteins:

- **complementary proteins**—incomplete protein combined with another incomplete protein to equal complete protein.
  Examples: peanut butter sandwich, beans and rice, chili, peas and rice, macaroni salad with peas, lentil soup with crackers, navy beans with cornbread, baked beans and brown bread, black bean tacos
- **supplementary proteins**—incomplete protein combined with a small amount of complete protein to equal complete protein.
  Examples: macaroni and cheese, rice pudding, egg salad sandwich, cheese pizza, cereal and milk

Protein Requirements

The total amount of protein needed daily is based on desirable body weight. Because infants are growing at an extremely rapid rate, their protein requirements are greater, relative to their size, than at any other period of life. (See Figure 12–3, Chapter 12.) Children's need for protein per pound of body weight continues to remain high during the preschool years due to continued growth. For example, an 8-month-old infant needs approximately 13.5 grams of protein daily, a 2-year-old requires 13 grams, and a 4-year-old needs 19 grams. Although school-age children are growing at a slower rate, they continue to require approximately 35–40 grams of high quality protein. To be

---

complementary proteins – *proteins with offsetting missing amino acids; complementary proteins can be combined to provide complete protein.*

supplementary proteins – *a complete protein mix resulting from combining a small amount of a complete protein with an incomplete protein to provide all essential amino acids.*

meaningful, these figures can be considered in terms of food amounts. The following food selections illustrate how easy it is for children to obtain adequate protein.

Food	Protein
2 cups of milk	16 grams
1 slice whole wheat bread	2.7 grams
1 ounce meat	7 grams
1 slice provolone cheese	7 grams
1 egg	5.5 grams
3 wheat crackers	0.5 grams
2 ounces cooked pasta	7 grams
	TOTAL = 45.7 grams

Table 14–1 illustrates a one day menu that would more than adequately meet the daily recommended protein requirement for a 4- to 6-year-old child.

Table 14–1 Menu Supplying Recommended Daily Allowances of Protein for 4- to 6-Year-Olds

Breakfast	**Grams of Protein**
1/2 c. fruit juice or 1/2 medium banana	trace
1/2 c. dry oat cereal	1
1/2 c. milk*	4
Midmorning Snack	
1/2 c milk*	4
1/2 slice buttered toast	1
Lunch	
1/2 fish taco (1/2 tortilla, 1½ ounces tilapia)*	15
4 cherry tomatoes	0.5
1/2 medium apple	trace
1/2 c. milk*	4
Mid-afternoon Snack	
1/2 c. fruit juice	trace
2 rye crackers	1
Dinner	
1 chicken leg (1 oz.)*	6
1/4 c. rice	1
1/4 c. broccoli	trace
1/4 c. strawberries	trace
1/2 c. milk*	4
	TOTAL: 41.5 grams of protein

*Complete protein.

Minerals for Growth

Minerals are inorganic elements that help to regulate body functions and build body tissue. The following discussion focuses on minerals that help to build body tissue. The regulatory functions performed by minerals will be addressed in Chapter 15. (See Table 15–4, for detailed information about important minerals.)

Minerals provide no energy and are required in far smaller amounts than are energy-producing nutrients. For example, the RDA for protein is 19 grams for a 4-year-old child; this amount is slightly more than 2½ servings of meat. In contrast, the RDA for calcium for that same child is 0.8 gram. Other minerals are required in even smaller amounts.

Specific minerals are involved in the process of building new body tissues. Two types of body tissues most dependent on minerals for growth are bones and teeth, and blood.

Building Bones and Teeth

Calcium and phosphorus are the major minerals found in bones and teeth. Bones are formed by the deposition of phosphorus and calcium crystals on **collagen**, a flexible protein base composed of amino acids. Young children's bones are relatively soft and pliable because they have not yet calcified. As growth occurs, the amount of calcium and phosphorus deposited in their bones increases, resulting in larger, denser, and stronger bones. Although bones appear to be solid and unchanging, calcium and phosphorus move in and out and are continually being replaced. The calcium content of adult bone, for example, is thought to be replaced every 5 years. Children need calcium not only for bone growth, but also for replacement of existing bone; adults require calcium only for replacement. Other minerals are also needed for normal bone and tooth formation, but they are rarely limiting factors in the development of these tissues.

Sources of Calcium Milk and milk products are the major food source of calcium. With the exception of vegetables such as broccoli, collard greens, kale, and Chinese cabbage, or the soy products tofu, miso, and tempeh, there are no rich sources of dietary calcium other than milk and dairy products. A 1-cup serving of the vegetables and soy products listed above will provide only about half the amount of calcium available in 1 cup of milk. Milk, cheese, and yogurt are excellent sources of calcium. Custards, pudding, and ice cream provide calcium, but they also contain varying amounts of added sugar and fat, which reduce their nutrient density relative to calcium.

Nonfat dry milk solids or cheese can be added to many dishes, such as casseroles, cooked cereals, breads, salads, and ground meats to increase their calcium content and improve the quality of incomplete proteins present in the grains (e.g., pastas, cereals, flours). All

Calcium and phosphorus are essential for healthy teeth and bones.

minerals – *inorganic chemical elements that are required in the diet to support growth, repair tissue, and regulate body functions.*
collagen – *a protein that forms the major constituent of connective tissue, cartilage, bone, and skin.*

Reflective Thoughts

A daily regimen of physical activity is important for children and adults. Improvements in muscle tone, cardiovascular health, and mental functioning can often be achieved in a short period of time. It is also important that some of the activities be weight-bearing in nature. What health benefits do weight-bearing activities offer? What are some examples of weight-bearing activities? How often must a person engage in this type of activity to have positive outcomes?

flours and some brands of orange juice are currently fortified with additional calcium. This is an ideal combination; the vitamin C in the orange juice improves calcium absorption. Many additional food products, such as breads, pastas, cereals, crackers, and soy milks, are also being enriched with calcium.

Sources of Phosphorus The highest concentrations of phosphorus are found in milk and milk-containing food sources, high-protein items such as meat, fish and eggs, and whole grain products. Phosphorus is easier to obtain than calcium because it is available in a wider variety of foods. Calcium and phosphorus occur in approximately equal amounts in milk, which improves the body's ability to absorb both minerals. However, this calcium-phosphorus balance may be upset if a child is permitted to drink large amounts of carbonated beverages that contain phosphorus. If the child drinks more carbonated beverages than milk, dietary phosphorus will outweigh calcium, and calcium absorption may be impaired (Olson et al, 2009; Wang, Bleich, & Gortmaker, 2008). This could result in reduced deposition of calcium in the bones and, in extreme cases, withdrawal of calcium from the bones. When carbonated beverages are substituted for milk in a child's diet, calcium consumption is further reduced (Wilson, Adolph, & Butte, 2009).

The Role of Fluoride Fluoride also plays an important role in bone and tooth formation. Many communities currently add fluoride to the municipal water supply in an effort to reduce tooth decay in children. Fluoride-containing toothpastes are also recommended for use by children and adults. Fluoride is incorporated into the growing tooth structure to increase the enamel's strength and resistance to decay. Fluoride applied to the exterior surface of the tooth is less effective in hardening tooth enamel, but it is thought to reduce the incidence of dental caries (decay) (Zero et al., 2009). However, excessive fluoride intake can cause mottling and brown discoloration of the teeth. Children who drink fluoridated water should be taught not to swallow toothpaste after brushing to prevent excess fluoride consumption.

The most consistent source of fluoride is the local water supply, either as naturally occurring fluorine or as fluoride added to a level of 1 p.p.m. (one part fluoride per million parts of water). Food sources of fluoride are variable and depend on the fluorine content of the soil in which they were grown.

Building Blood

Iron is a mineral that is essential to the formation of hemoglobin and healthy blood. **Hemoglobin,** the iron-containing protein in red blood cells, carries oxygen to the cells and removes waste

---

hemoglobin – *the iron-containing, oxygen-carrying pigment in red blood cells.*

Issues To Consider: Nutrient-Fortified Foods

Concerns about children's declining dietary calcium intake have prompted manufacturers to increase the number of calcium-enriched food products they offer and have also made us susceptible to their advertisements. For example, one bakery claims that its bread is better than another brand's because two slices of its product have the same amount of calcium as one glass of milk. Several commercial fruit juices are now fortified with enough calcium to make them nearly equivalent to 8 ounces of milk. However, questions are being raised about the potential for excessive calcium intake, especially among populations who already consume adequate amounts.

- Does fortification suggest that such products can be substituted for milk?
- Do these fortified foods give us the protein and vitamins A and D that milk provides?

The upper, adult tolerable level for calcium intake is 2,500 mg per day. An amount above this limit may increase the risk for kidney stone formation. Children's smaller bodies may reduce their tolerance level.

- Is there a need to regulate the types and amounts of nutrients used to fortify foods?
- What foods would be the safest to fortify with the least danger of exceeding tolerance levels?

(carbon dioxide) from the cells. Normal growth depends on a healthy blood supply to nourish an increasing number of cells.

Iron-deficiency anemia is caused by inadequate intake of dietary iron and is more common in children 1 to 3 years of age (Suskind, 2009). It is characterized by low levels of hemoglobin in red blood cells, which reduces the cells' ability to carry oxygen to tissues. The result is decreased growth rate, fatigue, lack of energy, reduction in learning ability, and reduced resistance to infections (Park et al., 2009; Peirano et al., 2009).

Sources of Iron The Meat and Beans group and the iron-fortified Grain group yield the best iron sources. Although liver is especially rich in iron, it is also exceptionally high in cholesterol (and not a food that is well-accepted by most adults or children). Milk, which is usually a major part of children's diets, contains very little iron. Consequently, a child who drinks large amounts of milk to the exclusion of iron-containing foods may not receive enough iron to support a growing blood supply.

Studies of children's nutritional status have repeatedly found their intakes of calcium and iron to be inadequate (Cogswell et al., 2009; Keller et al., 2009). One reason for this deficiency may be that neither calcium nor iron is widely distributed in foods. Also, many factors affect the absorption of calcium and iron. Therefore, the presence of either mineral in foods does not always ensure that they will be absorbed for use by body cells. Additionally, many foods containing calcium or iron, especially meats, may be more costly to purchase (Eicher-Miller et al., 2009).

Factors that *increase* the absorption of calcium and iron (Table 14–2):

- Vitamin C aids in keeping calcium and iron more soluble and, therefore, more readily absorbed by the body.
- Vitamin C maximizes the absorption of iron in foods when it is consumed in the same meal.
- Calcium and iron absorption increases at times when the body requires more calcium, such as when intake is inadequate or during periods of rapid growth.

---

iron-deficiency anemia – *a failure in the oxygen transport system caused by too little iron.*

Table 14–2 Factors That Affect Calcium and Iron Absorption

Calcium	Factor	Iron
↑	Adequate vitamin C	↑
↑	Increased need	↑
↓	Large dose	↓
↓	Fiber (bulk) in diet	↓
↓	High protein level	↑
↓	Physical activity	

Factors that *decrease* the absorption of calcium and iron:

- Large single doses of calcium and iron are not as well-absorbed as several smaller doses.
- Large amounts of fiber in the diet speed intestinal movement, decreasing the time calcium and iron are in contact with absorption surfaces.

Proteins also enhance the overall absorption of iron. Heme iron (the form of iron in meats) is especially high in red meats such as beef, and is absorbed more readily than the iron in grains and other nonmeat foods. However, young children often refuse this type of meat because it is more difficult to chew and swallow.

Although the child has a significant need for the minerals calcium, phosphorus, and iron, smaller amounts of "trace" minerals are also required for growth. Zinc and selenium are two such minerals that continue to attract media attention. Because these minerals are required in quite small amounts, their need can usually be met with the average diet—one that includes variety and adequate calories.

The Role of Water

Water is an important constituent of all body tissues and is essential for survival; humans can live much longer without food than they can without water. Water accounts for approximately 70–75

Reflective Thoughts

Single nutrients are often discussed as if functioning independently. Actually a single nutrient can rarely complete any function alone. A look at the critical needs of an actively growing child shows many nutrient dependencies. A protein deficiency is often looked upon as the only cause of retarded growth in children in some poor, underdeveloped countries. If that is true, how can their protein deficiency and growth retardation be so easily corrected by feeding the children generous amounts of flour and sugar? When a child is provided with sufficient energy, the small amounts of protein in their diet can be used for growth.

- How does vitamin C help maximize the availability of calcium from food sources?
- Why is growth depressed when a diet has adequate protein but lacks folic acid (or vitamin B12)?
- Lack of a single vitamin can keep carbohydrates from yielding energy. Explain how this can happen.
- How is calcium dependent upon vitamin D?
- Make a list of other known nutrient interdependencies.

percent of an infant's body weight and approximately 60 percent of normal adult body weight. This percentage gradually decreases throughout the life cycle. Several factors determine the body's need for water, including total body surface area, environmental temperature, and activity. Water is supplied to the body through drinking water and other beverages, digestion of solid foods, and water that results from energy metabolism.

Children absorbed in active play may need frequent reminders to drink water.

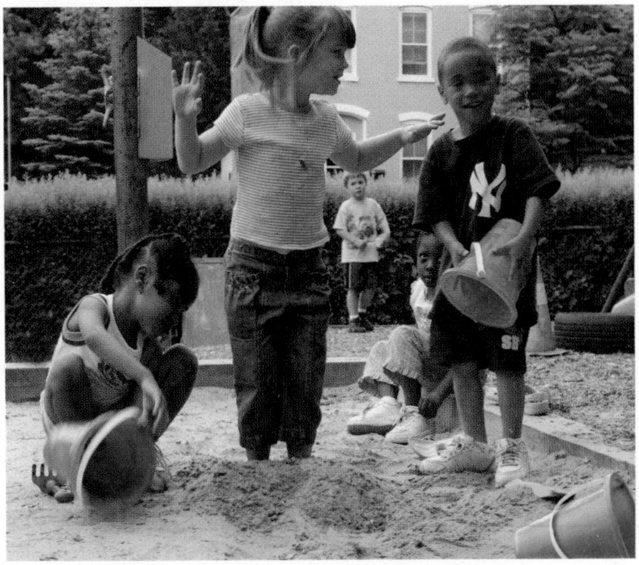

Vomiting and diarrhea cause an excess loss of water that can rapidly cause dehydration. This is an especially serious condition in infants, toddlers, and young children because the amount of water loss necessary to produce dehydration is small in comparison to that of an adult.

Children also experience more rapid water loss through evaporation and dehydration than do adults. Consequently, when children are busily involved in activities, they may need periodic reminders to drink fluids. This is important at any time but especially during periods of vigorous physical activity and when the weather is hot or humid. Children and adults should be encouraged to drink water rather than sugared beverages, since the presence of sugar can slow water absorption. Many children request fruit juice instead of water to drink but this practice should also be discouraged. Although 100 percent fruit juices contribute important nutrients to a healthy diet, excess intake can lead to a number of health problems in children, including:

- Stunted growth. Toddlers who fill up on fruit juice may not get the fuel they need to grow (Nicklas, O'Neil, & Kleinman, 2008). They have less room for milk and other foods that are richer in calories and other essential nutrients, including protein and fat, which should not be restricted in very young children.
- Diarrhea. Too much fluid in itself can cause loose stools. Some juices, notably apple juice, also contain sorbitol, a natural sugar that can be difficult to digest in large quantities, compounding that effect. Some children who drink large quantities of juice may experience occasional loose stools while others may develop diarrhea.
- Tooth decay. Toddlers sometimes use a bottle more for comfort than nourishment or refreshment. Overreliance on a bottle, especially as a way to fall asleep, can lead to baby bottle tooth decay (BBDT)—a form of dental decay resulting from prolonged exposure to sugars in juice or in milk (Nunn et al., 2009; Schroth, Harrison, & Moffat, 2009; Lim et al., 2008).
- Excess weight gain. Children who consume large quantities of fruit juices are also at risk for becoming overweight. Natural sugars in fruit juices can contribute to excess energy intake and resulting weight gain (Fiorito et al., 2009; Nicklas, O'Neil, & Kleinman, 2008).

The Supporting Role of Vitamins

Vitamins are not structural parts of growing tissue. However, some play critical roles in the way that minerals and proteins are used as building material for the body. For example, bones could not be properly formed or maintained without vitamins A, D, and C, and blood components could not be produced without vitamins C, B_6, B_{12}, and folic acid. (See Chapter 15, Table 15–1.) Vitamins, although not structural parts of any of the growth products, are essential for cell division that results in new cell formation and increased cell mass. Because infants and young children are undergoing rapid periods of growth, they require some vitamins in greater amounts relative to their body weight and size than do adults.

Focus On Families — Nutrients That Promote Growth

Calcium is a major mineral found in bones and teeth and is needed in the diet to support normal bone formation. Children ages 1 through 8 require 500 to 800 mg of calcium daily to meet nutritional needs. The calcium requirement for school-age children (9–12 years) increases to approximately 1,300 mg daily. Teachers can support calcium intake by regularly including calcium-rich foods into meal patterns and by encouraging families to provide these foods in the child's diet. Some excellent sources of calcium are:

Milk Group	***Serving Size***	***Calcium (mg)***
yogurt	1 cup	452
cheese (cheddar, Swiss)	1 1/2 oz.	300–400
milk	8 oz.	300
calcium-fortified orange juice	8 oz.	300
lasagna	1 cup	286
calcium-fortified cereal	1 cup	250
cheese pizza	1 slice	220
string cheese	1 ounce (1 slice)	214
cheeseburger	1	182
macaroni and cheese	1/2 cup	180

Classroom Corner — Teacher Activities

Calcium Helps to Make Strong Bones and Teeth...

(Grades 3–5; National Health Standards 6.5.1; 7.5.1)

Concept: Some foods supply calcium and calcium is important for strong bones and teeth.

Learning Objectives

- Children will learn how calcium helps to make strong bones and teeth.
- Children will learn about foods that are good sources of calcium.
- Children will monitor their calcium intake and take steps to achieve the Referenced Daily Intake (RDI) for calcium.

(continued)

Classroom Corner **Teacher Activities** *(continued)*

Supplies

- Two chicken drumstick bones (cooked; with meat removed)
- Two glass jars with lids
- Vinegar
- Internet connection and PowerPoint software
- A five-day chart/worksheet for each child

Learning Activities

- Have children place one chicken bone in each glass jar. Fill one jar with vinegar, the other with water and screw on the lids. Each day, have children observe the bones and note any changes (calcium crystals will gradually form on the bone immersed in vinegar). At the end of three weeks, remove both bones from their respective containers and let them air dry for at least 10–12 days. Have children break the bones and describe how they differ (in terms of strength and appearance). Discuss how calcium aids in building strong bones.
- Have children work in teams to conduct an Internet search for foods that are good sources of calcium. Each team should prepare a PowerPoint presentation highlighting their findings to share with the class.
- Provide each child with a five-day chart. Have them record the primary calcium sources they have consumed each day, total the number of daily servings, and compare this figure to MyPyramid recommendations. Older children can calculate the amount of daily calcium they have consumed (provide a worksheet with approximate values for serving equivalents: for example, 1 cup milk = 300 mg, 1 piece string cheese = 214 mg; ½ cup macaroni and cheese = 180 mg, and so on). Ask children to identify foods they can eat each day to continue meeting or to increase their calcium consumption; have them chart their progress toward achieving the recommended goals.

Evaluation

- Children will explain how calcium helps to make bones strong.
- Children will identify foods that provide calcium.
- Children will implement steps to achieve the Referenced Daily Intake (RDI) for calcium.

Additional lesson plans for grades PreK–2 are available on the premium website for this book.

Summary

- Growth involves an increase in size of the entire body or any part of the body.
- Proteins are components of all living cells; the amino acids they provide are essential for the synthesis of specific cellular proteins.
  - Meat, fish, poultry, and dairy products are complete proteins; grains, legumes and dry beans are incomplete proteins.
- Minerals are necessary for the regulation of body functions, building tissue, and blood formation.
  - Calcium and phosphorus are major components of bones and teeth; they cause structures to harden as crystals are deposited on a protein base.

- Calcium is found primarily in dairy products; phosphorus is found in milk and in meats, grains, beans, nuts, and cereal products.
- Iron is a critical component of hemoglobin, a protein found in red blood cells, that carries oxygen to all body cells. Best food sources are red meats and iron-fortified breads and cereals.

- Water is a major constituent of all living body cells; it makes up approximately 60 to 75 percent of total body weight. Water need is necessary for survival of body cells, especially during periods of active growth and physical activity.
- Vitamins play an essential role in cell division and an increase in cell mass (size).

Terms to Know

amino acids *p. 354*
nonessential amino acids *p. 354*
essential amino acids *p. 354*
complete protein *p. 354*
incomplete proteins *p. 354*
complementary proteins *p. 355*
supplementary proteins *p. 355*
minerals *p. 357*
collagen *p. 357*
hemoglobin *p. 358*
iron-deficiency anemia *p. 359*

Chapter Review

A. By Yourself:

1. Match the terms in **column II** with the definition in **column I.** Use each term in **column II** only once.

Column I	Column II
1. an essential amino acid	a. calcium
2. nutrient class that functions to build tissues and provide energy	b. Milk group
3. mineral component of hemoglobin	c. iron
4. major mineral component of bones and teeth	d. Meat and Beans group
5. food group that supplies the greatest amounts of calcium	e. lysine
6. food group that is rich in iron	f. minerals
7. nutrient class that helps to regulate body processes and build body tissue	g. protein
8. comprises approximately 60 percent of normal adult body weight	h. water
	i. collagen

2. Identify three food sources that are incomplete proteins.
3. Explain how supplementary proteins can be used to provide a complete protein.
4. List at least three non-dairy sources of complete protein.
5. Locate information about vegetarian diets on the Internet. Can all of a child's protein, iron, and calcium needs be met if he or she follows this type of dietary pattern? Explain.

B. As a Group:

1. Explain why an infant's and toddler's protein need is greater than that of an adult's.
2. Discuss why children are at-risk for developing iron deficiency anemia.
3. What problem(s) can occur from an excess intake of fluoride?
4. How could you provide calcium to a child who is allergic to milk and dairy products?

Case Study

The following chart shows a fairly typical daily intake for Timothy, age 4½. Consider this pattern in terms of the calcium-phosphorus balance.

Breakfast:

1 slice of toast

1 scrambled egg

1/2 cup orange juice

Midmorning Snack:

2 graham crackers (milk offered but refused)

Lunch:

2 fish sticks

1/4 cup peas

1/2 slice bread

water (milk offered but refused)

Midafternoon Snack:

1 small soft drink

Dinner:

hamburger

French fries

1 small soft drink

1. Which foods provide calcium?
2. Which foods supply phosphorus?
3. Change the above menu to eliminate the phosphorus/calcium imbalance.
4. What other foods would improve Timothy's calcium intake if he refuses to drink milk?

Application Activities

1. Compare the nutrition information labels from several prepared cereals. Common iron content levels are 98 percent daily value, 45 percent daily value, and 25 percent daily value. After reviewing the information in Table 14–2, discuss which cereal(s) would be the wisest choice in terms of iron absorption. What other step(s) could be taken to increase the absorption of iron available in the cereal?
2. Explain why early childhood is a time of risk for iron-deficiency anemia. Consider factors such as food groups in which iron occurs, typical food preferences, and relative ease of eating various foods. Develop a list of snacks that would provide children with additional iron.
3. Determine the recommended amount of protein for a child who weighs 42 pounds.

Helpful Web Resources

American Academy of Pediatrics	http://www.aap.org
American Dietetic Association	http://www.eatright.org
Dietitians of Canada	http://www.dietitians.ca
My Food-a-Pedia	http://www.myfoodapedia.gov
Nutrition Explorations	http://www.nutritionexplorations.org
U.S. Department of Agriculture, My Pyramid	http://www.mypyramid.gov
Vegetarian Resource Group	http://www.vrg.org

You are just a click away from additional health, safety, and nutrition resources! Go to www.CengageBrain.com to access this text's Education CourseMate website, where you'll find:

- glossary flashcards, activities, tutorial quizzes, videos, web links, and more

References

Cogswell, M., Looker, A., Pfeiffer, C., Cook, J., Lacher, D., Beard, J., Lynch, S., & Grummer-Strawn, L. (2009). Assessment of iron deficiency in US preschool children and nonpregnant females of childbearing age: National Health and Nutrition Examination Survey 2003–2006, *American Journal of Clinical Nutrition*, 89(5), 1334–1342.

Craig, W., & Mangels, A. (2009). Position of the American Dietetic Association: Vegetarian diets, *Journal of the American Dietetics Association*, 109(7), 1266–1282.

Eicher-Miller, H., Mason, A., Weaver, C., McCabe, G., & Boushey, C. (2009). Food insecurity is associated with iron deficiency anemia in US adolescents, *American Journal of Clinical Nutrition*, 90(5), 1358–1371.

Fiorito, L., Marini, M., Francis, L., Smiciklas-Wright, H., & Birch, L. (2009). Beverage intake of girls at age 5 years predicts adiposity and weight status in childhood and adolescence, *American Journal of Clinical Nutrition*, 90(4), 935–942.

Insel, P., Turner, R., & Ross, D. (2009). *Discovering Nutrition*. Sudbury, MA: Jones & Bartlett.

Keller, K., Kirzner, J., Pietrobelli, A., St-Onge, M., & Faith, M. (2009). Increased sweetened beverage intake is associated with reduced milk and calcium intake in 3- to 7-year-old children at multi-item laboratory lunches, *Journal of the American Dietetic Association*, 109(3), 497–501.

Lim, S., Sohn, W., Burt, B., Sandretto, A., Kolker, J., Marshall, T., & Ismail, A. (2008). Cariogenicity of soft drinks, milk and fruit juice in low-income African-American children: A longitudinal study, *Journal of the American Dental Association*, 139(7), 959–995.

Nicklas, T., O'Neil, C., & Kleinman, R. (2008). Association between 100% juice consumption and nutrient intake and weight of children 2 to 11 years, *Archives of Pediatric & Adolescent Medicine*, 162(6), 557–565.

Nunn, M., Braunstein, N., Kaye, E., Dietrich, T., Garcia, R., & Henshaw, M. (2009). Health eating index is a predictor of early childhood caries, *Journal of Dental Research*, 88(4), 361–366.

Olson, B., Chung, K., Reckase, M., & Schoemer, S. (2009). Parental influences on dairy intake in children, and their role in child calcium-fortified food use, *Journal of Nutrition Education and Behavior*, 41(1), 53–57.

Park, K., Kersey, M., Geppert, J., Story, M., Cutts, D., & Himes, J. (2009). Household food insecurity is a risk factor for iron-deficiency anaemia in a multi-ethnic, low-income sample of infants and toddlers, *Public Health Nutrition*, 12(11), 2120–2128.

Peirano, P., Algarin, C., Chamorrow, R., Reyes, S., Garrido, M., Duran, S., & Lozoff, B. (2009). Sleep and neurofunctions throughout child development: Lasting effects of early iron deficiency, *Journal of Pediatric Gastroenterology & Nutrition*, 48(S1), S8–S15.

Renda, M., & Fischer, P. (2009). Vegetarian diets in children and adolescents, *Pediatrics in Review*, 30(1), e1–e8.

Schroth, R., Harrison, R., & Moffatt, M. (2009). Oral health of indigenous children and the influence of early childhood caries on childhood health and well-being, *Pediatric Clinics of North America*, 56(6), 1481–1499.

Suskind, D. (2009). Nutritional deficiencies during normal growth, *Pediatric Clinics of North America*, 56(5), 1035–1053.

Wang, Y., Bleich, S., & Gortmaker, S. (2008). Increasing caloric contribution from sugar-sweetened beverages and 100% fruit juices among US children and adolescents, 1988–2004, *Pediatrics*, 121(6), e1604–e1614.

Wilson, T., Adolph, A., & Butte, N. (2009). Nutrient adequacy and diet quality in non-overweight and overweight Hispanic children of low socioeconomic status: The Viva la Familia Study, *Journal of the American Dietetic Association*, 109(6), 1012–1021.

Zero, D., Fontana, M., Martínez-Mier, A., Ferreira-Zandoná, A., Masatoshi, A., González-Cabezas, C., & Bayne, S. (2009). The biology, prevention, diagnosis and treatment of dental caries, *Journal of the American Dental Association*, 140(S1), 25S–34S.

CHAPTER

15

Nutrients That Regulate Body Functions (Vitamins, Minerals, Protein, and Water)

NAEYC Standards *Chapter Links*

- **#1 a, b, and c:** Promoting child development and learning
- **#2 a and c:** Building family and community relationships
- **#3 b, c, and d:** Observing, documenting, and assessing to support young children and families
- **#4 a:** Using developmentally effective approaches to connect with children and families
- **#6 c:** Becoming a professional

Learning Objectives

After studying this chapter, you should be able to:

- Name the primary functions that vitamins serve in the body.
- Discuss the major roles that minerals play in maintaining normal body functions.
- Describe how protein affects energy metabolism and growth regulation.
- Explain water's role as a regulator.

All body functions are subject to regulation by nutrients. For example, energy cannot be produced or released from carbohydrates, proteins, and fats without specific nutrients catalyzing the sequential steps. New tissues such as bone, blood, or muscles cannot be formed unless specific vitamins, minerals, and proteins are available to perform their primary functions in each of these processes. Nerve impulses will not travel from one nerve cell to another, nor will muscles contract, unless the required nutrients are available in adequate amounts at the appropriate times. The regulation of some body functions involves more than one or two nutrients and reactions. Other functions involve intricate sequences of reactions that require many nutrients.

The regulation of body functions is an extremely complex process. While much has been learned about nutrients' regulatory role, there is still much that is unknown. It is important to remember that nutrients and functions are intricately interrelated. No single nutrient can function alone; thus, regulation of body functions often depends on the availability of many nutrients. This unit briefly discusses four nutrient classes involved in regulating body functions:

- vitamins
- minerals
- proteins
- water

Protein has been discussed earlier in terms of both energy and growth. Minerals and water were introduced as tissue-building nutrients and will now be considered as regulatory nutrients. Vitamins are able to perform only regulatory functions. They do not yield energy directly, nor do they become part of body structure. However, no energy can be released or any tissue built without benefit of the specific regulatory activities performed by vitamins.

Vitamins and minerals are needed in extremely small amounts. In Chapter 12 (Table 12–2), you will find that their RDAs are measured in **milligrams (mg)**, which are one-thousandth of a gram, and in **micrograms (mcg or μg)**, which are one-millionth of a gram. One standard size metal paper clip weighs approximately 1 gram. Imagine that you smash that paper clip into 1,000 pieces or 1,000,000 pieces and try to envision one milligram or one microgram. Would you expect to see a particle that was one microgram in size?

The regulatory functions discussed in this chapter are crucial to children's normal growth and development (Table 15–1 and Table 15–4). Generally these functions are:

- energy metabolism
- cellular reproduction and growth
- bone growth
- **neuromuscular** development and function
- blood composition control

Although a number of additional functions are involved in the growth process, only those listed above will be discussed because of their critical relationship to children's health and learning potential.

Vitamins as Regulators

Vitamins are needed in extremely small amounts, but they are absolutely essential for normal body function (Ramakrishnan, Nguyen, & Martorell, 2009). Although each vitamin plays a specific role in a variety of body activities, they frequently depend upon one another to perform their functions (Table 15–1). For example, the vitamins thiamin and niacin are both needed as crucial coenzymes for the release of energy, but thiamin cannot function in the place of niacin, nor can niacin function in the absence of thiamin's action in a prior step. Study Table 15–1 and note that most vitamins are involved in several different functions; vitamin E may be one exception. It has only one main purpose, but this function is performed in almost every cell in the body.

Vitamins are also required and used in specific amounts. Large excesses do not serve any useful function and in some instances are known to be harmful. For example, toxic effects have long been identified for excesses of vitamin A and vitamin D (Stoffman & Gordon, 2009). Researchers have also identified neurological damage resulting from the ingestion of large vitamin B_6 doses

---

milligram (mg) – *a metric unit of measurement; one milligram equals one-thousandth of a gram.*
microgram (mcg or μg) – *a metric unit of measurement; one microgram equals one-millionth of a gram.*
neuromuscular – *pertaining to control of muscular function by the nervous system.*

Table 15–1 Vitamin Summary

Vitamin	Functions	Sources	Deficiency Symptoms	Toxicity Symptoms
Fat-Soluble Vitamins Vitamin A	Maintenance of: • remodeling of bones • all cell membranes • epithelial cells; skin • mucous membranes, glands Regulation of vision in dim light	Liver, whole milk, butter, fortified margarine, orange and dark green vegetables, orange fruits (apricots, nectarines, peaches)	Depressed bone and tooth formation, lack of visual acuity, dry epithelial tissue, increased frequency of infections related to epithelial cell vulnerability	Headaches, nausea, vomiting, fragile bones, loss of hair, dry skin Infant: hydrocephalus, hyperirritability
Vitamin D	Regulates calcium/phosphorus absorption mineralization of bone	Vitamin D fortified milk, exposure of skin to sunlight	Rickets (soft, easily bent bones), bone deformities	Elevated blood calcium; deposition of calcium in soft tissues resulting in cerebral, renal, and cardiovascular damage
Vitamin E	Antioxidant	Vegetable oils, wheat germ, egg yolk, leafy vegetables, legumes, margarine	Red blood cell destruction; creatinuria	Fatigue, skin rash, abdominal discomfort
Vitamin K	Normal blood coagulation	Leafy vegetables, vegetable oils, liver, pork; synthesis by intestinal bacteria	Hemorrhage	None reported for naturally occurring vitamin K
Water-Soluble Vitamins Vitamin C (ascorbic acid)	Formation of collagen for: • bones/teeth • intercellular cement • wound healing Aid to calcium/iron absorption Conversion of folacin to active form Neurotransmitter synthesis	Citrus fruits, strawberries, melons, cabbage, peppers, greens, tomatoes	Poor wound healing, bleeding gums, pin-point hemorrhages, sore joints, scurvy	Nausea, abdominal cramps, diarrhea, precipitation of kidney stones in susceptible person; "conditioned scurvy")
Thiamin	Carbohydrate metabolism Energy metabolism Neurotransmitter synthesis	Whole or enriched grain products, organ meats, pork	Loss of appetite, depression, poor neuromuscular control, beriberi	None reported

Riboflavin	Metabolism of carbohydrates, fats, and proteins; energy metabolism	Dairy foods, meat products, enriched or whole grains, green vegetables	Sore tongue, cracks at the corners of the mouth (cheilosis)	None reported
Niacin	Carbohydrate, protein, and fat metabolism; energy metabolism; conversion of folacin to its active form	Meat products, whole or enriched grain products, legumes	Dermatitis, diarrhea, depression, and paranoia	Flushing, itching, nausea, vomiting, diarrhea, low blood pressure, rapid heartbeat, low blood sugar, liver damage
Pantothenic acid	Energy metabolism; fatty acid metabolism; neurotransmitter synthesis	Nearly all foods	Uncommon in humans	None reported
Vitamin B_6 (pyridoxine)	Protein and fatty acid synthesis; neurotransmitter synthesis; hemoglobin synthesis	Meats, organ meats, whole grains, legumes, bananas	Can cause nervous system irritability, tremors, insomnia, convulsions (in infants)	Unstable gait, numbness, lack of coordination
Folacin	Synthesis of DNA and RNA: cell replication-protein synthesis	Liver, other meats, green vegetables	**Macrocytic anemia** characterized by unusually large red blood cells; sore tongue, diarrhea	None reported (large intake may hide B12 deficiency)
Vitamin B_{12} (cobalamin)	Synthesis of DNA and RNA: conversion of folacin to active form; synthesis of myelin (fatty covering of nerve cells); metabolism of carbohydrates for energy	Animal foods, liver, other meats, dairy products, eggs	Macrocytic anemia, nervous system damage, sore mouth and tongue, loss of appetite, nausea, vomiting (pernicious anemia results from faulty absorption of B_{12})	None reported
Biotin	Carbohydrate and fat metabolism; amino acid metabolism	Organ meats, milk, egg yolk, yeast; synthesis by intestinal bacteria	Nervous disorders, skin disorders, anorexia, muscle pain	None reported

macrocytic anemia – *a failure in the oxygen transport system characterized by abnormally large immature red blood cells.*

(Wiener et al., 2009). Kidney stone formation and destruction of vitamin B_{12} stores as a result of a vitamin C (ascorbic acid) **megadose** have also been described. Megadoses are defined as 10 times the recommended daily amount (RDA) for an adult. At present, there is not enough information available to define toxic levels of all vitamins for young children; however, it is certainly smaller than the amount required to produce **toxicity** symptoms in adults. Therefore, extreme caution should be used if giving children vitamin supplements, especially those containing iron, without a physician's advice because an excess can cause serious illness or death. "If a little bit is good, a lot is better" is a dangerous practice relative to taking vitamins.

Vitamins have been the subject of much media attention, having been promoted as "cures" for numerous conditions including cancer, common colds, fatigue, depression, and mental illness (Cassileth, Heitzer, & Wesa, 2009). Many people take vitamins and give them to their children as an "insurance policy" (Marra & Boyar, 2009; Shaikh, Byrd, & Auinger, 2009). Although vitamins can supplement a "hit-or-miss" diet, they should not be considered a substitute for adequate nutrient intake. There are several reasons why supplements, by themselves, cannot compensate for an inadequate diet. Vitamin and/or mineral supplements do not provide all of the nutrients known to be required by humans, nor do they provide any calories or protein, which are essential for growing children. In addition, diets often lack adequate fiber, essential amino acids, and/or essential fatty acids that cannot be corrected by vitamin/mineral supplements. Also, there may be substances as yet unknown, but essential, which are derived from foods that are not included in most vitamin/mineral preparations.

Vitamins are classified as fat-soluble (dissolved in or carried in fats) or water-soluble (dissolved in water). **Fat-soluble vitamins** differ from **water-soluble vitamins** both chemically and functionally. Consuming large doses of fat-soluble vitamins in supplements can cause toxicity because these substances are absorbed and stored in the body for later use. Fat-soluble vitamins are typically found in high-fat foods, such as meats, milk and milk products, eggs, nuts, avocados, and vegetable oils. Water-soluble vitamins dissolve in water and are absorbed directly into the blood stream and cells. Because the body is not able to store these vitamins, they are not considered to be toxic. Consequently, deficiencies of water-soluble vitamins can develop within a few days if they are not consumed on a regular basis. Water-soluble vitamins are readily available in fruits, vegetables, whole grain products, milk and milk products, and many meats. Table 15–2 summarizes the characteristics of these two vitamin classes.

Table 15–2 Characteristics of Vitamins

	Fat-Soluble Vitamins	Water-Soluble Vitamins
Examples	A, D, E, K	Vitamin C (ascorbic acid), thiamin, niacin, riboflavin, pantothenic acid, B_6 (pyridoxine), biotin, folacin, B_{12} (cobalamin)
Stored in body	Yes	No (B_{12} is an exception)
Excreted in urine	No	Yes
Needed daily	No	Yes
Deficiency	Develop slowly (months, years)	Develop rapidly (days, weeks)

megadose – *an amount of a vitamin or mineral at least 10 times that of the RDA.*
toxicity – *a state of being poisonous.*
fat-soluble vitamins – *vitamins that are dissolved, transported, and stored in fat.*
water-soluble vitamins – *vitamins that are dissolved and transported in water/fluids; cannot be stored.*

Vitamins in Energy Metabolism

A slow, steady release of energy is important to meet and sustain body needs. If energy is released in a haphazard fashion, much of it is lost as heat. Because young children require greater amounts of energy per pound, they cannot afford to lose energy in such a fashion. The primary vitamins involved in the regulation of metabolism for the release of energy are:

- thiamin
- niacin
- riboflavin
- pantothenic acid

These four vitamins are important coenzyme components that act as a team to release energy from carbohydrates and fats. However, they are not the only nutrients involved in this process; all of the other required nutrients must also be available in adequate amounts at the time needed.

Vitamins in Cellular Reproduction and Growth

Two vitamins that are absolutely essential for cell growth are folacin and cobalamin (B12) (Dror & Allen, 2008). Both vitamins participate in the **synthesis** of **DNA** and **RNA**, which are the chemicals that provide the pattern for cell division and growth. So crucial are these vitamins for cell division and growth that deficiencies are quickly noticeable in tissues that are frequently replaced, such as red blood cells or the cells lining the intestine.

Young children may be considered at risk for folacin and B_{12} deficiencies. Both vitamins are necessary for the synthesis of protein and are always required in greater amounts during periods of rapid growth. The fact that B_{12} is found only in food derived from animal sources must also be considered. Families must plan children's vegetarian meals carefully to be sure they include adequate vitamin B_{12} and other critical nutrients (Table 15–3) (Renda & Fischer, 2009). Vitamin B_{12} supplementation is usually recommended when no animal products are included in children's diet. Vegetarian diets are classified by the extent to which the diet includes animal foods:

Table 15–3 Non-animal Food Sources of Important Nutrients

Vegetarians who consume no animal products may lack several critical nutrients unless they pay careful attention to including alternative dietary sources. Nutrients that are most likely to be lacking and their non-animal sources are:

- **vitamin B_{12}**—fortified soy beverages and cereals
- **vitamin D**—fortified soy beverages and sunshine
- **calcium**—tofu processed with calcium, broccoli, seeds, nuts (almonds), kale, bok choy, legumes (peas and beans), lime products, and orange juice enriched with calcium
- **iron**—legumes (dried beans, peas, lentils), tofu, green leafy vegetables, dried fruit, whole grains, and iron-fortified cereals and breads, especially whole-wheat. (Absorption is improved by the presence of vitamin C, found in citrus fruits and juices, tomatoes, strawberries, broccoli, peppers, dark-green processed tortillas, leafy vegetables, and potatoes with skins.)
- **zinc**—whole wheat bread, whole grains (especially the germ and bran), legumes (dried beans, peas, lentils), nuts and nut butters, tofu
- **protein**—tofu and other soy-based products, legumes, seeds, nuts, grains, and vegetables

synthesis – *the process of making a compound by the union of simpler compounds or elements.*
DNA – *deoxyribonucleic acid; the substance in the cell nucleus that codes for genetically transmitted traits.*
RNA – *ribonucleic acid; the nucleic acid that serves as messenger between the nucleus and the ribosomes where proteins are synthesized.*

- lacto-ovo-vegetarian—dairy foods and eggs are included
- lacto-vegetarian—dairy foods are included, but not eggs
- ovo-vegetarian—eggs are included, but no dairy products
- vegan—no animal source foods are consumed, including items such as honey and gelatin

It was formerly thought that a vegan diet could not adequately meet children's nutrient needs. However, in their revised position paper on vegetarian diets, the American Dietetic Association (ADA) stated that, "Appropriately planned vegan, lacto-vegetarian, and lacto-ovo-vegetarian diets satisfy the nutrient needs of infants, children, and adolescents and promote normal growth" (ADA, 2009). The key point in this statement is the emphasis on well-planned diets that are based on sound nutrition information and meet children's nutrient requirements for growth, development, and health. Table 15–3 lists nutrients most likely to be deficient in the vegetarian diet and includes some alternative (non-animal) sources.

Some general recommendations for ensuring that children obtain the vitamins needed for optimal growth include:

- Minimize intake of less nutritious foods such as sweets and fatty foods.
- Choose whole or unrefined grain products instead of refined products.
- Choose a variety of nuts, seeds, legumes, fruits, and vegetables, including rich sources of vitamin C to improve iron absorption.
- Choose low fat varieties of dairy products, if they are included in the diet.
- Vegans should use properly fortified sources of vitamin B_{12}, such as fortified soy beverages or cereals, or take a supplement (Kirby & Danner, 2009).

Cellular reproduction and growth are dependent on the presence of proteins, folacin, and B_{12} (Chalouhi et al., 2008). One vitamin that is essential to the metabolism of proteins is pyridoxine (B_6). Pyridoxine **catalyzes** the chemical changes that permit the building of proteins from amino acids or the breakdown of proteins to provide needed amino acids.

Vitamins That Regulate Bone Growth

The minerals calcium and phosphorus are the major structural components of bones and teeth. However, bone growth also depends on a number of other nutrients as regulators, including vitamins A, C, and D.

Vitamin A regulates the destruction of old bone cells and their replacement by new ones. This process is known as "remodeling."

Vitamin C functions in two ways in the formation of bone tissue:

- maintains the solubility of calcium, making it more available for absorption
- aids in the formation of collagen, the flexible protein foundation upon which phosphorus and calcium are deposited

Vitamin D is necessary for the absorption of calcium and phosphorus, the major constituents of bones and teeth. It is also needed to ensure adequate blood levels of calcium and phosphorus that allow for deposition of these minerals in bones and teeth.

Vitamins That Regulate Neuromuscular Function

Vitamins play a role in neuromuscular functioning either through the synthesis of neurotransmitters (chemical messengers) or through growth or maintenance of nerve cells.

catalyzes – *accelerates a chemical reaction.*

Many nutrients are involved in the regulation of body functions.

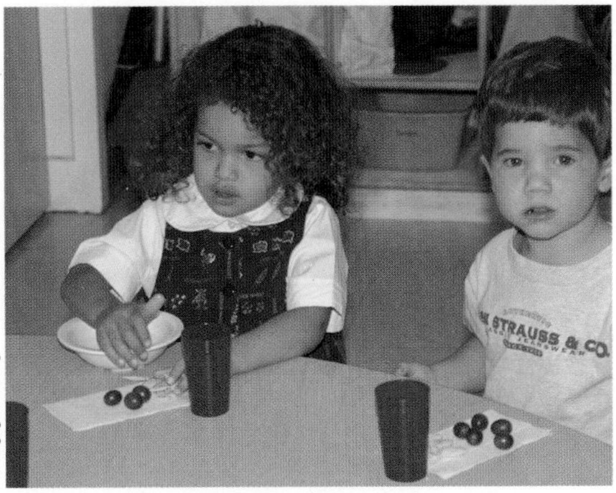

© Cengage Learning

Vitamin B_6 and vitamin C, thiamin, and niacin catalyze the synthesis of neurotransmitters that carry electrical messages to all organs and regulate nerve-muscle activities. Deficiencies of these vitamins can result in neurological abnormalities.

Vitamins B_6 and B_{12} are necessary for the formation and maintenance of the myelin sheath, the insulative layer surrounding nerve cells, and are, therefore, especially critical for developing infants and young children. Faulty myelin sheath formation and maintenance results in abnormal passage of nerve impulses, which may result in numbness, tremors, or loss of coordination.

Researchers have determined that maternal deficiency of folacin may result in the development of cleft lip, cleft palate, and/or neural tube defects during the first few months of fetal life (Bassuk & Kibar, 2009; Wolff et al., 2009). Neural tube defects, commonly known as spina bifida, result in an incomplete formation of the spinal column (nerves and bone) and brain. Folacin is readily found in fruits (oranges, strawberries), vegetables (spinach, asparagus), dried beans and legumes, and fortified whole grain products. Prenatal vitamins also contain folacin; however, neural tube defects often occur before the mother realizes that she is pregnant. Consequently, many foods and grain products are now being fortified with folacin as a preventive measure.

Vitamins That Regulate Blood Formation

Some vitamins play an important role in the formation of blood cells and hemoglobin. Hemoglobin, the red pigment of the red blood cells, carries oxygen to all cells of the body and carries the waste product, carbon dioxide, away from the cells to the lungs. Vitamins needed for the production of red blood cells and hemoglobin are:

- vitamin E
- pantothenic acid
- vitamin B_6 (pyridoxine)
- folacin
- vitamin B_{12} (cobalamin)

Minerals as Regulators

Many body functions also require the presence of specific minerals (Table 15–4). Minerals involved in regulatory processes are usually parts of enzymes or coenzymes or may catalyze their action and, therefore, are required in amounts considerably smaller than those needed for building or repairing body tissue.

Minerals in Energy Metabolism

Minerals also play an important role in the steady, efficient release of energy. This process of energy metabolism (production, storage, and release) depends on adequate amounts of:

- phosphorus
- magnesium
- iodine
- iron

Table 15–4 Mineral Summary

Mineral	Functions	Sources	Deficiency Symptoms	Toxicity Symptoms
Calcium	Major component of bones and teeth; collagen formation; muscle contraction; secretion/release of insulin; neurotransmitters; blood	Dairy products, turnip or collard greens, canned salmon or sardines, soybeans or soybean curd (tofu)	Poor growth, small adult size, fragile and deformed bones, some form of rickets	Unlikely: absorption is controlled; symptoms usually result from excess vitamin D or hormonal imbalance
Phosphorus	Major component of bones and teeth; energy metabolism; component of DNA and RNA	Dairy products, meats, legumes, grains; additive in soft drinks	Rare with normal diet	Large amounts may depress calcium absorption
Magnesium	Major component of bones and teeth; activator of enzymes for ATP use; required for synthesis of DNA and RNA and for synthesis of proteins by RNA	Nuts, seeds, green vegetables, legumes, whole grains	Poor neuromuscular coordination, tremors, convulsions	Unlikely
Sodium	Nerve impulse transmission; fluid balance; acid-base balance	Meats, fish, poultry, eggs, milk (naturally occurring sodium); high levels (sodium, salt, MSG) are present in many processed and cured foods	Rare (losses from sweat may cause dizziness, nausea, muscle cramps)	Linked to high blood pressure in some persons; confusion; coma

Potassium	Nerve impulse transmission; fluid balance; acid-base balance	Fruits (bananas, orange juice), vegetables, whole grains, fresh meats, fish	Weakness, irregular heartbeat	Unlikely from food sources
Iron	Component of hemoglobin; enzymes involved in oxygen utilization	Liver, oysters, meats, enriched and whole grains, leafy green vegetables	**Microcytic anemia** (characterized by small, pale red blood cells), fatigue, pallor, shortness of breath	Unlikely (may be due to genetic defect)
Zinc	Component of many enzymes involved in: protein metabolism; DNA/RNA synthesis; collagen formation; wound healing	Liver, oysters, meats, eggs, whole grains, legumes	Retarded growth, loss of senses of taste and smell, delayed wound healing	Excess supplementation may interfere with iron/copper metabolism and cause nausea, vomiting, diarrhea, gastric ulcers
Iodine	Component of thyroxin, which regulates basal metabolic rate; regulates physical and mental growth	Iodized salt, seafood, many processed foods	Goiter, hypothyroidism, infertility, stillbirth; inhibits fetal growth and brain development (cretinism)	Hyperthyroidism, abdominal pain, diarrhea, metallic taste (in mouth), seizures, thirst

microcytic anemia – *a failure in the oxygen transport system characterized by abnormally small red blood cells.*

Minerals are essential for proper neuromuscular development and function.

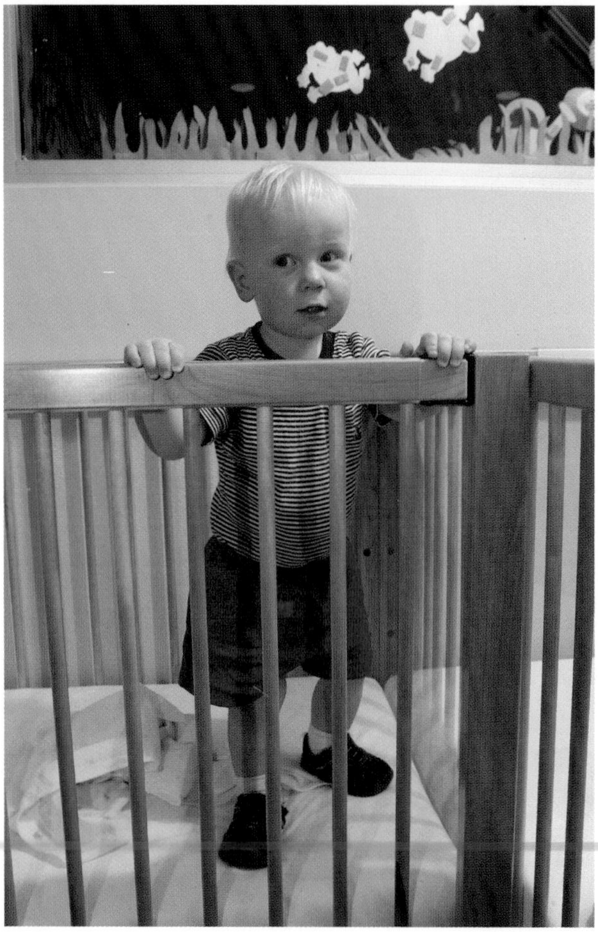
© Cengage Learning

Phosphorus is necessary for the production of enzymes and **coenzymes** required for energy-releasing metabolism, and also for the formation of **adenosine triphosphate (ATP)**, the chemical substance in which potential energy is stored in body cells. Another mineral, magnesium, is required for both the storage and the release of the energy trapped in ATP. Iodine is a component of the hormone thyroxin and plays an important role in controlling the rate at which the body uses energy for involuntary activities (the basal metabolic rate). Iron is a component in one of the key enzyme systems involved in the final stages of energy metabolism.

Minerals in Cellular Reproduction and Growth

Minerals required for cellular reproduction and growth include:

- phosphorus
- magnesium
- zinc

Phosphorus is a structural component of both DNA and RNA. Magnesium is required both for the synthesis of DNA and for synthesis of proteins from the pattern provided by DNA. Zinc functions as part of an enzyme system that must be active during DNA and RNA synthesis. DNA allows cells to reproduce and to synthesize proteins needed for growth.

A deficiency of dietary zinc can result in stunted growth, delayed sexual maturity, and decreased acuity of taste and smell that may further reduce appetite. Zinc is chemically related to iron so that its absorption is affected by many of the same factors. Excessive supplementation with calcium and/or iron can seriously reduce the availability of zinc.

Minerals That Regulate Neuromuscular Function

The transmission of nerve impulses from nerve cell to nerve cell or from nerve cell to muscle is dependent on the presence of:

- sodium
- potassium
- calcium
- magnesium

coenzymes – *a vitamin-containing substance required by certain enzymes before they can perform their prescribed function.*
adenosine triphosphate (ATP) – *a compound with energy-storing phosphate bonds that is the main energy source for all cells.*

Reflective Thoughts

What are your thoughts about vitamin and/or mineral pills? They are staples in the lives of millions of Americans, but are they necessary? Vitamin/mineral pills are safe for adults if they provide no more than 100 percent daily RDAs.

- Are they a wise purchase if they have only a placebo effect?
- Would you recommend vitamin/mineral pills for young children? Explain.

Think about the risks involved in giving vitamin/mineral supplements to children. Because they often look and taste like candy, it is easy for children to ingest an amount of supplements that could cause toxic symptoms and even death. However, there are circumstances when supplements can be beneficial for adults and children.

- Think of the benefit-risk ratio for both children and adults.

Sodium and potassium act to change the electrical charge on the surface of nerve cells, allowing the transmission of nerve impulses to muscle cells that, in turn, cause muscles to contract. Calcium is required for the release of many neurotransmitters from nerve cells and for the actual muscle contraction, while ATP, which contains phosphorus as a structural component, provides the energy that allows contractions to take place. Sodium, potassium, and magnesium promote the relaxation phase of muscle contraction. In addition, magnesium also helps to regulate neuromuscular activity.

Minerals in Blood Formation

Several minerals play an essential role in the formation and maintenance of a healthy blood supply, which is responsible for transporting all regulatory minerals throughout the body. Iron is a structural part of hemoglobin, which is a primary component of blood. Copper aids with the absorption of iron and its incorporation into hemoglobin. Calcium is also necessary for the production of substances that trigger blood coagulation.

Proteins as Regulators

Proteins are the only class of nutrients that can perform all three general functions of nutrients. They build and repair body tissue, regulate body functions, and provide energy.

Proteins in Energy Metabolism and Growth Regulation

Proteins (amino acids) are important components of enzymes and some hormones and, thus, play a major role in the regulation of energy metabolism. The body must have an adequate supply of protein in order to produce these critical enzymes and hormones.

All body functions depend on the presence and activity of enzymes, which are referred to as protein catalysts. A catalyst is a substance that regulates a chemical reaction without becoming part of that reaction. The sequential metabolism for release of energy requires many steps; each step requires at least one enzyme specific to the particular reaction. Many enzymes require vitamin-containing coenzymes to enable them to catalyze their specific chemical reactions.

Hormones are substances secreted by glands for action on tissue elsewhere in the body. As such, they regulate many body functions. Although not all hormones are composed of amino acids, two amino-acid-dependent hormones, thyroxin and insulin, are required in energy metabolism.

Thyroxin regulates the rate at which energy is used for involuntary activities and is secreted by the thyroid gland. Insulin is secreted by the pancreas and is necessary for the absorption of glucose by body cells so it can be utilized as an energy source for cellular activity. Insulin and adrenalin

Issues To Consider **Food Supplement Safety**

"Food supplements" are appearing in the food market in increasing numbers and are often in the news. Traditionally, food supplements were made of one or more essential nutrients believed to be needed in the diet in greater amounts, or they were promoted as cures for some disease or health condition. Now the term has been broadened to include products that are ingested to supplement one's diet, such as herbs and other plant-derived substances that might improve health. The magic of using the term "food supplement" is that it can be used legitimately to advertise a substance as a cure for a condition or disease without demonstrating any proof. Manufacturers do not have to submit their product to the Food and Drug Administration (FDA) for testing and approval before it can be offered for sale. Promoting herbs, often as pills, for the cure of numerous conditions is a concern of nutritionists, professional health care personnel, and pharmacists. A food supplement must now carry on its label the statement: "This product is not approved by the FDA."

- Will this label/statement adequately warn consumers that this product may not be safe to use?
- Does using the term "natural" ensure that a product is safe?
- Why is it important that a person check with his or her doctor and pharmacist before using any of these over-the-counter products?
- Why is there so much concern about the increasing use of herbs as food supplements?

Water is necessary for the regulation of many body functions.

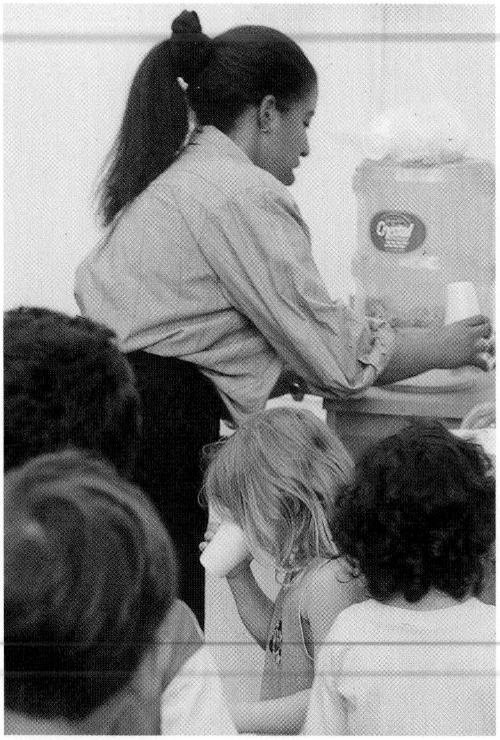

(another amino-acid-dependent hormone) act together to maintain normal blood glucose levels.

Water as a Regulator

When foods are consumed, they must be broken down into simple nutrients before they can be used by the body. This process is called digestion and involves a combination of mechanical (chewing) and chemical steps. Food composition is changed during chemical digestion as water is added at appropriate places in the protein, fats, and carbohydrate molecules to break them into units small enough to be absorbed and used by the cells. Thus, water is essential for many processes and serves as the medium in which chemical reactions take place.

After food is digested, nutrients are absorbed and carried in solution via the blood and lymph to the cells. Again, water serves as the main transporting agent and comprises all body fluids including blood, lymph, and tissue fluid. It also is the major component of body secretions such as salivary juice, gastric juice, bile, perspiration, and expirations from the lungs. Water also plays a major role in ridding the body of soluble waste materials that are carried out in urine, which is 95 percent water. Water also helps to regulate body temperature during changes in environmental conditions and activity-related heat production. It is important that children be given plain water rather than juice or other sweetened beverages because sugar greatly reduces water absorption.

Nutrient Functions: A Recap

Approximately 40 nutrients are recognized as essential for providing energy, allowing normal growth for the child and maintenance for the adult. Each nutrient has its special function(s). Some nutrients share functions and in many cases the function of any given nutrient depends on one or more other nutrients being present. Table 15–5 provides a summary of these functional relationships and highlights what nutrients really do in the body. You might make this a personal study by associating each functional unit with the part of your own body. For example, when listing nutrient needs for bones and teeth, envision your own bones and teeth and what these nutrients are doing for them.

Table 15–5 Summary of Nutrients and Their Biological Functions

Functional Unit	Nutrients Involved	Specific Function
Blood formation and maintenance	Calcium Vitamin K Protein Iron Copper	Blood clotting
	Vitamin B_6 Folacin	Hemoglobin production
	Folacin Vitamin B_{12}	Production of red blood cells
Bone and teeth development	Calcium Phosphorus Magnesium	Components of bones and teeth
	Vitamin C Vitamin A Vitamin D	Building and remodeling of bones
Nerve-muscle development and activity	Vitamin C Thiamin Niacin Vitamin B_6 Pantothenic acid Calcium Potassium	Transmission of nerve impulses
	Calcium Magnesium Potassium Sodium Thiamin Pantothenic acid	Regulates muscle contraction and relaxation
Growth and maintenance of cells and body organs	Protein Phosphorus Zinc Selenium Vitamin B_6 Folacin	Regulates cell division and synthesis of needed cell proteins
	Iodine	Regulates physical and mental growth

(continued)

Table 15–5 Summary of Nutrients and Their Biological Functions *(continued)*

Functional Unit	Nutrients Involved	Specific Function
Availability of energy for cellular activity	Carbohydrates Fats Proteins	May be "burned" to release energy
	Phosphorus Magnesium Thiamin Riboflavin Niacin Pantothenic acid Biotin	Roles in enzyme and coenzyme production to release energy
	Iodine	Regulates basal metabolic energy needs

Focus On Families — Nutrients That Regulate Body Functions

Water is essential for the regulation of many body functions. Although water is abundantly available, getting children and adults to consume adequate amounts continues to be a challenge. Water has many competitors such as sodas, fruit drinks, fruit beverages, and sport drinks that children often find more appealing. These beverages, however, are costly and provide little nutritional value while adding significant calories and sugar. Given the continuing increases in childhood obesity and dental caries, it is important that families and teachers encourage children to drink more water and set a good example for them to follow.

- Limit or avoid purchasing sweetened beverages. If these items are not readily available in the home, your child is more likely to drink water and other nutritious beverages such as milk and 100 percent fruit juice.
- Keep a pitcher of water available in the refrigerator with small cups where children can reach. Smaller cups are less intimidating and more manageable. Lemon or lime slices can be added for flavor interest and variation. Freeze ice cubes in fun-shaped trays.
- When traveling from home or participating in physical activities, encourage your child to carry a water bottle to quench his or her thirst. This is more economical than purchasing beverages from vending machines or convenience stores, offers more health benefits than sodas, fruit drinks, fruit beverages, and fruit-ades, and is eco-friendly.

Classroom Corner — Teacher Activities

Let's Make Pizza

(PreK–2; National Health Education Standards 1.2.1, 7.2.1)

Concept: Pizza can provide many of the nutrients your body needs.

Learning Objectives

- Children will learn how to make pizza.
- Children will learn that pizza can be a healthy food.
- Child will learn the names of the ingredients.

(continued)

Classroom Corner **Teacher Activities** *(continued)*

Supplies

- English muffins (one-half per child)
- One can of pizza sauce
- One red pepper
- One green pepper
- One package pepperoni or diced ham
- One can of black olives
- One can of pineapple chunks
- One bag of mozzarella cheese
- Two cookie sheets
- Seven plastic spoons
- Hand wipes

Learning Activities

- Read and discuss one of the following books:
  - *Pizza Party* by Grace Maccarone
  - *Pizza Pat* by Rita Golden Gelman
  - *Pizza* by Saturnino Romay
- Tell children they are going to make pizza. Ask children what kind of pizza they like to eat. Explain the process for making pizza (first get an English muffin, spread on pizza sauce, add remaining ingredients, cover with cheese). Have children name each ingredient.
- Set up ingredients on a table and have several children come up at a time to make their pizzas. Once pizzas are made, put them on a cookie sheet. (Be sure to identify each child's pizza so they can eat their own.)
- Talk about different ingredients they put on their pizza and how each can help their body.

Evaluation

- Children will follow the correct process for making a pizza.
- Children will explain that pizza can be a healthy food choice.
- Children will name several ingredients used to make pizza.

Additional lesson plans for grades 3–5 are available on the premium website for this book.

Summary

- Proteins, minerals, and vitamins are nutrient classes that regulate body activity.
- Vitamins function only as regulators, but they are essential for reactions involved with energy release, growth by cell division, bone and blood formation, and brain and nerve activities.
- Minerals are required for the same regulatory functions as vitamins in addition to regulating water balance in the body.

- Proteins function in many regulatory reactions in addition to providing energy and supporting growth.
- Water, as the medium in which most nutrient functions take place, regulates a majority of nutrient activity and transports all nutrients after they enter the body. Water is also the prime regulator of body temperature.

Terms to Know

milligram (mg) *p. 369*
microgram (mcg or μg) *p. 369*
neuromuscular *p. 369*
macrocytic anemia *p. 371*
megadose *p. 372*
toxicity *p. 372*
fat-soluble vitamins *p. 372*
water-soluble vitamins *p. 372*
synthesis *p. 373*
DNA *p. 373*
RNA *p. 373*
catalyzes (catalyst) *p. 374*
microcytic anemia *p. 377*
coenzymes *p. 378*
adenosine triphosphate (ATP) *p. 378*

Chapter Review

A. By Yourself:

1. What two minerals are required for energy metabolism?
2. What two minerals are required for cellular division and growth?
3. Name an important nutrient component of enzymes and some hormones.
4. Which nutrient is the prime regulator of body temperature?
5. What role(s) does water play in the body?

B. As a Group:

1. Read the revised position statement, "Vegetarian Diets," issued by the American Dietetic Association (http://www.eatright.org/About/Content.aspx?id=8357) (2009). What are the benefits and limitations of a vegetarian diet for young children?
2. Discuss why concerns about vitamin D deficiencies have been gaining increased public attention. How is vitamin D obtained (source)? What is its regulatory function?
3. Identify five non-dairy sources of calcium. Are they an adequate substitute?
4. Discuss why vitamins A and C are considered to be at-risk vitamins for young children.
5. React to the statement, "I take vitamins just to be sure I get everything I need."

Case Study

Evan, age 4½, is allergic to citrus fruits. Even a few drops of juice cause him to break out in hives.

1. For what nutrient should Evan's diet be closely monitored?
2. If Evan's diet is actually deficient in this nutrient, would symptoms appear rapidly or slowly? Explain why?
3. Suggest foods other than citrus fruits that would also provide this nutrient.
4. List two symptoms of deficiency that you might anticipate Evan to display.
5. Should Evan be given supplements of this nutrient to offset possible deficiencies? Why or why not?

Application Activities

1. Using the vitamin and mineral summaries in Tables 15–1 and 15–4:
   a. List two specific foods or types of foods that are rich sources of each of the following nutrients:
      magnesium   thiamin
      calcium   riboflavin
   b. What foods are good sources of more than one of these nutrients?
   c. Which nutrients occur in the same types of foods?
   d. Which nutrients do not occur in the same types of foods?
   e. Which nutrients are found mostly in animal-source foods?
   f. Which nutrients are found mostly in plant-based foods?

Helpful Web Resources

Action for Healthy Kids	http://www.actionforhealthykids.org/
Federal Citizen Information Center	http://www.pueblo.gsa.gov
Mayo Clinic Health Letter	http://www.healthletter.mayoclinic.com
MyPyramid for Kids	http://www.mypyramid.gov/Kids/
Nutrition Exploration (National Dairy Council)	http://www.nutritionexplorations.org/
United States Department of Agriculture (USDA)	http://www.fns.usda.gov

You are just a click away from additional health, safety, and nutrition resources! Go to www.CengageBrain.com to access this text's Education CourseMate website, where you'll find:

- a table summarizing the biological functions of major nutrients
- glossary flashcards, activities, tutorial quizzes, videos, web links, and more

References

American Dietetic Association (ADA). (2009). Position of the American Dietetic Association: Vegetarian diets. Accessed on January 7, 2010 from http://www.vgterre.net/wordpress/wp-content/uploads/2009/08./VegetarianPositionFINAL.pdf.

Bassuk, A., & Kibar, Z. (2009). Genetic basis of neural tube defects, *Seminars in Pediatric Neurology*, 16(3), 101–110.

Cassileth, B., Heitzer, M., & Wesa, K. (2009). The public health impact of herbs and nutritional supplements, *Pharmaceutical Biology*, 47(8), 761–767.

Chalouhi, C., Faesch, S., Anthoine-Milhomme, M., Fulla, Y., Dulac, O., & Chéron, G. (2008). Neurological consequences of vitamin B12 deficiency and its treatment, *Pediatric Emergency Care*, 24(8), 538–541.

Dror, D., & Allen, L. (2008). Effect of vitamin B12 deficiency on neurodevelopment in infants: Current knowledge and possible mechanisms, *Nutrition Reviews*, 66(5), 250–255.

Kirby, M., & Danner, E. (2009). Nutritional deficiencies in children on restricted diets, *Pediatric Clinics of North America*, 56(5), 1085–1103.

Marra, M., & Boyar, A. (2009). Position of the American Dietetic Association: Nutrient supplementation, *Journal of the American Dietetic Association*, 109(12), 2073–2085.

Ramakrishnan, U., Nguyen, P., & Martorell, R. (2009). Effects of micronutrients on growth of children under 5 years of age: Meta-analyses of single and multiple nutrient interventions, *American Journal of Clinical Nutrition*, 89(1), 191–203.

Renda, M., & Fischer, P. (2009). Vegetarian diets in children and adolescents, *Pediatrics in Review*, 30(1), e1–e8.

Shaikh, U., Byrd, R., & Auinger, P. (2009). Vitamin and mineral supplement use by children and adolescents in the 1999-2004 National Health and Nutrition Examination survey, *Archives of Pediatrics & Adolescent Medicine*, 163(2), 150–157.

Stoffman, N., & Gordon, C. (2009). Vitamin D and adolescents: What do we know? *Adolescent Medicine*, 21(4), 465–471.

Wiener, F., Schmidt, M., Munson, K., Khoury, P., Kalkwarf, H., & Daniels, S. (2009). Dietary intake of 3 year old children: Do they meet recommended intake? *Current Pediatric Reviews*, 5(2), 128–134(7).

Wolff, T., Witkop, C., Miller, T., & Syed, S. (2009). Folic acid supplementation for the prevention of neural tube defects: An update of the evidence for the U.S. Preventive Services Task Force, *Annals of Internal Medicine*, 150(9), 632–639.

UNIT 4

Nutrition and the Young Child

CHAPTER 16

Feeding Infants

NAEYC Standards *Chapter Links*

- **#1 a, b, and c:** Promoting child development and learning
- **#2 a, b, and c:** Building family and community relationships
- **#3 a, b and d:** Observing, documenting, and assessing to support young children and families
- **#4 a, b, and d:** Using developmentally effective approaches to connect with children and families
- **#5 a and c:** Using content knowledge to build meaningful curriculum
- **#6 c:** Becoming a professional

Learning Objectives

After studying this chapter, you should be able to:

- Explain how the feeding relationship helps to satisfy the infant's needs in other developmental areas.
- Discuss why the infant's nutrient requirements are greater during the first year.
- Demonstrate how to feed an infant correctly (e.g., food preparation, positioning, burping).
- Describe the factors that indicate when an infant is developmentally ready for semi-solid foods.
- Identify and discuss several health concerns associated with infant feeding.

Profile of an Infant

During the first year of a child's life, the rate of growth and development is more rapid than at any other period in the life cycle (Allen & Marotz, 2010). Infants will double their weight during the first 5 to 6 months and will approximately triple their birth weight by the end of the first year. Birth length typically increases by 50 percent as the child approaches his/her first birthday.

Infants depend on adults to protect them from environmental hazards, such as temperature change and pathogenic organisms, and to provide them with the necessary nutrients in a safe and useable form. Feeding must be coupled with physical contact, emotional connections, communication and social interchanges, and much tender loving care (TLC). Without this, infants' growth and development can be seriously delayed even when they are receiving all of the essential nutrients needed (Mueller-Nix & Forcad-Geux, 2009). Food and the feeding relationship play an important role in meeting many of the infant's developmental and early learning needs by providing a variety of tastes, colors, temperatures, textures, opportunities for physical contact, as well as visual, auditory, and social interaction. Within the first 12 months, infants quickly progress from a diet that consists solely of breast milk or formula to one that gradually includes semi-solid foods and finally to a modified adult diet that includes them in the family meal time (Table 16–1).

Meeting the Infant's Nutritional Needs

Infancy is characterized by a rapid rate of growth and development that must be supported by adequate nutrient intake—protein, carbohydrates, and fat. The infant's nutrient and caloric needs remain high, relative to their body size, throughout the first year but are greatest during the first 4 months when growth is most rapid. For example, a newborn requires approximately 50 calories per pound of body weight daily until 5 to 6 months of age. One-fourth to one-third of these calories is used for growth. As the infant progresses through the first year and becomes more mobile, fewer calories are needed for growth and more are required for physical activity. By 6 months of age, the infant requires only 40–45 calories per pound.

Meeting the infant's critical energy and nutrient needs presents a significant feeding challenge. Their small stomach capacity limits the quantity of food they are able to consume at a given meal. As a result, infants should be offered frequent, small feedings of nutrient-dense foods—sometimes as many as 6 to 8 feedings in a 24-hour period during the first few months.

Table 16–1 Recommended Infant Serving Sizes

Child Care Infant Meal Pattern		
	Breakfast	
Birth through 3 Months	**4 through 7 Months**	**8 through 11 Months**
4–6 fluid ounces of formula or breast milk	4–8 fluid ounces of formula or breast milk; 0–3 tablespoons of infant cereal	6–8 fluid ounces of formula or breast milk; and 2–4 tablespoons of infant cereal; and 1–4 tablespoons of fruit or vegetable or both
	Lunch or Supper	
4–6 fluid ounces of formula or breast milk 	4–8 fluid ounces of formula or breast milk; 0–3 tablespoons of infant cereal; and 0–3 tablespoons of fruit or vegetable or both 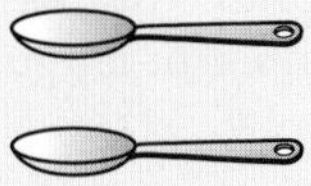	6–8 fluid ounces of formula or breast milk; 2–4 tablespoons of infant cereal; and/or 1–4 tablespoons of meat, fish, poultry, egg yolk, cooked dry beans, or peas; or ½–2 ounces of cheese; or 1–4 ounces (volume) of cottage cheese; or 1–4 ounces (weight) of cheese food or cheese spread; and 1–4 tablespoons of fruit or vegetable or both

Source: Child & Adult Care Food Program (CACFP)

A mother's nutrition during pregnancy influences her infant's early nutritional needs.

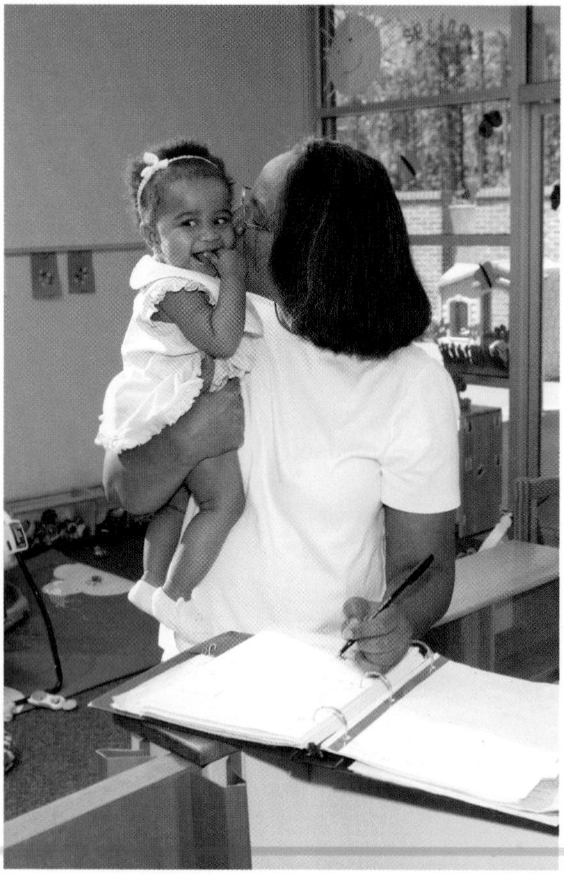

© Cengage Learning

Prenatal Influences on Infants' Nutritional Needs

An infant's early nutritional needs may be conditioned by the mother's nutritional status during pregnancy. A common consequence of poor **prenatal** nutrition is a **low-birthweight (LBW) infant**. The incidence of serious illness and premature death during their first year is especially high for low-birthweight infants. In addition, LBW infants are also at significant risk for many health problems such as:

- poor regulation of body temperature
- respiratory distress, including SIDS
- increased susceptibility to infection
- difficulty in metabolizing carbohydrates, fats, and proteins
- delayed development of kidneys and digestive organs
- poorly calcified bones—reduced bone density
- poor iron stores resulting in neonatal anemia
- vitamin deficiencies (especially vitamin E, folacin, and pyridoxine) during neonatal period (birth to 28 days)

Infants at highest risk for these problems are often those born to teenage mothers, who must meet their own nutritional needs for growth in addition to providing nutrients for the developing fetus. Women who smoke, are pregnant with multiple babies, or who fail to consume adequate calories and nutrients during pregnancy are also more likely to give birth to LBW infants.

Common prenatal nutritional deficiencies that produce low-birthweight babies include:

- protein
- energy
- folacin
- vitamin D
- pyridoxine

Prenatal nutrient deficiencies may be partially corrected, but rarely completely reversed, by supplementing for the infant's deficient nutrient needs immediately after birth. The WIC (Women, Infants, and Children) program, which provides food supplements for pregnant and breastfeeding women, infants, and children up to the age of 5, has been effective in reducing the incidence of prenatal, infant, and child malnutrition (Richards et al., 2009). WIC currently serves approximately 45 percent of all infants born in the United States and provides nutrition, health care, and child care information for families in a number of languages (Figure 16–1) (U.S. Department of Agriculture, 2009).

---

prenatal – *the period from conception to birth of the baby.*
low-birthweight (LBW) infant – *an infant who weighs less than 5.5 pounds (2,500 grams) at birth.*

Figure 16–1 Breastfeeding information is available in multiple languages from WIC.

MiPirámide en Acción:
Consejos para Mamás en Período de Lactancia

¿Cómo Puedo Adelgazar Después de que Nazca Mi Bebé?

Amamantar es lo mejor para las mamás y para sus bebés por muchas razones. Una de las razones es que la lactancia facilita la pérdida del peso que gano durante el embarazo, al quemar las calorías extras. Además, la leche materna ayuda a combatir infecciones y reduce las alergias, de modo que los bebés alimentados con leche materna se enferman con menor frecuencia.

Siga su Plan MiPirámide para Mamás (ver reverso) para elegir la cantidad adecuada de cada grupo de alimentos. Además, visite a su médico. Mientras está amamantando, su médico puede monitorear su peso y decirle si está perdiendo peso como debería. Si está perdiendo peso muy lentamente, disminuya la cantidad de calorías que está consumiendo. La mejor manera de ingerir menos calorías es reduciendo la cantidad de "calorías extras."

¿Qué son las "calorías extras"?

Las calorías extras son los azúcares agregados o grasas sólidas en los alimentos. Los siguientes son algunos ejemplos de alimentos con "calorías extras":

- Refrescos o gaseosas
- Golosinas
- Postres
- Galletas
- Cereales azucarados
- Alimentos fritos
- Queso
- Leche entera
- Yogur endulzado
- Salchichas
- Carnes grasas

Busque opciones que sean de bajo contenido graso, sin grasa, sin azúcar ni edulcorantes o sin azúcares agregados.

Source: USDA

The First 6 Months

During the first 6 months, the infant's nutritional needs can be met solely with formula or breast milk (with vitamin D supplementation). Breast milk and formula are both rich in fat and provide approximately 650 calories per quart to meet the infant's high energy needs. The full-term infant is born with a temporary store of iron and vitamin A that lasts for approximately the first 5 to 6 months. However, premature infants may need to be supplemented with these nutrients during this period because they have not had as much time to develop reserves. No semi-solid foods are needed or advisable until the infant is at least 5 months of age. Younger infants are not developmentally or physiologically ready to ingest solid foods. (This is discussed later in the chapter.)

The benefits of breastfeeding continue to gain increased attention and support (Walker, 2010). The American Academy of Pediatrics and the American Academy of Family Physicians (AAFP) urge mothers to breastfeed infants exclusively during the first 6 months and continue until they reach 1 year of age if possible (AAFP, 2007; AAP, 2005). Scientific evidence has shown a positive relationship between breastfeeding and a reduced risk of some childhood health problems, including SIDS, ear infection (otitis media), allergies and asthma, diabetes, and bacterial meningitis (James & Lessen, 2009; Wu & Chen, 2009). In addition, researchers have found that some children show small advantages in developmental and intellectual function (Tanaka et al., 2009). The advantages of breast milk are summarized in Table 16–2. Breastfeeding requires that mothers increase certain nutrients in their diet to maintain their own health and the quality of breast milk (Table 16–3).

Table 16–2 Advantages of Breast Milk

Breast Milk:

- has all of the nutrients needed by the infant for the first 6 months (with the exception of adequate vitamin D)
- contains proteins that are more digestible than cow's milk protein
- contains lactose, the main carbohydrate component, which aids in calcium absorption and in establishing beneficial intestinal flora
- provides **antibodies** (immunoglobulin) that protect the infant from some infectious illnesses
- has a higher content of the essential fatty acids
- provides taurine*
- provides dietary nucleotides**
- is less likely to cause food allergies
- reduces the risk of bacteria entering the infant's body from unsanitary formula preparation
- is inexpensive, convenient, and always available at the correct temperature
- contains less sodium (salt) than formulas
- fosters emotional bonding between mother and infant
- is a biologically active substance, changing in nutrient composition to meet the infant's changing needs

*Taurine is a free amino acid (not found in proteins) that is particularly important for the normal growth and development of the central nervous system. It is now added to many formulas, especially those for premature infants.
**Dietary nucleotides play a role in the infant's ability to produce antibodies in response to exposure to infectious organisms. The American Academy of Pediatrics currently recommends these be added to all prepared formulas.

Table 16–3 Breastfeeding and a Mother's Dietary Needs

Mothers who are breastfeeding need to increase their daily intake of nutrients, including:

- approximately 500 additional calories
- 15–20 grams of protein
- vitamins A, C, and folacin
- calcium (equivalent of one extra serving)
- an additional 4 cups of fluids
- vitamin B_{12} and D supplementation (if no animal products are consumed)

Some mothers may elect formula feeding as the best approach after giving careful consideration to their health and lifestyle factors. Conditions that might cause a mother to choose formula feeding are:

- maternal illness or surgery
- medications the mother may need to take
- demands that require the mother to be away from the child for long periods of time
- personal preference
- use of addictive drugs, including alcohol and tobacco

Regardless of the feeding method that is chosen, teachers must be accepting and willing to assist families in meeting their infants' nutritional needs. Mothers should never be made to feel guilty or that they have made the wrong decision.

antibodies – *special substances produced by the body that help protect against disease.*

The Teacher and the Breastfeeding Mother

The mother who is employed outside the home may choose to continue breastfeeding. She may use a breast pump or hand express her milk and refrigerate or freeze it so that caregivers can feed her baby breast milk while she is at work. Breast milk can be refrigerated (40°F) in a sterile container and used within 48 hours; it can also be frozen (0°F), preferably in hard plastic containers (to avoid breakage or tears) and used within 3 months from the time it was expressed. Frozen breast milk must never be refrozen once it has been thawed. Containers should be clearly labeled with the date and the baby's name.

Teachers should also be supportive and willing to assist the mother who is able to come and nurse her infant during the day (Table 16–4).

Safe Handling of Breast Milk Human milk varies in color, consistency, and odor, depending on the mother's diet and the container in which it is stored. Since breast milk is not homogenized, the cream may rise to the top of the container. Shaking it briefly before feeding helps to remix the layers. For safe handling, the teacher should always follow these steps:

- Wash hands well before touching any milk containers. Avoid touching the inside of bottles or caps.
- Request that mothers label containers with the date when milk was collected; use the oldest milk first.
- If breast milk is to be stored for more than 48 hours, it should be frozen. (See Table 16–5 for safe thawing instructions.)
- Frozen breast milk may be safely stored in a freezer (0°F) for up to 3 months.

The Teacher and the Formula-Fed Infant

Although breastfeeding offers important benefits, many infants in child care programs will be formula fed. The infant's family and health care provider will determine which formula is best for the infant. Commercial infant formulas are prepared to closely resemble breast milk in composition

Table 16–4 Teacher Checklist: Support for Nursing Mothers

Early childhood programs can provide an environment that will support mothers who wish to nurse their infants at the facility by:

- creating a private area that is quiet and comfortable
- having a place where mothers can wash their hands before and after nursing
- providing a comfortable chair (a rocking chair if possible) and a foot rest to relieve back strain
- making water or other fluids available for mothers to drink
- having the infant ready (e.g., awake, diapers changed, infant's hands cleaned) when mother arrives

Table 16–5 Thawing Frozen Breast Milk Safely

1. Wash your hands with soap and water before touching the breast milk container.
2. Place the sealed container of breast milk in a bowl of warm water for about 30 minutes, or hold the container of 4 ounces of human milk under warm running water for approximately four minutes. **NEVER MICROWAVE BREAST MILK!** Microwaving can alter the nutritional composition of breast milk and also cause burns to the infant due to uneven heating.
3. Swirl the container to blend any fat that may have separated and risen during thawing.
4. Feed thawed milk immediately or store in the refrigerator for a maximum of 24 hours.
5. **NEVER REFREEZE BREAST MILK.**

relative to the amount of protein, carbohydrate, and fat. Most infant formulas are made from modified cow's milk or soy products and are available in powder, liquid concentrates, or as ready-to-feed liquids. Infants who have difficulty tolerating milk-based formulas may be switched to one that is soy-based. Although soy-based formulas are considered to be safe for infants, there has been some concern expressed about the plant-based estrogens they contain and their effect on infant growth. Soy can also cause allergic reactions in some infants (Joeckel & Phillips, 2009; Fine & Sehgal, 2008). Unmodified cow's milk should not be given to infants prior to 1 year of age because it often causes digestive disorders including intestinal bleeding. Goat's milk is also not recommended as it does not contain adequate nutrients.

Preparation of Formula

Safe preparation of formula is primarily dependent on two factors:

1. Sanitation—Sanitary formula preparation using **aseptic procedures** prevents serious illness that could result when bacteria are introduced into the formula. This requires carefully sanitizing all utensils used in preparing formula and washing hands carefully prior to mixing the formula. Sterilized (boiled) or bottled water should be used when preparing formula from a powdered concentrate. Honey should never be added to any formula for an infant younger than 1 year of age.

   ⚠ **Caution: Honey contains *Clostridium botulinum* spores, which, in an infant's intestine, can produce a dangerous, life-threatening toxin.**

   Each formula type (ready-to-feed, concentrated liquid, powdered) requires different preparation techniques that must be followed precisely according to the manufacturers' directions on the label.
2. Accuracy—Accurate measuring and mixing of formula (according to directions) ensures that the infant will receive needed calories and nutrients in the amounts required for optimal growth and development. Adding too much water dilutes the formula and the amount of nutrients the infant receives and will cause malnutrition. Adding too little water results in an "over-rich" formula that may cause digestive problems, excessive caloric intake, and obesity over time. Skim or low-fat milks should not be used in formula preparation because their low fat content is inadequate to satisfy infants' daily caloric needs in the amount (volume) they are able to consume. It is recommended that 40 to 50 percent of the infant's calories come from fat. Adequate fat intake also plays a critical role in normal brain and central nervous system development and is needed to form the myelin sheath, or the insulation, around new nerve fibers. Essential fatty acids (linolenic and linoleic) in breast milk and formulas are also required for healthy cell growth and visual system development. The equivalent of 1 tablespoon of a polyunsaturated fat, such as corn oil or safflower oil, will meet the infant's need for these essential fatty acids. Table 16–6 provides a summary of common infant formulas.

Feeding Time for the Infant

How often an infant needs to be fed is determined by the family, infant, and health-care provider. On-demand feeding is usually recommended, as this allows caregivers to adjust the amount and frequency of feedings to meet an infant's unique needs. An infant will signal when he/she is hungry and is, therefore, the best source of information about when to feed or not to feed. It is important that parents and teachers learn to read an infant's cues because not all crying indicates a need for

---

aseptic procedure – *treatment to produce a product that is free of disease-producing bacteria.*

Table 16–6 Examples of Common Infant Formulas

Standard Formulas		
Enfamil & Enfamil with Iron; Similac & Similac with Iron; SMA & SMA Lo Iron; Carnation Good Start	20 cal./oz.	Modified cow's milk
Soy Formulas		
Isomil; Nursoy; ProSobee; Soyalac; Carnation Alsoy & Gerber Soy Formula	20 cal./oz.	Hypoallergenic formula
Therapeutic Formulas		
Nutramigen; Pregestimil; Alimentum	20 cal./oz.	Hypoallergenic formula
Phenyl-Free 2	22 cal./oz.	For phenylketonurics (PKU)
Pedialyte	3 cal./oz.	Electrolyte/fluid replacement
Mead Johnson Lactofree; Lactose-Free (Ross)	20 cal./oz.	Lactose-free milk
Enfamil Premature; Enfamil 22; Similac Special Care; Similac NeoSure Advance	20 or 24 cal./oz.	Premature infant formula

additional food (Vecchio, Walter, & Leary, 2009). Noting the infant's body language as well as the tone, intensity, and length of crying can be helpful in determining if he or she is indeed hungry, distressed about a wet diaper, or simply wants to be picked up and held. Although the frequency and amount of feeding varies from infant to infant, typical guidelines suggest:

0–1 months	6 feedings of 3–4 oz./feeding
1–2 months	6 feedings of 3–5 oz./feeding
2–3 months	5 feedings of 4–6 oz./feeding
4–5 months	5 feedings of 5–7 oz./feeding
6–7 months*	5 feedings of 6–8 oz./feeding
8–12 months*	3 feedings of 8 oz./feeding

*Also taking solid foods

An infant who is consuming adequate formula (liquids) will usually have at least six or more wet diapers a day.

Feeding an infant involves much more than simply getting the nipple into the mouth. Cleanliness at feeding time is of prime importance. The caregiver's hands must be soap-washed prior to every feeding. Formula should be tested against the inside of the wrist to make sure that it is the right temperature for the infant to drink.

⚠ **Caution: Infant formula in the bottle should not be heated in a microwave. The fluid formula may become dangerously hot while the outside of the bottle feels cool. This method of heating has severely burned some infants.**

Feeding time should be relaxed and preceded by a few minutes of talking and playing with the infant. When adults cuddle, maintain eye contact, and talk with the infant they are satisfying critical social, emotional, and communication needs. The feeding experience also meets the infant's need for close human contact (bonding).

The infant should be held in a sitting position with his/her head resting against the caregiver's upper arm. The bottle should be tilted slightly upward to keep the nipple filled with formula and

Feedings should be relaxed and a time for social and emotional engagement with the infant.

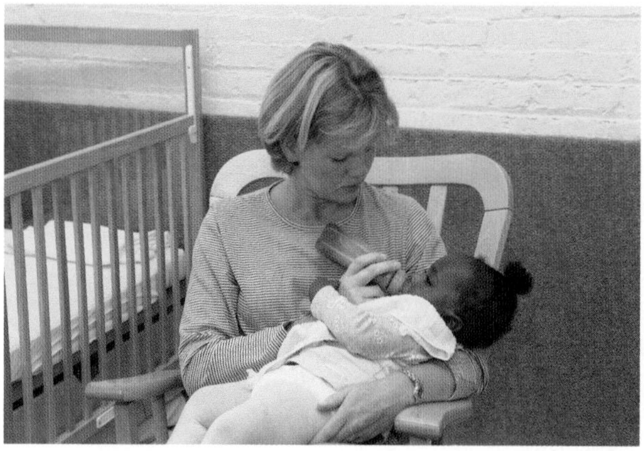

to prevent the infant from swallowing excess air, which can cause gas and **distention**. (See Figure 16–2 for examples of different nipples that can be used for bottle feeding.) Allow at least 20 minutes per feeding to avoid hurrying the infant. Infants will signal by turning their head away, releasing or playing with the nipple, or pushing away from the adult when they have had enough to eat. It is important to recognize these cues and not force the infant to take additional breast milk or formula.

Burping

Because infants naturally swallow air when sucking, they should be burped two or three times during the feeding and again when they have finished eating. The infant can be placed in either an upright position over the adult's shoulder or face-down across the adult's lap while gently patting or rubbing the infant's back. It is normal for infants, especially those who are formula-fed, to experience **regurgitation** and to spit up small amounts of their feeding. However, the frequency and amount of spit up generally decreases with age.

⚠ **Caution: An infant's bottle should never be propped up, nor should the baby ever be left unattended while feeding. Infants do not have sufficient motor control to remove the bottle from their mouth and may aspirate the breast milk or formula after they fall asleep. This practice also increases the risk of baby bottle tooth decay (BBTD) and ear infections.**

Figure 16–2 Different types of nipples.

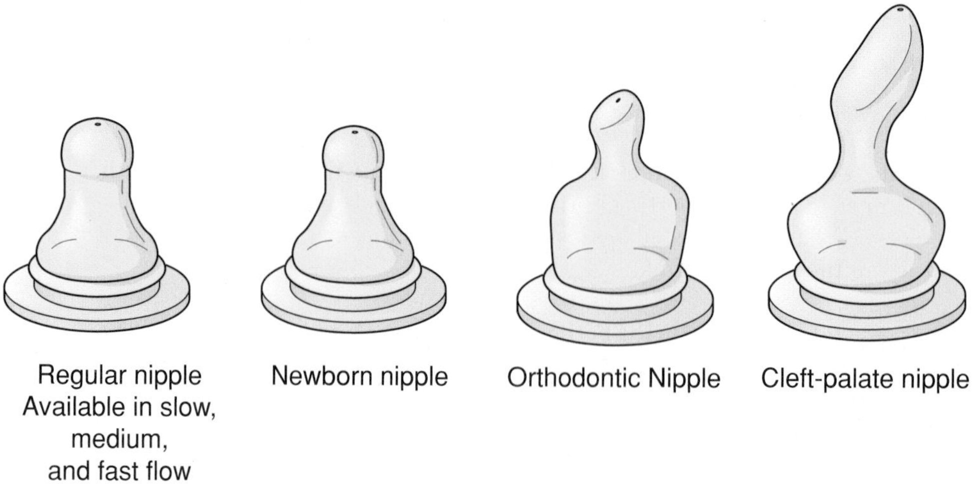

distention – *stretched or enlarged.*
regurgitation – *the return of partially digested food from stomach to mouth.*

Water

Until solid foods are added, breast milk or formula adequately meet the infant's water requirements. However, since infants have a greater need for water and are prone to dehydration, it is not safe to assume that formula will always meet their requirement. A thirsty infant often acts like a hungry baby. So, if the infant appears hungry shortly after feeding, a small amount of unflavored water can be offered. However, this amount should be limited to no more than 4 ounces daily so that it does not replace milk consumption. *Water sweetened with sugar or flavored drinks should not be fed to infants*; fluids with special **electrolytes** (salts and minerals) should only be given with a doctor's recommendation.

Infants should be burped during and after feedings.

Supplements

Vitamin and/or mineral supplements are sometimes recommended for infants. In general, breast milk or formula is adequate to meet most of the infant's nutritional needs with the exception of vitamin D and the mineral fluoride. Breastfed infants are usually given a vitamin D supplement; however, the formula-fed infant receives adequate amounts of this vitamin and should not be supplemented. Fluoride is present in breast milk in scant amounts and only added in low levels to concentrated and powdered formulas. However, the American Dental Association (ADA) and Academy of Pediatric Dentists (AAPD) do not recommend supplementation before 12 months of age because excess fluoride can have toxic effects and cause tooth discoloration (ADA, 2009). Infants who are breast fed longer than 6 months may require supplementation with iron because milk is a poor source of this mineral. Introducing iron-fortified foods around this time is also beneficial.

⚠ **Caution: Fluoride supplements combined with vitamin D are not safe to use with the formula-fed infant. Formulas are already fortified with vitamin D and excessive intake of this vitamin may have serious consequences for the infant.**

Introducing Semi-Solid (Pureed) Foods

The teacher, family, and health care professional must cooperate closely when infants are introduced to semi-solid foods. Finely cut, pureed foods high in fluid content, such as cereals, and pureed fruits and vegetables, can be introduced when the infant is around 5 and 6 months of age. Introducing semi-solid foods before this time is inappropriate because the infant does not demonstrate **developmental or physiological readiness**.

---

electrolytes – *substances that, when in solution, become capable of conducting electricity; examples include sodium and potassium.*

developmental or physiological readiness – *growth (both physical and cognitive) and chemical processes that lead to the ability to perform a function.*

Reflective Thoughts

Missy T. is the mother of 6-week-old Hayden. Hayden is Missy's first child. Missy's mother lives nearby and is happy to help out with Hayden's care. Missy complains of being tired and mentions to her mother that Hayden awakens several times during the night and acts hungry. Her mother advises her to add cereal to his bedtime bottle in order to "fill him up so he will sleep through the night." She also advises cutting larger holes in the nipple so the cereal won't block the opening.

- Should Missy follow her mother's advice?
- What are the dangers, if any, of feeding a 6-week-old baby cereal from the bottle?
- Do child care practices change from generation to generation?
- Consider possible short- and long-term consequences of feeding semi-solid food from a bottle.
- How would you respond if you were the teacher and a parent asked that you feed an infant in this manner?

Developmental Readiness

At approximately 5 months, infants develop the ability to move food to the back of their mouth and swallow without an initial sucking action. At this point, the baby is able to chew, to sit with some comfort, and to lean forward toward the spoon. At about 4 to 5 months, infants begin to show interest in touching, holding, and tasting objects—food and otherwise. It is important to note that at this age infants are able to turn their heads away from food when satisfied, signaling a desire to stop eating. This behavior should be noted, respected, and the offering of food stopped. Ignoring these signals can lead to overeating and obesity.

Older infants begin to show an interest in feeding themselves.

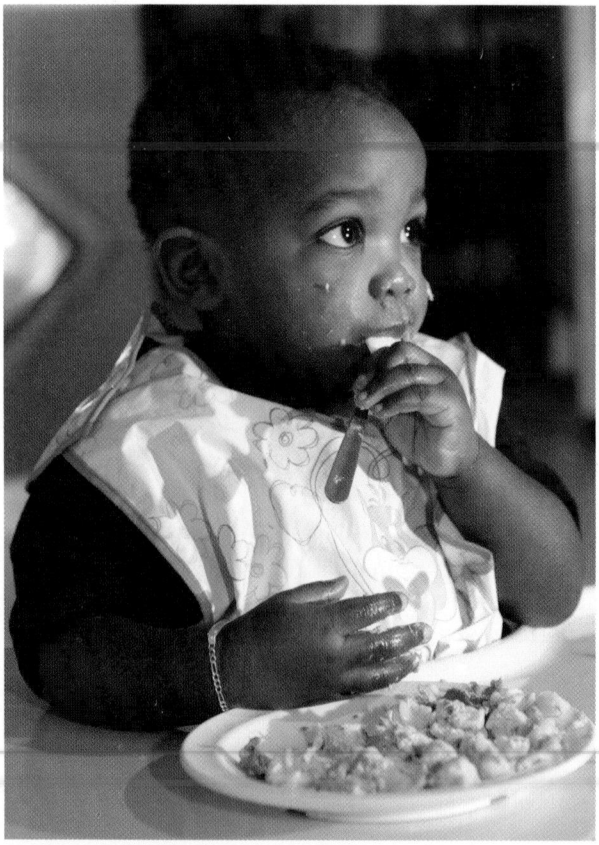

Physiological Readiness

By 5 to 6 months of age, the infant's digestive system has matured and is now able to metabolize complex carbohydrates and proteins other than milk protein. This is also about the time that the iron stores present at birth are nearly depleted. Semi-solid foods such as iron-enriched cereals and pureed vegetables and fruits can gradually be introduced into the infant's diet to replace iron reserves. High protein meat products should not be added until infants are approximately 6 to 8 months of age because their kidneys are not sufficiently developed to handle the nitrogen-containing wastes that result from digestion.

Table 16–7 presents age-related, developmental factors that may influence infant feeding behavior. However, it is important to remember that infants vary greatly in their rate of development (Allen & Marotz, 2010). Infants who have

Table 16–7 Age-Related Infant Eating Behaviors

Age	Common Infant Behaviors
1–3 months	• becomes fussy when hungry • turns face toward nipple • sucks vigorously but may choke on occasion
4–6 months	• assumes more symmetrical sitting position • grasps for objects • puts objects in mouth • may close hands around bottle • turns head away from food when no longer hungry • leans toward food-containing spoon
6–7 months	• teeth erupt • shows up and down chewing motions • grasps finger foods using entire hand (**palmar grasp**) and gets them to mouth • drinks small amounts of liquid from a cup • holds bottle with both hands
7–8 months	• sits alone with little support • uses finger and thumb (**pincer grip**) to pick up small food pieces • can better manipulate food in the mouth • is more successful when drinking from a cup • begins self-feeding with help
9–12 months	• can more precisely grasp and release objects • reaches for the spoon • feeds self with some help • drinks successfully from a cup • is more aware of surrounding environment • mimics motions and activities observed

developmental delays or special needs may take even longer to develop some of these skills. Differences in cultural practices may also influence when children are encouraged to attempt self-feeding (Pak-Gorstein, Haq, & Graham, 2009). Foods should be introduced according to the individual infant's abilities, interests, and nutritional needs.

New foods should be introduced slowly with only a few baby spoonfuls offered one or two times daily (see Table 16–1 for appropriate serving sizes). Iron-fortified infant cereals, such as rice or barley, are usually the first addition because they are less likely to cause allergic reactions. Cereals can be thinned with formula, breast milk, or water to make them more acceptable to the infant. Semi-solid foods should always be fed with a spoon and not from a bottle.

A suggested sequence for introducing solid foods is:

5–6 months	iron-enriched cereals
6–8 months	vegetables, followed by fruits
8–9 months	meat and meat substitutes

Initially, it is better to offer individual foods rather than mixtures. If an allergy or sensitivity develops, the offending food can be readily identified. Sugar, salt, and butter should not be added to an infant's food. Parents may choose to prepare pureed foods at home or purchase commercially prepared food. Either is acceptable as long as the foods are nutritionally adequate. Table foods (removed before they have been seasoned) can be pureed in a blender. For example, if the family is having baked

---

palmar grasp – *using the entire hand to pick up objects.*
pincer grip – *using the thumb and finger to pick up an object.*

Figure 16–3 Special labeling rules.

Nutrition Facts
Serving Size 1 jar (140g)

Amount Per Serving	
Calories 110	
Total Fat	0g
Sodium	10mg
Total Carbohydrate	27g
Dietary Fiber	4g
Sugars	18g
Protein	0g

% Daily Value	
Protein 0%	Vitamin A 6%
Vitamin C 45%	Calcium 2%
Iron 2%	

Nutrition Label for Foods for Children Under Four Years Old.

Nutrition Facts
Serving Size 1 jar (140g)

Amount Per Serving	
Calories 110	Calories from Fat 0
Total Fat	0g
Saturated Fat	0g
Cholesterol	0mg
Sodium	10mg
Total Carbohydrate	27g
Dietary Fiber	4g
Sugars	18g
Protein	0g

% Daily Value	
Protein 0%	Vitamin A 6%
Vitamin C 45%	Calcium 2%
Iron 2%	

Nutrition Label for Foods for Children Two to Four Years Old.

chicken, peas, and rice, an appropriate serving for the infant might be 2 tablespoons chicken, 2 tablespoons peas, and ¼ cup rice (all pureed). Preparing food in this manner can expose the infant to a wider variety of items and allows families to have more control over what is offered. Initially, it may be wise to limit high-fiber foods. Home-prepared pureed food can also be frozen in ice cube trays, removed after frozen and stored in a tightly sealed container, and thawed for use as needed.

If the decision is to use commercially prepared baby food, it is better to use plain fruits, vegetables, and meats rather than "dinners," or "desserts," which are often extended with starches and other additives. Information on the labels of commercially prepared infant and toddler foods should be read carefully in order to make healthful selections (Figure 16–3). Remember that ingredients on food labels are listed in descending order according to the amount present. The first ingredient in an acceptable infant food should always be fruit, vegetable, or meat—not water, cereal or other starch. When feeding a child prepared baby food, a small portion should be removed, placed in a bowl, and the rest of the jar's contents returned to the refrigerator. This reduces the chance of contaminating the remaining food with bacteria and enzymes found in the saliva, which can also cause the food to break down and become "watery."

Infants may begin to drink small amounts of liquid from a cup at about 6 to 7 months of age. An infant of such an age typically likes to help hold the cup and bring it to his/her mouth, although many spills should be expected. By 6 to 7 months, infants can pick up and chew on finger foods. Teeth are also beginning to erupt at this age, and the provision of "chew foods" such as dry toast or baby biscuits helps the teething process. (Refer to Table 16–1.)

Infants with Special Needs

Although eating appears to be a natural process, infants who are born prematurely or who have a range of health problems, including genetic disorders and congenital malformations, may present special feeding challenges and nutritional needs. For example, infants born with Down syndrome typically have weak facial muscles, which make sucking difficult and less efficient. Later, these children have a tendency to overeat and to gain excessive weight. Some infants may have conditions that require surgery, which can increase their need for certain nutrients at a time when they may not be receptive to food. It is especially important that infants with special needs obtain all of the nutrients necessary for healthy growth and brain development during the months following birth.

An infant's eating behaviors may be further challenged by infection, medication side effects, unpleasant medical treatments, swallowing difficulties, dental problems, special diets, and fatigue. These factors may make it difficult for the infant with special needs to eat and maintain an interest in food. Families may be referred to a feeding clinic where the infant's physical and nutritional needs can be evaluated and where they can receive assistance. Nutritional services are also available through Early Head Start, IDEA (Individuals with Disabilities Education Act, Part C), WIC (Special Supplemental Feeding Program for Women, Infants, and Children), hospital clinics, and other community-based programs.

Many infants with special needs are enrolled in early childhood programs today. Teachers must work closely with their families to learn as much about the child's condition, medical treatments, nutritional needs, and ways they can collaborate to assure the infant's healthy development.

Issues To Consider **Does Infant Formula Cause Type 1 Diabetes?**

Reports have identified a possible link between cow's milk-based formulas and an increased incidence of **type 1 diabetes** (Lempainen et al., 2009). The implication is that protein in cow's milk might precipitate type 1 diabetes; children who developed diabetes have shown elevated levels of antibodies to these proteins. The American Academy of Pediatrics strongly encourages breastfeeding and the avoidance of cow's milk and products containing cow's milk proteins during the first year, especially for infants with a strong family history of type 1 diabetes. The concern is even greater for infants who may have a sibling with diabetes.

- What implications does this study have for breastfeeding recommendations?
- If a family prefers to bottle feed an infant, what formula options are available?
- Why do you think the American Academy of Pediatrics recommends avoidance of cow's milk protein for just the first year?

Some Common Feeding Concerns

Allergies

One of the most common chronic conditions affecting infants is allergies. Allergic responses to food may cause a variety of symptoms such as runny nose, diarrhea, constipation, bloating, vomiting, hives, and eczema (Reda, 2009; Schroeder et al., 2009). These symptoms are not specific for any given food and should be discussed with the infant's physician.

If a family has a history of allergies, it is recommended that the introduction of semi-solid foods be delayed until the infant is at least 6 months of age (Anderson, Malley, & Snell, 2009). Certain foods such as citrus juice(s), eggs, cereal products other than rice, chocolate, nuts and nut butters, and fish/shellfish are common allergens and, thus, their addition to the infant's diet should be delayed.

If an infant seems to experience an allergic reaction to a specific food, it should be eliminated from the diet and reintroduced at a later time. If a milk-based formula seems to be the offending food, it may be necessary to replace it with one formulated from modified proteins or soybeans.

Children should be observed carefully for potential allergic reactions when new foods are introduced.

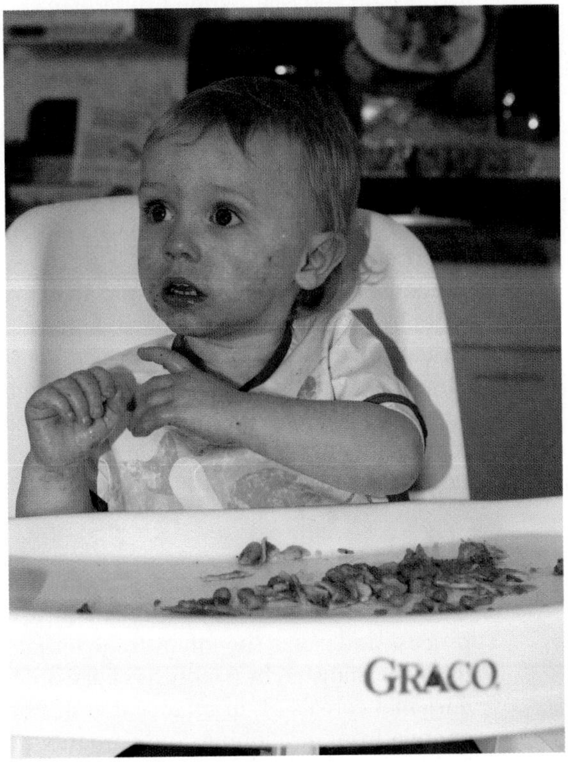

Colic

Some seemingly healthy infants (3–16 weeks of age) may develop colic, which causes abdominal discomfort, cramping, and prolonged periods of intense crying (O'Connor, 2009). The distress occurs most often in late afternoon and evening and at approximately the same time each day.

type 1 diabetes – *a disease distinguished by a lack of insulin production; usually diagnosed in childhood or young adulthood.*

Consoling these infants is difficult and typically ineffective. Although the exact cause of colic is unknown there is some evidence to suggest that reflux may be a contributing factor and that, if formula fed, changing the type of formula will sometimes relieve the infant's symptoms (Morin, 2009; Orenstein, 2008). Mothers who are breastfeeding should continue to do so, but may want to monitor their diet for highly spiced or strongly flavored foods that may trigger or contribute to the infant's discomfort. Fortunately, most infants outgrow colic at about 3 to 4 months of age.

Vomiting and Diarrhea

Common causes of vomiting and diarrhea in infants include:

- food allergies or food sensitivities
- overfeeding
- infections: systemic or food-borne
- eating food that the baby is not yet ready for
- incorrect formula preparation
- use of fruit juice
- swallowed air
- reflux

It is typical for young infants to spit up and/or to vomit. The muscle (sphincter), positioned at the stomach opening, is responsible for keeping stomach contents in place. This sphincter takes longer to develop and to function properly in some young infants (between 1and 6 weeks of age), causing them to spit up after almost every feeding. Back arching, difficulty feeding, and pulling away from the nipple are also common symptoms. This condition, known as gastroesophageal reflux (GER), is often resolved by feeding the infant in an upright position, changing formula type, and maturation. It is recognized as a disease (GERD) when it interferes with feeding and growth or causes the infant to wheeze, cough, or stop breathing (Smith, Ziegler, & Gladson, 2009).

Fluid and **electrolyte** replacement is a primary consideration when an infant has repeated vomiting and diarrhea. Infants who experience diarrhea should receive approximately 3 ounces of fluid per pound of body weight. There are also numerous ready-to-feed (RTF) rehydrating formulas available (Pedialyte, Infalyte, and Rehydralyte); parents should check with their health care provider before giving infants these solutions. Fruit juices, carbonated beverages, tea, or adult electrolyte formulas are not recommended because of their high sugar and low electrolyte content. The ultimate goal is gradual progression or return to the infant's normal diet.

Acute diarrhea due to an infection, and characterized by accompanying fever, must be attended to immediately. The infant's physician should be contacted for advice and consistent efforts should be made to replace lost fluids and electrolytes.

Anemia

Inadequate iron intake can result in low-hemoglobin-type anemia that may delay the growth process and cause the infant to be lethargic (Zhenyu et al., 2009). Iron stores present at birth are usually exhausted by 6 months of age unless the infant is on an iron-fortified formula. Adding iron-enriched cereals to an infant's diet at about 5 to 6 months of age is usually sufficient to prevent anemia from developing. Some infants may experience constipation or diarrhea when placed on an iron-fortified formula.

Baby Bottle Tooth Decay (BBDT)

Infants who are allowed to recline or sleep with a bottle or breast in their mouth may develop baby bottle tooth decay. This condition is characterized by a high rate of tooth decay caused by the pooling of sugar-containing formula, breast milk, or juices in the baby's mouth. Infants should finish feeding and have their gums cleaned before going down to sleep. Weaning infants to a cup at about 8 months of age also reduces the risk of developing this problem.

Ear Infection

Propping the bottle up so the infant may lie down and feed without being held can lead to a higher rate of ear infections (Morris & Leach, 2009). A child should be held in a semi-upright position during feedings to prevent milk from traveling back into the eustachian tubes and ear canals.

Obesity

Obesity results when energy intake exceeds an infant's need for energy for growth, maintenance, and activity. Infant feeding practices thought to play a role in obesity include overeating during bottle feeding, introduction of semi-solid foods too early, and feeding cereal from a bottle. (Butte, 2009; Griffiths et al., 2009).

It is important to be alert to signs that a baby is satisfied. Stopping periodically during the feeding gives the infant a chance to assess his/her own hunger and respond appropriately when the bottle is again offered. It is important to respect an infant's judgment of the amount of food needed at a given time. Urging an infant to finish milk remaining in a bottle may ignore his or her signs of fullness, which include:

- closing the mouth or turning away from the bottle
- falling asleep
- fussing at repeated attempts to continue feeding
- biting or playing with the nipple

Some authorities believe that continuously ignoring these signs may cause the infant to stop communicating signals and, thus, end an important means of regulating food intake. This could have serious consequences later on for children and adults who no longer know when to stop eating. To establish the point at which the infant is satisfied, the teacher might stop after a few minutes of solid-food feeding and play with the child before offering more food. This helps in determining whether the infant is eating because of hunger or to gain attention.

Introducing semi-solid foods to infants before they are old enough or giving them foods high in sugar and/or fat may cause them to take in more calories than are needed and can lead to obesity (Grummer-Strawn, Scalon, & Fein, 2008). Continuing to offer solid food after the infant seems satisfied also contributes to obesity and may set the stage for overeating later in life.

Choking

Choking can be avoided during breast or bottle feeding by holding the child properly with the head elevated as previously described. Allowing the infant to lie down with the bottle propped up greatly increases this danger. When 6- to 7-month-old infants begin to eat finger foods such as dry bread, crackers, or dry cereal, they must be monitored closely because these items may increase the risk of choking. This danger can be minimized by having the infant sit in an upright position and breaking foods into small pieces that are easy to chew and swallow. Offering semi-solid food that is finely ground and somewhat diluted will also minimize choking. Because the majority of choking instances occur in infants, it is essential that parents and teachers be prepared by completing CPR training.

Teething

Teeth begin to erupt around 6 months of age. This can be a stressful period for some infants and may temporarily disrupt their feeding pattern. As a result, some infants may begin to wean themselves from breast or bottle feedings. They may prefer foods that can be chewed such as dry cereal pieces, toast, or teething biscuits. Diarrhea accompanying teething is usually due to infectious organisms and is not caused by the teething process. Appropriate toys and food items should be made available to discourage infants from picking up and chewing on inappropriate or unsafe objects. In an early childhood program, it is important to ensure that toys are frequently sanitized to reduce the risk of spreading infectious organisms.

Constipation

Breast-fed infants are generally not troubled by constipation. Because breast milk is so easily digested, only a small amount of waste product remains to be excreted. Infants who are formula-fed, especially with soy-based or iron-enriched products, may experience more problems with constipation. Giving them additional water is often sufficient to address the problem. However, if the formula-fed infant fails to have a bowel movement for more than three or four days, the family should contact their health care provider for advice.

Focus On Families — Infant Feeding

A majority of food preferences carried into adulthood evolve from childhood and childhood eating experiences. Birth (or before) is the ideal time to begin addressing a child's nutritional well-being.

- Breast milk and/or infant formula is recommended as the infant's primary source of nutrition for the first year. Cow's milk cannot meet the infant's nutritional requirements for rapid growth rate and should not be offered during the first year.
- Always hold and bond with an infant during feedings. This practice fosters important emotional connections between the infant and adults. It also helps to prevent choking and baby bottle tooth decay.
- The first food introduced into an infant's diet should be a single-grain iron-fortified cereal. Introduce foods one at a time and for several days to detect possible allergies/intolerances.
- Be wary of food additives, especially in commercially produced baby food. "Desserts" and "dinners" often contain additives and offer less nutritional value than plain cereal, vegetables, fruits, and meats.
- 100 percent fruit juice can be introduced at approximately 6 to 7 months of age.
- Avoid fruit beverages, fruit drinks, sodas, and tea that provide no nutrients.
- Avoid foods that cause choking: grapes, peanuts, hotdogs, and popcorn.

Classroom Corner — Teacher Activities

Planning Healthy Snacks... **(PreK–2; grades 3-5; National Health Education Standards 1.2.1, 2.2.3, 6.2.1; 1.5.1, 2.5.5, 6.5.1)**

Concept: Concept: Healthy food choices provide important energy.

Learning Objectives

- Children will learn to plan healthy snacks.
- Children will identify foods that help bodies to stay healthy.

(continued)

Classroom Corner **Teacher Activities** *(continued)*

Supplies

- Paper
- Crayons or markers
- Computer and Internet access (for older children)
- Food Guide Pyramid poster (can be printed from http://www.mypyramid.gov)
- Magazine pictures of healthy snack items
- Glue sticks

Learning Activities

- Discuss the importance of choosing healthy snacks (e.g., growth, energy, staying healthy/not sick). Use the Food Guide Pyramid to talk about foods that are considered healthy and why it is important to select a variety of foods from each group, including some that are new.
- Draw a grid on a large sheet of paper (for each day of the week). Have younger children plan a week's worth of afternoon snacks; teachers can fill in the grid with foods that children name or children can glue food pictures from magazines onto the grid. Older children can explore the Food Pyramid online and learn about healthy food options before developing their menu. Ask the cook to prepare snacks from the children's menu; older children may be able to prepare their own snacks each day.

Evaluation

- Children will make healthy food choices and state why this is important.
- Children will use the menu to create a healthy snack plan.

Summary

- The first year of an infant's life is one of very rapid growth and change.
  - The infant will have tripled its birth weight and increased its length by 50 percent.
  - Growth and development are supported by meeting an infant's needs for all essential nutrients.
- Breast milk or formula will meet all of an infant's nutrient needs for growth and development during the first 4 to 6 months
- Infants are developmentally and physiologically ready for semi-solid foods at around 5 to 6 months of age.
  - Single-grain cereals are the first semi-solid foods added at around 5 to 6 months.
  - Vegetables, fruits, and meats are introduced over the next 3 months.
- Caregivers must anticipate common food-related problems, such as allergies, colic, vomiting and diarrhea, anemia, ear infection, obesity, and choking, that infants may develop.

Terms to Know

prenatal *p. 390*
low-birthweight (LBW) infant *p. 390*
antibodies *p. 392*
aseptic procedure *p. 394*
distention *p. 396*
regurgitation *p. 396*
electrolyte(s) *p. 397*
developmental readiness or physiological readiness *p. 397*
palmar grasp *p. 399*
pincer grip *p. 399*
type 1 diabetes *p. 401*

Chapter Review

A. By Yourself:

1. Provide a rationale for why an infant's bottle should not be propped up during a feeding.
2. In what order should the following foods be introduced?

   pureed peas   pureed meat products
   crisp toast   pureed peaches
   iron-fortified cereal

3. At approximately what age should each of these foods be introduced?
4. Describe three social factors that make feeding time more enjoyable for an infant.
5. Explain why unmodified cow's or goat's milk should not be given to an infant before 1 year of age.
6. Why should caregivers hold and talk to an infant while he/she is being fed?

B. As a Group:

1. Discuss why it is important not to feed infants semi-solid foods before 5 to 6 months of age.
2. Debate the advantages/disadvantages of breastfeeding versus formula feeding.
3. Describe several feeding practices that are considered to contribute to infant obesity.
4. Discuss baby bottle tooth decay (BBDT) and feeding practices that will prevent this condition.
5. Evaluate the nutrient contributions of several commercial baby foods using the website: www.nal.usda.gov/fnic/foodcomp/search. Make recommendations based on your findings.

Case Study

Lindsey, 5 months old, has begun attending a child care program as her mother recently returned to work. Lindsey was started on cereal mixed with pureed fruit prior to entering child care. Lindsey's mother pumps and freezes her breast milk and delivers it to the center to be thawed and fed as needed. Lindsey is now experiencing some diarrhea and apparent abdominal pain.

1. What are some possible causes of Lindsey's discomfort?
2. Do you know how the breast milk is handled at home?
3. What are safe procedures for handling breast milk at child care?
4. Given Lindsey's age, is she ready to have fruit added to her diet?
5. What other food/liquids could be used to mix in her cereal; what type of cereal should she be fed?

Application Activities

1. Mrs. Jones, mother of 2-month-old Kelly, has been on maternity leave from her job. She is preparing to return to work and has made arrangements for Kelly to stay in a nearby family child care home. Mrs. Jones wants to continue breastfeeding, but is concerned that she will have to change Kelly to formula. In what ways can the care provider support Mrs. Jones' interests in continuing to breastfeed?

2. Visit the baby food section of the local grocery store and read the ingredients listed on the food labels. Based on the ingredients listed, select several items that would be nutritious choices for a young infant.
3. Plan an instructional manual for new employees in an infant care facility. What social aspects of infant feeding should be addressed in addition to nutritional and sanitation factors?
4. If applicable, review state regulations relating to infant feeding guidelines in early childhood programs. Comment on the adequacy of information provided.
5. Review common problems associated with low-birthweight infants. What prenatal nutrient deficiencies often result in the birth of low-birthweight infants?

Helpful Web Resources

Administration for Children & Families	http://www.acf.hhs.gov
Healthy Children.org (AAP)	http://www.healthychildren.org
Keep Kids Healthy	http://www.keepkidshealthy.com
La Leche League	http://www.lalecheleague.org
National Network for Childcare	http://www.nncc.org
Women's Health.Gov	http://www.womenshealth.gov
Public Health Agency of Canada	http://www.phac-aspc.gc.ca

You are just a click away from additional health, safety, and nutrition resources! Go to www. CengageBrain.com to access this text's Education CourseMate website, where you'll find:

- glossary flashcards, activities, tutorial quizzes, videos, web links, and more

References

Allen, K., & Marotz, L. (2010). *Developmental profiles*. (6th ed.). Belmont, CA: Wadsworth Cengage.

American Academy of Family Physicians (AAFP). (2007). "Breastfeeding, family physicians supporting (Position Paper)." Accessed on February 20, 2010 from http://www.aafp.org/online/en/home/policy/policies/b/breastfeedingpositionpaper. html.

American Academy of Pediatrics (AAP). (2005). Breastfeeding and the use of human milk, *Pediatrics*, 115(2), 496–506.

American Dental Association.(ADA). (2009). "Fluoride and fluoridation." Accessed on January 10, 2010 from http://www.ada.org/public/topics/fluoride/fluoride_article01.asp#dosage.

Anderson J,, Malley K,, & Snell R. (2009). Is 6 months still the best for exclusive breastfeeding and introduction of solids? *Breastfeeding Review*, 17(2), 23–31.

Butte, N. (2009). Impact of infant feeding practices on childhood obesity, *Journal of Nutrition*, 139(2), 412S–416S.

Fine, B., & Sehgal, S. (2008). Caution with committee recommendations for soy protein-based formulas, *Pediatrics*, 121(5), 1062–1068.

Griffiths, L., Smeeth, L., Hawkins, S., Colel, T., & Dezateux, C. (2009). Effects of infant feeding practice on weight gain from birth to 3 years, *Archives of Disease in Childhood*, 94(8), 577–582.

Grummer-Strawn, L., Scalon, K., & Fein, S. (2008). Infant feeding and feeding transitions during the first year of life, *Pediatrics*, 122(2 Suppl.), S36–42.

James, D., & Lessen, R. (2009). Position of the American Dietetic Association: Promoting and supporting breastfeeding, *Journal of the American Dietetic Association*, 109(11), 1926–1942.

Joeckel, R., & Phillips, S. (2009). Overview of infant and pediatric formulas, *Nutrition in Clinical Practice*, 24(3), 356–362.

Lempainen, J., Vaarala, O., Mäkelä, M., Veijola, R., Simell, O., Knip, M., Hermann, R., & Illonen, J. (2009). Interplay between PTPN22 C1858T polymorphism and cow's milk formula exposure in type 1 diabetes, *Journal of Autoimmunity*, 33(2), 155–164.

Morin, K. (2009). Infant nutrition: The challenge of colic in infants, *The American Journal of Maternal & Child Nursing*, 34(3), 192–198.

Morris, P., & Leach, A. (2009). Acute and chronic otitis media, *Pediatric Clinics of North America*, 56(6), 1383–1399.

Mueller-Nix, C., & Forcad-Guex, M. (2009). Perinatal assessment of infant, parents, and parent-infant relationship: Prematurity as an example, *Child and Adolescent Psychiatric Clinics of North America*, 18(3) 545–557.

O'Connor, N. (2009). Infant formula, *American Family Physician*, 79(7), 565–570.

Orenstein, S. (2008). Crying in infant GERD: Acid, or volume? Heartburn or dyspepsia?, *Current Gastroenterology Reports*, 10(5), 433–436.

Pak-Gorstein, S., Haq, A., & Graham, E. (2009). Cultural influences on infant feeding practices, *Pediatrics in Review*, 30(3), e11–e21.

Reda, S. (2009). Gastrointestinal manifestations of food allergy, *Pediatric Health*, 3(3), 217–229.

Richards, R., Merrill, R., Baksh, L., & McGarry, J. (2009). Maternal nutrition-related behaviors and infant health outcomes according to homeless and WIC participation status from 31 PRAMS states/cities, *Journal of Nutrition Education & Behavior*, 41(4), S22– S32.

Schroeder, A., Kumar, R., Pongracic, J., Sullivan, C., Caruso, D., Costello, J., Meyer, K., Vucic, Y., Gupta, R., Kim, J., Fuleihan, R., & Wang, X. (2009). Food allergy is associated with an increased risk of asthma, *Clinical & Experimental Allergy*, 39(2), 261–270.

Smith, T., Ziegler, J., & Gladson, B. (2009). Pediatric gastroesophageal reflux disease, *Topics in Clinical Nutrition*, 24(2), 114–121.

Tanaka, K., Kon, N., Ohkawa, N., Yoshikawa, N., & Shimizu, T. (2009). Does breastfeeding in the neonatal period influence the cognitive function of very-low-birth-weight infants at 5 years of age? *Brain and Development*, 31(4), 288–293.

U.S. Department of Agriculture. (2009). "WIC Program data: National level annual summary." Accessed on January 10, 2010 from http://www.fns.usda.gov/pd/37WIC_Monthly.htm.

Vecchio, T., Walter, A., & Leary, S. (2009). Affective and physiological factors predicting maternal response to infant crying, *Infant Behavior & Development*, 32(1), 117–122.

Walker, A. (2010). Breast milk as the gold standard for protective nutrients, *Journal of Pediatrics*, 156(2 Suppl.), S3–7.

Wu, T., & Chen, P. (2009). Affective and physiological factors predicting maternal response to infant crying, *Infant Behavior and Development*, 32(1), 117–122.

Zhenyu, Y., Lönnerdal, B., Adu-Afarwuah, S., Brown, K., Chaparro, C., Cohen, R., Domellöf, M., Hernell, O., Lartey, A., & Dewey, K. (2009). Prevalence and predictors of iron deficiency in fully breastfed infants at 6 mo of age: Comparison of data from 6 studies, *American Journal of Clinical Nutrition*, 89(5), 1433–1440.

CHAPTER 17

Feeding Toddlers and Young Children

NAEYC Standards *Chapter Links*

- **#1 a, b, and c:** Promoting child development and learning
- **#2 a, b, and c:** Building family and community relationships
- **#3 a, b, and d:** Observing, documenting, and assessing to support young children and families
- **#4 a, b, and d:** Using developmentally effective approaches to connect with children and families
- **#5 a, and c:** Using content knowledge to build meaningful curriculum
- **#6 c:** Becoming a professional

Learning Objectives

After studying this chapter, you should be able to:

- Provide a word picture describing the characteristics of a typical toddler.
- Describe the physical and behavioral characteristics typical of preschool- and school-aged children.
- Explain why it is important to help young children establish healthy eating habits.
- Identify and discuss three health problems related to unhealthy eating patterns during early childhood.

Developmental Profile of Toddlers, Preschoolers, and School-Aged Children

Toddlers (1- to 2½-year-olds) are delightful individuals, but they can also be challenging at times. They are beginning to assert their independence yet need and want limits. They have an insatiable curiosity, yet prefer most things to be predictable and always done the same way. They are becoming increasingly mobile and active, but still need to be monitored closely and protected from unsafe conditions in their environment.

Many toddlers spend considerable time each day in early education programs while their parents work or attend school. These opportunities expose children to social and eating experiences that often differ from those they are accustomed to in their home. Children begin to learn that other people may do things differently but this doesn't necessarily translate into a willingness to join in.

Many toddlers also become avid television watchers. What they see is likely to affect their behavior, including their food preferences. Foods advertised on popular children's television programs are often of poor nutrient quality. Researchers have found that a majority of these commercials create a desire for foods high in calories, refined sugars, and fat (Dorey & McCool, 2009). Furthermore, hours spent sitting in front of the television reduce valuable time that toddlers should be spending involved in active play. Inactivity reduces the amount of calories that are burned and can ultimately contribute to childhood obesity (Cecil-Karb & Grogan-Kaylor, 2009).

Although toddlers are growing at a much slower rate than they did as infants, they continue to need adequate calories and essential nutrients to maintain growth and activity levels. However, the amount of food they are willing and able to eat often seems insufficient to adults. Because their stomach capacity is still quite small and their attention span is limited, it is best to maintain a consistent schedule for eating. Yet toddlers may resist this schedule and reject the foods served as they struggle for control. They have learned the power of the word "no" and use it repeatedly. They quickly learn to shape adults' behavior by refusing to eat or, at other times, by eating to gain adult favor.

The toddler is often described as being **neophobic,** especially when it comes to eating—that is, they exhibit a fear or reluctance of trying foods that are new or unfamiliar (Dovey et al., 2008). This behavior may limit the toddler's willingness to eat an increasing variety of foods. However, understanding that this behavior is characteristic of toddlers can help families and teachers be a bit more patient and ingenious as they begin to introduce new foods into children's diet.

Preschool-aged children (2½- to 6-year-olds) are generally more easygoing and cooperative. They are willing to listen and to follow adult directions in an effort to please, but are not always compliant. Although they prefer to do things for themselves, they may need a bit of adult assistance to be successful. Structure continues to be important for preschoolers, who are also more likely to respect it than did toddlers. They are learning more appropriate ways of expressing themselves, yet may still be somewhat hesitant to accept change at times. Families and teachers can anticipate that many of these developmental characteristics will be reflected in the preschooler's eating behaviors and responses to food.

Preschool-age children prefer to do things by themselves, but may still need adult assistance.

School-aged children are becoming increasingly aware of a much bigger world. They are energetic, curious, eager to learn, and able to understand situations that are more complex. Friends and friendships gradually replace time spent with family, although school-aged children still need and find comfort in knowing they can rely on their parents. Watching television, playing electronic games, and participating in organized activities now consume more of their time.

Family meal practices, including cultural eating habits and food preferences, remain an important factor in determining the school-aged child's mealtime behaviors (Deshmukh-Taskar et al., 2007). However, the favorite foods of friends and peers also begin to influence their food choices.

---

neophobic – *fear of things that are new and unfamiliar.*

School-aged children enjoy helping with meal planning, grocery shopping, and food preparation. Their appetite is generally good, but it also tends to fluctuate with growth spurts and activity levels.

The Challenge of Feeding Toddlers

Toddlers are beginning to assert their independence and to let their preferences be known. This includes their firm announcement of what foods they will or will not eat. Fortunately, their "will" and "will not" foods change almost daily. However, great care must be taken so that families and teachers do not become involved in a battle of wills over what the toddler will eat and when it will be eaten. Mealtime friction can be minimized by respecting adult and child responsibilities in the feeding relationship (Satter, 2000). Adults are responsible for:

- serving a variety of nutritious foods
- deciding when food is offered
- setting a good example by eating a variety of foods

The child is responsible for:

- choosing what foods will be eaten from those that have been offered
- deciding how much of the offered food to eat

What Foods Should Be Served and How Much

Families and teachers have a responsibility to provide children with a variety of nutritious foods each day. As discussed in Chapter 12, the Food Guide Pyramid guidelines are easy to follow and ensure that children's daily nutritional needs will be met (Figure 17–1, or visit www.MyPyramid.gov/kids). Table 17–1 presents a summary of recommended amounts that children should consume from each food group daily.

When feeding toddlers, it is preferable to serve slightly less than they are expected to eat. In this way toddlers are not overwhelmed by the amount of food on their plates and are able to assert their independence by asking for more. Appropriate serving sizes for toddlers are approximately one-fourth of an adult serving for each food group with the exception of the Milk group (see Figure 17–2):

Milk – 1/2 cup
Meat – 1 ounce
Fruits and Vegetables – 2 tablespoons
Breads and Cereals– 2 tablespoons rice, cereal, or pasta; 1/2 slice bread

The toddler's acceptance of foods is highly influenced by their sensory qualities, especially taste, texture, and temperature. Young children's mouths are very sensitive to temperature extremes; foods that are too cold or too hot will often be refused. Hot foods that are comfortable for adults may burn the toddler's mouth. Toddlers also have an abundance of taste buds that intensify the flavors of some foods. This may explain, in part, why toddlers often refuse vegetables such as broccoli, spinach, brussels sprouts, and beets. Food textures may also be challenging, especially as toddlers are transitioning from soft, pureed foods to table foods. They still have an active gag reflex and are also prone to choking. For this reason, foods must be cut into small pieces (1/4 inch) that are easy for toddlers to pick up and chew. They also prefer foods to be served individually (and not touching) rather than in mixtures. For example, instead of serving spaghetti and meatballs, green beans, and a mixed fruit salad, the same basic foods could be presented as:

- Ground beef patty
- Green beans
- Whole grain bread or pasta
- Diced peaches
- Milk

Figure 17–1 Food Guide Pyramid for children.

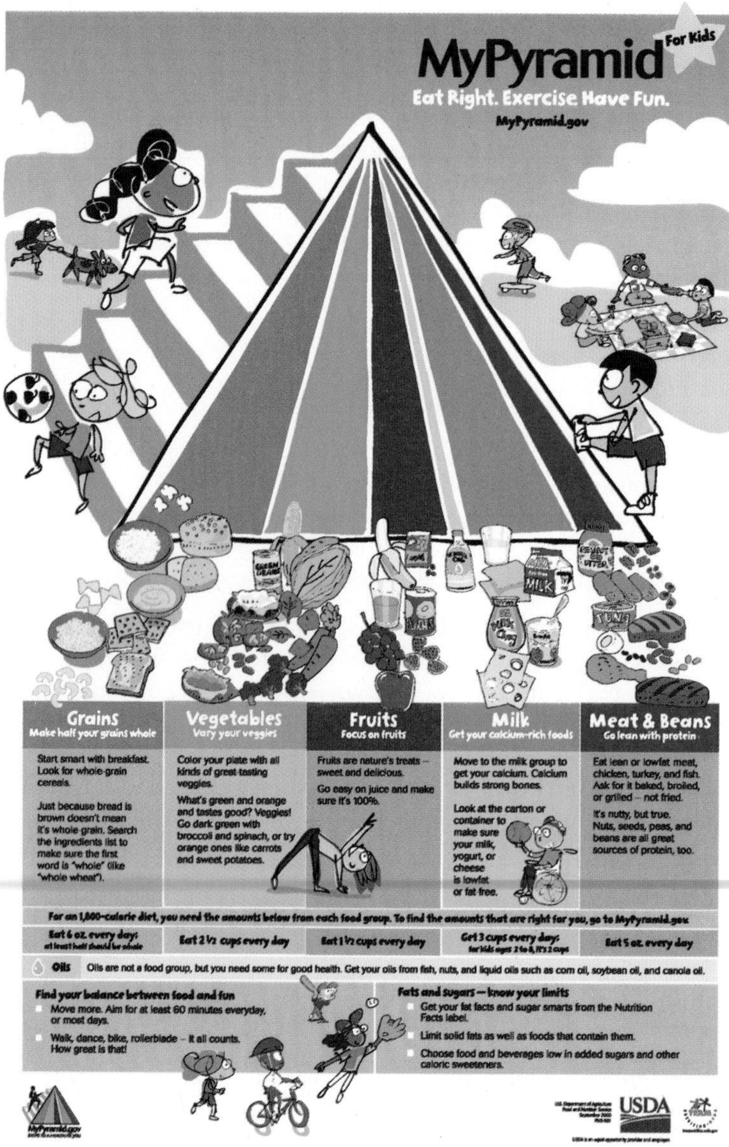

Table 17–1 Recommended Daily Food Group Intakes

Food Group	Toddlers	Preschoolers	School-Aged
Grains	3 ounces	4–5 ounces	5–6 ounces
Vegetables	1 cup	1½ cups	2–2½ cups
Fruits	1 cup	1–1½ cups	1½ cups
Milk	2 cups	2 cups	3 cups
Meat & Beans	2 ounces	3–4 ounces	5 ounces
Oils		use sparingly	

Figure 17–2 Sample menu with serving sizes for toddlers.

BREAKFAST	LUNCH	DINNER
Whole milk (1/2 cup)	Whole milk (1/2 cup)	Whole milk (1/2 cup)
Cream of wheat (1/4 cup)	Beef patty (1 oz)	Finely diced chicken (1 oz)
or	Broccoli (2 tbsp)	Cooked carrots (2 tbsp)
Whole wheat toast (1/2 slice)	Diced watermelon (2 tbsp)	Diced plums (2 tbsp)
Jam or Jelly (1 tsp)	Whole wheat bread (1/2 slice)	Rye bread (1/2 slice)
Diced peaches (1/4 cup)	Margarine (1 tsp)	Margarine (1 tsp)
MIDMORNING SNACK	**MIDAFTERNOON SNACK**	**EVENING SNACK**
Vanilla wafers (3)	Cheese cube (1/2 oz)	Applesauce (1/2 cup)
Orange juice (1/2 cup)	Whole wheat crackers (2)	Graham crackers (2)
	Water	Water

Remember that toddlers typically experience a decreased appetite due to their slower rate of growth so that adults should not become overly concerned if children are now eating less. It is important to avoid pressuring, nagging, or forcing children to eat more food than they want or need. Doing so can cause food to take on an emotional association and potentially lead to eating disorders.

Table 17–2 presents an overview of age-related eating behaviors that may be helpful in understanding children's changing responses to food. Adults can use this knowledge to establish realistic expectations and to create positive feeding experiences for children of all ages.

When to Serve Food

The timing of meals and snacks is an important consideration when feeding toddlers. Too much time between feedings will result in an overly hungry, cranky child who may lose interest in food when it is finally presented. Meals and snacks spaced too closely together will not allow ample time for a child to become hungry, again resulting in a poor eating response. Most young children also eat better at meals if they are not tired and if they have been given an advance warning so they can "wrap up" their play activities. Allowing time for a quiet story before mealtime can set the stage for a pleasant, relaxed, and more satisfying mealtime experience for everyone.

Because toddlers have a critical need for nutrients and a small stomach capacity, they must eat more often than the three-meal family pattern. An ideal eating pattern includes:

- breakfast
- mid-morning snack
- lunch
- mid-afternoon snack
- dinner
- bedtime snack, if needed

Snacks chosen from the Food Guide Pyramid can be planned to fulfill a portion of the child's daily nutrient intake. Foods commonly promoted on television as "snacks," such as chips, snack cakes,

Table 17–2 Age-Related Eating Behaviors

Age	Behavior
12–24 months	Has a decreased appetite Is sometimes described as a finicky or fussy eater; may go on food jags Uses spoon with some degree of skill Helps feed self
2-year-old	Has fair appetite Expresses strong likes and dislikes; may go on food jags Prefers simple food, dislikes mixtures, wants food served in familiar ways Learns table manners by imitating adults and older children
3-year-old	Has fairly good appetite; prefers small servings; likes only a few cooked vegetables Feeds self independently, if hungry Uses spoon in semi-adult fashion; may spear with fork and spread with a blunt knife Dawdles over food when not hungry
4- to 5-year-old	Eats well, but not at every meal May develop dislikes of certain foods and refuse them to the point of tears if pushed; often adapts to preferences of family and teachers Enjoys helping with meal preparation Uses all eating utensils; becomes skilled at spreading jelly or peanut butter, pouring milk on cereal, or cutting soft foods such as bread
6- to 7-year-old	Has good appetite; eats most foods Is willing to try new foods but is unpredictable Able to use eating utensils, but not always correctly Easily distracted; has difficulty sitting through a meal
8- to 9-year-old	Usually has a good appetite; boys eat more than girls Prefers to eat when hungry rather than at specified times Is open to trying new foods, but prefers certain "favorites" Enjoys cooking Eats quickly so they can resume previous activity
10- to 12-year-old	Always hungry; seems to eat non-stop and large amounts at one time Needs a big snack after school Dislikes few foods; interested in trying foods from other cultures and those seen on television Seems to forget manners that were previously learned

Adapted from Allen, K. E., & Marotz, L. R. (2010). *Developmental profiles: Pre-birth to twelve*. (6th ed.). Belmont, CA: Wadsworth Cengage.

frosted cookies, candy bars, fruit "drinks," and sodas have no place in the toddler's daily meal pattern. These foods consist primarily of empty calories and provide little if any nutritional value. Healthy snack choices include:

- cheese cubes and pita wedges
- crackers with peanut butter or hummus
- 100 percent fruit juice—orange or other juices fortified with vitamin C
- diced, raw vegetables—cucumber slices, cherry tomatoes, mushrooms, zucchini, red and orange peppers
- lightly cooked (steamed) vegetables—broccoli florets, green beans, carrots, edamame, sweet potato strips

- fruits—apple and orange wedges, bananas, applesauce, diced peaches, pears, plums, nectarines, kiwi
- whole grain crackers and breads
- dry, nonsweetened cereals
- yogurt

Making Mealtime Comfortable, Pleasant, and Safe

Children are more likely to eat in comfortable surroundings. Furniture should be of an appropriate size; table height should be comfortable for children to reach and chairs should permit their feet to rest flat on the floor. If a highchair or youth chair is used, it must have a stable base, washable eating tray, crotch safety strap, and support for the child's feet. Eating utensils should be child-sized and nonbreakable. Children's forks should have short, blunt tines and broad, short, easy-to-grasp handles. Spoons should also have short, blunt handles and shallow bowls for easy use. An upturned rim around plates provides a means for "trapping" elusive bits of food. Plates divided into two or three compartments can reduce frustration for toddlers as they develop self-feeding skills. Small (4–6 ounce) plastic cups with broad bases are easy for children to hold and also reduce spilling.

Toddlers are developing improved fine motor skills and hand/eye coordination that enable them to better handle utensils and to feed themselves. They should be encouraged to practice these skills but should not be given too many difficult-to-manage foods. Peas that roll off of a spoon or soups that spill before they reach the child's mouth can discourage even the most determined toddler. Finger foods served along with foods that require a fork or spoon encourage self-feeding and reduce mealtime frustration. Meats and cheeses cut into small cubes and vegetables and fruits sliced into small pieces are easier (and safer) for toddlers to pick up and chew. Although adults may not think that peas, mashed potatoes, and rice are finger foods, toddlers often do. A little flexibility in the choice of feeding methods can pay off in terms of the toddler's increased willingness to eat.

Sanitation is also an important consideration in feeding the toddler. The aseptic environment required when feeding infants is not necessary or possible to maintain with toddlers. However, cleanliness is of prime importance when preparing, serving, and eating food. Hand washing before and after meals is mandatory for toddlers as they often eat with their hands. Teachers must also wash their hands carefully before handling or eating food and again after cleaning up from a meal.

As the Toddler Becomes a Preschooler

As children mature, they also begin to eat more willingly. However, some preschoolers will have even firmer ideas of what they will and will not eat. During active growth periods the child's appetite and food acceptance are usually quite good. However, as growth slows, so does the child's appetite. It is during this latter stage that parents and teachers may become unduly concerned. (This concern may have the consequence of establishing a food–emotion link that can lead to feeding problems and eating disorders.) In most cases, there is no real cause for concern; growing, energetic children will usually eat when

Creating a comfortable eating environment encourages children's independence and ability to feed themselves.

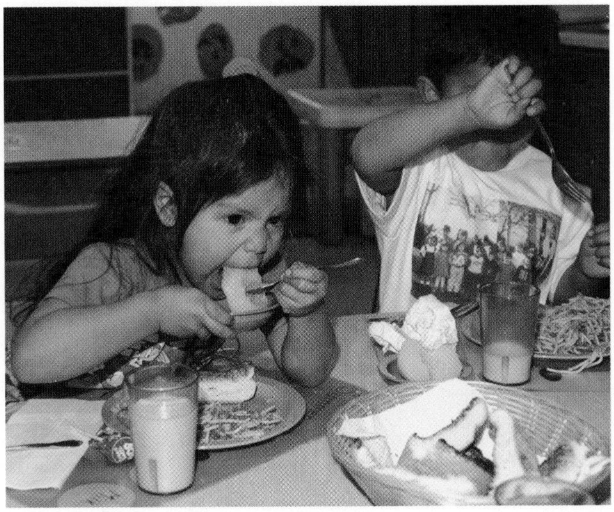

they are hungry. Remember that during this age, food should be offered frequently. If the child does not finish lunch, a nutrient dense mid-afternoon snack can make up for nutrients that may be lacking.

Attitudes formed about food and eating patterns during the preschool years are often carried over into adulthood. Teachers and families share responsibilities for promoting healthful eating practices and helping young children form positive feelings about food. Preschoolers like rules even though they may resist them at times. Rules about acceptable eating behavior should be enforced consistently but also allow some flexibility for both the adult and child in order to avoid a power struggle during mealtimes.

Guidelines for Feeding the Preschooler

As with toddlers, the Food Guide Pyramid provides a simple guideline for feeding preschoolers. Foods are needed from all of the food groups, but the amounts required are somewhat larger (Figure 17–3). Appropriate serving sizes for preschoolers are:

- 1/2 to 3/4 cup milk
- 1/2 to 1 slice of bread
- 1 tablespoon for each year of age for:
    - fruits (approximately 1/4 cup)
    - vegetables (approximately 1/4 cup)
    - meats and meat alternatives (approximately 1 1/2 ounces)

Food appearance and other sensory qualities still influence 3- to 5-year-olds. Foods presented in colorful combinations, shapes, and textures are attractive and invite children to try. Preschool-age children also prefer their foods served lukewarm, and are likely to reject or play with items that are

Figure 17–3 Sample menu with serving sizes for preschool-age children.

BREAKFAST	LUNCH	DINNER
2% milk (3/4 cup)	2% milk (3/4 cup)	2% milk (3/4 cup)
Cream of wheat (1/4 cup)	Beef patty (1 1/2 oz)	Diced chicken (1 1/2 oz)
or	Broccoli (1/4 cup)	Cooked carrots (1/4 cup)
Whole wheat toast (1/2 slice)	Diced watermelon (1/4 cup)	Diced plums (1/4 cup)
Jam or Jelly (1 tsp)	Whole-wheat bread (1/2 slice)	Rye bread (1/2 slice)
Diced peaches (1/2 cup)	Margarine (1 tsp)	Margarine (1 tsp)
MIDMORNING SNACK	**MIDAFTERNOON SNACK**	**EVENING SNACK**
Vanilla wafers (3)	Cheese cube (1 1/2 oz)	Applesauce (1/2 cup)
Orange juice (1/2 cup)	Whole wheat crackers (2)	Graham crackers (2)
	Water	Water

too hot or too cold until they reach an acceptable temperature. Serving portions that are slightly smaller prevents children from feeling visually overwhelmed and provides them with an opportunity to ask for more. Involving children in meal preparation often improves their interest in trying a new food or a meal they have helped to make.

Creating a comfortable mealtime environment for preschool-age children continues to be important. Appropriately sized furniture, dishes, and silverware encourage independence. Although many 3- to 5-year-olds still have difficulty managing eating utensils skillfully, they are becoming increasingly adept with continued practice. For example, a younger child may find it easier to handle a plastic knife when learning how to spread and cut their bread. Including a few finger foods in meals and ignoring unintentional messes also promotes a positive eating experience.

Nutrient Needs of School-Aged Children

Although energy expenditures and growth rates are highly variable from child to child, the need for a well-balanced diet continues to be critical for school-aged children. For the most part, they are eager eaters and open to trying new foods. Peers and groups outside of the child's family, including school and television, begin to compete with long-standing family eating patterns and food preferences. However, families still play an important role in terms of their expectations, the foods they make available at home, and the importance they place on eating meals together.

School-aged children are able to consume considerably more food at a sitting and, thus, require fewer in-between-meal snacks than when they were younger. Although many children receive a portion of their daily nutrients from meals eaten at school, they are usually eager for, and need, a substantial after-school snack. Having access to a supply of healthy fruits, vegetables, low-fat dairy products, and whole grain foods allows children to independently select and prepare nutritious snacks that also reinforce healthy eating habits. Appropriate serving sizes for school-aged children are:

1 cup milk (2%)

1 slice bread or 3/4 cup dry cereal

1/2 to 3/4 cup fruits/vegetables

1 ounce meat or meat alternative (snack); 2 ounces (meals)

The Food Guide Pyramid serves as an effective tool for ensuring that all essential nutrients are included in children's meals and snacks.

Children with Special Needs

Children who have developmental disabilities or special health conditions may present a range of unique nutritional needs and feeding challenges. Impaired motor abilities may make self-feeding and/or swallowing difficult. Medications, such as some antibiotics and those taken for seizure disorders, can increase a child's need for certain nutrients. Some genetic conditions, such as **Down syndrome** and **Prader-Willi syndrome**, increase the tendency for obesity and, thus, make it necessary to carefully monitor children's food intake. Other children may have difficulty recognizing and communicating when they are hungry or have had enough to eat. Children who experience autism spectrum disorders often restrict their food intake to a select few items and may require considerable coaxing before they will even take a few bits (Cermak, Curtin, & Bandini, 2010). Food intolerances and allergies to foods containing wheat, dairy, or gluten, for example, can make it challenging to ensure children's intake of essential nutrients.

Down syndrome – *a genetic disorder that is characterized by unique facial features, mental retardation, and motor delays.*

Prader-Willi syndrome – *a chromosomal disorder that causes learning and behavior problems, overeating that can lead to obesity, poor muscle tone, and short height.*

Children must always wash their hands before and after eating.

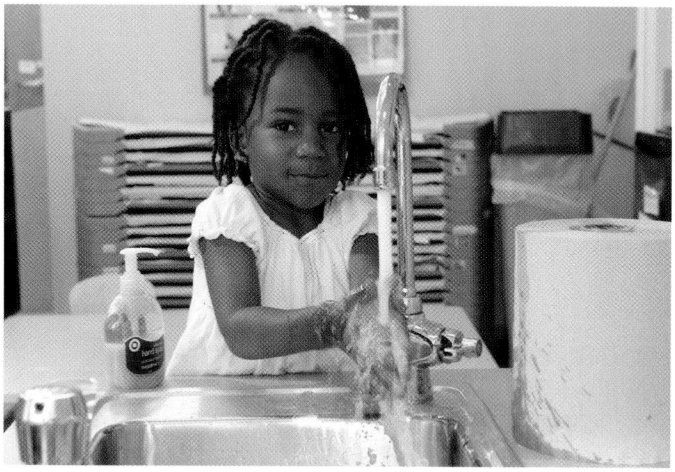
© Cengage Learning

Because nutrition is essential to healthy development and well-being, teachers must pay careful attention to identifying and meeting each child's unique nutrient needs. By partnering with the child's family, they can determine how the child's condition may affect eating ability and nutrient requirements. Teachers should also monitor children's growth patterns to make sure they remain within healthy limits. Families should keep teachers informed of any changes in the child's medical condition or treatments that might affect eating behavior. When teachers need advice or assistance with children's feeding problems, dietitians in hospitals or public health agencies can often be called upon.

Healthy Eating Habits

Children between the ages of 1 and 5 years are in the process of establishing lifelong eating patterns. This makes the feeding of toddlers and young children an especially important responsibility. Steps that families and teachers can take to promote children's healthy eating habits include:

- serving a variety of nutritious foods
- eating with the children and modeling an enjoyment of a variety of nutritious foods

One of the most important goals in helping children develop healthy eating habits is to increase the number and variety of foods they are willing to accept from each food group. It is especially important to cultivate their interest in the fruit and vegetable groups because these foods supply a wide range of important nutrients. Children should also experience familiar foods prepared in a variety of different ways in order to broaden their eating experiences and enjoyment.

Toddlers and preschoolers have a strong preference for sweet foods and a dislike for most vegetables. Knowing this, parents and teachers can downplay sweets in children's diets while increasing their exposure to fruits and vegetables. One way to approach this challenge might be to involve children in planting vegetables in containers or a small garden, harvesting the mature produce, and then helping to prepare the vegetables for a meal. Teachers can also set an example by eating a variety of vegetables in front of the children, commenting on how delicious they are, and indicating pleasure (such as smiling). This power of suggestion can have a contagious effect on children's willingness to at least try a few bites. Table 17–3 provides additional suggestions for introducing children to new or unfamiliar foods.

Children in group settings often begin to imitate the eating behaviors of their teachers and peers. For this reason, it is particularly important that adults sit and eat with the children at mealtime, engage in pleasant conversation, taste a variety of foods, and avoid displaying a dislike for any food. Children are quick to pick up and copy any negative reactions to foods.

Older children enjoy being involved in meal planning and preparation. For example, children in an after-school program might develop the weekly snack menu from a teacher-provided list of healthy foods rich in vitamins, minerals, and fiber. Children can also be assigned specific food preparation roles and trusted to perform them with skill and confidence. Not only does this acknowledgement appeal to the school-aged child's sense of responsibility, but it also fosters positive self-esteem. Involving school-aged children in food-related activities provides multiple opportunities to learn about foods and to reinforce healthy eating and physical activity habits. This is important since school-aged children are especially vulnerable to conflicting messages about body image and weight control. It also helps them

Table 17–3 Introducing New or Unfamiliar Foods

1. Introduce only one new food at a time.
2. Serve the new food along with other familiar foods.
3. Serve only small portions of the new food—begin with one bite or teaspoonful.
4. Introduce new foods when the child is hungry.
5. Talk about the new food—its taste, color, texture, where it comes from.
6. Let the child help to prepare the new food.
7. Encourage the child to taste the new food. If rejected, accept the refusal and try on another occasion. As foods become more familiar, they are also more readily accepted.
8. Determine what is not liked about a rejected food. Perhaps preparing it in a different manner will improve its appeal.
9. Let the child observe you eating and enjoying the new food!

to begin establishing important connections between well-being and eating behaviors.

Rewards should not be offered to children for trying a new food or for any other form of desired behavior. Adults are often tempted to use food (especially dessert or popular sweet snacks) as an incentive to get children to eat the nutritious portion of a meal. This practice causes desserts to assume undue importance for the child and is unlikely to result in any long-term acceptance of unfamiliar or disliked foods. Appropriate desserts, such as fresh fruits, should be nutritious (nutrient dense) and planned as a basic part of the meal. For example, a zucchini or carrot bar or slice of pumpkin bread may disguise vegetables that a child might otherwise refuse. Also, a child should never be asked to present a "clean plate" before receiving their dessert. This is one sure way to start the child on a road to obesity or eating disorders (Hilbran & Peterson, 2009).

Gardening helps children learn about where food comes from and improves their interest in trying vegetables they have grown.

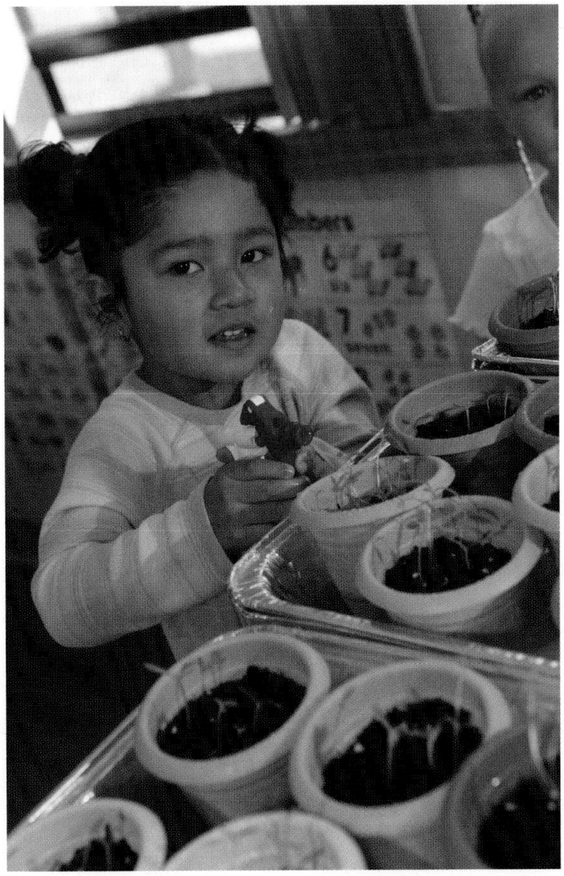

Health Problems Relating to Eating Habits

Teaching children healthful eating practices can have lifelong positive outcomes. A number of health problems are now thought to be directly or indirectly related to dietary patterns, including:

- **dental caries** (tooth decay)
- obesity (excess body fat)
- **hypertension** (high blood pressure)
- cardiovascular disease (CVD)
- diabetes mellitus

dental caries – *tooth decay.*
hypertension – *elevation of blood pressure above the normally accepted values.*

Dental Caries

Dietary sugars are known to increase the occurrence of dental caries. However, the type (soluble or not), its form (sticky or dissolved), how often, and the time of day (meals versus snacks) when sugar is consumed determine the decay potential more than does total sugar intake (Ruxton, Gardner, & McNulty, 2010). Providing sugar in the form of fruits and vegetables may actually offer protection from tooth decay while also supplying essential nutrients for the actively growing child.

Obesity

Prevention of obesity should begin with infant feeding. The infant's signals of **satiety** should be noted and feeding stopped when they occur. Toddlers and preschoolers will usually signal or stop eating when they have had enough food, unless eating or not eating is their best way to get attention. Forcing children to continue eating interferes with their ability to recognize when they are full and can contribute to excessive weight gain and obesity. However, children may be taking in more calories than needed because they have difficulty recognizing an appropriate serving as portion sizes have gradually increased (Croker, Sweetman, & Cooke, 2009) (Figure 17–4).

Approximately 47 percent of U.S. children are overweight or obese, an incidence that has nearly tripled over the past 20 years. Although a slight genetic potential for obesity exists in some families, this does not mean that it is inevitable for all family members. Thus, serving children nutritious foods, teaching them to make wise choices, involving them in physical activity, and limiting their sedentary activities, such as television viewing and computer/video games, is critical for maintaining normal body weight and reducing the risk of childhood obesity (Kim et al., 2010; Guyer et al., 2009) (Figure 17–5).

Hypertension

For many years hypertension (high blood pressure) has been correlated with a high intake of dietary sodium (salt) (Gillman, 2009). Children who have a family history of hypertension

Figure 17–4 Changes in portion size and calories.

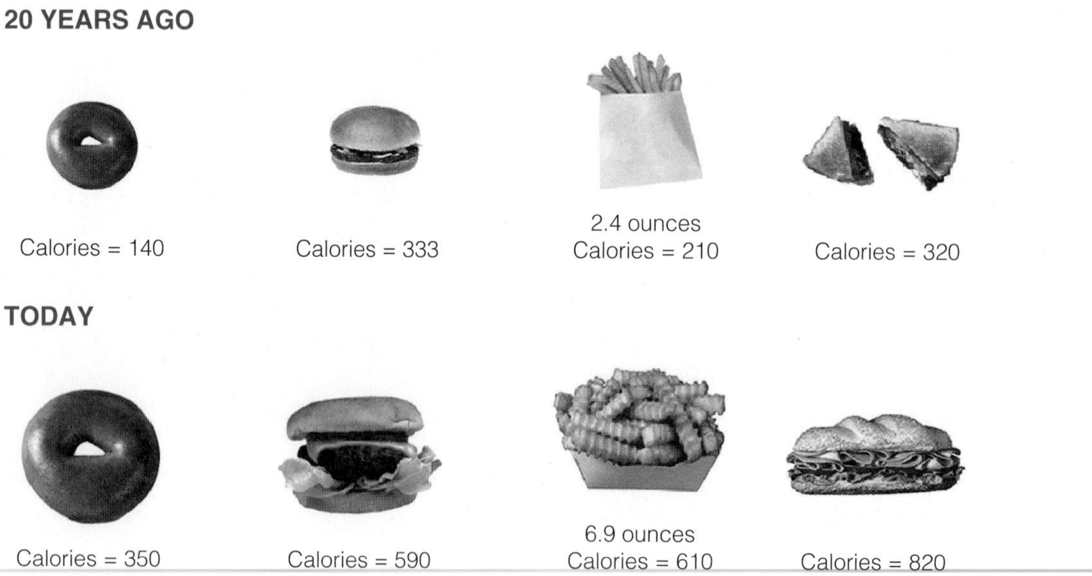

Source: Department of Health & Human Services, National Institutes of Health, National Heart, Lung & Blood Institute (http://hp2010.nhlbihin.net/portion).

satiety – *a feeling of satisfaction or fullness*

Figure 17–5 The Physical Activity Pyramid is designed to encourage children's fitness and health.

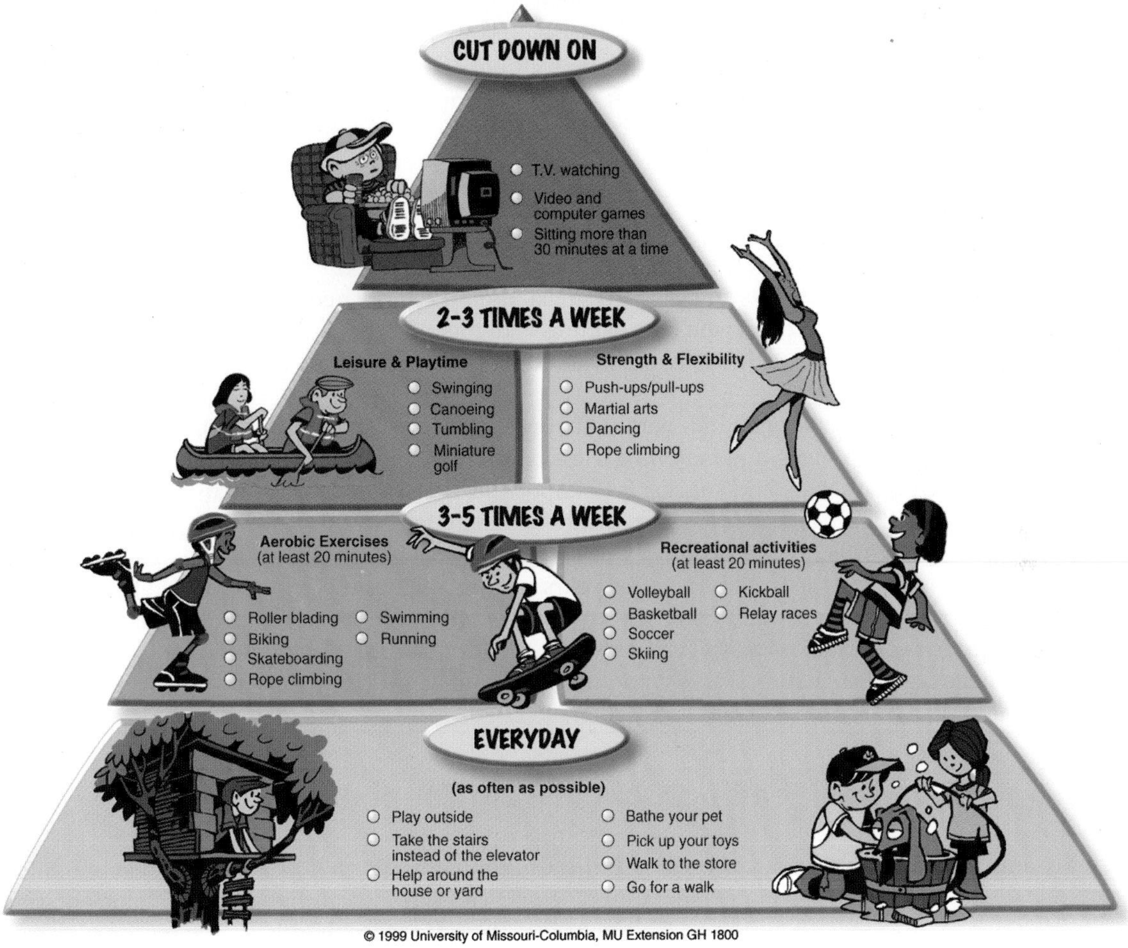

are at greater risk and may benefit from reducing their salt intake. Although sodium is an essential nutrient for infants and young children, this need can easily be met without the use of a salt shaker. Consumption of convenience, processed, and fast foods, which are often high in sodium, significantly increases a person's salt intake. The amount of salt added to foods prepared at home or by the school's cook can be controlled and often reduced with the same flavor outcome.

Cardiovascular Disease

Cardiovascular disease (CVD) is most often associated with high levels of certain fatty substances in the blood. Although cholesterol is cited most often as the culprit, the true causative agents are high intakes of dietary fat and saturated fatty acids. Over 60 percent of overweight children ages 5 to 10 already have at least one risk factor for heart disease that can be attributed to a high fat diet (Freedman et al., 2009).

Recommendations regarding the testing and monitoring of young children's blood cholesterol levels remain controversial. The American Academy of Pediatrics suggests that no cholesterol testing be done before the child is 2 years old. The 2- to 8-year-old child should be tested for cholesterol only if there is a strong family history of cardiovascular disease before the age of 55 years.

A child who has high blood cholesterol levels should have his/her diet monitored closely to include no more than 30 percent of calories from fat and 10 percent or less calories from saturated fat. However, fats, including cholesterol, should not be restricted in the infant or young toddler diet because they provide essential fatty acids necessary for normal nerve development. Any adjustments made in a child's diet must ensure that all nutrient requirements for normal growth and development are being met. In many cases, increasing the child's physical activity level is sufficient to lower blood cholesterol.

Diabetes

While type 1 diabetes is not caused by the quality of a child's diet, the disease does have a profound effect on a child's eating habits and growth (Hockenberry, 2008). There is no one "diabetic diet." The primary goal in feeding a child who has diabetes is to meet his/her essential nutrient needs and to achieve normal blood sugar levels by maintaining a balance between food, medication (insulin), and activity.

Typical meal plans for children with diabetes include limiting concentrated sugars, planning meals with food exchanges, and matching the amount of medication (insulin) taken to the amount of carbohydrates in meals and snacks. It is important that children with diabetes be able to eat foods similar to their peers so they don't always feel excluded.

Type 1 diabetes is usually diagnosed in children and adolescents, while type 2 diabetes typically develops during the middle- to later years in overweight adults. However, there has been a dramatic increase in the numbers of young children with type 2 diabetes in recent years due to the epidemic of childhood obesity (Weigensberg & Goran, 2009). Approximately half of all children newly diagnosed with diabetes have type 2 (Rosenbloom et al., 2009). This number was less than 4 percent in the 1990s (Pinhas-Hamiel & Zeitler, 2005).

Some Common Feeding Concerns in Younger Children

Consuming Excessive Amounts of Milk Children who drink milk to the exclusion of other foods may be at risk for iron-deficiency anemia and vitamin C (ascorbic acid) deficiency because it is a poor source of both nutrients. Children who consume more than 16–24 ounces of milk daily are usually not able to eat enough food from other food groups to adequately meet their nutrient needs. Offering children water between meals to satisfy thirst may help to address this problem. Special attention should also be paid to including iron-rich foods in daily meals to protect children from developing iron-deficiency anemia. Examples of foods high in iron are presented in Chapter 18 (Table 18–1).

Refusal to Eat and Selective Eating Toddlers and preschoolers may occasionally refuse food either because they are overly tired, asserting their newly found independence, or not hungry. If health problems do not explain a child's continued disinterest in food, it may be best to ignore the behavior. Remember that most active, growing children will soon become hungry and decide to eat. If nutritious food is provided for meals and snacks and if adults do not give in to children's requests for unhealthy food substitutions, hunger will eventually win over the challenge of refusal. However, it is also important that adults do not "try too hard" or attempt to coax or pressure children to eat because this can lead to unpleasant battles. Children with autism spectrum disorders often exhibit a significant aversion to foods and are especially sensitive to their textures. Prolonged cases of food refusal or selectivity may require professional behavioral intervention, close monitoring of children's nutrient intake, and nutrient supplementation (Williams & Seiverling, 2010).

Dawdling and Messiness These are the trademarks of young children and cannot be avoided although they can be controlled. Children dawdle for various reasons—they have eaten enough, they'd rather eat something else, or they have learned that it gets attention. Establishing and consistently enforcing mealtime rules will usually end dawdling behaviors. The teacher should decide upon an appropriate length of time for eating (approximately 20–25 minutes), warn the child when there is not much time remaining, and then remove the child from the table. This may result in some temporary unhappiness, but the young child quickly learns that they must eat when given the opportunity. However, it is always important to avoid hurrying children at mealtime and to allow sufficient time for eating.

Children need to learn to feed themselves and to manage eating utensils, even though some foods may present a real challenge (and should probably be limited). This process can result in understandable and forgivable messiness that should be overlooked. However, some children create messes to gain adult attention. In these cases, the child's behavior should be ignored to avoid reinforcing or encouraging it from being repeated. Continuous and avoidable messiness should not be tolerated and may be handled by removing the child from the table.

Food Jags Food jags are temporary phases during which children are willing to eat only a limited number of their favorite foods. These periods are not an uncommon occurrence among preschool-aged children and may simply reflect transitions in their tastes and interest in food. However, prolonged refusal of foods from all food groups can eventually result in nutrient deficiencies and the development of unhealthy eating habits. In most instances, adult patience and a few preventive measures offer the best approach. Meals and snacks served to young children should always include a variety of choices from all food groups. Serving the same few foods over and over strengthens children's preference for these items and narrows the range of foods they are likely to eat. Involving children in food preparation can also be effective for helping children to overcome food jags. Fortunately, children usually tire of these limited foods and will soon resume their normal eating pattern.

Inconsistencies in Adult Approaches to Feeding Problems This concern relates to several problems already cited. It is important that families and teachers communicate and agree on a consistent approach to handling children's food-related problems. It doesn't matter if the problem is weaning from excessive milk intake, decreasing dawdling and messiness behaviors, refusal to eat, or dealing with food jags. What is essential is that any interventions or strategies designed to address the child's eating behavior are enforced consistently by the teachers and family. The child cannot be expected to learn acceptable behavior if the rules constantly change.

Reflective Thoughts

Many families report that their children are allergic to specific foods. However, documented food allergies are known to affect only approximately 8 percent of children (Branum & Lukacs, 2009). Foods most commonly responsible for nearly 90 percent of all allergic reactions include milk, eggs, soy, peanuts, tree nuts (cashews and almonds), wheat, fish, and shellfish (The Food-Allergy & Anaphylaxis Network, 2009). However, not all food-related reactions are caused by allergies; some result from food intolerances. A **food intolerance** is a digestive system response to a given food while an allergic response involves an immune system reaction. Many symptoms of food intolerance are identical to those exhibited with a true allergy.

- How can you tell the difference between food allergies and food intolerances?
- Is the difference important in terms of meal planning?
- Review the list of common foods that cause allergic reactions. What similarities do you see between those foods and substances used to make infant formula?

---

food intolerance – *a digestive system response, such as nausea, vomiting, and/or diarrhea, to a given food.*

Food Additives and Hyperactivity Interest in the Feingold diet, initially published in 1973, and a potential link between sugar, food additives, and children's hyperactivity (ADHD) persists. However, several early double-blind studies have failed to demonstrate any relationship. Recent studies have suggested that a small number of children may experience allergic-type responses to some additives, which could explain their behavior (Sinn, 2008). For these children, eliminating the offending agent from their diet resulted in improvement. Sugar has also been thought to cause hyperactivity but this association remains unproven. Restricting a child's sugar intake has not been shown to improve behavior or learning. Actually, a biochemical case can be made for sugar as a calming and sleep-inducing agent (Sizer & Whitney, 2007). However, eliminating sugar and food additives, including dyes, from children's diet is certainly not harmful as long as sufficient amounts of nutritious foods from all food groups are provided.

Fast-Food Consumption The current cultural pattern of two-working-parents and single-parent families has led to significant changes in eating practices. More meals are eaten outside of the home today, especially in fast-food restaurants. Families have also increased reliance on convenience and processed foods from local grocery stores. These collective trends are raising public health concerns about children's food intake, especially of fast foods, and its effect on their health (Arredondo et al., 2009). Most fast foods are high in calories, cholesterol, fat, and salt, which over time can contribute to serious health problems such as cardiovascular disease, hypertension, diabetes, and obesity. Fast foods also tend to be low in vitamins A and C and calcium (unless milk is the selected beverage), and fiber. A too-frequent scenario is a mother and young child at a fast-food restaurant. The mother shares a few bites of her hamburger with the child, whose meal is rounded out with French fries and a small cola. An occasional fast-food meal for children is not a problem if care is taken to select healthy options and to provide nutritious foods at other times in the day to make up for any nutrient deficiencies.

Effect of Television on Food Preferences and Food Choices Advertising on television and in other media forms exerts a major effect on children's attitudes toward food. Many children spend more time watching television than they spend in school. It is estimated that a child is exposed to 3 hours of commercials per week and approximately 19,000–22,000 commercials each year (Kuo & Handu, 2009). Over half of these commercials are for food, particularly cereals (mostly sweetened), cookies, candy, sweetened beverages, and fast-food offerings (Bell et al., 2009). Most advertised foods are high in sugar and/or fat and are too calorie-dense to be healthful choices for young children. An additional concern is the extent to which adult food choices are influenced by the child's food preferences, which have been shaped by television food commercials. It is important to limit children's television viewing (and encourage active play) and to help them understand the persuasive nature of advertising.

Issues To Consider — "Surfing the Web" for Information

Many of us "surf the Web" for information. A report in the journal *Informatics for Health & Social Care* noted that a majority of families access the Internet at one time or another to obtain medical information (Hanif et al., 2009).

- Do you think all nutrition information available on the Internet is factual or reliable?
- Do you believe that you can judge what information is factual and what is not?
- What indicators would suggest that information on a given website may not be trustworthy?
- Where would you turn for reliable advice?

Focus on Families — Feeding Toddlers and Young Children

Mealtimes with children can be filled with many emotions and learning experiences. It can be a satisfying opportunity when families are able to spend time together and to establish positive bonds, or it can be a time when conflicts erupt and eating no longer becomes a pleasurable experience. Many families are faced with the latter if they have a child who is a "picky" or selective eater. Convincing these children to consume a healthy diet can be a challenging ordeal. However with patience and careful meal planning, a child's and family's eating experiences can gradually be turned into positive ones.

- Let children help with menu planning. Take them along to the grocery store and let them help to help pick out fresh fruits and vegetables. Challenge them to find a new food item for the family to try.
- Serve foods that a child does not like with a favorite or familiar food.
- Prepare foods in different ways to add fun and interest to meals. For example, try freezing fresh fruits and serving them frozen, incorporate a new vegetable into muffins and cookie bars, or make a tropical fruit salsa to top off grilled fish.
- Do not give up on a food if your child does not accept it the first time. It may take 10 to 15 exposures to an unfamiliar food before a child is willing to eat it.
- Serve meals and snacks at scheduled times. Children are more likely to eat if there is adequate time planned between their meals and snacks.
- Avoid sharing and passing your own food dislikes on to your children.
- Engage children in family conversations during mealtimes. By listening and showing interest in what they have to say, you are letting them know that they are valued family members.
- Finally, most children will get the nutrients they need, even if only small amounts of food are consumed. Continue to offer a wide variety of colorful foods and make mealtime a positive, pleasant experience.

Classroom Corner — Teacher Activities

Tasting Pears... (PreK–2; National Health Education Standards, 1.2.1, 1.2.2)

Concept: The same food can have different tastes and textures.

Learning Objectives

- Children will learn that pears come in a variety of tastes.
- Children will experience tasting three kinds of pears.

Supplies

- two Anjou pears; two Bosc pears; two Bartlett pears; hand wipes; small plates; napkins

Learning Activities

- Read and discuss the following book:
  - *Too Many Pears!* by Jackie French

(*continued*)

Classroom Corner **Teacher Activities** *(continued)*

- Tell children there are different varieties of pears. Talk about the importance of eating fruit each day (fiber, vitamins).
- Have children wash their hands with wipes and then pass around each pear for children to feel and look at the differences and similarities. Have children describe each pear's color, texture, and shape and talk about differences.
- Next, hand a napkin and a plate to each child. Place a small bite of each pear on a plate for children to taste; this can be done one at a time or the plate can have a sample of each pear on it.
- Give children an opportunity to taste each pear and talk about how each one tastes. Talk about the different tastes and textures.
- Repeat the activity using variations of other foods, such as vegetables, eggs, or grains.

Evaluation

- Children will state why pears are a healthy food choice.
- Children will taste a sample of each type of pear.

Additional lesson plans for grades 3–5 are available on the premium website for this book.

Summary

- Children's growth rate slows around their first birthday. They also begin to experience behavioral changes that are important steps for achieving a sense of independence.
- Mealtimes with toddlers can be challenging. To minimize potential friction, adults are responsible for: (a) serving a variety of nutritious foods, (b) deciding when to offer food, and (c) setting a positive example by eating a variety of nutritious foods.
- Children will decide: (a) what to eat and (b) how much to eat.
- Because lifetime food patterns are being formed during the toddler and preschool years, it is important that children be provided with a wide variety of nutritious foods to experience.
- Adults play an important role in shaping children's eating behaviors by planning and providing meals that include a variety of foods and also serving as positive role models.
- A nutritious diet can minimize children's risk of developing food-related health problems, such as dental caries, obesity, hypertension, heart disease, and diabetes.

Terms to Know

neophobic *p. 410*
Down syndrome *p. 417*
Prader-Willi syndrome *p. 417*
dental caries *p. 419*
hypertension *p. 419*
satiety *p. 420*
food intolerance *p. 423*

Chapter Review

A. By Yourself:

1. Name three ways to make mealtimes comfortable and pleasant for children.
2. Explain the teacher's major responsibilities in toddler feeding situations.
3. Suggest serving sizes for a 2-year-old and a 4-year-old for each of the following foods: bread, peas, applesauce, orange juice, banana, cooked chicken, noodles, baked beans.

B. As a Group:

1. Watch 1 hour of Saturday morning cartoons on television and discuss the following:
   a. What foods were presented in the majority of commercials?
   b. What adjectives did the announcer use to describe the foods being advertised?
   c. What other media effects were used to capture and maintain children's interest?
   d. Imagine that you are a 4-year-old. On your next trip to the grocery store with your mother, what products would you want her to buy? Why?
2. Visit a fast-food restaurant that features hamburgers and observe the following:
   a. How many toddlers and preschoolers are there?
   b. What are the children eating and drinking?
   c. What foods might have been ordered from the menu to provide a more nutritious or healthier meal?
   d. Ask the restaurant for nutritional information or visit its website. Are you surprised by any of the calorie and nutrient values?
3. Visit a local supermarket and observe the advertising techniques used to draw children's attention to certain foods and products.
   a. What cereals are shelved at a child's eye level? Describe features on the boxes that are used to capture children's attention.
   b. What types of foods are displayed at the end of aisles?
   c. What food items are typically displayed at the checkout counter?
   d. What types of free food samples are offered by the store to young children?

Case Study

Maria, age 7 years, is new to the community and has recently enrolled in your after-school program. She and her parents speak Portuguese, but very little English. The other children are intrigued with Maria and her "different" language. They eagerly attempt to teach her some English words by pointing to and repeating the names of foods and objects with exaggerated clarity. Although Maria seems to enjoy their attention and is responding to their efforts, you (teacher) are concerned that she still eats very little during snack time.

1. Why should you be concerned that Maria is not eating?
2. What steps can you take to learn more about her family's food preferences?
3. Where might you access information about foods and food preferences native to Maria's culture?
4. Where might you access materials to aid in Maria's care and your ability to communicate with her family?
5. Where might you locate an interpreter for assistance?

Application Activities

1. Eighteen-month-old Jason has recently been enrolled in an all-day early childhood program. His health assessment reveals that he is anemic. Observations of his eating habits suggest that he dislikes meat and vegetables but eats large quantities of fruits and drinks at least two cups of milk at every meal and snack. What changes in eating habits should the teacher try to foster to improve Jason's iron status?
2. Formulate plans for the dining area of an early childhood program that will promote children's self-feeding skills. Include a discussion of appropriate furniture and eating utensils. Plan a 1-day menu (one meal and two snacks) that will further enhance children's self-feeding efforts.
3. Traci, 4 years old, arrives at her family child-care provider's home every morning with a bag of doughnuts. Her mother informs the provider that it is okay for Traci to eat the doughnuts since she doesn't like what is being served for breakfast. The other children have also begun to ask for doughnuts. How should the provider handle this situation? What factors must be considered?
4. Prepare a 5-day snack menu for toddlers, preschoolers, and school-age children that features nutrient-dense foods.

Helpful Web Resources

American Diabetes Association	http://www.diabetes.org
American Heart Association (childhood obesity)	http://www.americanheart.org
Council for Exceptional Children	http://www.cec.sped.org
Food Allergy & Anaphylaxis Network	http://www.foodallergy.org
Nutrition Explorations	http://www.nutritionexplorations.org

You are just a click away from additional health, safety, and nutrition resources! Go to www.CengageBrain.com to access this text's Education CourseMate website, where you'll find:

- glossary flashcards, activities, tutorial quizzes, videos, web links, and more

References

Allen, K. E., & Marotz, L. R. (2010). *Developmental profiles: Pre-birth through twelve* (6th ed.). Belmont, CA: Wadsworth Cengage.

Arredondo, E., Castaneda, D., Elder, J., Slymen, D., & Dozier, D. (2009). Brand name logo recognition of fast food and healthy food among children, *Journal of Community Health*, 34(1), 73–78.

Bell, R., Cassady, D., Culp, J., & Alcalay, R. (2009). Frequency and types of foods advertised on Saturday morning and weekday afternoon English- and Spanish- language American television programs, *Journal of Nutrition Education & Behavior*, 41(6), 406–413.

Branum, A., & Lukacs, S. (2009). Food allergy among children in the United States, *Pediatrics*, 124(6), 1549–1555.

Cecil-Karb, R., & Grogan-Kaylor, A. (2009). Childhood body mass index in community context: Neighborhood safety, television viewing, and growth trajectories of BMI, *Health & Social Work*, 34(3), 169–177.

Cermak, S., Curtin, C., & Bandini, L. (2010). Food selectivity and sensory sensitivity in children with autism spectrum disorders, *Journal of the American Dietetic Association*, 110(2), 238–246.

Croker, H., Sweetman, C., & Cooke, L. (2009). Mother's views of portion sizes for children, *Journal of Human Nutrition & Dietetics*, 22(5), 437–443.

Deshmukh-Taskar, P., Nicklasm T., Yang, S., & Berenson, G. (2007). Does food group consumption vary by differences in socioeconomic, demographic, and lifestyle factors in young adults? The Bogalusa Heart Study, *Journal of the American Dietetic Association*, 107(2), 223–234.

Dorey, E., & McCool, J. (2009). The role of the media in influencing children's nutritional perceptions, *Qualitative Health Research*, 19(5), 645–654.

Dovey, T., Staples, P., Gibson, E., & Halford, J. (2008). Food neophobia and 'picky/fussy' eating in children: A review, *Appetite*, 50(2–3), 181–193.

Food Allergy & Anaphylaxis Network. (2009). *Allergens.* Accessed on January 17, 2010 from http://www.foodallergy.org.

Freedman, D., Dietz, W., Srinivasan, R., & Berenson, G. (2009). Risk factors and adult body mass index among overweight children: The Bogalusa Heart Study, *Pediatrics*, 123(3), 750–757.

Gillman, M. (2009). Childhood prevention of hypertensive cardiovascular disease, *The Journal of Pediatrics,* 155(2), 159–161.

Guyer, B., Ma, S., Grason, H., Frick, K., Perry, D., Sharkey, A., & McIntosh, J. (2009). Early childhood health promotion and its life course health consequences, *Academic Pediatrics*, 9(3), 142–149.

Hanif, F., Read, J., Goodacre, J., Chaudhry, A., & Gibbs, P. (2009). The role of quality tools in assessing reliability of the Internet for health information, *Informatics for Health & Social Care*, 34(4), 231–243.

Hilbran, A., & Peterson, S. (2009). Childhood weight status and food experiences impact adult food behaviors, *Journal of the American Dietetic Association*, 109(9), A52–A62.

Hockenberry, M. (2008). *Wong's essentials of pediatric nursing.* (8th ed.). St Louis: Mosby.

Kim, S., Adamson, K., Balfanz, D., Brownson, R., Wiecha, J., Shepard, D., & Alles, W. (2010). Development of the Community Healthy Living Index: A tool to foster healthy environments for the prevention of obesity and chronic disease, *Preventive Medicine*, 50(1S), S80–S85.

Kuo, J., & Handu, D. (2009). Content analysis of television advertisements aired during Saturday morning children programming, *Journal of the American Dietetic Association*, 109(9), A100–A110.

Pinhas-Hamiel, O., & Zeitler, P. (2005). The global spread of type 2 diabetes mellitus in children and adolescents, *The Journal of Pediatrics*, 146(5), 693–700.

Rosenbloom, A., Silverstein, J., Amemiva, S., Zeitler, P., & Klingensmith, G. (2009). Type 2 diabetes in children and adolescents, *Pediatric Diabetes*, 10(12 Suppl.), 17–32.

Ruxton, C., Gardner, E., & McNulty, H. (2010). Is sugar consumption detrimental to health? *Critical Reviews in Food Science & Nutrition*, 50(1), 1–19.

Satter, E. (2000). *How to get your child to eat . . . But not too much.* Palo Alto, CA: Bull Publishing Co.

Sinn, N. (2008). Nutritional and dietary influences on attention deficit hyperactivity disorder, *Nutrition Reviews*, 66(10), 558–568.

Sizer, F., & Whitney, E. (2007). *Nutrition: Concepts & controversies.* Belmont, CA: Wadsworth Cengage Learning.

Weigensberg, M., & Goran, M. (2009). Type 2 diabetes in children and adolescents, *The Lancet*, 3737(9677), 1743–1744.

Williams, K. & Seiverling, L. (2010). Eating problems in children with autism spectrum disorders, *Topics in Clinical Nutrition*, 25(1), 27–37.

CHAPTER

18

Planning and Serving Nutritious and Economical Meals

NAEYC Standards *Chapter Links*

- **#1 a, b, and c:** Promoting child development and learning
- **#2 b and c:** Building family and community relationships
- **#3 c and d:** Observing, documenting, and assessing to support young children and families
- **#4 a, b, c, and d:** Using developmentally effective approaches to connect with children and families
- **#5 b, and c:** Using content knowledge to build meaningful curriculum
- **#6 b, c, and d:** Becoming a professional

Learning Objectives

After studying this chapter, you should be able to:

- Identify criteria that must be addressed when planning menus for children.
- Explain how weekly and cycle menus differ.
- Plan snacks for toddlers, preschoolers, and school-aged children that meet their nutritional requirements.
- Create mealtime environments that are inviting for children.
- Outline a simple cost control plan to keep the menu within budget.

Eating is a sensory, emotional, and social experience that provides nourishment essential for human life. It should be an enjoyable time when children begin to establish positive attitudes toward food and healthy dietary habits. Teachers have many opportunities to encourage and support children in this process by planning nutritious meals and snacks and serving them in a pleasant atmosphere.

Meal Planning

A menu is a list of foods to be served and is fundamental to any food service. Menu planning requires time and a careful evaluation of the physical, developmental, and social needs of those for whom it is planned. Thoughtful planning is necessary whether the menu is designed to feed a family of three or an institution serving hundreds of meals a day. The difference between the two situations is largely one of scale. Creating menus for children requires that detailed attention be given to:

- meeting children's nutritional needs
- addressing any existing funding or licensing requirements
- providing sensory appeal (taste, texture, and visual interest)
- making children comfortable by including familiar foods
- encouraging healthy food habits by introducing new foods
- providing safe food and serving it in clean surroundings
- staying within budgetary limits
- providing alternatives for children who have food allergies, eating problems, and special nutritional needs

A Well-Designed Menu Meets Nutritional Needs

Children's nutrient and energy needs must be given priority during the initial steps of menu planning. For schools, this means determining what portion of children's daily nutrient requirements they will provide. Early childhood programs participating in federally funded food programs for children are required to meet at least one-third of the recommended daily requirements for calcium, iron, vitamin A, and vitamin C (these are considered at-risk nutrients for children; see Tables 18–1 through 18–4); supplying one-half of children's daily nutrient requirements is preferable. Schools serving older children should also aim to meet these recommendations. The Food Guide Pyramid and the Child and Adult Care Food Program (CACFP) guidelines, discussed later in this chapter, are excellent tools for determining what nutrients children require, what foods supply these nutrients, and in what amounts (serving sizes) they are needed

A Well-Designed Menu Meets Funding and/or Licensing Requirements

Several federally sponsored food assistance programs are available to schools and early childhood programs. Perhaps the best known of these are the School Lunch and the Child and Adult Care Food Programs (CACFP). The CACFP program reimburses participating early childhood centers and family child care homes for meals served to the children. The per meal/snack rate compensates programs, in part, for their food, labor, and administrative expenses. Funds are provided by the Food and Nutrition Service of the U.S. Department of Agriculture; in most states, the program is administered by the Department of Education. To qualify for reimbursement, programs must plan and serve meals according to specific CACFP guidelines (Table 18–5):

1. Minimum Breakfast Requirement
   - whole grain or enriched bread or grain alternate
   - fruit, vegetable, or full-strength fruit or vegetable juice
   - milk, fluid
2. Minimum Snack Requirement (choose two different components); refer to "Supplemental Foods."

Menus must be planned carefully to provide nutrients essential for children's growth and development.

- whole grain or enriched bread, or grain product
- milk, fluid
- fruit, vegetable, or full-strength fruit or vegetable juice
- meat, meat alternate, or yogurt

3. Minimum Lunch or Supper Requirement
   - meat or meat alternate
   - fruits and/or vegetables (two or more different kinds)
   - whole grain or enriched bread, or grain product
   - milk, fluid

Table 18–1 Sources of Iron and Suggested Preparations

Rich Sources
Beef liver – baked, braised with apple slices and onions
Beef – ground beef patty, meat loaf, roast beef, meat balls with spaghetti, stews, beef burrito
Dried Peas, Beans, and Lentils – with rice, with vegetables, in soup or salads, in a tortilla, on pitas (hummus), as soy curd (tofu)
Pumpkin and Sunflower Seeds – roasted, in salads or baked goods
Spinach – raw, in salad with bacon, cooked and tossed with parmesan cheese or hard boiled eggs
Whole or Enriched Grain Products – as tortillas, fortified ready-to-eat cereals, breads, crackers, pastas, bran or cornmeal muffins
Good Sources
Chicken – with rice, with noodles, baked, as chicken salad
Ham – baked and sliced, ham salad, ham and scalloped sweet potatoes, sandwich
Potatoes – baked, boiled in their skins
Raisins – in bread or rice pudding, plain, added to cereals or baked products

Table 18–2 Sources of Calcium and Suggested Preparations

Rich Sources
Milk – plain, in custards or puddings
Cheddar Cheese – sliced in sandwiches, cubed, in cream sauce, shredded in salads
Salmon (canned) or Sardines – as patties or loaf, plain with crackers
Soy Products (enriched) – soy milk, sautéed tofu, tofu in stir fry, in smoothies
Yogurt – plain, with fruit, as dips for fruit or vegetables, frozen, in smoothies
Good Sources
Almonds – plain, in baked products
Bok Choy (Chinese cabbage) – in stir fry, diced raw in salads, braised
Broccoli - raw as florets with yogurt dip, cooked plain or served with a light cheese sauce, in stir fry
Enriched Grain Products – as tortillas, fortified ready-to-eat cereals, breads, crackers, pastas
Oranges – raw, sections, juice

Table 18–3 Sources of Vitamin C and Suggested Preparations

Rich Sources
Broccoli – raw as florets with yogurt dip, cooked plain or served with a light cheese sauce **Cantaloupe** – sliced, cubed in mixed fruit salad **Cauliflower** – raw as florets with yogurt dip or in a tossed salad, cooked plain or served with a light cheese sauce **Green, Red, or Yellow Peppers** – strips, rings, or included in sauces and mixed dishes **Kiwi** – sliced, in mixed fruit salads **Oranges and Grapefruit** – juice, slices or wedges, juice added to gelatin **Strawberries** – plain, with milk, sliced in a fruit cup, in smoothies **Tomatoes** – cherry tomatoes, juice, stewed, broiled, cooked and added to mixed dishes; fresh and served as slices, wedges, or in tossed salads **Watermelon** – slices or chunks, added to mixed fruit salads
Good Sources
Brussels Sprouts – sliced in salads, cooked and lightly buttered **Cabbage** – raw in coleslaw or tossed salads, cooked and lightly buttered

Table 18–4 Sources of Vitamin A and Suggested Preparations

Rich Sources
Beef liver – baked or broiled **Sweet Potatoes** – baked, mashed, in breads **Carrots** – cooked, raw in salad with raisins, raw in sticks, curls, or "coins" **Pumpkin** – cooked and mashed, in breads or muffins, custard **Cantaloupe** – balls or cubes, in mixed fruit salad
Good Sources
Apricots – sliced fresh, canned in fruit juice **Broccoli** – raw as florets with yogurt dip, cooked plain or served with a light cheese sauce, in stir fry

Reflective Thoughts

The Food Guide Pyramid represents an idea that has become very popular. Several features, such as its interactivity, customized menu and physical activity tracker, menu planner, recipes and other resources have contributed to the website's success. Visit the Pyramid at www.MyPyramid.gov.

- What aspects of the Food Guide Pyramid do you personally find most useful?
- How might you use the Pyramid to plan your diet and set personal dietary goals?
- What changes do you plan to make in your diet and/or physical activity?
- What Pyramid food group do you have the greatest difficulty achieving? How might you change this?

Table 18–5 CACFP Meal Requirements for Children Ages 1 Through 12

Child Meal Pattern - Breakfast			
Select All Three Components for a Reimbursable Meal			
Food Components	**Ages 1–2**	**Ages 3–5**	**Ages 6–12[1]**
1 milk			
fluid milk	1/2 cup	3/4 cup	1 cup
1 fruit/vegetable			
juice,[2] fruit and/or vegetable	1/4 cup	1/2 cup	1/2 cup
1 grains/bread[3]			
bread or	1/2 slice	1/2 slice	1 slice
cornbread, biscuit, roll, muffin or	1/2 serving	1/2 serving	1 serving
cold dry cereal or	1/4 cup	1/3 cup	3/4 cup
hot cooked cereal or	1/4 cup	1/4 cup	1/2 cup
pasta, noodles, or grains	1/4 cup	1/4 cup	1/2 cup
Child Meal Pattern - Lunch or Supper			
Include Foods from All Four Components for a Reimbursable Meal			
Food Components	**Ages 1–2**	**Ages 3–5**	**Ages 6–12[1]**
1 milk			
fluid milk	1/2 cup	3/4 cup	1 cup
2 fruits/vegetables			
juice,[2] fruit and/or vegetable	1/4 cup	1/2 cup	3/4 cup
1 grains/bread[3]			
bread or	1/2 slice	1/2 slice	1 slice
cornbread, biscuit, roll, muffin, or	1/2 serving	1/2 serving	1 serving
cold dry cereal or	1/4 cup	1/3 cup	3/4 cup
hot cooked cereal or	1/4 cup	1/4 cup	1/2 cup
pasta, noodles, or grains	1/4 cup	1/4 cup	1/2 cup
1 meat/meat alternate			
meat, poultry, fish[4], or	1 ounce	1 1/2 ounces	2 ounces
alternate protein product or	1 ounce	1 1/2 ounces	2 ounces
cheese or	1 ounce	1 1/2 ounces	2 ounces
egg or	1/2 egg	3/4 egg	1 egg
cooked dry beans, or peas, or	1/4 cup	3/8 cup	1/2 cup
peanut or other nut or seed butters or	2 Tbsp.	3 Tbsp.	4 Tbsp.
nuts and/or seeds[5] or	1/2 ounce	3/4 ounces	1 ounces
yogurt[6]	4 ounces	6 ounces	8 ounces

[5] Nuts and seeds may meet only one-half of the total meat/meat alternative serving and must be combined with another meat/meat alternate to fulfill the lunch or supper requirement.
[6] Yogurt may be plain or flavored, unsweetened or sweetened.

(continued)

Table 18-5 CACFP Meal Requirements for Children Ages 1 Through 12 *(continued)*

Child Meal Pattern - Snack

Select Two of the Four Components for a Reimbursable Snack

Food Components	**Ages 1–2**	**Ages 3–5**	**Ages 6–12**[1]
1 milk			
fluid milk	1/2 cup	1/2 cup	1 cup
1 fruit/vegetable			
juice,[2] fruit and/or vegetable	1/2 cup	1/2 cup	3/4 cup
1 grains/bread[3]			
bread or	1/2 slice	1/2 slice	1 slice
cornbread, biscuit, roll, muffin, or	1/2 serving	1/2 serving	1 serving
cold dry cereal or	1/4 cup	1/3 cup	3/4 cup
hot cooked cereal or	1/4 cup	1/4 cup	1/2 cup
pasta, noodles, or grains	1/4 cup	1/4 cup	1/2 cup
1 meat/meat alternate	1/2 ounce	1/2 ounce	1 ounce
meat, poultry, fish[4], or	1/2 ounce	1/2 ounce	1 ounce
alternate protein product or	1/2 ounce	1/2 ounce	1 ounce
cheese or	1/2 ounce	1/2 ounce	1 ounce
egg[5] or	1/2 egg	1/2 egg	1/2 egg
cooked dry beans, peas, or	1/8 cup	1/8 cup	1/4 cup
peanut or other nut or seed butters or	1 Tbsp.	1 Tbsp.	2 Tbsp.
nuts and/or seeds or	1/2 ounce	1/2 ounce	1 ounce
yogurt[6]	2 ounces	2 ounces	4 ounces

[1] Children age 12 and older may be served larger portions based on their greater food needs. They may not be served less than the minimum quantities listed in this column.
[2] Fruit or vegetable juice must be full strength. Juice cannot be served when milk is the only other snack component.
[3] Breads and grains must be made from whole-grain or enriched meal or flour. Cereal must be whole-grain or enriched or fortified.
[4] A serving consists of the edible portion of cooked lean meat, poultry or fish.
[5] One-half egg meets the required minimum amount (1 ounce or less) of meat alternative.
[6] Yogurt may be plain or flavored, unsweetened or sweetened.

Source: Food and Nutrition Service, United States Department of Agriculture, 2009.

At this time, CACFP meal planning guidelines follow a food-based menu approach, using Nutrient Standard or Assisted Nutrient Standard Menu Planning, or adopting an alternate menu planning approach developed by a state agency or by the school food authority with state agency approval. The guidelines are quite specific as to the minimum amounts of food required to count as a full serving. Lists of alternative food items that qualify for reimbursement within each food group are also available (Table 18–6). The menu planner must work within these guidelines and take great care to keep up with current information as this program undergoes frequent and sometimes sweeping changes.

The National School Lunch Act requires that school meals comply with the *Dietary Guidelines for Americans*. However, many authorities are raising questions about the quality of school lunches, especially in light of concerns about high salt intake and childhood obesity rates, and have called for major reforms to provide children with healthier meals (Clark & Fox, 2009; Story, 2009). School food service personnel and child-care providers can access an extensive collection of healthy recipes and menu planning information on the U.S. Department of Agriculture's website, http://healthymeals.nal.usda.gov. (Click on "Recipes & Menu Planning.")

Early childhood programs must be licensed to participate in the CACFP program. Licensing of child care facilities is administered by state agencies, usually the Department of Health. Because each state establishes its own licensing nutrition and food service regulations, teachers who provide food for children should be familiar with the requirements for their particular state. Nutrition related areas that are typically addressed in state licensing regulations include:

Table 18–6 Acceptable Bread and Bread Alternates (serving sizes for children under 6 years)

Important Notes:

- All products must be made of whole grain or enriched flour or meal.
- Serving sizes listed below are specified for children younger than 6 years of age.
- A *"full"* serving (defined below) is required for children 6 years of age and older.
- USDA recommends that cookies, granola bars, and similar foods be served in a snack no more than twice a week. They may be used for a snack only when:
  - whole grain or enriched meal or flour is the predominant ingredient as specified on the label or according to the recipe; and
  - the total weight of a serving for children younger than 6 years of age is a minimum of 18 grams (0.6 ounces) and for children over 6 years, a minimum of 35 grams (1.2 ounces).
- To determine serving sizes for products in Group A that are made at child care centers, refer to "Cereal Products" in FNS–86, "Quantity Recipes for Child Care Centers."
- Doughnuts and sweet rolls are allowed as a bread item in breakfasts and snacks only.
- French, Vienna, Italian, and Syrian breads are commercially prepared products that often are made with unenriched flour. Check the label or manufacturer to be sure the product is made with *enriched* flour.
- The amount of bread in a serving of stuffing should weigh at least 13 grams (0.5 ounces).
- Whole grain, enriched, or fortified breakfast cereals (cold, dry, or cooked) may be served for breakfast or snack only.

Group A

When you obtain these items commercially, a *full* serving should have a minimum weight of 20 grams (0.7 ounces). The serving sizes specified below should have a minimum weight of 10 grams (0.5 ounces).

Item	Serving Size
bread sticks (hard)	2 sticks
chow mein noodles	1/4 cup
crackers (saltines and snack)	4 squares
lavosh	1/2 serving
melba toast	3 pieces
pretzels (hard)	1/2 serving
stuffing (bread)	1/2 serving

(continued)

Table 18–6 Acceptable Bread and Bread Alternates *(continued)*

Group B

When you obtain these items commercially, a *full* serving should have a minimum weight of 25 grams (0.9 ounces). The serving sizes specified below should have a minimum weight of 13 grams (0.5 ounces).

Item	Serving Size
bagels	1/2 bagel
biscuits	1 biscuit
breads (white, rye, whole-wheat, raisin, French)	1/2 slice
buns (hamburger, hot dog)	1/2 bun
cookie-crackers (graham, animal)	2 2¼ × 2¼ squares; 10 animal crackers
egg roll/wonton wrappers	1 serving
English muffins	1/2 muffin
pita bread	1/2 round
muffins	1/2 muffin
pizza crust	1 serving
pretzels (soft)	1 pretzel
rolls and sweet rolls (unfrosted)	1/2 roll
taco shells (whole, pieces)	1 shell
tortillas	1/2 tortilla

Group C

When you obtain these items commercially, a *full* serving should have a minimum weight of 31 grams (1.1 ounces). The serving sizes specified below should have a minimum weight of 16 grams (0.6 ounces).

Item	Serving Size
cookies	1/2 serving
cornbread	1 piece
croissants	1/2 croissant
pie crust (meat or meat alternative pies)	1/2 serving
popovers	1/2 popover
waffles	1/2 serving

Group D

When you obtain these items commercially, a *full* serving should have a minimum weight of 50 grams (1.8 ounces). The serving sizes specified below should have a minimum weight of 25 grams (0.9 ounces).

Item	Serving Size
doughnuts (all types)	1/2 doughnut
granola bars (plain)	1/2 serving
hush puppies	1/2 serving
muffins/quick breads (all except corn bread)	1/2 serving
sopapillas	1/2 serving
sweet roll (unfrosted)	1/2 serving
toaster pastry (unfrosted)	1/2 serving

(continued)

Table 18–6 Acceptable Bread and Bread Alternates *(continued)*

Group E

When you obtain these items commercially, a *full* serving should have a minimum weight of 63 grams (2.2 ounces). The serving sizes specified below should have a minimum weight of 31 grams (1.1 ounces).

Item	Serving Size
cookies (with nuts, raisins, chocolate pieces, fruit purees)	1/2 serving
doughnuts (all kinds)	1/2 serving
French toast	1/2 serving
fruit grain bars/granola bars (with fruit, nuts, chocolate pieces)	1/2 serving
sweet rolls	1/2 serving
toaster pastry (frosted)	1/2 serving

Group F

When you obtain these items commercially, a *full* serving should have a minimum weight of 75 grams (2.7 ounces). The serving sizes specified below should have a minimum weight of 38 grams (1.3 ounces).

Item	Serving Size
coffee cake	1/2 serving

Group G

When you obtain these items commercially, a *full* serving should have a minimum weight of 115 grams (4 ounces). The serving sizes specified below should have a minimum weight of 58 grams (2 ounces).

Item	Serving Size
brownies	1/2 serving

Group H

When you serve these items, a *full* serving should have a minimum of 1/2 cup cooked product. The serving sizes specified below are the minimum half servings of a cooked product.

Item	Serving Size
barley	1/4 cup
breakfast cereals (cooked)	1/4 cup
bulgur or cracked wheat	1/4 cup
couscous	1/4 cup
macaroni (all shapes)	1/4 cup
masa	1/4 cup
noodles (all varieties)	1/4 cup
pasta (all shapes)	1/4 cup
ravioli (noodle only)	1/4 cup
rice (enriched white or brown)	1/4 cup

Courtesy of USDA, 2009

Issues To Consider **CACFP and Positive Outcomes for Children**

Recent studies have concluded that meals planned according to CACFP guidelines have the potential to improve children's diets and health (Kaphingst & Story, 2009; Benjamin et al., 2008). Children attending programs that participate in the CACFP are more likely to be served meals aligned with recommendations outlined in the Dietary Guidelines for Healthy Americans. Programs are also better informed about the importance of increasing children's physical activity to help in establishing healthy lifestyle habits and discouraging childhood obesity.

- What are the potential implications and outcomes of these studies for families with young children in early childhood programs?
- Of what importance are the results of these studies to menu planners?
- What are the "take home lessons" from these studies for families and teachers?

1. Administration and record keeping
   - sample menus and appropriate menu substitutions
   - production records
   - number of meals served daily
2. Food service
   - specifications for kitchens and equipment
   - sanitation of dishes, utensils, and equipment
   - requirements for transport of food when kitchen facilities are not available
   - feeding equipment required for specific age groups
3. Staffing
   - requirements of person in charge of food service
4. Nutrition policies
   - number of meals and snacks to be served within the current week
   - posting of menus and their availability to families
   - seating of adults at the table with children
   - posting of food allergies in kitchen and eating area

A Well-designed Menu Is Appealing

The French say, "We eat with our eyes." Menu planners who take into consideration how food will look on a plate are likely to develop meals that are more appealing and acceptable to children. Figure 18–1 illustrates this principle: Apples can be sliced in various ways, some of which offer a surprise and may enhance their appeal for children. **Sensory qualities** to consider when planning children's menus include:

- color
- flavor (strong or mild; sweet or sour)
- texture (crisp, crunchy, or soft)
- shape (round, cubed, strings)
- temperature (cold or hot)

Figure 18–1 **Slice apples horizontally for a novel and magical surprise!**

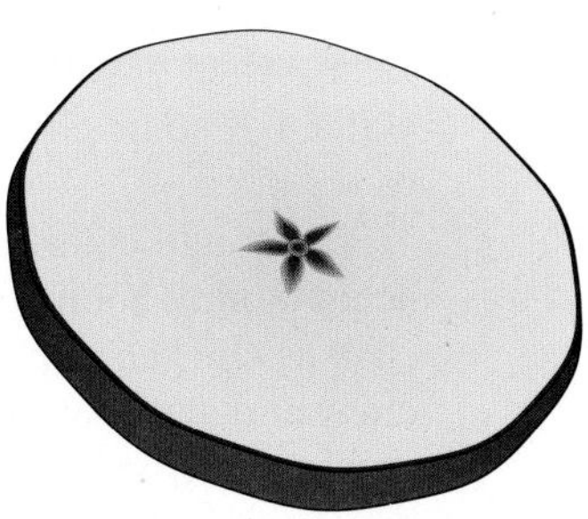

sensory qualities – *aspects that appeal to sight, sound, taste, feel, and smell.*

Sensory qualities affect children's food acceptance and choices (Mustonen, Rantanen, & Tuorila, 2009). Toddlers and young children think of foods in terms of color, flavor, texture, and shape rather than the nutrient content. Creating menus that incorporate a variety of sensory qualities improves their appeal and also reinforces children's developmental abilities to interpret the environment through their physical senses.

A comparison of the following two menus illustrates how color improves visual appeal:

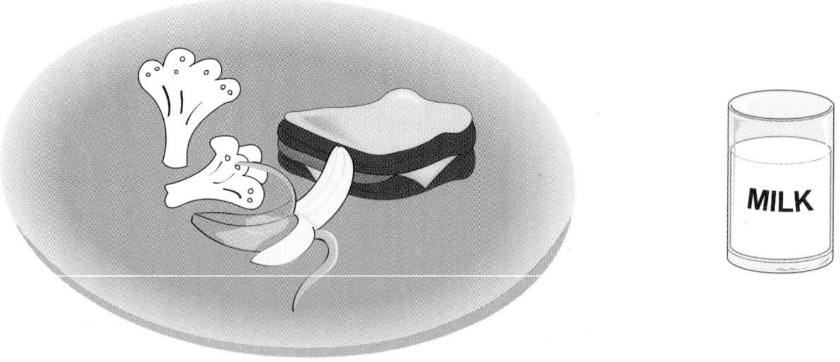

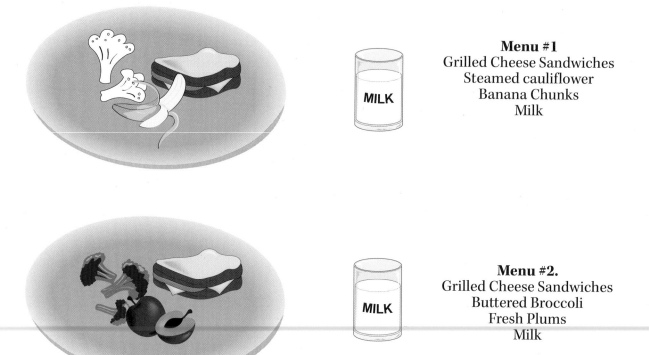

Menu #1
Grilled Cheese Sandwiches
Steamed cauliflower
Banana Chunks
Milk

Menu #2.
Grilled Cheese Sandwiches
Buttered Broccoli
Fresh Plums
Milk

Menu #1 is essentially a combination of yellow and brown tones. Substituting broccoli for cauliflower in Menu #2 adds color and also increases the amount of vitamins A and C. Substituting fresh plums for bananas also improves color contrast and adds yet another texture.

A meal's sensory qualities also provide opportunities for expanding children's language development. Children can be encouraged to identify and describe various food characteristics, such as being round or rectangular, red or yellow, hot or cold, smooth or rough, soft or crisp, sweet or salty. Songs and stories about foods also provide a fun way to reinforce language skills. For some children, simply talking about a food's qualities may improve their willingness to try it.

Although color is an important element in food appeal, other aspects also contribute to its acceptability. Young children often prefer simple foods that are mild in flavor. Softer textured foods such as chicken or ground meats are more likely to be eaten because they are easier for children to chew and swallow. Plain foods are often preferred over those served in combination dishes. Young children also have a preference for sweet foods. Since the basis for this may be biological, care should be taken to limit their availability and to offer fresh fruits and nutritious whole grain baked products instead.

A Well-designed Menu Includes Familiar Foods and New Foods

Although it is important to introduce children to new foods, a meal should also include some that are familiar. Much of this familiarity is learned from family eating practices, which help shape children's life-long food preferences (Aldridge, Dovey, & Halford, 2009; Hamilton & Wilson, 2009). Sharing information, menu plans, and recipes with families can be helpful for expanding children's choices and exposure to new foods.

When introducing new foods, it is preferable to include only one at a time and to serve it along with other familiar foods. This ensures that if the new food is rejected, children will not leave the table hungry. (See Table 17-3 for suggestions about introducing new foods to young children.) The menu planner might also consider introducing unfamiliar foods for children to try at snack time, which avoids the new food being labeled as a "breakfast food" or "lunch food." New foods should be introduced with little fanfare and in small amounts to entice children's interest. Involving children in the preparation of an unfamiliar food is also an effective strategy for improving its acceptance (Heim, Stang, & Ireland, 2009; Kalich, Bauer, & McPartlin, 2009).

When feeding young children, it is also wise to include a number of finger foods (Table 18–7). Children who may still have difficulty managing eating utensils will find comfort in having small pieces of foods that they can pick up. This also helps to promote children's independence.

Most classrooms include children from a variety of cultural and ethnic backgrounds. A sensitive menu planner draws on this diversity and incorporates foods that are familiar to a variety of cultures. Incorporating **ethnic** foods into the menu serves several purposes:

- Children from the featured culture are likely to be familiar with these foods. Their acceptance and enjoyment may encourage classmates to try foods that are unfamiliar.
- Foods that are representative of different cultural groups add variety and interest to children's meals. They also provide a valuable forum for helping children to learn about other cultures.
- Serving ethnic foods can help to reduce barriers and encourage rapport with the children and their families. Families can be asked to submit recipes for consideration.
- Educating children about various cultures fosters greater respect for children who are from a culture different from their own (Lam & Lehman, 2008).
- The sharing of food is often an effective way of helping children from different cultures and ethnicities gain acceptance and comfort in an unfamiliar group.

Table 18–7 Suggested Finger Foods

apricot pieces	grapefruit sections (seeded)
banana chunks	green grapes (halved)
blueberries	melon cubes
cauliflower buds	nectarines
cheese cubes	orange sections
cherry tomatoes	red and green pepper sticks
crackers	pineapple chunks
cucumbers	sliced mushrooms
diced fresh peaches	string cheese
diced fresh pears	strawberries, diced
kiwi slices	zucchini sticks

ethnic – *pertaining to races or groups of people who share common traits or customs.*

Steps in Menu Planning

Menu planning should be organized so that it proceeds efficiently and effectively. Materials should be assembled before beginning and include:

- menu forms
- a list of foods on hand that need to be used
- a list of children's allergies
- recipe file
- old menus with notes and suggestions
- calendar with special events and holidays noted
- grocery ads for short-term planning
- USDA list of available commodity foods

The menu form shown in Figure 18–2 can be used by a large center or small home-based program and modified to include only the meals that will be served.

Step 1 List the main dishes to be served for lunch for the entire week. These should include a meat or meat alternative. Be sure to note children's food allergies and plan for appropriate substitutes. Combinations of whole grain products (see Chapter 13), such as dried peas, beans, lentils, cheese, nuts, or nut butters, are acceptable protein-source substitutes for meat, poultry, eggs, or fish. However, many of these combinations do not contribute as much iron as does meat so that care must be taken to meet children's needs by including other iron-rich foods.

Bean burrito with cheese	BBQ beef	Scrambled eggs	Vegetarian chili	Macaroni and cheese	Protein

Step 2 List vegetables and fruits, including salads, for the main meal. Be sure to use fruits and vegetables in season. Fresh produce in season is often less expensive, more nutritious, higher in fiber, and lower in sodium than canned or frozen foods. Fresh fruits and vegetables also serve as excellent learning activity materials. If menus are planned months in advance, local County Extension Offices can provide information concerning seasonal produce and predicted supplies.

Zucchini Orange wedges	Broccoli Mango slices	Cherry tomatoes Banana	Carrots and celery Plum slices	Green beans Apple wedges	Fruits and Vegetables

Step 3 Add enriched or whole grain breads and cereal products.

Whole wheat tortilla	Enriched whole grain bun	Whole wheat toast	Corn muffin	Enriched macaroni (in casserole)	Bread

Step 4 Add a beverage. Be sure to include the required amount of milk.

Milk	Milk	Milk	Milk	Milk	Milk

Figure 18–2 A sample menu-planning form.

		Monday	Tuesday	Wednesday	Thursday	Friday
Breakfast	Fruit/Vegetable Bread Milk					
Snack (supplement)	Bread Fruit/Vegetable or Milk					
Lunch	Protein Fruit/Vegetable Fruit/Vegetable Bread Milk					
Snack (supplement)	Bread Fruit/Vegetable or Milk					
	# Served					
Notes						

Step 5 Plan snacks to balance the main meal. Pay special attention to providing adequate amounts of vitamin C, vitamin A, iron, and calcium.

A.M. Snack	Prepared oat cereal Milk	Bran muffin Apple juice	Pumpkin bread Milk	Raisin toast Orange juice	Rye crackers Milk
P.M. Snack	Watermelon Wheat crackers Water	Cheese crackers Peanut butter Milk	Pizza biscuits Pineapple juice	Oatmeal cookies Milk	Egg salad sandwich Cranberry juice

Step 6 Review your menu. Be sure it includes the required amounts from the Food Guide Pyramid.

- Does it meet funding or licensing requirements?
- Does it include a variety of contrasting foods?
- Does it contain familiar foods?
- Does it contain new foods?

Step 7 Note changes on the menu and post where it can be viewed by teachers and families (Figure 18–3). The menu serves as an important form of communication between the school and families and helps to ensure that children's daily and weekly nutrient needs are more likely to be met.

Step 8 Evaluate the menu. Did the children appear to eat and enjoy the foods that were served? Was there much plate waste? Do not eliminate a food from the menu because it was rejected. Repeated exposures to disliked foods, sometimes as often as 10–12 times, have been shown to improve children's acceptance over time (Aldridge, Dovey, & Halford, 2009). Children's likes and dislikes are continually changing and a rejected food this week may become a favorite in another week or two. However, be sure to note children's preferences and dislikes on your copy and keep for future reference.

Figure 18–3 **Menus should be made available to families.**

WEEKLY MENUS

Week of ____________

Lunch and Snacks

	Monday	Tuesday	Wednesday	Thursday	Friday
Snack	Bagel with cream cheese Orange juice	Blueberry muffin Milk	Mixed fresh veggies & dip Corn muffin Water	Waffles Applesauce Milk	Graham crackers Cranberry juice
Lunch	Turkey with gravy Mashed sweet potatoes Peas Apple slices Bread & butter Milk	Macaroni & cheese Broccoli Watermelon Milk	Scrambled eggs Green beans Plums Biscuits Milk	Beef barbecue Cooked carrots Whole wheat bread Pears Milk	Spaghetti with meat sauce Tossed salad Bread sticks Honeydew melon Milk
Snack	Peanut butter Bananas Milk	Yogurt Pineapple Smoothies Water	Cheese cubes Whole wheat crackers Grape juice	Oatmeal cookies Milk	Mini pitas Hummus Tomato juice

Writing Menus

There are several approaches to menu-writing that the planner may wish to consider: weekly menus, cycle menus, and odd-day cycle menus. The program's scheduled hours of operation, personnel available to prepare the food, and method of purchasing food and supplies will determine the menu planning style that is most efficient and functional. **Weekly menus** list foods that are to be prepared and served for an entire week. This approach can be time-consuming because it must be repeated each week. Preparing 2 or 3 weeks' worth of menus simultaneously is often a more efficient use of the menu planner's time and allows utilization of larger, more economical amounts of food. The menu planner is also better able to evaluate the menu's nutrient contributions over an extended time period and avoid frequent repetitions of the same foods.

Cycle menus incorporate a series of weekly menus that are reused or recycled over a 2- or 3-month period. Cycle menus are usually written to parallel the seasons and incorporate fruits and vegetables that are most available and affordable. Although a well-planned cycle menu requires a greater initial time investment, it also saves time in the long run. Food ordering is more efficient and less time-consuming. However, the planner should not hesitate to change parts of the cycle that prove difficult to prepare or are not well accepted by the children. Seasonal cycle menus can be reused year after year with timely revisions.

Odd-day cycle menus involve planning menus for any number of days other than a week (e.g., 4 days, 6 days, 9 days). This type of cycling avoids the association of specific foods with certain days of the week. It also requires careful planning to avoid serving dishes or foods that require advance preparation in Monday-to-Friday programs.

Nutritious Snacks

Snacks can be an effective strategy for meeting some of children's daily nutrient needs as long as the food choices are nutrient-dense (Matt, 2008). Snacks should contribute vitamins, minerals, and other nutrients essential for health, growth, and development (Figure 18–4). Calorie-dense snacks, high in sugars and fat, are not appropriate choices for young children because they do not provide any nutrients that may have been missing or not adequately consumed in previous meals.

Foods that are new or unfamiliar to children are best introduced at snack time. Tasting parties and learning experiences designed around new foods also help to increase children's interest and willingness to try something different.

Snacks can also be planned to meet children's high energy needs. Small stomach capacity and short attention spans often limit what children are able to consume at a given time and, thus, may not be sufficient to sustain them until the next meal. A nutrient-dense snack served about 2 hours between meals is usually the best spacing for most children. This amount of time prevents children from becoming overly hungry or spoiling their appetite for the next meal.

Suitable Snack Foods

Fresh fruits and vegetables are ideal choices for snack foods and are excellent sources of vitamin C, vitamin A, and fiber (which aids elimination). The crispness of fresh fruits and vegetables also aids in removing food particles that may cling to teeth and stimulates the gums so they stay healthy. Fresh fruits and vegetables should be sectioned, sliced, or diced into small pieces to make them easier for children to chew and to prevent choking.

---

weekly menus – *menus that are written to be served on a weekly basis.*
cycle menus – *menus that are written to repeat after a set interval, such as every 3 to 4 weeks.*
odd-day cycle menus – *menus planned for a period of days other than a week that repeat after the planned period; cycles of any number of days may be used. These menus are a means of avoiding repetition of the same foods on the same day of the week.*

Figure 18–4 Snack suggestions for school-aged children.

Active days and growing bodies make after-school snacks a must. Plan snacks that children can help to make. Encourage children to drink water—thirst may be disguised as hunger.

- Banana chunks dipped in yogurt and crispy rice cereal; freeze
- Yogurt "sundaes"—layer flavored yogurt with fruit pieces and granola
- Bagel melts—low-fat cheese slice on bagel half; microwave
- Baked pita chips (make your own) with salsa
- Tortilla rollups—roll a low-fat cheese and ham slice up in a tortilla; serve with fatfree ranch dip
- Fruit smoothies—blend yogurt with favorite fruits
- Trail mix—combine various cereals, dried fruit, and mini marshmallows
- Whole wheat tortilla spread with peanut butter and cinnamon sugar
- Raw veggies with homemade hummus
- Oatmeal raisin cookies or pumpkin bread (a great cooking activity)
- Egg salad on wheat crackers
- Apple wedges with peanut butter dip
- Chocolate tofu pudding

Whole grains or enriched breads and grain products are also ideal high-fiber snack choices. Foods from this group offer a variety of flavors, textures, and interest to children's diets. **Enriched** breads and cereals are refined products to which iron, thiamin, niacin, riboflavin, and folic acid are added in amounts equal to the original whole grain product.

Unsweetened beverages such as **full-strength** fruit and vegetable juices offer another healthy snack food option. Orange, grapefruit, tangerine, and tomato juices are rich in vitamin C. Many manufacturers add vitamin C to their apple, grape, cranberry and pineapple juices; however, always check juice labels to determine if they are indeed fortified with vitamin C. Carbonated beverages, fruit punches, **fruit drinks**, and fruit-ades are unacceptable options. These beverages consist primarily of sugar, water, and few other nutrients unless small amounts of vitamin C have been added.

Water plays an important role in maintaining a healthy body (Edmonds & Burford, 2009). It should be made available to children at all times and can be served with their meals and snacks. Allowing children to pour water from a pitcher, on demand, may encourage them to drink it more often. Special attention should be given to water intake following a period of physical activity and when environmental temperatures and humidity are high. A quick stop at the drinking fountain is an ideal way to replenish water lost during active outdoor play.

Serving Meals

A nutritious meal is of no value to a child if it is not eaten. The mealtime atmosphere in which foods are presented can either forestall, encourage, or further contribute to eating problems. Meals should be served in a peaceful, social atmosphere. Straightening up the classroom prior to mealtimes eliminates the distraction of scattered toys or an unfinished game. Quiet music playing in the background also helps children (and adults) to relax and focus on the meal.

---

whole grains – *grain products that have not been refined; they contain all parts of the kernel of grain.*
enriched – *adding nutrients to grain products to replace those lost during refinement; thiamin, niacin, riboflavin, and iron are nutrients most commonly added.*
full-strength– *undiluted (as in 100 percent fruit or vegetable juice).*
fruit drinks – *products that contain 0–10 percent real fruit juice, added water, and sugar.*

Care should be taken to make the table and settings attractive. Child-made placemats add interest and give children an opportunity to contribute to the meal. Children can also make centerpieces from objects gathered on field trips or nature hikes. Plates, cups, utensils, and napkins should be laid out neatly and appropriately at each place. Involving children in setting the table provides a positive learning experience, improves their interest in the meal, and also promotes self-esteem.

Food served in an attractive manner also contributes to its appeal for children. Cooking foods at proper temperatures helps to retain their color, shape, and texture. Arranging them neatly in serving dishes or on plates also improves their visual appeal. (White or warm-hued plates enhance food's natural colors; cool-hued dishes such as blues and greens detract from most food colors.) Fresh, edible garnishes may be used if time and budget permit. Contrived or "cute" foods are time-consuming to prepare and may actually result in the children wanting to save them as "souvenirs" rather than in eating them.

Food may be served in a variety of styles:

- plate service
- family-style service
- combination of the above

Plate service involves placing food on individual plates in the kitchen before serving. This style offers the best option for **cost control** as it permits the food server to manage portion size and results in fewer leftovers and waste.

In family-style service, food is placed on the table in serving dishes. Children are encouraged to help themselves and pass the dish to the next child. Beverages are placed in small, easily managed pitchers, and each child pours the amount desired before passing it to the next child. Although this method does not permit the same degree of portion control as plate service, it does promote children's independence. Because children determine how much food to take and to eat, they are learning important problem-solving, decision-making, and self-regulation skills. They are also practicing motor skills used to dip, serve, pass, and pour, as well as social skills such as cooperating and sharing. Many teachers believe the positive aspects of family-style service outweigh the benefits of portion and cost control associated with plate service.

Because both service styles offer distinct advantages, teachers may decide to use a combination of the two. For example, the teacher may place entrée servings on the plates (the amount determined by each child's request) while the children pass the bread, fruit, and vegetables. Thus, cost savings are maintained by controlling the

Important self-regulation and motor skills are learned when children are encouraged to serve themselves.

cost control – *reduction of expenses through portion control inventory and reduction of waste.*

Adults should sit and eat meals together with children.

more expensive entrée portions and children's safety is ensured because entrees often involve hot foods. If the vegetables are hot, the teacher may prefer to serve them also.

It is important that teachers eat meals with the children because they serve as role models for appropriate behavior and attitudes concerning foods (Pearson, Biddle, & Gorely, 2009). Teachers should sit at the tables and engage children in pleasant conversations about things of interest. Children should also be encouraged to talk with one another. Dwelling on table manners and proper behavior during meals should be avoided as much as possible. Desirable eating behaviors can be acknowledged while children's negative eating behaviors should be ignored if possible. Table 18–8 offers additional suggestions for making mealtime relaxed, happy times.

Table 18–8 Making Mealtime a Pleasant Experience

Creating a positive eating environment makes mealtime an enjoyable experience for children if you:
• Provide meals that are nutritious, attractive, and tasty. • Provide a transition or quiet time just before meals so children are relaxed. • Avoid delays so children do not have to wait. • Have children help set the table, put food on the table, and/or help to clean up after eating. • Make sure the room is attractive, clean, and well lit; limit distractions. • Get to know each child's personality and reaction to foods. • Provide tables, chairs, dishes, glassware, eating, and serving utensils that are appropriate scale for children. • Support and encourage children's efforts to feed themselves. • Avoid making children feel rushed or pressured. Allow plenty of time for children to eat. • Never force children to eat. They will be picky eaters at times. • Offer a variety of foods prepared in different ways. • Encourage social interaction.

The Menu Must Stay Within the Budget

While the menu lists what foods are to be served, the budget defines the resources allotted for implementing the plan. Items that must be addressed in the budget include food, personnel, and equipment. The food budget can be controlled through careful attention paid to:

- menu planning
- food purchasing
- food preparation
- food service
- recordkeeping

Cost control is essential if a food service is to stay within the budget. The goal is to feed the children appetizing, nutritious meals at a reasonably low cost. However, cost control should never be the defining factor at the expense of providing nutritious food.

Menu Planning

Cost control begins at the menu-planning stage. To plan menus that stay within a budget, it is important to begin by including inexpensive foods. To do so, the planner must be aware of current prices and seasonal supplies.

The menu planner can reduce food costs by utilizing supplies on hand and any remaining leftovers. (Note: *Leftovers must be refrigerated promptly and cannot be reclaimed for reimbursement.)* To ensure that quality foods are selected from supplies on hand, the **First-In-First-Out (FIFO) inventory method** should be used. Supplies are dated as they are brought into the storage area. Newly purchased foods are placed at the back of storage and older items are moved to the front so they are used first.

Food Purchasing

Food purchasing, or **procurement**, is a crucial step in cost control. Lowering food costs during the purchasing phase can be accomplished by utilizing food from local suppliers, using USDA donated foods, and keeping abreast of price trends and market availability of various foods. Purchasing too much food or inappropriate foods can turn a menu that is planned around inexpensive foods into one that becomes expensive. The key step is to determine as accurately as possible the amount of food that is needed to adequately feed everyone. The use of standardized recipes can make this process easier by determining how much and what kinds of food are needed. The U.S. Department of Agriculture has developed a series of healthy recipes, including ingredient lists and large group quantities, for use in school lunches and child care programs. (See "Helpful Web Resources" at the end of this chapter.)

Before purchasing food, a written food order should be prepared with the following specifications:

- name of product
- federal grade
- packaging procedures and type of package
- test or inspection procedures
- market units—ounces, pounds, can size, cases, and so on
- quantity (number) of units needed
- style of food desired—pieces, slices, halves, chunks

If foods are purchased from local retail stores, a simple form that follows the store's floor plan will make the task of shopping easier and more efficient. When preparing the market order,

---

First-In-First-Out (FIFO) inventory method – *a method of storage in which the items stored for the longest time will be retrieved first.*

procurement – *the process of obtaining services, supplies, and equipment in conformance with applicable laws and regulations.*

list the items that must be purchased for the entire menu period (e.g., 1 week, 4 weeks) in the following order:

- main dishes
- breads, cereals, pastas
- fruits and vegetables
- dairy products

Frozen foods should be purchased last to minimize thawing between the store freezer and food service freezer.

Food Preparation

The nutrients in food are best retained when appropriate food preparation methods are utilized. Fruits and vegetables should be washed under running water; the use of soap or detergents is not recommended. If produce must be peeled for very young children, only a thin outer layer should be removed as many important nutrients are present in the skins.

Utilizing correct heat and cooking times are also important factors in cost control. Foods cooked too long or at excessively high heat may burn or undergo significant shrinkage. In either case, this can increase costs because burned food is not usable and shrinkage results in fewer portions than originally planned. Equally important is the fact that some nutrients, such as thiamin and vitamin C, are readily destroyed when exposed to heat.

Standardized recipes, as previously described, help to ensure that correct amounts of ingredients are purchased and leftovers are minimized. Leftover foods that have not been placed on the table may be promptly frozen and used when serving the same dish at a later date. Leftovers should be reheated in a separate pan and not combined with freshly prepared portions, nor should they ever be reheated more than once to prevent food-borne illness.

Food Service

If a recipe specifies a serving size, for example, 1/2 cup or 1 1/2 × 1 1/2 inch square, that amount is what must be served. When a family-style method is used, teachers may serve children standard portions as a means of portion control. In programs where children are encouraged to serve themselves, each child should be asked to initially take only as much as can be eaten and then request more.

Special serving utensils designed to measure out preselected amounts can be useful for controlling food portions and costs. Examples of such utensils are soup ladles and ice cream scoops, which are available in a number of standardized sizes (e.g., 1/4 cup, 1/2 cup); such tools can be purchased online or from restaurant supply stores.

Recordkeeping

Records documenting actual food expenses are vital for determining whether the menu planner has stayed within the projected budget. The cost of feeding each child and adult (cost/person ratio) is also important information for the meal planner to determine:

- Calculate the total number of individuals served.
- Calculate the total food bills.
- Divide the total dollars spent on food by the total number of persons served to determine the weekly or monthly food costs per person.

The results of weekly or month-by-month expense records can be used to modify the following month's menu in order to stay within budget. An inventory of all foods remaining on hand should also be updated monthly (unless there is little variation from month to month).

Focus On Families — Meal Planning

Families should use the Food Guide Pyramid as the basis for planning healthy, nutritious meals. Although meal planning may require some additional time and effort in the beginning, there are important benefits that can be achieved:

1. You can ensure that all food groups from the Pyramid are included.
2. It helps you to balance meals (serving meat that is high in salt, such as ham, with foods that do not contain much salt, such as steamed vegetables or fresh fruits).
3. By using a grocery list, you will make fewer unnecessary trips to the store and be less likely to buy foods on impulse.

Preparing a grocery list for the first time may seem a bit intimidating, but following these principles can help get you started:

- Build the main part of your meal around complex carbohydrates (rice, pastas, whole grains).
- Add variety and try different ethnic cuisines.
- Use planned leftovers to save time and money. (Serve half of a beef pot roast for one meal and use the other half in a stew or for BBQ sandwiches.) If time allows, cook a double batch of your family's favorite dish and freeze part for another meal.
- Avoid purchasing foods high in fat (and trans-fats) such as doughnuts, croissants, pastries, snack cakes, high-fat cookies, high-fat crackers, and chips.
- Try purchasing these foods for healthy, nutritious snacks: animal crackers, fig bars, whole grain cereals, graham crackers, whole wheat pitas or tortillas, pretzels, whole grain bread sticks, fresh fruits and vegetables.

Classroom Corner — Teacher Activities

Exploring Pumpkins

(PreK–2; National Health Education Standards, 1.2.1, 1.2.2)

Concept: Pumpkins are a type of food that is abundant in the fall. You can eat their seeds or use them to make many other foods items.

Learning Objectives

- Children will learn about and explore pumpkins.
- Children will be given an opportunity to help make and taste two pumpkin products.

Supplies

- 1 large pumpkin
- knife (teacher use only)
- newspaper
- medium-sized bowl for seeds
- baking pan

(continued)

Classroom Corner **Teacher Activities** *(continued)*

- oil
- pumpkin muffin recipe and ingredients
- muffin tins
- hand wipes

Learning Activities

- Read and discuss one of the following books:
  - *Pumpkin Day, Pumpkin Night* by Anne Rockwell
  - *Pumpkins* by Melvin and Gilda Berger
  - *The Berenstain Bears and the Prize Pumpkin* by Stan and Jan Berenstein
  - *Pumpkin Pumpkin* by Jeanne Titherington
- Show the children a pumpkin and ask them to help describe its appearance. Ask children questions about the pumpkin (color, size, shape, what can be done with a pumpkin, if it is a vegetable, where it grows, and if it can be eaten).
- Tell the children you are going to cut open the pumpkin and see what is inside. While the teacher cuts open the pumpkin, have children clean their hands with wipes. Call children up one at a time to put their hands in the pumpkin and remove some of the seeds. After everyone has had a turn, put the seeds aside; let children know that you will wash the seeds and bake them in the oven later.
- Next, have the children help make pumpkin muffins. They can add ingredients, stir, spoon batter into muffin cups, and so on.
- Serve the pumpkin seeds and muffins for snack with a glass of milk.

Evaluation

- Children will describe several characteristics and uses for pumpkins.
- Children will name at least two foods that can be made from a pumpkin.

Additional lesson plans for grades 3–5 are available on the premium website for this book.

Summary

- The menu is the basic tool of food service. It should meet the nutritional needs of those it is intended to serve, introduce new foods, include some items that are familiar/well-liked, be prepared in sanitary surroundings, and planned within budgetary limits.
- Menus can be planned by the week (weekly menu) or for multiple weeks at a time (cycle menu), or an odd-number of days (odd-day menu).
- Snacks should be nutrient-dense and planned to address deficiencies in children's diet.
- Meals should be served in a comfortable environment with foods prepared and served in an attractive manner to enhance their appeal to children.
- Strategies for planning meals that stay within budget include: purchasing high-quality foods that are in season; storing foods promptly and at the correct temperature, cooking foods at correct temperatures; using standardized recipes and appropriate serving sizes; and accurate recordkeeping.

Terms to Know

sensory qualities *p. 439*
ethnic *p. 441*
weekly menus *p. 445*
cycle menus *p. 445*
odd-day cycle menus *p. 445*
whole grains *p. 446*
enriched *p. 446*
full-strength *p. 446*
fruit drinks *p. 446*
cost control *p. 447*
(First-In-First-Out) FIFO inventory method *p. 449*
procurement *p. 449*

Chapter Review

A. By Yourself:

1. State the appropriate serving size for a child 3 to 5 years-old for each of the following foods:
   a. milk
   b. dry cereal
   c. fruit
   d. vegetable
   e. bread
2. Where can a program director locate information about licensing requirements for nutrition and food services for young children?
3. Name four sensory qualities that improve food's appeal.
4. What are two advantages of using fresh fruits and vegetables in season?
5. List two strategies the menu planner can use to control food costs.

B. As a Group:

1. Outline three ways to control food costs when preparing food.
2. Discuss how environment affects children's mealtime behaviors. Identify steps that adults can take to create a positive eating atmosphere for children.
3. Discuss how you might handle the following mealtime behaviors:
   - child refuses to eat any vegetables
   - child eats only the macaroni and cheese on his plate and then asks for more
   - child belches loudly to make the other children laugh
   - child is too busy talking to finish eating by the time others are done
4. Evaluate and comment on the nutrient quality of the following snacks:
   - cheese pizza and water
   - oatmeal/raisin cookie and milk
   - grape juice and pear slices
   - fruit drink and graham crackers
   - apricot jam and whole wheat toast

Case Study

Richard is in charge of the menu-planning at a small private school that enrolls approximately 75 children between the ages of 3 to 8 years. He wants to build his weekly menus around the Food Guide Pyramid by featuring a variety of foods from a different food group section each week. He is working closely with the classroom teachers to achieve his goal of introducing the children to a number of less common foods. He has decided to begin with the grain group and features bagels, tortillas, fried rice, grits, and pita bread on the first week's menu. The next food group he wants to address is the vegetable group.

1. Suggest a list of new or less familiar vegetables that Richard might include in his menu.
2. What are some ways that Richard might prepare these vegetables to make them appealing to children?
3. How should refusals be handled?
4. What food group would you suggest that Richard address the following week? Why?

Application Activities

1. Plan a 5-day menu appropriate for 4-year-old children that includes morning snack, lunch, and afternoon snack. The menu should provide one-half of the foods needed according to the Food Guide Pyramid. Provide one strong source of vitamin C, calcium, and iron each day. Include at least three rich vitamin A sources during the 5-day period.
2. Four-year-old Jamie often comes to school without having had breakfast at home. (Both of his parents work so he leaves home early every day.) By mid-morning, Jamie is often inattentive, lethargic, and seems to be "off in his own world." He seldom plays games with the other children and spends most of his recess just standing around. At lunchtime, Jamie tends to select only milk and breads and is resistant to eating most vegetables and meats.
   a. What may be the cause of Jamie's mid-morning behavior?
   b. How would you characterize Jamie's nutritional status?
   c. What eating patterns need to be corrected?
   d. What steps should be taken to improve Jamie's participation in activities, as well as his nutritional habits and health status?
3. Review the menu criteria discussed in this chapter. Rank the criteria as you perceive their degree of importance. Are there other factors that you believe should be considered in planning adequate menus? Consider the needs of individual early childhood programs, home-based programs, or family homes. Are the important factors the same or different for each situation?
4. Eiswari, 3 years old, is allergic to eggs. Explain how this affects menu planning.
5. Plan a daily menu that would meet all of the nutrient needs of a child who follows a vegan vegetarian diet. Then, modify the menu for a child who is a lacto-ovo-vegetarian. Include appropriate serving sizes.
6. The following weekly menu is planned for an early childhood program during the month of January:

Meat loaf	Whole wheat roll with margarine
Fresh asparagus	Watermelon-blueberry fresh fruit cup
Milk	

a. Evaluate this menu and suggest changes that would make it less expensive to serve yet still be equally or even more nutritious.
b. How would the cost of this menu served in January compare to the cost of the same menu served in June or July?

7. Videotape children in a group setting while they are eating. Identify and describe an aspect of the mealtime that you would change based on what you have learned in this chapter. Observe the same videotape and describe children's eating be haviors from a developmental perspective.

Helpful Web Resources

American Dietetic Association	http://www.eatright.org
Child and Adult Care Food Program	http://www.cacfp.org
FoodSafety.gov	http://www.foodsafety.gov
Native American Food Pyramid	http://www.nal.usda.gov/fnic/Fpyr/NAmFGP.html
National Food Service Management Institute (see newsletters for menus)	http://www.nfsmi.org
USDA—Center for Nutrition Policy & Promotion	http://www.cnpp.usda.gov/
USDA Healthy Meals Resource System (click on "Recipes & Menu Planning")	http://healthymeals.nal.usda.gov/
USDA- Nutrition Assistance Programs	http://www.fns.usda.gov/fns

You are just a click away from additional health, safety, and nutrition resources! Go to www.CengageBrain.com to access this text's Education CourseMate website, where you'll find:

- CACFP meal requirements for children ages 1 through 12
- sample menu planning form
- glossary flashcards, activities, tutorial quizzes, videos, web links, and more

References

Aldridge, V., Dovey, T., & Halford, J. (2009). The role of familiarity in dietary development, *Developmental Review*, 29(1), 32–44.

Benjamin, S., Copeland, K., Cradock, A., Meelon, B., Walker, E., Slining, M., & Gillman, M. (2008). Menus in child care: A comparison of state regulations with national standards, *Journal of the American Dietetic Association*, 109(1), 109–115.

Clark, M., & Fox, M. (2009). Nutritional quality of the diets of US public school children and the role of the school meal programs, *Journal of the American Dietetic Association*, 109(2 Suppl.), S44–S56.

Edmonds, C., & Burford, D. (2009). Should children drink more water? The effects of drinking water on cognition in children, *Appetite*, 52(3), 776–779.

Hamilton, S., & Wilson, J. (2009). Family mealtimes....Worth the effort? *Infant, Child & Adolescent Nutrition*, 1(6), 346–350.

Heim, S., Stang, J., & Ireland, M. (2009). A garden plot project enhances fruit and vegetable consumption among children, *Journal of the American Dietetic Association*, 109(7), 122–126.

Kalich, K., Bauer, D., & McPartlin, D. (2009). "Early Sprouts": Establishing health food choices for young children, *Young Children*, 64(4), 49–55.

Kaphingst, K. & Story, M. (2009). Child care as an untapped setting for obesity prevention: State child care licensing regulations related to nutrition, physical activity, and media use for preschool-aged children in the United States, *Preventing Chronic Disease*, 6(1), 143–167.

Lam, V., & Leman, P. (2008). Children's gender- and ethnicity-based reasoning about foods, *Social Development*, 18(2), 478–496.

Matt, M. (2008). Plant part snack: A way to family involvement, science learning, and nutrition, *Young Children*, 63(6), 98–99.

Mustonen, S., Rantanen, R., & Tuorila, H. (2009). Effect of sensory education on school children's food perception: A 2-year follow-up study, *Food Quality & Preference*, 20(3), 230–240.

Pearson, N., Biddle, S., & Gorely, T. (2009). Family correlates of breakfast consumption among children and adolescents: A systematic review, *Appetite*, 52(1), 1–7.

Story, M. (2009). The Third School Nutrition Dietary Assessment Study: Findings and policy implications for improving the health of US children, *Journal of the American Dietetic Association*, 109(2), S7–S13.

CHAPTER 19

Food Safety

NAEYC Standards *Chapter Links*

- **#1 c:** Promoting child development and learning
- **#2 c:** Building family and community relationships
- **#3 a, c, d:** Observing, documenting, and assessing to support young children and families
- **#4 c:** Using developmentally effective approaches to connect with children and families
- **#5 b:** Using content knowledge to build meaningful curriculum
- **#6 b, c, d and e:** Becoming a professional

Learning Objectives

After studying this chapter, you should be able to:

- Describe the populations at greatest risk for food-borne illnesses.
- Outline food safety and sanitation practices that are critical to preventing illness.
- Identify common food-borne diseases, including their food sources, symptoms, and prevention methods.
- Discuss conditions that promote bacterial growth, and explain how food infections and food intoxications differ.

This unit introduces factors other than the menu that contribute to effective food service in schools and early childhood settings. The success of a carefully planned menu depends upon the food being safe to eat.

Food Safety Depends on Sanitation

The safety of foods and meals prepared for young children is of equal importance to their nutritional value. **Food-borne illness** is a major public health concern that poses an especially dangerous risk, including death, for young children (Maki, 2009).

food-borne illness – *a disease or illness transmitted by the ingestion of food contaminated with bacteria, viruses, some molds, or parasites.*

A **food-borne illness outbreak** occurs when two or more people become ill after ingesting the same food and a laboratory analysis confirms that food was the source of the illness. The United States Centers for Disease Control (CDC) estimates that 76 million people become ill each year as a result of food-borne illnesses (CDC, 2009). This accounts for 325,000 hospitalizations and 5,000 deaths annually. Those groups at greatest risk are:

- infants and children, especially under 4 years
- pregnant women
- individuals 50 years of age and older
- persons with chronic diseases and weakened immune systems

Our increased reliance on mass food production and restaurant meals has raised the risk of exposing large numbers of people to food-borne illnesses. However, while outbreaks of food-borne illnesses associated with fast-food chains and food processing plants receive extensive media coverage, many cases are caused by home-cooked meals. (Remember the Thanksgiving when the whole family had "the flu" after the holiday dinner?) The connection between food and illness is often overlooked because the symptoms are similar to those experienced with other common conditions. As a result, the true extent of food-borne illness in this and other countries is unknown.

Causes of Food-Borne Illness

Food can become unsafe in several ways. Hazards to food are present in the air, in water, in other foods, on work surfaces, and on a food preparer's hands and body. These hazards can be divided into three categories (Figure 19–1):

- biological
- chemical
- physical

Bacteria present in the environment pose the greatest threat to food safety. Some bacteria can cause serious and dangerous illnesses while others are beneficial (e.g., blue cheese, yogurt). The risk of environmental contamination of foods can be reduced through two basic approaches:

- following strict personal health and cleanliness habits
- maintaining a sanitary food service operation

Figure 19–1 **Examples of food-borne contaminants.**

Hazard	Examples
Biological 	Bacteria Parasites Viruses Molds, yeasts
Chemical 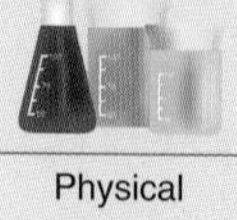	Pesticides Metals Cleaning chemicals
Physical 	Dirt Hair Broken glass Metal shavings Plastic Bones Rodent droppings

Hazard Analysis and Critical Control Point (HACCP)

- HACCP, or **Hazard Analysis and Critical Control Point**, is a food safety and self-inspection system that highlights potentially hazardous foods and how they are handled in

food-borne illness outbreak – *two or more persons become ill after ingesting the same food. Laboratory analysis must confirm that food is the source of the illness.*

Hazard Analysis Critical Control Point (HACCP) – *a food safety and self-inspection system that highlights potentially hazardous foods and how they are handled in the food service department.*

the food service environment. The U.S. Food and Drug Administration (FDA) recommends the implementation of HACCP because it is one of the most effective and efficient ways to ensure that food products are safe (Riggins & Barrett, 2008). A sound HACCP plan is based on seven principles:

1. **Conducting a hazard analysis**. In this phase, an HACCP team is assembled. The team should list all food items used in the establishment with the product code, preparation techniques, and storage requirements for each one. A flow chart should be developed that follows the food from receiving to serving in order to identify potential hazards during each step of this process (Figure 19–2).
2. **Determining the critical control point (CCP).** These are points during food preparation where potential and preventable hazards are identified (i.e., cooking foods to appropriate temperatures; using proper thawing techniques; maintaining proper refrigerator/freezer temperatures).
3. **Establishing critical limits.** Procedures and operating guidelines are developed to help prevent or reduce hazards in the food service area. Requirements should be established and monitored to ensure that they are being met.
4. **Establishing monitoring procedures.** This principle needs to be accomplished through consistent documentation in temperature logs, observation and measurement of requirements, and frequent feedback and monitoring by the food service manager.
5. **Establishing corrective actions.** Specific actions need to be developed and implemented if a critical control point procedure is not being met. These episodes should be accurately documented so that future occurrences can be prevented.
6. **Establishing recordkeeping and documentation procedures.** Records of importance include recipes, time/temperature logs, employee training documentation, cleaning schedules, and job descriptions.
7. **Establish verification procedures.** Management must be diligent in observing staff members' routine behaviors and provide continued training to address any deficiencies.

For the HACCP plan to be successful in any food service establishment, continuous monitoring and improvement are essential (USDA, 2010).

Personal Health and Cleanliness

Persons who are involved in food preparation and service must take great care to maintain a high level of personal health. Food handlers must meet health standards set by health department and child care licensing agencies in each state. Personnel who work in licensed early childhood or school-based programs are generally required to provide written confirmation that they are currently free of communicable diseases such as tuberculosis and hepatitis. Food handlers should also undergo periodic physical examinations to document their state of general health.

Everyone who is involved in food preparation and service should also be free of all communicable illnesses, such as colds, respiratory or intestinal types of influenza, gastrointestinal upsets, or acute throat infections. People who are experiencing even mild forms of these conditions often believe they are well enough to work, but in doing so they may transmit their illness to others. A person who is ill should refrain from handling food until he or she is symptom free for at least 24 hours (Figure 19–3). Programs should prepare for the possibility of a cook's absence by maintaining an emergency menu with easy-to-prepare foods, such as:

- canned soups
- peanut butter
- canned or frozen fruits and vegetables

---

critical control point (CCP) – *a point or procedure in a specific food system where loss of control may result in an unacceptable health risk.*

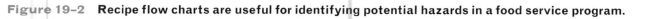

Figure 19–2 **Recipe flow charts are useful for identifying potential hazards in a food service program.**

BASIC BEEF CHILI

INGREDIENTS	AMOUNT	25	50	100
Lean ground beef	Lbs	7	14	28
Canned tomatoes	Qts	1 1/2	3	6
Canned kidney beans	Qts	1 3/4	3 1/2	7
Tomato paste	Cups	1 3/4	3 1/2	7
Water	Gals	1/2	1	2
Dehydrated onions	Ozs	1	2	4
Chili Powder	Tbsp	3	6	12
Sugar	Tbsp	1 1/4	2 1/2	5
Cumin	Tbsp	2	4	8
Garlic powder	Tbsp	1	2	4
Onion powder	Tbsp	1	2	4
Paprika	Tbsp	1	2	4
Black pepper	Tbsp	1/2	1	2

PREPARATION

1. **CCP** Thaw ground beef under refrigeration (41°F).
2. Place ground beef in steam kettle or in large skillet on stove top. Cook meat using medium high heat until lightly browned. While cooking, break meat into crumbs of about 1/2" to 1/4" pieces.
3. Drain meat well, stirring while draining to remove as much fat as possible. If desired, pour hot water over beef and drain to remove additional fat.
4. Mash or grind canned tomatoes with juice. Add to kettle or stock pot with cooked ground beef. Add remaining ingredients to mixture and stir well.
5. **CCP** Simmer chili mixture for 1 hour, stirring occasionally. Temperature of cooked mixture must register 155°F or higher.

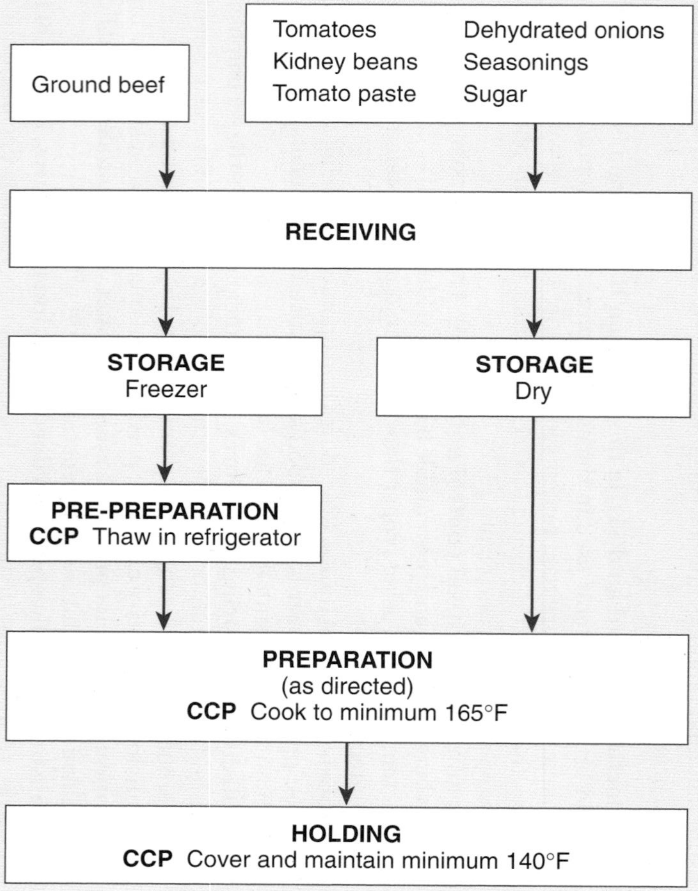

(continued)

Figure 19–2 Recipe flow charts are useful for identifying potential hazards in a food service program. *(continued)*

BASIC BEEF CHILI (cont'd)

PREPARATION (cont'd)

6. **CCP** Remove from heat and portion into service pans. Cover and hold for service (140°F).

7. Portion: 1 cup (8 ounces) per serving

SERVICE

1. **CCP** Maintain temperature of finished product above 140°F during entire service period. Keep covered whenever possible. Take and record temperature of unserved product every 30 minutes. Maximum holding time, 4 hours.

STORAGE

1. **CCP** Transfer unserved product into clean, 2-inch deep pans. Quick-chill. Cooling temperature of product must be as follows: from 140°F to 70°F within 2 hours and then from 70°F to 41°F or below, within an additional 4 hour period. Take and record temperature every hour during chill-down.

2. **CCP** Cover, label, and date. Refrigerate at 41°F or lower for up to 7 days (based on quality maintained) or freeze at 0°F for up to 3 months.

REHEATING:

1. **CCP** Thaw product under refrigeration, if frozen (41°F).

2. **CCP** Remove from refrigeration, transfer into shallow, 2-inch deep pans and immediately place in preheated 350°F oven, covered. Heat for 30 minutes or until internal temperature reaches 165°F or above.

   Discard unused product.

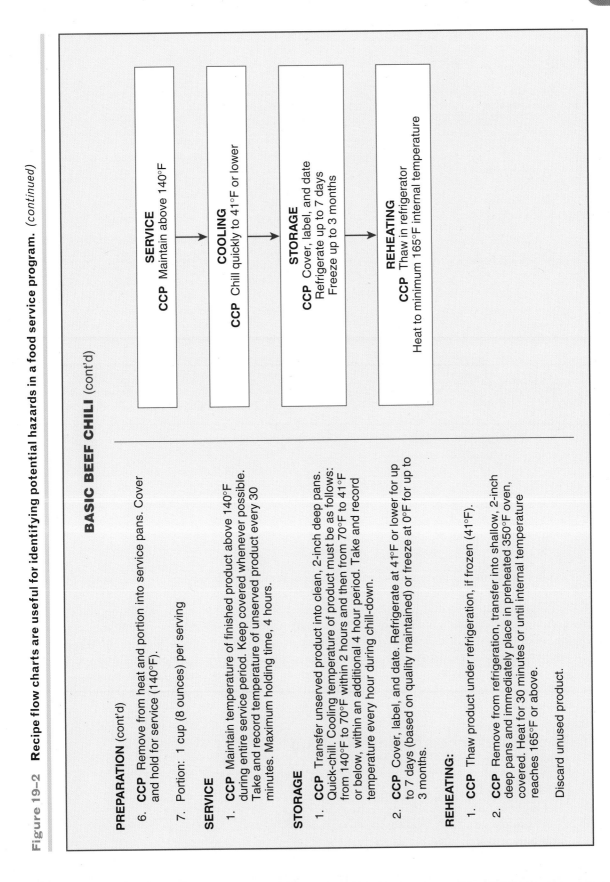

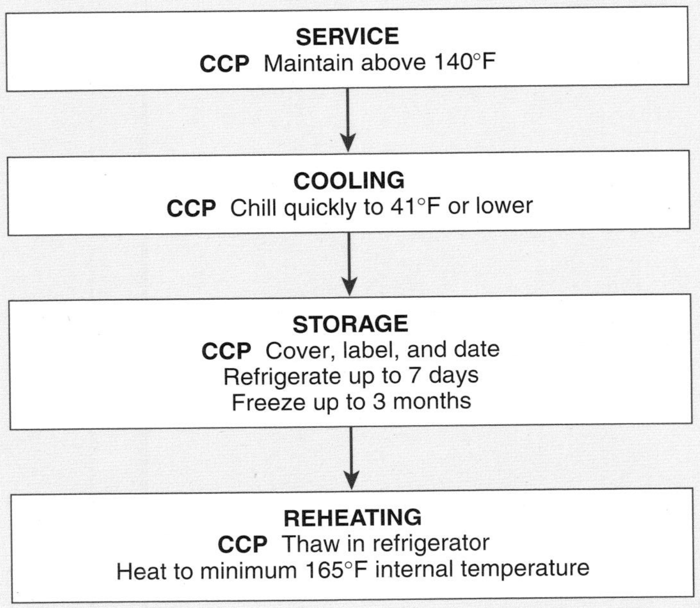

SERVICE
CCP Maintain above 140°F
COOLING
CCP Chill quickly to 41°F or lower
STORAGE
CCP Cover, label, and date
Refrigerate up to 7 days
Freeze up to 3 months
REHEATING
CCP Thaw in refrigerator
Heat to minimum 165°F internal temperature

Figure 19–3 Food handler's health and the potential for transmission of food-borne illness.

Condition	Guidelines
Abscess or skin infections	Avoid food preparation if lesions are open or draining. Plastic/latex gloves should be worn if sores are present on hands.
Cough, cold, or respiratory infection (without fever)	Avoid handling or working with food if coughing is uncontrollable or nose-blowing is frequent. Wash hands often and step out of food preparation areas when coughing or sneezing.
Cuts or burns (not infected)	Keep affected area(s) bandaged. Wear plastic/latex gloves if injuries are on hands or lower arms.
Diarrhea	Avoid contact with food, children and other personnel until 24 hours after diarrhea ends. Medical evaluation should be obtained for diarrhea lasting longer than 48 hours to rule out infectious diseases such as E. coli, giardia, salmonella, hepatitis A, and campylobacter. Contact local health department authorities if tested positive for any of these.
HIV/AIDS	No restrictions are necessary. Food handlers should practice good handwashing and personal hygiene.
Respiratory infections (with fever)	No contact should be had with food or food preparations until 24 hours after the fever ends. A throat culture may be needed to rule out strep infections.
Vomiting	Avoid contact with food, children, and other personnel until 24 hours after the vomiting ends.

- canned tuna or frozen, cooked chicken
- cheese (can be frozen)
- dried beans, rice, and pastas
- eggs

Meals that require a minimum of time and/or cooking skill can easily be prepared when adequate food supplies are kept on hand.

Food handlers should wear clean, washable clothing and change aprons frequently if they become soiled. Hair should be covered by a net, cap, or scarf while the worker is preparing food. Head coverings should be put on and shoulders checked carefully for loose hair prior to entering the kitchen. Fingernails should be properly maintained and no polish or artificial nails allowed. Jewelry should not be worn with the exception of a plain wedding band to prevent transfer of trapped food particles. Food handlers should also refrain from chewing gum or smoking around food to prevent contamination from saliva.

The Importance of Hand Washing

Hand washing is of utmost importance to personal cleanliness (Figure 19–4). Hands should be washed thoroughly:

- upon entering the food preparation area
- before putting on gloves to work with food
- before touching food
- after handling nonfood items such as cleaning or laundry supplies

Figure 19–4 Correct hand-washing technique.

1. Have paper towel ready.
2. Wet hands and wrists under warm, running water.
3. Apply soap and lather hands to loosen dirt and bacteria.
4. Rub hands together vigorously for at least 30 seconds,washing carefully between fingers and under nails.
5. Rinse thoroughly under running water.
6. Before turning off the water, dry hands carefully.
7. Use the paper towel to turn off the faucet.

- between handling different food items
- after using the bathroom
- after coughing, sneezing, or blowing the nose
- after using tobacco, eating, or drinking
- after touching hair or bare body parts (face, ears, nose)

Frequent and correct hand washing is essential for reducing the spread of food-borne illnesses.

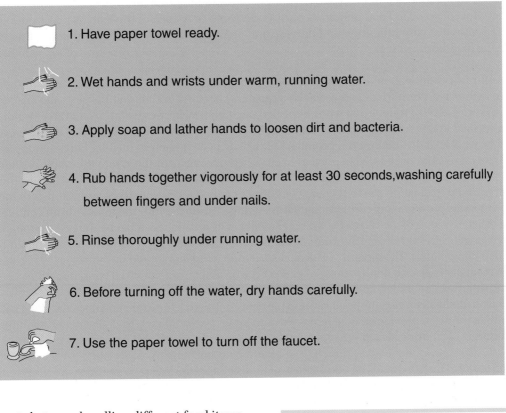

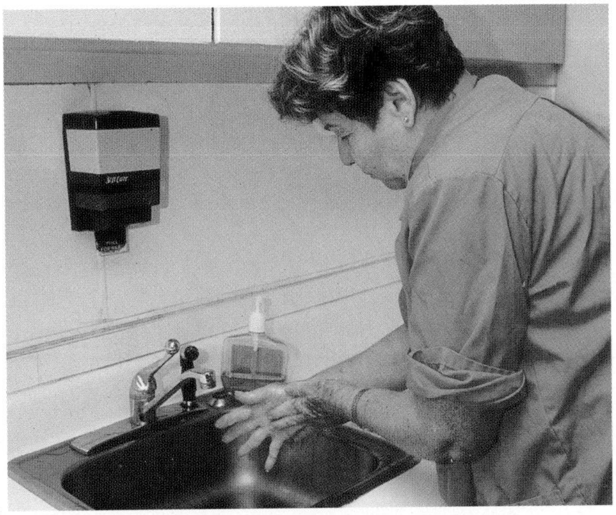

Careful hand washing is also mandatory after handling raw foods such as fish, shellfish, meat, and poultry to prevent cross-contamination with other foods. Latex gloves offer an additional measure of protection but hands must still be washed carefully following their removal. Current recommendations suggest that soap and water remains the accepted method of cleaning hands in non-health care settings (Liu et al., 2010). Although waterless, alcohol-based gels are increasingly being used in health care settings, they are never considered a substitute for proper hand washing. Disease prevention and control also depend on teaching children proper hand-washing technique. This can be accomplished by having children count to 20 and state their full name, or by singing the entire alphabet song while washing their hands. Any cuts or abrasions on the food handler's forearms, arms, or hands must be bandaged and covered with gloves (hands only). Gloved hands should be washed as often as bare hands because they also pick up and transmit infectious organisms.

Safe and Sanitary Food Service

The way in which food is handled, stored, transported, and prepared ultimately affects the health of those who consume it. Food preparers must understand how each of these steps may become a potential source of contamination and develop and practice safety measures to minimize the risk of causing food-borne illness.

Food All raw produce should be inspected for spoilage upon delivery and should be thoroughly washed before use. Fresh fruits and vegetables can carry bacteria and numerous pesticide residues (Katz & Winter, 2009). Produce that won't be peeled, such as strawberries, potatoes, and green onions, can be washed under running water and a small brush used to remove surface dirt. Lettuce leaves should be washed individually. Even produce that will be peeled, such as melons, bananas, oranges and carrots should be rinsed well to prevent bacteria from being introduced into the edible portions when cutting into the food or touching it with hands that have handled contaminated peel or rind. All dairy products must be **pasteurized**. The tops of canned foods should be washed before they are opened; this prevents any contaminants from being introduced into the food or from contaminating other cans or work surfaces via a dirty can opener. (Can openers must be washed thoroughly between uses to prevent cross-contamination). Food in cans that "spew" when opened should be discarded immediately. The integrity of all packaged food wrappers should be intact (e.g., no broken film on meat packages, no dented cans) to protect the product from potential contamination.

The sink, faucet handles, and drain should be cleaned with a disinfectant after any contact with raw meat, fish, shellfish, eggs, or poultry. Food particles trapped in the drain and disposal along with moisture in the drain provide an excellent environment for bacterial growth. A disinfecting solution (1 tablespoon of chlorine bleach per one quart of water) can be mixed and poured down the drain.

Food Storage Careful handling and storage of foods at appropriate temperatures are important safety measures that can be taken to prevent illness. Thermometers should be hung in the warmest area of the refrigerator and in the freezer to determine if appropriate temperatures are being maintained. Refrigerators should be kept at 38°F to 40°F and freezers at 0°F or below. Foods must remain frozen until they are ready to be used, and then thawed:

- in the refrigerator
- in cold water (place food in watertight, plastic bag; change water every 30 minutes)
- in a microwave oven
- while cooking

⚠ **Caution: Frozen food should never be thawed at room temperature! Once thawed, food should be used and never refrozen.**

Transport Food should be covered or wrapped during transport to help maintain temperature control and avoid the possibility of **microbial** contamination. When serving foods, each serving bowl, dish, or pan should have a spoon; spoons should not be used to serve more than one food. Caution should also be used not to touch serving spoons to a person's plate to prevent contamination from saliva.

Food Service Food that has been served should not be saved. An exception to this rule are fresh fruits and vegetables that can be washed after removal from the table and served later or incorporated into baked products such as muffins. Foods are safe to serve if they have been held in the kitchen at proper temperatures (160°F for hot food or 40°F or below for cold foods) for no longer

---

pasteurized – *heating a food to a prescribed temperature for a specific time period to destroy disease-producing bacteria.*
microbial – *refers to living organisms, such as bacteria, viruses, parasites, or fungi that can cause disease.*

than 2 hours. Foods that are to be saved should be placed in shallow pans (three inches or less in depth so they cool quickly) and immediately refrigerated or frozen.

Foods such as creamed dishes, meat, poultry, or egg salads are especially prone to spoilage and should be prepared from ingredients that have been cooked and chilled or maintained at temperatures below 40°F until they are used. Protein-based dishes such as these should also be assembled quickly and served or immediately refrigerated in shallow containers.

Sanitation of Food Preparation Areas and Equipment

Cleanliness of the kitchen and kitchen equipment is essential for ensuring food safety. Traffic through the kitchen should be minimized to reduce the introduction of dirt and bacteria. A schedule, such as that shown in Figure 19–5, is useful for assuring that all areas of the kitchen, including floors, walls, ranges, ovens, and refrigerators, are cleaned on a regular basis. Equipment used in the direct handling of food must also receive extra care and attention. Countertops and other surfaces on which food is being prepared should be **sanitized** or **disinfected** with a chlorine bleach solution (¼ cup bleach to a gallon of water or 1 tablespoon per quart of water) between every preparation of different food types (meat, salads, fruit). A fresh bleach solution must be mixed daily to retain its disinfecting strength.

> ⚠ Caution **Never mix bleach with anything other than water—a poisonous gas can result!**

Cutting boards should be nonporous and always washed with hot, soapy water and sanitized with a bleach solution after each use. Separate cutting boards should be designated for different food preparations (e.g., meat, raw poultry, salad, fresh fruits) to reduce the risk of cross contamination (Fravalo et al., 2009). Cutting boards can be labeled or color coded to indicate their specific purpose.

Figure 19–5 Frequent, systematic cleaning is essential for maintaining a safe and sanitary kitchen.

CLEANING SCHEDULE

Daily

- Cutting boards are sanitized after each use.
- Counter tops are washed and sanitized before food preparation is begun and between preparation of different foods.
- Tables are washed with sanitizing solution.
- Can openers are washed and sanitized.
- Range tops are cleaned and functional.
- Floors are damp mopped.
- Sink is scrubbed and disinfected.

Weekly

- Ovens are cleaned.
- Refrigerator is cleaned with soap and rinsed with vinegar water.

As Needed

- Refrigerator/freezer are defrosted.
- Walls are around countertops are washed.
- Floors are scrubbed and sanitized.

---

sanitized – *cleaned or sterilized.*
disinfected – *killed pathogenic organisms.*

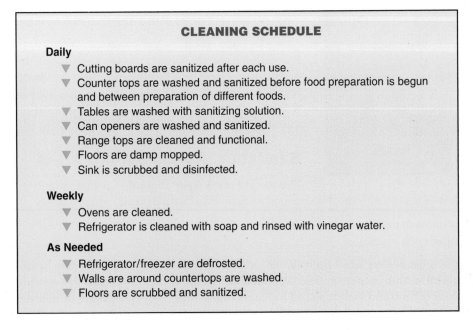

Reflective Thoughts

How safe is your personal kitchen? Although regulations are written for organizational kitchens, what about the kitchens in our homes?

Do you:

- sanitize counter surfaces and cutting boards each time they are used? Do you use an antibacterial product or dilute chlorine bleach?
- sanitize utensils? Do you immerse them in hot (170°F) water for at least 30 seconds? Do you wash them in the dishwasher?
- wash your hands frequently? Wash briskly with soap? Dry them with a clean towel or paper towels?
- sanitize spills from raw meats, fish, seafood, and poultry?
- avoid using sponges, or wash/sanitize them regularly?
- wash fruits and vegetables thoroughly?
- cook foods to proper temperatures?
- have a thermometer in the refrigerator, freezer, and oven to determine if appropriate temperatures are being maintained?

Tables should be washed and disinfected before and after meals.

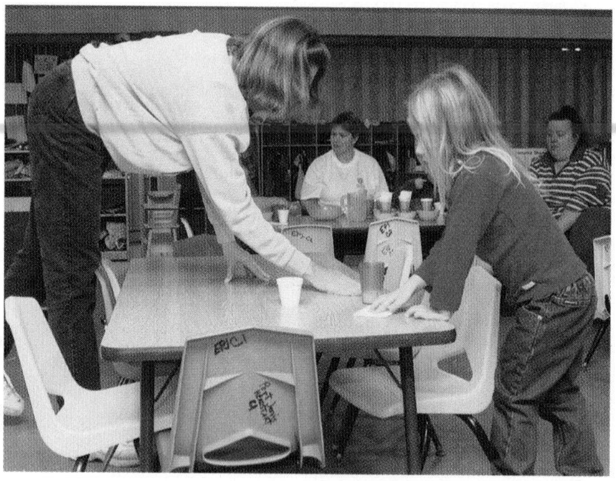

Dishwashing Dishes may be washed by hand or with a mechanical dishwasher. If washing by hand:

- Wash dishes with hot water and detergent.
- Rinse dishes in hot, clear water.
- Sanitize dishes with chlorine bleach solution or scald with boiling water.
- Air dry (not dried with a towel) all dishes, utensils, and surfaces.

If a mechanical dishwasher is used to wash dishes, the machine must meet local health department standards. Some state licensing regulations provide guidelines as to which dishwashing method is permitted based on the number of persons being served.

Sanitation of Food Service Areas

The eating area also requires special attention. Tables used for classroom activities must be washed and sanitized with a disinfecting solution:

- before and after each meal
- before and after each snack

Children and adults must always wash their hands carefully before eating and especially before they begin to set the table or to prepare and serve food. Children should also be taught that serving spoons are used to serve food and then replaced in the serving dishes. They must never be allowed to eat food directly from the serving dishes or serving utensils.

Continuous assessment of sanitation and food service conditions is essential for preventing food-related illnesses. A functional tool for monitoring the food environment and food handling practices is illustrated in Figure 19–6.

Figure 19–6 Checklist for evaluating sanitary conditions in food service areas.

SANITATION EVALUATION

	EX	GOOD	FAIR	POOR
FOOD				
1. Supplies of food and beverages must meet local, state, and federal codes.				
2. Meats and poultry must be inspected and passed for wholesomeness by federal or state inspectors.				
3. Milk and milk products must be pasteurized.				
4. Home-canned foods must not be used.				
FOOD STORAGE				
1. Perishable foods are stored at temperatures that will prevent spoilage: a. Refrigerator temperature: 40°F (4°C) or below				
b. Freezer temperature: 0°F (-18°C) or below				
2. Thermometers are located in the warmest part of each refrigerator and freezer and are checked daily.				
3. Refrigerator has enough shelves to allow space between foods for air circulation to maintain proper temperatures.				
4. Frozen foods are thawed in refrigerator or quick-thawed under cold water for immediate preparation, or thawed as part of the cooking process. (Never thawed at room temperature.)				
5. Food is examined when brought to center to make sure it is not spoiled, dirty, or infested with insects.				
6. Foods are stored in rodent-proof and insect-proof covered metal, glass, or hard plastic containers.				
7. Containers of food are stored above the floor (6 inches) on racks that permit moving for easy cleaning.				

(*Continued*)

Figure 19–6 Checklist for evaluating sanitary conditions in food service areas. *(continued)*

SANITATION EVALUATION

	EX	GOOD	FAIR	POOR
8. Storerooms are dry and free from leaky plumbing or drainage problems. All holes and cracks in storeroom are repaired.				
9. Storerooms are kept cool: 50°F to 70°F (10°C to 21°C)				
10. All food items are stored separately from nonfood items.				
11. Inventory system is used to be sure that stored food is rotated.				
FOOD PREPARATION AND HANDLING 1. All raw fruits and vegetables are washed before use. Tops of cans are washed before opening.				
2. Thermometers are used to check internal temperatures of: a. Poultry—minimum 170°F (74°C)				
b. Pork and pork products—minimum 160°F (66°C).				
3. Meat salads, poultry salads, potato salads, egg salad, cream-filled pastries and other potentially hazardous prepared foods are prepared from chilled products as quickly as possible and refrigerated in shallow containers or served immediately.				
4. All potentially hazardous foods are maintained below 40°F (4°C) or above 140°F (60°C) during transportation and holding until service.				
5. Foods are covered or completely wrapped during transportation.				
6. Two spoons are used for tasting foods.				
7. Each serving bowl has a serving spoon.				
8. Leftover food from serving bowls on the tables is not saved. An exception would be raw fruits and vegetables that could be washed. Food held in kitchen at safe temperatures is used for refilling bowls as needed.				

(Continued)

Figure 19–6 Checklist for evaluating sanitary conditions in food service areas. *(continued)*

SANITATION EVALUATION	EX	GOOD	FAIR	POOR
9. Food held in the kitchen at safe temperatures is reused.				
10. Foods stored for reuse are placed in shallow pans and refrigerated or frozen immediately.				
11. Leftovers or prepared casseroles are held in refrigerator or frozen immediately.				
STORAGE OF NONFOOD SUPPLIES 1. All cleaning supplies (including dish sanitizers) and other poisonous materials are stored in locked compartments or in compartments well above the reach of children and separate from food, dishes, and utensils.				
2. Poisonous and toxic materials other than those needed for kitchen sanitation are stored in locked compartments outside the kitchen area.				
3. Insect and rodent poisons are stored in locked compartments in an area apart from other cleaning compounds to avoid contamination or mistaken usage.				
CLEANING AND CARE OF EQUIPMENT 1. A cleaning schedule is followed: a. Floors are wet mopped daily, scrubbed as needed.				
b. Food preparation surfaces are washed and sanitized between preparation of different food items (as between meat and salad preparation).				
c. Cutting boards are made of hard nontoxic material, and are smooth and free from cracks, crevices, and open seams.				

(Continued)

Figure 19–6 Checklist for evaluating sanitary conditions in food service areas. *(continued)*

SANITATION EVALUATION

	EX	GOOD	FAIR	POOR
d. After cutting any single meat, fish, or poultry item, the cutting board is thoroughly washed and sanitized.				
e. Can openers are washed and sanitized daily.				
f. Utensils are cleaned and sanitized between uses on different food items.				
2. Dishwashing is done by an approved method: a. *Hand washed*—3-step operation including sanitizing rinse.				
b. *Mechanical*—by machine that meets local health department standards.				
3. Range tops are washed daily and as needed to keep them clean during preparation.				
4. Ovens are cleaned weekly or as needed.				
5. Refrigerator is washed once a week with vinegar.				
6. Refrigerator is defrosted when there is about 1/4" thickness of frost.				
7. Tables and other eating surfaces are washed with a mild disinfectant solution before and after each meal.				
8. All food contact surfaces are air-dried after cleaning and sanitizing.				
9. Cracked or chipped utensils or dishes are not used; they are disposed of.				
10. Garbage cans are leakproof and have tight-fitting lids.				
11. Garbage cans are lined with plastic liners and emptied and cleaned frequently.				
12. There is a sufficient number of garbage containers available.				

(Continued)

Figure 19–6 Checklist for evaluating sanitary conditions in food service areas. *(continued)*

SANITATION EVALUATION

	EX	GOOD	FAIR	POOR
INSECT AND RODENT CONTROL				
1. Only an approved pyrithren base insecticide or fly swatter is used in the food preparation area.				
2. The insecticides do not come in contact with raw or cooked food, utensils, or equipment used in food preparation and serving, or with any other food contact surface.				
3. Doors and windows have screens in proper repair and are closed at all times. All openings to the outside are closed or properly screened to prevent entrance of rodents or insects.				
PERSONAL SANITATION				
1. Health of food service personnel meets standards: a. TB test is current.				
b. Physical examination is up to date.				
2. Everyone who works with or near food is free from communicable disease.				
3. Clean washable clothing is worn.				
4. Hairnets or hair caps are worn in the kitchen.				
5. There is no use of tobacco or chewing gum in the kitchen.				
6. Hands are washed thoroughly before touching food, before work, after handling nonfood items, between handling of different food items, after using bathroom, after coughing, sneezing, blowing nose.				

Food-Borne Illnesses

Food poisoning refers to a variety of food-borne illnesses that may be caused by the presence of **bacteria**, **viruses**, **parasites**, or some forms of molds growing on foods. Descriptions of common food-borne illnesses, including the source of contamination, symptoms, and prevention methods, are presented in Table 19–1. Foods that are visibly moldy, soured, discolored, or beginning to liquefy should not be used; nor should food from bulging cans or cans in which the liquid is foamy or smells strange. However, many foods infected with disease-producing organisms provide the consumer with few notable clues. These foods may smell and appear safe, yet be capable of causing severe illness. Adhering to proper sanitation procedures, food preparation guidelines, and food handling techniques significantly decreases the risk of most food-borne illnesses (Ewen et al., 2009; Luber, 2009).

The introduction of **irradiation** as a food preservation technique has played an important role in reducing the incidence of some food-borne disease (Arvanitoyannis, Stratakos, & Tsarouhas, 2009). The U.S. Food and Drug Administration (FDA) has approved this technology as a "processing aid" for destroying illness-producing microorganisms, such as salmonella and E. coli in beef and poultry products, lunch meats, fresh fruits and vegetables, and processed foods containing eggs. It is also used to eliminate parasites and insects in spices and teas, slow the sprouting process (as in potatoes), delay ripening, and decrease spoilage. This procedure involves briefly exposing foods to low levels of gamma radiation; the amount of exposure and the types of foods that can be irradiated are closely regulated by the FDA (Trigo et al., 2009). The U.S. Department of Agriculture has approved the use of irradiated ground beef for the School Lunch Program since 2004.

Irradiated foods must carry the symbol and message shown in Figure 19–7. Irradiation is allowed in nearly 40 countries and is endorsed by the World Health Organization, the American Medical Association, and the CDC, among other groups.

Although some consumer groups remain skeptical about food irradiation, the practice is considered to be a safe and effective method for improving food safety. Irradiated foods are not radioactive, nor do they retain any radioactivity. Nutrient loss during irradiation, particularly of vitamins A, E, and C, and thiamin is minimal and significantly less than losses that occur during most conventional food preservation methods (Alothman, Bhat, & Karim, 2009).

Figure 19–7 Irradiated foods are required to display the radura symbol.

Irradiation serves an important role in improving food safety, but it is not the solution to preventing all food-borne illness. Concerns that irradiation will be used to cover up unsanitary food processing procedures or that consumers will depend on this process to prevent food-related illnesses have been raised by various groups. However, no technology will ever replace the need for consumers to follow safe food handling practices.

Steam pasteurization is another technique that has been developed to produce safer meat products. In this process, processed meats and animal carcasses are exposed to pressurized steam for 6 to 8 seconds to destroy harmful bacteria (Sommers, Geveke, & Fan, 2008). Researchers are also studying a variety of other preventive measures, including spraying baby chicks with antibiotic mist to reduce salmonella infections in poultry and changing cattle feeding practices immediately before slaughter to control E. coli in beef. Undoubtedly, new strategies for controlling and managing food contamination will continue to be developed in an effort to reduce food-borne disease.

---

bacteria – *one-celled microorganisms; some are beneficial for the body but pathogenic bacteria cause diseases.*
viruses – *any of a group of submicroscopic infective agents, many of which cause a number of diseases in animals and plants.*
parasites – *organisms that live on or within other living organisms.*
irradiation – *food preservation by short-term exposure of the food to gamma ray radiation.*

Table 19–1 Food-Borne Illnesses

Disease and Organism That Causes It	Source of Illness	Symptoms	Prevention Methods
salmonellosis *Salmonella* (bacteria; more than 2,000 varieties)	May be found in raw meats, poultry, eggs, fish, milk, and products made with them. Multiplies rapidly at room temperature.	Onset: 1–3 days after eating; symptoms may last 7 days; can be fatal. Nausea, fever, headache, abdominal cramps, diarrhea, and sometimes vomiting.	• Adhere to sanitary food handling practices. • Cook foods thoroughly. • Refrigerate foods promptly and properly.
E. coli *E. coli* 0157:H7 (bacteria)	May occur in undercooked beef (primarily ground beef), unpasteurized apple cider, raw milk, raw fruits and vegetables, and person-to-person contact. Organism is naturally present in animals raised for food.	Onset: 1–7 days; symptoms can last 7–10 days. Watery, profuse diarrhea, fever. Diarrhea may be bloody.	• Cook ground meats to 165°F, the temperature high enough to inactivate *E. coli.* • Pasteurization.
Staphylococcal food poisoning staphylococcal enterotoxin (produced by *Staphylococcus aureus* bacteria)	Toxins are produced when food contaminated with the bacteria remains too long at room temperature. Meats, poultry, egg products; tuna, potato and macaroni salads; and cream-filled pastries are ideal environments for these bacteria to produce toxin.	Onset: 1–8 hours after eating; symptoms may last 24–48 hours; rarely fatal. Diarrhea, vomiting, nausea, abdominal cramps, and prostration. Mimics stomach flu.	• Use sanitary food handling practices. • Cook foods to proper temperatures. • Refrigerate foods promptly and properly.
botulism *Clostridium botulinum* (bacteria)	Bacteria are widespread in the environment. However, bacteria produce toxin only in an anaerobic (oxygen-less) environment of little acidity. Types A, B, and F may result from inadequate processing of low-acid canned foods, such as green beans, mushrooms, spinach, olives, beef, and lunch meats. Type E normally occurs in fish.	Onset: 6–36 hours after eating, but can develop up to 10 days after ingestion. Recovery is slow, some symptoms may remain forever. Symptoms include muscle weakness, double vision, slurred speech, difficulty swallowing and breathing, and progressive paralysis. OBTAIN MEDICAL HELP IMMEDIATELY. BOTULISM IS OFTEN FATAL.	• Use proper methods for canning low-acid foods. • Avoidance of commercially canned low-acid foods with leaky seals or with bent, bulging, or broken cans. • Dispose of foods carefully to prevent animals from exposure.

(continued)

Table 19–1 Food-Borne Illnesses *(continued)*

Disease and Organism That Causes It	Source of Illness	Symptoms	Prevention Methods
Listeriosis *Listeria* monocytogenes (bacteria)	Raw animal and dairy products; fresh, soft cheeses; contaminated water.	Onset 7–21 days or longer; recovery time varies. Muscle aches, mild fever, diarrhea, and miscarriage; can spread to the nervous system, causing headache, stiff neck, loss of balance, and convulsions	• Pasteurization. • Adhere to proper cooking and refrigeration recommendations. • Wash hands to prevent cross-contamination.
parahaemolyticus food poisoning *Vibrio parahaemolyticus* (bacteria)	Organism thrives in warm waters and can contaminate fish and shellfish. Avoid eating raw fish and shellfish (e.g., mussels, oysters).	Onset: 12–24 hours after eating; lasts 1–7 days. Causes abdominal pain, nausea, vomiting, and diarrhea; can also bring on fever, headache, chills, and mucus and blood in the stools. Rarely fatal.	• Use sanitary food handling, including hand washing. • Cook seafood thoroughly.
gastrointestinal disease enteroviruses, rotaviruses, parvoviruses (virus)	Viruses exist in the human intestinal tract and are expelled in feces. Contamination of foods can occur in three ways: (1) when sewage is used to enrich garden/farm soil, (2) by direct hand-to-food contact during meal preparation, and (3) when shellfish grow in waters contaminated by sewage.	Onset: 1–2 days; usually lasts 4–5 days but may last for weeks. Causes severe diarrhea, nausea, and vomiting.	• Maintain sanitary handling of foods. • Use purified drinking water. • Ensure proper sewage disposal. • Cook foods adequately.
hepatitis hepatitis A virus (virus)	Chief food sources: shellfish harvested from contaminated areas, and foods that are handled a lot during preparation and then eaten raw (such as vegetables).	Onset 5–50 days (average 28 days); recovery takes several weeks. Causes jaundice, fatigue, headache, diarrhea, and dark urine. May cause liver damage and death.	• Maintain sanitary handling and cooking of foods. • Wash hands thoroughly. • Ensure proper sewage disposal.
mycotoxicosis mycotoxins (molds)	Produced in foods relatively high in moisture. Chief food sources: beans, grains, and peanuts that have been stored in warm, moist places.	May cause liver and/or kidney disease.	• Discard foods with visible mold. • Store susceptible foods properly.

giardiasis *Giardia lamblia* (parasite)	Parasites can reside in the intestinal tract of humans and animals and are expelled in feces. Parasites may be ingested from foods contaminated with sewage, from swallowing contaminated water (lake, pool, spring, river, spa), and from dirty hands and infected persons.	Onset 1–2 weeks; lasts 2–6 weeks with treatment. Diarrhea, abdominal pain, flatulence, and nausea.	• Maintain sanitary food handling. • Wash hands carefully. • Drink only from approved water sources.
Perfringens food poisoning *Clostridium perfringens* (bacteria)	Bacteria are widespread in environment. Generally found in meat and poultry and dishes made with them. Multiply rapidly when foods are left at room temperature too long. Destroyed by cooking.	Onset: 8–22 hours after eating (usually 12); symptoms last 1–2 days and are usually mild. Causes abdominal pain, diarrhea, nausea, and vomiting. Can be more serious in older or debilitated people.	• Maintain sanitary handling of foods, especially meat, meat dishes, and gravies. • Cook foods at appropriate temperatures. • Refrigerate foods promptly and properly.
shigellosis (bacillary dysentery) *Shigella* (bacteria)	Food becomes contaminated when a human carrier with poor sanitary habits handles liquid or moist food that is then not cooked thoroughly. Organisms multiply in food stored above room temperature. Found in milk and dairy products, poultry, potato salad, and contaminated water.	Onset: 1–7 days after eating; lasts 4–7 days. Causes abdominal pain, cramps, bloody diarrhea, fever, sometimes vomiting. Can be serious in infants, the elderly, or debilitated people.	• Maintain sanitary handling of food. • Cook food to proper temperatures. • Disposal of sewage and diapers properly. • Wash hands frequently and carefully.
campylobacterosis *Campylobacter jejuni* (bacteria)	Chief food sources: raw and undercooked poultry and meat, unpasteurized milk, and contaminated water.	Onset: 2–5 days after eating; lasts 6–7 days. Causes diarrhea (may be bloody), cramping, fever, nausea, and fever.	• Cook foods thoroughly. • Wash hands frequently and carefully. • Avoid unpasteurized milk.

(continued)

Table 19–1 Food-Borne Illnesses *(continued)*

Disease and Organism That Causes It	Source of Illness	Symptoms	Prevention Methods
gastroenteritis *Yersinia enterocolitica* (bacteria)	Bacteria multiply rapidly at room temperature, as well as at refrigerator temperatures of 39.2° to 48.2°F (4° to 9°C). Generally found in raw vegetables, undercooked meats (especially pork), water, and unpasteurized milk. Also transmitted person-to-person via dirty hands.	Onset: 4–7 days after exposure; lasts 1–3 weeks or longer. Flu-like symptoms, including fever, headache, nausea, diarrhea, abdominal pain, and fatigue. An important cause of gastroenteritis in children, but affects those of all ages. If not treated, can lead to more serious diseases (such as lymphadenitis, arthritis, and Reiter's syndrome).	• Cook foods thoroughly. • Sanitize cutting instruments and cutting boards before preparing foods that are eaten raw. • Avoid unpasteurized milk and unchlorinated water. • Wash hands carefully.
cereus food poisoning *Bacillus cereus* (bacteria and possibly their toxin)	Illness may be caused by the bacteria, which are widespread in the environment, or by an enterotoxin created by the bacteria. Found in raw meat, fish, milk, and vegetables. Bacteria multiply rapidly in foods stored at room temperature.	Can cause two types of illness: a) onset of nausea and vomiting 1–6 hours after eating; b) abdominal cramps and diarrhea 8–16 hours after eating.	• Maintain sanitary handling of foods. • Cook foods thoroughly. • Refrigerate foods promptly and properly.
cholera *Vibrio cholera* (bacteria)	Found in raw milk, fruits, and vegetables; contaminated water; fish and shellfish harvested from waters contaminated by human sewage. (Bacteria may also occur naturally in Gulf Coast waters.) Chief food sources: seafood, especially types eaten raw (such as oysters).	Onset: 1–3 days. Can range from "subclinical" (a mild uncomplicated bout with diarrhea) to fatal (intense diarrhea with dehydration). Severe cases require hospitalization and antibiotics.	• Maintain sanitary handling of foods. • Cook foods thoroughly, especially seafood. • Avoid drinking untreated water.

Issues To Consider **An *E. coli* Outbreak**

E. coli 0157:H7 is a deadly bacterium that is frequently in the news. It is commonly associated with outbreaks of contaminated and undercooked meats—especially ground beef. However, foods are not the only source of this infectious agent. A recent outbreak occurred at a popular water park when one of the children in attendance accidentally defecated in the wading pool. It was later determined that the chlorine levels had not been maintained at a level sufficient to destroy the bacteria. Twenty-six cases of 0157:H7 illness and one death were reported in several surrounding states. Other recent incidences of *E. coli* 0157:H7 infections have been traced to children's petting zoos and digging in beach sand (Goode et al., 2009; Heaney et al., 2009).

- Are your sanitation procedures adequate to prevent illnesses, such as E. coli, from spreading through water play?
- Are your food preparation and service methods safe?
- What sanitation precautions should you observe when taking children on an outing to prevent this type of illness?

Conditions for Bacterial Growth

Because our environment contains numerous bacteria, why do food-borne illnesses not occur even more frequently than they do? For illness to occur the following conditions must be present:

- *Potentially hazardous food*—bacteria generally prefer foods that are high in protein, such as meat, poultry, eggs, and dairy products.
- *Oxygen*—some bacteria require oxygen. Others cannot tolerate oxygen. A few bacteria can grow in environments with or without oxygen.
- *Temperature*—temperature is probably the most critical factor in bacterial growth. The hazard zone of 41°F–140°F is the ideal range in which bacteria grow most rapidly.
- *Time*—a single bacterial cell can multiply into one million cells in 5 hours under ideal conditions.
- *Water*—bacteria grow in foods with a higher moisture content.
- *Acidity*—bacteria prefer conditions that are near neutral (pH 7.0).

Food infections result when food containing large amounts of viable (live), disease-producing bacteria is ingested. Salmonella, E. coli, and campylobacter are examples of bacteria that commonly cause this type of

Protein-based foods, such as eggs, must be stored and cooked at proper temperatures to prevent disease-producing bacteria from growing.

food infections – *illnesses resulting from ingestion of live bacteria in food.*

Figure 19–8 Safe handling instructions are present on every package of meat and poultry.

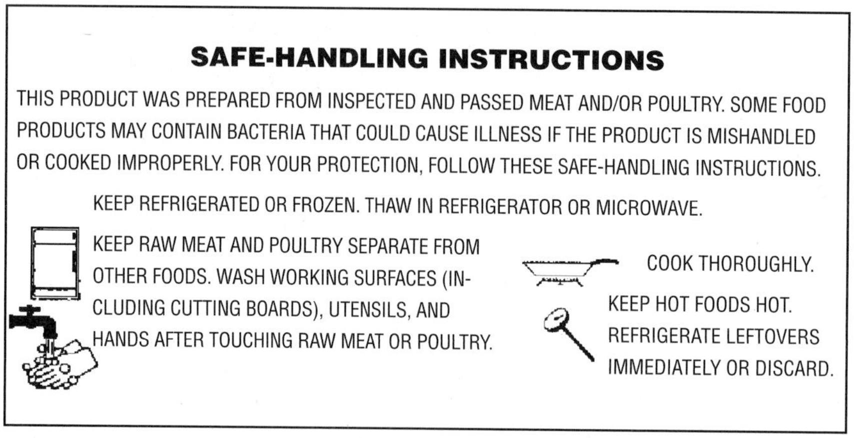
SAFE-HANDLING INSTRUCTIONS
THIS PRODUCT WAS PREPARED FROM INSPECTED AND PASSED MEAT AND/OR POULTRY. SOME FOOD PRODUCTS MAY CONTAIN BACTERIA THAT COULD CAUSE ILLNESS IF THE PRODUCT IS MISHANDLED OR COOKED IMPROPERLY. FOR YOUR PROTECTION, FOLLOW THESE SAFE-HANDLING INSTRUCTIONS.
KEEP REFRIGERATED OR FROZEN. THAW IN REFRIGERATOR OR MICROWAVE.
KEEP RAW MEAT AND POULTRY SEPARATE FROM OTHER FOODS. WASH WORKING SURFACES (INCLUDING CUTTING BOARDS), UTENSILS, AND HANDS AFTER TOUCHING RAW MEAT OR POULTRY.
COOK THOROUGHLY.
KEEP HOT FOODS HOT. REFRIGERATE LEFTOVERS IMMEDIATELY OR DISCARD.

food-borne illness. Symptoms typically develop within 12–24 hours after contaminated food has been ingested and bacteria have had sufficient time to multiply.

Food intoxications occur when food containing the bacterial toxins is consumed. Symptoms usually develop within a shorter time period (1–6 hours), with the exception of botulinum toxins, which take longer to cause illness (8–36 hours).

The incidence of food-borne illnesses remains a significant health threat to populations, especially young children, in the United States and worldwide (CDC, 2009). Large-scale food production and increased demands for exotic and out-of-season produce have made food-related diseases more difficult to control and prevent. International food inspection and production systems have also been slow to improve. In the United States, new legislation and resources have been added to increase food inspections and recalls, but they are still inadequate to address the complexity of the current food supply. For example, the USDA regulations allow federal meat inspectors to conduct brief (several second) visual examinations of animal carcasses. Because bacteria are not visible to the human eye, the results of any "inspection" must be questioned. Thus, the consumer must assume full responsibility for choosing, storing, and preparing these products to minimize the chances of becoming ill. Since protein-based foods such as milk, eggs, meat, fish, and poultry are the most common carriers of infectious agents and/or toxins, extra care must be taken whenever preparing these items. Safe-handling instructions attached to packaging should be followed carefully (Figure 19–8). Most bacteria and toxins are destroyed when foods are cooked to the proper temperatures (Figure 19–9). It is NEVER safe to allow young children to eat raw or undercooked eggs, meat products, fish, or seafood because their immature immune systems leave them more vulnerable to food-borne illness (Pesavento et al., 2010). Remember that cold temperatures **STOP** most (not all) bacterial growth, while heat **KILLS** most (not all) bacteria.

Figure 19–9 Safe cooking temperatures.

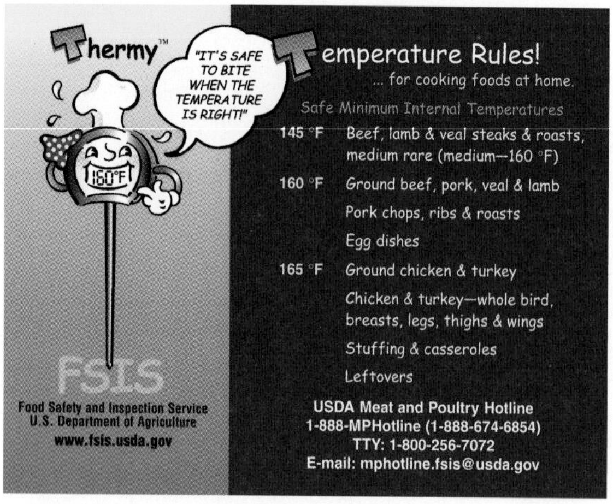

... for cooking foods at home.

It's Safe to Bite When the Temperature is Right. Food Safety and Inspection Service, USDA.

food intoxications – *illnesses resulting from ingestion of food containing residual bacterial toxins in the absence of viable bacteria.*

Focus On Families — Hand Washing

Food safety is everyone's responsibility, and it is never too early to introduce children to safe hygiene behaviors. Hand washing is the single-most effective tool for reducing illness caused by germs that have been transferred from people and surroundings. Teaching children the art of correct hand washing is an essential component of healthy eating behaviors and practices. As the primary role model for children, parents and teachers must also practice correct hand washing techniques and be consistent in helping children to adopt this behavior.

- Children should wash their hands with warm, soapy water before and after eating, after using the toilet, after playing with a pet, and after covering a cough or blowing their nose, or after playing in sand.
- Keep a step stool nearby to make it easier for the child to reach the sink.
- Post a chart near the sink and have children make a mark for every time he/she has washed their hands. Acknowledge your child for a job well done.
- Make hand washing fun. Purchase colorful soaps and soap dispensers; design special towels (use fabric paints to add the child's name).
- Be creative ... make up your own song using the melodies from favorite childhood tunes or nursery rhymes such as "Row, Row, Row Your Boat" or "Old McDonald Had a Farm." Have your child wash hands for the entire length of the song. They will have fun while ensuring that an appropriate amount of time is spent washing hands.

Classroom Corner — Teacher Activities

Cleaning and Setting the Table... **(PreK–2; National Health Education Standards 1.2.1; 7.2.1; 7.2.2)**

Concept: Cleaning the table before eating and touching the correct parts of cups, plates, and silverware when placing them on the table can prevent the spread of germs.

Learning Objectives

- Children will learn how to clean classroom tables before meals.
- Children will learn how to properly place cups, plates, and silverware on the table.

Supplies

- Soapy water and disinfectant water in spray bottles
- One dishcloth per table
- One paper towel per table
- Silverware, cups, plates, and napkins for meal time

Learning Activities

- Choose one helper per table and demonstrate how a table is to be washed and set for meal time.
- Have each child wash his/her hands carefully before starting.

(*continued*)

Classroom Corner **Teacher Activities** *(continued)*

- Fill a spray bottle with soapy water. Have the children take turns spraying and wiping the table surface where they are sitting. Next, the teacher should spray the disinfectant (bleach mixture or commercial product) and wipe it off.
- Have children wash their hands after cleaning the tables; explain that hands get dirty after touching a dirty table.
- Show children how to put one plate by each chair; they should only touch the outside rim of each plate.
- Show children how to handle silverware by touching only the handles and not the eating portion.
- Show children how to touch the lower part of the cup, not the rim. Have children place silverware, cups, and napkins at each place.
- Have children rewash their hands if they scratch their nose, cover a cough, and so on, while setting the table.
- Discuss how washing hands, cleaning the tables, and handling eating utensils correctly help to prevent the spread of germs.

Evaluation

- Children will demonstrate the correct procedure for cleaning the tables.
- Children will set the tables correctly and touch the plates, cups, and silverware appropriately.

Additional lesson plans for grades 3–5 are available on the premium website for this book.

Summary

- People whose immune system may be weakened by age, pregnancy, or a medical condition are most vulnerable to food-borne illnesses.
- Food service personnel must consistently follow basic food safety practices, including:
  - Implementing HACCP (Hazard Analysis and Critical Control Point), a food safety and self-inspection system
  - Maintaining personal health and cleanliness; avoid working around food if ill
  - Practicing correct and consistent hand washing
  - Handling and storing food items safely and at correct temperatures
  - Sanitizing all food service areas on a regular basis
- Food-borne illnesses are most commonly caused by bacteria, viruses, parasites, and some molds. High temperatures, irradiation, and pasteurization are some of the methods currently used to destroy harmful bacteria.
- Bacteria grow best in conditions that include a protein food source, oxygen, temperatures between 41°F–140°F, time, moisture, and a non-acidic environment.

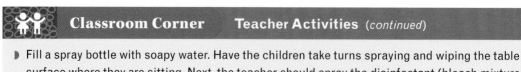

Terms to Know

food-borne illness *p. 457*
food-borne illness outbreak *p. 458*
HACCP—Hazard Analysis Critical Control Point *p. 459*
critical control point *p. 459*
pasteurized *p. 464*
microbial *p. 464*
sanitized *p. 465*
disinfected *p. 465*
bacteria *p. 472*
viruses *p. 472*
parasites *p. 472*
irradiation *p. 472*
food infections *p. 477*
food intoxications *p. 478*

Chapter Review

A. By Yourself:

1. List three methods for maintaining food preparation areas clean and germ-free.
2. Describe the proper care, uses, and handling of cutting boards that must be followed for safe food service.
3. How should ground meat be safely thawed if there is not time to defrost it in the refrigerator?
4. Terry, a chef, has a cut on her hand. John, a school lunch cook, has developed a sore throat and productive cough. Hanna, a cook's assistant, has experienced several days of unexplained diarrhea. What precautions must each of these food handlers take?

B. As a Group:

1. Describe the HACCP process. Develop your own HACCP plan—from the time you purchase a pound of ground beef until it shows up as a hamburger on your plate.
2. Identify and describe the personal sanitation practices that would be important to review with a newly hired cook.
3. Set up a debate, with one side arguing on behalf of irradiation while the other side argues against this technology.
4. Describe the audiences most likely to be sickened by food-borne illnesses and explain why they are at greater risk.

Case Study

The health department is investigating an outbreak of food poisoning at a local child care center. The children were served a menu that included tacos, tossed lettuce salad, fresh melon cubes, and milk. Annie, the cook, had forgotten to put the ground beef in the refrigerator to defrost a few days earlier, so she allowed it to thaw on the counter overnight. After dividing the partially thawed raw ground beef with her bare hands, she continued preparations for lunch and chopped the ingredients for a tossed salad. Using the same knife that she used to open the packages of ground beef, she cut the melon into cubes for the fruit salad.

1. What is the likely cause of this food-borne illness outbreak?
2. In what ways did the cook contribute to this situation?
3. How could this outbreak have been prevented?

Application Activities

1. The cook at your early childhood center has called in sick with strep throat. Using the emergency stock described in this chapter, plan a lunch menu that will meet the CACFP menu-planning guidelines outlined in Chapter 18.
2. Invite a laboratory technician to class. Ask him/her to make culture plates of a:
   a. hand before washing
   b. hand after washing with water only
   c. hand after washing with soap and water
   d. strand of hair

   Have the technician return with the cultures after they have incubated for several days.
   a. Is bacterial growth present on any of the culture plates?
   b. Which cultures have the most bacterial growth?
   c. Discuss how these results could be best utilized in terms of:
      1. food preparation and service procedures
      2. early childhood center meal and snack times.
3. Visit a local early childhood center or public school. Use the sanitation checklist in Figure 19–6 to assess the kitchen. Develop suggestions for correcting any problems noted and share your results with the program director.

Helpful Web Resources

Canadian Food Inspection Agency (CFIA)	http://www.inspection.gc.ca
Centers for Disease Control and Prevention	http://www.cdc.gov
Fight Bac!	http://www.fightbac.org
Food and Drug Administration	http://www.fda.gov
Gateway to Government Food Safety Information	http://www.FoodSafety.gov
USDA Food Safety & Inspection Service (FSIS)	http://www.fsis.usda.gov

You are just a click away from additional health, safety, and nutrition resources! Go to www.CengageBrain.com to access this text's EducationCourseMate website, where you'll find:

- sanitation evaluation checklist
- glossary flashcards, activities, tutorial quizzes, videos, web links, and more

References

Alothman, M., Bhat, R., & Karim, A. (2009). Effects of radiation processing on phytochemicals and antioxidants in plant produce, *Trends in Food Science & Technology,* 20(5), 201–212.

Arvanitoyannis, I., Stratakos, A., & Tsarouhas, P. (2009). Irradiation applications in vegetables and fruits: A review, *Critical Reviews in Food Science & Nutrition,* 49(5), 427–462.

Centers for Disease Control & Prevention (CDC). (2009). Preliminary FoodNet data on the incidence of infection with pathogens transmitted commonly through food—10 states, 2008, *MMWR,* 58(13), 333–337.

Ewen, T., Greig, J., Bartleson, C., & Michaels, B. (2009). Outbreaks where food workers have been implicated in the spread of foodborne disease, *Journal of Food Protection,* 72(1), 202–219.

Fravalo, P., Laisney, M., Gillard, M., Salvat, G., & Chemaly, M. (2009). Campylobacter transfer from naturally contaminated chicken thighs to cutting boards is inversely related to initial load, *Journal of Food Protection*, 72(9), 1836–1840.

Goode, B., O'Reilly, C., Dunn, J., Fullerton, K., Smith, S., Ghneim, G., Keen, J., Durso, L., Davies, M., & Montgomery, S. (2009). Outbreak of Escherichia coli 0157 – H7 infections after petting zoo visits, *Archives of Pediatrics & Adolescent Medicine*, 163(1), 42–48.

Heaney, C., Sams, E., Wing, S., Marshall, S., Brenner, K., Dufour, A., & Wade, T. (2009). Contact with beach sand among beachgoers and risk of illness, *American Journal of Epidemiology*, 170(2), 164–172.

Katz, J., & Winter, C. (2009). Comparison of pesticide exposure from consumption of domestic and imported fruits and vegetables, *Food & Chemical Toxicology*, 47(2), 335–338.

Luber, P. (2009). Cross-contamination versus undercooking of poultry meat or eggs—Which risks need to be managed first? *International Journal of Food Microbiology*, 134(1–2), 21–28.

Liu, P., Yuen, Y., Hsiao, H., Jaykus, L. & Moe, C. (2010). Effectiveness of liquid soap and hand sanitizer against Norwalk virus on contaminated hands, *Applied & Environmental Microbiology*, 76(2), 394–399.

Maki, D. (2009). Coming to grips with foodborne infection—Peanut butter, peppers and nationwide Salmonella outbreak, *New England Journal of Medicine*, 360(10), 949–953.

Pesavento, G., Ducci, B., Nieri, D., Comodo, N., & Nostro, A. (2010). Prevalence and antibiotic susceptibility of *Listeria* spp. isolated from raw meat and retail foods, *Food Control*, 21(5), 708–713.

Riggins, L., & Barrett, B. (2008). Benefits and barriers to following HACCP-based food safety programs in childcare centers, *Food Protection Trends*, 28(1), 37–55.

Sommers, C., Geveke, D., & Fan, X. (2008). Inactivation of Listeria innocua on frankfurters that contain potassium lactate and sodium diacetate by flash pasteurization, *Journal of Food Science*, 73(2), 72–4.

Trigo, M., Sousa, M., Sapata, M., Ferreira, A., Curado, T., Andrada, L., Botelho, M., & Veloso, M. (2009). Radiation processing of minimally processed vegetables and aromatic plants, *Radiation Physics & Chemistry*, 78(7–8), 659–663.

U.S. Department of Agriculture (USDA). (2010). Food Safety & Inspection Service. *Food safety in the kitchen: A "HACCP" approach.* Accessed on January 25, 2010 from http://www.fsis.usda.gov/fact_sheets/Food_Safety_in_the_Kitchen/index.asp.

CHAPTER

20

Nutrition Education Concepts and Activities

NAEYC Standards *Chapter Links*

- **#1 a, b, and c:** Promoting child development and learning
- **#2 a, b, and c:** Building family and community relationships
- **#3 a, c, and d:** Observing, documenting, and assessing to support young children and families
- **#4 a, b, c, and d:** Using developmentally effective approaches to connect with children and families
- **#5 a, b, and c:** Using content knowledge to build meaningful curriculum
- **#6 b, c, and d:** Becoming a professional

Learning Objectives

After studying this chapter, you should be able to:

- Summarize the four basic principles that are fundamental to children's nutrition education.
- Explain why families must be involved in children's nutrition education.
- Discuss how nutrition learning experiences can be planned to reinforce children's developmental skills in other areas
- Describe the steps and safety issues involved in developing an effective nutrition lesson plan.
- Understand the sources that typically shape children's ideas about nutrition.

In the simplest of terms, **nutrition education** is any activity that tells a person something about food. These activities may be structured, planned activities, or very brief, informal happenings. The primary goals of nutrition education designed for young children are to introduce them to a few basic nutrition principles and to encourage them to eat and enjoy a variety of nutritious foods.

---

nutrition education – *activities that impart information about food and its use in the body.*

Basic Concepts of Nutrition Education

Schools have a responsibility to promote children's health and nutrition knowledge. They can help children begin to make connections between healthy eating and wellness by conducting learning experiences that are ongoing and reflect basic nutrition **concepts:**

1. Children must have nutritious food for their bodies to grow and stay healthy.
   - All animals and plants need food.
   - Eating food helps children to grow, play, learn, feel happy, and stay well.
   - It is important to eat many different foods.
   - Food provides energy for play.
   - A healthy diet must be balanced with physical activity.
2. Nutrients come from foods. It is these nutrients that allow children to grow and be healthy.
   - After food is eaten, nutrients are set free to work in our bodies.
   - Nutrients perform different functions in our bodies.
   - Many different nutrients are needed each day.
   - Foods are the source of all of the nutrients that are needed.
3. A variety of foods should be eaten each day. No one food provides all of the nutrients needed.
   - Different foods provide different nutrients so we need to eat many kinds of food each day.
   - Nutrients need to work together in our bodies.
   - Children should be introduced to a variety of foods from each of the Food Guide Pyramid groups and be encouraged to at least try a small bite.
   - Children should explore how foods differ relative to color, shape, taste, and texture. They can learn to group and to identify certain food categories, such as vegetables, fruits, grains, and meats.
4. Foods must be handled carefully before they are eaten to ensure that they are healthful and safe.
   - Cleanliness of all foods and the people who handle foods prevents illness.
   - Hands should always be washed carefully before eating or touching food.
   - Some foods need to be cooked properly and eaten hot.
   - Some foods must be kept refrigerated and may be served cold.
   - Involving children in food preparation teaches important lessons about how food must be handled to keep it safe.
   - Eating food that has not been handled properly can make children ill.

These conceptual points require that the adults responsible for nutrition education have a basic knowledge of nutrition, in relation to both foods and nutrients.

Families often have nutrition-related questions that may either be about their child or something they have seen in a magazine, heard on television,

Daily participation in physical activity is an important component of a healthy diet.

concepts – *combinations of basic and related factual information that represent a more generalized statement or idea.*

or read on the Internet. Because much misinformation abounds, it is important that teachers be well-informed and able to provide accurate information. However, they may not always know the correct answer. In these instances, teachers can refer families to a variety of community resources and health professionals, including dietitians, public health departments, USDA extension service offices, and health educators.

Teachers can also access an abundance of information and educational resource materials on the Internet to use when planning classroom nutrition activities or for distributing to families. However, these materials (and their sources) must be evaluated cautiously to determine if they are accurate, free of bias, and appropriate for the purpose intended. Questions to consider include:

1. Is the resource known for its reliability in reporting?
2. What are the professional credentials of the author(s)?
3. Is the resource accurate and does it address nutritional facts rather than theories or biased opinion?
4. Are unsubstantiated health claims presented?
5. Is the resource trying to sell something?
6. Is the material presented at the appropriate level or is it adaptable?
7. Are the suggested nutrition education projects healthful?
8. Are the projects safe?

As a general rule, information posted on websites with a ".gov" or ".edu" extension will usually meet these criteria and is considered trustworthy.

Responsibility for Nutrition Education

An effective nutrition education program involves the cooperative efforts of directors, administrators, teachers, cooks or food service personnel, and children's families. Although the size and organizational structure may vary from program to program, everyone makes important direct and indirect contributions to children's nutrition education (Drake, 2009).

Administrators can play a supportive and influential role in this process. The value they place on nutrition education sends a powerful message to teachers and food service personnel. For example, a director who considers children's nutrition education a priority will make sure that financial support is available and that obstacles don't interfere. In contrast, a director who considers this unimportant may also care little about the nutritious quality of children's meals and snacks or whether teachers include any nutrition education in the curriculum.

Classroom teachers are usually responsible for planning and executing nutrition education experiences. For this reason, they should be familiar with the conceptual framework that validates the importance of nutrition education. They must understand the principles of effective instruction and utilize methods that are age- and developmentally appropriate, establish achievable objectives, and evaluate the outcome of any nutrition activity. Teachers must also be knowledgeable about the nutritional value of foods and know how to foster children's healthy eating behaviors.

Food service personnel are responsible for preparing and serving meals that are nutritious and appealing, and, in some programs, they may also plan the menu. These roles provide valuable opportunities to contribute to children's understanding of a healthy diet. In addition, food service personnel can also be instrumental in reinforcing classroom nutrition activities by including foods that children are learning about on the weekly menu (Chan et al., 2009). For this reason, teachers should work closely with food service personnel so they are aware of planned nutrition activities and can have the necessary foods and equipment on hand.

Underlying the effectiveness of all nutrition education for young children is one very simple, basic concept: *Set a good example.* Children who observe a teacher eating and enjoying a variety of nutritious foods will learn to eat more nutritiously than children who observe adults drinking soft drinks and consuming other calorie-dense junk foods.

Family involvement in children's nutrition education is essential for positive outcomes.

Family Involvement in Nutrition Education

Family involvement is vital to children's nutrition education. Teachers play an important role in this process by helping families to understand why a nutritious diet is necessary, how to meet children's nutrient needs, and how to encourage healthy eating and activity patterns (Blom-Hoffman et al., 2008). By establishing open lines of communication, teachers can support families' efforts to reinforce what children are learning about in school by:

- posting weekly menus and including suggestions for foods that provide nutritional complements to each menu
- providing families with a report of, and recipes for, new foods that children have recently been introduced to and tasted
- sharing information about nutrition education learning activities and food experiences with families; requesting feedback on children's reactions to these experiences
- presenting occasional evening meetings or workshops for families, which could include presentations or questions/answer sessions with local health agency personnel, demonstrations of food preparation by a local chef, or presentations by a parent who may have some food or nutrition experience to share
- inviting families to accompany children on food-related field trips
- encouraging families to join their children for lunch on occasion
- having a family volunteer to assist with menu planning
- asking families to share special recipes that are nutritious and family favorites
- inviting families to share ethnic or traditional foods with the class
- requesting that families assist with, and observe, one food experience activity with their child
- soliciting volunteers to develop guidelines/policy for acceptable (nutritious and safe) foods that families can provide for birthday or holiday celebrations

Remember that the ultimate goal of nutrition education is the promotion of children's health and development. Achieving this goal requires that effective communication and cooperation be established between school and children's homes.

Rationale for Nutrition Education in the Early Years

Young children are in the process of forming lifelong eating habits, and are thus more receptive to new ideas about food and food-related practices. Many everyday experiences, such as a trip to the grocery store or farmer's market or planting a garden, provide valuable "teachable moments." Impromptu as well as formal learning experiences should be based on sound pedagogical principles that support children's understanding, retention, and relevance to their personal well-being. This can be accomplished, in part, by thoughtfully integrating nutrition education across the curriculum to encourage children's development in all areas:

- *Promotion of language development and listening skills*
  Children learn and use food names, food preparation terms, and names of utensils. Children also use language to communicate with their peers and teachers throughout the nutrition activity. A variety of media sources, including children's literature, video clips, and music, can also be introduced to reinforce language, listening, and motor skills as well as nutrition concepts (Figure 20–1).
- *Promotion of cognitive development*
  Children learn to follow step-by-step directions in recipes. Math concepts are learned through activities that involve measurement of food (cups, ounces, teaspoons), counting, and time periods. Science concepts, such as changes in form (e.g., solids, liquids, gases), are reinforced through activities that involve heating, mixing, cooking, or chilling of foods. Children also begin to learn respect for other cultures, different food practices, where foods come from, and the ways in which foods are grown or produced.
- *Promotion of* ***sensorimotor*** *development*
  Hand-eye coordination and hand-finger dexterity are developed through measuring, cutting, mixing, spreading, and serving food. Sensory experiences involving shapes, textures, and colors are learned through an introduction to a wide variety of foods.
- *Promotion of social/emotional development*
  Children learn to work as part of a team in either large or small groups during nutrition activities. They begin to learn respect and acceptance of cultural differences through exposure to various ethnic foods and eating customs. Children also gain self-confidence and improved self-esteem when they master skills such as pouring juice into a glass, serving their own vegetables, or cutting up a sandwich by themselves. Educational activities centered around nutrition also provide opportunities for children to develop problem-solving, decision-making, cooperation, and communication skills.

Planning a Nutrition Education Program

The nutrition education program should be part of a coordinated plan that consists of well-designed activities leading to specific outcomes. Educational experiences should be planned to meet specified goals rather than simply being a way to fill time or to keep children busy. Measurable objectives should be developed and serve as guides in the selection of content, instructional method, assessment process, and desired behavioral outcomes. The National Health Education Standards are one example of a comprehensive framework that includes

---

sensorimotor – *Piaget's first stage of cognitive development, during which children learn and relate to their world primarily through motor and sensory activities.*

Figure 20–1 **Resources for teaching nutrition education.**

Action for Healthy Kids. **http://www.actionforhealthykids.org**

Albyn, C. & Webb, L. (1993). *The multicultural cookbook for students* (ages 9–12). Phoenix, AZ: Oryx Press.

Alliance for a Healthier Generation. **http://www.healthiergeneration.org/schools.aspx**

American Dietetic Association. *Five a day for children up to 2 years.* **http://www.eatright.org**

Berman, C. & Fromer, J. (2006). *Meals without squeals: Child care feeding guide & cookbook.* Boulder CO: Bull Publishing.

Coordinated Approach to Child Health (CATCH). **http://www.catchinfo.org**

D'Amico & Drummond, K. (1996).The science chef travels around the world: Fun food Experiments and recipes for kids. San Francisco, CA: Jossey-Bass.

Dodge, A. (2008). Around the world cookbook. New York: DK Publishing.

Dole Fresh Fruit & Vegetable Planner. **http://dpi.wi.gov/fns/pdf/dole_nov_09.pdf**

Eat Well and Keep Moving (interdisciplinary curriculum). **http://www.eatwellandkeepmoving.org**

Evers, C. (2006). *How to teach nutrition to kids.* Tigard, OR: 24 Carrot Press.

Food for Thought. University of Illinois Extension. **http://urbanext.illinois.edu/foodforthought/**

HeartPower Online. American Heart Association (lesson plans for preK through first grade; in English and Spanish). **http://www.americanheart.org/presenter.jhtml?identifier=3003345**

Kalich, K., Bauer, D., & McParlin, D. (2009). *Early sprouts: Cultivating healthy food choices in young children.* St. Paul, MN: Redleaf Press.

Kids Health in the Classroom. The Nemours Foundation. Weekly newsletter for educators with lesson plans. **http://classroom.kidshealth.org**

MyPyramid for Kids **http://www.MyPyramid.gov**

National Gardening Association. Kids Gardening (lesson plans and school projects) **http://www.kidsgardening.org**

National Dairy Council. *Nutrition Explorations.* **http://www.nutritionexplorations.org**

National Institute of Dental and Craniofacial Research (education resources). **http://www.nidcr.nih.gov/EducationalResources**

National Network for Child Care. Cooking with children: Kids in the kitchen. **http://www.nncc.org/Curriculum/fc46_cook.kids.html**

Nutrition Education of Texas (extensive lesson plans and resources for teaching nutrition education to children grades preK through high school) **http://netx.squaremeals.org**

learning materials, behavioral objectives, and evaluation criteria for grades PreK–12. (See Appendix A and the inside covers of this text.)

The overall program should be planned around some or all of the four basic nutrition education concepts described at the beginning of this chapter. Learning experiences should be age- and developmentally appropriate for children in the group. For example, young children are able to comprehend that food promotes growth, that eating a variety of foods is important for staying healthy, and that foods can be prepared in different ways. However, some 3-year-olds may not yet realize that a head of lettuce, a leaf of lettuce on a sandwich, and lettuce in a salad involve the same food. Tasting parties are an easy way to introduce children to new foods or to the same food prepared in different ways. Older children are able to understand the concept of food groups based on similar nutrient contributions and their relationship to health.

Ongoing evaluation enables the teacher to determine if nutrition lessons and activities have been effective in achieving the intended outcomes. Measurable objectives that describe expected behavioral changes should be developed during the initial planning stages and used for this purpose. Figures 20–2 and 20–3 illustrate how a nutrition concept can be outlined and translated into learning experiences for children. The CDC offers a Health Education Curriculum Analysis Tool (HECAT) on its website that teachers may also find useful for developing effective lessons and evaluating instructional outcomes (CDC, 2009).

Figure 20–2 Sample outline for incorporating nutrition education concept #1 into children's learning experiences.

CONCEPT: CHILDREN NEED FOOD TO GROW AND HAVE HEALTHY BODIES

OBJECTIVES: The children should learn that

- all living things need food
- food is important for growth and for good health

SUGGESTED ACTIVITIES

- caring for animals in the classroom with special attention to their diets
- taking field trips to the zoo or farm to learn what animals eat
- caring for plants in the classroom
- planting a vegetable garden in containers or a small plot of ground
- weighing and measuring the children periodically
- tracing outlines of each child on large sheets of paper

QUESTIONS FOR EXTENDING LEARNING EXPERIENCES

- What do animals eat?
- Do all animals eat the same foods?
- Do animals eat the same foods as people?
- Do animals grow faster or slower than people?
- What do plants eat?
- Can people see plants eating?
- Do plants eat the same foods as people?
- What does it mean to be healthy?
- Do people need food to be healthy?
- Do children need food to grow?

EVALUATION

- Children can name what animals and plants eat.
- Children can describe some effects of not feeding plants and animals.

Guidelines and Safety Considerations for Nutrition Education Activities

Nutrition education activities should contribute to children's improved understanding and practice of healthy lifestyle behaviors. In addition, lessons should reflect children's unique developmental needs, abilities, and interests.

1. Nutrition activities should be suitable for the children's developmental skills and abilities. Teachers should modify activities so that all children, including those who have special needs, can fully participate.

Figure 20–3 Sample outline for incorporating nutrition education concept #4 into children's learning experiences.

CONCEPT: FOODS MUST BE CAREFULLY HANDLED BEFORE THEY ARE EATEN

OBJECTIVES: Children should understand

- where foods come from
- how foods are handled

SUGGESTED ACTIVITIES

- Grow, harvest, and prepare foods from a garden.
- Sprout alfalfa, radishes, or bean seeds.
- Discuss and illustrate the different parts of plants used as food (leaves, roots, fruit, seeds).
- Conduct simple experiments that show change in color or form of food.
- Play "store" or "farm."
- Take children on a field trip to a farm, dairy, bakery, or grocery store.

QUESTIONS FOR EXTENDING LEARNING EXPERIENCES

- Where does food come from?
- Where do grocery stores get food?
- Is food always eaten the way it is grown?
- Who prepares different foods?
- Does all food come from the store?

EVALUATION

- Children can name sources of specific foods.
- Children can name who handles such foods as bread, milk, etc.

⚠ **Caution: Special consideration should be given to children's chewing ability, especially when fresh fruits, peanut butter, or raw vegetables are to be used in the activity.**

2. Actual foods should be used in nutrition projects as often as possible. These may be accompanied by pictures, games, and stories to reinforce what is being learned. Special consideration must be given to food safety, funding, available equipment, and children's known food allergies when planning educational experiences that involve real food.

⚠ **Caution: The teacher should always check for allergies to any foods (or similar foods) that will be used in the nutrition activity.**

3. The foods used should be nutritious. A variety of nutrient-dense foods should be chosen from the various Food Guide Pyramid groups. Foods (such as cakes, pies, doughnuts, frostings, and cookies) that are typically high in fat, sugar, and calories provide few essential nutrients and should be limited.
4. The end products of a nutrition activity should be edible and eaten by the children on the same day to effectively reinforce learning concepts. Pasta collages, vegetable prints, and chocolate pudding finger paintings are not suitable nutrition projects since it is not possible to eat the final product. These activities also convey the message that it is okay to play

Involving children in nutrition activities improves their ability to learn and remember.

© Cengage Learning

with or waste food; this is not an acceptable or desirable behavior for children to develop.

5. Children should be involved in the actual food preparation. **Hands-on** experiences such as cleaning vegetables, rolling dough, spreading butter, and cutting biscuits increase learning and help to develop a child's positive feelings about food (Aldridge, Dovey, & Halford, 2009).These activities not only enhance food experiences, but they also promote the development of other skills such as manual dexterity, counting, problem-solving, and learning to follow directions. Children are often more willing to taste an unfamiliar food if they have been involved in its preparation.
6. Once the nutrition activity is completed, the food should be eaten within a short period of time, preferably the same day. Delays between project completion and when the food is consumed reduces the activity's educational value.

Foods prepared during nutrition activities should be eaten shortly after the lesson is completed.

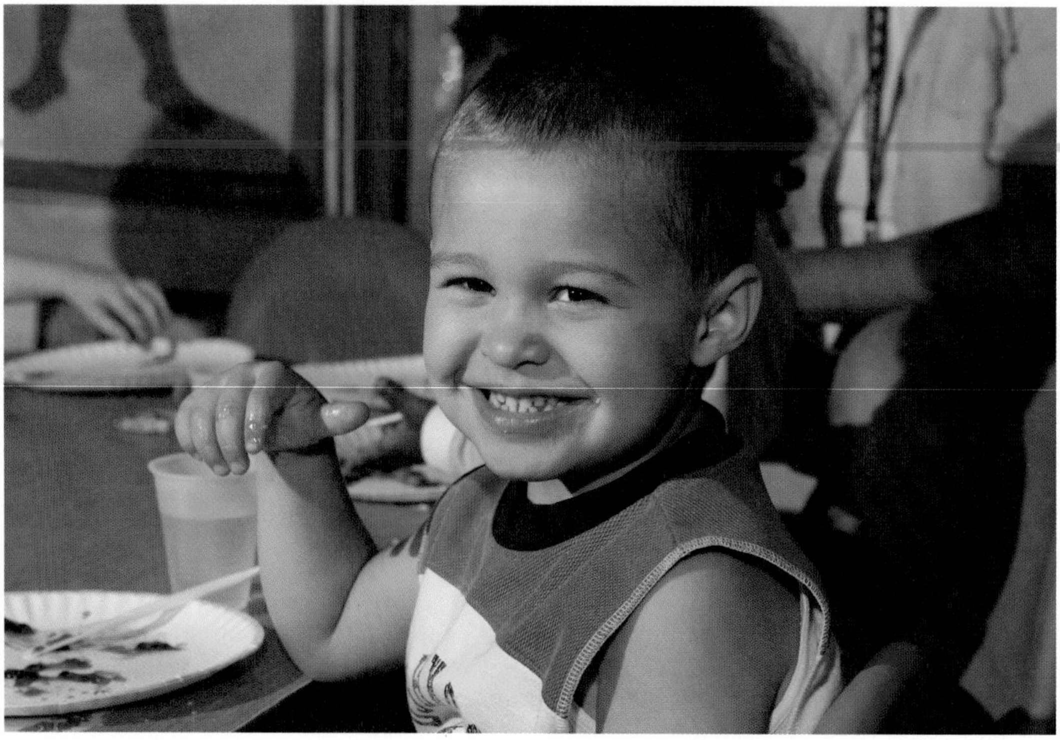

© Cengage Learning

hands-on – *active involvement in a project; actually doing something.*

Safety Considerations

The safety of nutrition activities must always be taken into consideration during the planning, set up, and implementation stages to ensure their success (Burney, Richards, & Draughon, 2009). Several areas that require special teacher attention are described here.

Basic Safety Guidelines

- Be aware of children's food allergies. Post a list of the children's names and the foods they must not eat. Foods that are common allergens include: wheat, milk and milk products, juices with a high acid content such as orange or grapefruit, strawberries, chocolate, eggs, soy, shellfish, and nuts.
- Avoid serving foods such as nuts, raw vegetables, peanut butter, and popcorn that may cause younger children to choke. These foods should also not be served to children who have problems with chewing or swallowing. Peanut butter and raw fruits and vegetables are appropriate to serve to older children under close adult supervision.
- Children should eat only when they are sitting down.
- Use low work tables and chairs.
- Use unbreakable equipment whenever possible.
- Supply enough tools and utensils for all children in the group to use.
- Provide blunt knives or **serrated** plastic knives for cutting cooked eggs, potatoes, bananas, and so on. Vegetable peelers should be used under supervision and only after demonstrating their proper use to the children.
- Have only the necessary tools, utensils, and ingredients at the work table. All other materials should be removed as soon as they are no longer needed. Plan equipment needs carefully to avoid leaving the work area during an activity, especially when there are utensils or foods present that may cause injury.
- **Preplan** the steps of the cooking project; discuss these steps with the children before beginning. Children should understand what they are expected to do and what the adults will do before the cooking ingredients are presented.
- Long hair should be pulled back and fastened; floppy or cumbersome clothing should not be worn. Aprons are not essential, but may help to protect clothing.
- Hands should be washed thoroughly at the start of the activity.
- Begin with simple recipes that require little cooking. Once children feel comfortable with basic cooking projects, move on to slightly more complex ones.
- Allow plenty of time for touching, tasting, looking, and comparing as well as for discussion. Use every step in the cooking project as an opportunity to expand children's learning.

Food Safety

- Wash hands before and after the cooking project; this also applies to teachers.
- Exclude any child or adult from participating in food preparation if they have a cold or other contagious illness.
- Bandage any cuts or open sores before beginning food preparation (use latex gloves over bandages on hands).
- Keep all cooking utensils clean. Have extra utensils available in case one is dropped or a child accidentally puts one into his/her mouth.
- Teach children how to taste foods that are being prepared. Give each child a small plate and spoon for this purpose. Never allow children to taste foods directly from the bowl or pan in which they are being prepared.
- Avoid using foods that spoil rapidly. Keep sauces, meats, eggs, and dairy products refrigerated.

---

serrated – *saw-toothed or notched.*
preplan – *outline a method of action prior to carrying it out.*

Cooking Safety

- Match cooking tasks to children's developmental skills and attention spans.
- Take time to instruct children about the safe use of utensils.
- Emphasize that all cooking must be supervised by an adult.
- Arrange for an adult to do the cooking over a hot stove or hot plate; always turn pot handles toward the back.
- Use wooden or heat-resistant utensils for cooking. (Metal utensils conduct heat and can cause painful burns.)

Reflective Thoughts

Americans are heavy and getting heavier. Our supermarket shelves provide the most extensive selection of foods in the world. Low-fat, fat-free, and sugar-free foods are available in increasing numbers. Yet books, magazines, and newspapers continue to feature the "Diet of the Week/Month/Year."

- What nutrition education experiences and activities could you suggest to promote children's healthy eating habits?
- What types of foods or eating patterns should be stressed?
- What additional lifestyle practices may be contributing to childhood obesity?
- In what ways might children's exposure to electronic media influence this problem?

Developing Lesson Plans for Nutrition Activities

The success of each classroom activity as it contributes to the total nutrition education program depends on comprehensive planning. The principles of curriculum design, including topic selection, development of **behavioral objectives**, instructional procedures, and **evaluation** are covered in depth in Chapter 11. Additional consideration should be given to developing lesson plans and activities that:

- Contribute to children's understanding of one or more of the four basic nutrition concepts.
- Involve hands-on experiences with actual food to improve learning and retention.
- Ensure that activities are safe and a positive learning experience for children. Most plans require a safe precautions list.
- Provide a sequencing of activities so that each new experience reinforces and advances concepts that have already been learned.
- Reflect improvements based on evaluation results from previous presentations.

---

behavioral objectives – *a clear and measurable description of a specific behavior that an individual is expected to learn.*
evaluation – *a measurement of effectiveness for determining whether or not educational objectives have been achieved.*

Activity Plan #1: Weighing and Measuring Children

CONCEPT Weighing and measuring children

LEARNING OBJECTIVES

- Children will be able to discuss how eating healthy foods helps them to grow.
- Children can explain how growth is determined by measurements of height and weight.
- Children will be able to recognize that people come in different sizes.

SUPPLIES

- A balance-beam scale or bathroom scale
- Yardstick
- Large sheets of paper and markers or crayons
- Samples of nutritious fruits or vegetables for children to taste

LEARNING ACTIVITIES

A. Weigh and measure each child. Encourage children to assist the teacher in reading his/her height and weight measurements. Record the information. Repeat this activity every 4 months to monitor children's growth rate and to make comparisons. Use this activity to reinforce the importance of healthy eating and activity habits.

B. Trace an outline of each child on large sheets of paper. Have children color their paper "selves."

C. Discuss individual differences among children, such as concepts of tall and short. (The discussion should be positive—these differences are what make each child special.)
   - Does everybody weigh the same?
   - Is everyone the same height?
   - Do children stay the same size? Do adults?
   - What makes children grow?

D. Prepare samples of several nutritious fruits or vegetables for children to taste. Use this activity to reinforce the concept that nutritious foods help children to grow.

EVALUATION

- Each child states his/her height and weight.
- Children name several nutritious foods that contribute to their health and growth.
- Children discuss why some people are taller or shorter than others.

Activity Plan #2: Making Hummus and Pitas

CONCEPT People from other cultures eat foods that may be different from those we typically eat.

LEARNING OBJECTIVES

- Children will learn that people from other cultures may eat different types of foods.
- Children will be able to describe correctly the ingredients used to make hummus and why hummus is considered to be a healthy food.

SUPPLIES

- Bowl
- Measuring spoons

- Spatula
- Potato masher
- Blender or food processor
- Ingredients (see recipe)
- Fresh vegetables
- Pocket pitas or flatbread cut into small wedges

LEARNING ACTIVITIES

A. Be sure teachers and children have washed their hands before proceeding. To make the hummus, assemble the equipment and all ingredients.
(For a picture recipe to use in the classroom, see Figure 20–4.)
1 15-ounce can chickpeas (garbanzo beans), drained
2–3 tablespoons warm water
2 tablespoons olive oil
2 tablespoons lemon juice

Figure 20–4 Picture recipe for making hummus.

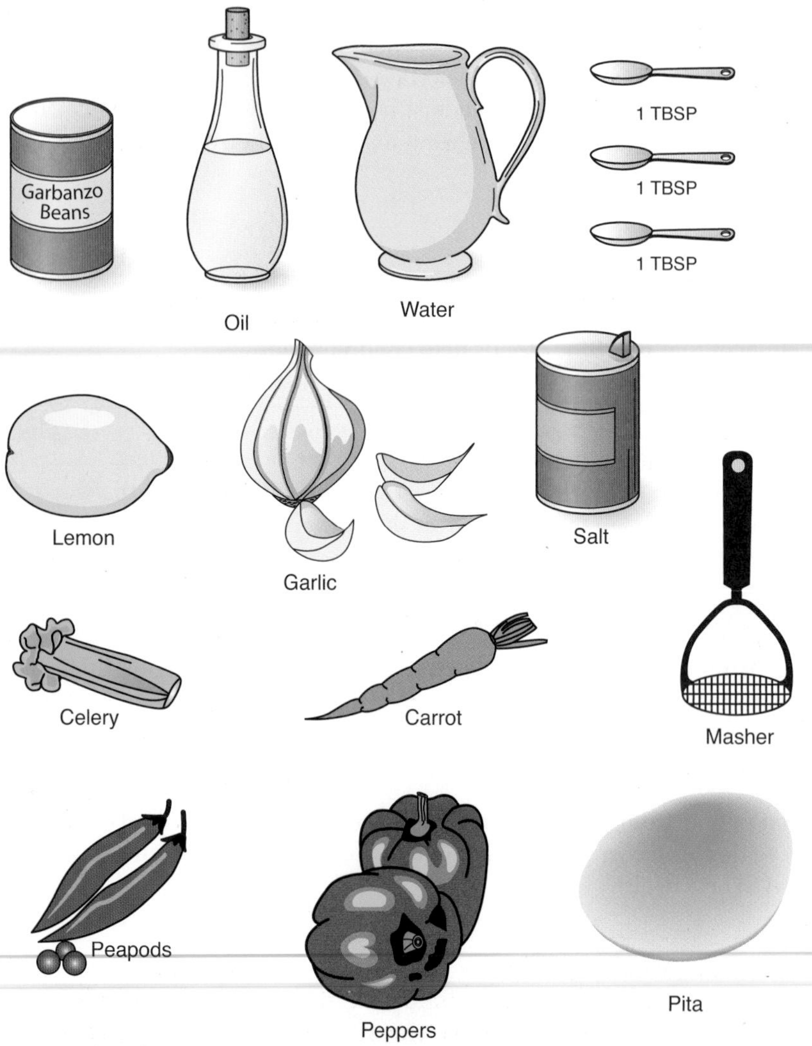

1 garlic clove, crushed salt to flavor
2 tablespoons sesame seeds or 3 tablespoons peanut butter (optional)
an assortment of raw vegetables (such as carrot and celery sticks, red/orange/yellow pepper strips, broccoli pieces)
pita wedges, pieces of flatbread, or crackers for dipping

Drain chickpeas; place them in a small bowl with the water, olive oil, and lemon juice. Let children take turns mashing the beans using the potato masher. After each child has had a turn, the teacher can scrape the mixture into a blender and add the remaining ingredients, blending until smooth. Place the hummus in a small bowl and serve with raw vegetables, pita wedges, pieces of flatbread, or crackers.

⚠ **Caution: Be sure to check for any food allergies before beginning this project.**

B. Read one or more of the following books and discuss the concept that people may eat many different kinds of foods:
Everybody Cooks Rice by Norah Dooley
Dumpling Soup by Jama Kim Rattigan
Dim Sum for Everyone by Grace Lin
The Tortilla Factory by Gary Paulsen

C. Have each child name his/her favorite food. Discuss why families eat foods that may be the same and/or different.

EVALUATION

- Children name some foods that are commonly eaten by people from different cultures.
- Children explain why some people eat foods that may be different from those that they typically eat.

Activity Plan #3: Tasting Party

CONCEPT Tasting party for dairy foods.

LEARNING OBJECTIVES

- Children will learn that common foods may be served in a variety of ways.
- Children will be able to identify foods that belong to the milk group.
- Children will be able to state why it is important to drink milk.

SUPPLIES

- Small pitcher of milk
- Unflavored yogurt
- Cottage cheese
- Cheddar cheese
- Ice cream
- 1 pint of whipping cream
- Small plastic jar with lid
- Plastic knives

LEARNING ACTIVITIES

A. Teachers and children should wash their hands before starting this activity.
Place the pitcher of milk, unflavored yogurt, cottage cheese, cheddar cheese (cut into small cubes), and ice cream on the table. Encourage children to describe the appearance and texture of each item. Do they look alike? Is cottage cheese like cheddar cheese? How is it

different? Point out that each food began as milk and has been changed as the result of different preparation methods. Have the children sample each food. Do they all taste alike? Why were these foods chilled before preparation and why should they be eaten immediately? Why is it important to drink milk and eat milk-based products?

B. Pour the whipping cream into a small, clean plastic jar, filling it only half full. Add a few dashes of salt and tighten the jar lid. Let the jar sit until the cream reaches room temperature. Have children take turns shaking the jar until the butter separates from the milk. When it is finished, pour away the milk and remove the butter. Let children spread the butter on a small cracker to taste.

> ⚠ **Caution: Check beforehand for any milk or dairy product allergies. Provide alternative foods if necessary. Stress that refrigeration and sanitation are very important when working with protein foods such as milk and milk products.**

C. Read and discuss one or more of the following books:
No Moon, No Milk by Chris Babcock
Milk Comes from a COW? by Dan Yunk
Milk: From Cow to Carton by Aliki
From Milk to Ice Cream by Stacy Taus-Bolstad

D. Additional activities can be planned, including making yogurt or cheese from milk, preparing fruit smoothies, and/or making ice cream.

EVALUATION

- Children identify foods made from milk.
- Children taste each food served.
- Children describe where milk and butter come from.

Activity Plan #4: Trip to the Grocery Store

CONCEPT Children will learn that many different types of fruits and vegetables are available.

LEARNING OBJECTIVES

- Children are encouraged to make decisions about foods and to taste a variety of foods.
- Children will select a fruit or vegetable with which they may not be familiar.
- Children will be able to name three new fruits or vegetables.

SUPPLIES

- Local newspaper with weekly food advertisements
- Paper and pencil
- Plastic foods
- Grocery bags
- Cash register and play money

LEARNING ACTIVITIES

A. Have children look at the produce section in the weekly food advertisements. Ask them to name the fruits and vegetables pictured in the paper. Find out if children have ever tasted each of the items and whether or not they liked them.

B. Plan a field trip to the grocery store. Be sure to secure parental permission in advance. Give each child a small piece of paper on which the name of a different fruit or vegetable is written. At the grocery store, help children locate their assigned fruit or vegetable. After purchasing the items and returning to the classroom, ask the children to help describe each food—its color and shape, whether or not it has seeds, how it grows, and if the skin is peeled or eaten. Finally, ask the cook to prepare the fruits or vegetables for the children to eat: a mixed fruit salad, a vegetable plate, or vegetable soup.

⚠ **Caution: Permission must be obtained from families before taking the field trip. Fasten restraints if driving to the store. If walking to store, review safety rules for walking, crossing streets, and so on. Check for food allergies and provide alternatives if necessary.**

C. Provide the children with various props—plastic foods, empty food containers, grocery bags, cash register, and play money—to create their own grocery store. Have some children act as grocers, some as clerks, and others as shoppers.

EVALUATION

- Children identify two varieties of red fruit.
- Children taste each of the prepared fruits or vegetables.
- Children name and describe three different fruits and/or vegetables.

Activity Plan #5: Safe Lunches

CONCEPT How to pack lunches that are safe and healthy.

LEARNING OBJECTIVES

- Children will learn how to select and eat food safely.
- Children will select at least one food with which they are not familiar.
- Children will include a variety of nutritious foods in their lunch.

SUPPLIES

- Empty lunch box with thermos
- Foods that may be available in school cafeteria/kitchen and are examples of items that children can pack in a lunchbox (e.g., sandwich, milk, juice, soup, carrot sticks or other fresh vegetables, cheese cubes, tortilla, apple, banana, yogurt, salad)

LEARNING ACTIVITIES

A. Display the food choices on a table. Have children wash their hands prior to selecting food. In groups of two, have children choose foods from those provided that they would pack in a lunchbox to bring to school. Encourage children to choose a variety of foods based on the Food Guide Pyramid. After each child has packed his/her lunch, have a discussion about the foods that were chosen. Let children eat the foods they have packed in their lunchboxes. Extend the discussion by asking:
   - Which foods need to be kept cold?
   - Which foods need to be kept hot?
   - Which foods need to be wrapped or stored in special containers to be kept safe?
   - Which foods need to be washed before they are eaten?
   - Are there any other foods you would choose for your lunch box that are not included here?

⚠ **Cautions: Check for children's food allergies prior to activity. Recommend sampling only those foods that do not require storage at extreme temperatures to avoid illness (i.e., avoid milk, yogurt, ice cream, soup).**

Children's willingness to try new foods is improved when they are involved in its preparation.

B. Take children on an actual picnic lunch. Involve them in the preparation and safe storage of foods for this event.

EVALUATION

- Children participate in choosing their own food at mealtime.
- Children select a variety of healthful foods from each of the Food Guide Pyramid groups.
- Children explain how foods must be handled and stored to prevent illness.

Activity Plan #6: Eating Different Fruits and Vegetables Each Day

CONCEPT It is important to eat several different fruits and vegetables each day.

LEARNING OBJECTIVES

- Children will learn that there are a wide variety of fruits and vegetables.
- Children will learn that a particular fruit or vegetable may be prepared and eaten in different ways.
- Children will understand that fruits and vegetables taste good and have vitamins that keep us healthy.

SUPPLIES

- Disposable plates and napkins
- A variety of fruits that represent different sizes, colors, and shapes (e.g., apples, bananas, oranges, kiwi, melons, star fruit, mangos)
- A variety of vegetables, emphasizing different preparation techniques (e.g., baked potato, mashed potato, French fries, scalloped potatoes)

LEARNING ACTIVITIES

A. Be sure that adults and children wash their hands prior to handling the food. Lay out the assortment of fruits and vegetables (that have been cut into small pieces) on a table. Give children paper plates and allow them to select a total of five fruits and vegetables. Encourage children to select and taste a variety of different foods, particularly those they have never eaten before. Talk about the general nutrients (vitamins, minerals) that are in fruits and vegetables. As a group, discuss these questions:

- What colors are the fruits and vegetables?
- What are some different ways of preparing the same food? Do you know of any more?
- Is there a food you tried today that you have never eaten before? Will you try it again?
- Did you know that eating different fruits and vegetables every day can help you from becoming sick? Discuss.

> ⚠ **Caution: Check beforehand for children's food allergies. Maintain foods at appropriate temperatures to avoid illness.**

B. On another day, have the cook prepare some of the same vegetables. Discuss how cooking affects the color, texture, and flavor of different vegetables.

C. Take the children to visit a local supermarket or farmer's market. Call ahead to make arrangements for a special tour that might include food sampling in the produce department.

EVALUATION

- Children explain why it is important to include a variety of fruits and vegetables in their daily diet.
- Children select a variety of fruits and vegetables to eat at mealtime.
- Children state why it is important to eat several different fruits and vegetables daily.

Additional Food Information Sources

Children learn about food from informal sources as well as from planned programs of instruction. Their families, teachers, peers, television, and websites serve as additional information sources about food and all have an effect on children's eating habits (Adams et al., 2009; Lingas & Dorfman, 2009) (Figure 20–5).

The Family

A family's food preferences and **attitudes** exert a strong shaping effect on the child's eating patterns and ideas about food (Aldridge, Dovey, & Halford, 2009). Family food choices are subject to cultural influences, regional differences, money available for food, education, and specific likes and dislikes of individual members. Children become familiar and comfortable with certain foods through repeated exposures (Williams et al., 2008). Since familiarity is one of the most influential factors affecting food choices, children whose families eat a wide variety of foods are often more receptive to trying new foods.

Teachers

Teachers also exert considerable influence over children's attitudes about food. For this reason, it is important that teachers display a positive attitude, through their actions and words and a willingness to try new foods (Cohen, 2009).

---

attitudes – *beliefs or feelings one has toward certain facts or situations.*

Figure 20–5 Additional sources of influence on children's eating habits.

ADDITIONAL FACTORS THAT INFLUENCE CHILDREN'S EATING HABITS

- Families of children who have a strong preference for high-fat foods have higher BMI scores than parents who do not have a strong preference for high-fat foods.
- Children are more likely to eat a certain food if they observe adults eating it.
- There is a strong relationship between the food preferences of toddlers and their mothers, fathers, and older siblings.
- Involving families in children's nutrition education programs increases the diversity and quality of student's diets.
- Involving families in children's nutrition education programs increases the diversity and quality of student's diets. In general, the more hours women work outside the home, the fewer hours they spend preparing meals, and the more meals their children eat away from home.
- The nutrition knowledge and practices of food service personnel in child care centers has a major influence on the quality of menus served (Chan et al., 2009).

Issues To Consider **Food Trend Predictions**

Food corporations are continuously engaged in developing and marketing new items aimed at the health-conscious consumer. Organic foods, herbal supplements, fortified waters, low- and fat-free foods, foods enhanced with phytochemicals for added health benefits, and nutrition products, such as juice bars, energy bars and shakes, and protein smoothies that can be eaten on the run, are predicted to be hot products.

- Do you perceive these trends to be positive or negative?
- What effect(s) might these trends have on families' ideas about what children should be eating?
- How might these trends influence children's ideas about nutritious food?
- How will these trends affect children in your care?

Peer Groups

Children's food choices are frequently made on the basis of **peer** approval or disapproval (Greenhalgh et al., 2009). A child with a strong personality who eats a variety of foods can be a positive influence on other children. In contrast, children who are "picky" or "selective eaters" may also spread their negative influence to others at the table. A simple statement from the teacher, such

peer – *one of the same rank; equal.*

as, "You don't have to eat the broccoli, Jamie, but I can't allow you to spoil it for Tara and Pablo," can be effective in limiting this negative environment. Although younger children often base their food choices on familiarity and taste, older children's (5 and up) eating patterns are more likely to be affected by peer influence.

Television and the Media

Television, the Internet, and print media such as magazines, newspapers, and books serve as major sources of nutrition information and misinformation for many children and their families (Kuo & Handu, 2009). However, the lack of oversight and quality control governing the accuracy of information provided through these channels can make it challenging for consumers to determine what is fact and what is fiction. Unfortunately, nutrient-dense foods are rarely featured in television commercials (Harris, Bargh, & Brownell, 2009; Elliott, 2008). Rather, foods that are chocolaty, highly sugared, loaded with fat, packed with calories, are really fun, or come with a prize appear most often. Families and teachers can be instrumental in counteracting television's negative influence by monitoring programs that children view and by pointing out differences between programs and commercials. Children often have difficulty understanding that a commercial's purpose is to convince people to buy a product that may not always be the most nutritious choice (Radnitz et al., 2009).

Focus On Families — More Fruits and Vegetables Please

Families can take an active part in ensuring that their child consumes a daily total of 2½–3 cups of five different fruits and vegetables. Serving a variety of fruits and vegetables each day can improve children's health and reduce their risk of developing diseases such as cancer, heart disease, hypertension, diabetes, and obesity.

Families can create activities that help to convey this important health message.

- Prepare homemade vegetable soup or a fresh fruit salad. Have your child name each vegetable or fruit contained in the recipe. This increases your child's awareness of how fruits and vegetables can be included in daily meal plans while providing a nutritious meal or snack.
- Visit the nearest farmer's market. Not only will your child develop an appreciation for fresh produce, but the experience is likely to generate curiosity and questions for learning.
- Teach your child the importance of eating seasonal fruits and vegetables not only for the taste, but also the cost savings it can provide for your family. Below is a sampling of fruits and vegetables that are often more plentiful during certain seasons.
  - Spring: apples, grapefruits, pears, strawberries, broccoli, cabbage, carrots, asparagus
  - Summer: berries, cantaloupes, melons, peaches, corn, green beans, cucumbers, okra
  - Fall: oranges, peaches, prunes, plums, brussels sprouts, tomatoes, peppers, zucchini
  - Winter: apples, grapefruit, oranges, beets, cauliflower, potatoes, spinach, squash
- Plant a small garden with some of the vegetables listed above. Vegetables can also be grown in containers set out on the deck or patio. Your child will learn about the growing process and where foods originate.

Summary

- A sound nutrition education program is based on four principles: (1) food is needed for a healthy body, (2) nutrients come from foods, (3) a variety of foods must be eaten, and (4) foods must be handled carefully so they are safe to eat.
- An effective nutrition education program requires the involvement and support of administrators, food service personnel, teachers, and families.
- Nutrition learning experiences can be used to reinforce children's language, cognitive, sensorimotor, and social/emotional development.
- Efforts to teach children about nutrition should be part of a coordinated framework or plan that continues to increase children's knowledge and health-promoting behaviors.
- Effective lessons are based on children's developmental abilities, the use of real foods that are nutritious and edible, and that involve children in food preparation.
- Safety must always be considered when conducting food-related experiences.
- Advanced planning is essential for ensuring that lessons will be meaningful.
- Children's ideas about food are shaped by family, teachers, peers, and the media.

Terms to Know

nutrition education *p. 484*
concepts *p. 485*
sensorimotor *p. 488*
hands-on *p. 492*
serrated *p. 493*
preplan *p. 493*
behavioral objectives *p. 494*
evaluation *p. 494*
attitudes *p. 501*
peer *p. 502*

Chapter Review

A. By Yourself:

1. Explain how children typically form their food preferences.
2. Describe how program directors, teachers, and families collectively contribute to children's nutrition education.
3. What role do teachers play in developing and implementing nutrition education for children?
4. What fundamental principles should guide nutrition education activities conducted with children?

B. As a Group:

1. Discuss the ways in which nutrition education experiences can promote children's development in other areas.
2. What criteria should be used for choosing appropriate nutrition education concepts for children?
3. Describe four ways that programs can involve families in children's nutrition education.
4. Why is it important to include nutrition education during children's early years?
5. What safety issues must teachers consider when conducting classroom food activities?

Case Study

Marcus, age 4 years, has been ill several times this spring with upper respiratory infections. His mother mentions that she is now giving him an herbal supplement to "boost his immune system" so that he won't be sick as often. She asks if you think the supplement will help Marcus and if it is safe for him to take.

1. Are you qualified to advise Marcus's mother on this issue?
2. What information do you need to know before answering her questions?
3. What resources are available to find the necessary information?
4. How will you determine if the information available to you is accurate and reliable?

Application Activities

1. Prepare lesson plans for a 2-day nutrition education activity. Plans may be for 2 consecutive days or for any 2 days within one week. The lesson plan for each day should be in the format presented in this unit.
2. Outline an equipment list and safety plan for a food experience in which 4- and 5-year-olds make pancakes in the classroom. Cooking will be done in an electric griddle on a table. What precautions should be taken? How should the room be arranged to ensure children's safety? What instructions should be given to the children beforehand?
3. Select 15 to 20 library books appropriate for young children. Note those instances where food is portrayed either in the story or pictures. What types of foods are shown? Chart these foods according to the Food Guide Pyramid. What percentage of foods was noted within each group? What was the general message about food presented in these books?
4. Watch 1 hour of children's television programs on Saturday morning.
   a. Determine the percent of observed advertisements that featured "sweets" (gum, candy, soft drinks, snack cakes, and pre-sweetened cereals). Calculate the percentage of advertisements featuring fast foods or those especially high in fat.
   b. Which food groups were least represented in these commercials?
5. Review an article about nutrition from a popular magazine. Apply the suggested criteria for determining the reliability of a nutrition resource. Is this a good article? Why or why not?

Helpful Web Resources

American Dietetic Association	http://www.eatright.org
Better Health Foundation	http://www.fruitsandveggiesmorematters.org/
MyPyramid for Kids	http://www.mypyramid.gov/Kids
PE Central	http://www.pecentral.org
School Health Education Resources (SHER)	http://apps.nccd.cdc.gov/sher
U.S. Department of Agriculture	http://www.usda.gov

You are just a click away from additional health, safety, and nutrition resources! Go to www.CengageBrain.com to access this text's Education CourseMate website, where you'll find:

- glossary flashcards, activities, tutorial quizzes, videos, web links, and more

References

Adams, J., Hennessy-Priest, K., Ingimarsdóttir, S., Sheeshka, J., Ostbye, T., & White, M. (2009). Food advertising during children's television in Canada and the UK, *Archives of Disease in Childhood*, 94(9), 658–662.

Aldridge, V., Dovey, T., & Halford, J. (2009). The role of familiarity in dietary development, *Developmental Review*, 29(1), 32–44.

Blom-Hoffman, J., Wilcox, K., Dunn, L., Leff, S., & Power, T. (2008). Family involvement in school-based health promotion: Bringing nutrition information home, *The School Psychology Review*, 37(4), 567–577.

Burney, J., Richards, J., & Draughon, A. (2009). Food safety in the classroom, *Journal of Nutrition Education & Behavior*, 41(4), S40–S49.

Centers for Disease Control and Prevention (CDC). (2009). *The Health Education Curriculum Analysis Tool (HECAT).* Accessed on December 5, 2009 from http://www.cdc.gov/healthyyouth/HECAT/.

Chan, H., Hesse, D., Arndt, E., & Marquart, L. (2009). Knowledge and practices of school foodservice personnel regarding whole grain foods, *Journal of Foodservice*, 20(3), 109–116.

Cohen, L., (2009). Cultural heritage in a kindergarten classroom, *Young Children*, 64(3), 72–77.

Drake, L. (2009). Nourishing choices: Implementing food education in classrooms, cafeterias, and schoolyards, *Journal of Nutrition Education and Behavior*, 41(4), 305.e7–311.e7.

Elliott, C. (2008). Assessing 'fun foods': Nutritional content and analysis of supermarket foods targeted at children, *Obesity Reviews*, 9(4), 68–77.

Greenhalgh, J., Dowey, A., Horne, P., Lowe, F., Griffiths, J., & Whitaker, C. (2009). Positive- and negative peer modelling effects on young children's consumption of novel blue foods, *Appetite*, 52(3), 646–653.

Harris, J., Bargh, J., & Brownell, K. (2009). Priming effects of television food advertising on eating behavior, *Health Psychology*, 28(4), 404–413.

Kuo, J., & Handu, D. (2009). Content analysis of television advertisements aired during Saturday morning children programming, *Journal of the American Dietetic Association*, 109(9), A100–A110.

Lingas, E., & Dorfman, L. (2009). Nutrition content of food and beverage products on websites popular with children, *American Journal of Public Health*, 99(7), 1–7.

Radnitz, C., Bryne, S., Goldman, R., Sparks, M., Gantshar, M., & Tung, K. (2009). Food cues in children's television programs, *Appetite*, 52(1), 230–233.

Williams, K., Paul, C., Pizzo, B., & Riegel, K. (2008). Practice does make perfect: A longitudinal look at repeated taste exposure, *Appetite*, 51(3), 739–742.

Epilogue

Looking Ahead. . .Making a Difference

As promised, this book has taken you on a journey. You have had an opportunity to learn about many topics that are important to children's health, safety, and nutrition. The new skills you have developed will improve your abilities to observe children and to detect the early signs of acute and chronic health conditions and impending illness. You have become more knowledgeable about children's health problems, including childhood obesity, communicable illness, chronic medical conditions, and sensory impairments and their impact on learning and development. You have learned how to modify environments in order to protect children from unintentional injury and unnecessary exposure to illness. Your knowledge of children's critical nutrient needs and ways to address them through thoughtful menu planning has also undoubtedly improved.

Most importantly, you have gained a better understanding of the preventive health concept, not only as it applies to the care and education of young children, but also its application to your own personal life. Knowing there are many things one can do to improve the quality of his or her well-being becomes a powerful incentive to help children establish healthful eating and physical activity habits at an early age. Undoubtedly, you have become more aware of the valuable role you play as a positive role model for children who look up to adults and often imitate their behaviors. As stated throughout the book, teachers are in an ideal position to promote children's health, safety, and nutrition and to make this a priority. Their dedicated efforts to achieving this goal through the development of meaningful learning experiences and their commitment to partnering with families will truly make a difference in children's lives.

The ultimate goal and true mark of learning is change. . .change in the way one thinks, change in one's behavior. Undoubtedly, your journey through this book has changed you in some way—to question, think, and/or act differently. However, the journey does not end here. New discoveries that affect our understanding of chronic diseases, nutrition, and safety practices are revealed almost daily. Our ideas and best practices for promoting children's lifetime wellness are continually being reshaped by this information. A few of the areas receiving special attention include:

- Improving the quality of early childhood programs.
- Planning and serving meals/snacks that provide essential nutrients, reduce unnecessary fat and calories, and are respectful of cultural differences.
- Reducing the incidence of childhood obesity.
- Maintaining the safety of food and food environments.
- Addressing and responding to the needs of children with special medical and developmental challenges.
- Building children's resiliency to stress, bullying, and everyday environmental pressures.
- Improving communication and partnerships with families.
- Increasing awareness and sensitivity to child and family differences.
- Recognizing environmental contaminants and their effect on children's health.
- Addressing the need for more family education.
- Encouraging physical activity as a lifestyle practice.

- Addressing the issues of child abuse and domestic violence.
- Advocating on behalf of children's interests.
- Improving children's access to medical and dental care.
- Reducing poverty and food insecurity.

This list is not inclusive. Some issues may be of greater concern and interest to particular communities or regions. Others have an appeal that is more universal and likely to affect the welfare of children everywhere. In either case, the future of children's well-being offers unique opportunities for innovative solutions and teacher commitment.

Continue this journey. Keep learning about new developments as they unfold, explore topics that pique your curiosity, and become an advocate for children's health, safety, and nutrition. Accept the challenge. . .look ahead and make a difference!

APPENDICES

Appendix A National Health Education Standards

Appendix B Monthly Calendar: Health, Safety, and Nutrition Observances

Appendix C Federal Food Programs

Appendix D Children's Book List

Appendix E Nutrient Information: Fast-Food Vendor Websites

Appendix A National Health Education Standards

NHES Standard 1: Students will comprehend concepts related to health promotion and disease prevention to enhance health.

Rationale: The acquisition of basic health concepts and functional health knowledge provides a foundation for promoting health-enhancing behaviors among youth. This standard includes essential concepts that are based on established health behavior theories and models. Concepts that focus on both health promotion and risk reduction are included in the performance indicators.

PreK–Grade 2 Performance Indicators, Standard 1

1.2.1 Identify that healthy behaviors impact personal health.
1.2.2 Recognize that there are multiple dimensions of health.
1.2.3 Describe ways to prevent communicable diseases.
1.2.4 List ways to prevent common childhood injuries.
1.2.5 Describe why it is important to seek health care.

Grades 3–5 Performance Indicators, Standard 1

1.5.1 Describe the relationship between healthy behaviors and personal health.
1.5.2 Identify examples of emotional, intellectual, physical, and social health.
1.5.3 Describe ways in which safe and healthy school and community environments can promote personal health.
1.5.4 Describe ways to prevent common childhood injuries and health problems.
1.5.5 Describe when it is important to seek health care.

NHES Standard 2: Students will analyze the influence of family, peers, culture, media, technology, and other factors on health behaviors.

Rationale: Health is affected by a variety of positive and negative influences within society. This standard focuses on identifying and understanding the diverse internal and external factors that influence health practices and behaviors among youth, including personal values, beliefs, and perceived norms.

PreK–Grade 2 Performance Indicators, Standard 2

2.2.1 Identify how the family influences personal health practices and behaviors.
2.2.2 Identify what the school can do to support personal health practices and behaviors.
2.2.3 Describe how the media can influence health behaviors.

Grades 3–5 Performance Indicators, Standard 2

2.5.1 Describe how family influences personal health practices and behaviors.
2.5.2 Identify the influence of culture on health practices and behaviors.
2.5.3 Identify how peers can influence healthy and unhealthy behaviors.
2.5.4 Describe how the school and community can support personal health practices and behaviors.
2.5.5 Explain how media influences thoughts, feelings, and health behaviors.
2.5.6 Describe ways that technology can influence personal health.

NHES Standard 3: Demonstrate the ability to access valid information, products, and services to enhance health.

Rationale: Access to valid health information and health-promoting products and services is critical in the prevention, early detection, and treatment of health problems. This standard focuses on how to identify and access valid health resources and to reject unproven sources. Application of the skills of analysis, comparison, and evaluation of health resources empowers students to achieve health literacy.

PreK–Grade 2 Performance Indicators, Standard 3

3.2.1 Identify trusted adults and professionals who can help promote health.
3.2.1 Identify ways to locate school and community health helpers.

Grades 3–5 Performance Indicators Standard 3

3.5.1 Identify characteristics of valid health information, products, and services.
3.5.2 Locate resources from home, school, and community that provide valid health information.

NHES Standard 4: Demonstrate the ability to use interpersonal communication skills to enhance health and avoid or reduce health risks.

Rationale: Effective communication enhances personal, family, and community health. This standard focuses on how responsible individuals use verbal and non-verbal skills to develop and maintain healthy personal relationships. The ability to organize and to convey information and feelings is the basis for strengthening interpersonal interactions and reducing or avoiding conflict.

PreK–Grade 2 Performance Indicators, Standard 4

4.2.1 Demonstrate healthy ways to express needs, wants, and feelings.
4.2.2 Demonstrate listening skills to enhance health.
4.2.3 Demonstrate ways to respond in an unwanted, threatening, or dangerous situation.
4.2.4 Demonstrate ways to tell a trusted adult if threatened or harmed.

Grades 3–5 Performance Indicators, Standard 4

4.5.1 Demonstrate effective verbal and nonverbal communication skills to enhance health.
4.5.2 Demonstrate refusal skills that avoid or reduce health risks.
4.5.3 Demonstrate nonviolent strategies to manage or resolve conflict.
4.5.4 Demonstrate how to ask for assistance to enhance personal health.

NHES Standard 5: Demonstrate the ability to use decision-making skills to enhance health.

Rationale: Decision-making skills are needed to identify, implement, and sustain health-enhancing behaviors. This standard includes the essential steps that are needed to make healthy decisions as prescribed in the performance indicators. When applied to health issues, the decision-making process enables individuals to collaborate with others to improve their quality of life.

PreK–Grade 2 Performance Indicators, Standard 5

5.2.1 Identify situations when a health-related decision is needed.
5.2.2 Differentiate between situations when a health-related decision can be made individually or when assistance is needed.

Grades 3–5 Performance Indicators, Standard 5

5.5.1 Identify health-related situations that might require a thoughtful decision.
5.5.2 Analyze when assistance is needed in making a health-related decision.
5.5.3 List healthy options to health-related issues or problems.
5.5.4 Predict the potential outcomes of each option when making a health-related decision.
5.5.5 Choose a healthy option when making a decision.
5.5.6 Describe the outcomes of a health-related decision.

NHES Standard 6: Students will demonstrate the ability to use goal-setting skills to enhance health.

Rationale: Goal-setting skills are essential to help students identify, adopt, and maintain healthy behaviors. This standard includes the critical steps that are needed to achieve both short-term and long-term health goals. These skills make it possible for individuals to have aspirations and plans for the future.

PreK–Grade 2 Performance Indicators, Standard 6

6.2.1 Identify a short-term personal health goal and take action toward achieving the goal.
6.2.2 Identify who can help when assistance is needed to achieve a personal health goal.

Grades 3–5 Performance Indicators, Standard 6

6.5.1 Set a personal health goal and track progress toward its achievement.
6.5.2 Identify resources to assist in achieving a personal health goal.

NHES Standard 7: Demonstrate the ability to practice health-enhancing behaviors and avoid or reduce health risks.

Rationale: Research confirms that practicing health-enhancing behaviors can contribute to a positive quality of life. In addition, many diseases and injuries can be prevented by reducing harmful and risk-taking behaviors. This standard promotes the acceptance of personal responsibility for health and encourages the practice of healthy behaviors.

PreK–Grade 2 Performance Indicators, Standard 7

7.2.1 Demonstrate healthy practices and behaviors to maintain or improve personal health.
7.2.2 Demonstrate behaviors that avoid or reduce health risks.

Grades 3–5 Performance Indicators, Standard 7

7.5.1 Identify responsible personal health behaviors.
7.5.2 Demonstrate a variety of healthy practices and behaviors to maintain or improve personal health.
7.5.3 Demonstrate a variety of behaviors to avoid or reduce health risks.

NHES Standard 8: Demonstrate the ability to advocate for personal, family, and community health.

Rationale: Advocacy skills help students promote healthy norms and healthy behaviors. This standard helps students develop important skills to target their health-enhancing messages and to encourage others to adopt healthy behaviors.

PreK–Grade 2 Performance Indicators, Standard 8

8.2.1 Make requests to promote personal health.
8.2.2 Encourage peers to make positive health choices.

Grades 3–5 Performance Indicators, Standard 8

8.5.1 Express opinions and give accurate information about health issues.
8.5.2 Encourage others to make positive health choices.

This represents the work of the Joint Committee on National Health Education Standards. Copies of *National Health Education Standards: Achieving Health Literacy* can be obtained through the American School Health Association, Association for the Advancement of Health Education, or the American Cancer Society. This information can also be accessed from the CDC's website (http://www.cdc.gov/healthyyouth/sher/standards).

Appendix B Monthly Calendar: Health, Safety, and Nutrition Observances

Teachers may find the following list helpful for developing educational lessons and activities that focus on national observances of children's health, safety, and nutrition concerns. Additional resources and information can be accessed on many web sites, including those that follow.

January

Healthy Weight Week	National Heart Lung & Blood Institute: *We Can* campaign http://wecan.nhlbi.nih.gov
Poverty Awareness Month	Children's Defense Fund http://www.childrensdefense.org

February

American Heart Month	American Heart Association http://www.americanheart.org
Burn Awareness Week	Burn Prevention Foundation http://www.burnprevention.org
Children's Dental Health Month	American Dental Association http://www.ada.org
Child Passenger Safety Week	National Highway Traffic Safety Administration http://www.nhtsa.dot.gov
Girls and Women in Sports Day	National Association for Girls and Women in Sports http://www.aahperd.org National Council of Youth Sports http://www.ncys.org
Random Acts of Kindness	Random Acts of Kindness Foundation http://www.actsofkindness.org

March

Brain Injury Awareness Month	Brain Injury Association of America http://www.biausa.org
Diabetes Awareness	American Diabetes Association http://www.diabetes.org
Inhalants and Poisons Awareness	National Inhalant Prevention Coalition http://www.inhalants.org
Nutrition Month	American Dietetic Association http://www.eatright.org
Poison Prevention Month	Poison Prevention Week Council http://www.poisonprevention.org
Save Your Vision Month	American Optometric Association http://www.aoa.org
School Breakfast Week	School Nutrition Association http://www.schoolnutrition.org/nsbw

April

Autism Awareness Month	Autism Society of America http://www.autism-society.org
Child Abuse Prevention Month	Children's Bureau Administration for Children and Families http://www.childwelfare.gov

National Playground Safety Week	National Program for Playground Safety http://www.uni.edu/playground
National Safe Kids Week	Safe Kids Worldwide http://www.safekids.org
Sports Eye Safety Month	American Academy of Ophthalmology http://www.aao.org
Youth Sports Safety Month	National Youth Sports Safety Foundation http://www.nyssf.org

May

Allergy and Asthma Awareness Month	Asthma and Allergy Foundation of America http://www.aafa.org http://www.foodallergy.org
Better Hearing and Speech Month	American Speech-Language-Hearing Association (ASHA) http://www.asha.org
Bike Safety Month	League of American Bicyclists http://www.bikeleague.org Pedestrian and Bicycle Information Center http://www.bicyclinginfo.org Safe Kids U.S.A. http://www.usa.safekids.org
Buckle Up America Week	National Highway Traffic Safety Administration http://www.nhtsa.dot.gov
Clean Air Month	American Lung Association http://www.lungusa.org
Healthy Vision Month	American Optometric Association http://www.aoa.org
Lyme Disease Awareness Month	Lyme Disease Foundation http://www.lyme.org
Mental Health Month (Children)	Mental Health America http://www.nmha.org
Melanoma/Skin Cancer Detection and Prevention Month	The Skin Cancer Foundation http://www.skincancer.org
Physical Fitness and Sports Month	President's Council on Physical and Sports Fitness http://www.fitness.gov

June

Fireworks Eye Safety Month	Prevent Blindness America http://www.preventblindness.org
Home Safety Month	Home Safety Council http://www.homesafetycouncil.org
Lightning Safety Week	National Weather Service http://www.lightningsafety.noaa.gov
National Safety Month	National Safety Council http://www.nsc.org
Sun Safety Week	Sun Safety Alliance http://www.sunsafetyalliance.org

July

UV (Ultra Violet) Eye Safety Month	American Academy of Ophthalmology http://www.aao.org

August

Children's Eye Health and Safety Month	Prevent Blindness America http://www.preventblindness.org
Immunization Awareness Month	National Immunization Program Centers for Disease Control and Prevention http://www.cdc.gov

September

America on the Move	America On the Move Foundation http://www.americaonthemove.org
Baby Safety Month	U.S. Consumer Product Safety Commission http://www.cpsc.gov
Family Health and Fitness	Shape Up America http://www.shapeup.org
Fruit and Vegetable Month	Fruit and Vegetable Program Office Centers for Disease Control and Prevention/Produce for Better Health Foundation http://www.fruitsandveggiesmatter.gov
Head Lice Prevention Month	National Pediculosis Association http://www.headlice.org
National Preparedness Month	National Safety Council http://www.nsc.org
Sickle Cell Awareness Month	Sickle Cell Disease Association of America, Inc. http://www.sicklecelldisease.org
Sports and Home Eye Safety	Prevent Blindness America http://wwwpreventblindness.org
Whole Grains Month	Whole Grains Council http://www.wholegrainscouncil.org

October

Dental Hygiene Month	American Dental Hygienists' Association http://www.adha.org
Eye Injury Prevention Month	American Academy of Ophthalmology http://www.geteyesmart.org/injuries
Fire Prevention Week	National Fire Protection Association http://www.firepreventionweek.org
Halloween Safety Month	Prevent Blindness America http://www.preventblindness.org
Health Literacy Month	National Institutes of Health (NIH) http://www.nih.gov
National School Lunch Week	School Nutrition Association http://www.schoolnutrition.org/nslw
School Bus Safety Week	National Association for Pupil Transportation http://www.napt.org
SIDS Awareness Month	First Candle/SIDS Alliance http://www.firstcandle.org

November

American Diabetes Awareness Month	American Diabetes Association http://www.diabetes.org
Epilepsy Awareness Month	Epilepsy Foundation http://www.epilepsyfoundation.org
National Adoption Awareness Month	National Council for Adoption Infant Adoption Awareness Program http://www.adoptioncouncil.org
National Healthy Skin Month	American Academy of Dermatology http://www.aad.org

December

National Handwashing Awareness Week	Henry the Hand Foundation http://www.henrythehand.com
National Safe Toys and Celebrations Month	Consumer Product Safety Commission http://www.cpsc.gov
Safe Toys and Gifts Month	Kids Health http://www.kidshealth.org

Appendix C Federal Food Programs

Federal food programs are funded and regulated by the U.S. Department of Agriculture and administered at the state level by the Department of Education or the Public Health Department. Information about food programs available in a given locality may be obtained from city or county health departments, state public health departments, or the state departments of education.

Child Nutrition Programs

Child nutrition programs provide cash and/or food assistance for children in public schools, nonprofit private schools, early education centers, home-based child care programs, and summer day camps.

National School Lunch Program (NSLP) (www.fns.usda.gov/cnd/Lunch)

The National School Lunch Program (NSLP) is the oldest and largest federal child food program in existence, both in terms of number of children reached (more than 30 million) and dollars spent. The NSLP is administered at the national level by the U.S. Department of Agriculture (USDA) and at the state level by the U.S. Department of Education. Participating public and nonprofit schools are reimbursed for serving children nutritionally adequate lunches. After-school and enrichment programs are also eligible to apply for reimbursement for the snacks they provide to children (through age 18 years). The amount of money schools receive per meal depends upon whether the student qualifies for free, reduced price, or full price meals. The families of students eligible to receive free or reduced price meals must submit financial statements and meet family size and income guidelines. These guidelines are adjusted periodically according to national poverty guidelines.

Meals funded by NSLP must comply with the Dietary Guidelines for Americans recommendations of no more than 30 percent of calories from fat and less than 10 percent of calories from saturated fat. In addition, meals must provide at least one-third of the recommended daily dietary allowances (RDAs) for protein, vitamins A and C, iron, calcium, and calories appropriate for the age group being served.

School Breakfast Program (SBP) (http://www.fns.usda.gov/cnd/Breakfast)

The School Breakfast Program was authorized by the Child Nutrition Act of 1966. This program also makes provision for free, reduced price, or full price meals. The same income eligibility and nutritional guidelines are used for the School Breakfast Program as for the School Lunch Program. The School Breakfast Program is available to public and nonprofit schools (through high school) and to licensed nonprofit residential child care institutions.

Child and Adult Care Food Program (CACFP) (http://www.cacfp.org)

The Child and Adult Care Food Program provides money for food and commodities for meals served to children in licensed early childhood centers, home-based child care programs, children in emergency shelters, and adults in adult group care programs. The program benefits children 12 years old and under, disabled persons in an institution serving a majority of persons 18 years old and under, migrant children 15 years old and younger, children 18 years or younger staying in emergency shelters, and adults with disabilities. The U.S. Department of Agriculture's Food and Nutrition Service (FNS) provides funding for the CACFP program, which is administered through the Department of Education in most states.

Programs are reimbursed for two meals and one snack or one meal and two snacks. Reimbursement levels are based on a family's income eligibility. The meal pattern follows the same guidelines required for the National School Lunch Program that are adjusted by age categories: infants, children 1–2 years, children 3–5 years, children 6–12 years, and adults.

Family Nutrition Programs

Two governmental programs that provide food assistance to eligible families are the Special Supplemental Nutrition Program for Women, Infants, and Children, better known as WIC, and the Supplemental Nutrition Assistance Program (SNAP).

Women, Infants, and Children (WIC) (http://www.fns.usda.gov/wic) WIC is administered at the federal level by the Food and Nutrition Service, which provides funding to local public health or nonprofit health agencies to operate this program. WIC offers nutrition education, and supplemental foods rich in protein, iron, and vitamin C to pregnant and/or lactating women, infants, and children up to 5 years of age who are determined to be at nutritional risk. Participants receive specified amounts of the following foods:

- iron-fortified infant formula and baby foods
- iron-fortified adult cereals
- fresh fruits and vegetables, including juices high in vitamin C
- whole grain bread
- fortified milk
- proteins, including cheese, eggs, peanut butter, tofu, and canned fish
- dried beans, peas, and legumes

Supplemental Nutrition Assistance Program (SNAP) (http://www.fns.usda.gov/snap) The SNAP program resulted from a complete overhaul of the Food Stamp Program in 2008. It is typically administered by either state or local welfare agencies and serves as the major form of food assistance for low income families in the United States. Eligibility is based on a combination of financial and nonfinancial factors. Monthly benefits are deposited electronically into a credit account that recipients are able to use for food purchases. The purpose of the electronic benefits transfer (EBT) is to reduce the potential for fraud. Funds may be used to purchase *allowed foods*, such as breads and cereals, fruits and vegetables, meats, fish or poultry, and dairy or seeds from which to grow foods. Items not allowed include soap, cigarettes, paper goods, alcoholic beverages, pet foods, vitamins, or deli foods that may be eaten on the premises.

Appendix D Children's Book List

Dental Health

Cousins, L. (2009). *Maisy, Charley, and the Wobbly Tooth: A Maisy First Experience Book*. Candlewick.
Katz, B. (2002). *Hello Reader: Make Your Way for Tooth Decay.* Cartwheel.
Keller, L. (2000). *Open Wide: Tooth School Inside*. Henry Holt & Company.
Lewison, W. (2002). *Clifford's Loose Tooth*. Scholastic.
Mayer, M. (2001). *Just Going to the Dentist*. Golden Books.
Miller, E. (2009). *The Tooth Book: A Guide to Healthy Teeth and Gums*. Holiday House.
Minarik, E. (2002). *Little Bear's Loose Tooth*. HarperFestival.
Munsch, R. (2002). *Andrew's Loose Tooth*. Scholastic.
Murkoff, H. (2002). *What to Expect When You Go to the Dentist*. HarperFestival.
Schoberle, C. (2000). *Open Wide! A Visit to the Dentist*. Simon Spotlight.
Schuh, M. (2008). *At the Dentist (Healthy Teeth series).* Capstone Press. (Also available in Spanish).
Smee, N. (2000). *Freddie Visits the Dentist.* Barrons Educational Series.
Ziefert, H. (2008). *ABC Dentist: Healthy Teeth from A to Z.* Blue Apple Books.

Illness/Germs

Berger, M. (1995). *Germs Make Me Sick!* HarperCollins.
Berger, M. (2002). *Why I Sneeze, Shiver, Hiccup, & Yawn*. HarperCollins.
Capeci, A. (2001). *The Giant Germ*. Scholastic Paperbacks.
Cole, J. (1995). *The Magic School Bus Inside Ralphie: A Book About Germs*. Scholastic.
Cote, P. (2002). *How Do I Feel?* Houghton Mifflin. (Spanish & English).
Dealey, E. (2002). *Goldie Locks Has Chicken Pox*. Scholastic.
Demuth, P. (1997). *Achoo! All About Colds*. Grosset & Dunlap.
Harvey, R. (2005). *Caillou: Is Sick*. Chouette Publishing.
O'Brien-Palmer, M. (1999). *Healthy Me: Fun Ways to Develop Good Health and Safety Habits: Activities for Children 5–8*. Chicago Review Press.
Oetting, J. (2006). *Germs*. Children's Press.
Rice, J. (1997). *Those Mean, Nasty, Dirty, Downright Disgusting but Invisible Germs*. Redleaf Press.
Romanek, T. (2003). *Achoo: The Most Interesting Book You'll Ever Read About Germs*. Kids Can Press.
Ross, T. (2006). *Wash Your Hands!* Kane/Miller.
Verdick, E. (2006). *Germs Are Not for Sharing*. Free Spirit Publishing.

Mental Health (feelings)

Aboff, E. (2010). *Everyone Feels Scared Sometimes*. Picture Window Books.
Agassi, M. (2000). *Hands Are Not for Hitting*. Free Spirit Publishing.
Anholt, C. (1998). *What I Like*. Candlewick Press.
Anholt, C. (1998). *What Makes Me Happy?* Candlewick Press.
Annunziata, J., & Nemiroff, M. (2009). *Sometimes I'm Scared*. Magination Press.
Baker, L. (2001). *I Love You Because You're You*. Cartwheel Books.
Bang, M. (1999). *When Sophie Gets Angry—Really, Really Angry*. Scholastic.
Blumenthal, D. (1999). *The Chocolate-Covered-Cookie Tantrum*. Clarion Books.
Cain, J. (2000). *The Way I Feel*. Parenting Press.
Carle, E. (1999). *The Very Lonely Firefly*. Philomel Books.
Carle, E. (2000). *The Grouchy Ladybug*. Scholastic.
Child, L. (2007). *You Can Be My Friend*. Grosset & Dunlap.
Cole, J. (1997). *I'm a Big Brother*. William Morrow & Co.

Cole, J. (1997). *I'm a Big Sister*. William Morrow & Co.
Cook, J. (2005). *A Bad Case of Tattle Tongue*. National Center for Youth Issues.
Crary, E. (1996). *I'm Scared*. Parenting Press.
Cruz, R. (1992). *Alexander and the Terrible, Horrible, No Good, Very Bad Day*. Aladdin.
Cutis, J. L. (1998). *Today I Feel Silly: And Other Moods That Make My Day*. HarperCollins.
Cutis, J. L. (2002). *I'm Gonna Like Me: Letting off a Little Self-Esteem*. Joanna Cotler.
Demi. (1996). *The Empty Pot*. Henry Holt & Co.
Gainer, C. (1998). *I'm Like You, You're Like Me: A Child's Book About Understanding and Celebrating Each Other*. Free Spirit Publishing.
Hammerseng, K. (1996). *Telling Isn't Tattling*. Parenting Press.
Hankinson, S. (2008). *Carrot-Walnut Pie*. AuthorHouse. (Bullying)
Henkes, K. (1996). *Chrysanthemum*. HarperTrophy.
Hudson, C., & Ford, B. (1990). *Bright Eyes, Brown Skin*. Just Us Books.
Krasny, L., & Brown, M. (2001). *How to Be a Friend: A Guide to Making Friends and Keeping Them*. Little Brown & Co.
Kubler, A., & Formby, C. (1995). *Come Play with Us*. Child's Play International, Ltd.
Lachner, D. (1995). *Andrew's Angry Words*. North South Books.
Lalli, J. (1997). *I Like Being Me: Poems for Children, About Feeling Special, Appreciating Others, and Getting Along*. Free Spirit Publishing.
Lewis, P. (2002). *I'll Always Love You*. Tiger Tales.
Lite, L. (2007). *A Boy and a Turtle: A Children's Relaxation Story to Improve Sleep, Manage Stress, Anxiety, Anger*. Stress Free Kids.
Lite, L. (2008). *The Angry Octopus*. Stress Free Kids.
Lovell, P. (2001). *Stand Tall, Molly Lou Melon*. Scholastic.
O'Neill, A. (2002). *The Recess Queen*. Scholastic.
Parr, T. (2001). *It's Okay to be Different*. Little, Brown.
Parr, T. (2009). *The Feelings Book*. Little, Brown Books for Young Readers.
Payne, L. (1997). *We Can Get Along: A Child's Book of Choices*. Free Spirit Publishing.
Pinkney, A., & Pinkney, B. (1997). *Pretty Brown Face*. Red Wagon Books.
Silver, G. (2009). *Anh's Anger*. Plum Blossom Books.
Spelman, C. (2000). *When I Feel Angry*. Albert Whitman & Co.
Tetik, B. (2009). *If You Are Mad Say It with Words*. BookSurge Publishing.
Thomas, P. (2000). *Stop Picking on Me*. Barrons.
Vail, R. (2002). *Sometimes I'm Bombaloo*. Scholastic.
Weninger, B., & Marks, A. (1995). *Good-bye Daddy*. North-South Books.
Willems, M. (2007). *My Friend Is Sad*. Hyperion Book CH.

Personal Health & Self-Care

Aliki. (1992). *I'm Growing*. HarperCollins.
Baker, K. (2001). *Brave Little Monster*. HarperCollins.
Berry, J. (2010). *Teach Me About I Love Getting Dressed*. Joy Berry Books.
Brown, M. (1991). *Good Night Moon*. HarperFestival.
Cason, S. (2008). *The Night-Night Dance*. Tate Publishing.
Civardi, A. (2005). Usborne First Experiences Collection: "*Going to School*," "*Going to the Doctor*," "*Moving House*," "*The New Baby*." Usborne Publishing Ltd.
Fox, L. (2010) *Ella Kazoo Will Not Brush Her Hair*. Walker Books for Young Readers.
Himmelman, J. (1995). *Lights Out!* Troll.
Katz, A. (2001). *Take Me Out of the Bathtub*. Scholastic.
Keats, E. J. (1992). *Dreams*. Aladdin Books.
Leonard, M. (1998). *Getting Dressed*. Bantam Books.
Murkoff, H. (2000). *What to Expect at Bedtime*. HarperFestival.

Murkoff, H. (2000). *What to Expect When You Go to the Doctor.* HarperFestival.
Pfeffer, W. (1999). *Sounds All Around.* HarperCollins.
Reidy, J. (2010). *Too Purpley!* Bloomsbury USA Children's Books.
Reidy, H. (1999). *What Do You Like to Wear?* Larousse Kingfisher Chambers.
Ricci, C. (2007). *Show Me Your Smile! A Visit to the Dentist.* Simon Spotlight Nickelodeon.
Rowland, P. (1996). *What Should I Wear?* Random House.
Showers, P. (1993). *The Listening Walk.* HarperTrophy.
Showers, P. (1997). *Sleep Is for Everyone.* HarperCollins.
Sykes, J. (1996). *I Don't Want to Go to Bed.* Tiger Tales.
Wood, A. (1996). *The Napping House.* Harcourt Brace & Co.

Safety

Berenstain, S., & Berenstain, J. (1999). *My Trusty Car Seat: Buckling Up for Safety.* Random House.
Boxall, E. (2002). *Francis the Scaredy Cat.* Candlewick Press.
Caviezel, G. (2007). *Policeman's Safety Hints.* Barron's Educational Series.
Committee, C. B. (2000). *Buckles Buckles Everywhere.* Palmetto Bookworks.
Cook, J. (2007). *SCOOP (Children's Life Skills).* National Center for Youth Issues.
Cuyler, M. (2001). *Stop, Drop, Roll.* Simon & Schuster.
Federico, J. (2009). *Some Parts Are Not for Sharing.* Tate Publishing.
Feigh, A. (2008). *On Those Runaway Days.* Free Spirit Publishing.
Hayward, L. (2001). *A Day in the Life of a Firefighter.* Dorling Kindersley Publisher.
Kelman, M. (2009). *Safety First!* Disney Press.
MacLean, C. K. (2002). *Even Firefighters Hug Their Moms.* Dutton.
Mattern, J. (2007). *Staying Safe in the Car.* Weekly Reader Early Learning Library.
Meiners, C. (2006). *Be Careful and Stay Safe.* Free Spirit Publishing
Mitton, T. (2001). *Down by the Cool of the Pool.* Orchard Books.
Palatini, M. (2002). *Earthquack!* Simon & Schuster.
Pendziwol, J. (2006). *Once Upon a Dragon: Stranger Safety for Kids (and Dragons).* Kids Can Press.
Prigger, M. (2002). *Aunt Minnie and the Twister.* Clarion.
Reasoner, C. (2003). *Bee Safe (The Bee Attitudes).* Price Stern Sloan Publishers.
Schwartz, L. (1995). *The Safety Book for Active Kids: Teaching Your Child How to Avoid Everyday Dangers.* Learning Works.
Spelman, C. & Weidner, T. (2000). *Your Body Belongs to You.* Albert Whitman.
Tekavec, H. (2002). *Storm Is Coming!* Dial.
Weeks, S. (2002). *My Somebody Special.* Harcourt, Inc.

Special Needs

Bunnett, R. (1996). *Friends at School.* Star Bright Books.
Fassler, J. (1987). *Howie Helps Himself.* Albert Whitman & Co.
Gaynor, K., Carswell, C., & Quirke, K. (2009). *A Birthday for Ben – Children with Hearing Difficulty.* Moonbeam Children's Books.
Gosselin, K. (1996). *Zooallergy: A Fun Story About Allergy and Asthma Triggers.* JayJo Books.
Gosselin, K. (1998). *Taking Diabetes to School.* JayJo Books.
Harrison, T. (1998). *Aaron's Awful Allergies.* Kids Can Press.
Lakin, P. (1994). *Dad and Me in the Morning.* Albert Whitman & Co.
London, J. (1997). *The Lion Who Had Asthma.* Albert Whitman & Co.
Maguire, A. (2000). *Special People, Special Ways.* Future Horizons.
Mayer, G., & Mayer, M. (1993). *A Very Special Critter.* Golden Books.
Millman, I. (2000). *Moses Goes to School.* Frances Foster Books/Farrar, Straus & Giroux.
Nausau, E. (2001). *The Peanut Butter Jam.* Health Press.
Powers, M. (1987). *Our Teacher's in a Wheelchair.* Albert Whitman & Co.

Shriver, M. (2001). *What's Wrong with Timmy?* Little Brown & Co.
Smith, N. (1999). *Allie the Allergic Elephant: A Children's Story of Peanut Allergies.* Jungle Communications, Inc.
Stuve-Bodeen, S. (1998). *We'll Paint the Octopus Red.* Woodbine House.
Weiner, E. (1999). *Taking Food Allergies to School.* JayJo Books.
White Pirner, C. (1994). *Even Little Kids Get Diabetes.* Albert Whitman & Co.

Nutrition

Appleton, J. (2001). *Do Carrots Make You See Better?* Red Leaf Press.
Brennan, G., & Brennan, E. (2004). *The Children's Kitchen Garden: A Book of Gardening, Cooking and Learning.* Ten Speed Press.
Brown, M. (1997). *D.W. The Picky Eater.* Little, Brown Books for Young Readers.
Brown, P. (2009). *The Curious Garden.* Little, Brown Books for Young Readers.
Caplan, J. (2009). *Gobey Gets Full: Good Nutrition in a Nutshell.* BookSurge Publishing.
Carle, E. (1986). *The Very Hungry Caterpillar.* Putnam.
Carle, E. (1998). *Pancakes, Pancakes!* Aladdin Books.
Charney, S., Goldbeck, D., & Larson, M. (2007). *The ABCs of Fruits and Vegetables and Beyond.* Ceres Press.
Compestine, Y. (2001). *The Runaway Rice Cake.* Simon & Schuster.
Cooper, H. (2005). *Pumpkin Soup.* Farrar, Straus & Giroux (BYR).
French, V. (1998). *Oliver's Fruit Salad.* Orchard Books.
Geeslin, C. (1999). *How Nanita Learned to Make Flan.* Atheneum.
Gershator, D. (1998). *Bread Is for Eating.* Henry Holt.
Gibbons, G. (2000). *The Honey Makers.* HarperCollins.
Gibbons, G. (2008). *The Vegetables We Eat.* Holiday House.
Hall, Z. (1996). *The Apple Pie Tree.* Scholastic..
Katzen, M. (1994). *Pretend Soup and Other Real Recipes: A Cookbook for Preschoolers and Up.* Tricycle Press.
Kelly, C. (2002). *Eat Health, Feel Great.* Little, Brown Young Readers.
Krauss, R. (2004). *The Carrot Seed.* HarperCollins.
Levenson, G. (2002). *Pumpkin Circle: The Story of a Garden.* Tricycle Press.
Lin, G. (2003). *Dim Sum for Everyone.* Dragonfly Books.
Lin, G. (2009). *The Ugly Vegetables.* Charlesbridge Publishing.
Leedy, L. (2007). *The Edible Pyramid: Good Eating Every Day.* Holiday House.
Paulsen, G. (1998). *The Tortilla Factory.* Harcourt Brace.
Priceman, M. (1996). *How to Make an Apple Pie and See the World.* Knopf.
Rabe, T. (2001). *Oh the Things You Can Do That Are Good for You!* Random House.
Reiser, L. (1998). *Tortillas and Lullabies.* Greenwillow Books.
Richards, J. (2006). *A Fruit Is a Suitcase for Seeds.* First Avenue Editions.
Rockwell, L. (2009). *Good Enough to Eat: A Kid's Guide to Food and Nutrition.* HarperCollins.
Russ-Ayon, A., & June, C. (2009). *We Eat Food That's Fresh.* OurRainbow Press.
Sanger, A. (2001). *First Book of Sushi.* Tricycle Press.
Schuh, M. (2006). *Being Active (Healthy Eating With My Pyramid).* Capstone Press.
Sharmat, M. (2009). *Gregory, the Terrible Eater.* Scholastic.
Wells, P. (2003). *Busy Bears: Breakfast with the Bears.* Sterling Publications.
Westcott, N. (1998). *Never Take a Pig Out to Lunch and Other Poems.* Orchard Books.
Woods, D., & Woods, A. (2000). *The Big Hungry Bear.* Child's Play Publishers.
Woomer, L. (2009). *Cookie.* Outskirts Press.

Physical Activity

Ackerman, K., & Gammell, S. (2003). *Song and Dance Man.* Knopf Books.
Blackstone, S. (2001). *Bear About Town.* Barefoot Books.
Blackstone, S., & Harter, D. (2007). *Bear on a Bike.* Barefoot Books.

Brown, M. (1991). *D.W. Flips.* Little, Brown Books for Young Readers.
Brown, M. (1996). *D.W. Rides Again.* Little, Brown Books for Young Readers.
Cole, J., Calmenson, S., & Tiegreen, A. (1990). *Miss Mary Mack and Other Children's Street Rhymes.* HarperCollins.
Cole, J., & Tiegreen, A. (1989). *Anna Banana: 101 Jump Rope Rhymes.* Harper Collins.
Davis, K. (2001). *Who Hops?* Voyager Books.
Doering-Tourville, A. (2008). *Get Up and Go: Being Active (How to Be Healthy).* Picture Window Books.
Esbensen, B., & Leffler, M. (2000). *Jumping Day.* Boyds Mills Press.
Fallon, J., & Stower, A. (2007). *Snowball Fight!* Scholastic Inc.
Flemming, D. (1995). *In the Tall, Tall Grass.* Henry Holt & Co.
Hutchins, P. (2007). *Barn Dance!* Greenwillow Books.
Isadora, R. (2000). *Isadora Dances.* Puffin.
London, J. (1999). *Puddles.* Puffin.
London, J., & Remkiewicz, F. (2001). *Froggy Plays Soccer.* Puffin.
London, J., & Remkiewicz, F. (2008). *Froggy Rides a Bike.* Puffin.
Miller, E. (2008). *The Monster Health Book: A Guide to Eating Healthy, Being Active & Feeling Great for Monsters & Kids.* Holiday House.
Rosen, M. (2009). *We're Going on a Bear Hunt.* Helen Oxenbury.
Schuh, M. (2006). *Being Active.* Capstone Press.
Shannon, G., & Trynan, A. (2000). *Frog Legs.* Greenwillow Books.
Stickland, P. (1996). *Dinosaur Stomp!* Dutton Juvenile.
Stickland, P. (2000). *Ten Terrible Dinosaurs.* Puffin.
Thomas, P., & Facklam, P. (2008). *Snow Dance.* Pelican Publishing.
Torrey, R. (2003). *Beans Baker Bounces Back.* Random House Books.
Walton, R., & Gorton, J. (2000). *My Two Hands, My Two Feet.* Puffin.
Winch, J. (2000). *Keeping Up With Grandma.* Holiday House.
Wood, A., & Wood, D. (1997). *Quick As a Cricket.* Child's Play International.

Appendix E Nutrient Information: Fast-Food Vendor Websites

Arby's	http://www.arbys.com
A&W	http://www.awrestaurants.com
Back Yard Burgers	http://www.backyardburgers.com
Baja Fresh	http://www.bajafresh.com
Blimpie	http://www.blimpie.com
Burger King	http://www.burgerking.com
Carl's Jr.	http://www.carlsjr.com
Chick-fil-A	http://www.chick-fil-a.com
Chipotle Mexican Grill	http://www.chipotle.com
Church's Fried Chicken	http://www.churchs.com
Dairy Queen	http://www.dairyqueen.com
Domino's Pizza	http://www.dominos.com
El Pollo Loco	http://www.elpolloloco.com
Einstein Bros. Bagels	http://www.einsteinbros.com
Hardee's	http://www.hardees.com
In-and-Out Burger	http://www.in-n-out.com
KFC	http://www.kfc.com
Krystal	http://www.krystal.com
Little Caesars	http://www.littlecaesars.com
Long John Silvers	http://www.ljsilvers.com
McDonald's	http://www.mcdonalds.com
On the Border	http://www.ontheborder.com
Pizza Hut	http://www.pizzahut.com
Quiznos Sub	http://www.quiznos.com
Sonic Drive-in	http://www.sonicdrivein.com
Steak 'n Shake	http://www.steaknshake.com
Subway	http://www.subway.com
Taco Bell	http://www.tacobell.com
Wendy's	http://www.wendys.com
White Castle	http://www.whitecastle.com

*For additional information on the nutritional value of most foods, visit the Food and Nutrition Information Center at http://www.nal.usda.gov/fnic.

Glossary

abdomen – the portion of the body located between the diaphragm (located at the base of the lungs) and the pelvic or hip bones.

absorption – the process by which the products of digestion are transferred from the intestinal tract into the blood or lymph or by which substances are taken up by the cells.

abuse – to mistreat, attack, or cause harm to another individual.

accreditation – the process of certifying an individual or program as having met certain specified requirements.

acute – the stage of an illness or disease during which an individual is definitely sick and exhibits symptoms characteristic of the particular illness or disease involved.

adenosine triphosphate (ATP) – a compound with energy-storing phosphate bonds that is the main energy source for all cells.

airborne transmission – when germs are expelled into the air through coughs/sneezes, and transmitted to another individual via tiny moisture drops.

alkalis – groups of bases or caustic substances that are capable of neutralizing acids to form salts.

amblyopia – a condition of the eye commonly referred to as "lazy eye"; vision gradually becomes blurred or distorted due to unequal balance of the eye muscles. There are no observable abnormalities of the eyes when a child has amblyopia.

amino acids – the organic building blocks from which proteins are made.

anaphylaxis – a severe allergic reaction that may cause difficulty breathing, itching, unconsciousness, and possible death.

anecdotal – brief notes describing a person's observations.

antibodies – special substances produced by the body that help protect against disease.

apnea – momentary absence of breathing.

aseptic procedure – treatment to produce a product that is free of disease-producing bacteria.

aspiration – accidental inhalation of food, fluid, or an object into the respiratory tract.

asymptomatic – having no symptoms.

attachment – an emotional connection established between infants and their parents or primary caregivers.

attitudes – beliefs or feelings one has toward certain facts or situations.

atypical – unusual; different from what might commonly be expected.

audiologist – a specially prepared clinician who uses nonmedical techniques to diagnose hearing impairments.

bacteria – one-celled microorganisms; some are beneficial for the body, but pathogenic bacteria cause diseases.

basal metabolic rate – minimum amount of energy needed to carry on the body processes vital to life.

behavioral objectives – clear, meaningful descriptions of specific behavioral outcomes; can be observed and measured.

calories – units used to measure the energy value of foods.

calcium – mineral nutrient; a major component of bones and teeth.

Note: Definitions are based on usage within the text.

catalyzes – accelerates a chemical reaction.

chronic – frequent or repeated incidences of illness; can also be a lengthy or permanent status, as in chronic disease or dysfunction.

coenzymes – a vitamin-containing substance required by certain enzymes before they can perform their prescribed function.

cognitive – the aspect of learning that refers to the development of skills and abilities based on knowledge and thought processes.

collagen – a protein that forms the major constituent of connective tissue, cartilage, bone, and skin.

communicable – a condition that can be spread or transmitted from one individual to another.

complementary proteins – proteins with offsetting missing amino acids; complementary proteins can be combined to provide complete protein.

complete proteins – proteins that contain all essential amino acids in amounts relative to the amounts needed to support growth.

compliance – the act of obeying or cooperating with specific requests or requirements.

concepts – combinations of basic and related factual information that represent more generalized statements or ideas.

conductive hearing loss – affects the volume of word tones heard, so that loud sounds are more likely to be heard than soft sounds.

contagious – capable of being transmitted or passed from one person to another.

convalescent – the stage of recovery from an illness or disease.

cost control – reduction of expenses through portion control, inventory, and reduction of waste.

critical control point (CCP) – a point or procedure in a specific food system where loss of control may result in an unacceptable health risk.

cryptosporidiosis – an infectious illness caused by an intestinal parasite. May be present in water (e.g., swimming pools, hot tubs, streams) contaminated with feces or from unwashed hands. Often causes severe diarrhea in children.

cycle menus – menus that are written to repeat after a set interval, such as every three to four weeks.

deciduous teeth – a child's initial set of teeth; this set is temporary and gradually begins to fall out at about 5 years of age.

dehydration – a state in which there is an excessive loss of body fluids or extremely limited fluid intake. Symptoms may include loss of skin tone, sunken eyes, and mental confusion.

dental caries – tooth decay.

development – commonly refers to the process of intellectual growth and change.

developmental or physiological readiness – growth (both physical and cognitive) and chemical processes that lead to the ability to perform a function.

developmentally appropriate practice (DAP) – learning experiences and environments that take into each child's abilities, diverse needs, and individual interests. DAP also reflects differences among families and values them as essential partners in children's education.

diagnosis – the process of identifying a disease, illness, or injury from its symptoms.

Dietary Guidelines for Americans – a report that provides recommendations for daily food choices, to be balanced with physical activity, to promote good health and reduce certain disease risks.

Dietary Reference Intake (DRI) – a plan that presents the recommended goals of nutrient intakes for various age and gender groups.

digestion – the process by which complex nutrients in foods are changed into smaller units that can be absorbed and used by the body.

discipline – training or enforced obedience that corrects, shapes, or develops acceptable patterns of behavior.

disinfected – killed pathogenic organisms.

disorientation – lack of awareness or ability to recognize familiar persons or objects.

distention – stretched or enlarged.

DNA (deoxyribonucleic acid) – the substance in the cell nucleus that codes for genetically transmitted traits.

Down syndrome – a genetic disorder that is characterized by unique facial features, mental retardation, and motor delays.

electrolytes – substances which, when in solution, become capable of conducting electricity; examples include sodium and potassium.

elevate – to raise to a higher position.

emotional abuse – repeated humiliation, ridicule, or threats directed toward another individual.

emotional or psychological neglect – failure to meet a child's psychological needs for love and attention.

endocrine – refers to glands within the body that produce and secrete substances called hormones directly into the blood stream.

energy – power to perform work.

enriched – adding nutrients to grain products to replace those lost during refinement; thiamin, niacin, riboflavin, and iron are nutrients most commonly added.

environment – the sum total of physical, cultural, and behavioral features that surround and affect an individual.

enzymes – proteins that catalyze body functions.

essential amino acids – amino acids that can only be obtained from protein food sources.

essential nutrient – a nutrient that must be provided in food because it cannot be synthesized by the body at a rate sufficient to meet the body's needs.

ethnic – pertaining to races or groups of people who share common traits or customs.

evaluation – a measurement of effectiveness for determining whether or not educational objectives have been achieved.

expectations – behaviors or actions that are anticipated.

failure to thrive – a term used to describe an infant whose growth and mental development are severely slowed due to lack of nurturing or mental stimulation.

fat-soluble vitamins – vitamins that are dissolved, transported, and stored in fat.

fecal-oral transmission – when germs are transferred to the mouth via hands contaminated with fecal material.

fever – an elevation of body temperature above normal; a temperature over 99.4°F or 37.4°C orally is usually considered a fever.

First-In-First-Out (FIFO) – a method of storage in which the items stored for the longest time will be retrieved first.

fluorosis – white or brown spots that form on children's teeth due to excessive fluoride intake.

food-borne illness – a disease or illness transmitted by the ingestion of food contaminated with bacteria, viruses, some molds, or parasites.

food-borne illness outbreak – when two or more people become ill after ingesting the same food. Laboratory analysis must confirm that food is the source of the illness.

food infections – illnesses resulting from ingestion of live bacteria in food.

food insecurity – uncertain or limited access to a reliable source of food.

food intolerance – unpleasant reactions to particular foods that do not involve an immune response and are usually outgrown.

food intoxications – illnesses resulting from ingestion of food containing residual bacterial toxins in the absence of viable bacteria.

fruit drinks and fruit-ades– products that contain 0–10 percent real fruit juice, added water, and sugar.

full-strength– undiluted (as in 100 percent fruit or vegetable juice).

gestational diabetes – a form of diabetes that occurs only during pregnancy; affects the way the mother's body utilizes sugars in foods and increases health risks for the baby.

Good Samaritan Law – legal protection afforded to an individual who renders emergency or first aid care in a reasonable manner.

gram – a metric unit of weight; approximately 1/28 of an ounce.

growth – increase in size of any body part or of the entire body.

hands-on – active involvement in a project; actually doing something.

Hazard Analysis Critical Control Point (HACCP) – a food safety and self-inspection system that highlights potentially hazardous foods and how they are handled in the food service department.

head circumference – the distance around the head obtained by measuring over the forehead and bony protuberance on the back of the head; it is an indication of normal or abnormal growth and development of the brain and central nervous system.

health – a state of wellness. Complete physical, mental, social, and emotional well-being; the quality of one element affects the state of the others.

health assessment – the process of gathering and evaluating information about an individual's state of health.

heat exhaustion – above normal body temperature caused by exposure to too much sun.

heat stroke – failure of the body's sweating reflex during exposure to high temperatures; causes body temperature to rise.

hemoglobin – the iron-containing, oxygen-carrying pigment in red blood cells.

heredity – the transmission of certain genetic material and characteristics from biological parents to child at the time of conception.

hormones – a special chemical substance produced by endocrine glands that influences and regulates certain body functions.

hyperglycemia – a condition characterized by an abnormally high level of sugar in the blood.

hyperopia – farsightedness; a condition of the eyes in which an individual can see objects clearly in the distance but has poor close vision.

hypertension – elevation of blood pressure above the normally accepted values.

hyperventilation – rapid breathing often with forced inhalation; can lead to sensations of dizziness, lightheadedness, and weakness.

hypothermia – below normal body temperature caused by overexposure to cold conditions.

immunized – a state of becoming resistant to a specific disease through the introduction of living or dead microorganisms into the body, which then stimulate the production of antibodies.

impairment – a condition or malfunction of a body part that interferes with optimal functioning.

incidental learning – learning that occurs in addition to the primary intent or goals of instruction.

incomplete proteins – proteins that lack required amounts of one or more essential amino acids.

incubation – the interval of time between exposure to infection and the appearance of the first signs or symptoms of illness.

infection – a condition that results when a pathogen invades and establishes itself within a susceptible host.

ingested – the process of taking food or other substances into the body through the mouth.

inservice – educational training provided by an employer.

intervention – practices or procedures implemented to modify or change a specific behavior or condition.

intestinal – pertaining to the intestinal tract or bowel.

iron-deficiency anemia – a failure in the oxygen transport system caused by too little iron.

irradiation – food preservation by short-term exposure of the food to gamma ray radiation.

language – form of communication that allows individuals to share feelings, ideas, and experiences with one another.

latch-key – a term that refers to school-aged children who care for themselves without adult supervision before and after school hours.

lethargy – a state of inaction or indifference.

liability – legal responsibility or obligation for one's actions owed to another individual.

licensing – the act of granting formal permission to conduct a business or profession.

linoleic acid – a polyunsaturated fatty acid, which is essential (must be provided in food) for humans; also known as omega-6 fatty acid.

linolenic acid – one of the two polyunsaturated fatty acids that are recognized as essential for humans; also known as omega-3 fatty acid.

listlessness – a state characterized by a lack of energy and/or interest in one's affairs.

low-birthweight (LBW) infant – an infant who weighs less than 5.5 pounds (2500 grams) at birth.

Lyme disease – bacterial illness caused by the bite of infected deer ticks found in grassy or wooded areas.

lymph glands – specialized groupings of tissue that produce and store white blood cells for protection against infection and illness.

macrocytic anemia – a failure in the oxygen transport system characterized by abnormally large immature red blood cells.

malnutrition – prolonged inadequate or excessive intake of nutrients and/or calories required by the body.

megadose – an amount of a vitamin or mineral at least ten times that of the RDA.

metabolism – all chemical changes that occur from the time nutrients are absorbed until they are built into body tissue or are excreted.

microbial – refers to living organisms, such as bacteria, viruses, parasites, or fungi, that can cause disease.

microcytic anemia – a failure in the oxygen transport system characterized by abnormally small red blood cells.

microgram (mcg or μg) – a metric unit of measurement; one microgram equals one-millionth of a gram.

milligram – a metric unit of measurement; one-thousandth of a gram.

minerals – inorganic chemical elements that are required in the diet to support growth, and repair tissue, and to regulate body functions.

misarticulations – improper pronunciation of words and word sounds.

mixed hearing loss – a disorder that involves a combination of conductive and sensorineural hearing losses

monounsaturated fatty acid (MUFA) – a fatty acid that has only one bond in its structure, and that is not fully saturated with hydrogen.

mottling – marked with spots of dense white or brown coloring.

myopia – nearsightedness; an individual has good near vision but poor distant vision.

neglect – failure of a parent or legal guardian to properly care for and meet the basic needs of a child under 18 years of age.

negligence – failure to practice or perform one's duties according to certain standards; carelessness.

neophobic – fear of things that are new and unfamiliar.

neurological – pertaining to the nervous system, which consists of the nerves, brain, and spinal column.

neuromuscular – pertaining to control of muscular function by the nervous system.

nonessential amino acids – amino acids that are produced in the body.

normal – average; a characteristic or quality that is common to most individuals in a defined group.

norms – an expression (e.g., weeks, months, years) of when a child is likely to demonstrate certain developmental skills.

notarized – official acknowledgment of the authenticity of a signature or document by a notary public.

nutrients –the chemical substances in food.

nutrition – the study of food and how it is used by the body.

nutrition claims – statements of reduced calories, fat, or salt on the food labels.

nutrition education – activities that impart information about food and its use in the body.

obese – a BMI over 30.

objectives – clear, meaningful descriptions of specific behavioral outcomes; can be observed and measured.

observations – to inspect and take note of the appearance and behavior of other individuals.

odd-day cycle menus – menus planned for a period of days other than a week that repeat after the planned period; cycles of any number of days may be used. These menus are a means of avoiding repetition of the same foods on the same day of the week.

ophthalmologist – a physician who specializes in diseases and abnormalities of the eye.

optometrist – a specialist (non-physician) trained to examine eyes and prescribe glasses and eye exercises.

overweight – a BMI greater than 25 and less than 30.

pallor – paleness.

palmar grasp – using the entire hand to pick up objects.

paralysis – temporary or permanent loss of sensation, function, or voluntary movement of a body part.

parasites – organisms that live on or within other living organisms.

pasteurized – heating a food to a prescribed temperature for a specific time period to destroy disease-producing bacteria.

pathogen – a microorganism capable of producing illness or infection.

peers – one of the same rank; equals.

Percent Daily Values (%DV) – a measure of the nutritional value of food; used in nutrition labeling.

physical abuse – injuries such as welts, burns, bruises, or broken bones, that are caused intentionally.

physical neglect – failure to meet children's fundamental needs for food, shelter, medical care, and education, including abandonment.

pincer grip – using the thumb and finger to pick up an object.

Prader-Willi syndrome – a chromosomal disorder that causes learning and behavior problems, overeating that can lead to obesity, poor muscle tone, and short height.

precipitating – factors that trigger or initiate a reaction or response.

predisposition – having an increased chance or susceptibility.

prenatal – the period from conception to birth of the baby.

preplan – outline a method of action prior to carrying it out.

preventive health – engaging in behaviors that help to maintain and enhance one's health status; includes concern for certain social issues affecting the population's health and environment.

procurement – the process of obtaining services, supplies, and equipment in conformance with applicable laws and regulations.

prodromal – the appearance of the first nonspecific signs of infection; this stage ends when the symptoms characteristic of a particular communicable illness begin to appear.

protein – class of nutrients used primarily for structural and regulatory functions.

PUFA (polyunsaturated fatty acids) – fatty acids that contain more than one bond that is not fully saturated with hydrogen.

punishment – a negative response to what the observer considers to be wrong or inappropriate behavior; may involve physical or harsh treatment.

recovery position – placing an individual in a side-lying position.

referrals – directing an individual to other sources, usually for additional evaluation or treatment.

registration – the act of placing the name of a child care program on a list of active providers; usually does not require on-site inspection.

regulations – standards or requirement that are set to ensure uniform and safe practices.

regurgitation – the return of partially digested food from stomach to mouth.

reprimand – to scold or discipline for unacceptable behavior.

resilient – the ability to withstand or resist difficulty.

resistance – the ability to avoid infection or illness.

respiratory tract – pertains to, and includes, the nose, throat, trachea, and lungs.

resuscitation – to revive from unconsciousness or death; to restore breathing and heartbeat.

retention – the ability to remember or recall previously learned material.

risk management – measures taken to avoid an event such as an injury or illness implies the ability to anticipate circumstances and behaviors.

RNA (ribonucleic acid) – the nucleic acid that serves as messenger between the nucleus and the ribosomes where proteins are synthesized.

salmonellosis – a bacterial infection that is spread through contaminated drinking water, food, or milk, or contact with other infected persons. Symptoms include diarrhea, fever, nausea, and vomiting.

sanitized – cleaned or sterilized.

satiety – a feeling of satisfaction or fullness.

sedentary – unusually slow or sluggish; a lifestyle that implies inactivity.
self-concept – a person's concept of who they are and how they fit in.
self-esteem – an individual's sense of value or confidence in himself or herself.
seizures – a temporary interruption of consciousness sometimes accompanied by convulsive movements.
sensorimotor – Piaget's first stage of cognitive development, during which children learn and relate to their world primarily through motor and sensory activities.
sensorineural loss – a type of hearing loss that occurs when sound impulses cannot reach the brain due to damage of the auditory nerve, or cannot be interpreted because of prior brain damage.
sensory qualities – aspects that appeal to sight, sound, taste, feel, and smell.
serrated – saw-toothed or notched.
sexual abuse – any sexual involvement between an adult and child.
shaken baby syndrome – forceful shaking of a baby that causes head trauma, internal bleeding, and sometimes death.
skeletal – pertaining to the bony framework that supports the body.
skinfold – a measurement of the amount of fat under the skin; also referred to as fat-fold measurements.
sleep apnea –temporary interruptions or stoppages in breathing during sleep.
speech – the process of using words to express one's thoughts and ideas.
sterile – free from living microorganisms.
strabismus – a condition of the eyes in which one or both eyes appear to be turned inward (crossed) or outward (walleye).
submerge – to place in water.
supervision – watching carefully over the behaviors and actions of children and others.
supplementary proteins – a complete protein mix resulting from combining a small amount of a complete protein with an incomplete protein to provide all essential amino acids.
susceptible host – an individual who is capable of being infected by a pathogen.
symptomatic control – treatment that controls symptoms but does not cure the condition.
symptoms – changes in the body or its functions that are experienced by the affected individual.
synthesis – the process of making a compound by the union of simpler compounds or elements.
temperature – a measurement of body heat; varies with the time of day, activity, and method of measurement.
thermic energy of foods – energy required to digest, absorb, transport, and metabolize nutrients in food.
toxicity – a state of being poisonous.
trans-fats – unsaturated fats that have been converted to a solid by a process called hydrogenation.
tympanic – referring to the ear canal.
type 1 diabetes – a disease distinguished by a lack of insulin production; usually diagnosed in childhood or young adulthood.
undernutrition – an inadequate intake of one or more required or essential nutrients.
underweight – a BMI of less than 18.5.
unintentional injury – an unexpected or unplanned event that may result in physical harm or injury.
universal infection control precautions – special measures taken when handling bodily fluids, including careful handwashing, wearing latex gloves, disinfecting surfaces, and proper disposal of contaminated objects.
urination – the act of emptying the bladder of urine.
values – the beliefs, traditions, and customs an individual incorporates and utilizes to guide behavior and judgments.
verbal abuse – to attack another individual with words.
viruses – any of a group of submicroscopic infective agents, many of which cause a number of diseases in animals and plants.
vitamins – organic substances needed in very small amounts to regulate many metabolic functions in the body.
water-soluble vitamins – vitamins that are dissolved and transported in water/fluids; cannot be stored.
weekly menus – menus that are written to be served on a weekly basis.
well child – a child in a good physical, mental, social, and emotional state.
whole grains – grain products that have not been refined; they contain all parts of the kernel of grain.

Index

ABCs for assessing emergencies, 240*t*
Abrasions, 254
Absence of breathing, 241–243
Absence seizure, 103
Abuse. *See* Maltreatment of children
Accidents, 208, 212
Accreditation, 174
Acquired immunodeficiency syndrome (AIDS), 141*t*, 272*t*
Activity plans, 298–311. *See also* Classroom Corner
  dental health, 303–304
  dressing appropriately for the weather, 302
  feelings (emotional health), 305–307
  fire safety, 310–311
  germs and illness prevention, 299
  hand washing, 300–301
  pedestrian safety, 308–309
  poison prevention, 309–310
  safety in cars, 307–308
  tooth brushing, 304–305
Acute illness. *See* Management of injuries and acute illness
Acute stage, 117
Adenosine triphosphate (ATP), 378
Adequate intake (AI), 320
Administration of medication form, 122
Administration of medicine, 120–121
Adrenalin, 379
Adult-onset diabetes, 96
Adults
  abusive/neglectful, 274–276
  body mechanics, 20
  role models, as, 24
Aerosol breathing treatment, 89
Aerosol sprays, 225*t*
Age-related eating behaviors, 399*t*, 414*t*
AI, 320
AIDS, 141*t*, 272*t*
Air pollutants, 190*t*
Air quality, 190–191
Airborne transmission, 116*f*
Airborne transmitted illnesses, 138–141*t*
Airway obstruction, 243–246
Alcoholic beverages, 323
Allergen, 85
Allergic diseases, 85–90
  anaphylaxis, 89
  asthma, 90–92
  classification, 86
  cold, compared, 86
  food allergies, 86–87
  management, 88–90
  signs/symptoms, 85–87
Allergy and Asthma Awareness Month, 515
Allergy shots, 89
Amblyopia, 63
America On the Move Foundation, 516
American Diabetes Awareness Month, 517
American Heart Month, 514
Amino acids, 354, 355
Anaphylaxis, 89
Anemia, 92–94
Anger management, 283
Animal bites, 254–255
Anthropometric assessment, 72
Antihistamines, 89
Apnea, 159
Art materials, 225*t*
Artificial lighting, 190
Artificial sweeteners, 343–344
Ascorbic acid, 370*t*. *See also* Vitamin C
Assessing children's health, 54–83
  child health histories, 56–57
  health records, 55–56
  hearing screening, 65–69
  height and weight measurements, 58–59
  medical and dental examinations, 57–58
  nutritional assessment, 71–73
  speech and language evaluation, 69–71
  vision screening, 59–65
Asthma, 90–92, 247–248
At-risk nutrients, 431–433
ATP, 378
Autism Awareness Month, 514

Note: tables, figures/illustrations, and boxes are denoted by a *t*, *f*, or *b* respectively, following the page number

Baby bottle tooth decay (BBTD), 21, 361, 402–403
Baby Safety Month, 516
Baby teeth, 13, 20
Bacillary dysentery, 475*t*
Back carrier, 222*t*
Bacterial growth, 477–478
Bark mulch, 197*t*
Basal metabolic rate (BMR), 338
Bassinet, 222*t*
Bathroom facilities, 185–187
BBTD, 21, 361, 402–403
Beans, 327–328
Better Hearing and Speech Month, 515
Bicycle helmets, 196, 196*f*, 252
Bike Safety Month, 515
Biotin, 371*t*
Bites, 254–255, 261
Bittersweet (vegetation), 193*t*
Black locust tree, 193*t*
Bleeding, 248, 250*f*
Blink reflex, 61
Blisters, 256
Blood-borne transmitted illnesses, 141–142*t*
BMI, 59
BMR, 338
Body mass index (BMI), 59
Body mechanics, 19, 20
Book list, 281–282*t*, 520–524
Booster seat, 199
Botulism, 473*t*
Brain Injury Awareness Month, 514
Bread/bread alternatives, 436–438*t*
Breast milk, 392*t*, 393, 393*t*
Breast pump, 393
Breastfeeding, 391–393
Breathing emergencies, 241–243
Bruises, 256
Brushing the teeth, 21, 22
Buckle Up America Week, 515
Building and site location, 182–184
Building blood, 358–360
Building security, 184
Bullying, 29
Burn Awareness Week, 514
Burns, 256–257
Burping, 396
Buttercup, 193*t*

CACFP, 431, 434–435*t*, 439, 518–519
Calcium
  absorption, 359, 360*t*
  deficiency symptoms, 376*t*
  functions, 376*t*
  labeling terms, 330*t*
  non-animal food source, 373*t*
  one cup of milk, 327
  sources, 357–358, 432*t*
  toxicity symptoms, 376*t*
Caloric value of food, 338
Calories
  discretionary, 328
  empty, 342
  fat-, 338
  labeling terms, 330*f*
  potential energy/energy cost, 338
Calories from fat, 329, 331
Campylobacterosis, 475*t*
Canada's Food Guide, 324
Cancer, 94–96
CAPTA, 268
Carbohydrates, 21, 323, 340–344
  complex, 343–344
  compound sugars, 342–343
  simple sugars, 341–342
Carbon monoxide detector, 185
Cardiopulmonary resuscitation (CPR), 242*f*
Cardiovascular disease, 421–422
Caring for Our Children: National Health and Safety Performance Standards: Guidelines for Out-of-Home Child Care, 5, 182
Carrier seat, 222*t*
Carrying heavy objects, 19
Case studies
  breast milk at day care, 406
  child abuse, 286
  developmental screening, 80
  field trip, 233
  food poisoning, 481
  food preferences - Portuguese family, 427
  herbal supplement, 505
  lesson planning, 314
  meals (allergy to citrus fruits), 384
  meals (calcium-phosphorus balance), 365
  menu planning (different food groups), 454
  menu planning (no refined sucrose), 350
  nutrition, generally, 334
  pinworms, 167
  seizure, 109, 265
  taking child to school, 133
  unhealthy meals/snacks, 33
  unlicensed in-home child care, 203
  vision disorder, 52
Castor bean, 193*t*
CCA-treated lumber, 195
CCP (critical point control), 459
Cellulose, 343
Cereus food poisoning, 476*t*
Changing table, 222*t*
Checking temperature, 155*t*
Checklists. *See* Teacher checklist
Chemical burns, 257, 258
Cherry tree, 193*t*

Chickenpox, 138*t*
Child abuse/neglect. *See* Maltreatment of children
Child Abuse Prevention and Treatment Act (CAPTA), 268
Child Abuse Prevention Month, 514
Child and Adult Care Food Program (CACFP), 431, 434–435*t*, 439, 518–519
Child care. *See* Early childhood program
Child health histories, 56–57
Child nutrition programs, 518–519
Child Passenger Safety Week, 514
Child safety seat, 199
Childhood cancers, 94–96
Childhood choking, 244–246
Childhood depression, 27
Childhood fears, 27–28
Childproof receptacle, 185
Children's book list, 281–282*t*, 520–524
Children's Dental Health Month, 514
Children's Eye Health and Safety Month, 516
Children's Health Insurance Program (CHIP), 5
Children's health records, 55–56
CHIP, 5
Chlamydia trachomatis, 272*t*
Choking, 244–246
Cholera, 476*t*
Cholesterol, 323, 345–347
Chronic medical conditions, 84–113
  allergic diseases. *See* Allergic diseases
  anemia, 92–94
  asthma, 90–92
  cancer, 94–96
  diabetes, 96–98
  eczema, 98
  excessive fatigue, 99
  factors to consider, 85
  lead poisoning, 100–101
  seizure disorder, 102–104
  sickle cell disease, 104–105
Classroom atmosphere, 24–25
Classroom corner. *See also* Activity plans
  burn prevention, 262–263
  calcium, 362–363
  cleaning and setting the table ..., 479–480
  everyone is special, 106–107
  feelings, 283–284
  fire safety ..., 230–231
  friendship, 31
  gear up for health ..., 164–165
  healthy snacks, 404–405
  hear with my ears ..., 50
  let's make pizza, 382–383
  my five senses ..., 77–78
  pumpkins, 451–452
  recycle everyday ..., 201
  roll the cube and move ..., 348
  tasting a rainbow ..., 332
  tasting pears ..., 425–426
  those invisible germs ..., 131
Clean Air Month, 515
Cleaning, 126–127
Cleft-palate nipple, 396
Climbing apparatus, 215*t*
CMV (cytomegalovirus), 142*t*
Cobalamin, 371*t*, 373
Coenzymes, 338
Cold sores, 143*t*
Colds, 138*t*, 148
Colic, 401–402
Collagen, 357
Color blindness, 64
Common cold, 138*t*, 148
Communicable and acute illness, 115, 136–170
  airborne transmitted illnesses, 138–141*t*
  blood-borne transmitted illnesses, 141–142*t*
  colds, 138*t*, 148
  contact transmitted illnesses, 142–145*t*
  control measures, 118–129
  diaper rash, 148–149
  diarrhea, 149–150
  dizziness, 151–152
  ear infection, 152–153
  fainting, 153–154
  fecal/oral transmitted illnesses, 145–174*t*
  fever, 154–155
  headache, 155
  heat rash, 157
  Lyme disease, 157–158
  modes of transmission, 116*f*
  SIDS, 159–161
  sore throat, 158
  stages of illness, 117–118
  stomachache, 158–159
  teething, 161
  toothache, 161–162
  vomiting, 162–163
  West Nile virus, 163
Complementary proteins, 355
Complete protein, 354, 355
Complex carbohydrates, 343–344
Compound sugars, 342–343
Conductive loss, 68
Condyloma, 272*t*
Confidentiality, 46
Conjunctivitis, 142*t*
Constipation, 404
Contact transmitted illnesses, 142–145*t*
Contactants, 86
Convalescent (recovery) stage, 118
Cooking temperatures, 478*f*
Coordinated School Health Program (CSHP), 6
Coordinated school health program components, 7*f*

CPR (cardiopulmonary resuscitation), 242*f*
Cradle, 222*t*
Creating high-quality environments, 172–206
  environmental safety. *See* Environmental safety
  features of high-quality programs, 176–182
  locating high-quality programs, 173–176
Crib toys, 222–223*t*
Critical control point (CCP), 459
Crocus bulbs, 192*f*
Crossed eyes, 63
CSHP, 6
Cubby, 187
Curriculum, 179
Cuts, 254
Cutting boards, 465
Cycle menus, 445
Cytomegalovirus (CMV), 142*t*

Daffodil, 192*f*, 193*t*
Daily health checks, 42–44
Daily health observations, 39–53
  benefits of health observations, 46–47
  confidentiality, 46
  daily health checks, 42–44
  family education, 49–50
  family involvement, 47–48
  gathering information, 41
  health education, 48–50
  observation as screening tool, as, 41–42
  recording health observations, 44–46
DAP (Developmentally Appropriate Practice), 179
Deciduous teeth, 13, 20
Decongestants, 89
Deer ticks, 157
Definitions (glossary), 527–533
Dehydration, 150
Dental caries, 420
Dental checkups, 22
Dental examination, 58
Dental fluorosis, 22
Dental health, 303–304
Dental Hygiene Month, 516
Desensitization therapy, 89
Development, 15, 16–17. *See also* Growth and development
Developmental milestones, 16–17*t*, 70*t*
Developmentally appropriate practices (DAP), 179
Diabetes, 96–98, 248–249, 422
Diabetic coma, 249*t*
Diaper rash, 148–149
Diapering and toileting areas, 127, 128*t*
Diarrhea, 149–150, 361
Dieffenbachia, 193*t*
Dietary assessment, 72
Dietary fiber, 326, 326*t*
Dietary Guidelines for Americans, 320–324, 331
Dietary reference intakes (DRIs), 319–320, 321–322*t*
Digital thermometer, 156
Direct transmission, 116*f*
Discipline *vs.* punishment, 268–269
Discretionary calories, 328
Diseases/disorders
  acute illness. *See* Management of injuries and acute illness
  chronic conditions. *See* Chronic medical conditions
  communicable illness, 115. *See also* Communicable and acute illness
  food-borne illness, 473–476*t*
  hearing impairment, 68
  nutritional problems, 72–75
  visual problems, 63–64
Dishwashing, 466
Dizziness, 151–152
Down syndrome, 417
Dressing appropriately for the weather, 302
DRIs (Daily Reference Value), 319–320, 321–322*t*
Drowning, 249–250
Dysentery, 145*t*

E. *coli*, 145*t*, 473*t*
EAR, 320
Ear, 68*f*
Ear infection, 18, 152–153
Early childhood program, 173–182
  curriculum, 179
  group size and composition, 178
  health services, 180–182
  locating high-quality programs, 173–176
  staffing ratios, 178
  teacher qualifications, 177–178
Eczema, 98
Education
  family. *See* 49–50
  health. *See* Health and safety education
  infectious disease, 129–130
  nutrition. *See* Nutrition education
Egg carton teeth, 304*f*
Electrical appliances, 224*t*
Electrical outlet, 185
Electrical shock, 250–251
Emergency ABCs, 240*t*
Emergency care, 240
Emergency contact information form, 181*f*
Emergency preparedness, 182*t*
Emergency response plan, 237–238
Emotional climate (classroom), 24–25
Emotional/psychological neglect, 270*t*, 273
Emotional/verbal abuse, 270*t*
Empty calories, 342
Encephalitis, 146*t*
Energy, 331, 337. *See also* Nutrients - energy sources
Energy utilization, 338–339
English ivy, 192*f*, 193*t*
Environmental factors, 9–10
Environmental lead, 101

Environmental safety, 182–201
  indoor safety. *See* Indoor safety
  outdoor play area, 189*t*, 191–198
  transportation, 198–201
Enzymes, 338, 379
Epilepsy, 102
Epilepsy Awareness Month, 517
EpiPen, 89, 90*f*
Equipment, 187, 193–196
Essential amino acids, 354, 355
Essential nutrient, 319
Estimated average requirement (EAR), 320
Ethnic foods, 441
Evacuation route, 185
Example cases. *See* Case studies
Excess energy, 339–340
Excessive fatigue, 93, 99
Exclusion policy, 119
Expressive vocabulary, 69
Extension cord, 185
Eye. *See* Vision
Eye injuries, 257–258
Eye Injury Prevention Month, 516
Eye safety, 76

Fact situations. *See* Case studies
Failure to thrive, 273
Fainting, 153–154
Families. *See* Focus on families
Family and environmental stresses, 275–276
Family education, 49–50
Family nutrition programs, 519
Farsightedness, 64
Fast food consumption, 424
Fast food vendor websites, 525
Fat-calories, 329, 331
"Fat-free," 330*f*
Fat intake, 323
Fat-soluble vitamins, 370*t*, 372
Fatigue, 93, 99
Fats, 323, 328*t*, 344–347
Fatty acids, 345
Fears, 27–28
Febrile seizure, 103
Fecal-oral transmission, 116*f*
Fecal/oral transmitted illnesses, 145–174*t*
Federal food programs, 518–519
Feeding infants, 388–408
  allergies, 401
  anemia, 402
  BBTD, 402–403
  breastfeeding, 391–393
  burping, 396
  colic, 401–402
  constipation, 404
  ear infection, 403
  first six months, 391–392
  formula, 393–394, 395*t*
  frequency of feedings, 394–396
  obesity, 403
  prenatal influences, 390
  semi-solid (pureed) food, 397–400
  serving size, 389*t*
  special needs children, 400
  supplements, 397
  teething, 403–404
  vomiting and diarrhea, 402
  water, 397
Feeding younger children, 409–429. *See also* Planning and serving meals
  age-related eating behaviors, 414*t*
  cardiovascular disease, 421–422
  common feeding concerns, 422–424
  dental caries, 420
  diabetes, 422
  feeding preschoolers, 415–417
  feeding school-aged children, 417
  feeding toddlers, 411–415
  healthy eating habits, 418–419
  hypertension, 420–421
  introducing new foods, 419*t*
  obesity, 420
  recommended daily requirements, 412
  special needs children, 417–418
Feelings (emotional health), 305–307
Fence, 192
Fever, 154–155
Field trips, 226
Fifth disease, 138*t*
Finger foods, 441*t*
Fire drill, 185, 186*t*
Fire Prevention Week, 516
Fire safety, 185, 186*t*, 230–231, 298, 310–311
Fireworks Eye Safety Month, 515
First aid, 238*t*, 239*t*, 240
First degree burns, 256
First-in first-out (FIFO) inventory method, 449
Floor plan, 184
Flossing, 22
Flower bed, 192
Flu, 151
Fluoride, 358
Fluorosis, 22
Focus on families
  administration of medicine, 130
  anger management, 283
  child care, 201
  Dietary Guidelines for Americans, 331
  evaluating health safety information, 311–312
  eye safety, 76
  feeding toddlers and young children, 425
  fruits and vegetables, 503
  hand washing, 479

Focus on families (*continued*)
  healthy families, 347
  infant feeding, 404
  meal planning, 451
  nutrients that promote growth, 362
  nutrients that regulate body functions, 382
  oral health, 49
  poison prevention, 262
  sun safety, 230
  West Nile virus, 106
  when to call the doctor, 164
Folacin, 371*t*, 373
Food allergens, 87*t*
Food allergies, 86–87
Food-borne contaminants, 458*f*
Food-borne illness
  at-risk groups, 458
  causes, 458, 458*f*
  defined, 457
  diseases, listed, 473–476*t*
  prevention, 472
Food-borne illness outbreak, 458
Food Guide Pyramid, 324–329, 412*f*, 433
Food handlers, 462, 462*f*
Food infections, 477
Food intolerance, 87
Food intoxication, 478
Food jags, 423
Food labels, 329–331
Food poisoning, 472, 473–476*t*
Food preparation, 450
Food preparation areas, 465–466
Food programs (federal), 518–519
Food purchasing, 449–450
Food safety, 324, 457–483
  bacterial growth, 477–478
  dishwashing, 466
  food-borne illness. *See* Food-borne illness
  food handlers, 462, 462*f*
  food preparation areas, 465–466
  food service, 464–465
  food service areas, 466, 467–471*f*
  food storage, 464
  HACCP, 458–459
  hand washing, 462–463
  personal health and cleanliness, 459, 462
  safe handling instructions, 478*f*
  transport, 464
Food service areas, 466, 467–471*f*
Food storage, 464
Food supplement safety, 380
Food trend predictions, 502
Fracture, 258
Friendship, 31
Frostbite, 258–259
Fructose, 342
Fruit and Vegetable Month, 516
Fruit juice, 361
Fruits, 323, 326, 500–501, 503
Furniture, 187
Future topics for discussion, 507–508

Galactose, 342
Gastroenteritis, 476*t*
Gastrointestinal disease, 474*t*
Gates and enclosures, 223*t*
Gathering information, 41
Generalized seizure, 103
Genital warts, 272*t*
German measles, 140*t*
Germs and illness prevention, 299
Giardiasis, 146*t*, 475*t*
Girls and Women in Sports Day, 514
Glass mercury thermometer, 154
Glitter, 225*t*
Glossary, 527–533
Glucose, 342
Glycerol, 345
Glycogen, 343
Golden chain tree, 193*t*
Gonorrhea, 272*t*
Good cholesterol, 347
Good Samaritan Law, 240
"Good source of calcium," 330*f*
Grains, 325
Gram, 338
Grassy areas, 192
Gravel, 197*t*
Grocery store, 498–499
Group size and composition, 178
Growth, 354. *See also* Nutrients - growth of body tissues
Growth and development, 12–15
  development, 15, 16–17
  factors to consider, 12
  infants, 12–13
  milestones, 16–17*t*
  preschoolers, 14
  school-age children, 14
  toddlers, 13–14
Growth charts, 58–59

HACCP, 458–459
Haemophilus influenza Type b, 139*t*
Halloween Safety Month, 516
Hand, foot, and mouth disease, 142–143*t*
Hand washing, 126, 126*t*, 300–301, 462–463, 479
Handling body fluids, 125*t*
Hazard analysis and critical control point (HACCP), 458–459
Hazardous art materials, 225*t*
HCCA, 5
HDL, 346, 347
Head circumference, 13, 57
Head injury, 251–252

Head lice, 143*t*
Head Lice Prevention Month, 516
Head Start, 174
Headache, 155
Health
  defined, 8
  environmental factors, 9–10
  factors to consider, 8–10
  heredity, 9
  interactive state, as, 9
  learning, and, 40
Health and safety education, 48–50, 217, 290–315
  activity plans. *See* Activity plans
  behavioral objectives, 295
  content presentation, 295–297
  evaluation, 297
  family involvement, 291
  teacher, role of, 292
  topic selection, 293–295
Health and safety videos, 234
Health education, 48–50
Health Education Curriculum Analysis Tool (HECAT), 293
Health histories, 56–57
Health history questionnaire, 57
Health initiatives. *See* National health initiatives
Health insurance, 48
Health Literacy Month, 516
Health observation checklist, 43*t*
Health observations. *See* Daily health observations
Health problems. *See* Diseases/disorders
Health records, 55–56
Health services, 180–182
Healthy Child Care America (HCCA), 5
Healthy eating habits, 418–419
Healthy People 2000: National Health Promotion and Disease Prevention Objectives, 4
Healthy People 2020, 4, 5
Healthy People guidelines, 324
Healthy snacks, 404–405, 414, 445–446
Healthy Vision Month, 515
Healthy Weight Week, 514
Hearing, 65–69
  additional information, 68
  behavioral indicators, 66*t*
  causes of hearing loss, 67
  diagram of ear, 68*f*
  disorders, 67–68
  infants, 66*t*
  management, 68
  methods of assessment, 65–67
  newborns, 67
  teacher checklist, 69*t*
  toddlers, 66*t*
Heat exhaustion, 259
Heat rash, 157
Heat stroke, 259–260
Heating and cooling system, 190
HECAT, 293
HECAT instructional modules, 293*t*
Height and weight measurements, 58–59
Heimlich maneuver, 246*f*, 247*f*
Helmets, 196, 196*f*, 252
Heme iron, 360
Hemoglobin, 358
Hepatitis A, 146*t*, 474*t*
Hepatitis B, 142*t*
Heredity, 9
Herpes simplex, 143*t*
Hib, 139*t*
High chair, 223*t*
High density lipoprotein (HDL), 346, 347
"High protein," 330*f*
H1N1 flu, 151
Holly, 193*t*
Home Safety Month, 515
Home visitor, 227*t*
Homelessness, 28, 75
Hook-on chair, 223*t*
Hormones, 338, 379
Hummus, 495–497
Hyacinth, 193*t*
Hydrogenation, 327
Hyperglycemia, 96, 249*t*
Hyperopia, 64
Hypertension, 420–421
Hypoglycemia, 248, 249*t*
Hypothermia, 259

Illness. *See* Diseases/disorders
Illustrative cases. *See* Case studies
Immunization, 121–124
Immunization Awareness Month, 516
Impetigo, 143*t*
Incidental learning experiences, 217
Incomplete proteins, 354
Incubation stage, 117
Indirect transmission, 116*f*
Individual injury report form, 229*f*
Indoor air quality, 190–191
Indoor safety, 182–191
  air quality, 190–191
  bathroom facilities, 185–187
  building and site location, 182–184
  building security, 184
  fire safety, 185, 186*t*
  floor plan, 184
  lighting and ventilation, 187, 190
  program security, 185*t*
  safety checklist, 188–189
  surface and furnishings, 187
Infant, 388–389
  brain, 13
  checking temperature, 155*t*

Infant (*continued*)
choking, 244–245
common behaviors, 399*t*
CPR, 242*f*
equipment safety list, 222–224*t*
factors to consider, 13
feeding. *See* Feeding infants
growth and development, 12–13
head, 13
health problems, 401–404
hearing abnormalities, 66*t*
injury prevention, 209*t*
milestones, 16*t*
mouth-to-mouth breathing, 241–243
play area, 191
risk of life-threatening injuries, 208
speech/language milestones, 70*t*
toy choices, 219*t*
transportation - safety restraint, 198–199
visual abnormalities, 61*t*
Infant equipment safety checklist, 222–224*t*
Infant formula, 394, 395*t*, 401
Infectious disease, 114–135
administration of medicine, 120–121
cleaning, 126–127
communicable illness, 115. *See also* Communicable and acute illness
control measures, 118–129
diapering and toileting areas, 127, 128*t*
education, 129–130
environmental control, 125–129
hand washing, 126, 126*t*
immunization, 121–124
modes of transmission, 116*f*
observations, 118
policies, 118–120
room arrangement, 128–129
stages of illness, 117–118
universal infection control precautions, 125–126
Influenza, 151
Information gathering, 41
Information release form, 56
Infrared forehead thermometer, 154
Ingestants, 86
Inhalants, 86
Injectables, 86
Injury prevention, 18, 209–211*t*. *See also* Management of injuries and acute illness
Injury reports, 228–229
Insect bites, 255
Insulin, 379
Insulin-resistant diabetes, 96
Insulin shock, 248, 249*t*
Internet sites. *See* Web resources
Introducing new foods, 419*t*
Iodine, 377*t*
Iris, 193*t*
Iron
absorption, 359–360
deficiency symptoms, 377*t*
functions, 377*t*
heme, 360
hemoglobin/healthy blood, 358
non-animal sources, 373*t*
sources, 359, 432*t*
toxicity symptoms, 377*t*
Iron-deficiency anemia, 359
Irradiation, 472
Issues to Consider features
bullying, 29
CACFP, 439
child abuse and cultural practices, 273
childhood asthma, 93
E. coli outbreak, 477
fire safety, 298
Food Guide Pyramid, 325
food supplement safety, 380
food trend predictions, 502
health and learning, 40
infant formula and diabetes, 401
nutrient-fortified foods, 359
obesity epidemic, 342
poverty, 75
seasonal and H1N1 flu, 151
security in early childhood programs, 183
surfing the Web for information, 424
transportation safety, 226
water safety, 251

Jonquil, 193*t*

Lacto-ovo-vegetarian, 374
Lacto-vegetarian, 374
Lactose, 343
Lactose intolerance, 343
Language development, 69
Latch-key children, 272–273
Lazy eye, 63
LBW infant, 390
Lead poisoning, 100–101
Legal issues, 227–229
Leukemia, 94
Liability, 228
Lice (head), 143*t*
Licensing, 175–176
Life-threatening conditions, 240–254
Lifting, 19
"Light or lite," 330*f*
Lighting and ventilation, 187, 190
Lightning Safety Week, 515
Lily-of-the-valley, 192*f*, 193*t*
Linoleic acid, 345, 346
Linolenic acid, 345, 346

Listeriosis, 474*t*
Locker, 187
Low-birthweight (LBW) infant, 390
"Low cholesterol," 330*f*
"Low-fat," 330*f*
Lyme disease, 157–158
Lyme Disease Awareness Month, 515

Magnesium, 376*t*
Malnutrition, 72, 74*t*, 319
Maltreatment of children, 267–289
  abuse and neglect, 269–273
  characteristics of abusive adults, 274–276
  children's books, 281–282*t*
  cultural practices, 273
  discipline *vs.* punishment, 268–269
  educating families, 282–284
  family and environmental stresses, 275–276
  historical developments, 268
  inservice training, 277
  latch-key children, 272–273
  program policy, 278–279
  protective measures, 276–277
  reporting laws, 277–279
  signs/symptoms, 270*t*
  teacher, role of, 279–284
Management of injuries and acute illness, 237–266
  abrasions, 254
  absence of breathing, 241–243
  airway obstruction, 243–246
  asthma, 247–248
  bites, 254–255, 261
  bleeding, 248, 250*f*
  blisters, 256
  bruises, 256
  burns, 256–257
  choking, 244–246
  CPR, 242*f*
  cuts, 254
  diabetes, 248–249
  drowning, 249–250
  electrical shock, 250–251
  emergency ABCs, 240*t*
  emergency response plan, 237–238
  eye injuries, 257–258
  first aid, 238*t*, 239*t*, 240
  fracture, 258
  frostbite, 258–259
  head injury, 251–252
  heat exhaustion/heat stroke, 259–260
  Heimlich maneuver, 246*f*, 247*f*
  hypothermia, 259
  injury prevention, 209–211*t*
  life-threatening conditions, 240–254
  mouth-to-mouth breathing, 241–243
  non-life threatening conditions, 254–261
  nosebleed, 260
  poisoning, 253–254
  seizure, 260–261
  shock, 247
  skin wounds, 254
  splinters, 261
  sprains, 261
  tick bites, 261
  tooth emergencies, 261
  what to do/what not to do, 238
mcg, 369
Meal/menu planning, 430–444
Measles, 139*t*
Meat and beans, 327–328
Media violence, 29–30
Medical and dental examinations, 57–58
Medication administration, 120–121
Medication recording form, 122
Melanoma/Skin Cancer Detection and Prevention Month, 515
Meningitis, 139*t*
Mental health
  depression, 27
  fears/nightmares, 27–28
  teacher checklist, 45
Mental Health Month (Children), 515
Menu-planning form, 443*f*
Menu writing, 445
mg, 338, 369
Microgram, 369
Milestones, 16–17*t*, 70*t*
Milk, 327
Milk sugar, 343
Milligram, 338, 369
Minerals, 357–360, 375–379
Minerals and fibers, 225*t*
Misarticulations, 69
Mistletoe, 193*t*
Mixed hearing loss, 68
Modified first aid kits, 239*t*
Mononucleosis, 139*t*
Monosaturated fatty acids (MUFAs), 346
Monthly calendar, 514–517
"More iron," 330*f*
Mouth-to-mouth breathing, 241–243
MUFAs, 346
μg, 369
Mumps, 140*t*
Mycotoxiocosis, 474*t*
Myopia, 64
MyPyramid, 324*f*

NACCRRA, 174
NAEYC, 174
NAFCC, 174
Narcissus, 193*t*
National accrediting organizations, 174

National Adoption Awareness Month, 517
National After School Association, 174
National Association for Family Child Care (NAFCC), 174
National Association for the Education of Young Children (NAEYC), 174
National Association of Child Care Resource and Referral Agencies (NACCRRA), 174
National Children's Agenda: Developing a Shared Vision, 4
National Children's Study, 6–7
National Handwashing Awareness Week, 517
National Health Education Standards (NHES), 293, 510–513
National Health Education Standards: Achieving Health Literacy, 513
National health initiatives
  CHIP, 5
  CSHP, 6
  HCCA, 5
  Healthy People 2020, 4, 5
  National Children's Agenda, 4
  National Children's Study, 6–7
  NCLB, 6
  web sites, 34
National Healthy Skin Month, 517
National observances (monthly calendar), 514–517
National Playground Safety Week, 515
National Preparedness Month, 516
National Safe Kids Week, 515
National Safe Toys and Celebrations Month, 517
National Safety Month, 515
National School Lunch Program (NSLP), 518
National School Lunch Week, 516
Natural light, 187, 190
NCLB, 6
Nearsightedness, 64
Neglect. *See* Maltreatment of children
Negligence, 228
Newborn hearing tests, 67
Newborn nipple, 396
Newborns. *See* Infant
NHES standards, 293, 510–513
Niacin, 371*t*
Nightmare, 27, 28
Nipples, 396
No Child Left Behind (NCLB), 6
Non-essential amino acids, 354
Non-life-threatening conditions, 254–261
Nosebleed, 260
NSLP, 518
Nutrient-fortified foods, 359
Nutrient functions, 381–382*t*
Nutrients, 318–319
Nutrients - energy sources, 337–352
  carbohydrates, 340–344
  fats, 344–347
  overview, 338–340
  proteins, 347
Nutrients - growth of body tissues, 353–367
  minerals, 357–360
  proteins, 354–356
  vitamins, 361–362
  water, 360–361
Nutrients - regulation of body functions, 368–386
  minerals, 375–379
  proteins, 379–380
  vitamins. *See* Vitamins
  water, 380–381
Nutrition
  defined, 10, 318
  disorders, 72–75
  education. *See* Nutrition education
  effect on children, 11
  energy. *See* Nutrients - energy sources
  factors to consider, 502*f*
  food safety. *See* Food safety
  growth. *See* Nutrients - growth of body tissues
  guidelines. *See* Nutritional guidelines
  nutrient functions, 381–382*t*
  regulation of body functions. *See* Nutrients - regulation of body functions
Nutrition education, 484–506
  activity plan (fruits and vegetables), 500–501
  activity plan (making hummus/pita), 495–497
  activity plan (school lunches), 499–500
  activity plan (tasting party), 497–498
  activity plan (trip to grocery store), 498–499
  activity plan (weighing and measuring children), 495
  administrators, 486
  basic concepts, 485
  books/web sites, 489*f*
  defined, 484
  evaluation of resource material, 486
  family involvement, 487, 501
  food service personnel, 486
  incorporating basic concepts, 490*f*, 491*f*
  lesson plans, 494
  objectives, 488
  peer groups, 502–503
  planning, 488
  safety considerations, 493–494
  setting a good example, 486–487
  teachers, 486, 501
  television and media, 503
  tips/guidelines, 490–492
Nutrition month, 514
Nutritional assessment, 71–73
Nutritional assessment questionnaire, 73*f*
Nutritional guidelines, 318–335
  Dietary Guidelines for Americans, 320–324
  DRIs, 319–320, 321–322*t*

Food Guide Pyramid, 324–329
food labels, 329–331
Healthy People guidelines, 324
Nutritional problems, 72–75

Oak tree, 193*t*
Obesity, 72, 74, 403, 420
Observations. *See* Daily health observations
Odd-day cycle menus, 445
Oils, 326–327
Oleander, 193*t*
Oral health, 20–22, 49
Orthodontic nipple, 396
Otitis media, 152–153
Outdoor play area, 189*t,* 191–198
Outdoor play equipment, 193–196
Overweight, 72, 74
Overweight children, 340*t*
Ovo-vegetarian, 374

Pacifier, 223*t*
Pantothenic acid, 371*t*
Parahaemolyticus food poisoning, 474*t*
Partial seizure, 103
Pathogen, 115
Pedestrian safety, 308–309
Perfringens food poisoning, 475*t*
Permanent markers, 225*t*
Personal health and cleanliness, 459, 462
Petroleum products, 253*t*
Pets, 226–227
Phenylketonuria (PKU), 344
Philodendron, 193*t*
Phosphorus, 358, 376*t*
Photographic chemicals, 225*t*
Photoscreening, 61
Physical abuse, 269, 270*t*
Physical activity, 20, 323
Physical activity pyramid, 421*f*
Physical arrangement (classroom), 128–129
Physical Fitness and Sports Month, 515
Physical neglect, 270*t,* 272
Pinkeye, 142*t*
Pinworms, 147*t*
PKU, 344
Public Law (PL), 93-247, 268
Planning and serving meals, 430–456
at-risk nutrients, 431–433
bread/bread alternatives, 436–438*t*
CACFP, 431, 434–435*t,* 439
cost considerations, 448–450
ethnic foods, 441
finger foods, 441*t*
meal/menu planning, 430–444
menu writing, 445
recordkeeping, 450
serving meals, 446–448
snack foods, 445–446
steps in menu planning, 442–444
Plant oils, 327
Play equipment, 215*t,* 218*t*
Playpen, 223*t*
Poison prevention, 309–310
Poison Prevention Month, 514
Poisoning, 253–254
Poisonous substances, 253*t*
Poisonous vegetation, 192*f,* 193*t*
Polyunsaturated fatty acids (PUFAs), 346
Pool water, 195
Posture, 18, 19
Potassium, 323, 377*t*
Potty training, 127, 128*t*
Pound, 338
Poverty, 28, 75
Poverty Awareness Month, 514
Powders, 225*t*
Prader-Willi syndrome, 417
Predisposition, 9
Preschoolers, 410
checking temperature, 155*t*
eating behaviors, 414*t*
fears/nightmares, 28
feeding, 415–417. *See also* Feeding younger children
growth and development, 14
health/safety concepts, 294
injury prevention, 211*t*
milestones, 17*t*
protein, 356
speech/language milestones, 70*t*
tooth brushing, 22
toy choices, 219*t*
transportation - safety restraint, 199
vision screening tests, 62*t*
Preventive health concept, 3
Preventive health practices, 3
Procurement, 449
Prodromal stage, 117
Professional accreditation, 174
Program curriculum, 179
Program security, 185*t*
Protein
body functions, 379–380
complementary/supplementary, 355
complete/incomplete, 354
energy source, as, 347
growth of body tissues, 354–356
non-animal sources, 373*t*
number of calories per gram, 347
one ounce of meat, fish, 328
Psychological neglect, 270*t,* 273
PUFAs, 346
Puncture-type wounds, 254
Pupil response, 61

Pureed food, 397–400
Pyridoxine, 371*t*

Quality supervision, 216–217

Radura symbol, 472
Random Acts of Kindness Foundation, 514
Rattles, 224*t*
RDA, 320
Receptive vocabulary, 69
Recipe flow charts, 460–461*f*
Recommended daily allowance (RDA), 320
Recording health observations, 44–46
Recordkeeping, 55
Recovery position, 243, 243*f*
Recycling, 201
"Reduced or fewer calories," 330*f*
"Reduced sugar," 330*f*
Referrals, 75–76
Refined sucrose, 342
Reflective thoughts
- BBTD, 21
- bicycle helmets, 252
- child abuse, 276, 278
- child care, 174
- childhood obesity, 494
- chronic health disorders, 87
- communicable illness, 120
- daily health checks, 44
- diversity, 8, 137
- emergency telephone call, 241
- exposure to blood-borne diseases, 256
- family involvement, 47
- fat intake, 344
- food allergies, 423
- Food Guide Pyramid, 329, 433
- friendships, 22
- health and safety education, 292
- infant feeding, 398
- kitchen (home), 466
- newborn hearing tests, 67
- physical activity, 358
- reporting suspected child abuse, 276
- resource material, evaluation of, 298
- safety, 184
- shutting off electrical power source, 251
- single nutrients, 360
- teacher calling in sick, 213
- teacher exposure to communicable disease, 130, 152
- toys and age guidelines, 220
- vision problems, 64
- vitamin/mineral pills, 379
- weight/height measurement, 59

Refusal to eat, 422
Rescue breath, 241
Resilience, 30–31
Resource and referral services, 174
Rheumatic fever, 140–141*t*
Rhododendron, 193*t*
Rhubarb, 193*t*
Riboflavin, 371*t*
Riding toys, 196
Ringworm, 144*t*
Risk management, 212–217
Rocky Mountain spotted fever, 144*t*
Role models, 24
Room arrangement, 128–129
Room temperature, 190
Roseola infantum, 140*t*
Rubella, 140*t*
Rubeola, 139*t*

Safe handling instructions (food), 478
Safe Toys and Gifts Month, 517
Safety, 10
- activity plans. *See* Activity plans
- cars, and, 307–308
- child abuse/neglect. *See* Maltreatment of children
- education. *See* Health and safety education
- environmental safety. *See* Environmental safety
- food. *See* Food safety
- injury prevention, 209–211t. *See also* Management of injuries and acute illness management. *See* Safety management

Safety management, 207–236. *See also* Safety
- advance planning, 213–214
- classroom activities, 221–225
- electrical appliances, 224*t*
- field trips, 226
- hazardous art materials, 225*t*
- home visitor, 227*t*
- infant equipment safety checklist, 222–224*t*
- legal implications, 227–229
- pets, 226–227
- play equipment, 215*t*, 218*t*
- quality supervision, 216–217
- risk management, 212–217
- safety education, 217. *See also* Health and safety education
- safety policies/guidelines, 214–216
- toys and equipment, 215*t*, 218–221

Safety policies/guidelines, 214–216
Salmonellosis, 147*t*, 473*t*
Sample cases. *See* Case studies
Sand, 197*t*
Sandbox, 195*t*
Sanitary diapering procedure, 128*t*
Saturated fats, 345, 346
Save Your Vision Month, 514
Scabies, 145*t*
Scarlatina, 140–141*t*
SCHIP, 5

School-age children
  checking temperature, 155*t*
  eating behaviors, 414*t*
  feeding, 417. *See also* Feeding younger children
  growth and development, 14
  health education, 48–49
  health/safety concepts, 294–295
  injury prevention, 211*t*
  milestones, 17*t*
  snack suggestions, 446*f*
  speech/language milestones, 70*t*
  transportation - safety restraint, 199
  visual acuity problems, 62*t*
School Breakfast Program (SBP), 518
School Breakfast Week, 514
School Bus Safety Week, 516
School lunches, 436, 499–500, 516, 518
Scrapes, 254
Screening procedures. *See* Assessing children's health
Seasonal flu, 151
Second degree burns, 256
Seizure, 260–261
Seizure disorder, 102–104
Selective eating, 422
Selenium, 360
Self-concept, 23
Self-esteem, 23
Semi-solid (pureed) food, 397–400
Senses, 77–78
Sensorineural loss, 68
Sensory system, 59
Serious injury and illness plan, 238*f*
Serving meals, 446–448
Sexual abuse, 270*t*, 271
Sexually transmitted diseases (STDs), 272*t*
Shaken baby syndrome, 269, 271
Shape Up America, 516
Shigellosis, 145*t*, 475*t*
Shock, 247
Shredded tires, 197–198
Sickle Cell Awareness Month, 516
Sickle cell disease, 104–105
SIDS, 159–161
SIDS Awareness Month, 516
Simple sugars, 341–342
Single parent, 28
Sitting, 19
Skin wounds, 254
Smoke detector, 185
Snack foods, 404–405, 414, 445–446
SNAP, 519
Social-emotional competence, 23–28
Sodium, 323, 376*t*
"Sodium-free," 330*f*
Solid fats, 327
Solvents and thinners, 225*t*
Sore throat, 158
Soybean, 354
Space, 184, 191–193
Special programs/dates (monthly calendar), 514–517
Speech and language evaluation, 69–71
Speech impairment, 71
Speech/language milestones, 70*t*
Splinters, 261
Sports and Home Eye Safety, 516
Sports Eye Safety Month, 515
Sprains, 261
Squeeze toys, 224*t*
Staffing ratios, 178
Standing, 19
Staphyloccal food poisoning, 473*t*
Starches, 343
State Children's Health Insurance Program (SCHIP), 5
State licensing requirements, 175–176
STDs, 272*t*
Steam pasteurization, 472
Stomachache, 158–159
Storage space, 187
Strabismus, 63–64
Strep throat, 140–141*t*
Streptococcal infections, 140–141*t*
Stress
  children, 25–27
  teacher, 25
Stroller, 224*t*
Strong acid and alkalis, 253*t*
Stunted growth, 361
Sucrose, 342
Sudden infant death syndrome (SIDS), 159–161
Sugar, 328*t*, 341–343
"Sugar-free," 330*f*
Sun safety, 230
Sun Safety Week, 515
Sunglasses, 76
Sunlight, 190
Supplemental Nutrition Assistance Program (SNAP), 519
Supplementary proteins, 355
Surface and furnishings (indoors), 187
Surfacing materials, 196–198
Surveillance camera, 184
Susceptible host, 115
Sweet pea, 193*t*
Swimming pools, 195
Swings, 194, 215*t*
Syphilis, 272*t*

Table sugar, 342
Tasting party, 489, 497–498
Teacher
  checklists. *See* Teacher checklist
  child abuse/neglect, 279–284

Teacher (*continued*)
- children's emotional health, 32
- children's social-emotional competence, 24
- daily health checks, 42–44
- emotional climate of classroom, 25
- health and safety education, 292
- illness, 119–120
- nutrition education, 486, 501
- referrals, 75–76
- role model, as, 24
- stress, 25

Teacher activities. *See* Classroom corner
Teacher checklist
- allergies/asthma, 92*t*
- burns, 256*t*
- cancer, 95*t*
- child abuse/neglect, 270*t*
- child abuse/neglect report, 279*t*
- childhood choking, 244*t*
- diabetes, 97*t*
- electrical appliances, 224*t*
- evaluation of resource material, 297*t*
- fire drill, 186*t*
- hazardous art materials, 225*t*
- health observation checklist, 43*t*
- hearing-impaired children, 69*t*
- home visitor, 227*t*
- hyperglycemia/hypoglycemia, 249*t*
- inappropriate behavior, 217*t*
- maltreatment, children books, 281–282*t*
- mental health problems, 45*t*
- nursing mothers, 393*t*
- positive behavior management, 277*t*
- safety checklist, 188–189*t*
- sandbox care and maintenance, 195*t*
- sickle cell disease, 105*t*
- SIDS, 160*t*
- STDs, 272*t*
- toys and play equipment, 218*t*

Teacher illness, 119
Teacher qualifications, 177–178
Teacher stress, 25
Teeter-totter, 194
Teeth, 20–22, 49
Teether, 224*t*
Teething, 161, 403–404
Telephone, 187
Temperature, 154–155, 156*t*
Terminology (glossary), 527–533
Tetanus, 145*t*
Thermic energy of food, 339
Thermometer, 154, 156*t*
Thiamin, 370*t*
Third degree burns, 256
Thyroxin, 379
Tick bites, 157*t*, 261
Titmus fly test, 61
Toddler, 409–410
- checking temperature, 155*t*
- dental checkups, 22
- eating behaviors, 414*t*
- feeding, 411–415. *See also* Feeding younger children
- growth and development, 13–14
- health/safety concepts, 294
- hearing abnormalities, 66*t*
- injury prevention, 209–210*t*
- milestones, 16*t*
- play area, 191
- risk of life-threatening injuries, 208
- speech/language milestones, 70*t*
- teeth, 13
- tooth brushing, 21
- toy choices, 219*t*
- transportation - safety restraint, 199
- vision abnormalities, 61*t*

Toilet training, 127, 128*t*
Tolerable upper intake level (UL), 320
Tonic-clonic seizure, 103
Tooth brushing, 21, 22, 304–305
Tooth decay, 361
Tooth emergencies, 261
Toothache, 161–162
Toothpaste, 21, 22
Tourniquet, 248
Toy chest, 224*t*
Toys and equipment, 215*t*, 218–221
Trace minerals, 360
Trampoline, 195
Trans-fats, 345
Transportation, 198–201, 226
Trees, 192
Trichomoniasis, 272*t*
Tricycle, 196
Trip to grocery store, 498–499
Tuberculosis, 141*t*
Tympanic thermometer, 156
Type 1 diabetes, 96
Type 2 diabetes, 96

UL, 320
Undernutrition, 319
Unequal pupils, 252*f*
Unintentional injury, 208, 212
Universal infection control precautions, 125–126
Universal newborn hearing screening and intervention programs, 67
Unsaturated fats, 346
UV exposure, 76
UV (ultra violet) Eye Safety Month, 515

Vaccine, 121–124
Vegan, 374

Vegetables, 323, 325–326, 500–501, 503
Vegetarian diets, 373–374
Ventilation, 190
Verbal abuse, 270*t*
Videos, health and safety, 234
Vignettes. *See* Case studies
Violence, 28–30. *See also* Maltreatment of children
Vision, 59–65
  acuity tests, 62*t*
  disorders, 63–64
  infants, 61, 61*t*
  injury prevention, 76
  management, 64–65
  methods of assessment, 60–62
  older children, 62*t*
  signs/symptoms, 61*t*, 62*t*
  toddlers, 61*t*
Vitamin A, 326*t*, 370*t*, 433*t*
Vitamin B_6, 371*t*
Vitamin B_{12}, 371*t*, 373*t*
Vitamin C
  absorption of calcium and iron, 359
  deficiency symptoms, 370*t*
  enriched food products, 358
  functions, 370*t*
  orange juice, 358
  sources, 327*t*, 433*t*
  toxicity symptoms, 370*t*
Vitamin D, 370*t*, 373*t*
Vitamin E, 370*t*
Vitamins, 369–375
  blood formation, 375
  bone growth, 374
  cellular reproduction and growth, 373–374
  deficiency symptoms, 370–371*t*
  energy metabolism, 373
  functions, 370–371*t*
  growth of body tissues, 361–362
  neuromuscular function, 374–375
  sources, 370–371*t*
  toxicity symptoms, 370–371*t*
Vocabulary, 69, 70
Vomiting, 162–163

Wading (swimming) pools, 195
Water, 360–361, 380–381, 446
Water safety, 251
Water-soluble vitamins, 370–371*t*, 372
Web resources
  assessing children's health, 81
  child abuse/maltreatment, 287
  chronic medical conditions, 110
  communicable and acute illness, 168
  daily health observations, 53
  energy food, 351
  environmental safety, 204
  fast-food vendor websites, 525
  feeding infants, 407
  feeding younger children, 428
  food safety, 482
  growth food, 366
  health and safety education, 314–315
  healthy eating, 75
  infectious disease, 134
  injury management, 265
  monthly calendar, 514–517
  national health initiatives, 34
  nutrients - regulation of body functions, 385
  nutrition education, 489, 505
  nutritional guidelines, 335
  physical activities, 75
  planning and serving meals, 455
  safety management, 233–234
  SIDS, 161
Weekly menus, 445
Weight/height measurements, 58–59
Weight management, 74–75, 320
West Nile virus, 106, 163
When to call the doctor, 164
Whole grains, 323
Whole Grains Month, 516
WIC, 519
Wisteria, 193*t*
Women, Infants, and Children (WIC), 519
Wood chips, 197*t*
Worth 4-dot test, 61

Yews, 193*t*
Youth Sports Safety Month, 515

Zinc, 360, 373*t*, 377*t*

Notes

Notes

Notes